THE LIFE AND TIMES OF COTTON MATHER

Also by Kenneth Silverman

A Cultural History of the American Revolution

The Life and Times of

COTTON

MATHER

Kenneth Silverman

Columbia University Press

New York

Columbia University Press
New York
Columbia University Press Morningside Edition 1985

This edition published by arrangement with
Harper & Row.
Printed in U.S.A.

Grateful acknowledgment is made for permission to reprint:

Excerpt from *The Collected Essays and Occasional Writings of Katherine Anne Porter* by Katherine Anne Porter. Copyright © 1970 by Katherine Anne Porter. Reprinted by permission of Delacorte Press/Seymour Lawrence and Joan Daves.

Excerpt from *Main Currents in American Thought, Volume One: 1620–1800* by Vernon L. Parrington, Jr., Louise P. Tucker, Elizabeth P. Thomas. Reprinted by permission of the publisher.

Excerpt from *The European Witch-Craze of the Sixteenth and Seventeenth Centuries and Other Essays* by H. R. Trevor-Roper. (Harper Torchbook edition, 1969). Reprinted by permission of Harper & Row, Publishers, Inc.

Designer: Sidney Feinberg

Library of Congress Cataloging in Publication Data

Silverman, Kenneth.
   The life and times of Cotton Mather.

   Reprint. Originally published: New York : Harper & Row, c1984.
   Bibliography: p.
   Includes index.
   1. Mather, Cotton, 1663–1728. 2. Puritans—
Massachusetts—Biography. 3. Massachusetts—History
Colonial period, ca. 1600–1775. I. Title.
F67.M43S57 1985   285.8'32'0924 [B]   85-387
ISBN 0-231-06125-0

p 10 9 8 7 6 5 4 3

For my teacher and friend, Lewis Leary
And for my brother, Alex

Contents

Illustrations follow page 306

Acknowledgments

MANY persons and institutions made this book possible by preserving, transmitting, and interpreting Cotton Mather's life and works for three centuries. Most of them must necessarily but unjustly go unnamed, yet to be able to acknowledge some publicly is a rich and complex pleasure. First, my thanks to the following for allowing me to use and to quote from manuscripts in their collections: the American Antiquarian Society, Worcester, Mass.; the Bodleian Library, Oxford, England; Department of Rare Books and Manuscripts, Boston Public Library, by courtesy of the Trustees of the Boston Public Library; Department of Manuscripts, the British Library, London; the Brown University Library, Providence, R.I.; the Francis A. Countway Library, Harvard Medical School, Boston; the Houghton Library, Harvard University, Cambridge, Mass., by permission of the Houghton Library; the Historical Society of Pennsylvania, Philadelphia; the Henry E. Huntington Library, San Marino, Calif.; the Massachusetts Historical Society, Boston; the National Library of Scotland, Edinburgh, with permission of the Trustees of the National Library of Scotland; Rare Books and Manuscripts Division, the New York Public Library (Astor, Lenox, and Tilden Foundations), New York City; the Royal Society, London; Mather Collection (#38-632), the Tracy W. McGregor Library, University of Virginia Library, Charlottesville; the Yale University Library, New Haven, Conn.

For various favors I also feel grateful to Alfred Owen Aldridge, Patricia Bonomi, Ursula Brumm, Everett Emerson, Mason I. Lowance, Patricia Thompson, Louis Tucker, James W. Tuttleton, and Aileen Ward. Christopher Jedrey found me a room in Lowell House at Harvard University when the inns were full, and Kathryn M. Carey guided me through the

Boston court records. Marcus A. McCorison and his superb staff at the American Antiquarian Society were, as always, lavish in both help and hospitality, especially Jo-Anne Beales, Bill Joyce, and Georgia Bumgardner. I am also obliged to my colleagues Josephine Hendin, for her encouraging comments on the work-in-progress, and Robert Raymo, for his expert advice on Mather's Latin. Michael G. Hall of the University of Texas very generously gave much time to a detailed reading of the manuscript. His unmatched knowledge of Increase Mather and of seventeenth-century New England political life spared me many errors.

Sometimes in the course of writing the book I have had in mind the rudderless ship where Whitman's captain chalks in large letters on a board, "*Be of good cheer, we will not desert you.*" For their large hearts I thank my friends Sacvan Bercovitch, Guen Chabrier, Tom and Gina Davis, Daniel Fuchs, Eugene Goldberg, Flora Kaplan, John Kuehl, Peter Shaw, and Jack Zipes. My final acknowledgments I hardly know whether to call debts or boasts, for I owe most to a beautiful young scholar and to a young man of rare integrity who happen also to be my children, Willa Zahava Silverman and Ethan Leigh Silverman.

K.S.

New York City
5 February 1983

... the *silent Saint* shall now *speak aloud* unto us: Even in *holding his Peace* he shall now *speak aloud* unto us: A *Dumb Man* shall now *speak* unto us. It shall be done, I will not say, *Miraculously,* but I hope, it will be done *Remarkably,* and very *Profitably.* The very *silence* will have in it a *Voice* to be greatly hearken'd to. And if I declare to you, That my Design is, to strike my Hearers *Dumb,* it will be a *Kindness* for them.

—*Silentiarius* (1721)

THE LIFE AND TIMES OF COTTON MATHER

I

COTTONUS MATHERUS
(1663–1686)

✌︎

He was perhaps the *principal Ornament* of this Country, and the *greatest Scholar* that was ever bred in it.

But besides his universal *Learning*; his exalted *Piety* and extensive *Charity*, his entertaining *Wit*, and singular *Goodness of Temper* recommended him to all, that were Judges of real and distinguishing Merit.

—*New-England Weekly Journal*, February 19, 1728

If young Mr. Mather publishes his father's Life I should be glad to see his memory honored with an Elogium wherein his Merits are touched with delicacy, so as to make them shine but not glare. That great Man was worthy of the utmost labors of the Muse. . . .

—ISAAC WATTS to Mather Byles, January 23, 1729

His Son . . . can have therefore no Occasion to invent any Additions to his Dear Father's History . . . indeed, if He had Published all that his Written Memorials would have enabled him, or that himself and others have been Witnesses of, He had not only swell'd the Volume to too large a size for the present Age to bear, and thereby hurt its Usefulness; but he must have also given such a full Account of this extraordinary Person as would have exceeded the Belief of those who were Strangers to him. The very bare Narration would have rather looked like the celebrated Life of *CYRUS,* and be disputed by Posterity whether it were design'd and drawn for a mixt Romance, or a real History.

—THOMAS PRINCE, Preface to Samuel Mather's *The Life of the Very Reverend and Learned Cotton Mather, D.D. & F.R.S.* (1729)

The man who is possessed of a power to act the tyrant when he thinks proper, let him become possessed of it as he may, is at least an USURPER of power that *cannot* belong to him in any free state—Power is intoxicating: There have been few men, if any, who when possessed of an *unrestrained* power, have not made a very bad use of it—They have generally exercised *such* a power to the terror both of the good and the evil, and of the good more than the evil. . . .

—"COTTON MATHER" (pen name of Samuel Adams), *Boston Gazette*, November 25, 1771

Ah pity the wretches that lived in those days,
(Ye modern admirers of novels and plays)
When nothing was suffered but musty, dull rules,
And nonsense from Mather and stuff from the schools!

—PHILIP FRENEAU, "Sketches from American
History" (1781)

When I was a boy, I met with a book entitled "Essays to do Good," which I think was written by your father. It had been so little regarded by a former possessor, that several leaves of it were torn out; but the remainder gave me such a turn of thinking, as to have an influence on my conduct through life; for I have always set a greater value on the character of a *doer of good,* than on any other kind of reputation; and if I have been, as you seem to think, a useful citizen, the public owes the advantage of it to that book.

—BENJAMIN FRANKLIN to Samuel Mather,
May 12, 1784

1

Quantum Nomen! Quanta Nomina!

⎯⎯⎯⎯⎯

ESTEEM, prestige, position, and respect belonged to Cotton Mather by birth, for his flesh and name united two of the most honored families in early New England, the Cottons and the Mathers.

Both his grandfathers were Moses-like figures, leaders and lawgivers during the great exodus of English Puritans from England to America. Richard Mather, his paternal grandfather, had studied at Oxford University and, like other Puritan ministers, was harassed for flouting the practices of the Church of England. When he admitted to an official of a church court that in his fifteen years of preaching he had never worn a surplice, he was told, *"It had been better for him, that he had gotten Seven Bastards."* Suspended from his pulpit, he migrated to Massachusetts in disguise and settled at Dorchester, where he preached for nearly thirty-four years. In addition to acting as a Harvard Overseer and working at the conversion of the Indians, he drafted the famous Cambridge Platform of 1648, by which the New England Puritans codified and published to the world their distinctive form of church government—known, because of its emphasis on the autonomy of individual congregations, as Congregationalism.

Cotton Mather's maternal grandfather, John Cotton, was also a renowned English minister, as well as a graduate of Cambridge University and the author of nearly three thousand pages of published sermons. When John Winthrop's historic fleet of four ships sailed to Massachusetts Bay in 1630, the vanguard of the Puritan hegira, it was John Cotton who preached the farewell sermon. He reminded the emigrants that after Jeroboam set up golden calves for worship, godly Israelites abandoned his kingdom and moved to Jerusalem. Thus, he implied, Scripture warranted the Puritans' own flight from idolatrous England to the New World, where they might have "liberty of the Ordinances"—liberty to observe the religious forms and ceremonies prescribed by God in the New Testament, purged of such merely human additions as the wearing of elaborate clerical vestments, the hearing of confession and praying to saints, the hierarchy of bishops and cardinals. Two years later Cotton was summoned to an ecclesiastical court to answer for his religious views. He went into hiding, and at the age of forty-eight emigrated. His congregation in England followed him to America, where he became the minister of the First Church of Boston.

The moral and political authority of Cotton Mather's grandfathers lived on in the next generation. Two of John Cotton's sons, and four of Richard Mather's, graduated from Harvard College and entered the ministry. The devotion of the two families to the Puritans' Christian Israel in America meant that eight of Cotton Mather's closest male relatives were ministers: both his famous grandfathers, five of his six uncles—and of course his father, Increase Mather.

*

Except for uncertain health, Increase Mather demonstrated even in youth that the eminence of Richard Mather would not diminish in him, but expand. Born in Dorchester on June 21, 1639, he learned Latin and Greek grammar from his father, and entered Harvard at the age of twelve. But his concerned parents withdrew him a while for private instruction, fearing the effect of the college diet, he said, on "my weak natural constitution of Body." At the age of fifteen he was first smitten by what became a lifelong ailment, "a sore disease, which was apprehended to be the stone, but I suppose it was a spice of the strangury [slow painful emission of urine]"—classic afflictions of the sedentary scholar. Terror of dying coupled with the death of his mother in 1655 produced an extremity of anguish in his soul, resulting in an experience of religious conversion followed by a considerable period of inward peace. On his eighteenth birthday he preached his first sermon; soon after he preached in Dorchester, from Richard Mather's own pulpit.

Increase improved his education and preparation for the ministry by spending the next four years abroad. His eldest brother, a minister in Dublin, encouraged him to come to Ireland. Increase wished to do so, and prevailed on his father for permission. Stricken after about a month abroad with measles and a month later with smallpox, he however recovered and took a Master's degree at Trinity College. His commencement exercises so pleased the scholars that they "did publicly *Hum* me; a vanity which I never saw practised before nor since; nor to any one but my self." For the next three years he preached in England and Guernsey. During this time he felt a troubled, prophetic intimation of impending change. The impression came with such strength that while preaching in the city of Gloucester, young as he was, he publicly prophesied that faithful witnesses of Christ must expect new suffering. Several weeks later, monarchy was restored in England after a decade of Puritan rule, bringing with it new demands for conformity to the ceremonies of the Church of England. Increase himself, as he recalled with gratification, was "persecuted out of two places . . . before I was 22 years of age." Hoping to find at least temporary shelter and greatly desiring to see his father again, he returned in September 1661 to New England. At the first sight of Richard Mather he wept abundantly—"I think the only time that I ever wept for Joy." His love was returned, for when Increase once again preached at his father's church in Dorchester, Richard Mather could hardly pronounce the blessing for his own tears.

Returned from England, Increase settled into public and domestic life. He found himself with invitations to preach from no fewer than twelve congregations. Often self-deprecating and with no very high opinion of humanity, he considered his popularity a result of his years abroad, which made him seem a stranger in Massachusetts, "and people are apt to run after strangers though they have little in them of real worth." He chose to settle where he believed he would be most serviceable for Christ and His people, in the Boston North Church. On March 6, 1662, he married Maria Cotton, the daughter of the great John Cotton, now dead. The families had been drawn together in 1656 when Richard Mather, widower, married Cotton's widow. As Increase described his marriage to his step-sister, he was "brought into acquaintance with her by means of my Fathers having married her mother."

*

The first eight years of their marriage, Increase Mather and Maria Cotton lived in the house where Maria had been born. It had been built on the slope of an eighty-foot hill known as Cotton's Hill—one of the three peaks of Trimountain, a high ridge on whose central peak a beacon was set to notify the surrounding country of danger. This ridge dominated a nearly islanded peninsula, almost completely surrounded by water but attached to the mainland by a skinny neck, so low that the spring tide sometimes washed its road. Below this ridge lay Boston.

Although settled only about thirty years, Boston was the largest town in North America, containing in 1663 about three thousand inhabitants. Most of the houses seem to have been small (not twenty of them, by a 1673 report, had ten rooms), built of wood, and set close together as in London. Many were built near the shoreline, with wharves extending into the harbor. Cobblestones paved some streets, but most were dirt, roamed by stray horses and swine. The outstanding building was the multipurpose Town House, the center of New England's civic and business life, containing the various courts of the colony and the town's free library, but serving as well for town meetings and an armory. Set at the main intersection of Boston and surrounded by many shops, it was a two-story structure with a projecting first floor upheld by ten-foot-high pillars, the spaces between which served as an open-air exchange for merchants and shipmasters.

The Mathers' house, perhaps a fifteen-minute walk from the Town House, stood on about an acre and a half of land, with fences, a garden, and fruit trees. Sir Henry Vane, an early governor of Massachusetts, had lived there and to the original building had annexed a second one. In this "double house" on a steep hill overlooking Boston, the couple's first child was born at a quarter past ten in the morning, February 12, 1663. Always mindful of the prestigious past, Increase named the child Cotton in honor of Maria's father, "the most Eminent Man of God that ever *New-England* saw."

Virtually nothing is known about Cotton Mather's early relation to his mother. Indeed very little is known about his first years as a whole, although much can be inferred from the hopes and anxieties of his father. Increase made a formidable parent: loving, encouraging, and principled, but also high-strung, morose, and mysterious. "Strong affections," as he remarked, "bring strong afflictions," and during Cotton's frequent childhood illnesses, the father's intense love for his son caused him equally intense anxiety. In October 1664 he recorded in his diary, "Fears of Cotton's death because so ill." A month later he wrote, "This day Cotton taken very ill of vomiting and purging. I troubled because loved him so strongly." The next June the child suffered "extreme pains," leaving Increase crying to God to spare his life. During a new illness with high fever two months later, Cotton, now two and a half years old and able to speak, said: "Father, Ton [i.e., Cotton] would go see God." The child's pious wish to die "went to my heart," Increase wrote, "lest Lord should take him away by death."

These and Increase's several other bouts of acute distress over Cotton's health arose not only from the child's actual illnesses and from the high infant mortality rate in New England, but also from a huge invest-ment of hope. Very early in his son's life he felt an inner supernatural conviction that Cotton had been specially chosen: "if ever Father had a particular Faith for a child, then I had so for that child, of whom I could with Assurance say, God has blessed him, yea, and He shall be blessed." And Cotton early bore out his father's certainty. By his own later account of his childhood, he learned to write before going to school and began to pray just as he began to speak, not repeating standard forms of prayers but inventing prayers for himself. In encouraging such hopeful signs, In-crease likely observed at home the parental practices he often urged on his congregation: to spend much time educating their children's minds and hearts; pray much for their conversion; explain to them sadly their corruption by nature; and charge them, with the greatest solemnity, "to know and serve the God of their Fathers."

While such nurture demanded much time and close personal supervi-sion, Increase was also often remote and forbidding. A deeply private man, he wrote on the title page of his diary some verses describing his melancholy yearning for solitude:

> Give me a Call
> To dwell
> Where no foot hath
> A Path
> There will I spend
> And End
> My wearied years
> In tears

Increase's love of withdrawal and his often-expressed dislike of visitors were in part vocational, a relish for prayer and reading that fitted him for the ministry, in keeping with the Hebraic and Puritan view of study as a form of worship. He said once that he "loved to be in no place on the Earth, so much as in my Study." Usually there by about seven in the morning, he sometimes stayed until after midnight, appearing only for meals or to supervise religious instruction and devotion in his family. He seldom spent fewer than sixteen hours a day in his study. "He lov'd this *Study,*" a contemporary wrote, "to a kind of excess, and in a manner *liv'd* in it from his Youth to a great Old Age."

Yet Increase Mather's love of privacy was personal as well. He carried the lonely austerity of his study into public life, being, as his son emphasized later, "HEART SERIOUS." While displaying the neatness, carriage, and conduct of a gentleman, his behavior was grave: *"His very Countenance carried the Force of a Sermon with it."* Contemptuous of loquacity and ornament, in both his preaching and his social life, he spoke little and plainly. This was no "Starch'd *Appearance,* and a *Tartuff* cover," his son later believed, but rather that, having a true fear of God, he guarded his heart. Some of his reserve in personal relationships he tried to foster in his children, teaching them to maintain a moderate disposition, suspect others, and suppress resentment. For instance, the "Rules of Behavior" drawn up by Cotton's brother Nathanael (born when Cotton was six) include such wary injunctions as: "Believe not all you hear, and speak not all you believe"; "Never impart that to a Friend, which may Impower him to be your Enemy"; "If you have an *Injury* done you, you do your Adversary too much Honour to take notice of it; and think too meanly of your self to Revenge it."

On larger, impersonal issues, however, Increase's solitariness assumed a militant aspect. The conviction of serving a sacred cause made many Puritans blunt, but Increase was unusual in the frequency and boldness of his displays of crotchety dissent. Indifferent to current opinion and defiant of majorities and authorities of every sort, he heeded his conscience. When he took his M.A. at Trinity College he refused to wear the customary ceremonial hood and cap. When the Restoration was proclaimed he refused to toast the new king's health, explaining he would "pray for the Kings health but drink for my own." When the celebrated aged minister Michael Wigglesworth was about to remarry—having in view a woman who was unbaptized, not yet twenty years old, and his serving maid—Increase told him tartly: "if there were an eminency of the fear of God discernible in your Damosel, notwithstanding her obscurity upon other accounts, there would be less of scandal in proceedings. But I do not hear any one but yourself speak much concerning that matter." Fearless as well, he acted as part of an underground, during Cotton's youth, hiding the regicides Goffe and Whalley from crown officials pursuing them in New England.

But Increase's inwardness went far beyond love of study, personal reserve, or feisty outspokenness. It was also a realm of mystical experience and of depressive longings for annihilation. Like others he believed that singular devotion to contemplation and prayer produced a heightened susceptibility to psychical events, *"Presagious Impressions."* Once he felt his soul strangely moved with thoughts of heaven; three days later he learned that "at *That very Time,*" a hundred miles away, his brother

Eleazer had died. Another time while praying in his study he found his heart exceedingly melted, "and me thought, I saw God before my eyes." The experience was so strong that he feared falling into a trance. Often he received strange intimations that he would shortly die; they sometimes arrived with guilty feelings of inadequacy in his ministry. On one such occasion, for instance, he recorded feeling "ashamed to think how little I have done for God and for Jesus Christ, and how short I have fallen of the obligations the Lord has brought me under." God, he sensed, "may now justly put an end to my days, and take me out of the world because I am (and ever have been) an unprofitable servant." These hints of mortality he often revealed in his published writings and sermons, and he often spoke from his pulpit, a contemporary said, "in the most solemn and affecting manner, of his *Desires to depart.*"

Whatever Increase's congregation made of his frequent announcements of his imminent death, his son can have taken them only as dreadful threats of abandonment. They already echo in Cotton's remarkable comment to him, at the age of two and a half, "Father, Ton would go see God." However loving and attentive, this was a father not easily pleased, whose attention was not guaranteed, and whose concern often seemed to lie elsewhere than here and now.

*

The years of Cotton's infancy and early childhood were for Increase Mather a period of turbulent dissatisfaction, for the church and place in which he settled left him feeling painfully unfulfilled. The North (or Second) Church had been formed in 1650, the first sermon there having been preached by his brother Samuel. The congregation had invited Increase to settle with them soon after his return from England, but he held out for two years, "finding a great averseness in my spirit to comply therewith." His aversion had several sources. Although he preached to the congregation regularly on a salaried basis, ordination meant a lifelong holy commitment to them. Distance probably also counted, for the church lay in the other, north end of Boston, perhaps a mile from his south-end home on Cotton's Hill. Many ministers in Increase's generation, too, were beginning to fall out with their congregations over such matters as salary and admissions policy. Above all, he was aware of his family's distinction and, having sampled the richness of cosmopolitan life abroad, he greatly hoped to return to England, if liberty toward Dissenters was granted.

The brethren of the church held a day of prayer asking God to incline

Increase to accept their call. The same day he felt a strong impression on his mind to do so, and relented. But he stipulated conditions: that if persecuted, insufficiently paid, in poor health, or called to greater service, he be free to move elsewhere or return to England—threats of abandonment in a different form. Obviously he accepted the invitation with intense repugnance, for the prospect of his ordination touched off a severe religious crisis. On four separate days between April 10 and 19, 1664, a month before his ordination, he recorded feeling "Dead in receiving sacrament," his heart "lifeless." Agonies of religious doubt made him listless and sleepless, fearful of being unable to preach, "Grieved, grieved, grieved, with temptations to Atheism." How long this crisis lasted is uncertain, but his son later wrote that "Furious and Boisterous *Temptations* unto *Atheism*" embittered "the more *Early Years* of his Ministry." In this mood he was ordained at the North Church on May 27, 1664, his father, Richard Mather, assisting in the ceremony.

Immediately Increase regretted his decision. He learned that some members of his church opposed offering him a substantial maintenance, and that a motion had even come before the legislature to ask the church to forbear ordaining him altogether. These "unworthy dealings" made him feel, just a month after his ordination, that he would rather suffer under prelacy in England than stay in Boston and "suffer under them that looked upon as godly *[sic]*." As he settled into his ministry, other members of the church criticized him for grousing over his pay, threatening to leave, or acting dictatorially, so that he found himself not only feeling unappreciated but also unable to study or to sleep, and owing money to his butcher. For three years he complained about his wretched situation in his diaries, his grievances alternating with anguished exclamations of religious doubt:

> Many thoughts of heart whether to continue in Boston. Strong inclinations to move to Connecticut.
> . . . much troubled and disturbed in my spirit to think how little encouragement and how much disrespect I have met with in Boston.
> Melancholy and inclination to leave Boston because of the miserable uncertain maintenance. . . .
> Heart full of sad thoughts.

His resentment of his inadequate salary was allayed when some wealthy persons joined his church and contributed extra money for his support. Later in life he grew more affectionate toward his flock, but he never wholly overcame or stopped speaking of his desire to return to England, "to follow my studies and increase learning, and where I might have suitable encouragement in outward respects."

What must have been a discontented household mood during Cotton Mather's first few years was aggravated by the inevitable bickering of a young couple, however pious, learning to live together. Not much is known about Maria Cotton, two years younger than Increase. Both her husband and her son later praised her affection, godliness, and self-sacrificing nature. Increase described her as a woman of a "very loving tender disposition" who strove never to displease him: "Her honor for me was too great. For She has said to many, that She thought I was the best Husband, and the best man in the whole world." Given his solitary temperament and vocation, he also saw her as an ideal wife: "I kept close to my Study, and committed the management of the affairs of the Family to her." Cotton clearly felt loved by her and later praised her as a pattern of piety: a woman who read over the Bible perhaps twice a year, performed private devotions perhaps six times a day, kept whole days of fasting and prayer, and was humble, modest in attire, and charitable to the poor.

But these eulogies came forty years later. Increase's diaries for the earliest years of his marriage offer few glimpses of Maria, and they all reveal less sugar than vinegar. Hardly three months after Cotton's birth, he found his wife also dissatisfied with him. When he asked her "in a loving way" to explain just how he had misconducted himself, she said she "expected no good either for soul or body" from him, for he "was never like to have any." Some people, she assured him, considered it "a 1000 pities" that she had married him; if she wanted, she "might have had better." Next month Increase recorded that Maria felt ill-requited in her esteem for him: "you set down my bad and I set down your good," she said. And she added a dash of venom: "if my bad ones be no more than your good ones they not very many." Another ambiguous entry suggests that Maria was distressed by Increase's complaints about Boston, and by living with her new husband and infant son in her father's house (and perhaps with her mother): "This morning my wife desired me with tears to leave her fathers house, wishing that I would rather leave Boston than live here, because her mother had spoken to her &c."

In the fall of 1669, when Cotton was six, Increase succumbed to serious emotional difficulties. They may have been precipitated by the death, that April, of his father. Now blind in one eye, Richard Mather became ill at Increase's house with a violent fit of the stone and was taken home to Dorchester to die a week later. That fall, Increase himself experienced extreme pain in his left side and a violent fever that "brought me to the gates of death." These subsided but gave way to "Hypochondriacal affection," that is, melancholy or depression. The depression shut Increase in for the winter, incapacitating him for preaching until March 1670, and then "very weak in body." Around the spring of 1671 he began suffering attacks of "Ephialtes," severe nightmares later described by his son as "little short of Mortal." His considerable medical reading taught him that victims of Ephialtes were vulnerable to apoplexy, epilepsy, or mania. He became persuaded (or, as he put it later, Satan took advantage of his melancholy to persuade him, "though there was no ground for it") that his own fate would be mania.

The possibility of going insane filled Increase with "inexpressible sorrows and fears." For several weeks he lodged at Lynn to drink from its noted spring, on the widespread theory that "melancholy Hypochondriacal vapors" originated in the spleen and might be remedied by mineral waters. But the nightmares returned almost every night, depriving him of rest and leading him to fear that his faith in God to relieve him would prove a delusion. Despite periods of revival and sound sleep, the nightmares persisted through the summer and fall, waking him before day, convincing him that "my Ephialtes would issue in a Mania." Pouring out his heart, he begged God either to answer his prayers for survival or to deny them. This prolonged bout of Ephialtes seems to have passed in the fall of 1671, but he suffered terrifying nightmares recurrently throughout the rest of his life.

During this period, probably in 1671, the family moved into a new house, in the other, north, end of Boston. What occasioned the move is unknown; perhaps Increase's emotional state or Maria's unhappiness over residing in her father's house, or simple convenience. The new house was only a short walk from the North Church, to whom it belonged, and the family was growing. By about the time of the move, Cotton was one of five Mather children, a new infant having arrived every two years: Maria (March 1665), Elizabeth (January 1667), Nathanael (July 1669), and Sarah (November 1671)—for each of whom Increase prayed each day and night by name, except when ill and unable to pray at all.

Cotton later called the North End "the Island of *North-Boston*." It was in fact a genuine island, roughly the shape of a reversed **P**. The stem of the **P** was separated from the South End of Boston by a canal, spanned by two drawbridges. Larger bodies of water surrounded the bowl of the **P**: the Mill Pond (which worked a grist mill and a saw mill), the Charles River, and Boston Harbor. This was a compact, brisk shipbuilding and commercial area with many wharves and coffee houses, described by a visitor in 1663 as "the most elegant and populous part of the town." In addition to the many merchants and shipbuilders who wished to live near their warehouses and wharves, the street traffic thickened with travelers to or from Charlestown, Cambridge, or the north, who needed to use the Charlestown ferry. The most conspicuous features of the neighborhood were the Mill Creek, in which butchers cast entrails and garbage, and windmill hill (later Copp's Hill), rising about fifty feet from the sea, the burial ground of the North Church. Increase's life and his family's centered in the part of the End known as Clark's Square, an important social district near which lived many families of wealth and consequence. Here, only a street or so from the wharves extending into Boston Harbor, stood the North Church, apparently built, like the two other Boston meeting-houses, of clapboards and shingles, its bell ringing out at nine each night and five each morning.

By moving near his flock Increase did not improve his relation to them. In debt and oppressed by "outward wants and Family straits," he began compiling a fresh list of resentments, praying to Christ either to move his people to give him a comfortable living or to "remove me to another people who will take care of me." The indifference of some members of his congregation to his welfare again stirred angry, sorrowful fantasies of departure and death. Only his absence would make him appreciated: "When I am gone, my poor people will believe that the grief which I sustained by their neglects of me and mine, was unprofitable for them." Worse, Increase's pinching circumstances hindered his studies and his ministry. He could be content to be poor, he wrote at the end of 1672, as long as he could serve God undistractedly: "but to be in debt to the dishonor of the Gospel, is a wounding killing thought to me; yea so grievous as that if it be not remedied in a little Time it will bring me with sorrow to my grave."

*

From the time of the family's move, just before or after 1671, come the first substantial details of Cotton Mather's life. Some survive in forms that invite omission and distortion, accounts written long after the events by family members with didactic, apologetic, or self-justifying motives. Even so, they make clear part of what it meant to grow up a Cotton and a Mather, and the son of Increase Mather.

Not surprisingly, Cotton's piety was precocious. Before he was able to take notes in church while listening to his father and other preachers, he would come home from the service and write out what he remembered.

He read Scripture ardently, for a time nothing less than fifteen chapters a day, divided into morning, noon, and night exercises. Presumably emulating his father's paternal and ministerial pedagogy, with a touch of his own ingenuity, he composed prayers for his school friends and "Obliged them to *Pray*." He also "Rebuked my Play-mates, for their Wicked *Words* and *Ways*." As a result, he learned at the age of seven or eight that part of the meaning of being a Mather was to undergo ingratitude. For his playmates did not always take his concern for their souls kindly: "Sometimes I Suffered from them, the persecution of not only *Scoffs*," he recalled, "but *Blows* also, for my Rebukes." Increase responded to this like someone whose father had been persecuted for not wearing a surplice and who had himself been harassed out of two places before the age of twenty-two. He seemed "very *Glad*, Yea, almost *Proud*, of my Affronts; and I then wondered at it, tho' afterwards, I better understood his Heavenly Principle."

In study and learning Cotton was equally precocious and equally a Mather. For his formal schooling he attended the public school in the South End run by the gifted poet Benjamin Tompson and then by the legendary Ezekiel Cheever, the first great schoolmaster in America. A teacher in Boston for thirty-eight years, Cheever combined in his teaching Christian piety and classical learning. A sort of "*Christian Terence*," as Cotton later described him, he not only labored to improve his sdents' Latin prose style but also prayed with them daily, catechized them weekly, and dressed plainly to set them an example of Puritan tradition. Cheever praised Cotton's diligence, but how much of his classical learning Cotton got from Cheever and how much from his father or on his own is unclear. Cotton's constitution being "Tender and Weakly," and the school being in the other end of Boston, the anxious Increase kept him home during the winter. Cotton spent the time reading church history and developing his budding facility and love for language. Able even earlier to write out what he remembered of sermons and to create prayers, by around the age of eleven he had read in Cato, Tully, Ovid, and Virgil, gone through a great part of the New Testament in Greek, "read considerably" in Homer, and begun Hebrew grammar. He now spoke Latin "so readily" that he could not only write notes of sermons as the preacher spoke in church, but even write them in Latin while the preacher spoke in English.

By 1674 Cotton had mastered the entrance requirements for Harvard College and was admitted, he wrote later, "upon a Strict Examination of the President and Fellows." No account of his examination remains, but the college laws required for admission a working knowledge of Latin and Greek, and signs of academic promise:

> When any Scholar is able to read and understand Tully Virgil or any such ordinary Classical Authors, and can readily make and speak or write true Latin in prose and hath Skill in making verse, and is Competently grounded in the Greek Language; so as to be able to Construe and Grammatically to resolve ordinary Greek, as in the Greek Testament, Isocrates, and the minor poets, or such like, having withal meet Testimony of his towardliness, he shall be capable of his admission into the College.

Increase Mather entered Harvard at the age of twelve; his son entered at the age of eleven and a half—the youngest student admitted to the college in its history.

Cotton's brilliant entrance, however, was flawed. He had developed a stammer. For a Mather, of course, such a handicap was all but ruinous. The firstborn son of a rising minister, the grandson of two famous ministers, and the nephew of five other ministers, there was no question but that he would be raised for the ministry himself. Yet the stammer, he wrote later, made such a career " a Thing as much despaired of, as anything in the World." Increase saw what his son's impediment meant for the tasks of preaching and public prayer, and worried "lest the Hesitancy in his speech should make him uncapable of improvement in the work of the ministry, whereunto I had designed him." On October 7, 1674, he fasted and prayed in concern over Cotton's stammer, calling him and Maria into his study, where they prayed together, and with "many Tears bewailed our sinfullness, and begged of God mercy in this particular." He resolved to trust in God and let Him do what He saw good, whether He chose to remove the impediment or not.

Just when and why Cotton Mather's stammer manifested itself is uncertain. However speculative, the question deserves brief discussion because feelings about his speech guided or colored many of his later activities, sometime subtly. Increase first mentions the stammer in his diary of October 1674, a few months into Cotton's freshman year at Harvard. Only portions of this diary have survived, however, and the diaries for the preceding six years, which may have contained entries concerning Cotton's stammer, are missing. Thus the affliction may have developed well before 1674. In fact stuttering, to use the current term, can begin even before the third year; most stutterers, eighty-five to ninety percent, begin stuttering before the age of eight. The notion of an onset to stuttering is itself misleading, since nearly all children have some natural disfluency of speech. A child "begins" stuttering when its disfluency first strikes a parent as abnormal, or when some provocations abruptly intensify it. The likelihood that Cotton's speech problems began several years before the age of eleven is strengthened by a later remark of his son Samuel. An *"uncommon Impediment in his Speech,"* he wrote about his father, appeared "from his Cradle."

In explaining the causes of stuttering, modern speech pathologists differ, some emphasizing the organic, others the psychological. Cotton's several childhood ailments may have contributed, since many stutterers seem to have had rheumatic fever and scarlet fever. But even most authorities who emphasize physiology grant importance to psychological influences. As the son of a father to whom great affections meant great afflictions, who spent sixteen hours daily in his study and welcomed his son's chastisement by the ungodly, Cotton Mather fits a widely accepted model of stutterers as "sensitive" children of overanxious and perfectionist parents who set lofty standards of achievement and conduct. That Increase Mather was a man who garnered invitations to preach from a dozen different congregations cannot have helped; extra pressure is created when a child's parents or siblings are endowed with particularly effective speech that is an object of family pride. Even if exceptionally good speech has never been demanded of some minister's or lawyer's or teacher's son, one authority writes, it is "reasonably sure that he inflicted on himself all of the consequences of such demands merely in the natural process of competing with his father."

Whether Cotton Mather's stutter began in early childhood or close to puberty, and whatever its causes, it exposed him to ridicule and made him highly self-conscious and highly sensitive to criticism of what he said. "I know one, who had been very much a *Stammerer,*" he wrote late in his life, " and no words can tell, how much his Infirmity did Encumber and Embitter the first years of his Pilgrimage." Speaking impersonally but evidently from distressing personal experience, he described the stutterer's tension and embarrassment in speech situations, "when he feels God continually *Binding* of him; and when Every *Business* and Every *Company,* wherewith he is concerned, puts him in *Pain,* how to get thro' the *Speaking Part* which he has before him." Even more painfully, people of no goodness or breeding subject him to *"Inhumane Derision,"* so that he feels unfit for, and perhaps averse to, the delights of human society. The "one" he knew, Mather wrote, poured out to Christ "Thousands of *Supplications* for a *Free Speech.*"

Christ was not the only Comforter, for the closeness of Puritan social and family ties meant that Cotton need not struggle with his humiliation alone. Besides praying at home with his concerned parents, he received a visit in his chamber at Harvard (probably after freshman year) from Elijah Corlet, an aged, famous schoolmaster and a sympathetic person. Corlet told him: "*My Friend,* I now Visit you for nothing, but only to Talk with you about the *Infirmity* in your *Speech,* and offer you my Advice about it; Because I suppose tis a Thing that greatly Trouble [*sic*] you." Observing that no one ever stuttered when singing psalms (many stutterers can sing fluently), he advised Cotton to speak very deliberately, with a "a *Drawling* that shall be little short of *Singing.*" He illustrated the method by reciting the first verse in Homer and prolonging every syllable. The drawling, he suggested, was at least preferable to stuttering, and would give him time to command his thoughts and to substitute a pronounceable word for one that he anticipated might be blocked. And by using the method for a while he would soon become habituated to speaking correctly, and by degrees grow able to speak at a normal pace, "Tho' my Advice is," he concluded, "Beware of *Speaking too fast,* as Long as you Live."

*

Other problems than his stutter faced Cotton Mather at Harvard. At the time of his admission, physical, demographic, and administrative problems had put the school in the sorriest state in its history. Because Harvard was the training ground for the New England ministry, its sinking condition long remained a matter of deep public concern. Set on a large plain, the physical college consisted essentially of the President's house, a small brick Indian school, and the College Hall, making a compact unit around the college yard. But the Indian college was little used and was maintained as a printing house. The College Hall, a two-story wood building enclosing most of the college facilities (library, recitation hall, dormitory, and study), was collapsing, and by 1677 became uninhabitable. A large new brick hall was under construction at public expense, but probably no students moved in until the spring of 1678, just months before Cotton's graduation.

No ampler facilities were in a sense needed, because the number of college-age boys in the families that had founded and used the school had dwindled, threatening its very existence. When Cotton attended, Harvard enrolled perhaps no more than twenty students all together; his own class had only four. Administration was erratic. Between 1672 and 1685 no fewer than thirteen official attempts were made to retain a president, resulting in a succession of short-term administrations. When Cotton entered, the president was Leonard Hoar, a Harvard graduate himself (1650), recently returned to Boston after taking a medical degree in England. A man with lively scientific interests and a friend of the English chemist Robert Boyle, he hoped to raise funds toward building an arboreum, a chemical laboratory, and an "ergasterium for mechanic fancies," and by these means to effect Harvard's "resuscitation from its ruins."

But in the depleted state of the college neither President Hoar nor Cotton Mather prospered. Cotton's student life under Hoar seems to have begun auspiciously. The president assigned him for his first declamation a topic that acknowledged his family's achievement and his own promise: "Telemacho *veniet, vivat modo, fortior AEtas*"—that the son of Ulysses might one day be even braver than his father. But at the moment Cotton Mather was an eleven-year-old boy and probably already a stutterer, among students whose ages ranged from about fifteen to eighteen. After only a month or two at college he returned home. He had received, Increase wrote, "some discouragement . . . by reason that some of the scholars threatened him, &c., as apprehending that he had told me of their miscarriages." Unfortunately the nature of the discouragement, the threats, and the miscarriages is entirely unknown. But Cotton may have stayed home the rest of his freshman year, studying with his father and on his own.

President Hoar fared even worse. The General Court (Massachusetts' bicameral legislature) held an extraordinary session in October 1674 to deal with the college's "languishing and decaying condition." Because of the paucity of students, it dismissed all of the school's salaried officers, and ruled that if by the next Court the college was in the same condition Hoar would be dismissed. Next month all but three students left. In March Hoar resigned his presidency and by the winter he was dead. Increase, prone to attribute death to ingratitude, believed Hoar was "brought into a consumption by the grief he sustained through afflictions when President of the college." By the time Cotton returned for his sophomore year the college had a new president, the minister of Cambridge, Urian Oakes.

The change in administration apparently did not ease Cotton's difficult situation at Harvard. His discomfort may even have grown, because a few days before Hoar resigned, Increase Mather accepted an appointment by the college Overseers as a nonresident Fellow of the college, and then became active in its affairs, not always helpfully. When he learned that students were saying he desired the presidency, he rode to Cambridge to complain to President Oakes, who assured him everyone knew he could have the presidency if he desired it and prayed him for the good of the college to bear with the students' "Jealousy." Increase made equally plain his anger over his son's treatment at the school. Less than a month into Cotton's sophomore year, Increase was troubled to learn that he had been "abused" by some students. Like the "discouragement" Cotton received as a freshman, the nature of this "abuse" is unknown—perhaps hazing and fagging, or some taunt for his stutter. But it was presumably what goaded Increase into riding to Cambridge to speak with Oakes and one of the Fellows about withdrawing his son again. Understandably, given the Mather name and the few students, they resisted. Increase did at least remove Cotton from under the instruction of his current tutor, and may have again kept him home a while. In September he also threatened to resign his position as Fellow because he too, he said, "had been so abused," and because the Corporation had dealt with him grievously in summoning students to ask them "who told tales to me"—which may have figured in Cotton's abuse. Deeply protective toward the young, however strict, he also complained to the Overseers about the general practice of hazing freshmen.

The demoralized atmosphere at the college during Cotton's sophomore year was deepened by a violent event, which his father claimed to have foreseen. Early in 1674 Increase felt persistent intimations that God would strike New England by sword. Believing that when God intended heavy judgments He often forewarned some servant, he preached two sermons on Ezekiel 7:7: The day of Trouble is near. The summer of 1675 fulfilled his prophecy. King Philip's War erupted, almost wholly destroying more than a dozen towns, and leaving many Indians from several tribes slaughtered, sold into slavery, or dead of exposure in what for them was a virtual war of annihilation. By one estimate almost every person in Boston lost a relation or near friend; the debt incurred by Massachusetts seems to have exceeded the value of the whole personal property of its inhabitants.

While Cotton was enrolled at the college in the winter and spring of 1675–76, towns such as Medfield, Groton, and Rehoboth suffered bloody and fiery raids. The fighting came within twenty miles of Boston; ongoing construction of the new College Hall was suspended. Cotton witnessed his father's many prayers to God for victory, and believed them efficacious. Increase set apart a special day to beseech God to cut off the Indian leader, King Philip, by a providential stroke. In "less than a Week, after This," Cotton recalled, *"the Thing was Accomplished."* Philip was shot and quartered, Boston receiving his hands, Plymouth his head. Cotton later recalled how with his own hands he detached Philip's jaw from his skull.

The war hardly ended when Cotton, now nearly fourteen, understood himself to have witnessed the accomplishment of another of his father's prophecies. Increase had become "strongly possessed" with fears that Boston would be punished by a judgment of fire. On November 19, 1676, he again preached his congregation a warning sermon. But he found them unmoved. When he went home he paced his study, weeping, saying, *"O Lord God, I have told this people in thy Name that thou art about to cut off dwellings, but they will not believe me."* Maria did not trust his prophetic sense either. He feared their house would burn, and urged her to move from it with him and the children. Unawed and unpersuaded, she considered his forebodings "only a phansy in my head."

Increase frequently suffered from insomnia, but the fact that he was awake at about five o'clock in the morning on November 27 he attributed to Providence: "God (and I believe his Angels) did so influence that I could not sleep that morning," he wrote. Smelling something, he rose and looked out the window. Then, "some began to cry fire."

Cotton Mather saw his family's house burn down, in a conflagration that also destroyed his father's meetinghouse and threatened to consume Boston. Breaking out in a building opposite the Mathers' house from a carelessly set candle, the fire headed on wind toward the Mathers' living quarters. Increase's immediate thought was to get the children out of the house. Next he tried to save his many manuscripts and his more than a thousand books, whose loss "would more afflict me," he said, "than to be deprived of all other outward effects." He went to his much loved study and—apparently with the house aflame—gave his most valuable manuscripts to Cotton to carry off. Then he began throwing books down the stairs as fast as he could. Before he managed to clear the study people called to him that if he stayed longer he would be killed.

Increase lost by fire about eighty books, his father's letters, a trunk of his mother's writings, the winter provision in the cellar, the clothing in the garret, and some English money and gold that were filched, seemingly while his goods lay in the street. But he rescued the beds, bedding, linens, most of the chairs, and—the "great mercy"—a thousand books and most of his manuscripts. Luckily for history these included a work he then had in his library, the manuscript of William Bradford's *History of Plymouth Plantation*. By one account the fire devoured about forty-five dwellings, the North Church, and several warehouses, leaving seventy or eighty families homeless. Except for a heavy downpour of rain it would probably have destroyed the whole North End and endangered Charlestown also, for fireflakes drifted over the river and fell there on houses and barns.

After the fire the Mathers stayed a few days with John Richards, a prominent member of the North Church, then moved for a while to another house. For six months Increase preached at the other Boston meetinghouses, until his church was rebuilt. In October 1677 he bought some land near the North Church, which probably became the site of what he called "the house which was built for me" (presumably by his congregation). Still standing in the nineteenth century, it was then described as a two-story building with dormer windows, complemented by a large garden and orchard.

*

No record remains of Cotton's childhood thoughts and feelings about King Philip's War, or the burning of his home, or his abuse by fellow students. But in later life he could study and work productively amid heavy personal burdens, and even as he reached puberty, his powers of concentration were great. Despite his trials he seems to have breezed through the required junior and senior curriculum at Harvard. Although the college trained ministers, it was not a divinity school, but rather aimed at educating both religious and civic leaders. Its 1650 charter declared that the school intended to educate young men "in all manner of good literature, arts, and sciences." While the first two years of study emphasized Greek, Hebrew, and logic, the third introduced ethics, and the fourth included metaphysics, mathematics, rhetoric, oratory and theology.

Cotton later wrote that before the age of fourteen he composed Hebrew exercises and "*Ran* thro' the other Sciences, that *Academical Studies* ordinarily fall upon"—apparently meaning that he completed most of the curriculum by the middle of his junior year. By then he had also composed systems of logic and physics that were used by other students; had advanced in arithmetic (never his strong subject, he admitted) "as far as was Ordinary"; and had learned "the Use of the *Globes*" (and drawn a map of New England that was sent to his uncle Nathaniel, a minister in Dublin). By following Elijah Corlet's advice to speak very deliberately he gained at least enough fluency to enable him to make the required declamations. Already a prodigious reader, he had also "read over" hundreds of books. Several of the first books he owned as a student have survived, such as Wilhelm Schickard's *Horologium Hebraeum* (1639; a Hebrew grammar) and Archibald Simson's *Hieroglyphica Animalium Terrestrium* (1622; on natural history). Passed from father to son, they bear Increase Mather's name as the previous owner and donor, and beneath that the inscription "Cottonus Matherus, 1674."

Cotton usually took for his student declamations some article of natural philosophy, that is, of science. Significantly for his later life, he was attending a school that sanctioned and taught the Copernican view of the universe, and that owned a three-and-a-half-foot telescope. His stutter played into his scientific interests, for at some time during his college years the impediment led him almost to despair of becoming a minister, and to apply himself to becoming a physician. As an unsought result, he began imagining he had "almost every *Distemper* that I read of, in my studies." To cure his fancied maladies he sometimes administered medicines to himself, not only needlessly but also hurtfully.

Cotton came down with a real malady as well. And as happened to his father when he was afflicted with urological ailments in adolescence, this illness, or another close to it in time, brought on a religious crisis. At about the age of fourteen he fell into "great Symptoms of an *Hectic*" (extreme emaciation), severe enough to make him think, "*I am going apace to the Gates of the Grave, I am deprived of the Residue of my Years.*" Even before he became ill, his "diverse Miscarriages" had made him suspect he had never truly been moved by God's Spirit, that he was but a "*Refined Hypocrite.*" With the onset of his illness, and of fear that he would die, his suspicions became gnawing. He trembled to think, he recalled later, that after his high hopes for himself and the commendation of others, he would turn out to be a "*Castaway.*" His life at Harvard may have aggravated his self-doubt. His first extant letter, likely written in his senior year, speaks not only of his "deceitful heart" but also of "residing in a place of much temptation" where he is "debarred the special opportunities of seeking and seeing the face of God, which have once been enjoyed." Apparently he meant that being at Cambridge he could not regularly hear his father preach, although during his last two years he very often returned to Boston for Increase's Sunday sermon, and occasionally for his Thursday lecture.

For whatever reasons, Cotton labored under a sense of his vileness and unacceptableness to God. He confided his worries to Increase, who told him there was no repentant sinner whom Christ would not freely accept. His father's assurances quickened his spirit. While praying and thinking of being reconciled to God he felt "Strange, and Strong, and

Sweet Intimations" that Christ had accepted him. Once while praying he experienced what seemed a genuine influx of divine grace: "I sensibly felt an unaccountable *Cloud* and *Load* go off my Spirit," he recalled, "and from that Minute I was as much altered, by a New *Light*, and *Life*, and *Ease* arriving to me, as the Sunrise does change the World, from the Condition of *Midnight*."

During his last two years at Harvard Cotton also began to expand and refine his religious life in general. In 1676 he started taking detailed notes on sermons he heard, and the next year began serving as an amanuensis for his father, transcribing important documents into his church records. Around the same age he began to observe entire days of private prayer and fasting, and seems to have seriously begun the Puritan devotional art of meditation, trying to devise a logical daily method and even writing a discourse on the practice. Now or perhaps in his first year after graduation, he also joined a society of pious young men who met the evening following every Sabbath to pray, sing psalms, and propose devout questions. At these meetings he made some "*Probationary Essays*" toward the ministry, presumably attempting to preach impromptu sermons.

*

At the Commencement Day exercises for the class of 1678, President Urian Oakes regaled the audience with a copious Latin oration, in which he remarked that Cotton Mather, at the age of fifteen, already showed signs that he would emulate and honor his father, his two prestigious grandfathers, and his five uncles. Part of his oration he addressed, in his wittily florid style, to the new baccalaureate himself, to "COTTONUS MATHERUS."

"*Quantum Nomen!*" Oakes said, What a Name! Or rather, he corrected himself, "*quanta Nomina!*" What Names! He would say nothing of the boy's reverend father, in the audience, since he did not wish to praise him to his face. But if this youth, he continued in Latin, brought back in himself the piety, learning, ingenuity, judgment, prudence, and gravity of his reverend forebears he could be said to have done his part well. And President Oakes believed that would happen:

> ...*nec despero futurum, ut in hoc Juvene*
> COTTONUS *atq;* MATHERUS *tam re quam*
> *Nomine coalescant et reviviscant,—*

"I do not despair that in this youth COTTON and MATHER shall in fact as in name coalesce and revive."

2

The Solemnest Work in the World

❦

THE MINISTRY, for which Cotton Mather had been designed since birth, was both the main public role in Puritan culture and a transcendent, sacred calling. *"To preach the unsearchable Riches of Christ,"* Cotton knew, to nurture in others that miraculous transformation of being signifying their salvation, was "the Solemnest Work in the World," and for five years he prepared himself with exhausting dedication.

In his sixteenth year Cotton was admitted by rite to the North Church and began preaching informally to neighbors. He inaugurated his formal career by acknowledging his dual Cotton and Mather descent. He preached his first public sermon, on August 22, 1680, at his grandfather Richard Mather's church in Dorchester; the next Sabbath he preached for his father in Boston; and the Sabbath after that he preached in the Boston church once led by his grandfather John Cotton. His early efforts won praise and notice. The brethren of Increase's church voted in September to have Cotton assist his father in preaching, as a ministerial candidate, once every two weeks or oftener. Flattering letters reached him and his father from ministers and church members in Ireland, the West Indies, and both Englands, praising him as a "hopefull sprout," observing his "extraordinary pregnancy," comparing him to young Timothy. One woman told Increase in 1681 that she had come into a Boston shop to buy spectacles when his son, whom she had never seen before, walked in. It surprised her to "so fix my eyes upon one I did not know," yet the boy seemed so grave and becoming that "I could not forbear asking him if he were not a Mather." Cotton was aware of it himself. *"Lord,"* he prayed, *"I know Thou will signalize me, as thou hast my Father, my Grandfathers, and my Uncles before me. Hallelujah."*

24

But that Cotton would be signalized was not so certain. For a day or two before preaching his first public sermons he felt "horribly *Buffeted* and *Unhinged,*" his efforts even to pray for deliverance hobbled by mental confusion. By crying earnestly to Christ he managed to perform the service comfortably, but at around the same time he was shaken, like his father, by Ephialtes or nightmares, which sometime "handled me so Severely" that he expected to become apoplectic, or to die. These too he alleviated by prayer, and by eating no meat and taking an herbal remedy made of peony. But there were other fears also, including, several times during his candidacy, the threat of his father's imminent death. Spitting blood and thought to be consumptive, Increase became so ill in 1680 that between mid-April and early September he could not administer communion, and had to baptize his daughter Hannah not in church but at home. Nor was Increase ever ill quietly. Dissatisfied with his ministry and feeling that his destiny lay in England, he often used his illness to repay the ungrateful, warning them that his soul was about to take flight. All New England prayed for him when he became ill in 1681; another illness in 1683 sent rumors throughout Boston and surrounding towns that he was dying or dead.

Cotton feared being left alone by Increase, partly because Puritan culture stressed entire dependence on one's father for a model of behavior. Ideal children, he remarked in a later sermon, "are not mere *Pictures,* which may have something of the figure and feature in them, but they are Children that will *talk* and *walk* just like their father." Thus when Increase fell ill, Cotton importuned that he "may not therewith be taken from us; but still be continued as our Watchman, many days." When Increase recovered, he often thanked God for "a *Father,* given me from the Dead." Often he prayed for the "Life and Health of my dear *Father,* whom I may reckon among the richest of my Enjoyments."

Increase's grave illnesses cannot have eased the burblingly confused state of love, envy, rivalry, and dependence in which Cotton prepared to join his father in the ministry of the North Church. In addition, Puritan culture prescribed that parents' love should be returned more largely. Preaching to some young people in 1683, Cotton urged: "You should endeavor to *requite* your parents, for whom, I profess to you, you can *never do enough.*" Feeling that he too could never do enough for his father, he frequently served as Increase's amanuensis, copying over his sermons and tracts, and transcribing some of the manuscript of his celebrated *Remarkable Providences.* By such means he no doubt wished to honor and repay the father who had counseled him and prayed fervently for his health and salvation. But to display loyalty and admiration might also secure Increase's uncertain devotion to him, perhaps magically insure his continued life. Voluminously he wrote down his father's words as Increase preached in church, his notes on his father's sermons from the beginning of 1683 to February 1684 filling around two hundred pages. The nature of some of his favors to Increase, too, suggests a desire to demonstrate to him his own disinterest in competition. For instance, he gave his father several gifts. At the age of eighteen he bought Increase a Spanish Indian servant. Two years later he and some acquaintances offered to pay for the publication in London of some of Increase's discourses. He also owned a watch with a "Variety of Motions," of which Increase was "desirous." Although very fond of the watch himself, he presented it to his father, thinking, *"I owe him a great deal more than this."*

Cotton was correct in believing he could *"never do enough"* for his father; although throughout his son's candidacy Increase often prayed for the preservation of his life and the success of his service to God, he opposed Cotton's joining him in the ministry of the North Church. The brethren appointed the young man as a probationary preacher to them in 1680, but he was not ordained for another five years. In that period the church voted seven times for his continuance with them and, with growing annoyance, for his permanent settlement. Their frequently expressed desire to have Cotton as a colleague with his father partly arose from the scarcity of New England–trained ministers, corresponding to the drop in enrollment at Harvard, and probably also from their apprehension of being left without a minister by Increase's death. But they desired Cotton also because he proved himself an effective preacher, as appears in the language of their votes, which "earnestly desire" his continuance, and praise "the ministerial gifts wherewith the Lord hath graciously endowed" him.

How intently the North Church sought Cotton became particularly clear in the fall of 1681, when the Harvard administration voted to make Increase president of the college. However dissatisfied with his congregation in relatively urban Boston, Increase disdained rustic Cambridge, and interpreted the vote as a slight. Exactly twenty years before he had preached his first sermons in Boston, he grumbled, "and now I am voted out of the Town." He did preside over the 1681 commencement, at which he handed Cotton his M.A. degree. But he told the Overseers he could not accept the presidency without the consent of his church. They opposed the appointment not only because they wished to keep Increase as their minister but also, they explained, because they hoped Cotton might be "settled among us with his father," and that for them to release Increase was "a likely way to be deprived of them both."

Yet Increase did not want the North Church to have them both. He antagonized his flock, many of whom, he noticed, "seemed to be troubled" at his opposition to Cotton's settlement. Indeed the family's pride in dynastic succession makes Increase's resistance puzzling. Considering that he felt mistreated by his congregation, he may have been galled by their enthusiasm for his son; or he may have feared Cotton's rivalry and possible dissent. Perhaps he simply wished to avoid any suspicion of nepotism. He may even have been speaking for Cotton, who may have felt unready for ordination at this time. That seems unlikely, but it jibes with the explanation later given by Cotton's son Samuel. Cotton declined ordination by the church, Samuel wrote, "*partly* because they were not in extreme *Want,* having his *Father* with them, who was hearty and strong [as Increase certainly was not], and partly from a *modest* Opinion, and low Apprehension of himself and his Talents." Perhaps it was true both that Increase opposed Cotton's ordination and that Cotton feared it. Whatever the case, Increase told his flock that he did not wish to share his pulpit with his son. When one of his illnesses led him to advise the brethren to seek his replacement, they unanimously elected Cotton. But Increase explained that he was "very backward in consenting to their desires because of my Relation to him."

Cotton also received many invitations in 1681 and 1682 from the church at New Haven. Citizens and public officials of the town wrote to Increase to say that having heard so much and so well of his son they would count it "a great favor from God, if we may enjoy his ministry among us." They recognized, however, that Cotton had become popular at the North Church, and told Increase that "your son is so dear and precious to your society that it will be a breaking thing to part with him." These warm and persistent invitations proved awkward for Cotton. He told the New Haven church that his removal from Boston would turn the flock against his father, "if after so many Importunate *Votes* of theirs, for my Settlement here, he had any way permitted my Removal from them." In at least one sense, and probably more, his reply was disingenuous. Having been taught to "walk and talk" like his father, he no more wanted to preach in rustic New Haven than his father to dwell in Cambridge. By birth and disposition he had been designed, and now designed himself, for larger service, for the North Church in Boston, "as *Great* a Place, as any in these Parts of the World."

Yet Increase seems to have advised his son to accept the second-rate offer from New Haven. Later in life Cotton wrote that his father "(I thought) Encouraged me, to Accept an Invitation to a *Small* and *Mean Congregation.*" Whether the church involved was at New Haven or somewhere else, and whether the uneasy parenthesis indicates skepticism or continued resentment, Cotton considered the offer beneath him and found his father's advice that he accept it deflating. The "Humiliations," he later wrote, of "Leading an obscure Life among the poor Husbandmen, assaulted my Mind with sore Discouragements."

*

Cotton spent much of the five years of his candidacy in battering, tireless self-examination. To accept ordination he must be sure he was no longer a creature driven unawares by sin, but one to whom God had granted the grace to perceive, and thus the desire to live for, God's goodness. And anguishingly he recognized, as all Puritans did, that to dispel unloving and rebellious feelings in himself—his portion of the universal legacy of original sin—was beyond his doing. No more than the blind can force themselves to see could he overcome his sinful nature by Scripture reading, self-persuasion, or any act of his will. To purge himself required the supernatural work of God's Holy Spirit on his heart, transforming his entire way of feeling about the world. "O undertake for me, Deliver me," he cried, "*My Diseases are so complicated, that I am not able so much as distinctly to mention them unto thee; much less can I remedy them.*"

To discern whether such a deliverance had taken place in him was the wracking, everyday work of Cotton's entire candidacy, especially from the age of eighteen when, he wrote, his "Mind was Exceedingly taken up, with the great Action, of, *A Closing with the Lord Jesus Christ.*" He strove now not to understand faith, repentance, and holiness, but rather to experience them. His method for attaining this "*Impressive*" knowledge began with trying to identify and rebuke his sins, then seeking pardon for them. The two-step process might last days, weeks, or months, and might falter in doubt and have to be repeated. Prostrate on his study floor he bewailed his listlessness, sloth, lukewarmness, and many other sins, especially lust and pride. He identified with an aging minister who had been found guilty of adultery, and feared that "I, who am a *young Man,* in my single Estate, should be left by God, unto some Fall, whereby His Blessed Name would suffer." Apparently guilt-ridden over masturbation performed or considered, he confessed to God the loathsome defilement of his soul: "*Lord, Wherewithal shall a young man cleanse his way?* . . . . . . I have certainly been one of the filthiest Creatures upon Earth." To halt the "irregularities which my Thoughts within me have hurried me into," he resolved to practice extraordinary austerities and to emulate Saint Augustine in perpetual celibacy.

Cotton also felt embittered and confused over his "cursed *Pride*, the Sin of *young Ministers.*" He wished to become what he understood his father to have been, the father whose fellow graduates publicly "hummed" him, " a Young Man every where Admired, and Applauded, and Accepted, and Flock'd after." Yet he recognized that his ambitious desire to become a famous preacher like Increase dishonored his sacred obligation to use his ministry to glorify not himself but God alone. Often he recorded his pleasure in preaching in a populous place, "the *Metropolis* of the whole English *America,*" and of garnering a great and growing reputation. But he just as often warned himself against his "abominably proud Fishing for popular Applause." In 1681 he spent a special day of humiliation to castigate his pride, indicting himself for desiring greater renown than his age or ability merited, and for congratulating himself when answering questions readily or preaching well. "*Proud Thoughts,*" he lamented, "fly-blow my best Performances!"

The stains on his soul tormented Cotton, producing anguished cries of his unworthiness for salvation. Summoning his sins into his mind in the hope of cracking his hard heart, he cursed himself for a "poor, broken, sorry despicable Vessel," a "rotten Stump." He was "feeble and worthless," "miserably defective," "crabbed, foolish, despicable," "*unsavoury Salt,* fit for nothing but the Dunghill." How could such a thing love God, much less lead others to love Him? His disfigurement made him worthy not of the ministry, but rather "worthy of *Death, Death, Death* forever."

But having identified and bewailed his sins Cotton prayed God to fill his soul with love, and as he hoped, his long bouts of self-condemnation and humiliation gave rise to an assured sense that God had forgiven him. One such cleansing epiphany occurred after much secret prayer in September 1681, when he felt that his heart no longer relished lust and pride: "*Oh! I feel! I feel! I feel! I love the Lord Jesus Christ; I love Him dearly, I love Him greatly, yea, I love Him above all.*" Another such moment arrived in August 1683, when he spent about two weeks preaching with his father in rural Lynn. While enjoying the solitude of the fields he felt "strong and strange *Assurances*" not only that God had pardoned him, but also that He designed to make him His instrument, "*not only to bless me, but also to make me a Blessing.*"

This certainty, however, Cotton found hard to sustain. Time and again, he soon worried whether it was illusory, then doubted the genuineness of his repentance, until his sureness dissolved into fresh doubts, leaving him where he began. Returning from Sabbath worship in March 1681, for instance, he felt an assurance that left him saying, "*I believe that I am a chosen Vessel, and that the Lord will pour mercy unto me . . . It will be so!*" But six days later his belief collapsed into "Discouraging Fears, that I should not be able to go thro' the work." His inability to believe in the reality of his conversion gave rise to self-accusations of heart-deadness and formality, of mimicking the conversion process without experiencing it: "I am but a very *Parrot* in Religion!" The inauthenticity of even his keenest epiphanies left him with a sense of desertion and rejection by God: "Oh! how hath He *broken my Heart,* and ground it . . . into Powder, before Him! How is the inflexible *Stone* turn'd into pliable *Flesh!*"

However brokenhearted, Cotton also knew that God's abandonment of him, like all forms of affliction, was intended to draw him closer to Himself. By raising then crushing his conviction, God meant to produce in him more perfect understanding of his sinful nature, preparatory to a genuine experience of conversion and a more able ministry. So he trusted: "I believe, that when the Lord has *broken* me, and fitted me for further Mercy, and laid me low before Him, He will *raise* me up, in bestowing of great *Comfort* on me and employing me in great *Service* for Him." For being broken the only remedy was to repeat the process of identifying and bewailing his sins in the hope of pardon, even should the pardon prove transient and illusory. Alternately rejoicing and despairing of his conversion throughout his candidacy, he was repeatedly forced to recommence the work of closing with Christ, and to "anew go over all the Sorrowful and Heart-breaking Hours."

Cycles of assurance and doubt were common, even formulaic, among Puritans. But Cotton saw himself as trying to serve God more strenuously than others, and as suffering more than others by His abandonment. God had favored him with two quickened faculties, which "(however *vile* I am) I cannot but acknowledge." First, God had given him "*A tender Heart,*" a sensitivity that made him unable to "live quietly under the smaller neglects of God, which the Generality of Christians give way unto." Second, "*an active Mind,*" an ingenuity that made him uneasy except when doing something to promote God's Kingdom. Now and throughout his life he believed deeply in a hierarchy of the pious, and aspired to join the elite. "My Heart is insatiably *pressing,*" he wrote at around the age of nineteen, "after the *High Attainments* of Religion."

Such high attainments differed greatly from what Cotton later called the "Low, Dull, Slothful Measures, of the *Common* and *Barren* Christianity." The distinction lay in vigorous constancy and imaginativeness. To press after high attainments of religion meant living in heaven while on earth, and Cotton resolved in 1685 "to be continually abounding in the Thoughts of God. Nor would I be one waking quarter of an Hour without them." Not only the abundance of devotion counted but also the manner. He wished, he wrote later, to use "my Wit, as well as my Grace" and to lend his devotions "a certain charming *Elegancy,* and Sacred *Curiosity.*" He strove to invent ever new, ever more ingenious and striking methods of praising God. Indeed, ingenuity or "curiosity" would become one of his distinctive values, a measure for him of all accomplishment. Devoting one's life to God involved for him a play of imagination that made it akin to art.

Some means of living in heaven while on earth Cotton performed daily or almost daily, often laying down schedules of devotion for himself. Secret prayer (private prayer, as opposed to public prayer in church or family prayer at home) he considered "the straight way to the City of God," a daily duty. He later recommended that it be practiced in a locked or barred room to prevent disturbance and permit intimate confession of secret sin, begging the Lord's mercy while lying prostrate on the floor, mouth in the dust. Occasionally he devoted entire days to secret prayer, and in 1683 even drew up an elaborate routine for them, in fourteen numbered steps. He began the day by expressing to God his belief that the Lord rewarded those who sought Him diligently. Then, in order, he read chapters of Scripture, meditated on his vileness, sang hymns, proposed profitable questions to himself, supplicated God for pardon of sin, sang another hymn, meditated, prayed again, sang a psalm—and so on until he ended the day by "renouncing all Apprehension of *Merit,* in my own Duties, and relying upon the Lord Jesus Christ alone, for Acceptance and Salvation." Twice a week or more, as mentioned earlier, he also recorded sermons in his voluminous notebooks, often adding his own resolves upon hearing them. Almost daily he also recorded his prayers, meditations, and religious experiences in a diary, with occasional comment on his domestic circumstances, or about social and political events. These diaries, the lengthiest surviving of any American Puritan, begin in 1681 and end in February 1725, although he probably began them earlier and kept them until his death: eighteen years have unfortunately been lost.

As if he had cast God Himself in the image of Increase Mather, for whom he could *"never do enough,"* Cotton invented literally thousands of other means of demonstrating his devoutness. Taking pleasure in the *"Variety* of *Contrivance"* that flooded from him he decided to spend at least a tithe of his income on pious purposes; to precede every act with the thought *"let me now do this* (or, *I will do this) for God"*; to preface the recording of every act in his diary with a statement that he did it for God's glory; to ask each morning, and review each evening, questions designed to strengthen grace in him; to sing hymns every morning and night, of his own composing; to make his rising thoughts concern some passage of Scripture, disposing him to fear God all day; to write letters to people needing help; to penalize himself if he omitted any religious exercise he had prescribed, or failed to annex a pious thought to each sentence of his prayers, or on the Sabbath spoke any word incongruous with the day—and to donate the self-imposed fines to the poor. He even set apart a special day on which to invent "Contrivances" on the question, What may I do for God? The answers, he said, issued in "Thousands of *Resolves."* He drew others into his contrivances as well. He often prayed and fasted with groups of religious young men, and from the age of seventeen he undertook the tuition of several scholars, some older than himself, in Hebrew, discoursing with them individually in his study about their salvation. When two people unexpectedly visited him during a day-long fast in 1685 he invited them to join his devotions, which included preaching them three sermons, each about an hour long.

Not even this was enough. Cotton wished to have God in his thoughts every waking moment. To attain that high end he practiced a "spiritual *Alchemy."* This meant ceaselessly creating brief petitions and supplications—"Ejaculatory Prayers"—and sending them to Heaven in an all-day stream of spontaneous praying. He often based the "ejaculation" on some present thing or person, viewing the entire world as a preacher: "The *Meanest Objects* in the House, or in the Street, have afforded me Thousands of Lessons, which I have immediately Sent up to Heaven." Transmuting his moment-to-moment sensory experience into a glorification of God, he could form prayers not only before acts of worship or while hearing sermons or singing psalms, but also while traveling in the road, eating dinner, walking down the street, or just sitting in his study. Although he chose to "not be so *pharisaical* as to show it," when encountering a tall man he might pray, *"Lord,* give that Man, *High Attainments* in Christianity"; seeing a black person he asked, *"Lord, wash* that poor Soul

white in the *Blood* of thy Son"; feeling unnoticed by someone (a revealing category) he said, "*Lord,* help that Man, to take a *due Notice* of the
Lord Jesus Christ." As the wit of these ejaculations suggests, his motives
in distilling thousands of brief prayers from mundane experience were
both devotional and aesthetic, aimed at glorifying God but also at "the
pleasing of my Fancy."

As Cotton noted in his diaries several times during his candidacy, he
was not always able to complete the devotional tasks he prescribed for
himself. Yet he found the prescribing a goad to the performance, and a
help in producing the "heavenly *Way of Living*" he sought. And it was
enough. He feared that by his "macerating Exercises" he had wasted his
strength, wounded his body, and thereby broken the sixth commandment. The "Excesses of my Devotions" atop his occasional, intense re-
gimes of secret fasting and prayer sometime did damage his health. In
January 1684 they brought splenetic maladies and the possibility of consumption, threatening his life, he believed. Wondering whether he had
made his duties into murders and injured the very service he intended to
glorify, he asked God to pardon and pity him for the sake of Jesus Christ.

*

"Give my Stammering Tongue leave to say; Oh! That we *knew the Day
of our Visitation.*" Thus Cotton urged immediate repentance upon the
audience of his first recorded sermon, preached when he was sixteen. As
his self-conscious candor indicates, Elijah Corlet's advice to him had not
wholly succeeded. Modern speech therapists would not recommend Corlet's method of speaking very deliberately, for the effort to scan approaching speech situations produces a strained vigilance, and the avoidance of
hard-to-pronounce words invites bizarre substitutions or odd circumven-
tions, not curing the inability but masking or avoiding it. Just the same,
Cotton managed to control the impediment effectively enough so that by
the time he gave his first formal sermons, in 1680, Increase observed
gratefully that despite his "natural Infirmity" he delivered himself in
preaching and prayer "without any considerable Hesitancy."

During the first three years of Cotton's candidacy the severity of his
stutter fluctuated. Shortly after his eighteenth birthday he recorded that
his preaching was free of it; but a year later it "threatened such a Return
upon me as to render me unserviceable." While following Corlet's advice, he spent on the matter "many Thousands of solicitous Thoughts,"
and sought help by prayer. Some solace he found in the fact that the

speech difficulties of Moses had continued even after he began his ministry:

> Oh! Thou that *madest Man's Mouth*, didst Thou not make the Mouth of
> the Stammering *Moses* to speak? Didst thou not open the Lips of *Jeremiah*,
> when he pleaded, *I cannot speak?* Did not my Lord Jesus cure a man that
> had *an Impediment in his Speech? Oh! Lord, Oh! Lord*, I am sensible, that
> one Touch, one Word of thine will relieve my Infirmity. Oh! touch my
> Tongue: Say, *Ephphatha* and my mouth will be opened!

On his knees in prayer he often received strong persuasions that the
Lord's Ephphatha—"Be Opened"—would be spoken, promising "*greater Supplies of Speech in store for me, than I ever yet received.*" But he
never fully conquered the impediment, and when it remitted he feared its
return.

Cotton tried as well to understand the cause and significance of his
stutter. Like any other affliction, it represented God's chastisement for
sin: "by my early Wickedness and Filthiness, I have provoked Thee," he
wrote at around nineteen, "to take away from me one of the greatest
Conveniencies, enjoyed by thy reasonable Creatures." In fact, God had
scourged him far more mildly than the depth of his depravity deserved:
"tho' thy *Rod* has been very heavy in this regard upon me. . . . Lord, I
deserve, not only a *Stammering, Slowness,* but also a total *Dumbness* in
my Speech." But as Cotton and other Puritans also understood affliction,
God's rod descended in loving concern. The purpose of his stutter was to
lead him to examine himself, become conscious of his sin, and renounce
it. God bound his tongue not to make him despair, but to make him
eminently holy, "yea, to make me more happy than other men."

In seeking the iniquitous causes of his stutter, Cotton fastened on two
related sins: pride and anger. He understood that his desire for fame
corrupted his obligation to use his tongue selflessly to serve God. His
stutter, then, was the ignominious mark of his "ambitious Affectation of
Praeheminencies." Determining to use his tongue as God's, not as his
own, he chastised its sins and declared in August 1683 that he "asked for
a *Tongue* only to serve Him, and bespeak the Loves and Lives of my
Neighbours for Him." In return for improvements in his speech he vowed
not to reach after improvements too high for him. The same year he drew
up "RULES OF SPEECH" in which he resolved not only to speak very
deliberately, but also to consecrate his speech to God, to rarely come into
company without seeking useful discourse, and to pray daily, "*Lord, let
my Mouth show forth thy Praise.*"

In fact, Cotton was probably correct in viewing his stutter as a punishment for his pride, only he applied the rod himself. The impediment may well have arisen in an attempt to block ambitious thoughts, dangerously charged with the thrill of showing up a father who had been invited to preach by a dozen different congregations. He was also probably correct in associating his stutter with anger. "*Stammerers* are often of too *Choleric* a Disposition," he wrote in later life, "and *Sooner Angry* than they should be; whereas they of all People, should always maintain the *Meekness of Wisdom*." The possibility that certain kinds of anger might themselves be linked to pride he set before himself at the age of nineteen, when he took notes on a sermon preached by his father. Increase observed that seemingly causeless anger is really caused: "pride is the spring whence causeless Anger does usually proceed." Cotton recorded in his notebook his father's view that to give vent to unprovoked anger by intemperate language reveals an unmanly spirit, while meekness is excellent and like to God, who is slow to anger. Judging from the "Rules of Behavior" composed by Cotton's brother Nathanael, Increase inculcated similar lessons at home, and they were borne in on Cotton again as he resolved to read books that might teach him "the Government of the Tongue." Out of one English work he copied at length injunctions against retorting when one is disparaged or defamed: "beware of a Transport of *Anger;* that you speak not harshly or unadvisedly against him; or too passionately for thyself"; "Watch against all bitter, and over-passionate Speeches against *malignant Opposers* of the Truth." While it remained Cotton's duty as a minister and a Puritan openly to denounce ungodliness, he repeatedly cautioned himself to speak ill of no one except for good reason and right purpose, and to be circumspect in his speech.

Cotton seems to have brought his stutter under satisfactory control a few months short of his twenty-first birthday, when he thanked God for the "miraculous Freedom of my *Speech*." Yet it recurred in later life, and his speaking seems to have become permanently marked by Corlet's advice: his son Samuel wrote that his father always spoke with "much *Deliberation*." There were other lasting effects of his long attempt to master the impediment, as he attempted to overcome its underlying anger and pride by demanding of himself the opposite behavior. However ambitious, he must appear selfless. However angry, he must appear mild, a conciliator. However much a stutterer, he must entrance large audiences. This wish to spellbind asserts itself in an utterly un-Puritan image which crops up several times in Cotton's early writing, that of a theater. Once, when concerned about the small size of his audience, he cautioned him-self, as if he were on stage, that the eye of God "shall be *Theatre* enough." Similarly, in a letter written around 1682, he apologized for his brevity by saying he "comes just like Cato on the stage . . . only to go off again." His desire to captivate seems equally apparent in his determina-tion to lend his devotional exercises "a certain charming *Elegancy,* and Sacred Curiosity," as if to entertain God Himself. In fact the youthful stutterer would become the most noted conversationalist of his time, much admired and sought after by contemporaries for his erudite and beguiling wit.

Meanwhile, Cotton had become highly sensitive to others' reception of what he said. When his speech was ignored he managed both to ac-knowledge and to deny his limitations by first denigrating and then con-gratulating himself, in a way that left him feeling at once big and small. Throughout a dinner he attended, for instance, he sat silently, creating ejaculatory prayers by "spiritual alchemy" in his mind. His youth, he felt, excluded him from conversation with his elders; and the other tabletalk, he decided next, was "too trivial to be Worthy of my Attention." Once, finding his congregation thinner than usual, he countered his discour-agement first by considering his unworthiness, then by adding that many ministers more excellent than himself "would count themselves happy, if they might preach quietly to a Company one quarter so big." Or he some-time soothed his hurt pride by glorying in defeat. In the voting to choose a preacher for the annual artillery sermon in 1686 he received few votes, even though he was closely connected to a captain in the militia, and was passed over. Out of this he made a show of gladly welcoming rejection, establishing his superiority by putting those who did not choose him to speak beneath his notice. "I took some Satisfaction, I hope," he wrote, "in being overlooked, as to that Choice."

Cotton's deliberateness and self-idealization in managing his speech extended to his writing as well. Even his childhood and adolescent script is neat, precise, in fact visually interesting; some is printlike, as if a substi-tute for publication. His fine handwriting made him serviceable through-out his middle and late teens as an amanuensis for many important church and government documents, most notably for writing up the deci-sions of the unprecedented Reform Synod which gathered in Boston in 1679–80 to discuss pressing social and moral reforms. Twenty eminent ministers of New England signed Cotton's lengthy document, the list headed by the signature of the legendary preacher to the Indians, John Eliot. From the viewpoint of Cotton's fears about his speech, the beautiful

clarity of the hand, the borderlike margins, bold capitals, and other carefully wrought devices all declare that surely this could not be the work of
a stutterer.

And beginning in youth, Cotton probably handwrote as much as any
human being ever has. The sermon notebooks alone which he kept between the ages of thirteen and thirty-two, with about two hundred and
fifty words per page, contain roughly seven thousand pages. Far lengthier
than the surviving sermon notebooks of any other American Puritan, they
summarize in detail around a thousand sermons by leading New England
ministers, about many of which little or nothing would otherwise be
known. They not only suggest unusual patience, stamina, and concentration, but also seem to flaunt an ability to produce unlimited numbers of
words with superb clarity, on a page if not by tongue. Later in life Cotton
would achieve such astonishing feats of language as the ability, he said,
to "write very good Spanish" by studying it only "a few leisure Minutes in
the Evening of every Day, in about a Fortnight, or three weeks Time"—
claiming in effect to have learned a language he also published in after
studying it about three hours. Later he also observed that stutterers' pride
in being able to speak a few words clearly makes them perversely loqua-
cious, so that "there is nothing more frequent, than for *Stammerers* to
speak Ten times more than they need to." Indeed by displaying his copious mastery of engaging language in every form, the youthful stutterer
would become one of the most prolific writers in American history.

Some connection between Cotton's written and spoken language was
noticed later by his friend Thomas Prince, who compared his prose with
his speech and described both as "very *emphatical*." A connection seems
clear enough in Cotton's first published work, his *Poem Dedicated to . . .
Urian Oakes* (1682), a funeral elegy on the recently deceased president
of Harvard. Having chosen to appear in print, at the age of nineteen, in a
classic New England form, he began the poem by cataloguing the New
England elegists who preceded him, starting with his grandfather John
Cotton. Like his comparable *Elegy on . . . Nathanael Collins* (1685, me-
morializing a Harvard-trained minister), the poem offers a summary of
the minister's virtues and assesses the meaning of his death to family,
friends, and community.

However traditional, Cotton's first poems record his highly personal
transference to writing of habits and attitudes connected with his difficulties in speaking. He presents himself as a mute: "I the *dumb* son of
Croesus." But as if in denial of his speechlessness, both poems are unusually long for American Puritan elegies, amounting together to thirty-seven

pages of verse: "My *Love*," he explains, "is Talkative." Despite the solemn elegiac occasions, too, he labors to entertain and impress by language, placing Collins's relatives on a "*Stage*" to comment on the "*Tragedy*." Exhibitions of cleverness choke or divert the forward flow of mourning verse—exclamations, rhetorical questions, italics, curious lore, classical references, esoteric allusions, half-page stacks of footnotes, and many puns. Cotton writes of his halting verse, "I strive to *run,* but then I want my *feet*"; the argument over how many angels can dance on the point of a needle, he says, is perhaps a "*needless Point.*" Wittily he compares Oakes's death to the loss of a tooth, and measures the depth of Collins's sermons by remarking that "*Elephants/* Might take content" in them. Both these rhapsodically insincere and pretentiously ornamental poems bespeak someone concerned less with what he is saying than with sounding copious and charming.

Cotton's stutter may echo more directly in the strange awkwardness of the elegies. Their gawky unmelodiousness suggests what he later described as the "broken and blundering" speech of stutterers, and seems not so much unmusical as pathological:

> Some *Elogyes* compose to try their Wits;
>   The Gout, (r) the *Feavour,* // yea & *Injustice,* (s)
> *Folly* (t) and *Poverty* (u) have in the Fits
>   Of Ranting Writers had a *comeliness.*

> My *Theme,* my *Humour* is not such an one:
>   Who to prove *Cicero* not eloquent,
> Pen'd Books (x) who *truth* & *worth* for *guards* disown
>   Such only count *Collins not excellent.*

Whether the inept clumsiness of Cotton's verse derived from his speech difficulties, he had no gift at all for rhyming or for verse rhythm, although he would attempt to write poetry throughout life. Increase sent copies of his son's first published work to several persons, one of whom replied bluntly that however hopeful Cotton's prospects as a minister, "in my thoughts he will never win the laurel for his poesy."

*

Cotton's affections and social sense were strong, his interests broad, his appetite for learning large, and while trying to live in heaven he also enjoyed earth. By the time of his family's move to the North End of Boston from Cotton's Hill he was one of five children; by 1684 he was one of ten, a new brother or sister having arrived about every two years: Samuel

(August 1674), Abigail (April 1677), Hannah (May 1680), Catherine (September 1682), and Jerusha (April 1684). Around the age of seventeen he undertook to engage his sisters Maria, Elizabeth, and Sarah in the service of Christ, calling them successively into his study and explaining in pathetical terms their obligation to give themselves to Christ.

Cotton says virtually nothing about the other Mather children in his diaries. But his closest relation seems to have been with his brother Nathanael, six and a half years his junior, to whom he presented a volume of manuscript sermons preached by their grandfather John Cotton. The gift was appropriate, for the extraordinarily pious Nathanael prayed constantly, tackled rabbinic learning and philological problems of Scripture, and wrestled soul-searchingly with the problem of his conversion. Cotton tutored Nathanael as well, but found that he was "forced often to chide him *to* his Recreations, but never that I remember *for* them." An unrelenting student, Nathanael was admitted to Harvard at the age of twelve, and four years later was suffering pains in his joints. Like his father he also experienced spells of depression, and sometime fashioned himself "*Deodatus Melancholicus.*" Increase also designed him for the ministry, but he felt unworthy and directionless, considered the prospect awesome, and wrote that "the Thoughts of it have almost amazed me so that I am much Perplexed in my Studies." Judging from his later biography of Nathanael, Cotton felt a little awed by his brother's grave piety and talent for learning but critical of his disregard for his health.

Among his numerous relatives Cotton most often visited his mother's brother, the minister John Cotton of Plymouth. A rather fat man with a "Handsome Ruddy yet grave Countenance," he could cite chapter and verse for almost any words of Scripture quoted to him. Although regarded as a "living Index to the Bible," something in him was quirky and unreliable. He had had the unhappiness, in 1664, to be excommunicated from the church of his own father, the famous John Cotton, for "lascivious unclean practises with three women." Perhaps because of this clouded reputation, Increase often took a high-handed, suspicious tone with him, as if John Cotton were seeking some advantage.

But the many surviving letters of John and his "comely fat" wife Joanna reveal a loving and good-natured couple, whose warmth extended to and was returned by Cotton. His uncle saluted him as "Endeared Cousen," while Cotton dubbed his aunt Joanna his "Plymouth-mother." He stayed with the Cottons in the summer of 1678, just after graduating from Harvard, studying industriously but delighting in the pleasant air. Because smallpox was then visiting Boston he considered his removal to

Plymouth "some special providence," although he feared, his uncle wrote, "going into the jaws of infection." When he did return to Boston, he, his brother Nathanael, and his sister Sarah all became mildly infected, his sister Maria more seriously. During another Plymouth sojourn he became a party to an obscure but farcical-sounding lawsuit, in which John Cotton brought a complaint against a man who allegedly had sold a watch belonging to him. The man denied having the watch, but Cotton Mather testified in court that he himself had delivered it to the man.

From Boston Cotton often wrote to his uncle, sending family news and political intelligence in a respectful but rather showy tone:

> Honored Sir,
>   You know I suppose how if a few of the eldest are *vocales,* then the rest either *semi-vocales* or mutes. Behold! how I make a virtue of necessity. Time and business have formerly forbad me to do that which at present it but just [as much?], *ut canis* [*ad nilum?*].

This, the opening of Cotton's first surviving letter, written when he was about fourteen, inaugurates a monumental correspondence he would cultivate throughout life.

Within his family Cotton also found precedent and encouragement for his keen scientific interests, already evident in his Harvard declamations and his flirtation with a career in medicine. His grandfather John Cotton, although steeped in medieval notions of physical reality, had considered it a divinely imposed duty to "study the nature and course, and use of all Gods works." His brother Nathanael read natural philosophy and the works of Francis Bacon, wrote up some experiments, investigated the "abstruse parts" of mathematics and astronomy, and expressed an allegiance to "the Mechanical Hypothesis of the Honorable Robert Boyle"— an atomistic view of the universe as composed of identical elementary particles. Increase Mather, after the spectacular appearance of Halley's comet in 1680, undertook a course of reading in the latest European astronomical studies, from which he emerged (or which perhaps confirmed him in being) a champion of observation and mathematical reasoning and an opponent of the abstract logic of Aristotle. Increase observed stars through the Harvard telescope, but found it irksome to travel to Cambridge and proposed in 1682 that a telescope and other scientific instruments be placed in the Town House. Although his *Kometographia* (1683) persists in treating comets as portents of coming events, it also recognizes that comets move like planets, cites the work of Johann Kepler, and dabbles in astronomical mathematics.

The Cotton and Mather families were hardly alone in their scientific interests. Many Puritans experimented with and encouraged science, and in Cotton's youth the Copernican system, the materialist philosophy of Descartes, and other revolutionary ideas that transformed the picture of the universe were beginning to take hold in New England. In 1683 was founded a Boston Philosophical Society, a step toward creating what became a Boston scientific community. Indirectly the group grew from the Royal Society of London, which tried to promote the new science in America and had corresponded with science-minded New Englanders since at least the mid-seventeenth century. But the specific proposal for a local scientific society came from Increase Mather, who hoped, he said, to lay "the foundation for that which will be for future edification." The Society first met in the spring of 1683, then fortnightly until 1688. No records of its meetings remain, if any were kept, so its membership and proceedings are largely unknown; but many persons in and near Boston had active scientific interests and may have participated. Cotton clearly became involved in the Society, for at least one meeting took place at his home, and he was befriended by one of the members, Dr. William Avery.

Cotton later described the Society's purpose as "Improvements in *Philosophy* and Additions to the Stores of *Natural History*." Evidently the members collected observations on novel natural phenomena in America, perhaps planning to compile a natural history of New England. Some such project may explain the obscure petition to the General Court in 1684, signed by Cotton, his father, and Dr. Avery, requesting an eight-mile tract of land "to make Some Essays towards the promoting of Learning together with and by the Improvement of Land among us." The Society also corresponded with at least one European scientist, Wolferdus Sanguerdius of Leiden, to whom it sent astronomical observations, and drawings of a parhelion and of a double rainbow which he published in his *Philosophia Naturalis* (2d ed. Leiden, 1685).

Although far older than Cotton, Dr. Avery enjoyed the young man's friendship. "I have longed more to have Commerce with your self," he wrote him in 1683, "than with most men that I know tho it be but in a little paper well blotted." One of the first physicians in America, Avery owned scientific apparatus and invented medical instruments himself. A contemporary described him as a "great inquirer," skilled in "chemical physick" generally and particularly in the work of the iatrochemist Jean Baptiste Van Helmont, a figure who would later become important to Cotton also. Avery described to Cotton his work on digestion, advised him on purchasing recent works on chemistry, and employed him as an amanuensis for some correspondence with the great English chemist Robert Boyle. Like many English scientists, Boyle was intrigued by the New World as a potential source of new and unusual material for investigation, and he asked Avery for observations about the air of New England, and expressed interest in its minerals. A letter from Avery to Boyle in August 1683 discusses at length chemicals and vessels to be used in various experiments. Cotton transcribed the letter for the elderly Avery, and may have written part of it himself, since some of the language sounds much like his own.

Cotton also took time during his candidacy to correspond with a Hartford minister about the change in polarity of a compass, and to observe Halley's comet through the Harvard telescope. He owned a microscope, too, and obviously found pleasure in viewing the "little *eels*," of which he could see "*incredible hundreds playing about in one drop of water.*" His first published work having been a poem, his second was a "mathematical Composure," *The Boston Ephemeris* (1683). Together with the dates of court sessions and elections, and a section on biblical chronology, this almanac contains the times and dates of eclipses, and a technical description of Halley's comet. It also includes an essay to encourage scripture knowledge "because," Cotton wrote, "if we design only to edifie the *Students* of *Astronomy* among us, Alas! there is scarce *One* of a *City* and two of a *Tribe* to be addressed." But in fact his observations through telescope and microscope were acts of devotion themselves, giving new grounds for praising the Almighty by enhancing his sense of the perfect design of things. "*Every Wheel* in this *huge clock*," he preached in his twentieth year, "moves just according to the *Rule* which the *All-wise Artist* [ga]ve it at the first."

*

The beginning of the end of Cotton's much delayed ordination came in July 1684, when he had preached at the North Church for four years. In that time, the brethren said, they had "more than once expressed their desire of his being settled," and with some irritation they now voted again that he "without further delays be ordained." Increase did not so much consent as give way. Ill once again, he had urged his flock to secure a second "Teaching officer." He accepted their choice of his son for the reason, he said, that they "could not agree in calling any other."

But Increase still did not consider Cotton an appropriate colleague for himself. A month or so later, after another illness, he preached a peculiar sermon, comparing his recovery to that of Hezekiah, the Old Testament king of Judah, who had fought against death although mortally ill. Hezekiah probably resisted death, Increase said, because he "had no son to succeed him, so that if God had taken him away, there must have been great Trouble in the Kingdom." He thus implied that he himself had struggled against his illness because his church had no successor to him, although the brethren's insistent votes for Cotton suggest they would have had no trouble choosing one. Cotton's ordination was postponed seven months more—and after another vote for it in April 1685, was nearly postponed again. This time the reason given for the delay was the shocking news that the king, as we shall see, was about to reorganize the government of New England. That, Cotton wrote, as if doubting the explanation himself, was how it had been "represented unto me."

Cotton's ordination was set, at last, for Wednesday, May 13, 1685. As the date approached he made fresh vows, promising the Lord to be a faithful pastor, contented with his condition and unresentful of slights. With his ordination only two weeks away, however, his "closing" with Christ remained incomplete. Woeful sights of his sinfulness alternated still with convictions that he was cleansed. Receiving assurances on May 4 that all controversy between God and his soul had ended, he wrote up and signed a covenant, engaging to renounce worldly vanities and to have Him as his chief Good. But like his many earlier assurances this one also waned. Days before his ordination he again felt confused and melancholy, doubtful of his fitness for the weighty work, apprehensive that God's supporting presence might be denied him, altogether "Buffeted, and mortified and macerated with Strong *Temptations*, and broken to pieces."

On the morning of his ordination, Cotton's assurances returned glowingly. He was in his study, praying on his knees and meditating on what the ministry entailed, when he experienced, in tears, an "astonishing Irradiation from Heaven," a guarantee that he would in his ministry enjoy a mighty presence of the Lord Jesus Christ. The exaltation, the "rapturous *Touches* and *Prospects*," became nearly unbearable: "I was forced most unwillingly to shake them off; they would have been too hard for me, and I would not have others take notice of any Effects thereby left upon me."

In this state of controlled rapture, his soul "inexpressibly irradiated from on High," Cotton entered the North Church. Here he beheld "one of the vastest Congregations that has ever been seen in these parts of the World." Exactly how many attended is unknown, but the church had three tiers of galleries, and a good congregation meant fifteen hundred to two thousand persons, one-third to nearly one-half the population of Boston. Many ministers and other dignitaries from churches in Boston and neighboring towns took part, as did the governor of Massachusetts and the revered, aged John Eliot.

Cotton began the daylong ritual by offering public prayers for about an hour and a quarter. Then to demonstrate, as the candidate customarily did, that he understood the work for which he was about to be separated, he preached for an hour and three-quarters. Nothing indicates that his stutter hampered him, but by the text he chose, John 21:17, he invoked his troubled "closing" and the frequent postponements. When the resurrected Jesus asked his disciple Peter whether he loved Him, Peter replied that he did; but as if doubting him, Christ repeated the question two more times: "Peter was grieved because he said unto him the third time, Lovest thou me? And he said unto him, Lord, thou knowest all things; thou knowest that I love thee. Jesus saith unto him, Feed my sheep."

Having spoken three hours in the morning, Cotton sat silent in the afternoon as Increase preached. He wrote down his father's words in his sermon notebook and, underlining certain statements, filled eleven pages. Increase took for his subject the nature of the ministry, emphasizing its solemnity and high demands. Occasionally referring directly to "My son Cotton Mather," he said that the ministry was a "Work." It was a work, first, in the sense of a difficult labor, requiring wearisome preaching, meditation, and study. It was also an awful work, for the minister in watching over souls does the Lord's work. Nor is everyone qualified for this work. Among the earliest Christians there were "extraordinary Ministers" called directly from Heaven, qualified for the ministry by being divinely endowed with miraculous gifts. But the age of miracles having ended, the qualifications now were ministerial, not miraculous: large knowledge, an ability to interpret Scripture, a desire to glorify God, and, most important, the experience of conversion, a calling from the Holy Ghost. Ministers, Increase concluded, must "addict themselves to the Ministry," must be spiritual in discourse and conversation, spiritual in preaching, indeed spiritually minded—for which Scripture compares them to angels.

Cotton's ordination as a minister followed. Such ceremonies well conducted could be moving and instructive, leaving, Cotton wrote later, "*Floods of Tears* in the affected Spectators, and lasting *Impressions of Piety* upon them." The custom in the New England churches was for the moderator to ask the visiting elders and messengers of neighboring churches whether they objected to the ordination; none objecting, the moderator then asked whether they knew of anything in the candidate's doctrine or morals that might forbid his ordination; nothing being named, the brethren were asked to signify with raised hands that they abided by their choice of the minister.

Now Increase Mather and the ministers John Allen and Samuel Willard lay their hands on Cotton's head. In this position Increase charged his son to feed dutifully the flock of God over which the Holy Ghost had appointed him shepherd, to give himself to meditation, reading, exhortation, and doctrine, and to make himself exemplary by his own purity, charity, and faith. If his son kept this charge, Increase said,

> ... the Lord of Hosts will give you a Place among His Holy Angels that stand by, and are Witnesses of this Days-Solemnity, and of your being thus solemnly apart to the special Service of God, and of Jesus Christ; And if you do thus, when the Lord Jesus shall appear, you shall appear with Him in glory. He, who is the chief Shepherd will then give unto you a Crown of Glory which shall never fade away.

After this dramatic "Imposition of Hands," a minister chosen to represent the elders and messengers of the churches customarily gave the new minister his right hand in token of fellowship in God's service, as James, Peter, and John to Paul and Barnabas.

The minister chosen to step forth was John Eliot. Now past eighty, he had lived in New England since it was an unchristian wilderness, for more than fifty years. Giving Cotton the "Right Hand of Fellowship" as the latest continuator of a sacred succession, he said to him: "*Brother, Art thou a Lover of the Lord Jesus Christ? Then, I pray Feed his Lambs.*" The solemnity and tradition of the event, Cotton wrote afterward in his diary, produced a "greater Number of moved Hearts and weeping Eyes, than perhaps have been at any Time here seen together."

Elevated into partnership with his father in a prestigious church, and to the honorable place designed for him in the line of Cottons and Mathers, Cotton felt small and weak. Some time after his ordination, he took the notes he had written on his father's sermon and, using a different pen, interlined his private responses to them. Where his father had said "Solomon my son is young and tender," he wrote, "The like here." Where Increase told the congregation, "I have been at the gates of the Grave," Cotton commented, "more than once within these four or five years." Increase may again have been ill at the time of Cotton's ordination, for he took the occasion to announce once more that his death might be near. He did so indirectly, referring in his sermon to the story in Numbers 20:26 of Aaron and his son Eleazar. The reference was not lost upon

Samuel Sewall, who noted in his diary that Increase had thereby intimated "he knew not but that God might now call him out of the World." Increase may have done no more than mention Aaron and Eleazar; to have applied the larger episode in which they figured to himself and his son, could be interpreted only as a gesture of bitter reproach. For Aaron the priest did not simply transmit his ministry to his son. Rather, an angry God stripped him of his priestly garments and put them upon Eleazar; immediately after his son replaced him, Aaron died. Whether or not Cotton interpreted Increase's reference to mean that his father considered himself demoted and mortally threatened by his ordination, he at least wrote in his notebook that *"When the priests garments were put upon Eleazar, then Aarons death was near."*

With this fearful prospect, and with how much guilt can only be conjectured, Cotton also recorded a resolve to find some method of extraordinary prayerfulness for his father's life. Increase himself told the congregation that if his son were left alone he would need their prayers. And Cotton concluded the afterthoughts in his notebook with a brief prayer of his own: "O mighty Redeemer by whose Spirit I am call'd unto the work of the Ministry in this time and place, Help Help a frail creature to discharge all the Duties of it."

*

Within about a year after his ordination Cotton had been initiated into most of the duties of the New England ministry. On June 28, 1685, he for the first time administered communion; in July he for the first time gave the "Country-Lecture"; beginning in October he participated in a formal excommunication, taking testimony of witnesses who had seen a member of the congregation, Ruth Fuller, holding on to the gate before her house, drunk; toward the end of the year he began catechizing visits, stopping by the houses of his flock each afternoon to catechize their young, seldom departing without "many *Tears* of Devotion dropt by all sorts of Persons" in the family, work he found rewarding but also fatiguing. As an ordained Boston minister he was also made an Overseer of Harvard, sometime in 1685. The same year, the Overseers unanimously devolved the care of the college on Increase, asking him to act as president until the establishment of a permanent administration. Still refusing to reside in Cambridge, he acted as "Rector," commuting between the North End and the Harvard Yard by ferry and horse.

Cotton preached extensively. Over two days in January 1686, he gave five sermons, and he filled pulpits in Watertown, Charlestown, Dorchester, and other places around Boston. One particular sermon called on his fullest abilities, brought him wide notice, and became the occasion, he said, "of my being *shown unto Israel*." In March 1686, a man named James Morgan, about thirty years old, was found guilty of murder and sentenced to be hanged. Condemned criminals were usually brought to church to be made the living objects of an exemplary sermon. Morgan himself asked Cotton to preach his execution sermon, as this genre became known, so that on March 7, Cotton found himself preaching at the North Church before a "vast Concourse of People." He addressed simultaneously the congregation and the criminal, who sat in the auditorium, probably chained, holding a Bible. Using Morgan as a frightening example of the results of brothels, swearing, and other prevalent vices, he exhorted him to look toward Christ:

> When the numerous crowd of *Spectators* are, three or four days hence, throng'd about the place where you shall then *breathe your last* before them all, then do you with the heart-piercing *groans of a deadly wounded man* beseech of your *Fellow-sinners* that they would *Turn now every one from the evil of his way.*

Cotton was not mistaken in predicting a large crowd, for on the morning of Morgan's hanging—the first execution in Boston in nearly seven years—Increase Mather preached to a gathering estimated, amazingly, at five thousand persons. Amidst this huge crush in the North Church a "crazed woman," as Samuel Sewall described her, either screamed that the gallery was falling, or else beat another woman, whose flight from her was mistaken for a rush to safety from a falling gallery. Either way, people fled the church in panic, and the governor moved the proceedings to the South Church. There Cotton took notes as his father preached on the nature of murder, praying at the same time that he might be as helpful as possible to "the poor man."

Morgan perhaps sensed compassion in Cotton or felt some bond with his youth, for he requested his company on the public march to the hanging. As they walked together to the gallows, about a mile outside Boston, they were followed by thousands of people. Some had traveled fifty miles to be present. En route, by Cotton's account, Morgan repeatedly thanked him for his help, and reviled himself for lying, drinking, breaking the Sabbath, and keeping evil company. Before a "huge Multitude" gathered at the place of execution, near which was a coffin, Cotton prayed with Morgan. Although he constantly pressed on his flock the need for immediate repentance, he believed that no repentance could come too late to make salvation possible, and he told Morgan to pray in his final moment on earth, that they might meet on Judgment Day at the right hand of Jesus. Morgan climbed the ladder to the noose. Cotton said to him, "*Farewell* poor heart, *Fare thee well.*"

Cotton's concern for Morgan's body and soul did not keep him from realizing that his role in the execution had brought him new prominence. His performance was so affecting, he recorded, that people throughout the country "very greedily desired the Publication," and the event produced his first published sermon, *The Call of the Gospel* (1686). It particularly pleased him that the sermon appeared together with the execution sermons by his father and by the Rev. Joshua Moodey, placing him, "a *sorry Youth,* in conjunction with *two* of the venerablest Men in the Land." As he noted proudly too, these sermons "sold exceedingly," calling for a second edition the next year, to which the publisher added a nine-page transcript of his conversation with Morgan on the death march. Having stepped impressively before the public, the same fall he was chosen for the first time to deliver the traditional "Artillery Sermon," marking the day for selecting leaders of the militia. In themselves such sermons were "things of considerable Observation." But Cotton took special pride in having been chosen to preach in Cambridge, to the artillery company of Middlesex County, while as a Bostonian he resided in Essex County. Never before had the Middlesex militia chosen for their Artillery Day preacher a minister from another county, "and this was my poor self." The event produced his second published sermon, *Military Duties* (1687).

While pleased by his early success Cotton was learning, however, that to be "shown unto Israel" meant also to be exposed unto Israel. Some found his florid language not entertaining but affected. Increase may have intended to warn him against verbal display when, in his sermon on Cotton's ordination, he told of an "Elaborate young Man" to whom someone said, "I wanted the Spirit of God in your sermon." To others, Cotton seemed unmistakably "elaborate." One minister congratulated Increase on his son's wealth of evangelical knowledge but added, "I only wish he delivered truths in your style, in that plainness of expression which the Gospel teach." Samuel Sewall too remarked that an otherwise excellent sermon by Cotton was found distasteful or "somewhat disgusted" for such expressions as "sweet-scented hands of Christ, Lord High Treasurer of AEthiopia, Ribband of Humility."

If Cotton's plush language hid from others his grave doubts about his ability, he was himself undeceived. Nearly a year after his ordination he again cautioned himself to watch his tongue lest he be punished by stuttering, and to use a "deliberate, considerable, profitable speech." Acutely conscious of being twenty-four years old in a role where venerableness was esteemed, he saw himself as "a young *person,* and a younger *pastor.*" His sense of his youthfulness also curbed any desire to outperform his father, toward whom he continued to act with respectful submission. When an address to the General Court was proposed, shortly before his ordination, he felt that "*Little can be done by so little* a person, as I am, in this matter," and he decided simply to "confer with my *Father, as a sorry Remembrancer.*" Increase fed this sense of subordinate littleness by his reluctance, even after Cotton's ordination, to acknowledge him as a colleague. When their execution sermons on James Morgan were published together in a single volume, Increase referred in the Preface, less enthusiastically than fatalistically, to "*my Son (whom the Lord Jesus has fixed in the same Church to which I am related)."*

Especially, Cotton feared that by his inexperience he might do something to bring the ministry into disrepute: "O Lord, " he prayed, "of all the Plagues in the World, I beseech Thee, do not suffer this to come upon me." A year after his ordination he took part in a church council at Malden which voted to temporarily suspend Thomas Cheever, a minister accused among other things of uttering obscenities at a Salem tavern. Sitting in a formal council and officially condemning the son of his old schoolmaster, Ezekiel Cheever, he felt not like one of the judges, but like the young offender: "having seen a poor *young Minister* terribly stigmatized for his Misdemeanours, by a Council, whereof I was myself a Member, I thought; *What if God should single me out now to be so publickly loaded with Shame for Sin?"*

*

Cotton completed his entry into the ministry, in mid-1686, by marrying. He chose very carefully, often seeking divine guidance, for a minister's wife was not only his companion but must also be a model of wifely, motherly, and neighborly behavior to the community. At the same time, bachelor ministers were much sought after, and its paternal authority lent the Puritan ministry a distinct erotic appeal, so that he found himself soon after ordination with "many Invitations" to marry. He seems to have considered several eligible women, promising that if God directed him to one who would honor his calling he would twice a year, every year, join her in keeping a private day of Thanksgiving to Him. Ministers in New England being, as Increase often complained, underpaid, he also prayed to be afforded through marriage a comfortable and well-provided home, "without the Distresses and the Temptations, which *Poverty* does expose unto."

Around his birthday in February 1686, Cotton began courting Abigail Phillips of Charlestown, the daughter of "worthy, pious, and credible Parents." Her father, Colonel John Phillips, a justice of the peace prominent in military affairs, owned houses and pastureland in and near Charlestown, plus an interest in a mill. Cotton pursued Abigail piously but vigorously. For three months he let scarce a week pass without spending a day of prayer for his success, and he fashioned his addresses to Abigail after Christ's methods of engaging souls. To remind himself that his courtship must serve the same purpose as all his other activities, to glorify God,he entered in his diary an anecdote concerning Rabbi Gamaliel, the teacher of Saint Paul, who, refusing to lay by the yoke of God's Kingdom a single hour, said over the scriptural passages in his phylacteries on his wedding night. What made the reminder necessary was perhaps that during his courtship, perhaps because of it, he felt the sting of disbelief, a weakening of faith, in fact the beginnings of a severe religious crisis. "O that the wonderful, Amazing, Everlasting Love of God to me," he cried in March, "might cause me to love Him again, with a Love as strong as Death."

Despite mounting spiritual turmoil, Cotton married Abigail Phillips on May 4, 1686. He was three months past twenty-three, she one month under sixteen. He found some renewal of spiritual strength on the morning of his wedding day, which he spent in secret prayer in Boston. Once again he experienced an assurance of Christ's love for him, and became tearfully certain that "in my *married Estate,* He had reserves of rich and great Blessings for me." Arriving in Charlestown with time to spare, he took his Bible into a garden and read the account in John 2 of the marriage in Cana, turning each verse into one pious thought and one supplication to God.

The wedding, Cotton decided, was an event—attended by many ministers and other prominent persons, celebrated with "Splendid Entertainments" at Abigail's house, withal marked by "many Circumstances of Respect and Honour, above most that have ever been in these parts of the World." After living a while with Colonel Phillips in Charlestown the couple moved to Boston around the early fall, to a house Increase had temporarily inhabited after the great fire of 1676 consumed his own. Here, as a very young college student, Cotton had many hundreds of times beseeched the Lord. "I could not but observe the Providence of God," he remarked, "in ordering my *Comforts* now, in those very Rooms, where I had many years before, sought Him with my *Prayers.*"

From the first, Cotton felt happy in his marriage to Abigail and thanked God for granting him "a *Meet Help,* an extremely desireable Companion for my *Joys* and *Griefs.*" As he had hoped, he was materially prosperous too, having received a good portion "*in,* as well as *with,* my Consort." He went from room to room of his house, deliberately gazing on the "Parcels of the *Estate,* whereof I am now become the owner"; rather, he reconsidered as he mentally gave back the parcels to God, the steward. The novel sexual license of marriage seems to have troubled him some, for he prayed to be freed from the "Slavery" of a "Lust seeming to assault me with a commission." But the household of course remained deeply devout. To aid Abigail in her so-far unconverted state, he offered conference and example, and prayed with her daily. The couple also invited neighbors for an hour of prayer and psalmody on Sabbath evenings, but their pious hospitality proved too inviting, bringing "such an unexpected Resort unto my House, that there was ordinarily near an hundred People at a Time, (and more than one Room could hold)."

Yet as happened to Increase just after his ordination, Cotton following his marriage underwent a tormenting assault of religious doubt, lasting about eight months. Only weeks after the wedding he found his soul "daily Enflamed" by the "fiery Darts" of atheism. The Christ he so often beseeched prostrate in the dust for his father's life and an unfettered tongue seemed now a dubious being: "O," he prayed, "That the foolish prejudices which my unbelief is ready to entertain against Jesus Christ, may be all removed." After his innumerable pious contrivances and ingenious devotions, his alchemizing street signs and flowers into prayers, he doubted the reality of Spirit: "O That my firm Belief of Invisible things may be as a shield unto me, defending me from those Temptations." The very soul whose sins of lust and pride he had striven in brokenhearted cycles of assurance and doubt to purge, might not exist: "O That I might beyond all Doubt or Darkness, be effectually convinced of the Immortality of my own soul." Indeed, he had arrived at the place appointed for him since birth, but as an unfamiliar being, disloyally changed: "O That I may not in any wise Lose that kindness to the Truths and ways of God, which I have had in my younger years."

A year before his marriage Cotton had visited his friend Thomas Shepard, a minister in Charlestown about four and a half years younger than himself. Ill, Shepard had said to him as they parted, "*Sir, I beg the Lord Jesus to be with you unto the End of the World!*" The next night Shepard died.

It was about four months after his marriage, in September 1686, that Cotton dreamed of being in a room with some other "Gentlemen," among them Shepard. He felt "somewhat shy" of him because he was dead and tried to slip out of the room. But Shepard "nimbly" approached him, took him by the hand, and said, *"Sir, you need not be so shy of me, for you shall quickly be as I am, and where I am."*

II

MR. COTTON MATHER

(1687–1703)

In the rear of the procession rode a figure on horseback, so darkly conspicuous, so sternly triumphant, that my hearers mistook him for the visible presence of the fiend himself; but it was only his good friend, Cotton Mather, proud of his well-won dignity, as the representative of all the hateful features of his time; the one blood-thirsty man, in whom were concentrated those vices of spirit and errors of opinion that sufficed to madden the whole surrounding multitude.

> —NATHANIEL HAWTHORNE, "Alice Doane's Appeal"
> (1834)

"It is difficult, my children," observed Grandfather, "to make you understand such a character as Cotton Mather's, in whom there was so much good, and yet so many failings and frailties."

> —NATHANIEL HAWTHORNE, *Grandfather's Chair*
> (1841)

Was Cotton Mather honestly credulous? Ever ready to dupe himself, he limited his credulity only by the probable credulity of others. He changes, or omits to repeat, his statements, without acknowledging error, and with a clear intention of conveying false impressions. He is an example how far selfishness, under the form of vanity and ambition, can blind the higher faculties, stupefy the judgment, and dupe consciousness itself. His self-righteousness was complete, till he was resisted.

> —GEORGE BANCROFT, *History of the United States*
> (12th ed., 1846)

. . . those who know only the eccentricities of Cotton Mather know little about him. Those who suppose they comprehend him, because they are familiar with the current anecdotes about him, or imagine that he could be fairly sketched by a few strong touches, could not be under a greater misapprehension. The truth is, few characters are less intelligible; few harder to describe; few are so many-sided; few have so little uniformity; few have so great a variety of qualities, in such strange admixture; few show such supposed inconsistencies; few present themselves in such ever-shifting positions and hues, such kaleidoscopic changes and combina-tions; few exhibit such surprising contrasts, such an apparent jumble of great and small, sharp and flat, wise and simple, saintly and ordinary. To group all these elements together, to arrange and blend them into any thing like a complete and satisfactory portrait, would be a task that requires more penetration and skill than have ever yet been exercised upon his biography. . . .

—CHANDLER ROBBINS, *A History of the Second Church* (1852)

. . . though, in my previous night-readings, Cotton Mather had but amused me, upon this particular night he terrified me. A thousand times I had laughed at such stories. Old wives' fables, I thought, however entertaining. But now, how different. They began to put on the aspect of reality. Now, for the first time it struck me that this was no romantic Mrs. Radcliffe who had written the *Magnalia,* but a practical, hard-working, earnest, upright man, a learned doctor, too, as well as a good Christian and orthodox clergyman. What possible motive could such a man have to deceive? His style had all the plainness and unpoetic boldness of truth. In the most straightforward way, he laid before me detailed accounts of New England witchcraft, each important item corroborated by respectable townsfolk, and, of not a few of the most surprising, he himself had been eye-witness. Cotton Mather testified whereof he had seen. But, is it possible? I asked myself.

—HERMAN MELVILLE, "The Apple-Tree Table" (1856)

3

The Glorious Revolution

❧

OVER THE NEXT fifteen years, three convulsive events shook the political, social, and religious life of New England. Of Cotton Mather's reaction to the first event, the Glorious Revolution of 1689, little is known, because his diaries between 1687 and 1692 are missing. That is doubly unfortunate because for most of the time his father was in London, leaving him in Boston alone. Although this biography otherwise narrates his life from inside, as he witnessed it himself, the present chapter perforce treats it largely as seen by others.

Yet in reacting to the upheavals of the time, Cotton Mather shared with many other New Englanders a single interpretive framework. He and they explained events according to a long lived public sense of vulnerability. As a persecuted minority in England, Puritans had grown used to expecting attack. Their settlement in America, however, did not ease their apprehensions. Instead, it demonstrated that their entire community was unstable and precarious, that troublesome and vast change could come at any time, and they lived under severe strain of invasion and disintegration.

*

The mentality of invasion arose from threats both external and internal. However the first settlers hoped to leave behind the corruptions and violence of Europe, they remained part of an international community. Holland, at war with England in the 1670s, made no distinction between mother country and colony, and seized vessels wherever New England traded; a day of public fasting was kept in 1673 to implore divine protection against Dutch attack. Invasion by a more potent and nearer enemy to

55

England, France, was a chronic threat, and Christian Israel had much to fear as well from its Indian neighbors, who raided often and bloodily. If not the Puritans' life and property, then their religious solidarity was menaced by incursions of other sects. Quakers—in the Puritan view, open heretics—first intruded on Boston in 1656 and kept returning despite severe punishments: for the first intrusion, loss of an ear; for the second, loss of the second ear; for the third, a hot iron through the tongue; for repeated intrusions, death: in the early 1660s three incorrigible Quakers were hanged. Baptists opened a church at Charlestown in 1665 and, although banished from the colony, managed to stay. And never far off was the prospect of a still more disruptive settlement in New England of Episcopal churches and an American bishop, backed by the crown.

The elements in New England were harsh and invasive also, protection minimal. An earthquake struck in and around Boston in 1663, transmitting six or more shocks over three days that moved objects on shelves and drove people in fright from their rocking houses. As a busy port Boston also awaited sudden calamities of the sea. The churches constantly invoked prayers for congregants then upon the waves; there were frequent reports of lost ships, and many widows. A combustible heap of contiguous houses, Boston lived under the constant threat of fire, too. Three years after the blaze that destroyed Increase Mather's house and church, a major fire destroyed eighty homes and seventy warehouses with a loss of £150,000, a toll proportionate to that suffered by London in the Great Fire of 1666. The very air threatened the community, bringing egg-sized hail, lightning to split houses, drought to blast wheat, and lethal measles, scarlet fever, and smallpox. As many as three of every ten infants in Boston died, compared with one in sixty in present America. The smallpox epidemic that struck just after Cotton Mather's graduation killed an estimated eight hundred persons; the coffins passed each other in the street.

The Puritans' habit of interpreting such events as judgments of God expanded their feeling of vulnerability. When houses rocked in 1663 it was thought, said one contemporary, that "these *Earthquakes* might portend the shaking the Foundations of our Churches, and of our Civil State." In the brilliant appearance of Halley's comet Increase Mather saw a portent of worse ahead:

> I am persuaded, that the floods of great water are coming. I am persuaded that God is about to open the windows of heaven, and to pour down the Cataracts of his Wrath, ere this Generation (wherein *Atheism* and *Profane-*

ness are come to such a prodigious height) I say, ere this Generation is passed away.

The idea that New England's plague of fire, war, disease, and drought represented divine punishment for its internal rot became more vehemently proclaimed the more the rot spread. And the 1680s, many felt, climaxed an insidious religious and social deterioration that had been evident for at least twenty years (see the note in Documentation) Writing in the eighteenth century, the minister Thomas Prince observed that a decay of piety occurred in New England a little after 1660, "And this increased to 1670, when it grew very visible and threatening, and was generally complained of and bewailed bitterly by the Pious among them; And yet much more to 1680, when but few of the first Generation remained." Sermons preached throughout New England bemoaned this decay and articulated the fear of the godly that, as one wrote, "New England hath seen its best days."

Among the chief signs that the moldering foundations of church and state might soon be overturned was the failure of many young persons to experience grace, that inward supernatural cleansing of perception which signified salvation. According to the original Congregational theory, only the gracious—the Saints—were entitled to full church membership, that is to taking the Lord's Supper and having their children baptized. The failure of many of the new generation to experience grace meant that fewer persons took communion and far fewer were being baptized. To deal with declining church membership, seventy church representatives met in March 1662 at the Boston First Church to discuss the question "Who are the subjects of baptism?" Their answer modified the original theory, extending baptism to the children of godly persons who were not full church members, that is, who had not experienced grace but had been baptized themselves and who professed an intellectual faith and submitted to church discipline. This famous Halfway Covenant carried at the Synod by better than seven votes to one, but resulted in a flood of controversial pamphlets and bitter divisions in many churches. Indeed, Increase Mather had refused to vote with the majority, although it included Richard Mather, his eminent father. From his deathbed Richard asked his son no longer to oppose the Halfway Covenant, but under Increase the North Church still stubbornly refused to baptize children of the unregenerate. At issue was simply whether to adhere to original Congregational theory and see church membership dwindle, or open the church to the ungracious and, in the minds of some, betray the Fathers.

Christian Israel felt equally threatened by the social expression of this

decay, a transformation of manners and morals that weakened the Puritans' strict sexual code and their devotion to family life. In 1672, a county
court convicted a woman named Alice Thomas "of great suspicion to
keep a brothel-house." This was apparently the first brothel in Boston,
although from 1670 to 1680 the Suffolk County Court sat on eleven more
cases of prostitution. Other signs of a growing sexual excess were more
violent, exotic, or unfeeling. Samuel Sewall mentions a Haverhill man
who raped Goodwife Nash of Amesbury in a pasture; a boy executed for
committing bestiality with a mare in broad daylight in an open yard; and,
in 1685, the discovery in the stall of a tobacco shop of an abandoned
infant pinned in a cloth: "So far as I can hear," Sewall remarks, "this is
the first Child that ever was in such a manner exposed in Boston." By the
1680s ministers had also to vie for attention with French and English
dancing masters, such as the Francis Stepney who held mixed dances on
lecture days and reportedly boasted that "by one Play he could teach
more Divinity than Mr. [Samuel] Willard or the Old Testament." Taverns
proliferated, and drunkenness, many alleged, was rampant; in April 1680
the selectmen approved licenses to sell beer, wine, cider or all three to
more than thirty different persons. Others complained of widespread
contention and a spirit of calumny, as if, Urian Oakes said in 1673, "there
were some Lying Office set up in New England." The deep, underlying
social change to which all these complaints and incidents point may have
contributed to an increase in suicide, against which several ministers
preached. In 1677, one diarist recorded within six months that a Plymouth woman who had nineteen children killed herself while pregnant
with the twentieth; a man named John Tomlin, of Boston, hanged himself
"under discontent"; an old man in Boston cut his throat; and another
Boston woman "in trouble of mind" starved herself to death.

The courts and churches struggled to repel this social blight, but it
only spread. The courts passed new laws ordering constables to present
to the selectmen the names of idlers, allowing county courts to fine wom-
en who disported naked breasts and arms, considering as riotous single
persons who rode out of town to drink and revel, empowering grand
juries to bring to trial men who wore long hair, their own or wigs. The
ministry took the part of the Old Testament Jeremiah, and joined in denouncing the degenerate younger generation, none more vigorously than
Increase Mather. "Where was there," he asked in one of his many jeremiads, "ever a place so like unto New Jerusalem as New-England hath
been?"—"hath been," however, for this was the New England, Increase
said, of the unconverted, not zealous for God "but luke warm and wofully

indifferent in the matters of Religion." The great Reform Synod of 1679–80 that gathered in Boston compiled a list of the "provoking Evils" of the land: pride in apparel, sleeping at sermons, neglect of church fellowship, Sabbath-breaking, lack of family prayer, naked breasts, mixed dances, unlawful gaming, lying, swearing, talebearing, litigiousness, drunkenness, overcharging. In these cankers, the Synod declared, was engrossed "this perishing people."

But however alarming it found the threat of war, elemental disaster, or inner decay, the mentality of invasion doted longest and most apprehensively on the undeclared intentions of the mother country. At the time of Cotton Mather's birth all New England waited anxiously to learn the disposition of the new monarchy, restored after more than a decade of Puritan rule in England. The new king, Charles II, sent a letter in June 1662, expressing satisfaction in the loyalty of the people of Massachusetts and promising to confirm and preserve their charter. But these gracious reassurances came with some demands. The king expected that liberty of conscience would be extended to Episcopalians. Congregational church membership, too, would no longer be required for voting privileges, but all landholders "orthodox in religion, (though of different persuasions concerning church government)" would be allowed to vote for civil and military officials. To be sure that Massachusetts complied, the king dispatched four observers, who arrived in July 1664. Ominously they came with about four hundred troops aboard two ships of war—the first vessels of the Royal Navy ever to enter Boston Harbor.

The royal commissioners were instructed to do more than observe. They also carried secret instructions to try to persuade the Massachusetts government to seek a "supplement" to the original charter of 1629. As Puritans understood this charter, it set forth and legitimated the purposes that had impelled the first immigrants to cross the Atlantic and found what John Winthrop called a City upon a Hill. To give up the charter was not only to deny their beginnings, however, but also to jeopardize their future. The charter, granted by Charles I, created a joint-stock trading company out of which the government of Massachusetts had evolved. Although the charter was little more than a commercial license for the Massachusetts Bay Company, the Puritans' view of their migration as a mission made the charter in their eyes sacred. It became, Michael G. Hall says, "illogically but in fact, a constitution as precious to the Boston Puritans in 1660 as the United States Constitution was to become for its citizens after 1789." Under the terms of the charter the Puritans had managed to live and to think of themselves as a small independent church-state, a purified American Israel separated from a corrupt Old World. The policy of the new king, however, was to make Massachusetts think of itself again—as did the other North American colonies—as a colony, existing to benefit the mother country.

The move against the charter was aimed particularly at empowering the king to appoint the governor of Massachusetts himself. The charter had granted the Massachusetts Bay Company the right, as a trading company, to choose its own officers; as the Bay Company became the Commonwealth of Massachusetts, the governor of the Company became in effect an elected political leader. Now to deny Massachusetts the right of electing its governor was to snap the tie between church and state on which the continuance of Christian Israel depended. In Puritan theory, church and state, Moses and Aaron, were coordinate authorities, strengthening each other jointly to enforce the moral law. The Cambridge Platform of 1648 assigned civil authority the duty of restraining and punishing idolatry, blasphemy, and heresy, and of coercing schismatical or corrupt individual congregations. Beyond that, government was charged with declaring days of public fasting and humiliation, passing laws against drunkenness or Sabbath-breaking, encouraging the college and schools, and supporting the ministry. Since a revocation of the charter almost certainly involved appointing a non-Puritan governor, it meant weakening the church and altering the Puritan character of the state.

In their own behavior the royal commissioners afforded a preview of what might be expected from a non-Puritan government in Massachusetts. They sent reports to London depicting New Englanders (with considerable accuracy) as rustic and antimonarchical, and warning that Harvard might continue to provide "schismatics to the Church" and "rebels to the King." They also set up as a court of appeals to review sentences already passed by the Massachusetts court. One was the case of John Porter, about thirty years old. This unruly man had been sentenced for saying, among other things, that he "cared not a turd" for Judge Hathorne. He also set fire to his father's woodpile, beat the man's servants, chopped down his fence, threatened to burn his house and kill his cattle, and called him a "liar, and simple Ape, shittabed." On top of that Porter tried to stab one of his own brothers, and cursed his mother as a "Rambeggur, Gamar Shithouse, Gamar Pisshouse," placing her as "the rankest sow in the town." For this oversized contempt of traditional filiopiety, the Massachusetts courts sent Porter to the Boston jail. He escaped, however, and presented himself before three of the commissioners, who granted him protection until his appeal could be heard.

Domestic and international political problems distracted the king's attention from New England until 1676. Then Edward Randolph, a leading advocate of strict royal control over Massachusetts, was sent on the first of his five portentous missions to America. He wrote home that the colony's losses and heavy expenses during King Philip's War made it ripe for a change in government. Yet the status of Massachusetts remained undecided for another decade. While Cotton Mather reached puberty, graduated from Harvard, and trained for his ministry, Randolph arrived and departed, composing censorious accounts of the Puritans' antimonarchical sentiments. Rumors often spread through New England that the charter was about to be revoked and a royal governor appointed. Massachusetts authorities fended off or made small concessions to demands from London, and reminded the king in petitions that for the liberty of living as they lived, "our fathers, and some of us with them, left their native land, with all their pleasant and desirable things."

In the public debate over how to deal with the long-threatening loss of autonomy, some urged submission, others compromise, others defiance. Perhaps the boldest spokesman for preserving the charter and its sacred privileges was Increase Mather. When the Rev. Samuel Willard denounced as madness a suggestion for resisting to the end, Increase told him that had Willard's grandfather heard him, "He would have Boxed his Ears." At a town meeting in January 1684, Increase spoke passionately to the question of whether, as he put it, to make "a full submission and entire Resignation of our charter and the privileges of it to the Kings pleasure." He answered that to submit was to "sin against God." Recalling the risky response of the biblical Naboth, when King Ahab demanded his vineyards—"God forbid, that I should give away the Inheritance of my Fathers"—he said he hoped "there is not one Freeman in Boston that will dare to be guilty of so great a sin." By one account he even excited his audience to defend the charter by arms. The meeting voted unanimously to resist the king's recent offer to "regulate" the charter for the mutual good of New England and the crown.

That New England's existence was precarious, Increase of course understood with special, visionary clarity. Foremost among the Jeremiahs recalling the rising generation to their Fathers' ways, he had publicly prophesied such other threats as King Philip's War, the smallpox epidemic that struck several of his children, and the fire that destroyed his home. A few weeks after his speech he spent a day of prayer and fasting in his

beloved study. Once more emerging from it prophetically moved, confident that God had heard his pleas, he called out: "*God will deliver New
England! God will deliver New England! God will deliver New England.*"

*

On Friday morning, May 14, 1686—ten days after Cotton Mather's marriage—Edward Randolph arrived in Boston from England for the fifth
time in a decade, bearing the revocation of the Massachusetts charter and
the king's commission for a new government.

The following Monday at the Town House the commission was shown
to the General Court, in a room filled with spectators. Some judges urged
a protest, but Samuel Sewall spoke against it: "the foundations being
destroyed," he asked, "what can the Righteous do." The possibility of
some form of resistance was discussed at small private meetings over the
next few days, but laid aside. A week later the General Court met for the
last time. The Rev. Samuel Nowell prayed God to pardon the magistrates
and deputies for capitulating, then thanked the Lord for the mercies He
had shown to Massachusetts in the fifty-six years it had existed. Those
assembled sang verses from Habakkuk. With "Many Tears Shed in Prayer
and at Parting," Sewall recorded, the marshal-general declared the court
adjourned until October. But it was a gesture. The charter of the Governor and Company of Massachusetts Bay had been nullified, together with
all the rights and privileges founded on it. Massachusetts, formerly a City
on a Hill, was now an English colony.

Until the arrival of the new governor later in the year, Massachusetts
was ruled by a council, under a native of Massachusetts, Joseph Dudley.
He understood his regime to be provisional and more or less preserved
established laws and customs. Edward Randolph, however, immediately
challenged the concept of a Puritan state. The Lords of Trade and Plantation in London had been advised for several years to create an outpost of
the Church of England in Massachusetts, if only to offset the authority of
the Puritan clergy. Randolph, now a councillor in the new government,
had brought with him to Boston an Anglican clergyman named Robert
Ratcliffe; ten days after arriving he suggested that Ratcliffe be allowed to
establish a ministry in one of the three Boston meetinghouses. That was
resisted, but Ratcliffe was allowed to preach in a room of the Town
House. The event, on Sunday, June 6, attracted a large audience, perhaps
because of its novelty, although at least one listener also found Ratcliffe's
preaching "Extraordinary; he being as well an Orator as a Preacher." For
the first time in New England's history a minister had worn a surplice and

had publicly read the liturgy from the Anglican Book of Common Prayer.

The full meaning to Massachusetts of the loss of its charter appeared with the arrival of the new governor on December 20, 1686. Edmund Andros was sent to rule over the Dominion of New England, an enlarged, newly unified territory that incorporated Massachusetts Bay, Plymouth, New Hampshire, Maine, and the Narragansett country; by 1688 it would include Rhode Island, Connecticut, New York, and the Jerseys as well. Bostonians scrutinized his arrival for clues to his intentions, but came away uncertain. Ominously he debarked, Sewall noticed, in a "Scarlet Coat Laced." Ominously too, when oaths were administered in the Town House he kept his hat on. To the ministers present he spoke about the need of Church of England worshipers for one of the Boston meeting-houses, and suggested it could be used by two congregations. The Boston ministers met next day to consider his suggestion and agreed they could not consent; Increase Mather and Samuel Willard delivered their answer "in great plainness," Sewall said. But instead of confronting them, Andros apparently hedged. "He seems to say," as Sewall reported his response, "will not impose."

Andros's seeming appeasement hardly lasted through the New Year. He decided that members of the Church of England needed a place of worship and, with Good Friday approaching, he sent Randolph to get the keys to the South Church. Sewall and some others waited on him and showed him a deed proving the land and house belonged to them and said "that we can't consent to part with it to such use." According to Increase Mather, Andros then threatened to seize all the meetinghouses in the country. On Good Friday the sexton of the South Church was "prevailed upon," in Sewall's phrase, to ring the church bell and open the door. For the first time a Puritan meetinghouse in New England was used for Anglican services. Thereafter the services were held jointly in the South Church with Congregational services. The arrangement pro-duced friction: Andros and other Anglican churchgoers were supposed to clear the meetinghouse by half past one; on one Sabbath they did not finish until after two, filling the street outside with Puritans "gazing and moving to and fro because had not entrance into the House"—a "sad Sight," Sewall found it. At the same time plans moved forward to build a separate Church of England chapel in Boston.

The new government affected not only the churches. It also abolished the Assembly (the lower house of the legislature), limited town meetings to one a year, and required juries to admit more non-Congregationalist jurors. Trade, which thrived on evasions of the Navigation Acts, was curtailed by the now strict enforcement of them. Andros also demanded the right to oversee the accounts of the college—to Puritans the nursery of the ministry, to the king's representative a seedbed of Congregational sedition. He sent the Anglican minister Ratcliffe to sit conspicuously in the pulpit during the 1687 commencement, with Increase Mather presiding. He gave the most injurious offense, however, by repatenting land titles, on the ground that they had been voided by the revocation of the charter. Land titles granted by the former government of Massachusetts, rather than by the crown, were invalid. When a sheriff was sent to dispossess a family inhabiting Deer Island in Boston Harbor and to take possession of the place in the king's name, two selectmen protested on behalf of the town of Boston. Andros's attorneys told them "there was no town of Boston, nor was there any town in the country." Those whose forefathers Christ had led as a chosen people into the wilderness now must petition for royal patents to land they already owned, and pay a fee for the repatenting service.

A possible means of protest arose around May 1687. Increase's prophetic assurance had been to some extent validated; on the same day that he cried *"God will deliver New England"*—as he observed—King Charles II died. Although Charles's successor, James, was a Catholic, the new king issued a Proclamation of Indulgence declaring liberty of conscience to both Roman Catholics and Dissenters, news of which came to Boston in May. Some ministers apparently took the Proclamation as a sign of James's sympathy to Dissenters, and saw in it the possibility of appealing to him directly, bypassing Andros. Increase proposed that the ministers send an address thanking James for the Proclamation. When the address came off "very seasonably" in London, he proposed a second address, not from the ministers only but from the churches. Andros, enraged, forbade holding a day of thanksgiving for the address, and threatened to set troops by the church doors to prevent it. But the message of thanks went ahead, with the added proposal that someone from Boston present it in London. When several persons advised Increase himself to bear the address he spent a day of prayer, asking God to declare His will in the matter through the brethren of the North Church. Next day he "mentioned the thing to the church," which unanimously consented to his mission.

Barely two weeks later, on December 24, Increase Mather was arrested. He was charged with having defamed Edward Randolph, but he and others considered the charge simply an effort to keep him in Boston.

Much mutual animosity had arisen between the two men, but the charge stemmed from some treasonable letters, allegedly written by Increase. One very lengthy letter, read to the king and Council and in part published in London, intimated that Randolph had set the great Boston fire of 1676 (which broke out the day after one of his arrivals) and charged the English people, including the king, with "whoring after their own lusts." Increase protested that "not so much as one line of it was ever written by me," and laid the forgery to Randolph, "a child of the Devil." The court that heard the case, on January 31, cleared Increase and required Randolph to pay the costs of the suit. Exultant, Increase preached a powerful sermon on Rom. 8:31, telling his congregation that "When God is for a Man, they that are Against him shall do him good; whether they will or no."

Increase now openly publicized his departure for England, while Andros tried again to hold him in Boston. On March 18 Increase delivered a farewell sermon, reminding his congregation that Christ's love for the Saints is indestructible and everlasting—as, implicitly, was his for them—and that although he had often rebuked his flock, Christ too may be wrathful over sin, "But a Father Loves in his Anger." Andros brought a new court action on the same charge of defamation, and on March 27 sent an officer to arrest Increase again. But the officer was denied entry to the house, even though Increase was unaware of his purpose. As Increase later reported the episode, he happened that morning to take some "working physic," which "caused me to refuse to speak with the officer altho I knew nothing of his design." Not until rumors circulated that he had been arrested did he realize that Andros was again seeking to detain him. Then he stayed home several days with the doors shut.

About ten o'clock on the night of March 30, Increase commended his family to God and left his house, disguised in a wig and white cloak. A man named Thurton, whom Randolph had appointed to spy on Increase and prevent his slipping away, saw him leave the house. But according to Increase, Thurton told him that he lost heart and felt powerless to lay hands on him. Increase spent the night in Charlestown, at the house of his son's father-in-law, Col. Phillips. With Randolph's men searching for him, however, he fled to Rumney Marsh.

About eleven o'clock on the night of April 3, some of Increase's friends and his sons Cotton and Samuel came to Rumney Marsh and escorted him to a ketch, which brought him to a ship bound for England, away from Randolph, Andros, and the others "whose names," Increase wrote, "will stink in New England to the worlds end." He took with him young Samuel, leaving Cotton behind and, for the first time, without him.

*

Because Cotton Mather's diaries from 1687 through 1691 are missing, virtually nothing is known of his reaction to these events. Luckily, a fragment of his 1688 diary remains, recording his feelings during and just after Increase's disguised flight. Increase had often warned of his departure, of course, and since childhood Cotton Mather had prayed earnestly for his health. With his father now departing in fact, and in dangerous circumstances, he responded with extreme anxiety.

While Increase was hiding in Charlestown, Cotton Mather prayed and sang psalms that applied to his situation, and "kept wrestling with God, for his Preservation." He held a daylong fast after his father's removal to the ketch, loathfully confessing his unworthiness for mercy but nevertheless asking it, "especially such a Mercy, as the Enjoyment of such a Father, as mine." News brought to him the same day of fresh perils menacing his father's escape produced such distress that he threw himself on his study floor and, mouth in the dust, begged for his father's deliverance. When his father-in-law, Col. Phillips, arrived at night to announce that a single wind had sped Increase forward and retarded his pursuers, and that Increase was now safely aboard ship, he believed the Lord had heard his prayers.

Cotton Mather's anxiety was not only for his father's safety but also for his own survival. Increase's mission put him in sole charge of a flock which had for years been denied his ordination, and thrust him to the front of grave political affairs. Even while absorbed in praying for his father's safety it occurred to him that "my Father had now left me, alone, in a great *Place* and in a great *Work.*" Above all he feared disgracing his ministry. The possibility that, deprived of his father's guidance, he might dishonor God, "was to me, the dreadfullest Thought in the World." He prayed for assistance, and felt an assurance that God would be with him. Yet like many earlier assurances this one faltered. Days or perhaps weeks after Increase left, he dreamed that, being left alone, he was put upon preaching a sermon for which he had no time to prepare. But as usually also happened, fresh confidence followed doubt. Forced in his dream to the "Extremity" of improvising a sermon, he chose the text "I will never leave thee, nor forsake thee." Parts of the dreamed sermon were so vivid that he remembered them after waking and used them in preaching the next Sabbath.

Other fragmentary evidence shows that however alarmed by the consequences of his father's political role, Cotton Mather was not wholly unprepared for them either. Moves against the charter, begun at the time of his birth, persisted through his teens and the period of his candidacy. At the age of seventeen, six years before Andros arrived, he took notes as John Eliot preached that the civil and religious liberties secured by the Fathers and enjoyed by their descendants might have to be defended: "shall we betray our Liberties . . . Let us do as our fathers have done—Die in the possession of these things." Intermittently over the next few years he recorded new threats with dismay, expressing scorn for Edward Randolph as a man "born to do mischief," reporting to his uncle John Cotton the royal attempts in New Hampshire to offer Anglican communion and baptism, praying mightily for "Deliverance for this poor Country." When the Catholic King James was proclaimed in Boston by military display, he withdrew for a day of private humiliation to lament the danger to Protestantism of his accession. He realized, too, that the troubled times might demand his public and active engagement. As news circulated in the summer of 1685 that Massachusetts was about to have a new governor, he underlined in his sermon notebook a statement by his father concerning times of persecution: "*The Ministers of God must then stand in the forefront of the battle, and be the first that shall be shot down.*"

Exactly how soon Cotton Mather came to stand on the front line is unknown, but it was no longer than five months after his father's departure. The occasion was the birth of a son to King James by his second wife. Previously, James's successor was his oldest daughter Mary, a Protestant married to the Protestant William of Orange. But the infant prince now took precedence, and would be reared as a Catholic. On September 1, Andros sent an order to Cotton Mather, beginning, "In his Majesty's name, you are hereby required. . . ." Andros demanded that he publicly read in the North Church a proclamation for a day of thanksgiving to honor the royal birth—the inception, that is, of a possible Catholic ruler of New England—and there "stir up your hearers to the solemn work of the day, as is required by the same." Andros made clear, also, that this was an order: "and hereof you are not to fail."

Andros had cause to impress on Cotton Mather his superior authority, but may not have known it fully. For one, Increase was relaying to his son in letters, now unfortunately lost, news of his successes at court. By June he had had two audiences with the king, in the second of which James asked him whether Andros had performed satisfactorily; he replied by naming all of the governor's violations of New England's rights. He spoke with James again in July and, very encouragingly, again in October, when the king told him that "property, liberty, and our College should all be confirmed to us." Andros had another reason for showing his authority, although he may have been unaware of it also. At some time or other, Cotton Mather somehow obtained and copied passages of letters from Randolph that made plain his animus toward New England. In the letters, sent to the Earl of Rochester and others in the English hierarchy, he described New Englanders as a "perverse people" amenable only to force, and said he considered it no crime "being the occasion of subverting their old Arbitrary government."

One month into the new year, 1689, a warrant was sent out to arrest Cotton Mather and hold him for trial. Details of the case are again missing, but he was accused of having been, in Randolph's words, "the abettor, if not the author, of a scandalous libel." This obviously contrived charge involved a work published in Cambridge more than two years earlier, *A Brief Discourse Concerning the unlawfulness of Common Prayer Worship.* The pamphlet appeared anonymously and was quite certainly written by Increase; Cotton, however, probably edited it and supervised its printing. The author of the *Brief Discourse,* identified only as a minister, attacked the Common Prayer Book and such Anglican practices as the use of a ring in marriage, making a sign of the cross in baptism, and kneeling at communion. These he condemned as superstitious and "*in a great measure Popish and Heathenish.*" According to one supporter of Andros, the thrust of the work was to insinuate "unto the Common People, that the Governor and all of the Church of *England* were Papists and Idolators, and to stir them up to Faction and Rebellion."

The Mathers' longtime friend Wait Winthrop, a member of the Council, managed to squash the order of arrest, although Cotton Mather became the target of new threats shortly after his birthday in February. The court now charged him with breaching the Act of Uniformity and began, he said, "tearing me to pieces, with their horrible *Talons.*" Under a "Storm of *Persecution* from the Church of England," he offered himself as an example of willing self-sacrifice for Christ. Amidst his troubles he preached to a congregation of nearly two thousand persons on the same text his father had used after being cleared of defaming Randolph—If God be for us, who can be against us—attempting to convey, he said, "a glorious Triumph, over Enemies and Sufferings."

The new threat of arrest apparently hovered over Cotton Mather for two months, until lifted by an event in England. The birth of James's son, and consequent prospect of a Catholic king, had induced William of Orange to land in England with a Dutch army, hoping to overthrow James and regain the throne for Protestantism. Rumors of his landing circulated in Boston early in the year, but dependable news seems to have come the first week in April 1689, when John Winslow (grandson of the Plymouth founder) returned from the West Indies with a copy of a document proclaiming William as king. When Andros learned of this inflammatory arrival he demanded Winslow's papers; Winslow refused, and was jailed for bringing into the country a treasonous libel. Andros issued his own proclamation, requiring the people and officers to be in a state of readiness should the usurper send forces to New England.

What remains of Cotton Mather's reaction to news of the Glorious Revolution in England are notes for a powerfully suggestive sermon he preached on April 14, entitled "The Mystery of Providence." He spoke on the cryptic prophetical text Ezekiel 1:16: "The fashion of the wheels and their work was like unto a chrysolite: and they four had one form, and their fashion, and their work was as one wheel in another wheel." He justified the Revolution by interpreting the wheels as the state of human affairs, intricately moved by God's providence "for the Best Issue and event that can be, His own glory." Perhaps more personally, he preached that those chosen by God are sometime brought low, but then "the wheel turns again, upon the Foes of God." His surviving notes leave unclear, however, whether he tried to rouse his congregation to rise against Andros. "Men do Gods Business," he told them, "when they go on their own Errands"—rather ambiguous counsel which might be construed as advising either rebellion or quietism.

Four days later, on April 18, Cotton Mather apparently was to be arrested. The same day, Boston took arms against Andros's government. Mather left no account of his direct part in the revolt, but Randolph later repeatedly accused him of being one of the "chief designers." Randolph claimed that although the uprising was defended as "the act of all the people," it was actually plotted by some prominent church members, some older magistrates, and six ministers: the Baptist minister Milborne, and the Congregationalist ministers Moodey, Morton, Allen, Willard, and "young Mather." (Mather was now twenty-six, while the average age of the other Congregationalist ministers Randolph mentions was nearly sixty.) Randolph even charged that on the night of April 17, Mather held a meeting of armed men at his house.

Whatever Cotton Mather's part in fomenting the revolt, on the morning of April 18 the captain of the frigate *Rose,* a warship guarding Boston Harbor, was seized, to prevent the ship's either firing on or sailing from

Boston. (Andros planned to escape on the ship to France, it was rumored, leaving the city open to French attack.) News of the captain's detainment, a contemporary said, ran "like Lightning" through Boston, inspiring "the most unanimous Resolution." Drums beat a call to arms, small groups rounded up supporters of Andros, and by midafternoon more than a thousand armed colonists swarmed in from Charlestown.

Cotton Mather spent much of the day in the Council chamber of the Town House, the pillared two-story civic center at the heart of the South End. There the Boston ministers and other prominent citizens formed a revolutionary council, including the octogenarian Simon Bradstreet, who had been governor before the charter was revoked. Around noon a statement was read from the gallery to a crowd assembled in the street below, entitled a "Declaration of the Gentlemen, Merchants, and Inhabitants of Boston and the Country Adjacent." Contemporary sources differ on whether this statement was prepared a few days before the uprising or in the heat of it. Mather's part in composing and delivering it is also highly arguable. Some later writers have ascribed it to him but no evidence whatsoever exists that he wrote it; the style sometimes sounds like his, sometimes not. The author or authors of the Declaration would be worth knowing, for he or they composed a deeply innovative political document. The Declaration marks a secular drift in New England political thought from the theological and providential treatment of affairs to constitutional and legal ones, and from a communal conception of the rights belonging to God's Chosen People to a conception of the rights of Englishmen. It also launches a New England revolutionary tradition that would culminate in 1776.

All that can confidently be said is that Cotton Mather enthusiastically approved of the Declaration. Its pacific sentiments appealed to his wish, in defiance of his underlying anger, to act the part of the meek conciliator. He also feared and disapproved rash action that might be both bloody and politically damaging to a New England already too well-known abroad for its alleged disorderliness. Especially, as a "Gentleman" himself, he scorned an armed rural mob. He and the other gentlemen hoped to contain the revolt, avoid bloodshed, and safeguard the political prisoners while awaiting instructions from England. As Mather later summed up their thinking, the gentlemen agreed that although New England had as compelling grounds for a revolution as Old England, yet they would if possible extinguish any popular attempt at an "*Insurrection*," awaiting orders from London. But "if the Country people, by any unrestrainable Violences" pushed toward revolution, then to prevent bloodshed by an "ungoverned *Mobile*" they would appear with and present the Declaration.

As later printed, the *Declaration of the Gentlemen* (1689) consists of twelve brief articles. They treat the Andros administration as part of a larger effort to extinguish Protestantism in the name of Rome, and rehearse familiar grievances against the Dominion government: jail for refusing to swear on the Bible, revocation of land titles, Joseph Dudley's infamous statement in Council that New Englanders "were all *Slaves* and the only difference between them and *Slaves* is their not being bought and sold," and so on. While the gentlemen offer these grievances as justification for the seizure of government officials, they painstakingly explain that they intended only to secure the officials for the fate decided upon at home, "for what Justice, Orders from his Highness with the *Parliament* shall direct." New Englanders, the document makes plain in every way, are not revolutionaries, but orderly, loyal subjects of the king.

Whether Cotton Mather wrote the Declaration or not, he probably delivered it from the gallery of the Town House. He went there, according to his son Samuel, when it became clear to the provisional council that the people had become "driving and furious," and he "reasoned down the Passions of the Populace." Had he "lisped" a syllable against those who had tried to jail him, Samuel said, perhaps "the People would by a sudden *Council of War* have try'd, judg'd and hang'd all those ill Men, who would have treated him otherwise."

Cotton Mather seems to have been at the Town House also when, apparently later in the day, Andros himself was brought from the fort on Fort Hill. When the governor demanded to know the reason for the uprising, he was told, by one account, that Bostonians would have his government and that he was now a prisoner. When asked to give orders for the surrender of the fort, he replied he would sooner die. Mather was certainly present when Randolph was brought in, for Randolph later recorded that he found Mather there "writing orders" along with four other ministers. Because Andros refused to command the fort to surrender, it was decided to have Randolph deliver the command in Andros's name. Someone clapped a pistol to Randolph's head and threatened to shoot him if he refused. He was forced to go, and the garrison at the fort surrendered. When Randolph's captors demanded that he deliver the same false message at Castle William, in the harbor, he did so, but those at the Castle held out for a day before capitulating.

By then apparently thousands on foot and horse had poured into Boston from the countryside, in "rage and heat," by one account, insisting that Andros be chained and imprisoned in the fort, as he was. Randolph and the interim governor Joseph Dudley were detained, together with as many as fifty other sympathizers and supporters. By nightfall the Dominion of New England had ceased to exist, and Boston again lay under Puritan rule, ending a revolt that was managed, Mather said emphatically later, "without the least *Bloodshed* or *Plunder,* and with as much *Order* as ever attended any *Tumult,* it may be, in the World."

*

Having filled his father's place at the front line during the revolt, Cotton Mather stayed there in the unsettled period afterward, especially in his role as peacemaker. The toppling of King James following the revocation of the charter left Massachusetts' form of government uncertain. Some New Englanders called for independence of the mother country, others for a military government; but most desired to return to the charter government that had existed before Andros. In the confusion, public affairs were conducted by the Town House group that styled itself a Council for Safety of the People and Conservation of Peace, most of whose members doubted the wisdom and legality of returning to the charter. Beset by demands for resumption, however, the council tried to resolve the issue by calling a convention of town representatives. The convention voted to reinstate the pre-Andros government, but because several towns had not submitted their views and others had failed to instruct their delegates, a second, larger convention was gathered. It began meeting in Boston on May 22, the time when for over fifty years, except under Andros, Massachusetts Puritans had held their annual election.

Cotton Mather preached to the convention the next day. The occasion was doubly momentous. Not only was Massachusetts to decide its form of government, but to give this annual election sermon was also one of the highest civic honors afforded the clergy. At twenty-six, Mather was by far the youngest minister to do so in the history of colonial Massachusetts. Conscious of addressing "as much of New England in this great congregation as can well be reach'd by the voice of one address," he acknowledged his youth: "For my own part, I confess my self but a *Child,* and among the meanest, the smallest of your *children* too." His feeling of inadequacy was probably compounded by uncertainty, for despite popular determination to reinstate the charter, he seems to have felt that it had been legally annulled, and to have grasped that the question must ultimately be decided by Parliament. He thus did not recommend a form of government to the convention himself, but rather described the spirit in which the debate should be conducted. The convention, as had been feared, opened in heated division and contention. This contention Mather depicted as itself the most dangerous of the many provoking evils for which God had been punishing New England by fire, drought, and civil strife. Passionately imploring each man to stop considering his scheme of government best and accept the other man's as next best, he pleaded for peace:

> He that Considers the Feverish *Paroxysms* which this Land is now raging in, through mere Misunderstandings about the *Means* leading to the *End* wherein we are generally agreed, and how ready we are to treat one another with fiery Animosities, had need cry, *Peace, Peace!* . . . I am old enough to cry *Peace!* and in the Name of God I do it. *Peace!* my dear Country-men; Let there be *Peace* in all our *Studies, Peace* in all our *Actions,* and *Peace* notwithstanding all our Differences.

Many who heard the sermon, his son Samuel wrote later, "fell into Tears and the whole Body of the People present immediately united in the *Methods of Peace* Mr. MATHER proposed unto them." Even so, Mather was probably not pleased by the outcome. Next day at least forty-two of the fifty-one towns represented voted to maintain the "rights and privileges" of Massachusetts by returning to the old charter, and reappointed the aged Simon Bradstreet as governor.

Whatever his doubts about the wisdom of the vote, Cotton Mather remained politically conspicuous under this restored but temporary government. From his pulpit he continued to justify the revolt against the "*Arbitrary disposals* of four or five Men, that beyond all measure hated us." He drafted a document proclaiming a day of Thanksgiving for the "Restoration of our Lately Invaded Liberties," and probably also had a hand in writing two addresses felicitating William and Mary on the success of the Revolution in England. He must also have helped produce *The Present State of New-English Affairs* (1689), a broadside containing a letter to him from his father. Here Increase described his interview with the new king in July, at which William "*kindly*" accepted the revolt in Boston and said, hedgingly, that New Englanders "*Should have their Ancient Rights and Privileges Restored and Confirmed unto them*"—if it were in his power.

Cotton Mather remained a prominent political figure also in the eyes of Andros's former underlings and supporters, some of whom referred to Mather privately as "the young Pope." Joseph Dudley, a native New Eng-

lander whose service under Andros made him much reviled, wrote to
Mather twice in June 1689 from jail, seeking his influence in "rolling
away the stone from the mouth of this Sepulchre, where I am buried
alive." Randolph, in jail himself, wrote to London complaining that
"young Mr. Mather" and "others of the gang" continued to promote antimonarchical principles, "and will oppose all commands from their Majesties which will not serve their interest (by them called the interest of
Jesus Christ)." Other supporters of Andros accused Mather of stirring up
hostility toward Church of England members in Boston. King's Chapel,
the Anglican church for which subscriptions were raised under Andros,
had opened for worship in June, just after the revolt. Its minister, Samuel
Myles, charged Mather with fomenting acts of desecration against the
building: "Young Mr. Mather informs the people that the reason of all our
Calamities is permitting of the high place [i.e., the Church of England]
among us, to this purpose hath he spoken in public several times of late."
The new chapel, he said, was already "battered and shattered," its windows no sooner mended than broken again.

In July the king sent an order recalling Andros, Randolph, Dudley,
and the others seized in the revolt to England, there to answer any complaints against them. Their removal did nothing to improve political affairs in Boston, for the temporary government under Simon Bradstreet
proved unstable and ineffectual, a continuing source of contention. Letters from Boston in the summer after the revolt abound in such comments
as "All is confusion here" or "Every man is a Governor." Compounding
the confusion, King William declared war on France in the summer of
1689, after only three months of his reign. The war spilled over into the
colonies, opening seventy years of European warfare in America and exposing New England to a new invasion, this time, Mather wrote, from
"whole Armies of Indians and Gallic Blood Hounds." Mather was dining
at Samuel Sewall's house in February 1690 when Governor Bradstreet
brought confirmation of news of the destruction of Schenectady by the
French and Indians, with the massacre of sixty persons, and reports of
pregnant women ripped up and of children having their brains dashed
out or freezing to death during a march to Albany. In mid-March came
news of a French-Indian attack on Salmon Falls, killing or capturing
eighty persons and burning all the houses.

To eliminate France from America became for Protestant New England
not only a victory over Catholicism and a dream of safety, but also a means
of showing loyalty to William and gaining his favor for a new charter.
Cotton Mather actively supported the Bradstreet government's decision to

launch expeditions against Canada, regarded by many, he said, as "the seminary of our troubles from the Indians." On March 20, 1690, he delivered a rousing speech to the General Court recommending the Canada expedition as "a great Service to be done for their Majesties: K. WILLIAM, and Q. MARY, whom God grant long to Reign." His language illustrates the underlying significance to him and others of the revolt of 1689: once stubbornly independent, Massachusetts was becoming an enthusiastic member of the English Empire.

The expedition was led by a member of the North Church, Sir William Phips. In May he took Port Royal and forced the inhabitants to swear allegiance to the English crown. His success emboldened more ambitious moves against Montreal and Quebec. These failed dismally. A large new fleet under Phips, thirty-two vessels with about two thousand men, sailed in early August, a month after alarming rumors of a French landing at Cape Cod, and near the end of a smallpox epidemic that took some 320 lives. Everything went wrong: smallpox erupted, commanders disagreed, supplies ran out, tempestuous weather mauled the ships. Phips estimated that by disease and casualty he lost two hundred men, but other estimates run as high as a thousand. The troops who survived returned to Boston unpaid and mutinous, and complaining of neglect, of men found dead in holes before they were missed, some having their eyes and cheeks eaten by cats. The treasury of Massachusetts, moreover, squandered fifty thousand pounds. To pay for the war the government levied heavy taxes. The disastrous expedition left Massachusetts at the end of 1690 feeling more vulnerable than ever, burdened by an unstable government, a depleted treasury, an exultant enemy on its borders, mourning in many homes, and the sense of a miserable defeat.

In this edgy atmosphere, dissatisfaction with Bradstreet's shaky interim government greatly increased. Despite his many calls for peace, Cotton Mather may have covertly contributed to the unrest, for he was accused of being the author of *Publick Occurrences,* sometimes called the first American newspaper. On its appearance in September, Bradstreet and the Council instantly ordered the paper suppressed, on the grounds that it was unlicensed, contained doubtful reports of events, and criticized the government. One specific objection seems to have been a report of the Canada expedition to the effect that the Mohawk Indians allied with the English failed to supply the canoes they had promised and lied about providing additional forces. The government, the paper suggested, had "too much confided" in these "miserable Savages."

Cotton Mather found that people believed he wrote the paper. The government, aware that his name was being "tossed about it," issued a severe proclamation, whose first line "thunders against *some*," Mather said (interpreting "some" as himself), "that had published that scandalous thing." Yet he admitted agreeing with the criticism of the Mohawks and said he considered the newspaper "noble, useful, and laudable." In fact, his denial, as he gave it to his uncle John Cotton, sounds slippery: "the publisher had not one line of it from me, only as accidentally meeting him in the high-way, on his request, I showed him how to contract and express the report of the expedition." Whether or not he wrote the paper, he took the accusation as an expression of ingratitude toward himself, "who have deserved so very ill of the country," and it awakened fears of tarnishing his ministry: "a few such tricks will render me uncapable of serving either God or man in New England."

*

The gap in Cotton Mather's diaries during this tumultuous time makes for a surprising contrast. Where his diaries break off in 1687 they depict a newly married young minister hungry for applause but agitated by religious doubt, worried about his father's health, cautious about his speech, and disturbed by morbid nightmares. But when he appears again in the accounts of others after his father's flight to England, he is a "young Pope," threatened with jail for seditious libels, "writing orders" on a revolutionary council, calming angry mobs.

Although this contrast, we shall see, is less drastic than it seems, these years did bring Cotton Mather several maturative experiences beside the political ones. Early in 1688, his and Abigail's five-month-old child, "perhaps One of the Comeliest Infants that have been seen in the world," died of "Convulsions." Committed to the idea that a minister must be an example to his flock, he preached the same afternoon on the nature of affliction, offering his hearers "such considerations as I would this day quiet my own tempestuous, rebellious heart with," namely that affliction is meant to induce us to seek the reasons for His chastisement. Yet he had looked often on the infant's "Lovely Features and Actions," and he acknowledged that "few outward, earthly anguishes are equal to these. The dying of a Child is like the tearing of a limb from us."

In October 1689, Cotton Mather also journeyed to Salem to attend his dying nineteen-year-old brother Nathanael. Endowed with the Mathers' prophetic streak, Nathanael had had a strange presage of early death, and since at least early fall had been seriously ill, apparently with a malignant tumor on his hip. A relentless scholar, he studied, in his own description, until "*He thought his Bones would all fall asunder.*" An incision had been made on his hip, which Cotton believed gave good hope of recovery; but Nathanael's continual sedentary studies, he said, had produced "*putrid Juices*" in his blood, which the incision circulated, giving rise to a fever which ended his life. Cotton admired his brother's learning, but saw in him a reprehensible contempt for his health. He disapproved of Nathanael's being less a pattern to young students than a caution, "for it may be truly written on his Grave, *Study kill'd him.*" Taking this "humble Self loathing Young-Man" as both a model of piety and a warning against self-abuse, within two weeks after Nathanael's death he had compiled a biography of him, *Early Piety Exemplified*, which he sent to his father for publication in London, the first of his works to be published abroad.

Never able to "*do enough*," Cotton Mather recognized a similar tendency to self-abuse in himself. Indeed, while embroiled in decisive political affairs and tending a large flock he did much else. He drafted documents for others, sat on church councils, joined an association of ministers in Cambridge, became in 1690 a Fellow of Harvard College, and partook in a pamphlet war against some Quakers (one of whom dubbed him "*The College-Boy of New-England*"). He also bought a new house and land, where he would live nearly the next thirty years, for the substantial sum of two hundred pounds. He had scarcely moved in before he invited to stay with him and Abigail a tormented young girl whom he tried by fervent prayer to depossess of devils (see the next chapter). Between 1689 and 1691 he also published some twenty-two titles, not to mention an extremely ambitious series of twenty connected sermons on typology which he composed and preached between August 1688 and November the following year. Increase felt that people were unreasonable in giving Cotton more work than his "weak" constitution could manage and that he was but "too apt to comply with their desires." Thus aware of his son's desire to please, he feared that his prolonged stay abroad might shorten Cotton's life. Twice from London he wrote to John Richards, probably the most prominent member of the North Church, imploring him: "do not Let him kill Himself. He will do it, if you do not hinder him." In fact the strain and overwork told. Partly by "excessive Toil" in his ministry, Cotton wrote in April 1692, "My *Health,* has been lamentably broken for diverse Years."

Much of this may suggest new boldness and authority in Cotton Mather during his father's absence. Yet when writing to Increase in May 1690, he seems hardly the same person who, two months earlier, had exhorted the government to attack Canada:

> But have you indeed come to resolutions of seeing New England no more? . . . I am sorry for myself, who am left alone in the midst of more cares, fears, anxieties, than, I believe, any one person in these territories, and who have just now been within a few minutes of death by a very dangerous fever, the relics whereof are yet upon me.

This whining manipulation of his father's concern for his health was apparently the reply to a prior letter from Increase, in which he raised before his son the dread prospect of his permanent settlement in England, because of criticism at home of his labors for the charter and inadequate payment. Identifying himself in his reply with "This distressed, enfeebled, ruined country," Cotton petitioned Increase to return on behalf of all New England, pleading that the country (himself included) had resolved not only to repay "our debts, which our affairs in your hands have made," but also such a requital "of all your pains for us, as would have been proper when you should have arrived here." Having learned Increase's lessons well, he closed with a veiled death threat:

> I confess that I write with a most ill-boding jealousy that I shall never see you again in this evil world; and it overwhelms me into tears which cannot be dried up, unless by this consideration, That you will shortly find among the spirits of just men made perfect, Your son. . . .

Cotton Mather's missing diaries in this period leave his inner life hidden. Yet this anxious, exploitative letter suggests that much of the difference between "the young Pope" and the uncertain young minister was that between others' view of Cotton Mather and his view of himself. While temporarily assuming his father's place in public affairs, he remained inwardly deferential and unconfident, and yearned for Increase to return.

While awaiting his father, Cotton Mather was nearly forced to flee to England himself. Rumors spread that the king would appoint as the new governor Sir Edmund Andros or Colonel Charles Kirk. The possible resurrection of Andros was frightening; he and his crew, Increase remarked later, would have "revenged themselves on and murdered the best men in New England." But the possible advent of "That Monster *Kirk,*" as Cotton Mather called him, was horrendous. To Kirk were attributed such atrocities as having hanged ninety wounded men and having executed thirty more by tens during an officers' dinner, upon successive toasts to the king, the queen, and Lord Jeffreys. When these rumors reached Boston, seemingly in the fall of 1691, they set off other rumors that Increase Mather had sent for his family, or that Cotton had been bound over in jail awaiting the new governor's vengeful pleasure. In fact Cotton awaited certain news, having decided that if Andros was returned, he and half a dozen important persons would flee to England.

The rumors came to nothing, for on Saturday evening, May 14, 1692, Increase Mather returned from London aboard the frigate *Nonesuch,* bringing with him his young son Samuel and the new governor, Sir William Phips, the former leader of the disastrous Canada campaign. Eight companies of troops escorted Phips to his house, then brought Increase to his. Cotton's pleasure and relief in his father's return was very likely dampened by illness, justifying his father's concern for his health. Just two weeks earlier he felt so overcome by "Vapour" and "an aguish Indisposition" that he could see "nothing but a *speedy Death* approaching." Ill or not, he wrote on the evening of his father's return: "*Oh! what shall I render to the Lord, for all his Benefits!*"

Increase's four years abroad had not made him less disgruntled, or less awesome to his son. Perhaps with both himself and Cotton in mind, only three months after his return he was again warning his congregation that the "faithful ministers of God are no less subject to death than other men," and that "Prophets may be killed by laying too great burdens on them." Dissatisfied anew with Boston, he began within a year having prophetic inklings of his return to England and prayed for encouraging signs, although now reluctant to leave because of the dangerous voyage and the anguish of departing again from his family, "and most of all the thoughts of leaving my son Cotton." Eight days after Increase's return, Cotton recorded in his notebook "My dear Fathers first Sermon, after his Arrival." In a blotchy, uncharacteristically infirm hand that suggests illness he took twenty-five pages of notes—the lengthiest entry among the hundreds of sermons he set down. And instead of entering the sermon serially with those of other ministers he had recorded during the year, he placed it in the middle of the notebook, numbering the page as "1," as if beginning a new year, a new existence. For eighteen months following he recorded virtually his father's sermons alone. A thirty-year-old man who had led a political revolt, he sat in church time after time writing down his father's words, taking over three hundred pages of notes on Increase's sermons.

If the Mathers had not changed, the governor had. Sir William Phips's speech upon landing, presumably in the candlelit Town House, made an auspicious contrast to the arrival of the scarlet-coated Andros. By one account he said that God had sent him to New England to serve his country, and that "all the privileges and laws and liberties as was practical [i.e., practiced] in the days of Old should be as they were before." Auspiciously too, as he was reading aloud his commission as governor he noticed that the sun was setting, marking the beginning of the Sabbath; he stopped reading, explaining that "he would not Infringe upon the lords day." It greatly pleased Cotton Mather also to have as governor a man "whom I baptised . . . and one of my own Flock, and one of my dearest Friends." (Phips had grown up in a frontier community lacking a settled minister, and had been baptized by Cotton Mather in adulthood.) That Increase and the other agents had been allowed to nominate several members of the governor's Council also promised renewed cooperation between the government and the clergy, Moses and Aaron: "instead, of my being made a Sacrifice to wicked *Rulers,* all the *Councellors* of the Province, are of my own Father's Nomination; and my *Father-in-Law,* with several *related* unto me, and several *Brethren* of my own church, are among them."

Cotton Mather also considered the new charter obtained by his father better than the former one. In fact, although Increase lacked diplomatic experience or training, his vigorous persistence had prevailed against court intrigues, wrangling, and betrayals to win what he considered a favorable charter for Massachusetts. In April 1691, he had presented New England's case personally before Queen Mary, stressing the country's willingness to enlarge the crown's dominion in America and its need for a settled government; the same month, in the king's bedchamber, he asked William "that they may be restored to their ancient privileges." On November 4, 1691, he formally accepted the new charter in the name of New England, in the king's presence. The best political minds he could consult, he said later, counselled him to "*Take your NEW CHARTER and be Thankful for it!*"

Encouragement to accept the charter was needed, for it differed from the old charter in undeniably essential ways. King William did not completely abandon the stricter colonial policy inaugurated by his predecessor, Charles II, at the Restoration. Although he allowed the Massachusetts agents to nominate Phips, the new charter empowered the sovereign to appoint a governor, lieutenant governor, and secretary. The appointed governor was given large powers himself, including a veto over acts of the General Court, and his consent was necessary for the appointment of all other officers nominated by the Court. The charter also granted liberty of conscience to all Christians except Catholics and eliminated religious

discrimination by tying suffrage to property. Even though the new governor belonged to the North Church, the irreducible meaning of the new
charter was that Massachusetts was not a Wilderness Zion but a royal
possession.

Opposition to the charter Increase accepted was widespread, including a faction that unrealistically insisted on nothing less than a restoration
of the old charter. Increase preached many sermons justifying what he
had done, scorning the ingratitude of New Englanders toward their public servants: "A Government has been settled among us. And, what an
ungrateful generation of Men may think of it, I know not; but I am sure,
Five years ago, such Favours, would have been of high Account with us."
Cotton, defending at once the charter and his father, preached on June 9
before Phips and the new General Court, praising the charter for securing
to the country "all *Christian Liberties,* and all *English Liberties."* He said
nothing, however, about what had once been considered the distinctive
liberties of New England, which now scarcely existed.

Cotton also wrote and circulated in manuscript, around 1692, four
Aesopian beast fables, works even more un-Puritan than his gaudy early
elegies but indicative of his love for entertaining tales and his unmistakable gift for narrative. One fable describes such favorable features of the
new charter as its confirmation of earlier land titles and its provision for
the election of the governor's Council by the lower house of the Assembly. Jupiter (King William) granted:

> that the birds might be everlastingly confirmed in their titles to their nests
> and fields. He offered that not so much as a twig should be plucked from
> any tree the birds would roost upon, without their own consent. He of
> fered that the birds might constantly make their own laws, and annually
> choose their own rulers. . . . He offered that it should be made impossible
> for any to disturb the birds in singing of their songs to the praise of their
> Maker, for which they had sought liberty in the wilderness.

Despite this benignly pastoral vision of freedom and security under the
new charter, in another fable Cotton presented Increase as Mercury at
Jupiter's court, laboring to rebuild the sheep's fold but finding it "necessary to comply with such directions as Jupiter . . . had given for the new
shaping of the folds; otherwise he saw the poor sheep had been left
without any folds at all." However Cotton wished to justify his father's
energetic and unselfish work, there was no denying that Increase had
accomplished not what he wanted but as much as he could.

The charter's full implications for Christian Israel would appear later.

For now, New England had another problem, unrelated but bedazzling. Increase Mather spoke of it in the first sermon he preached after his return, when he found the jails filled with accused witches. Recently invaded by Andros and Randolph, fire and smallpox, Quakers and Anglicans, French and Indians, New England amazedly faced a new invasion: "There is," as Cotton set down his father's dark words, "a power of Devils in our Air that are seeking to hurt us."

4

Letters of Thanks from Hell

‿✦‿

i

To COTTON MATHER and others, the enchantments that befell Salem Village early in 1692 seemed to repeat some earlier bizarre events in Boston.
Three and a half years before, soon after his father's flight to London,
Mather had visited the young daughter of a Boston mason named John
Goodwin. When he tried to pray with the girl she turned deaf and could
not hear again until the prayer ended. She and three more of Goodwin's
six children had become subjects of widespread comment and amazement. Scores of spectators saw their necks twist almost around or gazed
on such tortures as Mather described:

> One while their Tongues would be drawn down their Throats; another-
> while they would be pull'd out upon their Chins, to a prodigious length.
> They would have their Mouths opened unto such a Wideness, that their
> Jaws went out of joint; and anon they would clap together with a Force
> like that of a strong Spring-Lock. The same would happen to their Shoul-
> der-Blades, and their Elbows, and Hand-wrists, and several of their joints.
> They would at times ly in a benummed condition; and be drawn together
> as those that are ty'd Neck and Heels; and presently be stretched out, yea,
> drawn Backwards, to such a degree that it was fear'd the very skin of their
> Bellies would have crack'd.

These afflictions had begun after Goodwin's eldest daughter questioned
a laundress who was suspected of stealing family linens. The washerwom-
an's mother in turn "bestow'd very bad Language" on the Goodwin girl,
who was immediately taken with fits, which soon after seized three other
Goodwin children as well.

83

Thus Goody Glover, "an ignorant and a scandalous old Woman," as Mather described her, was tried for bewitching the Goodwin children. An Irish Catholic, she understood English but could speak only Gaelic, and conveyed her meaning through an interpreter. Small images were exhibited that had been found in her house, "Puppets, or Babies," Mather said, "made of Rags, and stuff'd with Goat's hair." She acknowledged that to torment objects of her malice she stroked the images with her finger, wetted with spittle. When she handled an image in court, one of the Goodwin children fell into fits. The judges asked whether she had assistants: "looking very pertly in the Air," Mather reported, she replied she had, and then confessed, "that she had One, who was her Prince." The court appointed five or six physicians to examine her and advise on her sanity. They found her sane, and she was sentenced to death.

As Glover lay in jail awaiting execution, Cotton Mather visited her twice. Driven by both curiosity and duty, he hoped to learn about the invisible world, to satisfy himself that her confession was credible, and to persuade her to repent her witchcraft. He asked many questions; after long silence, speaking through an interpreter, she said she wished to answer "but *they* would not give her leave." When he asked, "*They!* Who is that *They?*" she said "They" were her saints or spirits (the same Gaelic word, he noted, served for both). She never denied practicing witchcraft, but revealed little more to him than that she had attended meetings with five others, including "her Prince." He exhorted her to break her covenant with Hell and give herself to Christ. He asked a reasonable thing, she said, but she could not do it, nor without her spirits' permission could she desire or consent to his prayers. He prayed with her anyway, for which she thanked him with many good words. But he no sooner left, he recorded later, "than she took a stone, a long and slender stone, and with her Finger and Spittle fell to tormenting it."

Glover warned that because others cooperated in the witchcraft her execution would not relieve the Goodwin children. After her hanging their torments multiplied. They barked like dogs, purred like cats, fluttered like geese, "carried with an incredible Swiftness thro the Air, having but just their Toes now and then upon the ground, and their Arms waved like the Wings of a Bird." As though mad they climbed high fences. One of the boys groaned of being roasted on a spit run through his mouth and out his foot, shrieked that knives cut him, had his head invisibly nailed to the floor, "that it was as much as a strong man could do to pull it up." Although many observed these seizures, including several ministers, Mather was kept away by other business. Yet he wished to ease the tortured children, and hoped to gather eyewitness evidence to confute skeptics. He took the eldest Goodwin child, Martha, about thirteen years old, into the three-story home he had recently bought for himself and Abigail. The first few days she behaved normally, indeed seemed pious and industrious. But on the morning of November 20 she cried, "Ah, *They* have found me out!"

At once Martha Goodwin's fits resumed, only now in Cotton Mather's house. She would choke on a ball the size of a small egg; when she tried to bite a roasted apple her arms stiffened; she flew and dove, reeled and spewed as if drunk. They, she announced, were scheming a fall or blow or other harm to Abigail. Two phenomena fascinated Mather especially, the first involving an invisible chain. They would chain Martha and haul her from her seat toward the fire. When he stomped the hearth she screamed, protesting that he jarred the chain and hurt her back. He managed—as he would not be allowed to forget—to defend her from the chain: "Once I did with my own hand," he wrote, "knock it off, as it began to be fastened about her." They also brought Martha a horse, upon which she sprang and, settling in a riding posture, sometimes ambled, sometimes trotted, sometimes galloped furiously. "In these motions we could not perceive that she was stirred by the stress of her feet, upon the ground; for often she touch't it not." Once she rode up the stairs through the open door of his study, where she dismounted and exclaimed, "They are gone; they are gone! They say, that they cannot,—God won't let 'em come here!" Self-possessed again she sat in the study reading Scripture and pious books much of the afternoon. But when she returned downstairs "the Daemons were in a quarter of a minute as bad upon her as before, and her Horse was Waiting for her." Mather tried to return her to his study, but she became "twisted and writhen," weighed three times as much as before, was pulled from his hands and shoved on him, and he at last dragged her up the stairs only with help and by "incredible Forcing" while she screamed, "They say I must not go in!" As soon as she entered she stood up and said, in an altered tone, "now I am well."

However amazed by the workings of the invisible world, Mather remained alertly curious and made some wary experiments. He realized he might easily "be too bold, and go too far"; but he also saw an opportunity to propose and solve many "Problems which the pneumatic Discipline is concerned in." He tested the devils' telepathic abilities, although inconclusively. That devils can read thoughts was indicated when he called Martha by name, having in mind some religious expedient for her relief. Her neck went limp, as if broken, and he could not revive her until he "laid aside my purpose of speaking what I thought." A different experiment, however, indicated that devils had no telepathic power. When the Goodwin children were being undressed, the body part involved became so contorted there was "no coming at it." To see what would happen if one thing were thought but another thing said, an instruction was given to untie the child's neckcloth, followed by the untying of the child's shoe. Yet what became "strangely inaccessible" was not the shoe but the neckcloth. The conflicting results led Mather to speculate that some devils could read thoughts, others not, and that "Perhaps all Devils are not alike sagacious." He particularly wanted to determine Martha's ability to read religious books. Although such book tests were used as evidence of witchcraft or possession, he regarded them as a "fanciful Business" that devils might use as an ingenious trap. Just the same the book tests worked. When Martha tried to read the Bible her eyes became "strangely twisted and blinded." She could read from Quaker or Catholic books, but the sight of John Cotton's *Milk for Babes* convulsed her. And when she opened Increase Mather's *Mystery of Christ* she was "immediately struck backwards as dead upon the floor."

Even more than Cotton Mather hoped to learn about the invisible world he hoped to depossess Martha and the other "Haunted Children" by fervent and repeated prayer. But devotional exercises held for her relief were the worst of all the provocations that could be given her. When prayers were begun, "the Devils would still throw her on the Floor, at the feet of him that prayed." To drown out the prayers she whistled, sang, and made odd noises, beating and kicking whoever prayed although her fist and foot always recoiled a few hairs breadths from him, as if rebounding against a wall. As prayer continued she lay for dead, "her Belly swelled like a Drum, and sometimes with croaking Noises in it." Nevertheless, and despite several seeming cures followed by relapses, the prayers of Mather and the other Boston ministers ultimately restored the Goodwin children. John Goodwin, regretting that his daughter had been to Mather "but a troublesome guest," publicly thanked him, grateful that "his bowels so yearned towards us in this sad condition."

Mather's experience with Martha Goodwin had important results in his life. The five or six weeks she spent in his home brought him firsthand experience of evil spirits, and he resolved "after this, never to use but just one grain of patience with any man that shall go to impose upon me a Denial of Devils, or of Witches." In January 1691, too, Martha was herself admitted to membership in his church. He also produced his first important book-length publication, *Memorable Providences, Relating to*

Witchcrafts and Possessions (1689). He clearly intended to write an important book on an important witchcraft case, comparable to works by outstanding English ministers and demonologists. He succeeded, for his bout with invisible horses and chains inspired him to some of his most absorbing narrative writing and his cleverest organization, the brief sections and lively pace overcoming the repetitiousness of the events. The work appeared in a second edition in London in 1691 and a third edition in Edinburgh in 1697, and was often remembered later as it merged into a broad stream of tales of the supernatural. The London edition contained a recommendation by the prestigious Richard Baxter, who rejoiced, Mather learned, to leave behind someone "likely to prove so great a Master Builder in the Lords Work."

The book had another important effect also. About eighteen months after it appeared, some other young girls became topics of comment and amazement as they too succumbed to convulsive fits. According to the minister John Hale, they were "in all things afflicted as bad as John Goodwin's children at Boston, in the year 1689. So that he that will read Mr. Mather's Book of *Memorable Providences,* page 3 etc., may Read part of what these Children, and afterward sundry grown persons suffered by the hand of Satan, at Salem Village, and parts adjacent."

*

The linking of Cotton Mather with the Salem witchcraft trials began in his own time and persists to the present. In the popular imagining of the American past the man and the event are nearly synonymous. Yet the exact connection between the two remains obscure. Two questions are involved: did Mather excite accusations of witchcraft at Salem? and did he promote the trial and sentencing of the witches? For the first, John Hale's remark suggests that at least some contemporaries viewed the eruption at Salem as Mather had taught them to see cases of witchcraft. At one peak of the trials, in June 1692, a man named Brodbent wrote from Boston that "young Mather spoke pretty true when he preached a sermon about two years ago that the old landlord Satan would Arrest the Country out of their hands." Robert Calef, Mather's angriest and most dogged critic, charged that by being "the most active and forward of any minister in the country" in the Goodwin case, and by printing his account of it, Mather "conduced much to the kindling of those flames" at Salem that "threatened the destruction of this country."

Even ignoring Calef's debatable accuracy as a historian and his personal antagonism to Mather, there remains no doubt that in the eighteen months or so between the Goodwin case and the Salem outbreaks, Mather kept calling public attention to the existence of devils and witches. In a last-minute "Notandum" added to *Memorable Providences* sometime after June 1689, he informed readers that since he had completed his history another "very wonderful Attempt" had been made on a different family in Boston, "(probably by Witchcraft)," and he speculated that God may have permitted it in order to expose more witches. His preaching can be charted to show that he continually reminded his congregation of a hostile invisible world. In 1690 he described how Quakers at their meetings are "taken with a strange *Quaking,* which look'd so like a *Diabolical Possession.*" The same year he told a youth group that while he was preparing one of his works, "the *Devil* from the mouth of a possessed person, in the Audience of several standers-by, threatened me with much *Disgrace* for what I was about." Again in 1690, upon a new burst of fighting with the French and Indians, he preached that "The *Devils* are stark mad, that the *House of the Lord our God,* is come into these Remote Corners of the World; and they fume, they fret prodigiously." In 1691, warning against the public discontent that prevailed after the revolt, he asked, "How many doleful Wretches, have been decoy'd into *Witchcraft* it self, by the opportunities which their *Discontent* has given the *Devil,* to visit 'em and seduce 'em?" More examples from Mather's published and unpublished writings of 1690–92 could be cited. But these alone suggest that given the size of his congregation and the frequency of his preaching, he did much to keep alive in Massachusetts a sense of the malice of the invisible world.

Yet in preaching about devils in New England, Cotton Mather was not the first, and far from alone. Later history associates him with it because he published many of his sermons while other American Puritan ministers did not, although they held and preached similar ideas. The Charlestown minister Charles Morton, and three Boston ministers including Samuel Willard, wrote and endorsed a Preface to Mather's *Memorable Providences,* attesting that they had been "Eye and Ear-Witnesses" to many of the "most considerable things" in the Goodwin case as Mather described them. Morton, in one of his own sermons in 1688, told his congregation that in such disasters as droughts, God "improves Evil Angels as His Instruments and Executioners." Willard preached an entire series of sermons on devils in 1692. Increase Mather preached two such lengthy series, in 1683 and 1685.

More important, if obvious, belief in devils was not unique to Cotton Mather nor to New England Puritanism, but worldwide and ancient. According to a national Gallup poll taken in 1980, thirty-four percent of American adults believe in the devil as a personal being who directs evil forces. The possessed children in Boston and Salem represent only late, transatlantic instances of a vastly larger recurrence of witchcraft cases in Europe in the seventeenth century. In Bavaria, for example, a judge claimed the death of 274 witches in 1629; in Bonn, three- and four-year-old children were accused of having devils for lovers; at Bamberg a witch house and torture chamber were built and six hundred witches are said to have been burnt in ten years. Witchcraft cases were chronic in seventeenth-century America also, not only in New England but likewise in New York, Pennsylvania, and Virginia. Colonial courts tried more than eighty such cases from 1647 to 1691, resulting in twenty executions and many more fines, banishments, and whippings. Dozens of other episodes circulated by conversation and gossip. Their number clearly increased in New England during the 1680s, around the time of the Goodwin affair. Various sources tell of the devil appearing in 1684 to a Cambridge man, making a noise like a bird; of a 1683 case in Maine with ringing frying pans, mysterious arm bites, and floorboards buckled by invisible feet; of a fifty-year-old church deacon from Hadley who in 1684 suffered pinpricks and glossolalia, one of whose breasts was rendered like a woman's, and whose genitals were wounded or burned—and many more.

It must also be stressed that if the Salem possessions resembled those of the Goodwin children, both were in many features stereotypical. They conformed to a pattern classic in European outbreaks of witchcraft since at least the early sixteenth century. Almost invariably, the accuser and accused knew each other intimately, often as neighbors. The accuser had suffered some strange illness, accident, or other personal misfortune for which no natural explanation was apparent. He or she was aware, however, of having offended a neighbor, usually by having failed to discharge some hitherto customary social obligation, and accused the neighbor of having produced the illness or accident in revenge. The victims' symptoms were also stereotypical and monotonous—convulsions, speech difficulties, the sticking with or throwing up of pins and nails, appearances of cats, hogs, or other animals. On both sides of the Atlantic, finally, cases of witchcraft were distinctly community events. Whatever the behavior of ministers and magistrates, the responsibilty for prosecution and hanging ultimately rested on neighborhood people, who snooped on, accused, and gave evidence against each other. In their occasion, symptoms, and resolution, both the Goodwin affair and the Salem affair typify witchcraft cases throughout Europe and America throughout the seventeenth century. The enormous likelihood is that the girls at Salem would have become possessed, and their alleged tormentors would have been tried and hanged, had Cotton Mather never existed.

To us, the Goodwin children seem not possessed but turbulently rebellious. From the secular viewpoint of modern psychoanalysis and anthropology, their antics merely ventilated severely repressed desires and disapproved behavior. Similar demonic possessions of course still occur frequently in many cultures, preventing psychotic breaks with reality by affording underlying conflicts expression in a culturally shared idiom of spiritual beings which relates them to the people's larger religious life. Instead of driving the burdened person to an isolating private reality, the idiom of demonic possession allows inaccessible experiences to be made public and intelligible. Cotton Mather was unwittingly correct in equating diabolism with discontent, for much of the Goodwin children's behavior represented hostility toward Puritan standards. Through their fits they acted out with impunity the worst fears of those ministers who denounced the rising generation for wanting to explore sex, taunt their parents, and deride the ministry. "They" wanted Martha Goodwin "to keep Christmas with them!" so at Christmas Martha and her sister "were by the Daemons made very drunk." In Puritan New England, demonic possession was a culturally comprehensible and permissible assault on Puritan ideals, a jeremiad against the Jeremiad.

When read in the awareness of a society that demanded utter submission from the young, Cotton Mather's account of the Goodwin children becomes a tale of sassy adolescents who loathed washing their hands, going to bed, or doing their chores:

> If any useful thing were to be done to them, or by them, they would have all sorts of Troubles fall upon them. . . . at whiles, they would be so managed in their Beds, that no Bed-clothes could for an hour or two be laid upon them; nor could they go to wash their Hands, without having them clasp't so oddly together, there was no doing of it. . . . Whatever Work they were bid to do, they would be so snap't in the member which was to do it, that they with grief still desisted from it. If one ordered them to Rub a clean Table, they were able to do it without any disturbance; if to rub a dirty Table, presently they would with many Torments be made uncapable.

Puritan religious life also angered the children. When John Goodwin spoke to one of his sons about going to church, Mather wrote, "the Boy would be cast into such Tortures and Postures, that he would sooner Die than go out of doors." When Martha treated Mather with a "Sauciness that I had not been used to," when she knocked at his study door saying someone wished to see him although no one was there, when she called to him impertinently and threw small things at him, Mather rightly intuited that her tormentors designed "to disturb me in what I was about." These were no ethereal tormentors, however, but the restless spirit inside Martha and her generation, who would in his lifetime cease whistling and kicking and begin satirizing the ministry in essays, poems, and mock sermons. Martha Goodwin's heir in Boston, stripped of the grotesque legitimating guise of demonic possession, was the archetypal rebellious adolescent Benjamin Franklin.

Mather and his contemporaries of course located the source of Martha's behavior elsewhere, in an ever present, ever malicious world of invisible devils. Like others, Mather often wrote and preached about them, drawing his ideas from Scripture, patristic writings, demonological treatises, and notes on his father's sermons, but often adding his own speculations. Devils are the moving force in witchcraft, as Mather defined it: "the Doing of *Strange* (and for the most part *Ill*) Things by the help of *evil Spirits, Covenanting* with (and usually *Representing* of) the woful Children of Men." For him and most others the essence of witchcraft was this diabolic covenant, a parody of Christian practice, wherein witches promise to serve devils and devils promise to aid witches. The witch has no innate magical power, but can act only by virtue of the confederacy; not the witch but the devil produces the supernatural events in witchcraft.

Mather held the traditional Christian view that devils are fallen angels: "A *Devil* was once an *Angel,* but Sin has brought him to be a *Fallen* Angel; an Angel full of Enmity to God and man." Devils represent an entire order of creation, like human beings or animals, and can think and go about. They are confined as punishment to the several miles of dark air above the earth, where they mingle with the tormented souls of millions upon millions of the damned, excommunicated from the company of good angels, who dwell in heaven near God's throne. The fact that some men have been saved while they are damned fills the evil angels with tormented malice toward mankind, against whom they act with pitiless cruelty. Their number far exceeds the numbers of humanity, about whom they "*swarm* like the Frogs of *Egypt* in every chamber of our houses." Since the myriads of devils are united in one enmity, however, we speak as if there were one devil, "as we say, The Turk, or the Spaniard." One or many, they welcome an opportunity to do mischief in the world: "These are they by whom Witches do exert their Devillish and malignant Rage upon their Neighbours."

In their physical natures, devils as Mather conceived them were "a *spiritual* and a *rational* Substance." The definition may seem self-contradictory, but by "spiritual" Mather did not mean immaterial. Rather, like the Cambridge Platonists Joseph Glanvill and Henry More, he meant something between current popular conceptions of matter and spirit: the finest imaginable materiality, light and invisible, capable of being detached from or infused into more solid substances. To Mather, "spirit" also connoted vigor, and especially when he speaks of devils as spirits he intends not some limp fog but the acrid quickness of "spirits" of ammonia. Devils are vivacious agents who "dart" or "buzz" blasphemous thoughts into the mind, always in motion to undo men's souls, filling the air like midsummer flies.

Mather's view of the devil as "a *spiritual* and a *rational* Substance" intensified his desire to witness and publicize cases of witchcraft. To many persons of his time, the philosophical assumptions used to disprove a belief in witches threatened to deny the reality of Spirit itself. Disbelief in witchcraft joined declining manners, radical political theories, and the new science in becoming linked with forms of atheism. A logic that ran No Witches, No Spirit, No God, guides Thomas Browne's remark that those who deny witches "do not only deny them, but Spirits; and are obliquely and upon consequence a sort not of Infidels, but Atheists." As Mather himself told his congregation, "Since there are Witches and Devils, we may conclude that there are also Immortal Souls." He and others often identified doubts about Spirit with the ancient sect of the Sadducees, who in the time of Christ denied the resurrection of the dead and the existence of angels. Sadducism in the late seventeenth century became a code word for atheistical tendencies, and in the 1680s the target of a burgeoning literature in England. Mather's *Memorable Providences* belongs with such works as Nathaniel Crouch's *The Kingdom of Darkness: or The History of Daemons, Specters, Witches . . . obviating the common Objections and Allegations of the Sadduces [sic] and Atheists of the Age* (1688)—one of many works that assert the reality of supernatural phenomena as an indirect way of defending Christianity itself. Mather even reasons in *Memorable Providences* that God allowed devils to torment the Goodwin children expressly to give modern atheism the lie: "The Devils themselves are by Compulsion come to confute the Atheism and Sadducism, and to reprove the Madness of ungodly men."

Mather also longed to receive such "Letters of Thanks from Hell" because he sometimes doubted the reality of Spirit himself. Like every Puritan he found that during his conversion and his later growth in grace, the devil darted blasphemous thoughts into his mind. He had resolved at the age of eighteen to strive for a sharper sense of the *"Reality of Invisibles"* and had prayed during the religious crisis at the time of his marriage to be preserved from atheistic tendencies in himself: "O that my firm Belief of Invisible things may be as a shield unto me, defending me from those Temptations which, O Lord, Thou knowest, I find to be fiery darts." His intense curiosity about the Goodwin children was driven in part by a need to allay his own doubts. His dealings with them savor of *folie à deux,* as he played out his longing for evidence of Spirit while they played out their hostility to it. Once he tried to get Martha to own that she desired God's mercies and men's prayers, and to signify her desire by raising her hand. She refused, so he raised her hand himself and said, "Child, if you desire those things, let your hand fall, when I take mine away."

Mather's determined defense of spirit may seem to imply that he rejected the growingly materialistic view of nature in the late seventeenth century. Scientists of his time tried to dissociate the concept of matter from occult ideas with which it had been invested, so as to consider its purely physical properties. Ultimately the more precise formulation of celestial mechanics and the other triumphs of the scientific revolution did create skepticism about witchcraft, and discredited Spirit. But the effect was not immediate. In its early stages the experimental philosophy even dignified belief in the supernatural because, having seen many old ideas about nature upset by new discoveries, it held that no belief should be rejected out of hand and it regarded dismissive unbelief as a form of dogmatism. Also, the new science never completely discarded the older science it evolved from; even advanced thinking in the period was shot through with Pythagorean mysticism, cosmological fantasy, and Neoplatonist vitalism. Many scientists, being Christians as well, tried to harmonize older pneumatological views with new scientific theories. The chemist Robert Boyle wrote *Some Physico-theological Considerations about the Possibility of the Resurrection* (1675), discussing the Resurrection in terms of chemical transformations; Joseph Glanvill was both a preeminent demonologist and a member of the Royal Society, which he urged to investigate apparitions and demons.

In the style of the leading Christian scientists of his time, Cotton Mather dealt with pneumatological questions in both religious and scientific terms. Preaching about thunder in 1694, for instance, he proposed that thunder is produced according to "the Common Laws of Matter and Motion," perhaps by clouds clashing until their vapors take fire from contact. He also presented (and favored) the alternative chemical view that thunder results from decomposing vegetable matter on earth, which wafts to the atmosphere explosive "vapours of *Niter* and *Sulphur*." But neither account, he explained, denies diabolic agency: "it is a Scriptural and a Rational Assertion, That in the Thunder there is oftentimes by the Permission of God, the Agency of the Devil. The Devil is the prince of the *Air*, and when God gives him leave, he has a vast Power in the *Air*, and *Armies* that can make Thunders." God makes the mechanical or chemical laws, but may allow good or evil angels to mobilize them, although their influence is but the influence of instruments, "Instruments directed, ordered, limited by him, who is the *God of Thunders*." Mather used the same scientific-pneumatological thinking to explain how devils can use natural causes of disease to spread plagues, or why women more often become possessed than men (owing to the physiology of menstruation). He found nothing in new scientific ideas contrary to his belief in Spirit. At the height of the Salem crisis he wrote *Winter-Meditations* (1693), which discusses the formation of fossils and gives thanks that "we are Born in an Age of *Light*." For Mather devils and telescopes both proved the existence of God and confuted Sadducism.

Cotton Mather's concern for Martha Goodwin was rewarded by reassuring proof of an invisible world. But he also learned or became confirmed in methods of dealing with devils, which he would bring to the new cases at Salem. Like all Puritans he regarded holy water, crosses, and the entire Catholic rite of exorcism as gross superstition. He equally opposed the widespread efforts to relieve victims of witchcraft by popular magic. To conjure with bottles, horseshoes, and spells, he said, was "to *oppose Witchcraft* it *self* with Witchcraft." Such magic might even tempt the devil to intervene: "for ought I know, the frequent and constant Practice of certain *Magical Ceremonies* may have Invested many Persons with all the Diabolical ministry of Witches, who have not been well aware of what they have been adoing." Abjuring exorcism and magic, he followed Mark 9:29: "This kind can come forth by nothing, but by prayer and fasting." In Reformed tradition, the most powerful, and the only acceptable, method of depossession was prayer. In liberating Martha Goodwin Mather fought her devils with "no other weapons but Prayers and Tears, unto Him that has the Chaining of them."

The Goodwin case also confirmed Mather in certain ideas about detecting witches. For one, it persuaded him to abhor irresponsible accusations of witchcraft, such as apparently flourished in Boston: "An Ill-look, or a cross word will make a Witch with many people, who may on more ground be counted so themselves. There has been a fearful deal of Injury done in this way in this Town, to the Good-name of the most credible persons in it." In his jail visits to Goody Glover and his work with Martha he solemnly kept to himself the names of any other persons they implicated. In the "Discourse on Witchcraft" he preached during the case he also solemnly cautioned his congregation against taking reports of apparitions as evidence of witchcraft: "Suppose that a Person *bewitched* should pretend to see the Apparition of *such* or *such* an one, yet this may be no infallible Argument of their being Naughty people. It seems possible that the Devils may so traduce the most *Innocent,* the most praise-worthy."

The surest test for witchcraft, Mather believed, was credible confession. Here he followed the eminent English theologian and jurist William Perkins, who argued that *"Among the sufficient means of Conviction, the first is, the free and voluntary Confession of the Crime, made by the party suspected and accused, after Examination."* Goody Glover had herself demonstrated her hellish trade by handling her images in court, and her confession had stood up to the exactest scrutiny of her sanity by several physicians. Such confessions could not be disregarded without eliminating all judgment of human affairs and making a conviction for any crime whatsoever impossible: "all the *Murders,* yea, and all the *Bargains* in the World must be mere *Imaginations* if such *Confessions* are of no Account."

*

The new invasion from the invisible world began around February 1692, in Salem Village (now Danvers), Massachusetts. As described in *A Modest Inquiry* (1702), the classic account by the Rev. John Hale:

> . . . Mr. Samuel Paris, Pastor of the Church in Salem-Village, had a Daughter of Nine, and a Niece of about Eleven years of Age, sadly Afflicted of they knew not what Distempers; and he made his application to Physicians, yet still they grew worse; And at length one Physician gave his opinion, that they were under an Evil Hand. This the Neighbours quickly took up, and concluded they were bewitched.

Choked, convulsed, pinched, and rendered speechless by invisible agents, the girls were as badly afflicted as the Goodwin children had been, Hale said, yet "there was more in these Sufferings, than in those at Boston, by pins invisibly stuck into their flesh, pricking with Irons."

Despite the prayers of ministers at Salem and nearby towns the afflictions continued. Other young girls complained of being similarly molested, and identified three women or their shapes as the tormentors: a West Indian slave, Tituba; a bedridden old woman, "Gammer"Osborne; and a pauper who begged for food around the Village, Sarah Good. On February 29, warrants went out for their arrest on suspicion of witchcraft.

Pretrial examinations were held in Salem Village. Cotton Mather's old teacher, Ezekiel Cheever, recorded the examination of Sarah Good, on March 1, as conducted by the local officials. Good's examination has special importance because of her prominence in the subsequent trials, but also typifies the nature of the other examinations, and a part of it can stand for them all:

> Q. Sarah Good, what evil spirit have you familiarity with?
> A. None.
> Q. Have you made no contract with the devil?
> Good answered no.
> Q. Why do you hurt these children?
> A. I do not hurt them. I scorn it.
> Q. Who do you employ, then, to do it?
> A. I employ nobody.
> Q. What creature do you employ then?
> A. No creature. But I am falsely accused.
> Q. Why did you go away muttering from Mr. Parris's house?
> A. I did not mutter, but I thanked him for what he gave my child.
> Q. Have you made no contract with the devil?
> A. No.

H [Judge Hathorne] desired the children, all of them, to look upon her and see if this were the person that had hurt them, and so they all did look upon her and said this was one of the persons that did torment them. Presently they were all tormented.

> Q. Sarah Good, do you not see now what you have done? Why do you
>   not tell us the truth? Why do you thus torment these poor Children?
> A. I do not torment them.
> Q. Who do you employ then?
> A. I employ nobody. I scorn it.

Witnesses brought in against Good, including the other accused witches, offered plentiful evidence of her diabolic behavior. Tituba testified that Good had "a thing all over hairy," that she saw Good's name in the devil's book, and that she and Good rode together on a pole, holding each other. A man testified that Good appeared to him when he was in bed, bringing an "unusual light"; she sat on his foot, but when he kicked at her she and the light vanished. William Good, Sarah's husband, testified that the night before his wife's examination he saw below her right shoulder, and had never seen before, "a wart or tit." Good's own daughter Dorcas testified that her mother had three birds which afflicted the children and other persons.

A jury found Good and Tituba guilty of witchcraft. They were remanded on May 25 to the Boston jail and apparently chained. Good was then either pregnant or had recently given birth, for during her imprisonment she is known to have been nursing an infant, which died in the jail. Meanwhile, the number of afflicted and accused persons had jumped. By the third week in March the afflicted were not three but ten, including an old woman and four married women. More examinations were conducted in the thronged meetinghouse, where the cries of the enlarged group of the afflicted, one witness said, produced "an hideous scrietch and noise." Those examined included Sarah Good's daughter Dorcas. Only four or five years old, she had testified against her mother but was now accused of witchcraft herself. She was made to look upon the afflicted girls, who tormentedly complained of being bitten, and produced the marks of a set of small teeth. The court remanded Dorcas Good also to the Boston jail, where she would remain, chained, for about another eight months.

By April 11, the swelling numbers of afflicted and accused, and the growing uproar in the face of the Bradstreet government's uncertainty about what to do, meant that new examinations had to be moved from Salem Village to Salem town. They were held not only before local officials but before the deputy governor, six magistrates, and a large audience that included several ministers, who saw and heard the afflicted spasmodically swoon, cry, and scream when the accused looked upon them. How many persons were in jail by May 14, when at last the new governor, Sir William Phips, arrived with Increase Mather, is uncertain. Phips wrote that he found the prisons "full of people" and the number of complaints increasing daily. Having to deal not only with them, but also with the fighting against the allied French and Indians to the east, he decided to bring those who had been examined and jailed to trial. Before leaving for the east himself he appointed a seven-man commission of oyer and terminer, including Samuel Sewall, Wait Winthrop, John Richards, and, to head the court, William Stoughton—four very close friends of the Mathers.

As these events unfolded, Cotton Mather was seriously ill, his health "lamentably broken," as he wrote, in part by "excessive Toil." At some time he suggested that the afflicted girls be separated and scattered, and offered to take in six of them himself, as he had taken in Martha Goodwin, to "see whether without more bitter methods, *Prayer* with *Fasting* would not put an End unto these heavy Trials." His offer was not accepted, however, and his continued poor health kept him from accompanying John Richards to Salem for the court sessions, as Richards had requested: "the least excess of travel, or diet, or anything that may discompose me," he explained, "would at this time threaten perhaps my life itself, as my friends advise me."

However ill, Cotton Mather had pondered the happenings at Salem much and carefully, reflecting on his experience with Martha Goodwin. On the day the accused witches jailed in Boston were ordered returned to Salem for trial, May 31, he wrote Richards a long letter (five printed pages in modern editions), summarizing his views on the earlier examinations and offering firm, considered advice on the impending trials, where Richards would sit as a judge. The views he offered he probably kept throughout his life: first, that there are witches capable of enormous crimes, who should be executed; second, that witches who commit lesser crimes should be punished in a lesser way; third, that the identification and conviction of *all* witches demands the most extreme caution—although this last point, we shall see, he sometimes presented with disturbing qualifications.

Much as he cautioned his congregation at the time of the Goodwin case, Cotton Mather now particularly warned Richards about the use of so-called spectral evidence: testimony that mischief had been done by a specter or apparition of the accused. Such testimony had already been offered during the examinations at Salem, the Indian Tituba, for instance, testifying that Sarah Good afflicted the children "in her own shape." Such evidence was admissible in English witchcraft trials for a century before Salem, and as late as 1712, and was enthusiastically endorsed by the chief judge of the new court, William Stoughton. Yet Mather adamantly opposed using spectral evidence as proof of witchcraft. He reiterated to Richards that devils have sometime represented the shapes of innocent and even very virtuous persons, that spectral evidence lends itself to the accusation of people who have acted maliciously but not diabolically, and that the devil's chief means of creating havoc in society might 'be to cause the condemnation of the innocent:

> . . . if upon the bare supposal of a poor creature's being represented by a specter, too great a progress be made by the authority in ruining a poor neighbor so represented, it may be that a door may be thereby opened for the devils to obtain from the courts in the invisible world a license to proceed unto most hideous desolations upon the repute and repose of such as have yet been kept from the great transgression.

Mather felt that for advancing these cautions some might consider him a "witch advocate" himself—that is, a defender of witches. Nevertheless he urged Richards that persons accused by spectral evidence should not be reckoned "witches to be immediately exterminated," but that such evidence should be used only as a "presumption" that might justify a search for further evidence against them.

Such further evidence might consist of information an alleged witch could not have obtained without diabolical assistance, or of puppets used to torment victims, or of teats and similar body marks used for the devil's "cursed succages." But Mather cautioned that such evidence was also inconclusive. It should be taken rather as an intimation of guilt, leading to conviction only when found "in concurrence with other things." The most reliable evidence of witchcraft, he told Richards—again as in the Goodwin case—was credible confession. He emphasized "credible," forbidding the use of torture and dismissing confessions resulting from a "delirious brain, or a discontented heart."

On the ultimate question of punishment, Cotton Mather believed that unmistakably identified witches who had acted destructively in a spirit of intense malice should be executed. Just the same, he was deeply schooled in lessons of restraint and meekness, and except when meeting a direct military threat, as from the French or Indians, he abhorred violence. Only recently, in a sermon before the General Assembly, he had accused the Fathers themselves of overzealousness in sending Quakers to the gallows. He urged Richards to consider whether it was necessary to hang or burn "every wretched creature that shall be hooked into some degree of witchcraft." He recognized that the Mosaic law commanded "Thou shalt not suffer a witch to live." But he explained that devils easily convert "poor mortals" to witchcraft, particularly the forlorn or distempered—as he feared many had become, owing to the unsettled state of the country. Since devils easily lure the distressed into witchcraft he proposed lesser punishments for lesser witches, such as making a public renunciation of the devil.

*

By the standards Cotton Mather set forth to John Richards, the new court on which Richards sat was reckless and severe. Meeting for the first time in Salem on June 2 under Lieutenant Governor William Stoughton, it heard testimony against Bridget Bishop, the thrice-married owner of an unlicensed tavern, whose patrons drank late into the night and played shuffleboard. The testimony included spectral evidence by John Londer of Salem, aged thirty-two, that awakening in the dead of night he "did clearly see said Bridget Bishop, or her likeness, sitting upon my stomach." Two workmen testified that in Bishop's cellar they found puppets made of hog bristles and rags, stuck with headless pins. The court found Bishop guilty of witchcraft, and on June 10 she was led up a rocky elevation on the western side of Salem town and hanged—the first of the accused witches to be executed.

Bishop's execution alarmed many ministers, Cotton Mather among them. He drew up a statement entitled *The Return of Several Ministers* (1692), which was presented to Governor Phips and his Council around June 15. In behalf of the group of twelve ministers he expressed dissatisfaction with the court's incautious treatment of evidence, and argued that presumptions on which accused witches might be jailed, much less convictions on which they might be hanged, "ought certainly to be more considerable, than barely the Accused Persons being Represented by a *Spectre* unto the Afflicted." He also criticized two other features of the trials. Regarding evidentiary tests in which the accused witches were made to touch or look at the afflicted, he and the other ministers said they could not "esteem Alterations made in the Sufferers, by a *Look* or *Touch* of the Accused to be an Infallible Evidence of Guilt; but frequently Liable to be abused by the Devils Legerdemains." Regarding the crowded, noisy courtroom, he also cautioned the judges to admit "as little as is possible of such Noise, Company, and Openness, as may too hastily expose them that are Examined."

Had this document—and Cotton Mather's feelings—ended here, Mather might never have become a villain to history. But the document concludes with a flabbergasting "Nevertheless." Its final clause, as if discarding the preceding attack on the court's methods, urges the Phips government to push on the trials:

> Nevertheless, We cannot but humbly Recommend unto the Government, the speedy and vigorous Prosecution of such as have rendered themselves obnoxious, according to the Direction given in the Laws of God, and the wholesome Statutes of the English Nation, for the Detection of Witchcrafts.

The obscure, semiliterate Bostonian Robert Calef, soon to become Mather's antagonist, remarked that although the *Return of Several Ministers* appeared anonymously, its nature plainly identified the author as Mather. For the document, he said, was "perfectly ambidexter, giving as great or greater encouragement to proceed in those dark methods, than cautions against them." Mather himself seems to have recognized the startling inconsistency, for in later reprinting the document he omitted the final, blatantly contradictory clause.

Calef's very astute comment points to complexly intertwined features of Cotton Mather's personality and situation that would frustrate him throughout the Salem trials. What in part betrayed him into offering "ambidexter" advice were feelings of deference, loyalty, and youthful subordination to the judges. These often break through his earlier letter to John Richards, which speaks of "your honorable hands" or "your most worthy hands" while offering "my poor thoughts" and "my little skill." In fact, the judges were not only older, prominent men but also longtime family friends. Richards was not only a wealthy merchant, captain of the militia, selectman, and treasurer of Harvard, but also a property owner in the Mathers' neighborhood and a member of their church for nearly thirty years, as long as Increase was its minister. When Cotton Mather became an assistant to his father in 1680, Richards was the largest contributor to his salary; when Cotton married Abigail Phillips, Richards performed the ceremony; whenever some important church matter pended, Cotton consulted Richards, whose approval he deemed essential to gaining the brethren's consent. Cotton's ties to the other new judges were similarly close. Wait Winthrop, who had squashed an order to arrest him during the Andros administration, he ranked "among the Best of my Friends"; Adam Winthrop and John Foster were important members of his church; Samuel Sewall often went to hear him preach and admired his sermons, and they frequently dined together and corresponded.

And, in particular, Cotton Mather recognized "a real friend to New-England" in William Stoughton, the chief justice of the trials and the most vigorous prosecutor. This never married man, by whose signature on a warrant of execution witches were taken from jail and hanged, was intimate with both Mathers. Before entering the magistracy he had preached together with Increase; when Cotton was sixteen he inscribed to him a gift copy of Theophilus Gale's *The Court of the Gentiles* (1672); he attended Cotton's ordination as a representative of the Dorchester church; he was one of the judges before whom Edward Randolph lost his suit against Increase for defamation; and it was through Increase's influence that, when Phips became governor, Stoughton received a commission as lieutenant governor. In writing to and about the Salem court, Cotton Mather was addressing not only judges whom he felt were abusing evidence, but simultaneously neighbors, old friends, members of his church, persons to whom he owed favors and "for whom," he wrote, "no man living has a greater veneration."

Cotton Mather's relation with these judges was doubly compromised, however, for they also embodied the new government his father had all but created. Richards, Sewall, Foster, and the two Winthrops were members of the Council; Stoughton was lieutenant governor; and the man who appointed them, Sir William Phips, was "one of my own Flock, and one of my dearest Friends." To oppose the court meant opposing a government for whose existence a revolt had been waged, and to open again the breach, only recently healed, between ministry and magistracy, Aaron and Moses. Among the blessings of the new charter, Cotton had argued, was to have "our *Judges as at the First* . . . and that no *Judges,* or *Counsellors,* or *Justices* can ever hereafter be Arbitrarily Imposed upon us." Moreover, in the murmuring between the revolt and the arrival of Phips, and the more recent disquiet over the charter, Mather had spoken and labored strenuously and publicly to still jealousies, contentions, and factions by pleading that the new government be respected. On almost the same day he wrote to John Richards urging caution at the trials, he lamented in a sermon to the General Assembly how "every *Public Servant* must carry two *Handkerchiefs* about him, one to wipe off *Sweat,* of Travail, another to wipe off the *Spit* of Reproach." And he insisted that "'tis of inexpressible importance, that *Public Servants* be not abused for what they do." Whatever his own views on identifying and trying witches, he was not about to pillory public officials for theirs. An inveterate peacemaker, a leader of the revolt, and Increase Mather's son, he felt obliged to defend the new government, which meant he must also "wipe off the *Spit* of Reproach" from the court that was its first creation.

The "ambidexterity" of Cotton Mather's position had a less personal source as well. He genuinely believed that "most of the *Judges*" acted prudently and patiently, under "*Agony* of Soul" themselves. His respect for their honest efforts only complicated his conflict: "tho' I could not allow the *Principles,* that some of the Judges had espoused," he wrote, "yet I could not but speak honourably of *their* Persons, on all Occasions." His belief that the judges had acted prudently caused people to revile him, he said, "as if I had been the Doer of all the hard Things, that were done, in the Prosecution of the *Witchcraft.*" The charge was particularly unjust in the sense that he was himself deeply uncertain about the meaning of the events at Salem, an uncertainty compounded by chronic self-doubt, by his view of the devil as a uniquely subtle adversary, and by his longing for proofs of the invisible world to allay his own atheistical thoughts and to combat Sadducism. Salem was, he admitted, a "thorny affair," and to determine guilt in this "work of darkness" was itself a matter "much in the dark."

Indeed, Cotton Mather was not firmly convinced that the Salem girls had been bewitched. Just before the trials began, he told Richards, in extremely circumspect language, that the girls' afflictions might be due to possessions initiated not by witches but by devils themselves: "the devils may (tho' not often, yet sometimes) make most bloody invasions upon our exterior concerns, without any witchcrafts." A revised passage in his diary suggests that for a long while he remained uncertain whether the girls' symptoms came from devils invading their bodies or tortures inflicted from outside, whether they represented, that is, possession or witchcraft. Originally he wrote that houses at Salem were "filled with the horrid Cries of Persons possessed by evil Spirits"; at some time he deleted the word "possessed" and substituted the word "tormented." Even here he remained uncertain, for in explaining the revision he added that "There seem'd"—still a qualification—"an execrable *Witchcraft,* in the Foundation of this wonderful Affliction." Other possibilities occurred to him also. He speculated to Richards that the Salem outbreak might represent neither witchcraft nor incidental possession, but the approaching millennium, since Scripture foretold that at the time of the Second Coming Christ would dispossess the devils of their aerial abode to make a New Heaven. Agitated signs of his uncertainty fill his early letter to Richards—"I suppose," "I believe," "I do suspect," "Perhaps," "'tis probable," "I am ready to think," "'tis worth considering." Indeed, hardly a statement by him in this early period of the Salem outbreak is free from doubts, and from qualifications and reservations within and atop them.

In sum, the situation created by Salem called on Cotton Mather for answers he did not have, and he found it unmanageable. Any action might be wrong, no action was very certain. Emotionally and intellectually zigzagging every way betwixt disapproval of the trial methods, reverence for the judges, desire to defend the new government, longing for signs of the invisible world, uncertainty over the meaning of events, fear of speaking rashly, and lack of self-assurance, he on the one hand continued to urge caution on the judges, and on the other continued to defend their rash judgments, meanwhile continually hoping they would turn out to be right.

*

The court turned out, however, to be energetic. By one contemporary account, perhaps exaggerated, ten days after the hanging of Bridget Bishop more than seven hundred persons stood accused of witchcraft and over a hundred accused witches lay in prison. On June 28, Stoughton's court met for the second time, and in one day tried five accused witches. They included one of the original three accused witches, Sarah Good, who had been in the Boston jail for a month.

Despite the cautions of Mather and the other ministers against spectral evidence, Governor Phips wrote, Stoughton "persisted vigorously in the same method, to the great dissatisfaction and disturbance of the people." Much of the evidence presented at Good's trial was spectral, but it was overwhelming. Among others, Sarah Bibber, aged thirty-six, testified that one night she found Good's "apparition . . . standing by my bedside, and she pulled aside the curtain and turned down the sheet and looked upon my child 4 years old and presently upon it, the child was struck into a great fit that my husband and I could hardly hold it." Johanna Childen testified that the apparitions of Good and her infant appeared to her, and the infant's apparition accused Good of murdering it; Susannah Sheldon, aged about eighteen, testified that Good's apparition "most violently pulled down my head behind a Chest and tied my hands together with a whale band and almost Choked me to death." Others connected Good with mysterious and strange deaths of cows or the transportation of a broom into an apple tree, and much more. The court condemned Good and the four other accused women to death, and they were hanged at Salem on July 19. Before her execution Good reportedly said to the assistant minister of the Salem town church, Nicholas Noyes, "I am no more a Witch than you are a Wizard, and if you take away my Life, God will give you Blood to drink."

Considering Cotton Mather's adamant warnings about convicting suspected witches on spectral evidence and rushing them to the gallows, he might be expected to find the five hangings shocking. Instead, he found the judges' sentences "miraculously" confirmed. Hardly were the five hanged, he wrote, "impudently demanding of God a miraculous vindication of their innocency," when God produced evidence of their guilt. It arrived in the form that he, and William Perkins behind him, considered most reliable, as "credible confession." "Immediately upon" the hangings, five persons from the town of Andover made "a most ample, surprising, amazing confession" of witchcraft, and declared the five newly executed to have been of their company.

The confession of the Andover witches is among the least-known incidents of the Salem witchcraft trials, but for Cotton Mather it was a turning point. Sometime in the early summer of 1692, an Andover man named Joseph Ballard sent to Salem for some of the possessed girls, hoping they could identify the specters afflicting his wife, who was ill and later died of a fever. Others in Andover enlisted the girls for similar purposes. The girls acted in the Andover sickrooms as they had in the Salem court· they fell into fits and named the persons whose specters they saw tormenting the sick. Fifty persons in Andover were soon accused of witchcraft and thirty to forty sent to prison. Children, parents, grandparents, husbands and wives, accused and implicated each other. They were probably motivated by fear. Many who confessed reasoned that so far only witches who had refused to confess had been hanged. Six Andover women later drew up a statement explaining that they had confessed because "there was no other way to save our lives." According to an accused Salem witch, John Proctor, a statement implicating the Salem witches was drawn from two of the Andover witches by torture. He wrote from the Salem prison to "Mr. Mather" (probably Increase, but possibly Cotton) and four other Boston ministers, that his own son and two of the confessing Andover witches had been tied "Neck and Heels till the Blood was ready to come out of their Noses."

Cotton Mather may have attended some of the trials of the Andover witches himself, for he wrote, seemingly in August, that he had "lately seen; Even poor Children of several Ages, even from seven to twenty, more or less, *Confessing* their Familiarity with Devils." The confessing witches divulged much information about the workings of the invisible world. They denied from firsthand experience that devils could take the shape of innocent persons without their consent. Cautions against the admission of spectral evidence were discarded at the Andover trials. The local minister, Francis Dane, surmised that the reason family members turned on each other was that "the Conceit of Spectre Evidence as an infallible mark did too far prevail with us."

Virtually all the confessed Andover witches offered the same account of the devil's operation. The devil, they unanimously agreed, was a small black man. He got them to undo their allegiance to the Congregational church by renouncing their baptism, and had them seal their covenant with him by signing his book. Sixteen-year-old Richard Carrier, for instance, was one of many confessed witches who described the devil as a black man with a "high Crowned hat" who promised to reward his service with new clothes and a horse: "he told me also that he was Christ, and I must believe him, and I think I did So, I Set my hand to his book it was a little Red book I wrought with a Stick and made a red Colour with it and I promised to Serve him." The confessed witches all also described the devil's methods of rebaptizing people and of giving communion, offering only minor variations on whether his book was red or made of birchbark, and whether he dipped heads to baptize or flung initiates bodily in the water.

But the most spectacular revelations concerned a diabolic conspiracy. Witch after witch testified to riding poles to meetings where as many as five hundred witches plotted New England's ruin. Here too the evidence was overwhelming. When Mary Lacey, Jr., was asked why the devil wished to hurt the people of Salem, she replied, "the Devil would set up his Kingdom there and we should have happy days." William Barker, Sr., testified that at a meeting of about a hundred witches in Salem Village he learned that "Satans design was to set up his own worship, abolish all the churches in the land." Susannah Post testified that she had attended a witch meeting of two hundred, where she heard there were five hundred witches in the country. Mary Toothaker said that at a Salem Village witch meeting "they did talk of 305 witches in the country. She saith their discourse was about the pulling down the Kingdom of Christ and setting up the Kingdom of satan." Many of the confessed Andover witches who had attended these large meetings, moreover, identified the two ring-leaders of the conspiracy—a woman named Martha Carrier and a former minister named George Burroughs.

To Cotton Mather the Andover confessions not only tended to confirm the justice of the new court but also suggested that the Salem witchcraft horribly and drastically differed from the Goodwin case, representing not the possession of some young energumens but war from the invisible world aimed at destroying Christian Israel. This conspiratorial view of witchcraft outbreaks was common among European ecclesiastics. Indeed the notion of a diabolic plot against Christianity can be traced to antiquity, in fantasies of the existence within society of another small and secret society threatening its existence. Like cases of individual possession, such fantasies disburden repressed material, in this instance unacknowledged hostility to Christianity. Whether or not the Andover witches were projecting their covert animus against Congregationalism, their confessions struck deep and resoundingly into New England's mentality of invasion. Their talk of a plot to throw down all the churches in the land was entirely familiar, only it attributed to diabolic agency what had recently been laid to Andros and Randolph, and what for years had been decried as the inevitable result of exposed bosoms, dancing masters, and public drunkenness.

Cotton Mather himself was led to conclude that a diabolic plot was afoot to destroy New England: "more than One Twenty have Confessed that they have Signed unto a Book, which the Devil show'd them, and Engaged in his Hellish Design of Bewitching and Ruining our Land." Knowing the devil to be a wily adversary, skilled at sophistry, parody, and inversion, he had some doubt about the credibility of the Andover confessions. But the sheer number of them, and the support they gave to each other and to other evidence from Salem, persuaded him that they must in essentials be true. Satan may have woven delusions into some circumstances of the confessions, he allowed, "but one would think, all the Rules of Understanding Humane Affairs are at an end, if after so many most Voluntary Harmonious Confessions, made by Intelligent Persons of all Ages, in sundry Towns, at several Times, we must not believe the main strokes wherein those Confessions all agree."

On August 4, Mather made known to his congregation his changed understanding of the outbreak at Salem. It was a portentous day. The North Church was holding a special fast, as examinations of the Andover witches proceeded amidst continuing confessions. New trials of six more witches were scheduled at Salem the day after. And in the morning came news of a tremendous earthquake in Jamaica that reportedly killed over two thousand persons, sent the sea flowing across the island in a few minutes, and sank the iniquitous town of Port Royal. Appropriately, Mather chose the text Revelation 12:12: "Woe to the Inhabitants of the Earth, and of the Sea; for the Devil is come down unto you, having great Wrath; because he knoweth, that he hath but a short time."

Like other Puritan ministers, Cotton Mather usually did not preach at length on biblical prophecy. Its obscurities invited reckless predictions of the place and time of the Second Coming that often discredited its study, so that the subject was usually confined to discourse among the learned. Yet he had speculated in his early letter to Richards that Salem might be a harbinger of the end of time, and now from his pulpit he recalled the notion that the span allotted from the first Sabbath at the creation of the world to the founding of the New Jerusalem was twenty-three hundred years, of which at the time of Christ's resurrection seventeen or eighteen hundred years remained. The present, then, was near the time Revelation signified as the "*Evening* of the World," when the "*Evening Wolves* will be much abroad." Then people shall hear often about "*Apparitions* of the Devil, and about poor people strangely Bewitched." Then the devil, knowing Christ's Kingdom was at hand, would offer baptism and communion and make other despairing efforts to erect his own kingdom, "with a most Apish Imitation." Then, with the devil clapped up prisoner in or near the bowels of the earth, there would come repeated earthquakes, "and this perhaps by the energy of the Devil in the *Earth*," such earthquakes as had been reported this morning, whereby Jamaica "was at once pull'd into the Jaws of the Gaping and Groaning Earth."

Knowing his time was near, the devil fretted especially, Mather told his congregation, over New England. There the Puritans had claimed "a corner of the World, where he had reign'd without any controul for many Ages." Mather here referred to a popular notion, elaborated as early as 1634 by the English divine Joseph Mede, that before the coming of Christ the devil led the Indians to the New World as his own Chosen People, hoping to put at least some part of mankind beyond the reach of the gospel. Many persons thus viewed America at the time of its settlement as uniquely the land of the devil, an image reinforced and enhanced by the Indians' well-known practice of ceremonial magic. When a band of Puritans built evangelical churches and brought the gospel to the devil's domain, Mather continued, New England became to him a "vexing *Eyesore*," and he essayed by every means to "undermine his Plantation, and force us out of our Country." Indian powwows "used all their Sorceries to molest the first Planters"; fires often "laid the chief Treasure of the whole Province in ashes"; Andros and others schemed "to deprive us of those *English Liberties*, in the encouragement whereof these Territories have been settled." The outbreak at Salem was the latest of the roiled devil's frantic attempts to invade and reclaim New England. At the hellish meet ings revealed by the Andover witches, "these Monsters have associated themselves to do no less a thing than, *To destroy the Kingdom of our Lord Jesus Christ, in these parts of the World.*"

Mather's sermon indicates that however convinced he had become of the existence of a diabolic conspiracy, he remained bewildered over the question of how infallibly to detect and prosecute the other conspirators, for his remarks on the matter were again perfectly ambidexter. He assured his congregation that the judges had used spectral evidence only as a basis for further inquiry, but that God had providentially strengthened it by supplying other evidence, so that "some of the *Witch Gang* have been fairly Executed." Speaking as if fully convinced himself that the spectral shapes were those of guilty persons, he told his congregation that all of the witches "have their *Spectres*, or Devils, commission'd by them, and representing of them," and he summarized at length the testimony of the Andover witches:

> In the Prosecution of these Witchcrafts, among a thousand other unac-
> countable things, the *Spectres* have an odd faculty of clothing the most
> substantial and corporeal Instruments of Torture, with Invisibility. . . .
> These wicked *Spectres* have proceeded so far, as to steal several quantities
> of Money from diverse people, part of which Money has, before sufficient
> Spectators, been dropt out of the Air into the hands of the Sufferers, while
> the *Spectres* have been urging them to subscribe their *Covenant with
> Death.*

Mather's dozens of sober, unqualified references to "Spectres" torturing,
filching, or molesting, however, confusingly give way to assertions of
doubt concerning the justice of accusations and convictions based on
spectral evidence. He warned that in this obscure affair the devil might
be trying to shame New England with "perhaps a finer Thread, than was
ever yet practised upon the World," and beside his assurances that those
executed had been indeed guilty, he expressed continuing bafflement;
"The whole business is become hereupon so *Snarled,* and the determina-
tion of the Question one way or another, so *dismal,* that our Honourable
Judges have a Room for *Jehoshaphat's* Exclamation, *We know not what to
do!*"

The judges who met the next day, August 5, could have taken Mather's
sermon as either encouragement or warning. In either case they sentenced to death six accused witches, five of whom were hanged on August 19: John Proctor, George Jacobs, Sr., and John Willard of Salem Village; George Burroughs of Maine; and Martha Carrier of Andover.
Another condemned witch, Proctor's wife, Elizabeth, was pardoned because pregnant.

For the first time, Cotton Mather attended the executions. Until now,
he seems to have avoided any direct contact with the judicial proceedings. He did preach to some accused witches imprisoned in Boston, and
he may have attended some of the examinations at Andover; his diary
mentions, too, that his compassion for the judges' difficulty was increased
"by my Journeys to *Salem*"—presumably only to speak with them, since
he attended none of the trials. His presence at the hangings on August 19
is the only documented instance of his personal participation in the proceedings.

The two surviving accounts of Cotton Mather's appearance both make
it seem that he tried to justify the hangings, but both accounts are open to
interpretation. In the first, Samuel Sewall, who attended also, recorded

that before a "very great number" of spectators, George Burroughs prayed and made a speech protesting his innocence, which moved "unthinking persons" present to speak "hardly" about his sentence. All those about to be hanged also protested their innocence, Sewall said, but "Mr. Mather says they all died by a Righteous Sentence." In the second account, by Robert Calef, Burroughs spoke so solemnly and seriously from the gallows ladder as to win "the Admiration of all present." His fervent prayers, concluding with the Lord's Prayer, moved many to tears, "so that it seemed to some, that the Spectators would hinder the Execution." But as soon as Burroughs was turned off, Calef continued, "Mr. Cotton Mather, being mounted upon a Horse, addressed himself to the People, partly to declare, that he was no ordained Minister, and partly to possess the People of his guilt; saying, That the Devil has often been transformed into an Angel of Light; and this did somewhat appease the People, and the Executions went on."

Both these accounts, from which Mather's reputation has permanently suffered, have been questioned. Sewall refers only to "Mr. Mather," leaving it open whether he means Cotton or Increase; Calef disliked Cotton Mather, is often misleading, and wrote after the event. Yet it seems likely that the accounts refer to Cotton Mather and are essentially accurate. That Increase would have defended Burroughs' hanging is improbable because, even though he attended Burroughs' trial earlier in the month, he objected even more strenuously than did his son to the trial methods, and had interviewed several Andover witches in prison, where he heard them retract their confessions. Calef's account, secondly, squares with Cotton Mather's consistent defense of the judges. Just two days before the hangings Cotton wrote a rather incoherent letter to one judge, John Foster, ending, "I entreat you that whatever you do, you strengthen the hands of our honorable judges in the great work before them." Moreover, Cotton despised murmuring countryish mobs, such as he tried to pacify during the revolt of 1689. In political terms the spectators at the hangings were to him essentially the same mob, a threat to the stability of New England's fragile government. The one unconvincing note in Calef's account is that to assure the crowd of Burroughs' guilt, Mather told them the devil often appears as an angel of light—meaning that Burroughs might be a witch even though he had ostensibly been a minister. Whenever Mather invoked this idea he applied it to specters, never to persons. When he spoke of the devil taking an innocent shape he always meant it as a warning against condemning someone on the basis of spectral evidence. To have invoked the same idea to condemn someone presumed guilty implies a vicious perversion of justice out of keeping with Mather's personality.

Although the accounts do remain open for interpretation, the strongest argument for crediting them is that Cotton Mather's new understanding of the conspiracy against New England made the hangings for him unique. Two of those executed, Burroughs and Martha Carrier, were identified by the Andover witches as the very heads of the diabolic plot. Burroughs' trial produced testimony that, as the "chief of all the persons accused for witchcraft," he sounded the trumpet to call other witches together. Martha Carrier's own children, as well as other witches, testified that "the Devil had promised her, she should be *Queen of Heb.*" Mather himself called Burroughs the "Ringleader" and Martha Carrier a "rampant Hag." For him, the persons being executed included the veritable King and Queen of American Hell.

*

With apparently hundreds of witches accused or jailed, reports of torture, and new trials scheduled for early September, the hard words spoken at the Salem gallows spread. Public opposition to the trials had been evident for months. In late June, the Baptist minister William Milborne, a leader in the revolt against Andros, was arrested for circulating a petition to the General Assembly asking them to weigh the validity of spectral evidence. The accusations, moreover, had reached notable persons, including the eminent Boston minister Samuel Willard, several members of Governor Phips's Council, and Phips's own wife. Some of the original afflicted girls had accused the prominent shipmaster John Alden, a founder of the South Church and son of the Plymouth settlers John and Priscilla Alden; he was jailed in Boston for fifteen weeks before escaping to Duxbury. It was even said that the accused included Cotton Mather's mother, Maria, although he denounced the story as a lie fabricated by a Quaker.

Accustomed to putting down rebelliousness in himself, Cotton Mather saw in the mounting opposition to the trials a need to defend the new government more vigorously both at home and abroad. Four days before new trials were to begin, he offered to assist William Stoughton in "the weighty and worthy undertakings wherein almighty God has employed your Honor as His instrument for the extinguishing"—the word seems lethal—"of as wonderful a piece of devilism as has been seen in the world." He sent for Stoughton's approval part of a work-in-progress in which he sought, "even with something of designed contrivance," to end contention and restore peace, to "flatten that fury which we now so much turn upon one another." Aware of New England's reputation in London for disorder, he asked Stoughton's permission to include a digest of the trials, to vindicate the country as well as the judges and juries. Unwilling to misrepresent current dissatisfaction with the trial methods, however, he told Stoughton gingerly that he would submit for his correction any places where he had "let fall, as once or twice, the jealousies among us, of innocent people being accused." Anticipating criticism of the book, he hoped not only for Stoughton's permission but also for his protection, and ended with a blushing request for his endorsement:

> For me to beg that either Your Honor singly, or the judges jointly, would in a line or two signify unto the world that my labors have your approbation. . . . This were an arrogance whereupon I dare not presume. Although a favor of that kind bestowed upon me would somewhat lay before the world an intimation of that holy, pious, fatherly frame of spirit, with which you are herein concerned for us, yet, I say, I dare not aspire so far as to ask it.

This manipulative tactic of getting-by-renouncing, probably derived from his relation to his father, he would use increasingly to extort favors from austere or influential persons on whom he felt dependent.

While Cotton Mather wrote on in defense of the trials, the death sentences multiplied. New trials began in Salem on September 9; the court condemned nine persons. One of them, eighty-year-old Giles Corey, refused to plead his indictment; on September 19, heavy stones were laid on him in a field until he was crushed to death. According to Robert Calef, Corey's tongue came out of his mouth and "the Sheriff with his Cane forced it in again, when he was dying."

The next day, Cotton Mather wrote to the clerk at Salem, Stephen Sewall, saying he was beset by objections against the proceedings but willing to "expose myself unto the utmost for the Defense of my Friends with you." He asked Sewall to send narratives of a half-dozen or more trials to include in his book. However willing to expose himself, he also understood the risk in defending an increasingly unpopular cause. Wanting the court to share the risk with him, he asked that the trial account come in some quasi-official form, such as a letter to him. His request was strengthened, he told Sewall, by Governor Phips himself having "laid his positive commands upon me to desire this favor of you"—perhaps, he seems to hint, because of spectral accusations against his wife. Phips's intervention suggests that he in some degree oversaw the writing of Mather's book, and may even have coaxed him into producing it. Or Phips may have wished to take over the direction of the work from Stoughton, of whose conduct he now wholly disapproved. In any case, two days after writing to Sewall, Mather met with him and Stoughton in Boston to discuss publication of the book.

The same day, September 22, the trials at Salem neared a crisis with the hanging of eight of the nine witches condemned earlier in the month: Mary Easty, Alice Parker, Ann Pudeator, Margaret Scott, Wilmott Reed, Samuel Wardwell, Mary Parker, and Martha (the wife of Giles) Corey. A week after this, the most numerous of the Salem executions, Governor Phips returned from Pemaquid, Maine, where he had visited the scene of combat against the French and Indians. Throughout the examination and trials, the fighting in the east had heightened the frenzied atmosphere by producing apprehensive rumors of expected raids on Massachusetts. On his return, Phips found general dissatisfaction with the court and a widespread belief that some of those executed had been innocent.

Advice came to Phips, perhaps at his request, from a group of ministers, in the form of a short treatise written by Increase Mather and now or later subscribed by the others, published afterward as *Cases of Conscience Concerning Evil Spirits Personating Men* (1693). ("Cases of Conscience" refers to works of casuistry, that is, resolutions of moral dilemmas by skilled theologians.) In a postscript added for publication, Increase praised the judges as "wise and good Men" acting "with all Fidelity according to their Light." But their light he saw as darkness, what the ministers in their Preface impugn contemptuously as "*something vulgarly called* Spectre Evidence, *and a certain sort of Ordeal or trial by the sight and touch.*" No less than his son, Increase believed unquestioningly in the invisible world. In *Cases of Conscience* he speaks solemnly of "bewitched Water" that rubbed on the eyes affords supernormal vision. But unlike his son, he desired not to put down a diabolic conspiracy—which the treatise fails to mention—but to prevent innocent persons from disgrace or hanging. It became his vocation, he wrote, "to be very tender in Cases of Blood, and to imitate our Lord and Master, *Who came not to destroy the Lives of Men, but to save them.*" Refuting the court methods on scriptural, philosophical, and commonsense grounds, he made his meaning personal and unmistakable: "This then I declare and testify, that to take away the Life of any one, merely because a *Spectre* or Devil, in a bewitched or possessed Person does accuse them, will bring the Guilt of innocent Blood on the Land." To show their concurrence with Increase's views, fourteen ministers signed their names to his work—perhaps all the leading ministers in and near Boston, except one.

The one was Cotton Mather, who took this occasion to publicly dis-sent from his father for the first time. He declined the subscription, he said, "with all the modesty I could use" and explained to his colleagues that his own book, now in press, had his father's approval and would "sufficiently declare my opinion." But his certainty of a diabolic plot and his scorn for popular unrest gave him larger reasons as well, which he confided to his uncle John Cotton. For one, he feared that by concentrat-ing on the weakness of spectral evidence, his father's treatise might serve to halt the trials but divert attention from the conspiracy which made them necessary: "our witch-advocates" would be able to "cavil and nib-ble" learnedly at the proceedings against one or another witch, "while things as they lay in bulk, with their whole dependences, were not ex-posed; but also everlastingly stifle any further proceedings of justice." He also feared that the treatise might, unwittingly, turn public wrath against and thus endanger the judges, "who would (tho' beyond the intention of the worthy author and subscribers) find themselves brought unto the bar before the rashest *Mobile.*" Finally he hoped to uphold the authority and stability of the new government and to contain the growing quarrel be-tween it and the ministry. As usually happened, his efforts to bring peace increased contention. He found that his refusal to subscribe gained him "raging asperity" and filled the country with a "great slander"— *That I run against my own father and all the ministers in the country,* merely because I run between them when they are like mad men running against one another."

Around mid-October, just as popular and ministerial clamor against the trials was bringing them to a halt, Cotton Mather's *Wonders of the Invisible World* (1692) appeared in print, defending them. He made no secret of having written the book under wrenching stress: "None, but *the Father, who sees in secret,*" he said, "knows the Heart-breaking Exercises, wherewith I have composed what is now going to be exposed." Describ-ing himself as "One of the least among the Children of *New-England,*" he opened with a nervously self-justifying "Author's Defence" that gives an agonized explanation of his motives:

> . . . there may be few that love the Writer of this Book; but give me leave to boast so far, there is not one among all this Body of People, whom this *Mather* would not study to serve as well as to love. With such a *Spirit of Love,* is the Book now before us written: I appeal to all *this World;* and if *this* World will deny me the Right of acknowledging so much, I appeal to the *other,* that it is *not written with an Evil Spirit.*

Mather's distress may account for the book's formlessness. It is a jumble of sermons and parts of sermons, snippets from English works, letters, attestations, "Matchless CURIOSITIES," heaped without beginning, middle, or end around a digest of five of the Salem trials. Mather made no attempt to conceal the vicissitudes of composition. Having apparently garnered his material while impatiently awaiting trial transcripts from the Salem clerk, he made the reader wait with him, promising in the text to present the trial accounts next, and failing to. After the first hundred pages he writes, "I shall no longer detain my Reader from his expected Entertainment, in a brief account of the Trials." But what follows is another stall, a narrative of some English witchcraft trials in the 1680s.

Although the book remains a mélange, Mather supplied an opening statement of design. His main purpose, he said, was to extract fruitful improvements from the "amazing Dispensations now upon us." These appear as exhortations to reform the provoking causes of God's Controversy with New England. The "subordinate Ends"—to which he devoted by far the bulk of the book—were three. First, to expose the diabolic conspiracy: "I have indeed set myself to countermine the whole PLOT of the Devil, against *New-England,* in every branch of it, as far as one of my *darkness,* can comprehend such a *Work of Darkness.*" This purpose he realized by giving more than a third of the book to an expanded version of the apocalyptic sermon he had preached following the Andover confessions. Insensitive or indifferent to redundancy, he here repeated much of what he said in a previous section titled "Enchantments Encountered." Mather's second "subordinate" end was dual: to contribute to the ongoing work of such noted English pneumatologists as Richard Baxter, and to reassure the mother country that New England was orderly. In one, reserving for a moment the other, he succeeded, for *Wonders* was advertised in large type in the *London Gazette,* reviewed and summarized at length in the *London Compleat Library,* and published quickly in three English editions.

Mather's final "subordinate" end, however, outreached him, that of clarifying his views, "taking off the false Reports, and hard Censures about my Opinion in these Matters." The book clarifies much less than it screens. The assemblage of redundant fragments and the repeated stalls make everything seem the prologue to a prologue, creating an effect of endless jerky beginnings, obscured by tedious verbosity and an insuperable difficulty in getting to the point. A simultaneous saying and unsaying, the book resembles a gigantic stammer. Cries of conspiracy alternate with appeals for calm, and these with doubts that Satan might spread havoc by using genuine witches to implicate the blameless. Mather seems to leave unquestionable that in the five cases he treats at length, real and malicious witches were executed. To vindicate the methods of the court he shows that the evidence against the accused, in the sheer numbers who testified for the prosecution, was conclusive. To reassure readers in London that the court followed established precedent, he prints prominent English legal opinions on detecting and convicting witches, and summarizes important English witchcraft trials.

Yet even this defense, straightforward in itself, seems in context halfhearted and forced, for Mather hedged it around with hints of coercion, warning winks at the reader, tipoffs to his discomfort. Although he had asked Stoughton's permission to publish an account of the trials, he presents the account as if written on command. One of his several prologues confesses that he has no prejudice against the persons convicted, "But having received a Command so to do, I can do no other than shortly relate the chief *Matters of Fact,* which occur'd in the Trials." With a similar plaint of duress, his account of Burroughs' trial begins: "the Government requiring some Account of his Trial to be inserted in this Book, it becomes me with all Obedience to submit unto the Order." And his digest of the trials concludes, "Having thus far done the Service imposed upon me. . . ."

These insistent disclosures of unwillingness make the whole book seem a sort of bluff. The likelihood is that sometime between conceiving and publishing the work, Cotton Mather became disenchanted by Stoughton, whose tenacious trust in spectral evidence was under attack even from Richard Baxter in England. In the book he clearly tried to disengage himself from Stoughton. For instance, instead of the "line or two" of approbation he had requested, Stoughton provided a page-and-a-half panegyric to Mather as his defender, beginning:

> Such is your Design, most plainly expressed throughout the whole; such your Zeal for God, your Enmity to Satan and his Kingdom, your Faithfulness and Compassion to this poor People; such the Vigour, but yet great Temper of your Spirit; such your Instruction and Counsel, your *Care of Truth,* your Wisdom and Dexterity . . . that all Good Men must needs desire the making of this your Discourse public to the World . . . [italics reversed.]

Mather included this self-interested endorsement, but placed it just before his embarrassed statement of purpose, which begins: "I LIVE by *Neighbours* that force me to produce these undeserved Lines." In his

"Author's Defence" too he carefully distinguished his own parts of the book from the trial digests composed, he implied, at Stoughton's behest: "For the Dogmatical part of my Discourse, I want no Defence; for the Historical part of it, I have a very Great One; the Lieutenant-Governour of *New-England* having perused it, has done me the Honour of giving me a Shield, under the Umbrage whereof I now dare to walk abroad." But his actual uneasiness under Stoughton's self-serving protection he confided to his diary: "The Shield given by the Lieut. Governour, of the Province, under which, That Book is walk'd abroad, is enough, and, I confess, too much."

Cotton Mather's book appearing just as, to almost everyone's relief, the trials were halting, the result was predictable. *Wonders of the Invisible World* became, and remains, as Mather called it, "that reviled Book." Inopportunely also, his father's *Cases of Conscience* appeared in print just after *Wonders,* and many "besotted People" believed that Increase had written in deliberate opposition to it. In a postscript to *Cases of Conscience,* Increase asserted that he had approved his son's work before it was printed, and that "nothing but my Relation to him, hindred me, from recommending it unto the world"—his explanation also of his failure to support his son's ordination with him. Yet father and son always tried to present a united front when they disagreed, as here they undeniably did. The drift of *Wonders of the Invisible World* is that devils have broke loose in New England, of *Cases of Conscience* that at Salem innocent people are being killed. Having refused to drink one king's health, and having spoken with two other kings and a queen in their own quarters, Increase did not find a William Stoughton awesome, unlike his deferential son, whose crime, morally, lay not in promoting the trials but in doing nothing to stop them.

But Cotton Mather had again been hauled in every direction. Finally wary of Stoughton but still certain that real witches had been hanged, he was also at odds with his father, hopeful of making a place for himself among noted pneumatologists, and apparently under conflicting pressures from the governor and lieutenant governor, while remaining, as before, apprehensive of the devil's subtlety, cautious about contributing to public discontent, hopeful of combatting Saducees, fatally anxious to please, and simply baffled. A passage of his manuscript autobiography which seems to have belonged to his original diary for 1692 speaks of his "Fear, Lest under my Extraordinary *Trials* from the *Invisible World,* I have at any time gratified the *Hidden Desires* of *Evil Angels,* or Entertained any Disposition to see broken the Good, Wise, Right *Order* wherein *Humane Affairs* are fixed by the Lord."

Cotton Mather did receive some praise for *Wonders of the Invisible World,* and later in the year he entered in his diary some approving, vindicating comments by others. Yet he remained unhappy over what he had done, and wrote in the margin the hesitant, ambidexter consolation: "(Upon the severest Examination, and the solemnest Supplication, I still think, that for the main, I have, *written Right.*)"

*

About ten days after the publication of Cotton Mather's book, on October 26, a bill was sent to the Assembly calling for a fast day and a convocation of ministers to determine what to do next in the trials. Because of the "season and manner" of presenting the bill, Samuel Sewall wrote, the Salem court considered itself dismissed. The court was due to end anyway, since it had been established before the legislature could meet under the new charter to arrange a system of courts, and it became defunct when the legislature established a superior court for the whole province. A further session of the Salem court had been scheduled, however, and on October 28 Stoughton went to discuss its fate with Phips and the Council. They met him, Sewall said, with "great silence," and next day Phips declared that Stoughton's court "must fall." Phips estimated that at least fifty accused witches were still in prison, some of whom he released on bail. Because some judges now conceded that the trials had been too violent and agreed to adopt a different method of evidence, Phips permitted the scheduling of a new court in Salem—the last—just after the new year.

Despite the suspension of the trials and his reservations about *Wonders of the Invisible World,* Cotton Mather hoped to "do yet more, in a direct *opposition* unto the Devil." Late in the year he wrote to John Richards, now not as a judge but as a leading member of his church, asking his support in making an important change in church policy. He told Richards that the information given by the Andover witches about the devil's parodic rites of baptism and communion had "increased my uneasiness, under that sin of omission wherein I reckon myself to live." The "sin" was the failure of the North Church to conform to the requirements for baptism proposed by the Halfway Covenant Synod of 1662. To recall: the Synod met to deal, among other things, with the decline in membership threatening the existence of the New England churches. It voted to alter the original Congregational ideal, by which only the children of parents who had experienced regenerating grace were to be baptized and admitted to the church. Instead it recommended that the children of persons who were Virtuous Christians but had not received grace could also be baptized and admitted, declaring their desire to attain a state of grace.

Increase Mather had strenuously opposed the compromise, and until the time of the Salem trials the North Church admitted only children of the regenerate.

Because of Increase's opposition, the North Church evidently contained a large number of unbaptized adolescents and adults. And the claims on such people by legions of devils, Cotton told Richards, made the problem of their baptism urgent. He had been forced to turn away "scores of godly people" who sought baptism, because of antagonism to halfway membership by two people, of whom Richards was one. He did not ask Richards to support the new policy, but only to continue as a member of the North Church if it were adopted. Those who offered themselves for baptism, he assured him, would be examined rigorously. They would have to be "instructed and orthodox" in Christianity, bring testimony signed by more than one full church member that they were of a "virtuous conversation," and declare their "study to prepare themselves further for the table of the Lord." Richards presumably agreed, as Increase Mather must have also, for on January 15, 1693, Cotton entered in the church records the admission of Mary Sunderland and the baptism of her son John, "the first, so Admitted" under the Halfway Covenant proposed thirty years earlier. Baptisms in the church quickly doubled, from 54 in 1692 to 104 in 1693. Although it pleased Mather that his church had peaceably resolved a long-vexing issue, the resolution also gave him more work, and he noted that "my Charge of such as now submitted themselves unto my *ecclesiastical Watch,* was exceedingly increased."

About three years earlier, it should be added, Cotton Mather had decisively addressed the related issue of grace. Disappointingly to those who had invented the tradition-breaking compromise of 1662, many children of the unregenerate who were baptized under the Halfway Covenant also failed to experience grace and were denied communion, thus kept from full church membership and voting privileges. To help bring such persons to the Lord's Table, Mather published in 1690 his extremely important *Companion for Communicants,* copies of which were distributed at the North Church on May 25, the day when John and Martha Goodwin, parents of the depossessed children, were admitted to full membership. This work marks the beginning of an evangelistic sacramental piety in New England intended to bring more worshipers to communion, thus to fill the churches again with Visible Saints, a movement climaxed by the Great Awakening of the 1730s.

The crux of Mather's *Companion* is the test he provided by which worshipers might decide whether they can rightfully approach the Lord's Table. The issue contained hazards on either side: to stay away from communion while in a state of grace and to take communion lacking a state of grace were alike sinful. Mather's test is answerably elusive, as are those of other ministers in the period who tried to relax requirements for admission so as to fill the thinning churches while preserving an illusion of maintaining the Fathers' pristine requirement that only Saints could take communion. "We are to *Examine* our selves," Mather wrote, "and if upon the *Examination* we do not find full cause to pronounce ourselves *Unregenerate,* we are to come, tho' we have many *Fears,* whether we be indeed *Regenerate* or no." The principle that worshipers may take communion if certain they are not *un*regenerate did prove effective in filling out the communion table of the North Church. One church member, Joseph Green, took to heart Mather's rule that, as he put it, "if a person could not conclude themselves to be unconverted they ought to approach," and found that Mather's *Companion* "so moved me to come to the Lords table that I began to think of closing wholly with Jesus Christ." However practical, Mather's principle of "Probable" regeneration had little in common with the endless wrestling, doubts, and devotions he had undergone in his youthful closure with Christ, or with the exacting admissions standards of the earlier New England churches.

The acceptance of the Halfway Covenant by the North Church coincided with the ending of the Salem trials. The new court appointed by Phips met in Salem in January 1693, and using a different method of treating spectral evidence, acquitted forty-nine of the fifty-two persons under trial. The king's Attorney General advised Phips that the remaining three should also be cleared. Stoughton, however, signed a warrant for their execution. Openly at odds with Stoughton now, Phips sent a reprieve, which so enraged Stoughton that he refused to sit longer on the bench. By February 21, Phips felt confident enough that the witchcraft crisis was over to write home that the elimination of spectral evidence had "dissipated the black cloud that threatened this Province with destruction."

Now Cotton Mather's face-to-face engagement with the invisible world could begin.

ii

On November 29, with the Salem trials suspended, Cotton Mather took several people to keep a day of prayer with a seventeen-year-old energumen named Mercy Short. An orphan, she had been redeemed from Indians in the east, who had killed her father, mother, brother, and sister, and carried her captive to Canada. In the summer of 1692 she was sent on an errand to the Boston prison, where the convicted Sarah Good, awaiting execution, asked her for a little tobacco. Mercy threw a handful of shavings at her, saying, "That's Tobacco good enough for you." Good cursed her, producing fits that disappeared and recurred for several months. Mercy seems to have been taken in by a family in Mather's neighborhood, in the "Haunted Chamber" of whose house groups of five to fifty persons came to fast, pray, or simply observe her possession. When Mather arrived on November 29 she lay insensible, but when he began preaching on Mark 9:29—"And he said unto them, This kind can come forth by nothing, but by prayer and fasting"—she sprang at him and tore a page out of his Bible.

With the trials ending, Mather felt reluctant to publicize the case. Although he wrote and apparently circulated an account of it, entitled "A Brand Pluck'd out of the Burning," he did not publish the manuscript, for Mercy Short provided much information that confirmed the necessity and justice of the trials. She gave fresh evidence against Sarah Good and Martha Carrier, corroborating evidence that French and Indians attended witch meetings to "concert the methods of ruining New England," news that the devil planned to burn all Boston, and vindication of the judges' use of spectral evidence. Even in his manuscript Mather forbore comment on Mercy Short: "such is the froward, flouting sidred [cidered, i.e., soured], and proud Humour, whereunto the people are now Enchanted, no man in his Wits would fully expose his Thoughts unto them, till the charms which enrage the people are a little better Dissipated."

Yet Mercy Short's possession had several unique features that Mather could not ignore. Her devils, like those of the Goodwin children and the Salem girls, pinched and scorched her, and showed their contempt for the ministry by stopping her mouth and ears during prayer, attacking her with special violence when she attended Mather's church. But Mercy Short was not merely afflicted: she seemed borne to Hell itself. The devils cut off her sight and hearing from the visible world and routed them into direct communion with the Powers of Darkness, her open but unreceptive eyes visualizing only "the Hellish Harpies that were now fluttering about her." Cast into Outer Darkness she argued tremendously with her tormentors: "Oh You horrid Wretch! You make my very Heart cold within me. It is an Hell to me, to hear You speak so! Are you *God?* No, be gone, you Devil! Don't pester me any more with such horrid Blasphemies!" In Mercy Short, haunted by evil angels and tortured by cruciating fires,

Mather beheld the very state of the damned itself. In other ways too Mercy brought him and the other spectators close up to the invisible world. Once when invisible flames flashed on her the room smelled of brimstone; when devils stuck pins in her, "those we took out, with Wonderment"; when a hot iron plunged down her throat, "we saw the Skin fetch'd off her Tongue and Lips."

These and many other drawings-near to the realm of spirit led Mather to further pneumatological speculations, for instance that long fasts were "strangely Agreeable" to persons who "have something more than Ordinary to do with the Invisible World." His most far-reaching speculation concerned the presence in Mercy's room of "a Substance that seem'd like a Cat, or Dog," experienced by several onlookers as invisible but palpable. In trying to explain this quasi-material presence he invoked a concept that would, we shall see, fascinate him all his life: the view that spirit contains "an Innate Power by which it can attract suitable matter out of all Things for a Covering or Body, of a proportionable Form and Nature to itself." He had already used this concept in *Wonders of the Invisible World* to expand the traditional understanding of witchcraft as a diabolic covenant: "*Witchcraft* seems to be the Skill of Applying the *Plastic Spirit* of the World, unto some unlawful purposes, by means of a Confederacy with *Evil Spirits.*"

The notion of a plastic spirit—essentially an old idea new-named, similar to classical ideas of a vegetative soul—had the allegiance of nearly every important thinker in England at the time. In effect the last hold on the supernatural, it appealed to those who, like Mather, recognized the new mechanistic picture of nature but clung to Christian belief. Plastic spirit was a DNA-like program for matter, an immaterial agent pervading the universe, creating and upholding animated substances as a sort of surrogate of God, whom it at once involved in and disengaged from running the universe. Instead of overseeing the creation and growth of every leaf or ant, God imbued the universe with the plastic spirit, a vital force acting for ends God assigned it, but not conscious of so acting. Mather recognized that the concept in effect explained one unknown by another and could be attacked. Yet it was something to go on, and as an intermediary between the visible and invisible worlds it offered a satisfyingly materialistic explanation of the means by which devils could take material shapes.

Just as important, Mercy Short brought Mather information that the devils had laid designs against him. She revealed that at one of their meetings the witches used a Catholic book of devotion, written in

French, fetched from his own study. When he examined the book he found to his surprise a leaf of it doubled over. A night or two later he left the book on a table in his study, careful to see that every page lay flat, yet next morning he found three pages unaccountably folded. A commonplace of demonology held that the devil most plagues the best men. The rebukes of his playmates had taught Mather as much in childhood, but since the time of the Goodwin case he had come to feel with increasing certainty that the devils had chosen him as a special victim of their wrath. Even before he said so himself, he heard it remarked during the Salem outbreak that the assault of evil angels was "intended by *Hell,* as a particular Defiance, unto *my* poor Endeavours, to bring the Souls of men unto Heaven." He had spent a day virtually every week during the summer of the trials in a private fast, asking God for both a good issue from the amazements of Salem and for his own preservation "from the Malice and Power of the *evil Angels.*" In August, after the wildly spreading Andover accusations, he twice raised to one of the judges, John Foster, the possibility of God permitting "such a terrible calamity to befall myself as that a specter in my shape should so molest my neighbourhood as that they can have no quiet."

On March 28, 1693, the devils assaulted Cotton Mather lethally. Between four and five in the morning, Abigail gave birth to the couple's first son, whom they named Increase. The infant looked comely and hearty but its bowels were obstructed, preventing the elimination of feces. Unnamed correctives were made but the infant languished "in its Agonies" until the night of April 1, when it died. An autopsy disclosed that, in Mather's words, the "lower End of the *Rectum Intestinum,* instead of being *Musculous,* as it should have been, was *Membranous,* and altogether closed up." The imperforate anus, he felt, gave "great Reason to suspect a *Witchcraft.*" A few weeks before her delivery, Abigail had been accosted by "an horrible *Spectre,* in our Porch, which Fright caused her Bowels to turn within her."

Mather may have expected some tragedy to befall him, for the specters which tormented Mercy Short boasted of having frightened Abigail, "in hopes, they said, of doing Mischief unto her *Infant* at least, if not unto the *Mother.*" But to Mather the most remarkable and portentous feature of Mercy Short's case concerned her deliverance. In addition to the evil angels buzzing about her she was attended by another spirit. It never became visible, or more audible than a whisper; rather it communicated "chiefly by an Impulse, most powerfully and sensibly making Impressions upon her Mind." Mather compared it to the spirit New Foundlanders call "White-Hat," which before a dangerous storm appeared on shore crying "Hale up!"

Mercy's "Wonderful Spirit" told her how to answer the devils' temptations and assured her she would triumph. It induced her to leaf through a Bible randomly and alight at the most pertinent possible place, and told her that on Thursday evening, March 16, between nine and ten o'clock, she would be delivered. Mather, present that evening, reported that the specters tried all night to torture her, but could not; she was "Hedged by some unseen Defence." When at last, in the name of Christ, she bid the devils be gone, "they flew away Immediately, striking another young Woman down for Dead upon the Floor as they went along." Her troublers never returned. In January 1694, she was admitted to the North Church in full communion, not only depossessed, that is, but having experienced grace.

Such good angels as assisted Mercy Short, Mather noted, had made themselves known during some important European witchcraft cases as well. During the notorious outbreak at Mohra, Sweden, bewitched children talked of being forbidden to carry out the devil's commands by a "White Angel." Good angels lingered in the background at Salem also, where one of the afflicted girls testified to seeing "a man in white, with whom she went into a Glorious Place . . . where was no Light of the Sun, much less of Candles, yet was full of Light and Brightness, with a great Multitude in White Glittering Robes."

Mather began longing for communion with good angels himself. Around two and a half months after the depossession of Mercy Short, he kept a fast day whose special purpose was to petition for angelic favors. He asked God "please to grant unto me, the Enjoyment of those *Angelical* Kindnesses and Benefits, which use to be done by *His Order,* for His *Chosen Servants.*" Wary of slipping into an antinomian disregard for Scripture, sermons, and other means provided by God for human worship and understanding, he cautiously asked for only the angelical assistances mentioned in Scripture as belonging to the elect, although in some heightened form, "in a Manner and Measure, more *Transcendent,* than what the great *Corruptions* in the generality of *Good Men,* permitted them to be made Partakers of." He also promised that if granted any direct angelical communication he would not forsake the written Word, but on the contrary would contemplate it more reverently than before. And he would be discreet, concealing "with all *prudent Secrecy,* the *Extraordinary Things,* which I may perceive done for me by the *Angels,* who love *Secrecy* in their Administrations." Having prayed and resolved, he wrote in his diary: "I do now believe, that some *great Things* are to be done for me, by the *Angels* of God."

Mather's prayers for communication with angels were highly unusual for a Puritan. Reformed tradition of course maintained that angels existed, and he often spoke of their nature and function to his congregation. Like evil angels, good angels, as he described them, are "Spiritual and Rational Substances," forming a mighty host, *"Ten thousand times Ten Thousand."* In heaven they throng around the throne of Christ, serving as ministers to His pleasure, having in custody the souls of departed Saints, who with quiet expectation await the restoration of their bodies. When they fly to earth they perform many of the same tasks as evil angels, but in reverse, curing diseases evil angels may spread, guarding the faithful some evil angels molest. As regents of the Prince of the kings of the earth, they mobilize decisive political events: "When Monarchs fall, and Nations and Empires have Amazing Changes brought upon them, the Angels of God accomplish it." Especially they love to visit places of secret prayer, as on the other side it tortures devils to be there. So earth, like heaven, teems with good angels, invisible but ever present.

While Mather's views on good angels were entirely traditional, his hope for close communion with them was not. Since the time of Christ, according to the general Reformed position, good angels, but not evil angels, had ceased to appear. Increase Mather himself argued strenuously that although the angelic ministry continues, "it is an unwarrantable and a very dangerous thing, for men to wish, that they might see, and that they might converse with Angels." Indeed Richard Baxter considered the non-appearance of angels a boon, for such appearances invite idolatry, fear, and error: angels "act according to their spiritual nature, without deceit; and they serve us without any terrible appearances . . . whereas if they appeared to us in visible shapes, we might easily be affrighted, confounded, and left in doubt, whether they were good angels indeed or not." The problem of distinguishing movements of good spirits from those of evil spirits—St. Paul's *diakrisis pneumatōn* or spiritual discernment—particularly argued against the desire for angelic communion. Converse with angels, Baxter warned, was very probably "converse with Devils that are Transformed into seeming Angels of Light."

However it risked mistaking diabolical imposture for angelic visitation, Mather's hope of receiving "great Things" from the good angels was quickly realized. One Sabbath about a month after his special day of prayer, he went to preach on an island in Boston Harbor, to some troops from a warship returned from the West Indies. Enroute to the island aboard Governor Phips's barge he became "vehemently *sick*." His companions insisted that he return to Boston, and as soon as he came home he recovered. It turned out that his sudden illness may have rescued him from death. The troops he nearly visited were stricken with yellow fever, which became epidemic in Boston: "had I gone, and Conversed among So Infectious a Company," he wrote, "it would probably have Cost me my Life, as it proved Mortal unto very many others of my Neighbours." He felt he knew, too, how to interpret his deliverance: "I believe, 't was a *Good Angel*, which there struck me *sick*."

Mather made another surprising journey the first week in September, to Salem. He hoped to collect material there for an ambitious new book, *Magnalia Christi Americana*, and to help preserve the trial record, so that the "complete History" of the recent witchcraft might not be lost. For the sake of public peace he had kept largely to himself confirming evidence of the justice of the trials, which now was reinforced. While in Salem he spoke with a woman named Carver, who had been strangely visited by "some *shining Spirits*, which were *good Angels*, in her opinion of them." He kept secret some things she intimated, but recorded in his diary her assurance that a new storm of witchcraft would break out, for the purpose of chastising the "Iniquity that was used in the wilful Smothering and Covering of *the Last*." Many who had fiercely opposed the discovery of the Salem witches, she said, would at last be convinced. Once again the evil angels assaulted Mather. He had taken with him three sermons to preach in Salem but they were "*stolen*," under circumstances "that I am somewhat satisfied, The Spectres, or Agents in the *invisible World*, were the *Robbers*."

As if in fulfillment of Mrs. Carver's prophecy, when Mather returned to Boston he found that a pious young woman in his congregation, Margaret Rule, had become "horribly arrested by *evil Spirits*." Her specters boasted of having stolen his sermon notes but confessed they could not suppress them. (The notes were returned to him on October 5, although in eighteen separate quarters of sheets found scattered about the streets of Lynn.) Margaret Rule's afflictions lasted more than five weeks, during which Mather assisted her and prayed for her deliverance as a sister of his flock. Among other things her tormentors tried to get her to sign a thick red book (narrow but about a cubet long), and "before a very Numerous Company of Spectators" once levitated her to the ceiling. Another time spectators thought they saw something stir on her pillow; a man set his hand there and, to his horror, believed he felt, but could not see, "a living Creature, not altogether unlike a Rat."

In its other manifestations, Margaret Rule's affliction resembled Mercy Short's, including the appearance to her of "a wonderful *Spirit,* in White and bright Raiment, with a *Face unseen.*" Comfortingly it stood by her bedside, counselling her to keep faith in God and resist the temptations of the evil angels. The spirit also bid her consider Mather her father, and obey him, "for he said, the Lord had given her to me." Mather's several pneumatological experiments had convinced him that an expulsion of demons could not be achieved until the holding of a third fast, when Rule's miseries had lasted more than five weeks, the white spirit notified her that Mather had now kept a third fast, and said: "be of good cheer you shall speedily be delivered." The evil angels as they approached her now found themselves forced to recoil, unable to stick pins in their puppets. Rule could see their "Black Master" strike and kick them, "like an Overseer of so many Negro's" until tiring of their useless attempts they said furiously, "Well you shant be the last," and flew from the room.

It was probably during the possession of Margaret Rule—between roughly September 10 and the end of October, 1693—that there occurred to Cotton Mather *"Res Mirabilis Et Memoranda,"* a strange and memorable thing. He recorded it in Latin, on a separate page of his diary, probably because of his earlier promise to respect the angels' love of secrecy. But he probably also wished to conceal the account from others. For this experience—although it far surpassed in intensity his many castings-out of demons, and although after long seeking it at last introduced him to the invisible world himself—this experience contained the greatest possibility of self-deception.

Mather wrote: *Post Fusas, maximis cum Ardoribus, Iejuniisque* Preces—After outpourings of prayer, with the utmost fervor and fasting—*apparuit* ANGELUS, *qui* Vultum *habuit solis instar Meridiani* Micantem—there appeared an Angel, whose face shone like the noonday sun—*Caetera* Humanum, *at prorsus* imberbem: Caput *magnifica* Tiarâ *obvolutum;*—He was completely beardless, but in other respects human, his head encircled by a splendid tiara;—*In* Humeris, Alas:—On his shoulders were wings:—*Vestes deinceps Candidas et Splendidas;* Togam *nempè* Talarem: *et* Zonam *circà Lumbos, orientalium cingalis non absimilem.*—His garments were white and shining; his robe reached to his ankles; and about his loins was a belt not unlike the girdles of the peoples of the East.

The angel that appeared to Mather explained that he had been sent by Christ to answer *cujusdam Juvenis precibus*—the prayers of a certain youth—and to bear back his reply. Many things the angel told him Mather thought it improper to transcribe. But among other things not to be forgotten the angel prophesied the great work he would do for the church *in* Revolutionibus *jam Appropinquantibus*—in the revolutions now at hand. He declared that the destiny of this youth was best expressed in the words of the prophet Ezekiel. Mather wrote down the texts of Ezekiel 31: 3, 4, 5, 7, and 9 as spoken to him by the angel, a prophecy of fruitfulness, power, and fame:

> *Behold, he was a Cedar in Lebanon, with fair branches, and with a Shad-owing Shroud, and of an High Stature, and his Top was among the Thick Boughs. The waters made him great, the Deep Set him up on High with her Rivers running about his plants. His Height was Exalted above all the Trees of the Field, and his Boughs were multiplied, and his Branches became Long, because of the multitude of waters, when he shot forth.*
>
> *Thus was he fair in his greatness, in the Length of his Branches, for his Root was by the Great Waters. Nor was any Tree in the Garden of God like unto him, in his Beauty. I have made him fair by the multitude of his Branches, so that all the Trees of Eden, that were in the garden of God, envied him.*

Interpreting the text for him as it applied to his future, the angel explained that the lengthening of the tree's branches referred to *de* Libris *ab hoc Juvene componendis et non tantum in* America, *sed etiam in* Europa, *publicandis*—the books to be composed and published by this youth, not only in America, but also in Europe.

The appearance of the figure whose shoulders were wings left Mather feeling both astonished and perplexed. Domine Jesu!, he wrote, *Quid sibi vult haec Res tam Extraordinaria?* Lord Jesus! What is the meaning of this marvel? *Servum Tuum Indignissimum,* a most unworthy servant, he prayed to be delivered and defended from the wiles of the devil.

*

However extraordinary, Cotton Mather's angelic visitation seems comprehensible, even inevitable. It climaxed years of ever closer contact with the invisible world, beginning with the two-and-a-half-year-old's wish to "go see God," through his adolescent closure with Christ, his grappling with Martha Goodwin's invisible chains, the diabolic death of his malformed infant. The visitation may have been more immediately induced by Mather's preceding period of fervent prayer and fasting, since extreme sensory deprivation, as in persons locked in a room or adrift at sea, can produce hallucinations. Mather himself remarked on a connection between fasting and supernormal experience in Mercy Short's case, and he later wrote guardedly that he knew "*Certain Measures*" which might produce "Amazing Acquaintance with the Angelical Assistances."

As a Puritan, also, Cotton Mather was born into a society that daily felt the nearness of the invisible world and wove magical and supernatural notions into the very texture of his thinking, beginning in childhood. His particular childhood may have specially shaped him for a visitation, for adult beliefs in ghosts, spirits, and other supernatural beings sometime begin in childhood fantasizing about absent parents, such a parent as Increase often threatened to be and often was. It seems significant that the time of his visitation, the fall of 1693, coincided with an again renewed prospect of Increase's return to England as an agent for Massachusetts, at the suggestion of Governor Phips. When Increase prayed about the matter, he himself received extraordinary suggestions that he must go abroad, suggestions he considered "either divine or Angelical." As these impressions lasted, he started a course of reading on angels, and around March began preaching an impressive series of sermons on angelology, lasting into February 1694, on which Cotton took twenty-three pages of notes. While angels were intimating to Increase Mather that he should leave Boston, an angel appeared to his son predicting that his lengthening branches would reach Europe.

Like the demons who denounced ministers through the mouths of teen-aged energumens, the figure whose shoulders were wings spoke Cotton Mather's own thoughts. Among other things, the angel gave expression to the "ambitious Affectation of Praeheminencies" that had troubled him since youth, the much censored longing for applause and fame which the childlike view he maintained of himself helped restrain. Mather's need to demonstrate copious productivity appears as early as his youthful stammer, of course, and all of his writings teem with images of size. The angel merely articulated these while omitting the guilty reproofs that otherwise accompanied them, forecasting that a "certain youth" would enjoy some enormous potency: he would be set on high, his height exalted above all the trees of the field, his branches become long because of the multitude of waters when he shot forth. Explaining Ezekiel's prediction of the "*greatness, in the Length of his Branches,*" as referring to the books Mather would publish not only in America but also in Europe, the angel in effect promised him a transatlantic penis.

Mather's need at this time for reassurance against his feelings of littleness may have been due not only to the renewed prospect of his father's return to England but also to mounting criticism of his activities. Already under attack for his behavior during the trials and for his "reviled Book," he drew added criticism for his recent labors to depossess Mercy Short and Margaret Rule and for his continued preaching about devils. He deserved it, too, because now he acted on his own, without government coercion or the pressure of confused loyalty, having come to believe that he had conspired in obstructing justice. He had always warned against releasing the names of persons identified by the afflicted as their spectral tormentors. But he now also believed that some specters, identified by persons who had become afflicted since the trials ended, represented genuine witches. And he worried that his extreme caution had led him "to Sin in what I have done, such have been the Cowardice and Fearfulness whereunto my regard unto the dissatisfactions of other People has precipitated me." Thus he continued to withhold names while feeling "able to Convict some such Witches as ought to Die."

As Mather usually did when his judgment and his inclination conflicted, he adopted an inflammatory compromise. Although he accused no one by name, for eighteen months after the trials ended he kept alluding in his sermons to "the matchless *Enchantments* and *Possessions,* that have abounded in our Neighborhood" and kept warning that "the DEVIL, is more desirous to Regain poor *New England,* than any one *American* Spot of Ground." His remarks evidently provoked outrage, for he speaks in various places of the "cursed *Reproaches*" of "this unworthy, ungodly, ungrateful People" or of the "hard representations wherewith some Ill Men have given my conduct." The hostility toward him confounded his belief that he continued to act with enormous restraint for the sake of public peace, doing far less to expose witches than he could or should. It plainly touched on old, sore feelings of ingratitude, which the angelic visitation, and its promise of future honor and potency, may have allayed. "The very *Angels* of God," he told his congregation, "they take notice how we do acquit ourselves under any of our *Trials.* It is no matter whether *our Neighbours* do see our virtuous Carriage or no; *Gods Angels,* they see it."

Mather's most vigorous and persistent accuser was the otherwise obscure Robert Calef, probably a merchant, clothier, or dyer with whom Mather had some earlier acquaintance. However socially inconspicuous, it was Calef who had correctly observed in Mather the dangerous ambidexter habit of "carrying both fire to increase, and water, to quench, the conflagration." Calef saw the Salem trials as an unmitigated horror, a "tremendous judgment of God upon this country," the trial methods such "that most would have chosen to have fallen into the hands of the barbarous enemy, rather than . . . into the hands of their brethren in church fellowship." And now, as Calef saw this sequel to the Salem trials, now after the greatest blemish to religion that ever befell New England, after the governor with the crown's approval had stopped the executions, after it began being acknowledged that a mistake had been made, now Cotton Mather was sitting beside Margaret Rule surrounded by spectators, inquiring "Who is it that Afflicts you?"

On September 13—near the probable time of Mather's angelic encounter—Calef visited Rule's house, drawn by curiosity "and so much the rather because it was reported Mr. M_____ would be there that Night." He found the energumen lying still and speaking little, attended by thirty or forty people, including both Mathers. Shocked by what followed, he wrote out the same night an account highly discrediting to Cotton, who tries to get Rule to name her specters publicly, asks her leading questions, and lewdly feels her body:

> . . . they being sat, the Father on a Stool, and the Son upon the Bedside by her, the Son began to question her, Margaret Rule, how do you do? then a pause without any answer. *Question.* What, do there a great many Witches sit upon you? *Answer.* Yes. *Q.* Do you not know that there is a hard Master? Then she was in a Fit; He laid his hand upon her Face and Nose, but, as he said, without perceiving Breath; then he brush'd her on the Face with his Glove, and rubb'd her Stomach (her breast not covered with the Bedclothes) and bid others do so too. . . . *Q.* Who is it that Afflicts you? *A.* I know not, there is a great many of them (about this time the Father question'd if she knew the Spectres? An attendant said, if she did she would not tell; the Son proceeded) *Q.* You have seen the Black-man, hant you? *A.* No. *Reply;* I hope you never shall. *Q.* You have had a Book offered you, hant you? *A.* No. *Q.* The brushing of you gives you ease, don't it? *A.* Yes. She turned her self and a little Groan'd. *Q.* Now the Witches Scratch you and Pinch you, and Bite you, don't they? *A.* Yes. Then he put his hand upon her Breast and Belly, *viz.* on the Clothes over her, and felt a Living thing, as he said, which moved the Father also to feel, and some others; *Q.* Don't you feel the Live thing in the Bed? *A.* No. . . .

Calef secured two persons willing to verify his account, which he showed to several of his and of Mather's friends.

This "lying *Libel,*" as Mather called it, presented him doing exactly what he strove mightily not to do, disparaged him for discharging the solemn obligations of his ministry, and produced "*Paroxysms* in the Town." According to Calef, Mather made the episode "Pulpit news," called him "one of the worst of Liars," and threatened to have him arrested for slander. Mather's indignation must in this instance have been partly justified. Calef's memory cannot have served him well enough to write up at home, hours later, what poses as a verbatim transcript of the dialogue between Rule and the Mathers, occupying nearly two closely printed pages. Just the same, Mather seems to have been uncertain how to respond. Calef was brought before a justice of the peace on a warrant issued by Increase and Cotton Mather, to answer at the next court for "Scandalous Libels." But when Calef appeared no one appeared against him, and he was dismissed. Why Mather dropped the suit is unclear. Always wary of his tendency to blurt out resentment, he perhaps came to feel that he had overreacted in bringing the suit: "I did at first," he confided in his diary, "it may be too much resent the Injuries of that Libel."

Instead Mather indignantly attacked Calef's account in a lengthy letter to him on January 15, 1694. Calef's "pretended Narrative," he said, presented nothing about him or his father either truly or fairly. Where Calef portrayed them as coaxing new accusations from Rule, they on the contrary always charged her to "rather Die than tell the Names of any whom she might Imagine that she knew." Where Calef attributed to them such leading questions as "how many Witches sit upon you?" they on the contrary never used and deliberately avoided such questions. Especially, where Calef said that Cotton Mather "rub'd Rule's stomach, her Breast not being covered," spectators could confirm the charge to be "a gross (if not a doubled) Lie," a lie contrived to besmirch him. You "cannot but know," he told Calef, "how much this Representation hath contributed, to make People believe a Smutty thing of me."

Calef, however, retracted nothing. Replying to Mather's letter three days later, he reiterated his accusations but denied having said that Rule's breast was uncovered. Mather in paraphrasing his account, Calef said, omitted "those material words 'with the Bed-Clothes'"—an unfair retort, since Calef's account clearly implies that Rule was partly naked. The suggestion of prurience, he added, was created by Mather himself, in publicly discoursing about the event at dinner at the home of Governor Phips. Chiefly Calef indicted Mather for evading the potentially explosive social implications of the episode, "as if I were giving Characters, Reflections, and Libels, etc. concerning your self and Relations."

Mather and Calef continued their dispute through an exchange of lengthy letters and documents lasting into 1696, debating in detail many more pneumatological issues than can be discussed here. The entire epistolary duel evinces class antagonism: Mather the Harvard-educated ministerial son of a prestigious family writing to a semi-literate clothier with a condescension that makes evident his suppressed contempt, Calef writing with a cuttingly exaggerated respect occasionally breaking into open denunciation that makes equally plain his irritation with Mather's assumption of superiority. Although Calef's expression of his ideas is often elliptical and murky, it conveys, sometime eloquently, his conviction that at Salem innocent people had been legally murdered, and that by continuing to cast out alleged demons and to promulgate his pneumatology, Mather was brewing new Salems.

On his side of the debate, Calef hammered with impassioned insistence at a fundamental point which he pressed Mather, and other Boston ministers, to answer. Shifting his focus from spectral evidence to an issue prominent in earlier witchcraft literature—that of God's permission of witchcraft—he accused the judges of attributing to human beings, and punishing them for, powers belonging only to devils or to God. The judges acted on the principle that a witch can commission the devil to afflict mortals; but for Calef "only the Almighty that sets bounds to his rage . . . can commission him to hurt and destroy." With Mather more particularly in mind, he also challenged the notion that devils can invisibilize matter. His letters to Mather are pervaded by scorn for his credulousness and gleeful taunts for his memorable statement that with his own hands he had knocked off Martha Goodwin's invisible chains. Over and over with grinding sarcasm, Calef proposed to Mather that the methods used to defeat supposed witches savored of witchcraft themselves, such as "knocking off invisible chains."

Calef kept needling Mather to deal with his "Fundamentals," but Mather ignored him until February 1695, when he sent a thirty-two page treatise on witchcraft. Written as an epistle to someone else, as if he disdained addressing Calef directly, it was his last substantial work on the seven-year-long invasion of spirits. He devoted about a third of the treatise to elaborating a "preliminary *Position*": that by their fall, the evil angels did not lose all their angelical powers. He offered both scriptural and *"experimental"* proofs—"the *pinches* that I have seen given to them; the *Blisters* that I have seen Rais'd on them"—and concluded by explaining manifestations of the invisible world, more assuredly than before, in terms of the plastic spirit:

> That there is a *Plastic Spirit* permeating of the World, which very powerfully operates upon the more corporeal parts of it: and . . . the *Angels*, both good and bad, are on the account of their *Natures*, the most Able of all creatures, to Apply that *Spirit* unto very many and mighty purposes.

He devoted another third or more of the treatise to such miscellaneous questions as the form of witch-covenants, and most of the rest to the question of God's justice in permitting diabolic attacks on mankind.

But to Calef's fundamental question, whose importance he acknowl-edged, Mather allowed about one page of obfuscation, evasion, and con-tradiction. Indeed, Calef's question exposed a serious confusion in Math-er's understanding of the invisible world. If, as Mather remarked himself, "The *Devils* can do *no Evil,* without a special permission from our Great God," how could mortal witches "Commissionate" them? In his sketchy answer, Mather agreed with Calef that God limits the devils' power and must permit them to act. But he suggested, in characteristically elastic language, that "It seems possible that the *Devils* having a sufficient and antecedent Permission to do mischiefs may yet Hook in cursed *Witches* to consent with them." As Calef later pointed out to Mather, if the devils "Hook in" the witches then the witches do not commission them. Mather also proposed that if witchcraft is the "*Skill of Applying the plastic Spirit of the World unto unlawful Purposes,*" then the witches' consent as much contributes to the effects wrought by the devils as the longings of a preg-nant woman, by means of the plastic spirit also, contribute to shaping the fetus. Here Mather simply forgot or disregarded his own earlier defini-tion, quoted in the last paragraph, which assigns the power of using the plastic spirit not to witches but to devils. Finally, Mather speculated that God "seems to have made a *Grant* unto those Destroying Spirits, that when they are with such and such wicked *Ceremonies* called for, they *shall* make a mischievous Descent." This very slippery statement of what God "seems to" have done glides by the real question of whether, having made their descent, the devils also carry out the witches' desires. In this feeble, final show of answering Calef, Mather managed to be no more lucid or persuasive than in *Wonders of the Invisible World.*

Mather loaned his treatise to Calef with the condition that he return it in two weeks and promise not to copy it. After reading it, Calef replied that he did not wonder at Mather's stipulations, considering its "crude matter and impertinent absurdities." Before returning the manuscript he covered the margins, in most cases justly, with about a hundred jeering annotations for Mather's perusal. He accused Mather of begging the ques-tion by bare assertions, of evading it by lengthy discussion of the power of fallen angels, and of confusing it by introducing the occult concept of plastic spirit. In outraged marginalia he spat out his horror over the Salem hangings and slashed Mather for his credulous innocence: "You have told the world that already in your several books . . . Plastic Spirit, whats that. Sure some inkhorn term. . . . An easy trick for any Salem hocus to perform . . . turning men to cats and dogs riding a pole through the air, and the rest of such ridiculous and brutish stuff . . . . is this worse than knocking off invisible chains with the hand. . . ."

*

The good angels who appeared to Mercy Short, Margaret Rule, and Mrs. Carver of Salem made their largest descent on Boston in the fall of 1694, about a year after Cotton Mather's own visitation. This epilogue to the Salem trials is very little known, mainly because Mather's diaries for 1694 and 1695 are missing, and the events survive only in fragmentary and sometimes considerably later accounts. But by August 1694, the number of reported visitations, it seems, prompted the Cambridge Association of ministers to propose for discussion the topic, "Whether angelical visits by visible appearance to the people of God in these days are wholly ceased; or, if not ceased, what are the marks whereby we may distinguish them from diabolical?"

The counterdescent of good angels apparently coincided with, and perhaps inspired, a religious revival in the North Church. On a single day in September 1694, Cotton Mather entered in the church records thirteen admissions to full membership (that is, thirteen recent experiences of grace)—exceeding the number of admissions to the church for most entire *years*. (In all of 1695, only eight persons were admitted.) "In the Air," Increase observed the same month, "Angels have been descending and there making melody to the Lord." The angelic music seems to have rung loudest in October, when there occurred in the North End, Cotton wrote later, "a strange Descent of *Shining Spirits,* that had upon them great marks of their being such *Angels* as they Declared themselves to be." The angels told the persons they visited that Increase Mather need not perplex himself about going to England, for God would bring to pass what would be most for His Glory, *"And the Angels of* GOD *will attend him, wheresoever His Providence may dispose of him."*

Both Mathers regarded these visitations warily, alert to diabolic imposture. In one case a spiritually troubled woman in the North Church applied to Cotton for advice. While in his study she fell into a lifeless trance, eyes transfixed. When she revived she pointed to a place in the room where, she said, she had seen a "a most Glorious Appearance of An Angel in a Shining Apparel." Fearing a trick of the devil, Mather told her to be very cautious. But at a private religious meeting of young women she again became entranced and was told, she said, "Our Friend Mather is Apt to doubt we are good Angels, but tell him for to Convince him that we are these things, for he'll be here in half an hour, that he's now

Studying Such a Sermon on Such a Text." When Mather arrived he revealed that he had indeed been thinking of a sermon on that text. Ultimately the angels told the woman, however, that because their appearance puzzled Increase Mather, "we will because we loath to grieve him, never visit you any more."

A second young woman in the North Church heard a voice offering her religious counsel. Cotton Mather at first suspected a "*loose Imagination,*" but again learned that the "*Invisible Whisperer*" disclosed to her secrets which he knew to be true and she did not. Yet two features of her story disturbed him. She balked at visiting him as her pastor, and when she did visit she developed a strange inability to relate her experiences, suggesting that she was "under the Enchantments of a *Spirit* who was lothe, I should examine too narrowly his *Devices.*" Also, the spirit revealed to her some hidden miscarriages of others and commanded her to speak with them about their iniquities. Mather knew these persons to be innocent and foresaw that her accusations would endanger neighborhood peace. On balance he concluded the woman's voices "had no Angelical Aspect" and he required her to discountenance the unseen speaker and be afraid of hearing from him. When the spirit returned next she told it: "*I desire no more to hear from you; Mr.* Mather says *you are a Devil, and I am afraid you are. If you are an Angel of the Lord, give me a Proof of it.*" The spirit did not answer, and never returned, persuading Mather that his skepticism had aborted a "*Begun Witchcraft* of the most *explicit* sort."

However cautious about his own and other visitations, Mather never doubted that his life had been "wondrously Signalized, by the Sensible Ministry of those *Angels.*" Loath to be guilty of ungratefully neglecting the angels, as did "the Generality of the Faithful," he kept a day of secret thanksgiving, probably late in 1694, to offer extraordinary praises to God for them and obtain "a more Notable Share of their Influence, than had ever yet been granted me." In the morning, aside from singing many hymns relating to angels, he contemplated with the aid of Scripture the existence, properties, and relations of the good angels, and the honor owing to them. In the afternoon he searched his diaries for entries concerning divine mercies which might have been subordinately executed through the operation of angels.

Reinterpreting decisive moments in his life in view of his recent understanding of angelic agency, Mather listed fourteen particular mercies. Among them were the wise parental governance afforded him in childhood, which "had a *Bias* very often given to it, by the *Angels* of God"; his childhood preservation from dangers, "by the *Angels* Looking after me";

the kind conduct of his tutors, "which doubtless the *Angels* influenced";
his preservation from epidemical illnesses, "by an Hedge of *Angels* about
me." His call to the ministry in so remarkable a place as Boston, too, was
"full of *Angels*." He found many more angelically guided mercies in his
later life also, which he similarly avowed from his study floor with rapturous Hallelujahs. In the surprising opening of his "Door of *Utterance*," in
the "astonishing *Impulse*" that often impinged on his mind when speaking
and writing, in his marriage, family, and household provision, here too "I
were Blinder than a Stone, if I should not see *Angels* my Providers."

Nor, ever mindful of repaying gifts, did Cotton Mather fail to consider
what returns he should make to God for these angelic benefits. A proper
return, he decided, was to become angelical himself, like the angels continually to behold and to admire God's glories, continually to study the
mysteries of redemption and the approach of the millennium, continually
to aid the churches of Christ, continually post on God's errands. Indeed he
closed his special day of thanksgiving with something itself "a Little *Angelical*," making a list of poor people in his flock and resolving with some
care to have their necessities relieved against the approaching winter.

5

The Parter's Portion

~·⊙·~

SIR WILLIAM PHIPS was not John Winthrop. The first royal governor under the new charter, he had been baptized in adulthood by Cotton Mather and was a member of his congregation; Mather looked for close association with him. But Phips had spent his life adventurously at sea, and whatever he imbibed of the piety of the North Church did not extinguish in him the temperament of a corsair.

Six months into his governorship, Phips brawled on Scarlett's Wharf with a man named Richard Short. Phips was uncommonly tall, as Mather described him, "and *Thick* as well as *Tall,* and *Strong* as well as *Thick*." Short, at the time Phips called him a liar, was lame in one hand and had been ill in bed for a week. When Short denied being a liar, Phips struck him with his cane, and when Short fell over a gun, Phips kept striking him until his head was fractured. Phips exploded again when he came across a customs collector named Brenton unloading seized goods. According to one witness, Phips began caning Brenton and pushing him around the wharf, calling him villain, demanding that he return the goods immediately or "he would beat him until he broke his Bones."

The governor treated members of his own government hardly more subtly. When the Speaker of the Assembly opposed him he declared the man "no more Speaker." The Speaker protested, but Phips stopped him, saying, "I have declared you to be no more Speaker, and so I do not allow you to speak." Having governed less than three years Phips was ordered home in 1694 to answer complaints against him, including some £20,000 in damages. On November 17, Mather and others accompanied him aboard his yacht as he departed. About three months later he died in

London, and the affairs of Massachusetts again passed to a temporary ruler, the lieutenant governor and former chief justice of the Salem court, William Stoughton.

The unreliability of the government under the new charter was borne in on Mather again by the arrival in May 1699 of the second crown-appointed governor, the Irish peer Lord Bellomont. Except for Andros, he was the first person to govern Massachusetts as neither a native nor an immigrant. Being also the first who was a nobleman, he received a lavish welcome—military guard, toasts, drums beating, trumpets sounding, fireworks, colors displayed, ordnance booming, "such a vast Concourse of people," one Bostonian said, "as my poor eyes never saw the like before." Five days later the ministers, hoping for the governor's favor, waited on him as a body. Cotton Mather prepared an address, which Increase handed to Bellomont; but the governor, Cotton wrote proudly, "immediately gave it back into my Hand; asking me to read it unto him," as he did, requesting Bellomont's goodwill toward the churches and toward languishing Harvard.

Cotton Mather's hope for renewed influence in government proved doubly short-lived, first because Bellomont quickly came to regard him as given "to preach moderation, and not to practice it," then because as governor of both New England and New York Bellomont spent only fourteen months of his three-year reign in Boston. In his absence, the government again devolved on Stoughton. Stoughton himself died in 1701, however, and after fifteen years of bobbing and flux the government of Massachusetts passed, again temporarily, to the Council.

The succession of brief and sometime exotic governments showed that in one of its concerns the old mentality of invasion had not been unrealistic, for the loss of the charter and the accession of William and Mary were transforming the meaning of New England. As the imposition of royal government began being defined in practical political terms, local politics were reshaped along English lines, and Massachusetts adjusted itself to the tone and demands of the mother country. Mather was keenly aware that an exclusivist Christian Israel could no longer exist, and he tried strenuously to adapt the New England churches to these drastically changed circumstances. Despite his cries about the devil reclaiming a uniquely sanctified New England for his own, in the decade following the trials he continually proclaimed that New Englanders were not a special purified remnant but were, above all, loyal colonial Englishmen. "It is no Little Blessing of God, that we are a part of the *English*

Nation," he told the General Assembly in 1700. "Our Dependence on, and Relation to, that brave *Nation,* that man deserves not the Name of an *English man,* who despises it."

In this spirit of reunion, Mather also proclaimed New England Congregationalism restored to the Church of England, and sought a rapprochement with other English Protestants, particularly Presbyterians. The two sects had long been divided by their view of a national church. Presbyterians viewed local congregations as part of the Church of England, responsible to church courts; Congregationalists insisted on the independence of local churches, joined only by informal fellowship and advice. But upon William's accession, leaders of the two groups met in London, with the active participation of Increase Mather, and tried to effect a union. They produced in 1691 a document that demonstrated their agreement on basic articles of faith and abolished the distinction between them: *Heads of Agreement Assented to by the United Ministers In and About London: Formerly called Presbyterian and Congregational.* Cotton Mather joined in giving up the identity of Congregationalism, whose name had been conferred by his own grandfather John Cotton. The Nonconformist churches, he wrote in 1700, "have needlessly been sometimes Distinguished into *Presbyterian* and *Congregational,* but are now, I hope, losing the Distinction, in that more *Christian* Name of *United Brethren.*"

Mather moved even further from Congregational exclusivism in response to King William's Toleration Act of 1689. The Act profoundly affected English Nonconformists, for in legally recognizing their right to worship it left them without a cause to fight, sapped their zeal, and sped their decline. In abolishing religious persecution, the Act in effect also made New England Puritanism unnecessary, for it removed what had impelled the first settlers to flee old England. The Toleration Act emboldened in Mather a latent ecumenism. Not long after his father's return from England he had run "the Hazard of much Reproach" by preaching to the General Assembly against civil punishment for conscientious religious dissent, making him, he believed, "the only *Minister* Living in the Land, that have testified against the *Suppression* of *Heresy,* by *Persecution.*"

To show himself a true Englishman, respectful of English law, Mather would now no more regard Episcopalians as a danger to New England, any more than Episcopalians after the Toleration Act would regard Nonconformists as a threat to them. Indeed he took pleasure in observing that the New England churches welcomed Episcopalians and others to transient communion: "we have with delight seen godly Congregationals and

Presbyterians, and Episcopalians, and Antipaedobaptists [i.e., Baptists], all members in the same churches; and sitting together without offence about their Lesser Differences, at the same Holy Table." Beginning around 1692 he began urging Congregationalists not to "*Monopolize* all Godliness to our own *Little Party*," since Christians who keep differing modes of worship can still be in a state of salvation: "every *Difference in Religion,* does not make a *Different Religion*. And if we think our own *Understandings* to be a *Standard* for all the Rest of Mankind, we do certainly, *Think of our selves above what we ought*."

While opening Christian Israel to non-Congregationalists and reaching beyond it for union with English Presbyterians, Mather also forwarded important innovations in the relation of the Congregational churches to each other. For one, he tried to promote interchurch councils and synods. His desire to strengthen the churches through cooperation was influenced by Presbyterian practice and probably by the new charter, which weakened the churches in depriving them of dependable government support. In recommending various unions of churches he ventured on dangerous ground, however, for Congregationalism stressed the autonomy of individual churches and viewed overseeing bodies as a move toward episcopacy and even papacy. Largely because Increase Mather feared a drift in that direction, it was said, no church synod was held in New England for forty years.

Yet in an unpublished essay on the utility of synods, written around 1699, Cotton Mather professed his "Abhorrence of unaccountable *Independency*" in churches and depicted the congregations of New England as "bound up" with each other in the "Same Common Interests of Christianity." He recommended that each church respect the advice of prominent ministers, pledge to maintain intimate association with other churches, and freely account for its practices to any church inquiring after them. He also recommended the calling of church councils to consult on inflammatory disputes in individual churches. If the council when called failed to reclaim an erring church, it could declare the church unfit for communion with other churches and deprive it of the legal privileges they enjoyed—for instance, forbidding members of the wayward church to take communion at other churches. In fact, such councils and assemblies were multiplying at the turn of the century, and Mather attended several himself in Salem, Marlborough, and other places.

In the same spirit of innovation, Mather also promoted clerical associations. Congregationalists had long mistrusted these also: several New England ministers who gathered fortnightly at one of their homes, Governor John Winthrop recorded in 1633, met with objections and stirred fear that they might become a presbytery. On the other hand, many ministers among Cotton Mather's generation saw in clerical associations a means of reaffirming the importance and independence of their office. In 1690 twenty-two ministers meeting in Charlestown had founded a Cambridge Association of Ministers, modeled after similar groups in England. With Cotton Mather often acting as secretary they met at Harvard every six weeks to discuss religious topics and hear cases from individual churches or persons. Drawing material from their records, Cotton published *Thirty Important Cases* (1699), in the Preface to which he noted that such meetings had been approved by the United Ministers in England, "formerly called *Presbyterian* and *Congregational*," and encouraged ministers elsewhere to hold regular meetings on the Cambridge model. While recognizing that no more than occasional meetings could be expected, he saw no danger, he said, of "overwhelming the *Rights* of *Particular Churches* by *Classical* Combinations."

Mather also wished clerical groups to test ministerial candidates, to prevent the ordination of the unqualified or fraudulent. Two cases illustrate the need. The first Mather recounted in a delightful narrative, *A Warning to the Flocks* (1700), which tells the adventures of a preacher named Samuel May, who arrived with his wife from England in 1699. May's "Ragged, Wretched, Forlorn Circumstances" at first moved Mather's compassion. Mather found him work preaching to private religious meetings, and soon May had a large following. Soon also, Mather found him unable to name a single minister in London. Mather's suspicions mounted when he received from May a short note containing eighteen misspellings. He declared May "a BARBER" and prayed that he would be exposed. The chance came when he heard May preach at a private meeting and identified his sermon as a plagiarism. May not only denied it but also induced his followers to requite Mather's defamation of him by throwing into his house "insolent, bitter, bloody *Libels*." After May at last "went off with a Stink" to England, several Boston women deposed that if a young woman became affected by his ministry he spent hours counseling her to lie with him, "which he said, was *no Sin,* for *David* and *Solomon* did as much." They need not fear becoming pregnant by him, he added, "*for none ever were so!*" May's alleged wife turned out to be his mistress, and the impostor himself turned out to be Samuel Axel, a Hampshire brickmaker. The case notified churches, Mather said, to beware of hiring "*New Preachers,* of whose Endowments and Principles, they have not had a Reasonable Attestation."

A more dolorous case occurred in Mather's own family. His uncle John Cotton—the son of the great John Cotton, and his dearest relative since childhood—was charged in 1697 with what Samuel Sewall called "Notorious Breaches of the Seventh Commandment" or what a Plymouth shipbuilder described as "attempting to be too Familiar with one of his Church Members Wife." A council of neighboring churches recommended that the Plymouth church dismiss him, as it did. Although greatly distressed over the "terrible and amazing Circumstances, of my poor Uncle," Cotton Mather considered the recommendation just. A few months after the dismissal he apparently sent the Cotton family, as he often did, one of his recent publications. But it arrived with an anonymous letter, John Cotton lamented, with "no superscription to it, no inscription no subscription . . . neither is there a word who sent the Book." The snub hurt the more because he had damaged his standing with the church council by defending Mather, although one of the council members "very much" despised him. (Desolate and confused, John Cotton managed to secure a ministry in South Carolina. En route he visited his nephew in Boston and "very peremptorily," Cotton Mather said, denied "the most, and the worst" of the charges against him, but in less than a year he was dead, of an epidemic of yellow fever in Charleston that killed nearly two hundred people.)

In or out of his family such cases worried Mather, and in hopes of ensuring a learned and ethical clergy he published *Proposals for the Preservation of Religion in the Churches, by a Due Trial of Them that Stand Candidates for the Ministry* (1702). Here he recommended giving groups of ordained ministers a part in the process of candidacy and ordination, otherwise the concern of individual churches. He proposed that every ministerial candidate be examined by and preach before such a group, and obtain from four or five already ordained ministers testimonials to his knowledge of learned languages, skill in preaching, theological learning, soundness of principle, and ability to refute error. Although concurred in by nearly thirty ministers, Mather's proposals were not adopted. In fact they lay well outside the spirit of primitive New England Congregationalism, amounting to a crypto-Presbyterianism by which more or less formal panels of ministers might if not license ministerial candidates, at least police them.

In calling for more frequent church councils and for clerical associations, Mather departed from Congregational principles in the name, of course, of preserving Congregational orthodoxy. The inconsistency is uncomfortable but understandable. It becomes perplexing, however, if one adds that while calling for a Congregational-Presbyterian merger and for hospitality to all Protestant sects, Mather at the very same time continued to act the part of a Jeremiah, bemoaning and chastising the decline from the religion of the Fathers, for example in *Things for a Distress'd People to Think Upon* (1696):

> *New England* once abounded with *Hero's* worthy to have their Lives written, as Copies for future Ages to write after; But, *These are Ancient Things!* A *Public Spirit* in all that sustained any *Public Office*, and a fervent *Inclination* to Do Good, join'd with an Incomparable *Ability* to do it, once ran through *New England;* But, *These are Ancient Things!* . . . There seems to be a shameful *Shrink,* in all sorts of men among us, from that *Greatness,* and *Goodness,* which adorned our Ancestors: We grow *Little* every way; *Little* in our Civil Matters, *Little* in our Military Matters, *Little* in our Ecclesiastical Matters; we dwindle away, to *Nothing.* . . .

In fact, during the same years that he forwarded ecumenism and toleration, Mather published more works than ever before on the urgent need for reformation, aimed at restoring (if it ever existed) a special, spiritually minded Puritan community of praying families, children who did not play at the rear of the meetinghouse on Sabbaths, boys and girls who shunned mixed dances, cheerfully obedient servants catechized by caring masters, and sailors who sang psalms instead of bawdy songs.

Mather did not concede, or perhaps could not see, the conflict between his simultaneous calls for openness and exclusiveness. But the discrepancy has led modern historians to offer directly contradictory interpretations of his views in these years. Richard Lovelace, for instance, argues that Mather "put himself on record in favor of toleration in his earliest published sermons" and that he "seems to have been considerably in the vanguard of the conservative leadership of the colony." Contrarily, Robert Middlekauff writes that Mather's endorsements of toleration in the early 1690s were "undoubtedly insincere" and that he in fact "confined the guarantees of toleration as tightly as possible."

If not insincere, Mather's several innovations may at least have been politic. The demonstration of New England's loyalty to the empire was an old game. Mather's many expressions of loyalty to the crown often came in the presence of crown officials such as Lord Bellomont, and several of his ecumenical writings were published in England, perhaps to show New England's appreciation for William's policy of toleration. Mather had other compelling reasons for urging a reconciliation with England, including strong ecumenical tendencies that had long existed within Puritanism (Richard Baxter was a pioneer ecumenist), the hope of regaining a voice in English affairs, the need for allies in the raging struggle against Catholic Europe and the looming war against rationalism, and his prophetic sense, as we shall see, of impending revolutions that would unite all of Christianity.

It is more likely, however, that Mather's insincerity (or political trimming) lay in the other direction, that his simultaneous calls for liberalism and orthodoxy deferred not to English Protestantism but to Boston Puritanism. His policy on admission to communion was more liberal than his father's, and he may have been genuinely attracted to ecumenism and church union but maintained a show of greater orthodoxy than he felt out of respect to his father's ideals. However that may be, he undoubtedly in many ways enjoyed the more various and cosmopolitan world in part created by the new charter. While he deeply respected the Wilderness Zion of the Fathers, his yearnings for bigness and fame, his lively sympathy with new fashions and ideas, and his identification with the more aristocratic and urbane sections of society did not relish the sense of living in some isolated city on a hill. Something of unashamed worldliness appears in his attitude toward the wearing of large perriwigs, which became fashionable in New England around 1690, as they had in England thirty years earlier. The English Puritan William Prynne denounced those who "purchase the hairy excrements of some other person," for to him and most other Puritans wigs smacked of effeminacy, pride, and affectation, suggesting Stuart courtiers, theatrical costumes, and old men trying to look young. Yet in his one surviving portrait Cotton Mather wears a profuse perriwig, nearly shoulder length. Samuel Sewall considered wigs a profane abomination and was surprised when in 1691 he understood Mather to be defending them in a sermon as "an innocent fashion, taken up and used by the best of men." "I expected not," Sewall said, "to hear a vindication of Perriwigs in Boston Pulpit by Mr. Mather."

Sewall's surprise, in what it registers about Cotton Mather, does not differ from the contrary interpretations of Mather's ideas offered by modern historians, nor from Robert Calef's earlier perception that Mather brought both fire to increase and water to quench the conflagration. In fact, hardly a trait of Mather's maturing personality is more striking than his preoccupation with seeming irreconcilables and his view of himself as a peacemaker between warring factions—originating, it seems clear, in his unsuccessful youthful attempt to settle conflicts in himself, of which an earlier expression was his stammer. The discrepancy now between his twin attraction to the metropolitan world of London and the world of his grandfathers indeed seems a continuation of the earlier conflict between the pride and ambition he recognized in himself, and his dutiful wish to use his ministry in God's service alone.

Whether trying to calm contending political factions after the revolt or running between Moses and Aaron during the Salem trials, Cotton Mather's conciliatory efforts often brought him enmity from both sides, what he called the "*Parter's Portion*." He suspected, as he wrote in *Blessed Unions* (1692), that his current calls for toleration of rival religious claims and his attempt to close the gaps between different Protestant sects would get him the "*Parter's Portion*" also. That happened, his dole arriving through what he saw as a new invasion of the New England churches.

*

In another dozen years, Lydia Lee George would become the chief delight of Cotton Mather's life, and his greatest torment. But in 1701 she was the young wife of a prosperous organizer of a new Boston church, concerned that she had spent too much time and thought on her apparel and indulged the vanity of vying with others. Reassuringly her twenty-eight-year-old pastor, Benjamin Colman, counseled that her dress suited her birth, rank, age, and education. He criticized those who equate religion with plainness and "morosely judge all that wear more buttons, than they allow themselves." Since she had been brought up to dress richly, and her wealthy husband approved it, he said, "it is not offensive nor grievous to sober Christians: It is not good to indulge scruples too much, for they will grow upon you apace to your great discomfort."

This genial advice typified the young minister, who was known for his courtly tenderness toward women, and for powdering his hair. Those who knew Benjamin Colman invariably depicted him as pious but polished—a tall, spare figure neatly dressed, with a fair complexion and kindly mien, notable for his "Politeness and Elegance in Conversation" and his "inimitably soft and tuneful" voice—in short, a ministerial man of fashion. He had begun life less genteelly. Born in Boston and a member of the North Church, he had his early schooling from Mather's schoolmaster, Ezekiel Cheever, graduated from Harvard in 1692, preached a while at Medford, and added an M.A. in 1695. Shortly after, he went to England where, like many later Americans, he underwent a sea change. French privateers seized his ship, put him in the hold, and imprisoned him in France. Set free, he reached England with a few shillings in his pocket, of which a spark in Portsmouth bilked him. Finally settled in London, he preached there and in other English cities, attended the conference at which Increase Mather worked for the union of Congregationalists and Presbyterians, and wrote a poem on his flirtation with the daughter of the Massachusetts agent, Sir Henry Ashurst, comparing her to a candle and himself to a fly.

A Presbyterian board appointed Colman minister at Bath—a choice situation because of the resort there of the gentry. In his two years at Bath he met many fashionable families, including that of the poet "Philomela" (Elizabeth Singer), a "Heavenly maid," as he called her. "Music, poetry, and painting were her three beauties and delights." Upon visiting the family's home he versified the paradisal beauty of its grounds, viewing them as an eligible bachelor:

> Such Eden's streams, and banks, and tow'ring groves;
> Such Eve herself, and such her muse and loves.
> Only there wants an Adam on the green,
> Or else all Paradise might here be seen.

Such an Adam Elizabeth's family seem to have desired Colman to become. But he responded instead to a call that came in the summer of 1699 from the organizers of the new Boston church, inviting him to be their pastor. Apparently suspecting that opposition to their church might prevent his ordination in Boston, they advised him to be ordained by a board in London. Their advice defied Congregationalist principles, by which a minister could be ordained only by a particular church. But like some other ministers in his generation, Colman saw his identity as a minister less in terms of native tradition than in terms of English modes of religious life. When he returned to Boston in November 1699, he had been ordained, though still a member of the North Church, by the London Presbytery, in the Presbyterian manner.

The organizers of the new church were a group of Boston merchants, several of whom had subscribed in 1689 toward building a Church of England chapel. Led by the wealthy Thomas Brattle, the church later became known as the Brattle Street Church. The organizers claimed that a new church was needed because the older meetinghouse lacked enough "convenient seats." In fact, their new building—in the South End, about two streets from the Town House—was meaningfully innovative. Instead of the central turret distinctive to earlier New England meetinghouses, it had a full tower and spire at one end, like the churches of England. The building stood out from the other Boston churches in more than architecture, for the organizers also desired to make what they said were needed changes in worship.

In December, shortly after Colman's return, the organizers published a three-page *Manifesto* setting forth their principles. Calling in their defense upon the recent spirit of ecumenism, they said they intended only the true and pure worship of God as revealed in Scripture but conformable to the "Churches of the UNITED BRETHREN in *London,* and throughout all *England.*" Only in a few particulars, they said, did they "see cause to depart from what is ordinarily Professed and Practised by the Churches of CHRIST here in *New-England.*" The particulars included the reading of Scripture by the minister without explication; the omission of a public relation of converting experience as a requirement for entry to communion; and the extension of the power of choosing a minister beyond communicants to every baptized adult person. (In psalm singing the church also very soon abandoned the custom of "lining-out," that is, of alternately reading and singing psalms line by line—an important step toward the development of musical literacy in New England.) A contemporary later described the Brattle church as "midway between the Church of England and Dissenters." That seems correct, for the new church tried to retain its Congregational roots but inclined to benignity rather than zeal, sought contact with moderate Anglicans, and identified the church more with the entire congregation than with the core of Saints.

In fact the Brattle church was a somewhat advanced version of the vision of transatlantic and intersectarian harmony Cotton Mather had been popularizing for the last half-dozen years. Mather's response, however, was not welcoming but wrathful. He denounced the new church as the work of "Head-strong" men whose *Manifesto,* coming in the wake of Andros and the evil angels, attempted once again to "utterly subvert our Churches." In seeing "another *Day of Temptation* begun upon the Town and Land," he resembled the man to whom promiscuous means someone having one more affair than himself. He damned as dangerous innovations ideas only slightly left of innovations he had introduced himself. Having relaxed admissions requirements in his own church, he scorned the new church's still more lax failure to require a relation of conversion experience. While speaking proudly of sharing the communion table with Presbyterians, Baptists, and moderate Anglicans, he had no desire to create them out of Congregationalists, as Colman had in effect been in accepting Presbyterian ordination. Chiefly he seems to have objected to the Brattle group's rejection of church covenants—explicit public agreements by groups of Saints to worship together—not so much for its democratizing tendency as for making the operation of the church secretive and unneighborly. Ministers who would be faithful to Christ, he believed, would have to appear on the front lines again, and no little part must "unavoidably fall to my Share."

As a first maneuver, Mather sent the *"Innovators"* a long monitory letter. Although "most lovingly penn'd," he said, it only raised their "impetuous Lusts, to carry on the *Apostasy.*" Colman, while not yet formally dismissed from the Mathers' church, was installed as minister of the new church on December 12. On December 24 the Brattle church worshiped for the first time in its new meetinghouse and apparently drew, as it did afterward, a large crowd; Sewall remarked that his own congregation was "pretty much thin'd by it." The Brattle organizers had requested Colman to ask the other Boston ministers, as a token of fellowship, to join them in a day of fasting. Perhaps thinking it futile to resist Colman's influence, and perhaps serving his sense of himself as a peacemaker, Mather drew up a letter to Colman on December 28, signed also by his father and by the Boston minister James Allen, offering to preach and pray with the Brattle congregation provided they lay aside their *Manifesto* and simply declared their adherence to the *Heads of Agreement* of the United Brethren. Otherwise they could not join in fellowship, "Lest we partake in the guilt of those great Irregularities whereby you have given just cause of offence." The Brattle group's response has not survived but must have been unfavorable, since a week later Mather denounced them afresh in his diary as "ignorant, arrogant, obstinate, and full of Malice and Slander, and they fill the Land with *Lies,* in the Misrepresentation whereof, I am a very singular Sufferer."

With Sewall and some others acting as intermediaries between the Mathers and the Brattle church—"Was some heat," Sewall said, "but grew calmer" —a compromise was reached whereby the church agreed to announce its adherence to the *Heads of Agreement* and to follow Congregational practice in making a public declaration of church covenant. A "wonderful Joy fill'd the Hearts of our good People, far and near," Mather wrote, "that we had obtained thus much from them." On January 28 he formally dismissed Colman from the North Church and three days later he and his father joined the young minister in a public fast at the Brattle church. Increase, who did not easily put bygones to rest, preached on the doctrine that we must follow peace—so far as it consists with holiness. Cotton, Sewall recorded, prayed "excellently and pathetically for Mr. Colman and his Flock. Twas a close dark day."

But the darkness had only begun. While negotiating with the Brattle church, the Mathers had prepared for press a lengthy blast at it. Cotton speaks of the book as a joint effort, but it seems to have been very largely

Increase's work. After devising a compromise with the church, Cotton wrote, "we laid aside what was in the Press; resolving in a more comfortable, and I hope, effectual Way, to endeavour the Establishment of our Churches." But Increase decided to publish the book anyway, perhaps because the Brattle Street innovations seemed more dangerous to him than they seemed to his son. Although Increase had already preached and prayed at the new church, his book attacking it appeared in March, entitled *The Order of the Gospel* (1700). In 144 pages he argued against seventeen distinct principles of the Brattle church, defending the right of churches to demand written or oral evidence of regenerating experience before admitting a member to communion, questioning the ordination of ministers without the approbation of neighboring churches, and concluding that to espouse Brattle principles was to "give away *the whole Congregational cause* at once, and a great part of the *Presbyterian Discipline* also."

By coincidence, Increase's arguments against the Brattle church anticipated the announcement a few months later of some new but related innovations which gave the controversy redoubled intensity. This time the apostate was not a youth but a nearly sixty-year-old member of Increase's generation, the Northampton minister Solomon Stoddard, whose *Doctrine of Instituted Churches* appeared in London in the spring or early summer. Stoddard was, and remains, a highly controversial figure in the development of New England, whom some historians have seen as an early voice of democracy. His book gave comprehensive expression to views he had been promoting in western Massachusetts for twenty years, particularly that communion should not be limited to those who had experienced grace. In this he probably intended no more than to halt the widely lamented decline, where other attempts at reform had failed. But to open the communion table to all church members was to discard the most fundamental ideas of Puritan theology and church government, the distinctive Congregational understanding of the church as an elite group of Saints. Some saw Stoddard's views as the fatal outcome of the undermining doctrine of halfway membership promulgated since 1662, and Increase Mather had attacked Stoddard as early as 1677 for advancing notions certain to "corrupt Churches and ruin all in a little time."

Now, atop the opening of the Brattle church, Stoddard argued in print the even more extreme idea that communion might itself lead to Sainthood, might be "a means also to work saving Regeneration." Some eminent Presbyterians had advocated this view earlier, but to most Congregationalists it conjured up a communion table surrounded by thieves, drunkards, and adulterers hoping to drink and eat their salvation. To his very radical proposal, Stoddard added an astonishing concept of the church. He would conceive a congregation not as a coterie of Saints but as merely a group of people assembled by God in the same place. Since a church was only a neighborhood phenomenon it deserved no independent ecclesiastical power. Stoddard forthrightly advocated Presbyterianizing the churches, subjecting them to collective governance under synods composed of representatives from various churches. Even more broadly he questioned the whole vision of a supposed primitive Congregational church of uniquely pure principles. Many mistakes in church government, he said, had been made by people who "have a Veneration for antiquity and adopt the sayings of Ancient Fathers for Canonical."

Having seen vast changes in the political and social life of his childhood, Cotton Mather now began to witness the transformation of its religious life as well. Although dismayed by the appeal of Stoddard's "wretched *Novelties*" to a "carnal, giddy, rising Generation," he noted sorrowfully that hardly any but himself and his father dared "appear with any Strength of Argument, or Fortitude, in Defence of our invaded *Churches.*" Undaunted himself, when Stoddard visited Boston in the summer to assert his views before an assembly of ministers, he stood up and spoke at length against "a *Book* of a reverend Person, here present." In choosing the "*Parter's Portion*" he found himself having somehow to denounce Stoddard's and Colman's Presbyterian ideas plausibly while continuing to celebrate the Congregationalist-Presbyterian union. He attempted this feat by identifying them as Presbyterians-*manquè,* observing that "the Gentlemen in the Design against our Churches, will needs be call'd *Presbyterians:* but they very unjustly arrogate that Name. . . . Our Controversy with them indeed is, because they will not be *Presbyterians.*" He warned that of the continual attempts to unhinge the New England churches, none was more daring and explicit than Stoddard's. In creating national synods Stoddard would divest individual churches of their power of self-reform, and give over their governance to synods whose decrees would be impotent in New England, lacking "a *civil Magistrate,* that will make them *cut.*" Wishing to abolish conversion as a requirement for communion, Stoddard would have "those that *know themselves* ungodly Wretches come to the *dreadful Mysteries.*" The devil's initial plot against New Englanders, now far advanced, was to extinguish their godliness: "The *next plot* of Satan, is to confound our Holy *Church-Order,* and make us, with our own Hands pull down our House."

Caught in the odd logic of his situation, Mather turned his dispute

with Stoddard and Colman into a bizarre quarrel over which Congregationalists were the true Presbyterians. He prepared a Boston edition of
the work of a well-known English Presbyterian, John Quick's *Young Mans
Claim unto the Sacrament of the Lords-Supper*. In doing so he hoped to
show the close similarity between true Presbyterianism and orthodox
New England Congregationalism, to vouch for which he added to the
work signed attestations by such Puritan elder statesmen as John Higginson. At the same time he also tried to show how Stoddard and Colman
exploited the name Presbyterian to cloak their "*Disorderly Undertakings*" and, while nominally Congregationalists, "would not have Things
to be as the Eminent *Planters,* and General *Synods,* of our Churches have
left them unto us." He prefaced Quick's work with a fifty-nine-page essay,
signed by him and his father but seemingly written by himself, entitled
"A Defense of Evangelical Churches." While he felt "Tenderness" for
Stoddard he characterized him caustically as an "Ingenious and Contem-
plative Gentleman, in his Retirements" and condemned "the *Presbyterianism* that runs down *Connecticut* River." Lunging also at Colman and
other "Raw youths . . . under the name of *Presbyterians,*" he labeled both
men "*Presbyterian Formalists,*" as opposed to the true or "*Reforming
Presbyterians.*" Stoddard's call for national synods of clergymen—as opposed to his own call for clerical associations—he attacked as a move
toward episcopacy and thence to papacy. Stoddard's wish to open communion to the knowingly unregenerate—as opposed to his own (liberal)
view that a "probable hope" of grace qualifies for admission—he called a
"*Popish Fancy,*" rejected by Presbyterians and even Episcopalians as undoing the very form and matter of the churches. Those most eminent for
holiness, he concluded, had failed to stand up against the "*New model-
lers* of our Churches," leaving him and his father to do so though they
"bring all the raging Obloquy imaginable upon us."

Raging obloquy, however, was hardly Benjamin Colman's style, which
inclined rather to well-bred reasonableness, with a reserve of saucy wit.
In mid-December appeared a delayed reply to Increase's *Order of the
Gospel,* a pamphlet entitled *The Gospel Order Revived.* Published anonymously, it was taken as the work of Colman and some others sympathetic
to the Brattle church, whose principles it defends on scriptural, logical,
and historical grounds against Increase's charges. Through these patient
arguments, however, runs a vein of rather sneeringly sly personal attack.
The writers refer to Increase repeatedly, with accumulating irony, as the
"Reverend Author." Where Increase objected to what he called "*Dumb
Reading*"—the Brattle practice of reading Scripture without explica-

tion—they snip at the "complicated . . . Malignity in the Phrase" and at Increase's immodesty in thinking "any one of his Sermons or short Comments, can edify more than the reading of twenty Chapters." Sometimes thus needlingly and sometimes brusquely, they accuse Increase of misrepresenting the authorities he cites, treating as the practice of all the New England churches what are simply his own views, and crying up Presbyterian principles in London but denouncing them in Boston, where his own interest is touched. Particularly they deride his overzealousness in storming over niggling issues and wailing "*Oh Apostacy! Apostacy!*" In scoffing at Increase's emotionalism, Colman and the others in effect repudiated the whole theory of decline. They note that a generation ago the change in baptismal policy was decried as a woeful declension, but the present generation feel "the happy effects of it, and rising up at the Reformers names, do call them blessed." Declaring themselves not apostates but simply "less Rigid than others of the Reverend Authors severity," the writers end by vowing not to answer any further charges, however noisy.

The publication of *The Gospel Order Revived* created new issues between the Mathers and the innovators, calling attention to the Mathers' political influence in Boston. The pamphlet had been published in New York, as Stoddard's *Doctrine of Instituted Churches* had been published in London. The Brattle group charged that the Mathers' control of the Boston press was responsible for the New York imprint, and a six-month delay in publication, Boston printers being "so much under the awe" of Increase Mather that the printer Bartholomew Green refused to issue the work. Green denied the charge in a ten-page pamphlet, to which Cotton Mather supplied an anonymous endorsement. Green said he neither refused to print the pamphlet nor was told anything by Increase to discourage its printing. When members of the Brattle church brought him the manuscript, he explained, he agreed to print it; but when they insisted that it be published anonymously he asked them first to secure the governor's approval, at which they went away angrily. Two of those who brought the manuscript to Green, however, attested that they asked him if he would print it with the permission of Cotton Mather; Green readily said he would, and they told him "it was a shame so Worthy a Minister as Mr. *Stoddard* must send as far as *England* to have his Book printed, when young Mr. *Mather* had the Press at his pleasure."

The publication of *The Gospel Order Revived* exposed a far deeper issue as well. Although Increase refused to answer Colman, considering it beneath his dignity to notice, he said, "the impotent *Allatrations* of so little a thing as that *Youth* is," Cotton retaliated against the "Young *Pseudo-presbyterian*" in a twenty-four-page pamphlet entitled *A Collection, of Some of the Many Offensive Matters, Contained in . . . The Order of the Gospel Revived* (1701). To damn the Brattle group in their own words he simply listed the "vile Things" in their pamphlet, "barely to *Recite* which is enough to *refute* them." But in his controversy with the new church he had come to detect a more profound threat to New England than any dispute over ordination or church membership—a growing temper of disrespect. Colman and the others did not so much oppose the Gospel Order as "Elegantly *Scoff*" at it. The inner meaning of the Brattle church, he now saw, was that New England having just repulsed devils was being invaded by satirists.

The two were of course the same, for those who tweaked Increase Mather as the "Reverend Author" crying "*Oh Apostacy!*" embodied spirits akin to those who prodded the Goodwin children to howl and stomp at the ministers who prayed for them. The organizers of the new church, Cotton wrote, "have not only *departed from* the Religion of their Fathers but are become *Mockers* of it." Slightly exaggerating the actual language of their pamphlet, he denounced Colman and the others for their "*Squib*" on "*The Old Men and Women, that are for the Good Old Way,*" their treating public relations of conversion experiences as "*Talkative Brethren Standing up to Relate Experiences.*" "*Mocking is Catching,*" he warned, and having often preached against disrespect for elders, he foresaw that the children of New England might learn from the innovators to deride "the most Serious things that are done in our Churches, and carry on the *Mocking Humour.*" Nothing in the Brattle church seemed to him more dangerous than its airiness toward authority and tradition: "There is no one thing, which does more threaten or disgrace *New-England,* than want of due Respect unto *Superiors;* even that Abomination, *In thee they set Light by Fathers.*"

All of the issues dividing the Mathers and the new church were summed up deliciously in some anonymous verses written on a copy of *The Gospel Order Revived* and handed around Plymouth. "Blackman," in the first stanza, is Colman; the second stanza puns on the names of the ministers Bradstreet, Woodbridge, and Stone—taken by some to be the authors of the pamphlet; "Relations," in the third stanza, refers to public relations of conversion experiences; in the last stanza, "Mico" is John Mico, a wealthy founder of the new church. The writer depicted the Mathers defending the religion of the Fathers against Brattle Street's romanizing tendency and gentility:

A Simple Poem on the Authors and Designs of This Book.

Begging Manifesto proves but a great Pesto.
   Blackman is Synodalian.
Pray stay there and stop, lest next hap & hop
Ben't Peters chair Italian.

The old strait Gate is now out of Date,
The street it must be broad;
And the Bridge must be wood, tho not half so good
As firm Stone in the Road.

Relations are Rattle with Brattle & Brattle;
Lord Brother mayn't command:
But Mather and Mather had rather & rather
The good old way should stand

Saints Cotton & Hooker, o look down, & look here
Where's Platform, Way, & the Keys?
O Torey what story of Brattle Church Twattle
To have things as they please

Our merchants cum Mico do stand Sacro Vico;
Our Churches turn Genteel:
Parsons grow trim and trigg with wealth wine & wigg
And their crowns are covered with meal.

More revealing than the content of the poem is its bantering treatment of both the innovators and the Fathers, both Blackman and Saint Hooker. The lighthearted tone confirms Cotton Mather's insight that the Brattle Street controversy foretold the erosion not only of the Gospel Order but more deeply of Puritan gravity, of the particular sensibility of New England, of not just the Fathers' principles but of their spirit.

Despite the uproar over the "great Pesto," within a year or so Mather's enmity toward Colman gave way to what became lifelong cooperation with him, and slightly tense respect. The circumstance that resolved their quarrel is one of several important details lacking in what information about the controversy remains, another being Colman's part in writing *The Gospel Order Revived.* Their reconciliation probably involved no dramatic event or change of principle, for Mather's behavior toward Colman resulted as much from personal feelings as from religious ideals. As we shall see, in Mather's later life his stifled feelings of competition with Colman and envy of his popularity erupted. They may have existed from the first, for throughout the controversy his bitterest attacks on Colman, ten years his junior, dwell on youthful brashness, intimating resentment over Colman's indulging expansive qualities he shared but harnessed.

Indeed Colman and Mather may have been drawn together by simple affinity, for they were in many ways alike—learned, courteous, pious, conciliatory, and fancying themselves among the better sort. Raised in Mather's church, Colman greatly respected the founders of New England. But acknowledging himself to be "something of a *Presbyterian* under our Congregational Form," he felt no disloyalty in adjusting the founders' vision to changed times. Mather, adding constant professions of reverence for the Fathers, did the same. In preaching a new toleration, calling for councils and associations, and offering an attenuated test for communion, he surely fostered a climate of innovation where ideas like Colman's and Stoddard's could thrive, and conspired in creating what he condemned. Rather guilty acknowledgment of siding more with the innovators than he made known appears in his keeping his quite Presbyterian essay on the utility of synods unpublished. At a convention of ministers in Boston in 1705, however, he openly joined Colman in recommending standing councils of ministers to determine church affairs in a geographical area—a real move toward Presbyterianism. Increase Mather did not endorse the proposal, and later publicly declared his opposition to it.

If Cotton Mather restrained his views out of respect for his father it was ironic, for the New England Increase held up against the innovators, the primitive Congregationalism of the Gospel Order, was a New England whose destruction many people accused him of having negotiated. Cotton's defense of his father's acceptance of the charter rightly placed him in some minds among the innovators himself, while his attack on Colman and Stoddard made him seem conservative to others—The Parter's Portion. But his quarrel with the Brattle church was less over their innovations than over their flaunting them. Without a show of loyalty to the Fathers and an appearance of historical continuity, he feared, all authority and all forms of social order would collapse.

*

Because of its public nature, Mather's quarrel with Colman and Stoddard is the most conspicuous event in his life in the decade following the Salem trials. Yet it stands out only as a boulder in a stream, for other deep concerns flowed around and beyond it. The next chapter describes how for years following his visitation by the angel, Mather experienced exhilarating but finally disillusioning psychical phenomena. In the same period he also conceived two magisterial works, including the book for which he remains best known, his history of New England, *Magnalia Christi Americana.*

Mather proposed the work to himself in the early summer of 1693 and in July received formal encouragement from the Cambridge Association of Ministers, which offered him all necessary assistance for the "exact forming" of it and requested a monthly progress report. The dying off of first-generation American Puritans, however, had long made the need for such a history a subject of public discourse. Increase Mather considered it "one of New England's Sins that no better course hath been taken that the memory of the great things the Lord hath done for us be transmitted to posterity." Several people encouraged Increase to undertake the work himself. In writing *Magnalia,* Cotton answered a call that had sounded for nearly twenty-five years and had seemed likely to be answered by his father. A simultaneous call had gone out since the 1670s for a related history of God's providences toward New England, proposals for which were drawn up by a group of church elders in 1681. In March 1694, Increase in conjunction with the Harvard Fellows and some other ministers issued renewed proposals for compiling such a history, asking ministers around the country to submit credibly attested accounts of deliverances of the distressed, judgments against the wicked, fulfillments of scriptural prophecies, "*Apparitions, Possessions, Inchantments,* and all Extraordinary Things wherein the Existence and Agency of the *Invisible World,* is more sensibly demonstrated." Cotton Mather filled this call also by including as Book VI of *Magnalia* a history of memorable divine providences in New England.

Mather having begun writing the book toward the end of 1693, it was prematurely announced for publication in London as early as 1697. But he did not ship the heavy manuscript until June 1700, near the height of his quarrel with Colman. While working on *Magnalia* and trying to arrange its publication, he published parts of it as independent short works, no fewer than seventeen of which he reprinted virtually verbatim in the book. For two years after sending the manuscript he lived in repeatedly thwarted hope of seeing the book in print. One ship from London after another brought him no news at all or reports of ceaseless clogs, delays, and possible failure—the London booksellers were "cold" toward the project, subscriptions were "uncertain," everything stood in "extreme Hazard of Miscarrying." Sometimes resigned, sometimes painfully disappointed, Mather now consented to "so humbling a Trial, as the Loss of my Church-History," now fretted over the waste of "the vast Pains I have taken in composing it." Even the news of its imminent publication, as it came to Mather in a letter from the London Presbyterian minister John Quick, was discouraging. Quick told him that because the presswork had been given to the London printer Thomas Parkhurst, truncations could be expected, and interpolations, and textual errors, and type and paper that would "afflict" him. That had been Quick's own experience with Park-hurst, who "horribly maimed and wounded" one of Quick's works, send-ing it into the world as his when, he told Mather, "Sir, it's no more mine, than if you should chop off my hands, arms, and legs, and [binding?] pieces of wood to those parts, you should say, this is whole Mr. Quick."

As published in London in 1702, *Magnalia Christi Americana* did contain perhaps three hundred typographical errors. Just the same it was unmistakably a grandly imagined and formidable work: about eight hun-dred folio pages of double columns, divided in seven substantial books— history of the settlement of New England; lives of the governors; lives of the leading ministers (the longest book); history of Harvard College, with the lives of eminent graduates; account of the New England manner of worship; "Remarkables of Divine Providence"; and a history of the inva-sion of the New England churches by heretics, Andros, devils, Indians, and others. Mather gathered this information industriously and from many sources: surviving diaries, letters, and other papers; his father's cor-respondence; the manuscript histories of New England by William Hub-bard and William Bradford; personal acquaintance with surviving mem-bers of the earlier generations, the sermon notebooks in which he had taken down their words firsthand, informants who had known them. The minister Samuel Stone seems to have loaned him the "Chronological Decads" he composed, fastened by rings so they could be hung up away from rodents. It amounted to less information than Mather desired, and he complains several times in *Magnalia* of having to scant a subject be-cause people failed to send him adequate material. But of course he never felt he had given enough, and despite his apologies the enduring importance of his book partly lies in its sheer amassment of precious information about the early history of New England—about leaders in church and state, Puritan relations with the Indians, the development of Harvard, the 1689 revolt, the expeditions against Canada, the Salem trials. He also included many significant documents (for instance, relating to the Halfway Covenant), and verses (usually elegies) by such leading Puri-tan poets as Benjamin Tompson, so that *Magnalia* also contains a docu-mentary history of early New England and a small anthology of early American Poetry.

What unifies this seven-vault archive of fact, reminiscence, document, verse, and legend is Mather's ever present narrative voice—learned, face-tious, emphatic, at once intimate and grand, distinctively showmanlike, as if history were some banquet and he the master of ceremonies. His ge-niality again suggests the conciliator, and indeed the vast, miscellaneous materials take shape under two not very harmonious intentions. First he conceived the work as a contribution to his ceaseless call throughout the 1690s for reform, as a way, he wrote, "of keeping *Alive,* as far as this poor *Essay* may contribute thereunto, the interests of *Dying Religion* in our Churches." To do so, as Sacvan Bercovitch, the most profound interpreter of his works, remarks, he lifted New England history into the realm of heroic action. Beginning with the epical opening, modeled on the open-ing of the *Aeneid,* he created an archaic-seeming World of the Fathers. Before the appearance of his life of John Eliot in 1691, only two biogra-phies of New England ministers had been published: of his grandfather John Cotton (by John Norton) and of his grandfather Richard Mather (by Increase Mather). But *Magnalia* contains, depending on how one defines the term, about fifty biographies of eminent New Englanders, ranging from a few pages to nearly book length, plus perhaps dozens of brief biographical sketches. The subjects of this Puritan pantheon are mostly dead or aged members of the earlier generations, called to life as embodi-ments of standards from which the present generation has fallen away. The book's most pervasive image is probably resurrection: to halt the "visible *shrink* in all Orders of Men among us, from that *Greatness,* and that *Goodness,* which was in the *first Grain,*" Mather decided, "I'll show them, the *Graves* of their *dead Fathers.*" The lives accordingly take exem-plary patterns, illustrating the behavior of ideal Saints, ministers, and magistrates. Yet Mather's unfailing zest for the curious also provides indi-vidualizing scraps of memorable conversation, and such enlivening vi-gnettes of personal conduct as Thomas Hooker closing his eyes with his own hand just before dying.

Typical of Mather's revival of the heroic past is his fine biography of John Eliot, the first Puritan preacher to the Indians, whom he had known and revered since a child. Having come to Boston in the first wave of emigration and died in 1690 at the age of eighty-six, Eliot appears in Mather's ideal portrait as a *summa* of New England Congregationalist ideals—a model father, a great Bible student and Sabbath keeper, a com-forter of the poor and distressed, a skilled spiritualizer of earthly objects, and a prophet, a majestic man who walked all day in the light of God's countenance and grew more heavenly and savory toward his end. As Mather describes him, Eliot preached without froth, carrying Christ with him wherever he went, so that "like *Mary's* opened Box of *Ointment,* he fill'd the whole Room with the Perfumes of the *Graces* in his Lips." As an evangelist he personally catechized blacks, whose brutal treatment he deplored, and brought the Indians no diluted Christianity but pure Scripture worship, the creed of primitive believers. Above all he was a man although pleasant and affable yet uniquely mortified, "so nailed unto the *Cross* of the Lord Jesus Christ, that the Grandeurs of this World were unto him just what they would be to a *dying Man.*" He ate but one plain dish for supper, never drank wine, spoke with "*boiling Zeal*" against men who wore their hair with "Luxurious, Delicate, Feminine Prolixity," and dressed himself utterly without adornment, his loins, like John the Baptist's, circled with a leather girdle. When he saw a minister looking self-satisfied he told him, "*Study Mortification Brother, Study Mortification!*"

Eliot's wonderful rebuke, however, speaks from a world which the new charter had forever doomed to silence. While Mather resurrected the vanishing first generation as a model for the degenerate present he did not share its zeal for separation and did not cherish the tribal myth of a Chosen People that once gave New England meaning. He also intended the book specifically for an English audience, anxious again to exhibit New England's affection for the mother country, aware, and not distressed, that New England's place in history was that of one outpost in a taut new transatlantic imperial network. *Magnalia* accordingly looks back at the World of the Fathers across the Glorious Revolution, the Act of Toleration, and other dramatic events that made its heroism seem not so much epically nation-building as superfluous.

Virtually the whole book qualifies the Virgilian opening sentence: "I WRITE the *Wonders* of the CHRISTIAN RELIGION, flying from the Depravations of *Europe,* to the *American Strand.*" What drove Christianity to America, Mather shows repeatedly, were not the "Depravations of *Europe*" but, far less cosmically, a knot of high-Church romanists acting in an aberrant moment of English history. His "General Introduction" defines his subject as the history of "PROTESTANTS that highly honoured and affected *The Church of* ENGLAND, and humbly Petition to be a *Part* of it." The theme of flight from English persecution becomes a matter less for tribal mythologizing than for apology:

> Good men in the Church of *England,* I hope, will not be offended at it, if the *Unreasonable Impositions,* and Intolerable Persecutions, of certain Little-Soul'd *Ceremony-Mongers,* which drove these worthy Men out of their Native Country, into the horrid Thickets of *America,* be in their *Lives* complained and resented. For, distinguishing between a *Romanizing*

Faction in the Church of England, and the *True* Protestant Reforming *Church of* England . . . the First Planters of *New England,* at their first coming over, did in a Public and a Printed Address, call the Church of *England,* their *Dear Mother.* . . . Nor did they think, that it was their *Mother* who turned them out of Doors, but some of their angry *Brethren,* abusing the Name of their *Mother,* who so harshly treated them.

Many individual biographies similarly emphasize the forefathers' allegiance to England. Mather records John Higginson telling emigrants about to leave in 1629 for America, "*We will not say as the Separatists were wont to say at their leaving of* England, Farewel, *Babylon!* Farewel *Rome!* But *we will say,* Farewel Dear *England!* Farewel the Church of God in *England* and all the Christian Friends there!" The world of the Fathers recreated in *Magnalia* is populated not only by doctrinal purists but also by loyal Englishmen pining for home. Although the book has justly been described as a monument of New England orthodoxy, the greatest of the Jeremiads, it disharmoniously embodies another form at which New England had also become adept, the petition to the throne.

Indeed Mather recreates even the world of doctrinal purity in the light of his current vision of toleration and reunion. He depicts New Englanders as model ecumenists who "dare make no Difference between a *Presbyterian,* a *Congregational,* an *Episcopalian,* and an *Anti paedo-baptist,* where their *Visible Piety,* makes it probable, that the Lord Jesus Christ has received them." In the course of *Magnalia* he frequently promotes the Congregationalist-Presbyterian union, significantly including in Book Five, among such essential Congregational documents as *The Cambridge Platform,* the London *Heads of Agreement,* declaring it the best exposition of existing Congregationalism and placing it in the very mainstream of New England Puritanism. He remarks that he expects to be criticized for what he has done not only by the High Church party in England and the degenerate young at home, but in effect by the Fathers themselves, by "some among us, who very strictly profess the *Congregational Church-Discipline,* but at the same time they have an unhappy Narrowness of Soul, by which they confine their value and Kindness too much unto their own Party; and unto those my *Church History* will be offensive."

Although Mather set out on one hand to halt the "visible *shrink*" from the Fathers' grandeur, the Puritans of *Magnalia* exist as a Chosen People in only a sorely diminished sense. The Fathers' role in history, he speculates, may have been to serve as a model to Protestant churches elsewhere in the impending worldwide Reformation (see the next chapter), illustrating the qualifications needed in those attempting the reformation and the solutions for problems that might obstruct it. To play this illustrative role may have been why Christ brought His servants to America, that "He might there, *To* them first, and then *By* them, give a *Specimen* of many Good Things, which He would have His Churches elsewhere aspire and arise unto." But in the reformed, panchristian world it might inspire, New England itself would not survive as New Jerusalem; indeed it might have no place. "*This* being done," Mather speculates, "He knows not whether there be not *All done,* that *New-England* was planted for; and whether the Plantation may not, soon after this, *Come to Nothing.*"

Perhaps no feature of the book more dramatically reveals Mather's drift from the Fathers than his devoting the longest section of "The Great Works of Christ in America"—eighty pages in the most recent edition of *Magnalia*—to Sir William Phips. Before becoming governor and caning people on Scarlett's Wharf, Phips made his mark in the world as a rowdy treasure hunter commanding a debauched crew: "for swearing and cursing," one sailor said, "I bless God I never heard the like before in all the ships as ever I have sailed in." Phips did not hold himself aloof. A decade before becoming governor he made a ten-week stay in Boston with his crew, some of whom began brawling in a tavern. When constables ordered the crew members to return to ship, Phips defied them. They promised to tell Governor Bradstreet but he said "he did not care a t___d for the governour for he had more power than he had," and when brought to trial and rebuked by Bradstreet he threw his orders at him.

Yet Mather gave this choleric adventurer star billing in his gallery of *Ecclesiarum Clypei*—Shields of the Churches. His reasons for doing so are largely obvious. At the time Increase Mather was allowed to nominate Phips as the first governor under the new charter, he represented for better or worse the future of New England. As a member of the North Church, we have seen, he also represented the Mathers' hope of renewed access to government circles. While Mather did not conceal from his readers Phips's hot temper, he emphasized his piety and his concern for New England. Eligible for important posts at home, he preferred to live among the people of God in Massachusetts, invariably desiring their good, sharing the motto of the Emperor Hadrian, "NOT FOR MY SELF, BUT FOR MY PEOPLE."

Mather had a less obvious reason for featuring Phips as well: he relished his derring-do. Phips's dashing assaults and squeaky escapes inspired his capacity for imaginative identification with his subjects and gave scope to his considerable gift for narrative. As a result, his biography of Phips often reads like something less from Foxe's *Book of Martyrs* than from *Les Trois Mousquetaires*. Mather retails, for instance, Phips's repulse of an attempted mutiny:

> One day while [Phips's] Frigot lay *Careening*, at a desolate *Spanish* Island, by the side of a Rock, from whence they had laid a Bridge to the Shore, the Men, whereof he had about an *Hundred*, went all, but about Eight or Ten, to divert themselves, as they pretended, in the *Woods:* Where they all entered into an *Agreement*, which they Sign'd in a Ring, That about seven a Clock that Evening they would seize the Captain, and those Eight or Ten, which they knew to be True unto him, and leave them to perish on this Island, and so be gone away unto the *South Sea* to *seek their Fortune*. Will the Reader now imagine, that Captain *Phips* having Advice of this Plot but about an Hour and half before it was to be put in Execution, yet within *Two Hours* brought all these Rogues down upon their Knees to beg for their Lives? But so it was!

The mutinous knaves, Mather continues, fetched the ship's carpenter to the woods and asked him to join them. He begged for time to think it over and was returned to the ship, with a spy to keep watch over him. Pretending to be seized by a fit of cholic, he ran to Phips's cabin for a dram. Instead he told Phips of the plot. Phips gathered his seven or eight remaining crew, including his gunner, and

> demanded of them, whether they would stand by him in the Extremity, which he informed them was now come upon him; whereto they reply'd, *They would stand by him, if he could save them;* and he Answer'd, *By the help of God he did not fear it.* All their Provisions had been carried Ashore to a Tent, made for that Purpose there; about which they had placed several Great Guns to defend it, in case of any *Assault* from the *Spaniards*, that might happen to come that way. Wherefore Captain *Phips*, immediately ordered those Guns to be silently Drawn'd and Turn'd; and so pulling up the Bridge, he charged his Great Guns aboard, and brought them to Bear on every side of the Tent. But this time the *Army of Rebels* comes out of the Woods; but as they drew near to the Tent of Provisions, they saw such a change of Circumstances, that they cried out, *We are Betray'd!* And they were soon confirm'd in it, when they heard the Captain with a stern Fury call to them, *Stand off, ye Wretches, at your Peril!*

The mutineers fell on their knees to beg Phips's pardon, but he seized their weapons, took them aboard, then got rid of them in Jamaica.

Although *Magnalia* places Phips as a successor in the honored gubernatorial line of William Bradford and John Winthrop, he seems an exemplar not of the Governor but of the Self-Made Man. "Reader, enquire no further who was his *Father?*" Mather writes. "Thou shalt anon see, that he

was, as the *Italians* express it, *A Son to his own Labours!*" As the story of
the son of a gunsmith in a frontier village on the Kennebec River who
"rose from so *little*," the life of Phips falls between such Puritan spiritual
biographies as that of John Eliot, and the *Autobiography* of Benjamin
Franklin. In Phips the Fathers' piety can be seen overlaid with "Enterpriz-
ing *Genius*," the Puritan Saint has shaded off into the "*Knight of Honesty;*
for it was *Honesty* with *Industry* that raised him." To the several differences between Mather's viewpoint and that of the world he resurrects, the
life of Phips adds another, which Mather equally celebrates—the growth
of business enterprise in America.

Like John Eliot, Phips enjoyed prophetic foresight, but what it assured
him of was material success. When he was eighteen his friends urged him
to settle permanently in Maine, but he had, Mather writes, "an Unaccountable *Impulse* upon his Mind, persuading him, as he would privately
hint unto some of them, *That he was Born to greater Matters.*" Instead he
bound himself apprentice to a ship's carpenter, which trade he followed a
while in Boston, where for the first time he learned to read and write. He
also married the widow of a "well-bred Merchant." He confided to her
his belief that "the Providence of God" would ultimately make him the
"Owner of a *Fair Brick-House* in the *Green-Lane* of *North-Boston.*"
Phips's assurances, like John Eliot's, came true, not after fervent prayer
but after six years hunting sunken Spanish galleons. Mather describes
with zestful wonder how in January 1687 Phips reached a wreck in Porto
Plata, Hispaniola, and after diving three months brought up thirty-four
tons of treasure. This fantastic horde included copper guns, silver candlesticks and stirrups, gold chains and cups, and more than 37,000 pounds
troy in silver pieces-of-eight. The find was reported in newsletters and
pamphlets, communicated to the kings of Europe, and made the talk of
London. As his share Phips received more than £11,000, some of which
he invested in Boston real estate, plus part of the spoils. His wife received
a gold cup worth nearly £1000. In consideration of his services to the
crown he was knighted. The turning point in Mather's account of Phips's
fabulous strike is the remarkable cry of this Shield of the Churches, after a
diver disclosed to him a lump of silver at last dredged from the deep:
"*Thanks be to God! We are made.*"

The disparate voices of Phips's "*Thanks be to God! We are made*" and
Eliot's "*Study Mortification Brother, Study Mortification!*" together or-
chestrate *Magnalia Christi Americana* and define a historical moment.
Mather's attempt to make them both bespeak "The *Wonders* of the

CHRISTIAN RELIGION" dramatizes the survival in fact and memory of the first generation's mortified living, reverence toward ministers, and relation of conversion experiences into the new epoch of commercial enterprise, imperial expansion, and perriwigs. They survived tenuously, of course: mortification was not the style of young ministers like Benjamin Colman, and Phips was the last governor for at least twenty years who could be included without deliberate mockery among the Shields of the Churches. That Mather could comfortably celebrate both Eliot's leather girdle and Phips's golden cups testifies also to how much he remained drawn to both heaven-mindedness and worldly ambition. It seems likely that he welcomed the new atmosphere of toleration and reunion exactly because it legitimized his suppressed urbanity. In his life of Eliot, he first tells how the saintly evangelist hated men's wearing long hair, then remarks indulgently, "Doubtless, it may be lawful for us to accommodate the *length* of our *Hair* unto the modest *Customs* which vary in the *Churches of God*."

For all its ideological weight, *Magnalia* is a deeply literary work. Whether bringing to life the mortified piety of the Fathers or defending long hair and the *Heads of Agreement,* Mather was above all bidding for international attention as an American writer. Mixing the largest political and eschatological events with "Entertainments for the Curious," the book abounds in such vivid narratives as the captivity of Hannah Duston and the depossession of the Goodwin children, in wonder stories of ghosts and strange premonitions of death. With his appetite for believe-it-or-nots, Mather could not resist appending to his life of the minister Thomas Thacher a long account of a deaf and dumb member of Thacher's church who learned to convey her understanding of the doctrine of the Trinity in sign language. Mather's literary ambitions also declare themselves with stentorian gorgeousness in his "Massy" style—the copious matter, the intricately witty, graceful, or dense openings (the first sentence of the life of Phips runs 254 words), the formal invention, the trilingual puns and quotations and universal allusions. The style itself reveals much about New England at the turn of the century, rendering the first generation's heaven-mindedness in a language that reaches for cosmopolitan elegance but attains provincial grandioseness. If the epic ambitions of *Magnalia,* its attempt to put America on the cultural map, recall such later American works as *Moby-Dick* (to which it has been compared), its effort to rejoin provincial America to the mainstream of English culture recalls rather *The Wasteland.* Genuinely Anglo-American in outlook, the book projects a New England which is ultimately an enlarged version of Cotton Mather himself, a pious citizen of "The Metropolis of the whole English America."

For all its aspiring bulk, *Magnalia* is dwarfed beside the leviathan Mather "set upon" at about the same time, "*another,* and a *greater*" book on which he would labor the rest of his life. In this gigantic "Biblia Americana" he intended nothing less than to interpret all of Scripture in the light of "all the Learning in the World." The dazing scope of the work was probably inspired by the angel's prophecy of the books he would publish to exalt his height above all the other trees of the field. Its content, however, derived from his opinion that none of what he called the "*professed Commentaries*" on Scripture had yet afforded "a thousandth Part of so much *Illustration* unto it, as might be given."

In several ways the project uniquely suited Mather's temperament and talents. It satisfied his vaulting ambition, his taste for combining piety and elegance, and his continuing need to allay feelings of smallness and show extraordinary fecundity in producing language. It also put to use his ability to read with unusual speed, which several persons who knew him observed:

> In two or three Minutes turning thro' a Volume, he cou'd easily tell whether it wou'd make Additions to the Store of his Ideas. If it cou'd not, He quickly laid it by: If otherwise, he read it, passing over all those Parts which contained the things he had known before, perusing those Parts only that represented something *Novel,* which he Pencil'd as he went along . . . and all this with wonderful Celerity.

Swift and wide reading was essential, for he hoped to create, in contrast to the "*professed Commentaries,*" something at once entertaining, modern, and comprehensive. He would gather in one work more scriptural glosses from the "*scattered Books* of learned Men, than in any of the *ordinary Commentators.*" He would also search out strikingly pungent or fresh illustrations, "more entertaining for the *Rarity* and *Novelty* of them, than any that have been hitherto seen together." Since he and many others considered their age one of abundant new insight into the meaning of biblical texts, he would include as well all the "*Improvements,* which the *later Ages* have made in the Sciences." Approaching Scripture from every conceivable angle—scientific, patristic, classical, chronological, philological, theological, typological, historical, geographical—he would assemble "in *one Heap,* Thousands of those *remarkable Discoveries of the deep Thing[s] of the Spirit of God,* whereof one, or *two,* or a few sometimes, have been, with good Success, accounted *Materials* enough to advance one into *Authorism.*" He does not exaggerate: for the Mississippian flood of handwriting he disgorged in composing the work he might have published two hundred separate titles.

Mather began the trunk-sized manuscript in the late summer of 1693. He secured six huge folio volumes and divided them according to books of the Old and New Testaments. Then he laboriously entered glosses on various texts, in double columns and in catechistic form ("Q. Some Remark, I pray you, upon that great word, HALLELUJAH?"). He did not work serially through separate books of the Bible but on the entire Bible at once, filing glosses here and there in his folios as he came across them in his reading. Nearly every page of the manuscript thus shows several distinct stages of his handwriting over thirty years or more. He also began, but at some time gave up, separate double-columned auxiliary notebooks to list his authorities for each chapter of every book in Scripture, intending an eight-hundred page index of his sources. Originally he planned to write one gloss each morning, believing that in seven years—a godlike number—he would have a set of "learned, charming and curious *Notes* on His Word, far beyond any that hath yet seen the Light." Praying often for divine aid in coming upon apt illustrations, he found by 1697 that he already had "an huge Number of *golden Keys,* to open the *Pandects* of Heaven, and some Thousands of charming and singular Notes." In 1702 he included in the Preface to *Magnalia* a sort of progress report on his work to the learned world.

Later chapters will follow Mather's woeful frustrations with "Biblia Americana." But one earlier written section deserves notice here because its date makes it evident that although the political turmoil of the late 1680s ended the Boston Philosophical Society (the fledgling scientific group founded by Increase), Mather's scientific interests remained strong. His treatise-length illustration on the first chapter of Genesis occupies over fifty-one double-columned folio pages, written over a decade or more. A portion of it dated 1702 represents his summary of Edmund Dickinson's *Physica Vetus et Vera,* published the same year. In a manner typical of all of "Biblia Americana" he follows Dickinson's ideas closely but clothes them "very much in my own Expressions," trying to show that current atomistic ("corpuscularian") conceptions of matter not only agree with the biblical account of creation but in fact offer one of the chief proofs of God.

"Let it not surprize you now, if, I tell you," Mather writes, "That the *Mosaic philosophy,* was no other than the *Corpuscularian.*" Following

Dickinson, he interprets the "Water" mentioned at the opening of Genesis as in fact referring to atoms, on the ground that in Moses' time the word ordinarily meant an immense multitude. Then he gives a wholly atomistic account of creation, beginning with the first day:

> In the Beginning was universal Matter by God first created of nothing; a wondrous congeries of all sorts of particles, unform'd, and unmov'd; and Every where separated from one another with Empty Spaces. This Universal Matter was put into Motion, by the Spirit of God, and not Left unto a fortuitous Motion and Concourse. Thus was there given unto Matter, that Force which we call Nature; for Nature is nothing but that Motion which the Spirit of God has imprinted upon Matter, and which He perpetually governs with his infinite Wisdom.

In forwarding Dickinson's view of Genesis, Mather was following a somewhat conservative train of scientific thought. The corpuscularian philosophy, devised and named by Robert Boyle, was widespread in England before the end of the century, but soon outmoded by Newtonian ideas—some of which Mather entered into later-written portions of his illustration on the same text. But although conceived in the spirit of Descartes and Boyle rather than of Newton, this early portion of "Biblia Americana" looks forward to Mather's becoming probably the most influential spokesman in New England for a rationalized, scientized Christianity.

In many sermons of the time and in two notable published works—Winter-Meditations (1693) and Christianus per Ignem (1702)—Mather also popularized for American audiences the language, discoveries, and habits of thought of the new science. The same capacity for wonder that he invested in his accounts of devils, Indian captivities, or treasure hunts he here devoted to such current matters of scientific study as fossils, volcanoes, and the formation of snow, and to rapt descriptions of the miracles unveiled by microscope and telescope, from the "exquisite workmanship" in the eye of a frog to the "Innumerable Millions" of stars—"How Regular to the Hundredth part of a Minute, are they in their Motions?" Such discoveries of modern science, he told his readers and listeners, "Declare the Glory of God, and show forth His Handy work," and invite our meditation on the deity revealed in the creation.

6

Particular Faiths

‿๑๑౷

UNTIL MAY 1702, Abigail Mather is a shadowy figure in Cotton Mather's diaries, disembodied but clearly loved, "My dear Consort." But in May, ill, she miscarried of a son after a four or five months' pregnancy. Mather observed that it was the very week of their sixteenth anniversary, and at the time of their marriage Abigail herself had been just sixteen. He told his father: "*I seem to feel in my Mind, the Bodings of a dark Cloud hanging over my Family.*" Lapsing into a serious illness that puzzled the ablest physicians, Abigail became the central figure of her husband's diary as, with a few illusory remissions, she lay dying over the next seven months.

Cotton Mather's bodings both heralded grave doubt about his prophetic powers and climaxed nearly a decade of heightened psychic awareness, an agitated inner drama played out privately against his public conflict with Colman and Stoddard and the other events of the 1690s. In the years following his angelic visitation he spent much time fasting, often melted to tears by his psychical intimations, exalted but also unnerved by his nearness to the invisible world. Whether the angel itself returned is uncertain, owing to his caution in speaking of the event and to the loss of his diaries for 1694 and 1695. If no angels became visible they at least came close. Praying on the evening of his birthday in 1697 he found that "the *good Angels* of the Holy Spirit, were so near unto me, in my rapturous Praises of my Lord-Redeemer, that the Prae-Libations of Heaven which I enjoy'd . . . are *not fit here to be uttered.*" Another time he received a promise that an angel would appear to him in the future. He recorded the message in Latin, as he had done before, so that if Abigail looked at his diary she could not read it. In June 1698, it was infused (*infusum*) into him that a heavenly angel of my dearest Savior—*quod Coelestis quidam charissimi mei Salvatoris Angelus*—would at some time before his death when it seemed good to God show himself to me visible—*mihi se visibiliter exhibuerit.* The angel would appear in order to reveal certain matters *de Ecclesia, et Rebus novissimis*—concerning the church and the Last Things.

Such revelations would be of the keenest interest to Mather, for he prized the study of Last Things, of eschatology. His millennial expectations had been aroused by the Revolution of 1689, the invasion of devils, and his own angel, who prophesied the great works he would do "in the revolutions that are now in hand." A belief that the millennium might be near had also quickened his calls for reform and his enthusiasm for such signs of the extension of Protestantism as the Act of Toleration. The long series of European conflicts that began soon after the accession of King William, often pitting Protestant against Catholic interests, brought Mather many prophetic intimations of the collapse of infidelism and papacy and the establishment of God's true Kingdom. Several times he received "a strong Persuasion, that some very *overturning Dispensations* of Heaven, will quickly befall the *French* Empire," or felt a "marvellous Impression upon my Spirit" about a great religious revival in England, Scotland, and Ireland. He often prayed fervently for the fulfillment of these intimations, believing that secret prayer does "an incredible deal, towards Jogging the *High Wheels of Providence,* and Shaking of Churches, and Empires." Suspecting that the Lord might be preparing to take possession of the Spanish Indies he published a catechism of basic Protestant beliefs in Spanish (*La Fe del Christiano,* 1699, seemingly the only work in Spanish produced in seventeenth-century America), and also addressed an open letter "To the JEWISH Nation," bidding them desist from "your Damnable *Rebellion* against the CHRIST of GOD!" His prayers and publications were rewarded, he noted in 1698, with "astonishing Answers," such as the revival of Protestantism in the principality of Orange, "in the Bowels of *France.*" He thanked Christ for having "informed, inclined, and assisted . . . a vile Sinner, in a Corner of *America,* to foresee, and put on that Work of His."

Like many others, Mather read such events in the light of the prophetic books, especially Daniel in the Old Testament and Revelation in the New. He tried to fit them to the obscure imagery of vials, seals, beasts, woes, and candlesticks in which the scriptural prophets were understood to have laid out the approach of the millennium and of the Second Coming of Christ. Many viewed the revival of Protestant persecution in France upon revocation of the Edict of Nantes, for instance, as the realization of the Slaying of Witnesses described by Revelation. Mather fully appreciated the weakness of human learning in penetrating the dark language of the prophetic books, and the likelihood of interpretive error. He always approached them cautiously, and although he encouraged his congregation to read them he regarded eschatology as a subject for the elite: "*Apocalyptical Studies* are fittest for those Raised Souls," he wrote, "whose *Heart-Strings* are made of a Little *Finer Clay* than other mens."

At this time Mather's eschatological views followed those of his father and of the learned Joseph Mede of Christ's College, Cambridge. He set them forth in a ninety-one-page manuscript which he completed in 1703 but did not publish, entitled "Problema Theologicum." Here he drew a sort of schedule for the Second Coming, whose harbingers would be, among other events, the collapse of the papacy, the ceasing of Turkish hostilities against Europe, and the enlargement of the church by the conversion of the Jews. Increase Mather mentioned the same preconditions in his many sermons on the subject in the same years, but added the appearance of such awful works of God as famines, eclipses, pestilences, and huge earthquakes. Cotton's eschatology put less emphasis on natural upheavals, although in an almanac published in 1699 he too observed that the course of nature had recently been "every where most Wonderfully Altered"—plagues raging, the sun beginning to darken (according to astronomers), the seasons not as they used to be, "*Earthquakes* prodigiously multiplied," all suggesting "Further and Greater CHANGES upon the World." Mather shared these eschatological intimations with his congregation, filling his sermons of the period with prophecies of "a REVOLUTION *and a* REFORMATION *at the very Door.*"

Together with hints of the impending fulfillment of Daniel and Revelation, Mather received other strange intimations and providential favors, sometime less cosmic than comic. Several times when on journeys he found that threatened storms would be delayed until he returned home. Once, traveling to Salem and Ipswich, his road became swarmed, to everyone's alarm, by a "strange Descent of Hundreds of Bears"—"but I met none of them." When suffering heartburn he found it "darted into my Mind" to apply "*Philip Paris*'s Plaister" to his chest, which he did and was cured. His acts of self-sacrifice were mysteriously repaid. Lacking money to buy a new cloak although he needed one, he recalled Christ stripped of His garments and assured himself he would never want proper clothing: "Immediately after these Thoughts," a woman in his congregation surprised him with a present of a handsome and costly cloak. Again, after leaving some pious books or pamphlets behind during a pastoral visit, as he usually did, he reflected that no other minister in New England would put himself to such expense, and perhaps he should not do so either. Feeling a mental "Impulse" that something would happen to encourage his practice, he gave way to a "sudden inclination" to step in the house of a certain widow. She had come into part of the library of the famous Charles Chauncey, and pressed him to accept some forty books— not only an encouragement to continue distributing free religious works but also a help, he added, in filling his "Biblia Americana."

If the caliber of Cotton Mather's psychical experiences did not quite match his father's supposed ability to predict wars and other major events accurately, they did cause surprise. Once he felt God incline him to mention in public prayers the name of a church member held in captivity; the same afternoon that very person arrived home safe, "whereof much Notice was taken by the people of God in the Place." It seemed to him also that his intimations had their price, and that his moments of communion with heaven were often followed by some illness, public dispute, or other vexation. In one such case, he received what he considered intimations about the time and manner of his death. While he was preaching the next day, a chimney on his house caught fire, threatening his and his neighbors' homes. The large congregation ran from the church to quench the blaze, "and I was thus mark'd out for Talk all over."

With these many unsettling paranormal experiences seems to have come a return of Mather's youthful speech difficulties. How or whether the two were related—indeed, whether the difficulties did recur—is again uncertain because Mather's 1694 and 1695 diaries are missing. After the gap, however, his 1696 diary suddenly contains much new concern about fluency. On a day of secret prayer in March he asked Christ for "a more free, and fit, and useful *Speech.*" Lying prostrate on his study floor in May he received a vivid assurance, as if "spoken from Heaven," that speech would be supplied him, "and a greater *Freedom* of it . . . than ever I yet enjoyed." In October, for the first time in years, he set down rules for the governance of his tongue, reminiscent of the measures he once laid on himself to control his stammer: to let fall from his tongue only thoughts that glorified Christ, to avoid loquacity but on the contrary to "affect much *Deliberation.*" Whatever the origin of these renewed speech difficulties—if that is what the entries represent—they seem to have recurred over several years, for again in August 1699 he particularly thanked God "that I should be a great *Stammerer,* and yet be made not only a Preacher of the Gospel, but also my *Utterance* in preaching be not the least *Ornament* of it."

*

One sort of psychical experience came to Mather more often than any other, and more troublingly: the Particular Faith. He meant by the term "a little degree of the *Spirit of Prophecy*" granted by God to the devotional elite for abounding in secret prayer—some divinely sent intimation, perhaps conveyed through the invisible ministry of good angels, that a particular prayer would be answered. He seems to distinguish the Particular Faith from other forms of prayerful assurance by its quasi-hallucinatory definiteness. It is a vivid persuasion that one shall "Receive this *Particular Mercy* from the Lord: And this persuasion is not a mere Notion, and Fancy, but a *Special Impression from Heaven.*" The impression comes with a "certain powerful, Heart melting, Heavenly *Afflatus,*" quite as if an angel had spoken directly. Being entirely sensory, its actuality defies description: "*How do I know this Operation from a counterfeit?* My Answer is, That no words of mine can answer the Question; I *know* it, as I know the *Fire* to be the *Fire;* I *feel* it, but no words of mine can express, how it *feels.*"

Most of Mather's Particular Faiths concerned subjects of his secret prayers, often his own family, especially his children. Prayer was needed, given Boston's susceptibility to high infant mortality, fatal accident, and epidemic disease. By early 1696, when Mather was thirty-three, he and Abigail had had six children, of whom four were already dead, all but one in infancy. His firstborn child, Abigail, had died in 1687, aged five months; the most recent to die, in February 1696,was his infant daughter Mehetabel, probably smothered accidentally in its swaddling clothes by its nurse. Understandably his other children became the subject of fervent prayer, and then of Particular Faiths. In January 1699, his daughter Hannah ("Nancy"), about a year old, fell into the fire, so badly burning the right side of her face and her right hand and arm that her life seemed threatened. The fire that burned her, Mather wrote, only fired the zeal of his prayers for her, which God raised to a "Degree of a *Particular Faith* in her behalf." Nancy lived, but the following year she became ill of a pain in her bowels, which grew extreme. Again Mather found himself "Irradiated from Heaven with a *Particular Faith,* for some Help to be sent from Heaven unto the dying Child." Nancy began vomiting, however, and one of the physicians concluded she would certainly die. Astonishingly, on a

Sabbath, she began "running and laughing the whole Forenoon, about the House," and survived.

Only two months later, Mather's newborn son Samuel was taken with convulsions. Since Samuel's birth Mather had often tried to get his "Heart Raised, unto a *Particular Faith* for that Child," assuring him that God would accept Samuel, his only son, for the ministry. His failure to receive such a Particular Faith, however, made him continually apprehensive that the child, though hearty, would die in infancy. After Samuel survived more than a hundred convulsive fits, as Mather put it, "an odd thing" happened. Coming out of a fit about midnight, Samuel "most unaccountably fell a Laughing, yea, into a very great *Laughter,* and this held for diverse Minutes." The spectators were amazed, "indeed were so amazed, that they could hardly keep from Swooning." After its laughter the infant had no more fits until about ten o' clock in the morning, when it was seized with another fit and died.

Mather's longing for Particular Faiths regarding his children was most fervent on behalf of the son whose development, we shall see, would preoccupyingly both cheer and darken much of his later life—Increase, Jr., born to him and Abigail on July 9, 1699. In several ways Increase, Jr.'s, birth seemed portentous. Years before, Mather wrote, "A Son had been foretold unto me, in an Extraordinary Way." He always felt acute empathy, close to fear, with women's labor pains, and as signs of Abigail's approaching travail grew on her he set aside the day for prayer and fasting in his study. Abigail did not give birth, however, and to be fit for church services the next day, a Sabbath, he commended her to God and retired. At around one in the morning he awoke, feeling a "Concern upon my Spirit." He returned to his study, threw himself on his knees, and implored God's mercy on Abigail in her distress. At about a quarter to two, while he was pleading with God, "the People ran to my Study-door with Tidings, *that a Son was born unto me.*" As he continued praising God, on his knees, he received wonderful advice from heaven. The boy, he was told, would become a minister to continue the tradition of Cottons and Mathers, already three generations long, "a Servant of my Lord Jesus Christ throughout eternal Ages."

The Christ-like birth announcement makes clear how much hope Mather invested in the boy—the first of his male children to survive— from the beginning. This was a "Son given to me in answer to many Prayers among the People of God, and a Son of much Observation and Expectation." The day of the birth he entered in his church records, in large letters, his baptism of "My INCREASE." He decided on the name in honor of his father, as he had done before in naming the infant which died of an imperforate anus. (Increase, Sr., commented that he preferred a different name, but his neighbors "would not be satisfied except his Name were Increase.") To mark the baptism Cotton preached a sermon on the duty of parents to bring their children to Christ, especially since their children derived through them the misery of original sin. In hope of creating a son of unceasing heaven-mindedness, he began writing for him an exemplary, book-length autobiography, on which he worked over the next three years, relating his own spiritual development from childhood to the time of Increase, Jr.'s, birth. Entitled "Paterna," it consists largely of his methods of private devotion and his search for new ways of praising God, depicting his inner life as a continuous hum of praise.

Increase, Jr., became the subject of Particular Faiths as Cotton learned his father's lesson that strong affections bring strong afflictions. In his eighth month, the child was also taken with dangerous convulsions. Mather fasted two entire days, praying for his son's life yet resigning him to God. In one of his fits Increase somehow sucked in a pin through the silver nipple of his bottle and almost choked to death. Mather continued his prayers, awaiting a sign; once "a strange Thing was from Heaven said unto me: my Son shall yet live." But for at least another month Increase's convulsions returned, ceased, and then returned again, as Mather now feared the death of "My little and lovely and only Son" and then heard it told him from heaven that the child would live. In late April Increase's convulsions grew extreme and seemed incurable. Still Mather received assurances from heaven that his son would recover—"The good Angel of the Lord has told me so!"

Increase, Jr., did survive, confirming his father's Particular Faiths. But at the same time Mather received a surprising disappointment, in this case involving his father, and the older Increase's decade-long struggle over the Harvard presidency. The complex details of the episode—which drew in several governors and governmental bodies, the Harvard Corporation, and many influential persons—belong more to the biography of Increase Mather than of Cotton. They became subjects of Cotton Mather's Particular Faiths as they affected his father's desire, as acting president or "Rector" of Harvard, to obtain a charter for the college in England.

Under the Phips government, Harvard had been declared a corporation, with power to receive gifts and grant degrees; but this charter was disallowed in England, largely because it failed to provide for royal visitation and royal oversight of the college. Two further charters were drawn up in Boston and also disallowed. Supporters of Increase Mather urged that he be returned to England to seek a college charter. But they met opposition from a party headed by Elisha Cooke—a Boston physician and the town assessor—who adamantly held out for the old Massachusetts charter and reviled Increase for having negotiated the new one. Increase's own desire to take up the new agency went beyond the college. Uncomfortable in Boston since his education abroad, he wished to be sent to England because he was a peevish man of sophisticated intellect and worldly experience who felt cramped and unappreciated in provincial circumstances. Also, his discontent swelled on accusations that he had betrayed the country, and the prospect of leaving it became more tempting with the Act of Toleration, granting new liberty in England to Dissenters like himself. As he said in one of his continuing threats of desertion, his congregation well knew "that I have had a strong bent of spirit to spend (and to end) the remainder of my few days in England."

For years after Increase returned from his original charter agency, moreover, the belief that he would return to England had come to him, often and repeatedly, as a Particular Faith—for him also, a cherished phenomenon of devotional life. Cotton, having made a team with his father in almost every other aspect of their ministry, now joined him in experiencing Particular Faiths concerning his agency. They came for the first time in June 1699, as the General Court again considered the settlement of the college. He had prayed over the matter many times, without having his mind lifted to a Particular Faith one way or the other. But this day he for the first time experienced it: "it was in a powerful Manner assured me from Heaven, that my Father shall one Day be carried into *England . . .* and that the *Particular Faith* which had introduced it, shall be at last made a matter of wonderful Glory and Service unto the Lord." Probably spurred by his Particular Faith, he drew up an address on July 7, signed by some other ministers, asking the governor and General Assembly to consider sending an agent abroad for Harvard. The Assembly again took up the question of a college charter on the 18th, which Cotton reserved for a day of fasting and prayer. About noon, as he was crying to heaven to arrange his father's voyage, and while the Assembly was voting or debating, there came to him an unutterable assurance from heaven that his father would be carried into England, "and that at this very Time there was occurring that which would one Day accomplish it."

This time Mather's Particular Faith was answered by "a most unintelligible Dispensation." At just noon, as he received his assurance, the bill for the college was not being enacted by the Assembly but vetoed by Governor Bellomont. Bellomont apparently tried to get the Assembly to reconsider the matter, but the members had sat for many weeks and were anxious to return home, as many had done already; they refused to take further action until their next session. The confused outcome—occurring, Mather believed, even as he was receiving a contrary Particular Faith in his study—left him troubled. "Lord," he called, "preserve my Faith, and assist me to wait with an holy and humble Patience, for the Issue of these mysterious Things!" The issue was nearly a year in arriving, however, and meantime his father also, he recorded, became discouraged "about the accomplishment of the *Particular Faith,* which had seemed so often infused from Heaven into our Minds." On the last day of 1699 he once more lay the matter before God in his study, at noon. He failed to have a Particular Faith, however, until, as he ended his petitions, his mind "suddenly felt a strange and a strong Operation from Heaven upon it," causing him to say aloud: "*The Lord will do it, The Lord Will do it, my Father shall be carried into* England."

The test of this Particular Faith came the following June. During the Mathers' controversy with the Brattle church, the question of a college charter again arose in the Assembly, in such circumstances that if it failed it was unlikely to be revived again. Cotton's conviction having been several times aroused then defeated, he found himself "in extreme Distress of Spirit." His distress also grew, he recognized, from his knack for landing in uncomfortably conflicted situations. "My *Flesh,*" he observed, would be "on all Accounts imaginable against my Father's Removal from me"; but "my Faith" having been "so supernaturally raised for it, the Thoughts of that's being wholly disappointed, were insupportable." He cast himself on his study floor, pleading that he had always believed a Particular Faith to be a work of heaven on the minds of the devout, telling God that if his belief proved wrong he would be thrown into confusion. His distressed plaints failed to rouse him—"my Heart had the Coldness of a Stone"—until he suddenly felt the inexpressible afflatus: "if an *Angel* from Heaven had spoken it articulately to me, the Communication would not have been more powerful and perceptible." It was "told" him that God "had not permitted us to be deceived in our *Particular Faith.*" Assured that God delighted in him and his father as faithful servants, he called out in tears, "*He will do it, He will do it!*"

But it, Mather added lugubriously, "All came to nothing!" Governor Bellomont, who had favored Increase's agency, deserted it, and instead was allowed to present the case for the charter in England himself: "all Expectation of a Voyage for my Father into *England* on any such Occasion," Mather wrote, "is utterly at an End." The end, although real, was hard to accept. "*Wait!*" he advised himself. "*Wait!*"

But by the next month there was less than ever to wait for, as the General Assembly began ousting Increase from the Harvard presidency altogether. The Council had several times voted a requirement that the president reside in Cambridge, and had repeatedly pressed Increase to move there. He had sidestepped their resolves by threatening to resign, and by offering such objections as his unwillingness to give up preaching to fifteen hundred souls in Boston "only to expound to 40 or 50 children few of them capable of edification by such exercises." Although during his sixteen years as president Increase had resided in Cambridge only six months, he had been able by staying in Boston to consult often with the governor and legislature, and had helped reshape Harvard's policies and halt its slide. At the same time, his abhorrence of Cambridge became an effective weapon for Elisha Cooke, who together with some supporters of the Brattle church tried to oust him from Harvard by forcing him to live there. In July, the General Assembly voted that the president must reside in Cambridge, and appointed a committee to tell Increase it was expected that he repair to and reside at Cambridge as soon as possible.

Perhaps because there no longer seemed a hope of his going to England, and because friends advised him that if he resisted he would be widely reproached and would die with infamy, Increase hastened disconsolately to Cambridge, the place, Cotton said, "which of all under Heaven, was most abominable to him." Cotton felt as he had when his father escaped to England, "left alone, in the Care of a vast Congregation," concerned lest he fail to perform his duties adequately. His worry underestimated his father's disgust with Cambridge, for in three months Increase was back in Boston, having preached only once in the College Hall. He held out until the following March, when the House approved a new order providing that if he refused the presidency the governance of the college should go to the Rev. Samuel Willard. Increase moved to Cambridge again. On his father's birthday, June 21, Cotton found "to my Astonishment" a new hope of Increase's charter agency to England, "which had such a Sentence of Death upon it, about a year ago." He recorded experiencing no Particular Faith about it, however, and it too came to nothing. Increase, after living in Cambridge another three months, asked the General Court to choose a new president and delivered a farewell sermon to the scholars, telling them to expect for their service to Christ not honor but "rather to be *Despised and Rejected of Men;* rather to have all manner of *Indignities* heaped upon you."

Both Mathers felt the effects of Cooke's success in maneuvering Increase into resigning the presidency. Added to the uncertain dependability of the government and the popularity of the Brattle church, it meant to them a serious loss of influence. Cotton later viewed the episode as having ended his father's public life. Increase, stricken with gout and feeling himself aging, not only gave up hopes of returning to England; something gone of his old sour vitality, he also became, he said, "desirous to die where I am." He speculated, too, that the angels who transmit Particular Faiths might actually be ignorant of "some" future events. They might cause motions in men's spirits not according to what will certainly happen but according to what might come to pass "in probability."

*

Abigail Mather had already been ill when in May 1702 she miscarried of a son. The illness worsened, so that not even the most capable physicians, Mather wrote, knew "what to judge of or what to do for." She seems to have had breast cancer, later probably complicated by an infectious disease. Mather says little of her in his diaries until this illness, but in choosing her he had sought a wife who would honor the ministry and be a model to the community. From the beginning of their marriage he had resolved to help her toward her conversion by example, conference, and joint prayer, and his efforts succeeded in the fall of 1689, when she was admitted to the North Church as a full member. He praised not only her piety, however, but also her "obliging Deportment" to him, her discretion in ordering their affairs, "and the Lovely *Off-Spring* I have received by her." Later he would add that she also had a "melancholy Temper," her spirit having been broken by her father's second marriage, "bringing home a Mother-in-law, tho' he did well in it."

A week after Abigail's miscarriage Mather fasted and prayed for her in his study, hoping for an irradiation from heaven concerning her recovery. Instead, deprived of "the agreeable Charms of her *Person*," he found his mind buffeted by sexual longings, "*impure Thoughts*, which exceedingly abased me before the Lord." He set apart another day of fasting and prayer, this time with Abigail in her room. And this time, thankfully, he felt "the blessed Breezes of a *Particular Faith*, blowing from Heaven upon my mind." The breezes returned when he prayed alone in his study that afternoon, and encouraged him to assure Abigail that she would live longer.

Yet the very next day Abigail seemed to have in fact died. A physician was summoned from church. Although Abigail revived, Mather was called to her room the next night because she again seemed to be dying. About one or two in the morning he held a vigil in his study, and assurances came to him that God intended to restore her, and came again the next morning with hope, joy, and wonder when he prayed with her. That day, indeed, a "critical Salivation" began in Abigail. The salivation was auspicious, for it reduced her fever. But it did not stop, it became profuse and continued for a week and left her drained. Mather observed another day of prayer and fasting on June 24, and his Particular Faith was astonishingly renewed despite the extremity of Abigail's condition: "God, and His good Angel, has assured me from Heaven, that tho' my Consort be in such dying Circumstances, yet she shall not die, but live." But next Friday, she grew still worse, "if it could be," and her progressive deterioration, in defiance of his heavenly promises, was unmistakable, leaving no likelihood of anything after all but her death. For Mather the likelihood was dreadful enough, "But Lord!" he wrote, "how aggravated a Calamity must be her Death, if such a Sting, as the Disappointment of my *Particular Faith*, must be added unto it!"

Instead of dying, Abigail continued languishing through midsummer. Mather knew well enough the Puritan lesson of weaned affections, that we must love this life as children who although they cling to their mother's breast must give it up inevitably. Yet while he freely gave his wife up to the Lord, he admitted, "I could not *give her over*." If God spared her he would do much in return—study new methods of family prayer, use his ordeal to glorify Christ, try to be more exemplarily chaste and holy than ever. Part of one night he spent calling on God from his bedroom floor, "with so little of Garment on as to render my lying there painful to my tender Bones." Once he allowed himself a respite of bitterness: "I am kept up all Night, that I may see her die, and therewith see the terrible Death of my Prayer and Faith." But again prophetic certainty returned and, on the evening of August 23, with visionary intensity. As he sat in his study it was said to him, "*Go into your great Chamber and I will speak with you!*" He did so, confessing from the floor his loathsome worthiness to be thunderstruck into dust and ashes, until the inexpressible afflatus came, leaving on his agitated soul a sweet, calm, and sanctifying impression that caused him to say:

> My Father loves me, and will fill me with His *Love*, and will bring me to Everlasting *Life*. *My Father* will never permit anything to befall me, but what shall be for *His Interest*. . . . The Condition of my Dear *Consort, my Father* will give me to see His Wonderful Favour in it.

At the end of August, after fourteen weeks of pain and continued salivation, and now with feverish scurvy as well, Abigail took such a bad turn that she terrified him "with extreme Apprehensions of her Dissolution."

The weeks—as Mather began tallying the ordeal—of September passed amid the same wearing counterpoint of assurances from heaven and alarms from the sickroom. News arrived of the death in London of Abigail's second brother, a young merchant, "her Darling." Ill himself, he had gone abroad in hopes of a curative sea voyage, but after he left, Mather wrote, Abigail said with a "more than ordinary Passion and Agony, *that she desired, God would never let her live to hear of the Death of that young man!*" When the news of his death arrived, Mather and the rest of the family put on mourning costume but by "prudent Management" kept Abigail uninformed. He tried meanwhile to keep up his many other activities—writing, preaching at other towns and before the recently arrived new governor, Joseph Dudley, awaiting with great consternation the long-delayed publication of his *Magnalia*.

Mather pondered, too, this latest engagement with the invisible world. Perhaps, he considered, God had designed by these trials a special exercise of his prayer and faith. Or perhaps he had interpreted too casually the meaning of the Holy Ghost and His angel in the Particular Faiths they had given him. It might be that God, in demonstrating His being loathe to deny anything Mather importunately asked, intended not to prevent Abigail's death but only to delay it until she and he were better prepared. Or when God says "*that He has heard me,*" He might intend something other than Abigail's recovery, a future blessing he could not possibly anticipate, but in which the Particular Faith would be accomplished.

By October, after more than twenty weeks' languishing, Abigail fell into the symptoms of a "hopeless *Consumption*" and was now "wasted." Yet the end of the month seemed to bring one ground for hope and one for thanksgiving. Abigail had a prophetic dream, perhaps a visitation. A "grave Person" appeared to her—in her sleep, she supposed ("in her sleep, no doubt," Mather wrote years later)—accompanying a woman in such wretched circumstances that Abigail praised God for making her own condition less so. The grave person told her that the intolerable pain in her breast could be eased by applying to it warm wool cut from a living sheep, and that her continued salivation would be stemmed if she strengthened her glands by drinking gum mastic and gum isinglass dissolved in a tankard of spring water. She told the dream to her main physician, who encouraged trying it. To Mather's great surprise she revived quickly. Twice she managed to get up from her sickroom and visit him in his study, where they gave thanks together to God. A week later, on Thursday, October 29, at last arrived from England a copy of *Magnalia*

Christi Americana. For a change Mather set apart the next day for thanksgiving, praising God for "His watchful and gracious Providence over that Work, and for the Harvest of so many Prayers, and Cares, and Tears, and Resignations, as I had employ'd upon it."

Pleased with seeing his large book in print, Mather learned, the same day, that Abigail's namesake, their eight-year-old daughter "Nibby," had smallpox. The deadly disease had arrived in Boston in June, for the first time in thirteen years. The town selectmen had tried to contain it, moving an infected family, isolating an infected black person, quarantining some infected seamen, but in its sweep through Boston, twice-envenomed by a simultaneous epidemic of scarlet fever, it would kill more than three hundred persons. "God prepare me, God prepare me," Mather cried, "for what is coming upon me!"

Within a month Mather's house became a hospital, where to attend Abigail and now his children also, he ultimately used "near one hundred Watchers." Soon the maid became "horribly full" of pocks and distracted; five-year-old Nancy succumbed; three-year-old Increase, Jr., was smitten "pretty full and blind, and sore; tho' not so bad as his Sister." Although it was a large house, Mather decided that no room was better suited to caring for his sick children than his study—a "large, yet a warm chamber" filled with books, from which his "little Folks" called him to pray with them scarcely less than ten or a dozen times a day, as he did.

Always busy, Mather became doubly so. He also prayed with his sick neighbors, large numbers of whom he visited. Finding it impossible to visit them all, but considering it his duty to counsel them in the epidemic, he had three men distribute to the many stricken families in his neighborhood copies of his *Wholesome Words; or, A Visit of Advice to Families visited with Sickness* (1702?), which he had published at his own expense. While Abigail and the children lay ill, he also continued preaching elaborate sermons from his pulpit. "Our afflictions," he told his congregation in November, "must not prevent, no, they must promote, and provoke our glorifying of God." He interpreted the epidemic as he did all untoward events. That his study happened to serve ideally for the children's sickroom he saw as God's humiliation for not serving Him as he should have done in his study, "which provokes Him to chase me out of it." With the same reasoning he urged the afflicted to examine their condition, to see whether "perhaps the Spotted Faces of the *Sick* in the Family, are such as our Heavenly Father has been *Spitting* upon: Shall *He Spit in our Faces, and shall we not be Ashamed?*" In facing death too, he counseled, the family's duty was to exhibit, as a token of faith, the profoundest resignation: "Whatever Flower in our Garden be Cropt, tho' it be our *Isaac,* yet Resign it, and let it be said of us, Gen. XXII. 12. *Now I know that thou Fearest God, because thou hast not witheld* any thing from Him!"

Whatever Mather's fears for his children, still "the most exquisite of my Trials," he wrote, "was the Condition of my lovely Consort." Abigail had decayed for six months and her condition was hopeless. Obviously aware that her enfeeblement had taxed those around her, she once said, "*I shall make you all weary!*" Seemingly aware of her husband's pride in his capacity to give inexhaustibly, she added, "*I don't mean you,* Mr. Mather!" He felt unsure how to glorify God to her amid the enclosing distress and confusion, yet set himself to doing so "after my sorry Manner"—praying with her, catechizing her, discoursing on heaven, preparing her for death, which came on December 1. "At last, the black Day," Mather wrote. "I had never yet seen such a black Day, in all the Time of my Pilgrimage. The *Desire of my Eyes* is this Day to be taken from me."

Abigail lingered in pain the whole morning. Presumably because of his grief, Mather was later unable to recall his conversations with her. He did remember asking her to tell him what fault she had observed in his behavior that she would advise him to correct; she replied, to his wonder, that she knew of none, but that his behavior had helped bring her nearer to God. As she began dying Mather wished to signify his acquiescence, as he counseled others to do, thereby to glorify God. It occurred to him to kneel by her bedside and take her hand, "a dear Hand, the dearest in the World." Then he showed his Savior his utter resignation to His will: "I gently put her out of my Hands, and laid away a most lovely Hand, resolving that I would never touch it any more!" It was, he said, "the hardest and perhaps the bravest Action, that ever I did." To acknowledge his resignation, Abigail, who had called for him continually, ceased to call for him during the two hours she remained alive. Immediately after her death he prayed with her weeping father and the other mourners in her room.

Mather took pride in the many who honored Abigail, the next Friday, at her funeral: "Indeed, I do not know of a Gentlewoman, who has died in this Land, these many years, more generally esteemed and lamented." Her five infants and young children by Mather who had died before her had been buried with common grave stones, but now some members of the North Church built a costly tomb to contain Abigail's and the children's remains together. At the funeral Mather gave each person who had attended her a copy of one of his works, containing a twelve-line poem, pasted in on a paper, that began, "Go then, My DOVE, but now no longer *mine;* / Leave *Earth,* and now in *heavenly Glory* shine." Two days later he preached her funeral sermon. Taking for his text the death of the prophet Ezekiel's wife—Son of Man, Behold I take away the Desire of thine Eyes with a Stroke—he presented himself as a sad commentary upon it: "Your Eyes do behold," he said, "what it is, for the God of Heaven, to take away from a Son of Man, the Desire of His Eyes with a Stroke."

While stressing such customary pulpit themes as the need for self-examination under affliction, Mather did not conceal his own mood of sorrowful deprivation. He composed for the occasion perhaps the loveliest of his several paeans to married love, in the tradition of Anne Bradstreet's intimately domestic but scriptural poems to her husband. Some relatives, he remarked to his congregation, do not like each other. But the consorts in a loving marriage know a special joy at once erotic, spiritual, and natural. They can never see each other enough, for the sight of the beloved is the very condition of their happiness:

> The God of Love sometimes does dispose them whom He has made Consorts in the Conjugal Relation, greatly to Love and prize one another. The Consorts are to each other the Desire of their Eyes, and they so love each other that they Love to be as much as may be in the Sight of each other. . . .
> They live together Like Abraham and Sarah; Like Isaac and Rebeckah; Like Jacob and Rachel. They Live together in such Love that they could freely Die for one another; and when either of them does Die, it gives a thousand Deaths to the Survivor. . . . He loves her and her Love, and rejoices in his loving Hind, and his pleasant Roe. He had rather lose all his possessions, than suffer the loss of one whom God has thus Enriched him withal. He can scarce Relish any thing in his House, if his Eyes have not her also before him.

If the passage suggests the strength of Mather's attachment to Abigail, the unusually many blots and strikeouts in the surviving manuscript betray his strain in recalling it. He wrote the sermon, he said, under "the most grievous Desolations of his *Mind,* as well as of his *House,* that ever were upon him."

As the year ended, Mather reviewed the events of the last eight months to see what mercies they contained to balance his heavy loss. For one, his children had almost been consumed in the *"Fiery Furnace* of the *Small pox,"* but had all emerged alive; he had made many pastoral visits to "venomous, contagious loathsome Chambers," and had been preserved as well. Abigail's death could itself be considered a mercy, he decided, for it spared her painful knowledge of reverses in her family.

Given her melancholy temper, she would have suffered greatly to learn of the death abroad of her second brother, as she nearly did. Oddly, Mather thought, a letter addressed to her from London containing an account of his death arrived at the house about three hours after she died. There was more bad news to oppress her also. Her youngest brother had recently been captured by the French, and her sottish eldest brother was disgracing his family and hastening to his ruin. All this had been concealed from Abigail during her illness but would, Mather believed, "without a Miracle, have brought such a Disorder of Mind upon her, as would have rendered my Condition insupportable."

Mather's concern for "my Condition" perhaps sounds selfishly uncomprehending, icy. But he recognized and admitted that he himself felt relieved by Abigail's death. Her illness, on display before helpless physicians, attendants, and children, had been long and dehumanizing, six months of wasting fevers, incapacitating feebleness, severe breast pains, and bedridden hallucinations. So at last after her death Mather acknowledged, with weariedly grim realism, "all the Fatigues, which her long Illness obliged me to go through, and with all possible Tenderness." Had she gone on as she was, "my Health would infallibly have been destroy'd, if she had recovered a little more, and so far that I should have run the venture of sleeping with her, My feeble Constitution, would undoubtedly have run into a Consumption. And my Children would also have suffered miserably in their Education."

Still, it was a sore death, more trying by far, Mather felt, than the earlier deaths of his children. He had resignedly "laid away a most lovely Hand." Perhaps Abigail's extreme weakness, or the children's education, and his own vulnerable health made her death a mercy; but, he added, "my extravagant Fondness for her, would upon any Terms have detained her here." Until recently, he realized in January, he had rarely cried except when thinking of salvation, and then in joy. "But now, scarce a Day passes me without a Flood of Tears, and my Eyes even decay with weeping."

To the extent that Mather could escape his grief over Abigail's death he only ran into what locked him back in it, the "*Miscarriage of a Particular Faith!*" Abigail had died despite repeated assurances from heaven that she would live. "Truly, nothing has ever yet befallen me, that has come so near to it." He had many thoughts on this "astonishing Sting." He believed that in her misery Abigail had prayed, at cross-purposes from him, for her release, which in the court of heaven had overruled the effect of all his own prayers and hopes for her recovery. Or perhaps as God does nothing without purpose, He may defeat Particular Faiths as a warning against pride. Mather observed that the phrase "Son of Man," stressing human limitation, is used nearly a hundred times about Ezekiel, even though the prophet was admitted to familiarity with angels. God may have taken Ezekiel's wife to remind him that despite his angelic converse he was mortal: "The Angels of God, would have this brave man see That he was but a Son of Man," and they supplied "Enough in that one point, I take away the Desire of thine Eyes with a Stroke, to convince him of his being so."

Or, Mather speculated, God may have confounded him so that he could be serviceable in cautioning others about self-deceit. He conveyed this message in a sermon he preached two weeks after Abigail's death, on the doctrine, "*Tho' Faith be no Folly, yet Faith may be mixed with Folly.*" When we pray for some worldly thing, he told his congregation, God sometime favors us with "so much of a *Particular Faith,* as to say, *the Lord hath heard the Voice of my Weeping.*" But our strong desire for the thing may lead us to interpret the Particular Faith too literally, as if meaning that "*the Thing must be done in just such or such a manner.*" All that is meant in a Particular Faith, he cautioned, is that something will be done toward the blessing we desire which will demonstrate God's willingness to gratify us.

Yet Mather's puzzling over God's purpose in raising then frustrating his hopes produced no answer. He contented himself with thinking that God might allow him in the future to understand the working of a Particular Faith. And meanwhile he would be wary: "I have met with enough, to awaken in me a more exquisite Caution, than ever I had in my Life, concerning it."

*

Only two months after Abigail's death, a young gentlewoman wrote several letters to Mather, then visited him at his house. He had just turned forty, she was twenty-three, and she proposed that he marry her. She confessed to him that, his widowerhood having allowed her more liberty to think of him, she found him irresistible, "charmed with my Person, to such a Degree, that she could not but break in upon me, with her most importunate Requests, that I would make her mine." She assured him that what impelled her was the more than ordinary value she placed on his ministry, and that her highest consideration in wanting to be his wife was her eternal salvation.

Mather never names this young gentlewoman, so forward for her salvation, but she was almost certainly Katharine Maccarty, the daughter of a

Boston landholder and shopowner who had helped found King's Chapel. Mather thought Kate attractive and suitable, "a young Gentlewoman of incomparable Accomplishments . . . . one of rare Wit and Sense; and of a comely Aspect; and extremely Winning in her Conversation." Yet he tried to discourage her, portraying his life to her as a regimen of prayers, fasts, and "macerating Devotions and Reservations." But Kate told him she desired nothing so much as to share his macerations; his macerated way of living was exactly what "animated" her, she said. Considering her youth, and that she had been a "very airy Person," Mather was not entirely convinced. Yet he remained drawn to her and flattered by her attention, and suggested they take time to see if the question could be resolved. For himself he would pray and fast, and wait and see: "What Snares may be laying for me, I know not."

As Mather pondered this "odd Matter" he saw clearly that his wishes and his ministry conflicted. In himself he found "a mighty Tenderness for a person so very amiable." Breeding required that she be treated with honor and respect; religion required that instead of rashly rejecting her he continue the relationship so as to make her Christ's. But he foresaw violent opposition to the match, worried about the example he might set to young people in his flock, and feared making a bad mistake. His confusion sent him to his study floor often, calling for God's assistances until after midnight, and so wracked and wasted him that in mid-February he wrote Kate to "vehemently beg, as for my Life" that she end her pursuit. But to give up seeing her was not so easy: "such was my flexible Tenderness, as to be conquered by the Importunities of several, to allow some further Interviews." He determined to make these interviews revolve around her conversion, drawing from the "witty Gentlewoman" her tearful consent to the articles of the covenant of grace.

Gossip about the piquant affair tightened Mather's agitation. His "Relatives" (probably his father) believed he overvalued Kate, took the situation with extreme distaste, and treated him strangely and harshly. As the "ingenious Child" continued pressing him, news went around Boston that he was courting her. With most people Kate had a bad name, he discovered, partly because of "the Disadvantages of the Company which has continually resorted unto her unhappy Father's House." People also blamed him for his earliness in courting. The noise made him suspect a design of Satan to destroy his ministry—"Is it because I have done much against that Enemy?"—a possibility which as always left him overwrought: "There is Danger of my dying suddenly, with smothered Griefs and Fears." By mid-March, after long deliberation, he saw unquestionably

that marriage with Kate would damage his name and vocation. He resigned himself once again to laying aside a lovely hand, a person who
"for many charming Accomplishments, has not many Equals in the *English America*." In thus giving himself to Christ, howbeit in novel form,
he discerned "no unhappy Symptom, I hope, of Regeneration in my
Soul."

Sign of grace or no, Mather's decision only sharpened his distress. The
stubborn appeal of Kate's physical attractiveness and social charms evidently aroused severe guilt and anger. A highly sexual man, Mather became tempted, he wrote with indefinite frankness, to "*Impurities*" and,
worse, sometime to blasphemy, atheism, "and the Abandonment of all
Religion, as a mere Delusion; and sometimes, to self-Destruction itself."
His imagination began giving shape to a new trouble: Kate might retaliate
for being rejected. Apparently he had not let her down lightly, for he
speaks of the "coarse, tho' just, Usage that she has had from me." This
might provoke her to a "thousand Inventions" to scandalize a town
where new lies about him and the broken courtship were being invented
daily anyway. Despite his disappointment in Particular Faiths he sought
relief from his misery by pleading the question to heaven. On April 13 he
decided to spend no less than three successive days fasting and praying in
his study, something he believed had never been done before by anyone.
The extraordinary devotions produced "Extraordinary Things . . . that
cannot be related. I will only say, the Angels of Heaven are at work for
me." He set aside other days of fasting and prayer of similar fervency,
whose rapture exhausted his spirit, "made me faint and sick; they were
insupportable; I was forced, even to withdraw from them, lest I should
have swoon'd away."

Mather's heavenly messages had to contend, however, with Kate's
mother, Elizabeth—a woman, he thought her at first, "of an extraordinary
Character for her Piety." While he was out of town on a trip to Salem, she
and her daughter both wrote to and visited his father, and some of his
neighbors, to renew their suit. By now he was bent on hearing nothing
more of it, whatever the risk of revenge. But Elizabeth wrote to him herself; if her letter is any clue to her daughter's personality, Mather's jitteri-
ness is understandable, for although semiliterate, its pious flattery is
crafty, winning, and exquisitely manipulative. Elizabeth blessed him and
God for the little conversation the minister had granted her daughter
because it concerned, she knew, "that noble Design of bringing her nearer
to the Lord-Redeemer." Her daughter's interest in Mather was wholly
soteriological: "I am sure, Heaven knows, that was her whole Design, in

Addressing your worthy person." Her daughter thought, she said, that heaven might have ordered for the everlasting good of her soul "a Relation to so Heavenly a man (which she always thought more Like an Angel than a man)."

Susceptible to flattery but not to idolatrous armbending, Mather seems to have sent back a stiff warning that the Maccartys' hounding him was both unwanted and dangerous to his strained health. His letter is lost but its content reverberates in the reply Elizabeth wrote on June 7, which she delayed sending, she said, knowing it was his day for administering the Lord's Supper and concerned lest anything in it "might in the least discompose you at such a time." She had never, she said, received "any of the like unkind Letter from any person." Her own letter is poorly preserved and difficult to read, but seems to imply that Mather had sent other no-nonsense letters as well, which she sat on her couch afraid to open, crying to God that "this holy man means thus to distress me." In one letter he apparently spoke of his dying by excessive perturbation, so that she drenched "the paper throwly with my tears," hoping God would not suffer "such a star of the first magnitude to be removed from us, by which a great part of the world will be darkened." Mather's show of resentment and nervous strain seems to have convinced Elizabeth to retreat, for she assured him her greatest grief would be to be shut out of his and his father's prayers. In closing she presented Kate's thanks for a book Mather had given or sent her, presumably by him. Her daughter was reading his works, she added, "with the greatest Delight imaginable."

Mather felt that the Maccartys, in affirming that he had treated them honorably and righteously, had fully vindicated his behavior. Yet more than ever impertinent stories spread through Boston that made him contemptible, tales that he was actively wooing Kate, insinuations that he had gone too far in the suit to abandon it decently. The falsehoods and notoriety atop months of frazzling temptation and resistance swelled his anger: "these things do exceedingly unhinge me; and cause me sometimes to *speak unadvisedly with my Lips.* Tis well, if they do not perfectly kill me."

Unexpectedly Mather found relief just two houses from his own. His neighbor Mrs. Elizabeth Hubbard, widowed four years and nearing thirty years of age, offered the sobriety and respectability Kate lacked. She was "a Gentlewoman of Piety and Probity, and a most unspotted Reputation; a Gentlewoman of good Wit and Sense, and Discretion at ordering an Household; a Gentlewoman of incomparable Sweetness in her Temper, and Humor; a Gentlewoman honourably descended and related; and a very comely person." Yet Mather had reservations, among them that Elizabeth had a son, about the age of Increase, Jr. He reasoned that he had often urged Abigail to take some fatherless child into their family, feed and clothe it that God might bless his own children: "Why then should I think much to educate the Son of a Gentlewoman from whom I expect so much service to mine?" Visiting Elizabeth's house the first time on July 14, he found himself entertained if not exactly like an angel, yet with "more than ordinary Civility, Affection, and Veneration." His reservations also faded some, as Elizabeth turned out to be "an abundantly more agreeable Person, than ever I imagined," a reparation for his grief in Abigail's death, his disappointment in Particular Faiths, the resignations of the last fifteen months.

The lingering possibility that Kate might demand revenge for her "defeated Love" had kept Mather uneasy, and now came to life. Enraged, she threatened to be a thorn in his side, to contrive every possible way "to vex me, affront me, disgrace me, in my Attempting a Return to the married State with another Gentlewoman." Now able to see unconfusedly that she was a person perhaps of rare wit but of little grace, he did not try to mollify her. Instead he carried the matter to Christ, who this time answered; Kate wrote to him promising not to execute "those Disquietments, which in her Passion she had threatened." Astonished at this work of heaven, he offered God a sacrifice of love and praise.

His engagement, it also amazed Mather to think, created satisfaction in town and country alike. He too felt satisfied, and eager. Having lived celibate more than a year, it pleased him to think of "arriving speedily to the Enjoyment of a most lovely Creature," although in connection with this prospect a strong fancy troubled him, smacking of guilt, that before he could be married he would die. Rather, on the evening of August 18, he was married. He spent the entire day in his study in thanksgiving, tendering particular thanks to God for "my astonishing Preservations, from undoing myself, my Ministry, and my Family, under the amazing Temptations, which in the Time of my Widowhood, I have met withal." By God's help he had not made some scandalous, unredeemable mistake.

But he had come close; Kate had had her attractions. With his genius for compromise, he offered thanks too, if not exactly fervent ones, that God had provided "the most agreeable Consort (all things considered) that all *America* could have afforded me."

III

THE REVEREND COTTON MATHER
D.D. & F.R.S. (1703-1713)

Cotton Mather came galloping down
All the way to Newbury town,
With eyes agog and ears set wide,
And his marvellous inkhorn at his side;
Stirring the while in the shallow pool
Of his brains for the lore he learned at school,
To garnish the story, with here a streak
Of Latin, and there another of Greek:
And the tales he heard and the notes he took,
Behold! are they not in his Wonder-Book?

> —JOHN GREENLEAF WHITTIER, "The Double-Headed
> Snake of Newbury" (1859)

*A field near the graveyard. GILES COREY lying dead, with a great stone on his
breast....*

MATHER

O sight most horrible! In a land like this,
Spangled with Churches Evangelical,
Inwrapped in our salvations, must we seek
In mouldering statute-books of English Courts
Some old forgotten Law, to do such deeds?
Those who lie buried in the Potter's Field
Will rise again, as surely as ourselves
That sleep in honored graves with epitaphs;
And this poor man, whom we have made a victim,
Hereafter will be counted as a martyr!

> —HENRY WADSWORTH LONGFELLOW, *Giles Corey of the
> Salem Farms* (1868)

The tendency of the stately old families of New England to constitutional melancholy has been well set forth by Dr. Cotton Mather, that delightful old New

England grandmother, whose nursery tales of its infancy and childhood may well be pondered by those who would fully understand its far-reaching maturity. As I have before remarked, I have high ideas of the wisdom of grandmothers, and therefore do our beloved gossip, Dr. Cotton Mather, the greatest possible compliment in granting him the title.

—HARRIET BEECHER STOWE, *Oldtown Folks* (1869)

In 1721, this disease [smallpox], after a respite of nineteen years, again appeared as an epidemic. In that year it was that Cotton Mather, browsing, as was his wont, on all the printed fodder that came within reach of his ever-grinding mandibles, came upon an account of inoculation as practised in Turkey, contained in the "Philosophical Transactions." He spoke of it to several physicians, who paid little heed to his story; for they knew his medical whims, and had probably been bored, as we say now-a-days, many of them, with listening to his "Angel of Bethesda," and satiated with his speculations on the *Nishmath Chajim*.

The Reverend Mather,—I use a mode of expression he often employed when speaking of his honored brethren,—the Reverend Mather was right this time, and the irreverent doctors who laughed at him were wrong. . . .

—OLIVER WENDELL HOLMES, "The Medical Profession in Massachusetts" (1869)

7

Joseph Dudley

As THE NEW century opened, Cotton Mather was newly remarried, nearing forty, and about to replace his father as the most prominent minister in America. Increase's declining role in public life was partly owing to his ouster from the Harvard presidency and his decision to abide in New England, but also to his advancing age and failing health. In 1704, aged sixty-five, he had fits of what he understood to be apoplexy. He also suffered kidney pains and began urinating blood and stones. Over the next half-dozen years he recorded having insomnia, cholic, and pains in his jaw and teeth, and took to wearing fur gloves for the gout in his hands. To treat his losses of memory he administered to himself sixty drops of oil of lavender and a mouthful of gingerbread. Extremely fearful that his mind would fail, he hoped to die soon: "If I die quickly some few will lament my death. Whereas if I live a while longer I shall be useless. It is a great mercy for a minister not to outlive his work."

Increase conspired in his decline by his inveterate view of himself as moribund, now to a degree justified by objective conditions of his health. His announcements of his imminent death multiplied: "It is but a very little Time that I have now to be in the World," he told his congregation in 1703, "I am wasting continually." "*I must shortly put off this my Tabernacle,*" he told his readers in 1705. "The Time of my Departure hence, drawing on apace," he prefaced another work in 1711. In 1704 he considered choosing his successor, a partner to his son. Not anyone would be suitable for their large congregation, and he found the younger candidates not as loyal to the Cambridge Platform as he wished, and grown accustomed, lazily he thought, to reading all their sermons. He believed the most suitable choice was Cotton's younger brother Samuel, now in his mid-twenties and preaching in England. But Samuel was disinclined, and Increase decided to promote his candidacy no further, leaving the matter of his successor open.

Ironically, Increase's waning effectiveness and the troubled events of the next decade brought Cotton Mather not only greater prominence but also lessened influence in Boston. Cotton's pain over the discrepancy may be more complexly appreciated by sketching, before the narrative resumes, the more intimate side of the ministry he had established twenty or so years after his ordination—not its shifting involvement in public affairs, but something of its little-changing daily color and routine.

The congregation Mather served remained probably the largest in New England, containing about fifteen hundred people. Of these about four hundred were admitted to the Lord's Supper. He preached, that is, to a largely unregenerated audience, hoping to supervise their conversion, although in the more than forty years of his ministry the new admissions to communion amounted to only 574 women and 342 men. The congregation included such prosperous and notable persons as John Richards and Samuel Scarlett; a large number of maritime people (perhaps a quarter of his flock); a large number of widows (about a sixth of the communicants); many children; and numerous blacks. At least after 1711, he and his father received identical salaries of £3 per week, raised from weekly contributions at the church that averaged around £10, the remainder buying wood, bellropes, or casks of communion wine, or paying the numerous guest preachers, who received £1. Increments over the succeeding years brought Cotton's salary to £4 by 1725. These meager salaries were filled out by free repairs and firewood for their homes and gifts of money customarily left them in the wills of wealthy congregants, or occasionally donated by the church itself or by wealthy and pious friends who belonged to other churches.

Mather approached his ministry with thoughtful devotion and exceeding care. He strove to preach "as excellent and well studied Sermons as ever I can and contrive all my public Exercises in the most edifying manner that I am able." He undoubtedly succeeded; much other evidence confirms his several comments that when he preached outside Boston people flocked to hear him, and that in his own church he attracted very large audiences: "Few Ministers in the World, preach unto the like; it would be beyond the Strength of a mortal Man, to preach unto much bigger." Preaching once on Sunday, and often a second time at the so-called Thursday Lecture (a practice introduced to New England by his grandfather John Cotton), he produced seventy or so formal sermons a year, neatly handwritten in small booklets. In his earlier, and perhaps also his later, ministry he composed part of the sermon kneeling at his chair in a prayerful position, writing on a *"Table-Book"* of slate open before him—carefully weighing the meaning of his texts in their original languages, consulting scriptural commentaries, and praying much. In preparing each sermon, he reckoned, he usually spent seven hours.

Differing considerations dictated Mather's choice of sermon subjects. Occasionally he preached on a text "assigned" him in a dream or took his cue from a local event. Once as a thunderstorm broke outside his church he began preaching extemporaneously on thunder and later published the sermon. Other times he addressed his sermon to a particular public occasion—an execution, a funeral, Election Day—or to a specific group in his congregation, to sailors or children or merchants or women, by this means making his pulpit a forum for commenting on the life of the town. Sometimes he preached a series of connected sermons on the same text. His ministry required him to return again and again to such crucial points as conversion, prayer, and affliction, both to remind older congregants and instruct new ones who had not heard his message before. His ingenious aesthetic sense enjoyed the challenge of varying the presentation while repeating the substance. He noted in the Preface to one published sermon that he had published many sermons on youthful piety, using "a *Variety of Tunes,* for the Engaging of *Young* Minds. . . . And yet the *Tunes* are not *All Spent;* Early Piety is here Set unto a *New* one." The otherwise bewildering fact that much of his published writing repeats the same ideas is partly explained by his practical need to keep driving home the same essential ideas over forty years while varying the "tune" to keep the same congregation interested.

Mather devoted equally energetic care to delivering his sermons, which usually ran an hour and a half or an hour and three-quarters, about average for New England sermons. When he began his ministry his uncle Nathaniel urged him to follow other ministers in the family in preaching without notes. Yet sermon notes came into general use in Mather's lifetime and, as his many surviving manuscript sermons indicate, he often wrote out in full the major portion of his sermon—the lengthy exposition of doctrine—with brief notes for the concluding application, to encourage a freer, semi-improvised delivery for the ending. Just the same, he distinguished between the "*Neat using* of *Notes,* and the *dull Reading* of them," and advised other ministers to use notes only for reference:

> Let your *Notes* be little other than a *Quiver*, on which you may cast your
> Eye now and then, to see what *Arrow* is to be next fetch'd from thence;
> and then, with your Eye as much as may be on them whom you speak to,
> Let it be shot away, with a *Vivacity* becoming *One in Earnest*.

As this comment suggests, he endeavored to leave his congregation both
instructed and stirred. To begin preaching in a heightened spiritual state,
he urged ministers to "go directly from your Knees in your *Study* to the
Pulpit." Beginning neither too fast nor too loud, he tried to make his
sentences short enough to be intelligible to the listeners and transcriba-
ble by those who wrote as he preached, speaking deliberately and emphasizing key words. He followed conventional Puritan theory in also
urging ministers to conclude vigorously, to abandon exposition and argument and in parting strike by lively questions, appeals, and expostula-
tions for the worshiper's own conscience, "that flaming *Preacher* in the
Bosom of the Hearer." Pouring similar fervor into the public prayers he
offered before and after sermons, he once became so enraptured that he
prayed aloud before his congregation the better part of two hours, his
soul "soaring and flaming towards Heaven." He apologized for the unusual length, in the sermon that followed.

However demanding, preaching comprised only part of Mather's ministry. He also faithfully kept the church records, made pastoral visits, baptized and catechized children, married couples (fifty-two of them in
1709), appeared at funerals, wrote letters of recommendation, and promoted private religious societies, of which he was connected at one time
to more than twenty. Many hours he spent comforting the afflicted and
dying; by the age of thirty-four, he estimated, he had beheld the death
agonies of others hundreds, perhaps thousands of times. As a member of
the clerical fraternity he also preached at ordinations and sat on church
councils, still occasionally writing up their decisions. But in fact he performed as a minister all the time, his congregants ever in mind, ever
aware of serving them as a model. He prayed for them in his study and
tried to say something serviceable when passing them on the street.
Once, in addition to other devotions of the day, he prayed for each of the
full communicants of his church distinctly and by name—nearly four
hundred of them.

Some at least of Mather's efforts were rewarded, for many people
loved and honored him for his ministry. They often commented in their
diaries or to others on his soul-saving power and warmth, appreciatively

left him small bequests in their wills, or wrote to him commending his "Compassionate Regard for the Good of Souls" and asking for his help. A distressed man named Edward Goddard, for instance, wrote him a touching letter concerning his son, a ministerial candidate who had been doing poorly at Harvard. The boy had been suffering head and stomach pains so that his father had to remove him from school. Goddard seemingly sensed that his son's problems were as much emotional as physical, for he told Mather that the boy felt depressed by his intellectual limitations and had a habit of "looking at things as Almost Insuperable to make them really so." He prayed Mather's advice and assistance in finding some method to release his son's abilities by making him feel less discouraged. Nor is there reason to doubt the several stories Mather tells himself of deathbed thanks for his ministry, such as the expiring person who cried to him: "*Oh! Dear Sir, you are the Man! You are the Man, that have brought me home unto God! It is by your Means, that the Lord has brought me home to Himself. I must love you dearly; I shall do so, to my last Breath.*"

But no aspect of his ministry brought Mather greater prominence than the prodigious number of his publications. He quite outdid the angel's prophecy in 1693 that a certain youth would compose and publish many books in America and Europe, for from then through his quarrel with Colman he published around 90 works, and from 1702 to 1713 no fewer than 135 more, for the rest of his life averaging each year 10 published works. Ultimately he would publish some 388 separate titles. Viewed in comparison with the output of other New England ministers the total seems even more incredible, for publication was seldom more than a small part of a minister's work and most ministers eschewed it altogether. Of the over five hundred ministers born in New England before 1703, 66 percent never published anything, 11 percent published only a single work, only 5 percent published ten or more. Mather not only published far more than any other New England minister; he probably published more than all the New England ministers before his time combined. The titles range greatly in nature and length from a batch of funeral sermons on women (containing paeans to New England womanhood), to a long affectionate elegy on his old schoolmaster, Ezekiel Cheever (notable for the relative smoothness of its rhyme and meter), to the magisterial *Magnalia*. Intermittently he seems to have tried to pace or stamp some design on this deluge, for instance by deliberately publishing one title a month, or by roughly alphabetizing his titles over two years, producing in 1710, for instance, *Bonifacius, Christianity Demonstrated, Dust and Ashes, Eliz-*

abeth in her Holy Retirement, and so on.

One reason Mather published so much is that he often left one of his brief works behind on pastoral visits, with the caution: *"Remember, that I am speaking to you, all the while you have this Book before you!"* These household tokens of his ministry, he felt, enabled him to preach to his flock every day. He sometime published a new work only because the impression of an earlier work on the same topic had run out, a practice which again helps explain the large amount of repetition among his works, for he must have exhausted printings of his works quickly. In a day of pastoral visits he usually gave away half a dozen copies, and he estimated that he gave away at least six hundred copies of his works annually. In the first decade of the new century he also tried to expand greatly the distribution of his inexpensive religious books and pamphlets outside Boston, "sprinkling the *Salt* of Religion," as he said, "about the World." Thus he had a bundle of one thousand copies of his *Family-Religion, Excited and Assisted* (1705) sent for distribution to prayerless families in "every Town in all these Colonies, and to some other Places," and had his *Sailours Companion* (1709)—reproving smutty talk, masturbation, and sodomy—lodged in every sizable ship sailing out of New England. Concerned that his own behavior might fail to exemplify his widely disseminated advice, he reminded himself to read over his own works on Sabbath evenings, "lest my own Books, do not at last prove my own Condemnation." Considering that many of his other publications were bought briskly—*Good Fetch'd Out of Evil* (1706), a collection of captivity narratives, sold a thousand copies in a week—it is imaginable that numerous people overseas, many people in the colonies, most people in New England, and nearly everyone in Boston owned some of his works. By 1710 he may well have become the best-known man in America.

The sheer number of Mather's works, however awesome, misrepresents in several ways the nature and actual scope of his writing. He wrote many thousands of pages which were not published in his lifetime, and they include such ambitious works as the dozen connected, lengthy sermons he preached between March 1701 and April 1703, on the first two chapters of Ephesians (texts he considered of "a peculiar Excellency"), covering such basic Christian doctrines as original sin, providence, predestination, and communion—enough for a sizable volume of theology. Between 1700 and about 1723 he also cultivated a series of commonplace books or "Quotidiana," about six hundred pages of which remain. Valuable as a guide to his very wide reading, the books contain choice passages in English, French, Latin, and Greek about geography, science, demonology, Martin Luther, religious customs among the Jews, as well as maxims, comments on prose style, and rather surprising quotations from Dryden, Waller, and Cowley, and references to the Louvre and to Holbein. As before he also kept detailed diaries, wrote (sporadically now) after the preacher in church, and swelled his mammoth ongoing "Biblia Americana."

Mather also maintained a voluminous correspondence. There is no knowing how many letters he wrote, for many have been lost, but by a single ship to England in 1712 he sent more than thirty letters. His six hundred or so surviving letters make the largest extant correspondence of any American Puritan, but represent only the remains of what may have been more than five thousand letters, sent literally around the world. Through his European correspondence he tried to keep informed on religious and intellectual developments abroad, but also to extend his reputation and influence and to show the Old World what an American could do. He wrote to Germany, Holland, India, France, the West Indies, Scotland, and often to England, where his correspondents included such luminaries as Daniel Defoe and Isaac Watts, and perhaps Joseph Addison and Sir Isaac Newton. At home he kept in touch with other ministers and with friends far and near, such as John Winthrop, Jr., in Connecticut and even Samuel Sewall at the other end of Boston, with whom he often exchanged by mail ideas about scriptural prophecy, bits of verse, translations. To some friends he sent very lengthy news letters, commenting for pages on recent European events as reported in America's first genuine newspaper, *The Boston News-Letter,* begun in 1704. Conscious of often addressing, he said, "the politer sort of Persons," he read attentively the letters of other learned men, gathered into a commonplace book for his own use some of their "taking Flowers" of rhetoric, and worked many of his letters into polished, bantering literary epistles. And he seems to have made a preliminary draft of nearly every letter he sent.

Mather alternately gloried in and condemned his vast verbal fecundity, still troubled in middle age by "that particular Lust, my Pride . . . affectations of Grandeur, and Inclinations to be thought Somebody." Writing in the 1690s, he at one time thanked God for "publishing more of my Composures than any Man's, that ever was in *America,*" and at another time blamed himself for publishing too much: "I *do* confess, That I have written too many *Books,* for one of my small Attainments." Recurrently he discovered that other people, too, were "prejudiced against me for printing so many Books," including his own father. In print Increase often condemned the publishing of many books as a "*Vanity* which the

Earth Groans under"; less indirectly, in his Preface to one of Cotton's own works he chided those who neglect the Bible "and go to the *endless Writings of Men.*"

The intensity of Mather's conflict over his writing may be judged from the evident abundance in his works of unconscious strategies for resolving it, stammerlike devices that at once express and cancel. In trying to make peace between his ambition and his guilt, he often simultaneously concealed and revealed his authorship. To give one of many examples: he published his *Decennium Luctuosum* (1699) anonymously, and in some introductory remarks asked the reader's indulgence for not revealing the author's name: "All the *Favor* he desires of you, is, That you would *not Enquire after him;* or ask, *who he is?* but that, as he is at best, but an *Obscure* Person, he may continue in yet more *Obscurity.*" In short space he repeated this request three times, asking that the book be read like the writing on Belshazzar's wall, "where the Hand only was to be seen, and not who's it was"; reporting the existence of an academy of *"Innominati"* at Parma, into which "the Author of this *History*, would be glad of an Admission"; citing a Ludovicus Nihili (*"Lewis of Nothingham"*) and repeating that "the Author will count himself not a little favoured, if he may pass for one of no more Account, than a, *No body.*" As if the facetiously learned style of these requests for anonymity were not enough to identify the work as his, Mather managed to litter the book with clues to his authorship. The *"Nameless Writer"* includes a dialogue between a Quaker and a Puritan identified as "Friend M.," reveals himself to be a Harvard graduate, refers to the *Life of Phips* and *Wonders of the Invisible World*, and compares his father to a famous rabbi who had an also famous rabbi for a son. The book ends by announcing publication of a new work "by Mr. *Cotton Mather.*"

In a variant of this ambidexter tactic, Mather several times published in the character of an anonymous friend of Cotton Mather's, for instance reprinting one brief piece as the work of "Mr. Mather the Younger, as I have been inform'd." A charming instance of Mather's ability to preen himself even in hiding appears in his diary for 1700. He wrote down a quatrain, presumably sent him by an admirer, interpreting his name as greater than the sum of its Cotton and Mather parts:

> For *Grace* and *Act* and an Illustrious *Fame*
> Who would not look from such an *Ominous Name*,
> Where *Two Great Names* their Sanctuary take,
> And in a *Third* combined, a *Greater* make!

Through these four lines of tribute he ran a threadlike line of ink, striking them out in a way that presents no obstacle to their being read. Beneath the (un)obliterated verses he wrote an explanation, in whose parenthesis his conflict only surfaces again in fresh form: "Too gross Flattery for me to Transcribe; (tho' the Poetry be good.)"

Most revealingly of all, Mather often presented himself as being asked, begged, or virtually forced to produce a work. His *Small Offers* (1689), for example, begins with a statement that he is publishing the work unwillingly, on command of his patron:

> It is indeed a piece of *Self-Denial* that your Commands have obliged me unto; for whatever others may think of *Appearing in Print,* my own Opinion of it is, that unless a man be extremely unacquainted both with himself, and with the world, he will be rather *Afraid* or *Asham'd* of it, than *Taken* with it.

This denial of responsibility for his own writings seems mirrored in many facets of Mather's career and of the style and form of his works. As an amanuensis for others, a dedicated recorder of others' sermons, an anthologist of others' choice comments, a practitioner of a "massy " style woven of allusions to others and quotations from others, he often produced with great labor works at once his own and not his own, the extreme case being of course his "Biblia Americana," a gigantic collection of the works and words of others, at once toweringly self-aggrandizing and utterly self-effacing, distinctively by Cotton Mather and not by him at all.

Whatever his misgivings about the extent of his writings, Mather felt none about the busyness of his larger ministry, and took sly pleasure in identifying himself with the Spanish bishop named Fructuosus—Be Fruitful. To get through his "vast Variety of Employments" he arose at seven or eight in the morning (and, constantly accusing himself of sloth, constantly resolved to rise earlier), and usually retired around eleven at night or later, taking an agreeable book with him to read until he fell asleep. A general picture of his activities, leaving aside his also-busy family life, appears at the end of his diary for 1711. Every day of the year, he wrote, he had spent something on pious uses and had recorded some deed for someone's benefit; nearly every day he had written illustrations for "Biblia Americana," many more than a thousand for the year. During the year he had also preached many sermons to private societies in addition to his public sermons, published nearly as many works as there are months (and prepared others yet unpublished), made "many hundreds" of visits, managed "scores of Correspondences," performed "number-less" devotional exercises, and read over "many scores" of books. It was a year, he added, in which "I have been a most unprofitable servant."

Unlike his father, Mather accepted his heavy load with uncomplaining zest, at least in this period of his life. Indeed, although the two men continued working as a ministerial team, their personalities had come to differ distinctly. Both were deeply devout, studious, sensitive to criticism, inwardly taut; but while Increase remained disgruntled, private, laconic, melancholy, Cotton, although moody himself, was very often sociable, ornamental, jocose, amiable. The difference stamps their handwriting—Increase's brambled to the point of illegibility, Cotton's gracefully lucid, meant to be read—and appears perhaps most winningly in a facet of Cotton Mather's personality now beyond reach. Everyone who knew and liked him commented on his ability to extemporize, to convert his vast learning and tenacious memory entertainingly into inventive and fanciful conversation. The "Abundance within his *lips* overflow'd," Benjamin Colman wrote. "Here he excell'd, here he shone; being exceeding communicative, and bringing out of his *Treasury* things new and old, without measure." Atop Mather's inner conflicts and unceasing activity, the strain it must have cost the youthful stammerer to become the best-remembered conversationalist of his time can only be guessed, and was successfully masked. His protégé Thomas Prince later remarked that anyone who knew Mather casually might suppose from his erudition that he spent all his life studying, but on becoming aware of his constant instruction of others would decide he spent all his time in conversation, and on knowing him more intimately and learning of his numberless labors would conclude he had no time for study or talk but must spend his whole life in action. Yet while giving out the energy of three lives, Prince wrote, "He never seemed to be in a *Hurry*. . . . He would always entertain us with Ease and Pleasure, even in his Studying Hours, as long as we pleas'd, or cou'd venture to hinder Him."

*

The political influence otherwise owing to Mather for his prominence was denied him by the arrival of a new governor. Under the administration of Joseph Dudley he became more estranged from the government than at any other time since the reign of Sir Edmund Andros fifteen years earlier.

Both Mathers had been friendly with Dudley long before he became governor, and were related to him through marriage. His family's renown in New England's political history, indeed, was only slightly less than theirs in its ecclesiastical history. Dudley's father, Thomas (seventy years his senior), was the second governor of Massachusetts; his sister Anne married another governor of Massachusetts, Simon Bradstreet, and became famous as the poet Anne Bradstreet. Joseph Dudley himself, born in Roxbury in 1647, had been graduated from Harvard and trained for the ministry. Increase Mather, whom he regarded as a spiritual adviser, at one time recommended that his congregation call Dudley as his assistant in the North Church. But Dudley entered politics, became a representative to the General Court from Roxbury, and was invested with several important public trusts.

With the appointment of Governor Andros, Dudley lost the respect not only of the Mathers but also of most of New England. Under Andros he willingly became censor of the colony press and chief justice of the Superior Court. To him was attributed the infamous remark, delivered from the bench, "that the people in New England were all slaves, and that the only difference between them and slaves was their not being bought and sold." How the son of a former governor of Massachusetts might come to consider his countrymen all slaves was perhaps explained by Dudley's colleague, Edward Randolph, who accused him of misappropriating funds, and wrote that he would "cringe and bow to anything; he hath his fortune to make in the world."

Particularly because of his judicial role in enforcing laws passed under Andros, Dudley was scorned by many as a traitor to Massachusetts. When Andros was overthrown he became, by one account, "in a peculiar manner the object of the people's displeasure," and was jailed in Boston. To help get himself released, we have seen, he called on Cotton Mather's "steady friendship and respect," and sent him a lengthy letter from jail justifying his past. He claimed that he had worked to preserve the original charter, refuted charges that he had become tainted with popery, denied he had taken bribes, and insisted he privately had argued with Andros against repatenting lands. What if anything Mather did toward Dudley's release is unknown; popular enmity with Dudley left little to do. While imprisoned, Dudley fell ill and the Council allowed him to return to Roxbury under a guard; the same night, two to three hundred Bostonians broke open his house and, it was said, "led him back to gaol like a dog." When he was at last returned to England he was confronted with a list of charges prepared by a committee of colonists accusing him of 119 illegal acts.

Dudley's political career seemed finished. But he greatly desired to return to office in New England, and clearly understood that he might turn the growth of royal authority in the colonies to his advantage. And he abounded in one indispensable quality of a politician, resilience. When Sir William Phips was recalled to England, Dudley succeeded in having him arrested in an action for twenty thousand pounds. To his disappointment, however, upon Phips's death the government of Massachusetts passed not to him but to the Earl of Bellomont. Instead Dudley was made deputy governor of the Isle of Wight; he also obtained a commission, after which he was known as Colonel Dudley. Returning to England as a member of Parliament, he used his position to satisfy his intellectual curiosity and cultivated taste, and to gain a place in English society. He became friendly with Sir Richard Steele and with John Chamberlayne, gentleman-in-waiting to Prince George and a member of the Royal Society, to which Dudley submitted two scientific papers, one about the circulation of juices in fruit trees. He also seems to have made a fourth in a string quartet with what he called a "gang of halfpenny viol-players." He wished to be regarded as an English gentleman, had indeed become an Englishman. Yet he remained also a pious and affectionate husband and father, and missed his family, who remained in Roxbury. He often wrote longingly to his wife, "My Dearest Soul," describing his life in England as an "exile" and asking that God "in his Mercy restore me to my family and country."

Dudley began determinedly pushing his return to New England in the summer of 1701, apparently upon the death of the perennial acting governor, William Stoughton. Dudley enlisted support in London by advertising himself as a loyal servant of the king, who designed as governor to foster the Church of England, enforce the Acts of Trade, and keep New England "in a strict dependance upon the Crown and Government of England." He neatly parried criticism against him, the most slashing and persistent of which came from the Massachusetts agent in London, Sir Henry Ashurst. Ashurst made opposition to Dudley virtually a crusade, "standing at the sluice alone," he said, "and fencing against friends and enemies in the cause." Ashurst reiterated in conversation and letters his passionately certain belief that if Dudley became governor, New England would be ruined. "You must, gentlemen, look about you," he wrote to Boston, "I think your all is in danger." Dudley charged Ashurst with spreading a smear that he had promised the Bishop of London that, if he became governor, he would immediately make every man in New England conform to the Church of England. To counter such charges Dudley got several London Presbyterian ministers to sign and send to Increase

Mather a letter approving him as prudent and sober, respected by the present government, and loyal to his birth, a man whose "family Estate and Interest is in your Country."

Dudley also sought support for his governorship from New England itself, especially from the Mathers. That took skill, for it had been said in Boston that "both the Mr Mathers Intend to deal with him for his wickedness." Ashurst, moreover, had warned Cotton Mather that Dudley's "soul is as black as his hat and would ruin both you and I if in his power." Undeterred, Dudley began corresponding with Cotton Mather early in 1701. Mather seems to have ignored his first few letters but Dudley wrote a particularly well-calculated letter in May, chiding his silence and deftly working the carrot and the stick. Ingratiatingly, he suggested that he had personally mellowed and wanted peace, reminded Mather that he was a New Englander by birth and education, and assured him that his long exile abroad had given him "a New Value of my Country and the Religion and Virtue that dwells in it." Threateningly, he reported that the House of Lords was debating a new bill to repeal the Massachusetts charter and that many pretenders to the government of New England had come forward, many of whom might feel far less affection for the country than himself.

Mather of course had no little gift for transmitting crossed signals, and he sent Dudley an exceedingly wary reply. To Dudley's chiding his initial silence, he responded in an excessively polite tone which could be taken as flattery should Dudley succeed in becoming governor or as contempt should he fail: "I have obtained for myself a most agreeable pleasure in the rebuke which I have incurred from you. For what can be more pleasant than to be rebuked, when the rebuke itself is the greatest expression of kindness and service, only to chastise me and fall the more sensibly upon me." Fudging masterfully, Mather said that "the tribes of New England are now generally conspiring in their wishes to see Your Honour brought back in the highest capacity of usefulness unto them,"—leaving Dudley to decide whether "generally conspiring in their wishes" meant "wish" and whether "highest capacity of usefulness" meant the governorship, and in effect telling him he was both wanted and not wanted. Just the same, having suffered under Andros and Bellomont and having had before him the prospect of the murderous Kirke, Mather acknowledged Dudley's basic argument that unless he were appointed a worse governor might be. He told Dudley that he and his father had often declared that if Dudley were returned he would serve the mutual interest of the crown and of New England "beyond what could be expected from any other person."

Like his defense of the Salem judges, Mather's endorsement of Dudley, however it insinuated his displeasure, remained an endorsement. Apart from its pragmatic recognition of the realities of imperial politics, it probably reflected his and his father's hope that Dudley's avowals of personal change were sincere, and their sense that his return was probable, so his goodwill worth cultivating. They also had a common enemy with Dudley in Elisha Cooke, who as an adamant supporter of the old charter opposed Increase Mather and Dudley both. The Mathers' support for Dudley incensed the still battling Sir Henry Ashurst. He described to Increase his audience before the king and Council, himself on one side, the hated Dudley on the other. The king had been unwilling to appoint Dudley, Ashurst said, believing the people disliked him; but Dudley produced and read a letter from Cotton Mather (perhaps the one discussed above), as evidence that all the ministers in the land, and the whole Assembly, were "impatient for his coming." By one account, Ashurst accused Cotton Mather of betrayal, claiming he once described Dudley to him as "the cause of the Evil that has come upon this Country" and now calls him "the fittest person to be our Governour." When Ashurst demanded to know the reason for Mather's conversion, according to this account, Mather pronounced him a "madman" and denied having written anything against Dudley in seven years.

However recent or tactical, Mather's conversion was premature, as Dudley's arrival in Boston intimated. Memories of Dudley's conduct under Andros made a cordial welcome uncertain; some people said publicly they would oppose his landing. Still, convoyed by two armed vessels, Dudley reached Scarlett's Wharf on June 11, 1702, saluted by cannons from ships in port, Castle William in the harbor, and forts in town. Samuel Sewall, always adept at reading character out of attire, noticed disapprovingly that he arrived wearing "a very large Wig." Dudley was accompanied, too, by an elderly minister, George Keith, who he explained had been sent to America by the Bishop of London. After being congratulated in the name of the Council, Dudley was escorted by a large entourage of troops and prominent gentlemen from waterside to the Court chamber in the Town House, where before the court, the ministers, and as many others as could crowd in, his commission as governor was read. Then Increase Mather, Sewall recorded, "crav'd a Blessing" and Cotton Mather "Return'd Thanks." Dudley in taking his oath laid his hand on and kissed the Bible, contrary to Puritan custom. When he addressed the representatives in the chamber he made no apology for his career under Andros, nor did he try to conciliate the men who had imprisoned him in 1689. He departed for Roxbury in a coach drawn, Sewall added, by six horses "richly harnessed."

Five days later Cotton Mather was afforded another spectacle, this of his own gullibility. When Dudley visited him on June 16, he advised the new governor to adopt a bipartisan policy amid the various squabbling local factions. Ever the peacemaker, he offered his opinion that Dudley would be wise to treat the different parties—"if in our case, I may use so Coarse a Word as Parties"—evenhandedly, including himself and his father. In this connection he mentioned Nathaniel Byfield, a longtime member of the Executive Council, and Byfield's father-in-law, John Leverett, the Speaker of the House. Dudley should act, he recommended, so that no one could say "*you take all your Measures from the two Mr. Mathers*" or by the same token that "*you go by no Measures in your Conduct, but Mr.* Byfield's, *and* Mr. Leverett's." He gave this advice, he explained, not from prejudice against the two men but as a service to Dudley, considering that in their attitude toward the new government the people already stood divided. The value Dudley attached to Mather's advice became known to him quickly. "The Wretch," he groaned, "went unto those Men, and told them, that I had advised him, to be no ways advised by them: and inflamed them into an implacable Rage against me."

*

Dudley proved divisive, and largely unpopular, from the day he landed. Far from heeding Mather's bipartisan advice, he granted office only to his own supporters, and favored a narrow group composed of Anglicans, overseas merchants dependent on their British connections, and religious liberals such as Brattle, Leverett, and Colman.

From the beginning and repeatedly over the next few years, Dudley clashed with the House of Representatives. He fought them over his salary, over some pressing issues of defense, and over their choices for Speaker and for members of the governor's Council. His instructions from Queen Anne requiring him to see that the Council was "well affected" to the crown, he tried to purge it of diehard defenders of the old charter, men presumably tainted by antimonarchical sentiment. He vetoed five councillors chosen by the House in the 1703 elections, all supporters of the old charter, including Elisha Cooke. Cooke and another of the five were elected again the following year, and again Dudley vetoed the choice, and vetoed Cooke again a third time in 1706. Loftily he explained to the House that in choosing councillors they had passed over men of ability and station who were disposed to serve the crown, for others less qualified and in some cases of "little or mean estate." Cooke in fact was allied to the best families in Massachusetts and had a greater estate than Dudley; but in England he had zealously prosecuted complaints against Dudley and Andros. To some, the real irritant between Dudley and the House seemed to be the unhealable wounds of 1689. One contemporary wrote in 1703 that Dudley "hath given several instances of his remembering the old quarrel, and they [the House] resolve on their parts never to forget it; so that it is generally believed he will never gain any point from them."

Dudley offended others by his favor to the Church of England. Mather's ecumenical vision of Episcopalians joining Congregationalists at communion never included High Churchmen, whom he counted as virtual papists. But Dudley's governorship paralleled the reign of Queen Anne, whose tone—by contrast with that of the deceased Calvinistic King William—was High Church. George Keith, the Quaker-turned-Anglican minister who had accompanied Dudley, published soon after his arrival in Boston a sermon listing six rules which would bring Dissenters into the Church of England. The Church of England chapel, surviving but seemingly quiescent since the time of Andros, flourished under Dudley. The governor headed a petition in 1703 to the Archbishop of Canterbury asking assistance in erecting a new building; a decade later the congregation numbered about eight hundred persons and the chapel had been doubled in size by the addition.

Dudley's patronage encouraged others to extend the Church's influence in New England. The ministers of King's Chapel set about trying to open other Church of England chapels in neighboring towns, and the Anglican Society for the Propagation of the Gospel relayed to Dudley in 1705 the idea of enticing Harvard students to take holy orders in England and work for the SPG. Members of King's Chapel repaid Dudley for his support by countering complaints against his administration that reached London. In 1706 they addressed the Lord Bishop of London (a member of the queen's Privy Council) testifying to the success of his leadership and promising that his continuance in government would be "most Acceptable to all her Majesty's Good Subjects, Merchants and Planters, that have their Dependance on the Government of England as well as the Church here."

Quid pro quo was not only the reward for Dudley's support of the Church but clearly also one of the motives. For all his polish, warmth, and other attractive personal qualities, Dudley had his fortune to make in the world, as Edward Randolph said, and his politics could be whorish. Much of his favor to the Church amounted to obeisance to people of possible influence. George Keith returned to England after only about a year in Boston, complaining that Dudley after inviting him along on the crossing took not the least notice of him from the day he left England. Dudley's support for the chapel seems to have been ideological and personal as well as political, part of his dedication to the imperial ideal of an English colonial administrator, of a piece with his profuse wig and large outlays for food, his wish to marry his children into prominent families, his permitting public celebrations of coronation day or the queen's birthday even when they fell on the Sabbath. "Let us," he told the Council, "be English-men."

At first the Mathers treated Dudley characteristically, Increase direct, Cotton ambiguously indirect. Increase, dismayed that Dudley nominated "very ungodly men to be in place of power," bluntly and publicly told him that he believed the governor still brooded over his earlier imprisonment in Boston and still sought revenge. He dedicated to Dudley a sermon on *The Excellency of a Publick Spirit* (1702), in which he asked leave "to speak freely to you," and advised him to put memories of his jailing behind: "In some Remarkables you have been like *Joseph.* Let me pray you to imitate *Joseph,* not only in Seeking the good of those under your Government, as He did; but in a perfect forgetting whatever may have seemed grievous unto you." He also warned Dudley away from the "wicked men that solicited to have our *former Charter* taken from us," and, calling attention to his alleged Anglicanism, reminded him that people still spoke of his honored father, the former governor, as "*one that loved the true Christian Religion, and the pure Worship of God.*" When opposition to Dudley later mounted, Increase told him to his face that in his position "I would sooner go 3000 miles than continue to be a governour." Increase also took on George Keith in a pamphlet war and, with Cotton, preached and prayed publicly against attempts to open other Anglican churches outside Boston.

By contrast, Cotton Mather approached Dudley sounding complex harmonies of respect for his family, scorn for his untrustworthiness, gratitude for his treatment of the old-charter faction and, above all, recognition of his power and its usefulness to the ministry. In the sermon he preached to the General Assembly two weeks after Dudley's arrival he neither reproached the governor nor flattered him; with Dudley present, and the occasion demanding a panegyric, he described an ideally good man without mentioning him. In emphasizing that a good man governs his resentments and forgives his enemies, however, he drew a pattern of vengefulness to which Dudley could fit himself if he chose:

> There are men of an implacable and inveterate *Malice;* If once they appre-hend that another man has, it may be, stood in the way of their little Interests, they will pursue that man, with an immortal *Malice* and *Venom;* They will never be Reconciled unto one, whom they imagine to have some way or other Lessen'd them; No, but watch all occasions to vent their Spite against him, though they should go contrary even to themselves in doing it.

Actually the Mathers' and others' fear of Dudley's vengefulness was prob-ably misjudged, and in Cotton's case probably intensified by projection. The nineteenth-century historian John Gorham Palfrey was closer to the truth in seeing Dudley as an adroit politician who had "schooled himself to humiliations," and understood too well the conditions of success to seek to satisfy his pride at the expense of his effectiveness.

Mather and Dudley managed to acknowledge both their mutual dis-like and their mutual recognition of each other's usefulness by keeping their contacts politely tart. The flavor can be sampled in two letters Dud-ley sent Mather around 1706. Mather evidently gave him part of "Biblia Americana," hoping Dudley might use his influence abroad to have the work published. In reply Dudley sent an amiable and pious letter pervad-ed by mocking self-assurance, at once respectful and cutting. In telling Mather that he profited greatly from men of learning, for instance, he rebuked his halfhearted support: "if such men knew the value I have for their Conversation and the benefit I have by it, They would give it me more." In return for the perusal of "Biblia Americana" he offered, outra-geously, corrections of its biblical learning, explaining that "If I should not offer at these two or three [trifles?], you would not believe I had read it." In language rivaling in fuzziness Mather's own pseudo-assurances to him, he described the mountainously rising "Biblia" as "an Elaborate work, which I should be glad to see made public"—leaving Mather to decide whether "elaborate" meant "good," whether "I should be glad" meant "I will help," and whether "made public" meant "published."

While playing now-you-see-it-now-you-don't with Dudley personally and publicly, privately Mather dubbed him "a *fop* in *boots*" and worked to overthrow him. Efforts to remove Dudley began virtually as he stepped ashore; a month after his arrival, rumors circulated of a plot to assassinate him. New Englanders complained continually to London of the gover-nor's hot temper, violations of the charter, packing of courts, attempts to secure offices for his son. Sir Henry Ashurst, having tirelessly fought Dudley's appointment, just as tirelessly spent money and sought allies to remove him.

Mather's main choice to replace Dudley was Sir Charles Hobby—a choice no less pragmatic than his initial endorsement of Dudley, since Hobby's morals were considered loose and he belonged to the Church of England. But Mather believed that Hobby treated Nonconformists respectfully and seems to have felt he might wean him to Congregationalism. In November 1703, he sent a florid letter to the parliamentary leader Lord Nottingham, recommending Hobby as governor because "the gentleman who is our present governor has rendered himself so universally unacceptable that there is a likelihood of his removal." As governor, Mather urged, Hobby would not cut himself off from other branches of government, as Dudley had done, by so "trampling on them, as to render them intractable." His efforts to promote Hobby, however, were tempered by fears of enraging Dudley. When in 1704 he saw a possibility for getting Hobby the governorship by piling up complaints against Dudley in London, he advised Hobby against making the complaints lest they "unhinge" Dudley. Mather's hopes for Hobby were thus aroused and then thwarted repeatedly. In January 1706 he looked forward to Hobby's appointment by May, but May brought news that just when Hobby was to receive his commission Dudley's official life became "wondrously revived" by the arrival of five thousand pounds of Portuguese gold, "with advantageous representations."

This hint of bribery foreshadows Mather's eventual break with Dudley, which resulted in part from the governor's conduct of Queen Anne's War. Dudley's appointment coincided with the outbreak of over a decade of fighting between England and the combined French and Indians in America—one theater in a far larger struggle between the France of Louis XIV and a coalition of England, Austria, Prussia, and several minor states. For Bostonians the war meant French privateers capturing vessels almost in sight of the town and recurrent frightening rumors of a massive French invasion of New England. The war also brought Indian attacks on outlying towns and villages, such as the 1704 nightime raid on Deerfield, when fifty French soldiers and two-hundred Indians killed fifty of the three-hundred inhabitants and carried off more than a hundred, including the Rev. John Williams and his wife, Eunice, Cotton Mather's cousin, who remained with her captors and married into the tribe. It meant, too, a further threat to the loosening moral atmosphere by the presence in Boston of English and American sailors, increased numbers of poor, the depletion of the Massachusetts treasury at the rate of about thirty thousand pounds a year, and the making of many private fortunes through wartime commerce.

Mather preached and published much on the attendant social and economic problems. In *The Souldier Told What He Shall Do* (1707) and *Frontiers Well-Defended* (1707) he animadverted against prostitution, gambling, and other "VICES OF THE CAMP" and provided an anti-Catholic catechism for use in frontier communities who might be exposed to French papists. Some of Mather's beliefs could only encourage economic individualism, for instance that social distinctions were ordained by Providence and that wealth might be used for pious ends. Yet in his preaching he always tried to Christianize the marketplace, and now he fervently denounced cutthroat or questionable business practices. In such wartime sermons as *Lex Mercatoria. Or, the Just Rules of Commerce Declared* (1705) he blasted as "detestable *Hobbianism*" the "General *Scramble*" of unbridled economic exploitation, of men reverting as if in a state of nature to "*Sharks,* that are all for themselves, and that would gladly make *Minims and Morsels* of all mankind beside themselves."

That Dudley's handling of the war gave his enemies a noisy issue against him was ironic, for the need of wartime unity reduced factional struggle in Boston, and whatever his other limitations, Dudley made an effective wartime governor. Patriotically dedicated to eliminating the menace of France, and much experienced in Indian affairs, he tried vigorously to raise troops, introduced the use of snowshoes (enabling scouting parties to operate in winter), and strengthened fortifications in Boston Harbor, a labor involving hundreds of tradesmen, artisans, soldiers, and slaves in digging trenches and building a blockhouse and powderhouse.

Nevertheless, in the early summer of 1706, some men employed by Dudley to effect a prisoner exchange with the French were said to have been trading with them, including Dudley's friend Captain Samuel Vetch. Allegations of this illegal trade with a despised enemy, Mather wrote, "raised a mighty Flame among the People." Those accused were stiffly fined by the General Court, despite doubts over whether the crime, committed if at all in Nova Scotia, came under the jurisdiction of a Massachusetts court. More fateful, Dudley himself was accused of allowing and perhaps profiting from the trade. In June 1707, twenty New Englanders, headed by the respected Salem merchant Nathaniel Higginson, petitioned the queen to remove Dudley from office for having "countenanced a private trade and correspondence with the French of Canada and the Indians in their interest, and furnished them with ammunitions and provisions."

Mather and Sir William Ashurst seem now to have joined in a major attack on Dudley, a forty-six-page pamphlet entitled *A Memorial of the Present Deplorable State of New-England . . . by the Male-Administration of their Present Governour* (1707). Probably written and compiled by Mather and published in London by Ashurst, the work appeared anonymously and under a Boston imprint. Despite his pleas to Dudley to forget the past, Mather began by rehearsing charges of twenty years ago, that under Andros Dudley had given offices to cronies, silenced opponents by threatening to seize their estates, called New Englanders slaves. Then Mather brought a plethora of new charges against Dudley, supported by many letters and affidavits: that Dudley sold public offices; extorted letters of support for his administration; accepted bribes to grant tavern licenses; raised three times as much money to prosecute the war as was needed; hushed up the discovery of bullets, bought in Massachusetts, found concealed among peas in a French ship; and, most damaging, that he "countenanced" the sale of gunshot and other supplies to the French and Indians by his son William and his friend Vetch, under cover of redeeming captives. One letter Mather included drew on the old mentality of invasion, making Dudley seem not just corrupt but sinister. The writer gave his belief that Dudley was deliberately leading on the French and Indians to destroy all they could, thereby to put New England "to such vast Charges, as will Ruin the whole Government, by Killing some and Impoverishing the rest." The *Memorial's* many charges and attestations in effect build a case against Dudley for high treason.

Copies of Mather's pamphlet and of the petition to the queen did not reach Boston until late October or November, by which time Dudley had become the target of new charges. He had proposed to the General Court in March an expedition against Port Royal, in French Acadia. Mather, entirely sharing Dudley's hatred of the Sun King's France, enthusiastically approved the assault, which was accompanied, he wrote, by "as great an army of prayers to Heaven as we had employed on any occasion." Dudley mustered fifteen transports and eight sloops, defended by guard ships. The large fleet anchored off Port Royal near the end of May, but found itself barricaded by thick woods and marshes from the fort, whose strength had been underestimated. Instead of besieging the fort the expedition turned aside and attacked nearby French settlements, burning houses, drowning corn, destroying cattle and sheep. The utter failure to attempt the fort produced uproar in Boston. Officers returning from the expedition were met at Scarlett's Wharf by several women, who gave them large wooden swords, calling to each other, "Is your piss-pot charg'd, neighbor? So-ho, souse the cowards. Salute Port Royal." A drove of jeering children and servants followed the soldiers to the Town House, and by afternoon hundreds of boys with wooden swords and daggers or old gunstocks were marching through town crying "Port Royal! Port Royal!" to drumbeat. The debacle inspired new rumors about Dudley, this time that he had tried to restrain the expedition, hoping to preserve the fort for more lucratively treacherous trade with the French.

The new accusations put Dudley in no mood to act the forgiving Joseph when copies of the anonymous *Memorial* and of the petition reached Boston. Whether he attributed the pamphlet to Mather is unknown, but enraged in any case, he sent off for publication a counterpamphlet in his defense. He also demanded a vote from the Council clearing him of charges in the petition. Here his determination and his canniness at infighting triumphed. Samuel Sewall, a member of the Council, asked that the question of the petition be delayed until after the Sabbath, but Dudley wanted action. He ordered the Council secretary to draw up a vote, which was rushed through and sent to the House for confirmation. The House delayed, however, until Dudley himself assured it that the Council had unanimously voted to vindicate him—which "gall'd me," Sewall wrote, "yet I knew not how to contradict him before the Houses." According to Sewall, Dudley read before a House conference extracts of "many" letters by Cotton Mather—letters dated later than the *Memorial* but "giving him a high character." The House too cleared Dudley by voting that the charge against him of trading or allowing a trade with the French and Indians was a "scandalous and wicked accusation." To clinch Dudley's case, one subscriber to the petition to the queen, being brought before the Council, said he knew nothing of the truth of the charges, had signed "under provocation," and was sorry for what he had done.

Dudley's remarkable comeback left Mather sputtering in private. "Everything," he wrote, "is betrayed." The governor's official vindication he saw as a case of the best lacking all conviction and the worst being full of passionate intensity: indecisive opposition and delays in the House, "voting, and unvoting, in the same day, and at last the squirrels perpetually running into the mouth open for them," attempts to "blanch Ethiopians and blacken honest men," the "castration of all common honesty." Dudley's vindication, he told a correspondent, represented a debasement of civic morality: "Bribery, a crime capital among the Pagans, is already a peccadillo among us." If the climate of Dudley's administration continued, there would soon be "not so much as a shadow of justice left in the country."

The justness of Mather's indignation is debatable. Dudley's scrupulous biographer, Everett Kimball, argues that the accusations against him rested on doubtful rumor and malicious suspicion, and that the House probably voted his innocence because they had no evidence of his complicity. Yet Samuel Sewall came to believe that Dudley at least knew of illegal trading and, resentful as well of Dudley's steamrollering, he publicly withdrew his vote of vindication on the Council. Suspicions of bribery, also, hung continually over Dudley, who undoubtedly understood well-placed money. Once when someone remarked in Council that no man in England was made a captain without giving the Duke or Duchess of Marlborough five hundred guineas, Dudley observed that "there had not been any admitted these thousand years but in a way like that." Hints of securing places for friends and squeezing money from New England also appear in letters to Dudley from others during his governorship. His friend at the Royal Society, John Chamberlayne, for instance, suggested to him that "a little provender from New England will make my horses look plumper and slicker . . . and your land Sr., I hear, is famous both for oats and hay!" Dudley, he said, "is so great an husbandman and knows so well how to cultivate the most barren and ungratefull grounds, that next harvest you will not only have a crop sufficient to supply your own occasions, but even to export to the most remote and distant regions."

Dudley did send Chamberlayne what may have been some "provender"—gifts of precious and costly walnut, for making into cabinets. At the least, Dudley's long experience in colonial administration made him aware of the perquisites a governor might enjoy, and his genuine devotion to the crown entailed a sense of station that required concern for his and his family's comfort.

*

In the added uproar of one further fracas, Mather's wary restraint toward Dudley at last cracked. He and his father both realized that Dudley's connections could be helpful in securing from London a permanent charter for Harvard, without which the school could not give the doctorate degree, and the legitimacy of its B.A. and M.A. was questionable. The hope of obtaining a charter was very likely one of his strongest motives for avoiding a break with the governor. But on October 28, a few days before the Council met to vindicate Dudley, the Harvard Fellows chose as their new president Dudley's own candidate, John Leverett. The choice virtually ended Mather's influence at the college. It had declined anyway because the temporary president, Samuel Willard, was Dudley's brother-in-law, and because since his father's ouster he had absented himself from meetings of the Harvard Corporation and was regarded as having abdicated his place, which the Corporation filled.

But the man Dudley supported as president and helped elect was in Mather's mind close to the worst possible choice. John Leverett was the grandson of a governor of Massachusetts, and at one time or other had occupied nearly every important public office short of the governorship. But as he was also a lawyer by profession and, at the least, an Anglican sympathizer, Mather considered him unqualified and potentially danger-ous. It was preposterous, he said, "to make a Lawyer, and one who never affected the study of Divinity, a president for a College of Divines," and given Leverett's religious leanings, it would be less hypocritical for the college to be "directly Voted in the hands of the Bishop of London." He saw Leverett's election as an overt effort "to betray the College, and to destroy all the Churches of New England."

In behalf of Leverett's credentials it could be said that he had studied law rather for public service than personal profit, had served as a Harvard tutor for a dozen years, and that although never ordained he read divinity and could preach. As for his menace to the Congregational identity of Harvard, Leverett himself dismissed the charge as a scare, an attempt to "put every body into Terrour that I have led the voyaging Israelites back to Egypt." Some recent scholars have agreed, seeing Leverett as at most a religious liberal on the model of Benjamin Colman or as a complex man not very different from Mather himself in remaining doctrinally orthodox but magnifying Reason and moving toward the idea of a benevolent deity.

Yet Mather's view of Leverett as basically an Anglican was shared by many contemporaries, including Leverett's supporters. The Massachusetts agent Henry Newman had been a pupil at Harvard under Leverett, and wrote approvingly that while Increase Mather as president thundered against all who went over to the Church of England, tutors Leverett and Brattle dared to recommend the reading of Anglican writers and "made more Proselytes to the Church of England than any two men ever did that liv'd in America." As president, Leverett stayed closely in touch with the Anglican Society for the Propagation of the Gospel, which hoped to re-cruit potential Anglican ministers from New England youths at Harvard. Sir Henry Ashurst, a benefactor of Harvard, became unwilling to support the New England schools because under Leverett, he said, Harvard was "bringing up a strange generation," and because Dudley was using the president to "defeat the religious designs of founders and benefactors." Mather's vision of a Harvard supervised by the Bishop of London was exaggerated but not irrational.

In one of the several deft political maneuvers of his administration, Dudley while pushing through his own vindication by the House also forwarded Leverett to the presidency. Probably at Dudley's instigation, thirty-nine ministers signed an address recalling that it was under Leverett as their tutor that most of the "now Rising Ministry in New England were happily Educated," and affirming that no one else would be so acceptable to them as president. With two exceptions, however, all the ministers who signed came from towns outside Boston. Mather scoffed at this "Sham-recommendation" as having been concocted in the "most fallacious and fraudulent manner, that ever was heard of." It misrepresented the Corporation's choice of Leverett as unanimous when in fact only seven or eight members voted for him, he said, and Dudley's "Tools" used lying insinuations to collect the signatures.

However Dudley obtained the testimonial, he presented it to the Council on November 11, amidst his own struggle for vindication, and on January 14 met with the Council again, in the College library, to install Leverett as president. Taking Leverett by the hand, Dudley led him into the College Hall, where he ceremonially transferred to him the College seal, keys, and records. With a "Noble Fire" lighted and before an audience including Colman, Sewall, and ministers from six neighboring towns, the erudite governor delivered a Latin address, observing that Leverett's appointment had been approved by the ministry, hoping that an again flourishing Harvard would benefit New England, and promising that the new president could depend on the government for patronage and counsel.

For Mather, who of course did not attend, the ceremony could have seemed only a grisly parody of his hoped-for cooperation between Moses and Aaron. Coming atop Dudley's resilient recovery from accusations of treason, it ended Mather's six-year dalliance with the governor and unfettered his much guarded tongue. Both Mathers joined the attack. A week after Leverett's inauguration, Increase sent Dudley a long letter charging him, among other things, with the failure of the College to obtain a charter. This time Cotton outdid his father in frankness. The same day he sent Dudley a letter over twice as long, some seven full pages in modern printed editions. Coming from him, this essay-length malediction was unprecedented, for in his writings and from his pulpit he had always preached obedience to rulers. Indeed, except under Andros, probably no other minister in the history of New England spoke as vehemently against a governor as Mather did now. Aware of this himself, he began by explaining that he had always offered his earlier reproaches in "the language of the tribe of Napthali," pastorally counseling Dudley rather than reviling him. But he had learned the futility of applying to him "modes of addressing used among persons of the most polite education." Now he felt compelled to speak in a manner befitting rather "an ignorant mob."

It was his own letter, read to King William, Mather began, which helped deliver Dudley the governorship—a letter sent in the belief that Dudley repented his "wicked and horrid things," a letter sent despite the "venoms" Dudley streamed against him following the 1689 revolt, a letter that earned him nothing but "extreme displeasure in the country." And it was his duty to tell Dudley wherein he had not pleased the Lord: "Sir, your snare has been that thing, the hatred whereof is most expressly required of the ruler, namely *covetousness.*" The many ways in which Dudley's administration declared his "disposition to make haste to be rich" he would now specify. There was, he said, bribery, in which Dudley's son joined; there was, many believed, his countenancing "unlawful trade with the enemies"; there was the sham vindication by a House which voted several times over to "generally declare that they could not clear you from that unlawful trade."

And there was, more recently, the fort at Port Royal—an easy capture but that Dudley "absolutely *forbad*" it, "preemptorily *forbad*" it. But here the history of Dudley's covetousness grew "too black" to be pursued, darkened into treason:

> The expedition baffled. The fort never so much as demanded. The forces retreating from the place as if they were afraid of its being surrendered. . . . And all possible care taken that after all, *nobody shall be to blame!* I dare not, I cannot meddle with these mysteries. . . . All I say is, the country is ruined, and the premises declare whose conduct very much of the ruin is owing to.

And there was also, Mather did not forget, the governor's abuse of him. Dudley intercepted and distributed his correspondence, told lies about him in public, affronted people for no other reason than their living in his part of town. By his covetous deceit, plotting, and manipulation the governor had brought himself on ill terms with heaven and for the sake of his soul must reconcile himself with the Divine Majesty before the coming Judgment, when the Lord would demand to know how far he had aimed in his government at serving Him. In concluding, Mather called up his former ambidexter politeness with Dudley, but raised to a key of gracious bitchiness: "if the troubles you brought on yourself should procure your abdication and recess unto a more private condition, and your present parasites forsake you, as you may be sure they will, I should think it my duty to do you all the good offices imaginable."

Taken aback by Mather's bluntness, Dudley did not reach for spiteful, or any other, courteousness. "Yours of the 20th instant I received," he began his reply, "and the contents, both as to the matter and manner, astonish me to the last degree." In astonishment he was not alone, for Mather's letter created commotion and expectation. Samuel Sewall, to whom Mather lent a copy, waited with concern to see "what the issue of this plain home-dealing will be!"; Dudley's supporter Ebenezer Pemberton, the minister of the South Church, said that if he were governor he would "humble" Mather "though it cost him his head." Dudley tried to do that, reminding Mather of the Christian forbearance appropriate in a minister and the respect due a governor:

> I must think you have extremely forgot your own station, as well as my character; otherwise it had been impossible to have made such an open breach upon all the laws of decency, honour, justice, and christianity, as you have done in treating me with an air of superiority and contempt, which would have been greatly culpable towards a christian of the lowest order, and is insufferably rude towards one whom divine Providence has honoured with the character of your Governour.

As Mather had invoked for Dudley the ghost of Andros, Dudley brought back some specters himself. He said the Mathers based their charges against him on town gossip, that they intended "to withdraw the Queen's liege people from that duty and subjection which the laws of our holy religion do enjoin," and that they had concealed their animosity toward him for twenty years, awaiting a time when "you thought you could serve yourselves by exposing me"—the old case against the Mathers as credulous, antimonarchical, and self-interested. And authoritarian: their rage at him, Dudley said, betrayed their selfish insistence on having their own way—"the college must be disposed against the opinion of all the ministers in New England, except yourselves, or the Governour torn in pieces." While offering to satisfy their complaints if they visited him in a respectful spirit, the governor also laid down the law: "In the mean time, I expect you as subjects to the Queen, as christians, as messengers of the gospel of peace, to lay aside all methods that tend to blow up sedition."

Dudley's stiff personal rebuke to Mather was followed by the governor's public ridicule of him. Sometime later in the year appeared Dudley's earlier-written *Modest Inquiry into the Grounds and Occasions of a Late Pamphlet* (1707), published in London in response to the *Memorial* probably put together by Mather and Ashurst. Dudley countered vigorously the various affidavits they brought against him, for instance retorting that the Boston-made bullets found in the French peas amounted to enough smallshot "to shoot a few sea Fowl." At the same time he castically derided Mather's "*Hereditary Rancour,*" his boasts about his large number of publications, and his opposition to all government, "even though it were *Angelical.*" To show up Mather's "seeming Sanctity" he also dragged into print Kate Maccarty, the young woman who had courted Mather five years earlier, before his remarriage to Elizabeth Hubbard Clark. In Dudley's version of the affair—offered as factual but seemingly an old joke refurbished—Mather frequently called on a local "Gentlewoman of *Gayety.*" Because his visits offended some of his congregation he promised to avoid her, but his "*Vicious* Inclinations" sapped his good intentions. The intrigue went on, Kate and Cotton mutually swearing that "NEITHER OF THEM SHOULD CONFESS THEIR SEEING EACH OTHER." Their clandestine visits, however, again became public news, and this time Mather was accused by his own father, a scene Dudley undertook to reproduce. Cotton, "after two or three HEMS to recover himself," said to Increase: "INDEED, FATHER, IF I SHOULD SAY I DID SEE HER, I SHOULD TELL A GREAT LIE."

Later generations can savor the ironic rightness of this canard—Mather existing in the American imagination as a sort of un–George Washington—but Mather's own reaction is unknown. Some time during the year appeared a forty-eight-page fusillade entitled *The Deplorable State of New-England.* The pamphlet more amply documents earlier charges against Dudley, and implicates Leverett in reducing the charges against the convicted traders; but the range of the barrage also takes in the Council and many of the New England clergy for supporting them both. Mather was suspected of having a hand in writing the pamphlet, earning him the "Malice" not only of Dudley, he said, but of his Council and of the clergy as well. While the other North End ministers sat "feasting with our wicked Governor" in September 1709, he was excluded because, he felt, of his "provoking Plainness and Freedom, in telling this *Ahab* of his wickedness." Banished from the table of the governor, he took his reproofs to the pulpit. A scriptural anecdote he related to his congregation was understood by Samuel Sewall to mean that "not the prophet, but the K[ing] was hurt by his Estrangement." As Sewall also understood, Dudley responded with conspicuous absence: "Dr. Cotton Mather Preaches from those words, That which is Crooked cannot be made Straight. . . . Governor not at Lecture."

*

For Mather, the cost of his exchanges with Dudley was increasing isolation. This itself may explain why many others were now emboldened to attack Mather as well. Their freedom with him, unimaginable thirty years earlier, also sprang from the vast change of mores in his lifetime, occurring too organically to be traced step by step but palpable to members of his generation. In 1688 it was "They" who wanted Martha Goodwin to keep Christmas with them and got her "very drunk"; by 1711, boys and girls in the North Church, without becoming energumens, openly celebrated Christmas with a frolic, a reveling feast, and a ball.

Pranks had often been played on Mather; in 1703 someone threw at his gate a picture of a hanged man with his name over it. But in his growing prominence, in the increasingly permissive social atmosphere, and now with his public chastisement by the government, he became frequently the butt of scurrilous letters, defamatory broadsides, derisive gossip, and even physical threats. To mention only a few in 1711 and 1712: he learned, for instance, that some "Finished Rake" was making it a point in his travels to "load me with his lying Calumnies, wherever he has come." A ship captain, a stranger to him, imagined himself the subject of some reproofs Mather delivered from his pulpit and came to his house drunk about nine at night with a drawn cutlass, swearing he would be "content to lie a year in Hell, if he might have the Satisfaction of killing me." Several times "knots of riotous Young Men" gathered under his window at night to sing "profane and filthy Songs," on one occasion attacking people with clubs taken from his woodpile.

Abuse issued from abroad also. Some Quakers printed in London in 1710 a broadside entitled *A Just Reprehension of Cotton Mather,* accusing him of "*Scribling* against the said People, tho' *Covertly,* as if *ashamed* of his *Work*." John Winthrop came across a "sort of farce or comedy" about him and his father, "pretended to have been acted at the play-house in

London," where it was apparently written and printed. To Mather the most enduringly hurtful of these stabs, by far, came in the historian John Oldmixon's two-volume *The British Empire in America* (London, 1708). In mocking *Magnalia Christi Americana* as resembling a schoolboy's exercise, Oldmixon unknowingly turned his knife in a still livid ulcer, the place Mather probably remained most sensitive, his use of language:

> The *History of New-England* written by *Cotton Mather,* a Man of Fame in his Country, as appears by the barbarous Rhimes before it in Praise of the Author, is a sufficient Proof, that a Man may have read hundreds of Latin Authors, and be qualify'd to construe them, may have spent his Youth in a College, and be bred up in Letters, yet have neither Judgment to know how to make a Discourse perspicuous, nor Eloquence to express his Sentiments so that they may please and persuade. . . .

No other work of history ever published, Oldmixon continued,

> is so confus'd in the Form, so trivial in the Matter, and so faulty in the Expression, so cramm'd with Puns, Anagrams, Acrosticks, Miracles and Prodigies, that it rather resembles School Boys Exercises Forty Years ago, and *Romish* Legends, than the Collections of an Historian bred up in a Protestant Academy.

Throughout his life Mather alluded to these remarks in letters and published works, reviling with the sarcasm of smothered fury "the malicious and satanic pen of one *Oldnixson* (some such name)," whose own history, he added, has "far more lies than pages in it."

Mather of course had many admirers also, and his isolation in Boston was to some degree offset by prestigious recognition abroad—compliments about *Magnalia* from the Anglican Lord Mayor of London, unexpected letters and gifts from Sir Richard Blackmore and other eminent persons he had not met. Most comfortingly of all, in May 1710, the University of Glasgow awarded him a Doctor of Divinity degree, representing the highest scholastic honor attainable. Mather considered this a distinction to be greatly cherished, the "apex and summit of academic dignities." Besides, he esteemed the Church of Scotland for its notably pure worship and outstandingly able ministry, "a Set of Burning and Shining Lights . . . no where to be Equalled on the Face of the Earth." As the first American recipient, moreover, he took special pride in being shown such proofs of international respect as no person in America had won before him, and as news of the award spread he received many letters of congratulation.

Inwardly Mather always sought acclaim, but how deeply in this difficult time he craved it appears in his response, which was both guilty and
effusive. It was "proposed and advised" to him, he said—as if rationaliz-
ing one of his too numerous publications—to wear a ring in token of his
honorary doctorate. Inscribed on the ring were a tree and a quotation
from Psalms 1:3. ("And he shall be like a tree planted by the rivers of the
water"), the whole encircled by the words *GLASCUA RIGAVIT*—Glasgow
waters, or irrigates. To convince himself that he might wear the ring without pridefulness, he drafted more than a page of possible justifications,
for instance that the sight of it would continually prompt him to cry, "*O
make me a very fruitful Tree, and help me to bring forth seasonable Fruit
continually!*" Apparently still unconvinced, several weeks after making a
case for himself he added that if prideful thoughts arose he would quash
them by considering his humiliating circumstances, "and alas, I have
enough of these!"

But however guilty Mather felt, he felt far more grateful. His reply to
the University of Glasgow—a learned, gracious letter promising to prove
himself worthy—was published in Boston as a pamphlet of twelve pages.
Thus began his voluminous, years-long correspondence with members of
the University and of the Church of Scotland. The depth of his appreciation can be gauged by the obligatory character of his earlier letters. He
wrote in August 1713, for instance, that "I have not much material to add
unto my Last, which I wrote three or four Months ago." The reason he
wrote when he had little to say, he explained, was to "just Let you see,
that we can't forget you"—as if the esteem accorded him had to be repaid
every other day. Later, however, Mather settled into an unusually rich
correspondence with divines and academicians in Scotland, sending long
discussions of biblical prophecy or detailed news of missionary work, and
receiving lengthy admiring letters in return. The learned Scottish minister and ecclesiastical historian Robert Wodrow relished his own exchanges of letters with Mather as "one of the greatest satisfactions kind
Providence has allowed me." The correspondence not only demonstrates
Mather's eminence abroad but also marks the beginning of a century-long
and mutually fruitful communion between Scottish and American intel-
lectuals—men drawn together by their sense of shared problems in living
in cultural provinces of the British empire.

However honored abroad, Mather could do little right in Boston at
this time. Detractors jumped on his degree. A man named John Banister
published verses on what he called Mather's "Diploma," hailing him not

as a distinguished fellow citizen but as a verbose megalomaniac:

On C. Mr's. Diploma

> The mad enthusiast, thirsting after fame,
> By endless volum'ns thought to raise a name.
> With undigested trash he throngs the Press;
> Thus striving to be greater, he's the less.

In Banister's account, the degree was not awarded to Mather but whee-
dled by him, to restore his crushed pride after the publisher of *Magnalia,*
Thomas Parkhurst, fed up with Mather's outmoded theology and history,
refused to publish "Biblia Americana": "Parkhurst says, *Satis fecisti,* / My
belly's full of your Magnalia Christi." Thwarted, and envious of the doctorate his father "stole" from Harvard, Mather longed for a doctorate himself, but was repulsed by President John Leverett (the "Keeper" below);
rather than go unhonored, he decided to beg a degree abroad:

> Daz'd with the stol'n title of his Sire,
> To be a Doctor he is all on fire;
> Would after him, the Sacrilege commit
> But that the Keeper's, care doth him affright.
> To Britain's Northern Clime in haste he sends,
> And begs an Independent boon from Presbyterian friends;
> Rather than be without, he'd beg it of the Fiends.
> Facetious George brought him this Libertie
> To write C. Mather first, and then D.D.

The writer and publisher of these verses were brought before Judge Samuel Sewall, who fined them and bound them over to the Sessions Court.
Mather's enemies John Leverett and Ebenezer Pemberton visited Sewall
to protest his action. Leverett reminded him that in their letters the Mathers had treated Governor Dudley "barbarously," and the animated Pemberton began "capering with his feet," Sewall reported, and exclaimed
that if the Mathers ordered it Sewall would shoot him through. The libel
case came before a grand jury, to whom Mather seems to have sent a
message in Banister's defence, but the outcome is unknown.

The question of the respect due Mather for his honorary degree stayed
alive another year, because the Harvard Corporation voted to cite the
degree next to his name in a forthcoming cumulative catalogue of Harvard graduates. Hugely grateful for this recognition also, Mather sent the
Corporation a long florid Latin letter making clear that he prized their
acknowledgment, but characteristically assuring them that, despite his

recognition from Glasgow, Harvard retained its own: "once alumnus, always a son most observant and most obedient." President Leverett, forced to decide whether to insert the title beside Mather's name, asked Dudley about some "dutifull Letters" that, he heard, Mather had recently written the governor; but Dudley was "pleased to assure him" he had received no letters from Mather "since the undutiful One" of 1708. When Leverett learned, however, that Dudley told Pemberton he would not have the title omitted on his account, Leverett "Upon the whole of All Considerations" ordered a "D.D." printed beside Mather's name.

The addition did nothing to restore Mather's influence at Harvard, any more than Dudley's tacit consent restored his place at the governor's table. Since the 1689 revolt, Mather had grown accustomed to having a say in the political affairs of New England; a decade later, the sphere of his influence had shrunk to the North Church. And in the spring of 1712 this began slipping from him also. To deal with some crowding in his church, resulting from a growth in the population of the North End, he apparently allowed the building of some pews, contrary to earlier practice in New England meetinghouses, where people sat on benches. Some members of the North Church—perhaps objecting to the idea of pews, or wanting pews for themselves, or simply feeling crowded—resented the new seating arrangements and, Mather wrote, "made me the object of many Calumnies." There began to be talk of leaving his ministry, D.D. or no, and building a new church. Wary of doing something intemperate that might make things worse, he decided not to oppose the move. But the prospect of losing part of his congregation stunned him, and in the privacy of his diary he excoriated these "Uncivil, Uncourteous, Unthankful, Unhelpful, Disobliging People."

Within a year a fourteen-man committee of the North Church had asked and received permission from the brethren to form a new church. Anticipating that many others might follow this nucleus out, Increase told the swarmers that if they set their meetinghouse at a healthy distance from his own, he would "do all for them that a Father could do for his children." They erected the New North Church about three streets away, provoking him to predict that "a blasting from God will be upon them first or last." How many persons left the Mathers' ministry is unknown, but they made a visible emptiness. To Cotton the congregation seemed in "very diminutive Circumstances," even approaching "something of a Dissolution." He worried not only about the possible design of Satan to destroy the North Church but also about the intensity of his aging father's grief, and cautioned himself to stay calm. As a gesture of amity he preached to the swarmers, on whom his "courteous and candid way" made such an impression that they volunteered to publish the sermon although, he added with suppressed spite, "I were hardly six minutes preparing it"—compared to his normal seven hours.

Publicly forbearing, Mather raged in his diaries against the "Proud Crew, that must have Pews for their despicable Families." Behind scenes he tried to frustrate them. The new congregation desired for its pastor John Barnard, himself a member of the North Church. According to Barnard, the Mathers feared that his selection would entice prominent members of their church to desert them and flock to him. Cotton Mather told him candidly, he wrote: "Mr. Barnard, do you think we could easily bear to have the best men in our house leave us. . . . No, sir, we cannot part with such men as these." Increase Mather, he said, styled him a "*manifesto man*" because of his friendship with Benjamin Colman and blocked his election by persuading five members of the fourteen-man committee not to vote for him. The new minister, John Webb, was chosen by a minority of the committee.

At Webb's ordination in the nearby New North Church, Increase and Cotton Mather nevertheless assisted in the ceremonial laying on of hands, and Cotton Mather offered the ceremonial hand of fellowship—for them a humbling occasion at which Governor Joseph Dudley, not humblingly for him, lent his dignifying presence to the strayed sheep.

8

Bonifacius

❧

"THE MINISTER'S *Tongue,*" said Cotton Mather, "is the chief Instrument of his profession. . . . How extremely difficult is it, for a man that speaks much and often so to govern his Tongue, as to speak nothing amiss." His own tongue had always given him trouble, of course, not only by stuttering. Once after a rumor reached him that Samuel Sewall had criticized his father before the Council, he denounced Sewall so loudly in a Boston bookshop that people could hear him in the street. And now as the many humiliations, snubs, and desertions of Dudley's administration weighed heavily on his fragile self-esteem, they severely tested his impulse, when he felt unappreciated, to snarl. Always defiantly struggling to master his temptation to speak rashly, he now made the governance of the tongue a major topic of his ministry and diaries, while his isolation in Boston emphasized perhaps the most distinctive features of his personality and redirected some of his energies for a decade.

With unrelenting, sometimes ferocious, sternness, Mather admonished himself not to let fly when excluded from the governor's table, or faced with a depleted congregation, or versified as a drone. Impatient with his weakness in suffering slights, he constantly scolded his inability to "preserve that Sedate, and Serene, and Comfortable Frame of Mind which belongs to the *Peace* of God," constantly fretted that "I am too ready to express my Resentment," constantly resolved to "Keep a mighty Guard on my Language, that I may not Speak unadvisedly with my Lips." Preoccupied with his own self-control, he became more condemnatory than ever of angry reviling and gossip in others. For men, even good men, to speak evil of one another was the "special Vice" of Boston, he believed, and he lashed his townspeople with the same hard reproaches he

227

laid on himself: "On your Knees," he commanded in one sermon, "Abhor your selves, Condemn your selves, for the Sin of your *Unruly Tongue*." And again: "beware of *Rash Words* in your *passion. . . . Cursed is the Anger,* for it is raging, it is Hellish." Hellish it would, yet again, be punished in Hell: "O *Tongues, that are set on Fire of Hell. . . .* The *Owners* of such *Tongues . . .* must one Day *gnaw their Tongues* for Anguish, and Cry out, '*Oh! For a drop of Water to cool my Tongue!*' "

In whole works devoted to the problem of temperate speech, such as *Golden Curb for the Mouth* (1707; rpt. 1709), Mather counseled two methods of treating insult. First, conformity to Christ in mortification— becoming invulnerable by becoming nothing: "Be always really, heartily, inwardly *loathing your self;* really esteem others *Wiser* and *Better* than your self; really shun *Honours,* be averse to them, afraid of them; never be uneasy at being *over-looked* by other Men." Second, unrelaxing self-control: "Upon the first *advice* of any *Abuse* offered unto you, resolve . . . *I will keep my Mouth with a Bridle, while I have before me what the unbridled Mouth of Wickedness has uttered of me.*" When abusive letters arrived he received them emotionlessly, adding them to the large tied bundle on which he had written "*Libels: Father, forgive them!*" As in following Elisha Corlet's "Method of Deliberation" he once paused before every syllable, he now scrutinized every word. "I so took heed against Sinning with my Tongue," he noted approvingly in 1712, "that I did not Utter One Word all the Day, (though I Spoke on many occasions,) but what, I think, I may say, I did well to utter it."

In his mighty effort to wall in his outraged sense of rejection, Mather also hit upon one strategy that altered his life and in part determined his particular place in American history. He decided to deal with malice and betrayal by Doing Good. The design of Doing Good, of course, was hardly a novelty in Christianity or in Mather's career. His early notebooks record several sermons on the theme by Boston ministers, including his father; he preached on it himself during his earliest ministry, telling his congregation in one youthful sermon that "We all came into the World upon a very important *Errand,* which *Errand* is, To *Do* and to *get* Good." Indeed, the question "*What Good may I do?*" had been, he recalled in his autobiography, the subject of his daily thoughts "ever since I was a Lad."

Yet Mather's acts of Good beginning around 1710 differed from these earlier preachings and resolves in being specifically prompted by feelings of isolation and disregard. He made it a practice Tuesday mornings of each week, for instance, to single out his personal enemies, "as many of them, as I can know of," and to consider "*what good may I do unto them?*" He applied this method of substituting good for evil to his own thoughts and fantasies as well, promising himself that whenever he perceived the upwelling of some ill thought he would "extinguish it, and contradict it, with forming a good Thought, that shall be directly contrary unto it." Somewhat later he came to see Doing Good as God's reward to well-intentioned men enfeebled by rage. A good man, he wrote,

> if he should happen to be of an *Ill Temper*, the *Grace* of GOD in him overcomes and mortifies this *Ill Temper;* 'Tis a *Burden* to him; and he takes a *Revenge* upon it, by multiplying Acts of *Goodness*, that shall repair the *Errors* into which Base Passions have betray'd him.

This description of an inherently good man betrayed by strong inclinations of which he disapproves, not only conveys the way Mather had come to see himself but also comes near summarizing the man he was.

With incitements to his ill temper multiplying, Mather's effort to contain it became virtually a way of life. He returned to the straining generosity of his adolescence, when because one could "*never do enough*" for one's father he transcribed Increase's manuscripts and gave him a cherished watch, or poured forth novel devotions to God with boundless ingenuity. Now again he would be fertile and inventive, but in Doing Good. "Oh! may we be men always devising of Good!," he exhorted his congregation in 1709, "May our Devices of Services wherein we shall do good be Exquisite, be Numberless! May we be full of that wisdom which will find out well devised Inventions, to do good in the world."

How fully Mather now dedicated himself to this "virtuous *Epicurism in Usefulness*" is registered dramatically in the changed form of his diaries. Previously he had kept a separate daily record of attempts to Do Good, from which he annually culled the most important and transferred them to his diary at the end of the year. But now he resolved that each day of his life he would ask the question, "*What shall I render to the Lord,*" and he would enter the answer in his diary as a "GOOD DEVISED," abbreviated as "G.D." Beginning in 1711, he overhauled the entire format of his diaries, making the heart of each day's entry a "G.D.," some particular, intended act of Good. A five-day sample will illustrate the whole:

> 2. [Second day of the week, in February 1711] G.D. Unto the Sacrifices of the Lord's-Day Evening in my Family, I would often add this; take a Book of Piety, and make each of the capable Children read some short pungent Passage in the hearing of all. . . .
> 3. G.D. I have a little Nephew, for whom I have not hitherto done all

that I have to do, towards his Conversion and Salvation. . . . I will send for him; and bestow on him the little Book of the *Religion of the Morning*. . . .

4. G.D. By a vessel now going for *Carolina,* and thence for *Scotland,* I would send some Instruments of Piety. . . .

5. G.D. One of our *Societies for the Suppression of Disorders,* have thro' I know not what Feebleness, disbanded. I would, by the means of an active Person or two, try to revive it. . . .

6. G.D. An aged and pious Man, fallen into great Penury. . . . I will procure needful Garments for him. . . .

Although Mather continued to memorialize his prayers and fasts, for at least the next several years he wrote far less than before about his inner spiritual struggles and far more about his services in the world. "The grand Intention of my Life is," he declared conclusively in 1713, "*to Do Good.*"

Mather's numberless acts of Good did not escape contamination from the contrary feelings of envy and resentment from which they often arose, a subject to which the end of this chapter will return. Just the same, he was a deeply charitable man, whose keen sympathy for others' distress pervades his many earlier, empathetic accounts of persons captured by Indians, vexed by evil angels, or hounded by ecclesiastical authorities. Outcast himself during Dudley's administration, he grew more and more to identify with other outcasts. "I see no Person miserable," he wrote in 1705, "but my Heart is very sensibly touched with their Miseries, I would, if I could, with all my Heart, help them in their Miseries." The growth in the numbers of poor during Dudley's reign, largely as a result of the long war effort, inspired him also to keep a "Catalogue of the Poor," to visit imprisoned debtors, send money to indigent persons in neighboring towns, provide books for impoverished ministerial candidates or clothing for a poor Indian and his wife. His humane concern was well enough known so that when the Boston selectmen ordered a town meeting in 1710 to take up the question of poor relief, they specifically desired his presence. His whole life substantiates his later statement to his son that his ability to write in seven languages, his pleasure in feasting on "the Sweets of all the *Sciences,*" his enjoyment of history ancient and modern—none of this afforded him as much delight "as it does, to Relieve the Distresses of any one Poor, Mean, and *Miserable Neighbour.*"

Mather's program for Doing Good gained confidence and direction from his reading of the German Pietists, one of the most pervasive spiritual and intellectual influences on his adult life. Their names begin appearing in his diaries in late 1709, as he also begins mentioning "the *Devices of Good* which I form and write in the Morning." He shared the Pietists' concern that the Reformation of the sixteenth century had reformed doctrine without reforming society. To complete this partial Reformation the Pietists hoped to abolish slavery, refine social justice, ameliorate the condition of the poor, and curb exploitative business practices in the emerging commercial state. Mather admired much else in German Pietism as well: its emphasis on pastoral work and involvement in community life, its far-flung missionary work, perhaps especially its ecumenical attempt to reduce dogma to essentials. Elements of these of course existed in Mather's religion already, and there had been much earlier interchange between German Pietists and English Puritans.

Some more personal sources of Mather's attraction to the Pietists at this time are implied in his admiration for John Arndt, often considered the founder of Pietism. The true Christian described in his *True Christianity* (*De Vero Christianismo,* London, 1708)—a work Mather praised for bringing "Millions of Souls into the Life of GOD"— was someone Mather wished and felt compelled to become, combining profound ethical concern with self-denying Christ-mysticism. For Arndt, true faith fructifies into good works organically, by its inward impulse and nature. In language Mather well understood, the Preface to the English edition of *True Christianity* describes good works as *"fruits of the Spirit, rivers of living water;* because they are brought forth by a believer as *freely* as a good tree yields its fruits, and a plentiful fountain its water. The true christian is constantly employed about doing good, and laying out what he has received." Mather understood equally well Arndt's complementary stress on benign deadness to the world, "heroic meekness." Having tasted true love, Arndt wrote, the true Christian is gentle, courteous, and patient, "not apt to conceive any bitterness, much less to utter it by cursing and railing speeches, which even unman a man; but to imitate Christ Jesus, who did not cry out, or so much as open his mouth against the wrath of his crucifiers, but spake from the cross mere benediction and life."

One other side of Pietism that deeply appealed to Mather was the spiritual entrepreneurship of its organizer, "the incomparable Dr. Franckius." Just Mather's age, August Hermann Francke served for thirty-six years as both a minister and a professor of Greek and Oriental languages at the University of Halle, the most famous theological center in Europe in its time. With something of Mather's own zealous ingenuity, Francke erected at Halle an exemplary educational-philanthropic community, devoted not to transmitting information but to creating ideal Christian adults—persons who would be pious, well-mannered, honorable in business, and sensitive to human needs. Mather found the size, boldness, and success of Francke's enterprise dazzling, and initiated a fifteen-year correspondence with him in Germany. Around March 1711, he sent Francke a long adulatory Latin letter declaring that Francke's piety had crossed the Atlantic and "inflamed the same piety in American churches." As proof he enclosed some of his own sermons which he said reflected Francke's ideals, plus a donation for Francke's school and an appeal for his friendship. Francke responded, magnificently, with a Latin letter seventy pages long—a further demonstration to Mather that he was better appreciated abroad than at home.

Mather publicized Francke's remarkable institution in his own *Nuncia Bona* (1715), largely based on Francke's own account of it to him. Seeing in Francke much of himself, he depicted the German as erudite and pious, but above all a man of "peerless *Industry,*" the inventor and overseer of more vast projects in thirty years than a succession of equally capable men could have completed in a century and a half. Emphasizing the numbers and the scale, he described with wonder the components of Francke's benevolent utopia: the sixteen-hundred-scholar German school; the Latin, Greek, and Hebrew school where "Vast numbers" of poor children received free tuition; the Tynaecium for young gentlewomen and the Cherotrophea for poor widows; the printing presses that dispatched pious books as far off as Siberia and in a few years issued more editions of the Bible—some in modern Slavonic and other lesser tongues—"than in the whole Period of the Time, from the *Reformation* until *Now,*" and never before so cheaply; especially the five-hundred-student *Orphano-Tropheum* or orphan house, with its huge auditorium and dining room, and its *Officina Pharmaceutica,* where "the noblest Remedies upon Earth are known"—and many and much more. In sum, Mather depicted Francke as a seminal force in modern Christianity: "The Vast Number of Souls brought Home to God and made Instances of *Serious Piety!*—the Vast Number of *Instruments* qualified here to do good abroad in the World! More than all *Europe* will soon feel, yea, has already felt the precious Effects of the *Franckian* Education."

The impact of Arndt's self-abnegating charity and of Francke's imaginative enterprise marks several other works by Mather at this time, such as *The Heavenly Conversation* (1710; an essay in "AMERICAN PIETISM") and *Orphanotrophium* (1711), but especially *Bonifacius* (1710), one of his major writings and a representative product of American culture. First published in Boston as a book of just over two hundred pages, it was quoted by the Pietists themselves and, remaining popular into the nineteenth century, appeared in more than fifteen later editions. Although Franckean ideas are here tempered by Mather's elitism and indignation, the work exudes enthusiasm for the vast opportunities of Doing Good. The world, Mather notes with Franckean zest, now contains by some computations more than seven hundred million people—"an ample field among all these, to *do good* upon!" These large numbers need three essential kinds of good:

> There needs abundance to be done, that the great GOD and His CHRIST may be more known and served in the world. . . . There needs abundance to be done, that the *evil manners* of the world, by which men are *drowned in perdition,* may be reformed. . . . There needs abundance to be done, that the *miseries* of the world may have *remedies* and *abatements* provided for them; and that miserable people may be relieved and comforted.

The Good Mather intends, that is, consists of spreading the Reformation, correcting provoking evils, and relieving those in need.

Mather offered his suggestions for doing these three sorts of Good in chapters addressed to individual social groups, such as ministers, physicians, and rich men. To spread Christ and reform manners, for instance, he recommended that ministers distribute books of piety, that the wealthy devote a tithe of their income to pious purposes, and that neighbors exhort prayerless families among them. But he more prominently emphasized relieving the poor and miserable: he advised, for instance, that the wealthy provide scholarships for orphans and that lawyers undertake *pro bono* work to help the poor and needy. His concern in the book often extends beyond such immediate objects of relief to the long-range welfare of humanity, in terms already touched by Enlightenment ideals of progress. In addressing physicians, for instance, he urged them not to rest content with the present state of medicine but rather to read and think much, so as "to *find out,* and *give out,* something very considerable for the *good of mankind."* Presciently, he also suggested that physical ills may be related to emotional distress, and advised physicians to treat the patient's "*interior state*" as well as body. Citing the Italian physician Georgi Baglivi, he recommended that physicians experiment with "*the art of curing by consolation,"* using artful conversation to discover "what matter of anxiety, there may have been upon the mind of his *patient,"* and then using "all the ways he can devise to take it off." Mather concluded with a "CATALOGUE OF DESIRABLES" that specifies such large-scale

Franckean Goods to be performed as christianizing heathen places like Malabar and building charity schools.

Among the several facets of its importance, *Bonifacius* is a revealing biographical document. It records a period in Mather's life when he diverted his attention from the supernatural to the civic, from New England to the world, from regeneration to progress. The traits and events that led him in these directions were many: disappointment in his Particular Faiths, admiration for the Pietists, sympathy for the poor and ill, kinship with Enlightenment ideas, encroaching middle age—and isolation in Boston. For Mather in part took up Pietist ideas to outflank Joseph Dudley. *Magnalia,* written only a dozen years earlier, views the history of New England as being embodied in and transmitted through three groups of men: governors, ministers, and presidents of Harvard. But now the governor was a "wretch," the ministers sat feasting at his table, and the Harvard president was an Anglican lawyer. No longer appealing solely to them, *Bonifacius* enlists lesser social authorities and people of prestige—heads of household, men of wealth, minor officialdom—to whom Mather would in effect now entrust the continuance of New England history. For the advance of the larger Reformation the book looks outside New England altogether, reposing its hopes for the future of Protestantism not in a Puritan City on a Hill which might be its vanguard, nor even in an alliance of all English Protestants, but in a worldwide Pietistic evangelical movement.

In recognizing the need to enlist the voluntary support of others in philanthropic enterprises, Mather also hit on a method destined long to characterize movements for social betterment in America. Many commentators have recognized in *Bonifacius* the nascent spirit of Benjamin Franklin, contributor to the Philadelphia hospital, promoter of subscription libraries, organizer of discussion groups for mechanics, founder of the Union Fire Company, devotee of civic improvement. Four years old when *Bonifacius* appeared, Franklin himself later wrote that it produced "such a turn of thinking, as to have an influence on my conduct through life; for I have always set a greater value on the character of a *doer of good,* than on any other kind of reputation; and if I have been . . . a useful citizen, the Public owes the advantage of it to that book."

Franklin's remark should not be read backward to mean that Mather himself had drifted into secularism or felt content to be a "useful citizen." Both he and the Pietists maintained a delicate synthesis of engagement with the prevailing culture and mortification to life. He insisted at the opening of *Bonifacius* that only the regenerate could Do Good, for only those who had experienced grace could know what Good is, which largely meant advancing the Reformation. Franklin emulated Mather's ingenuity in contriving projects for Doing Good, but he lacked Mather's fervor for private mystical conversion and worldwide evangelical reformation, and he conceived goodness as making life more comfortable. When Mather begins sounding like Franklin in *Bonifacius,* it is not because he has abandoned inward piety but because he has moved away in thought from New England, as Franklin later did in person. Missing from *Bonifacius* is what the charter took away and Governor Dudley put beyond reach, the unhesitating cooperation of government in satisfying important needs and impulses of Congregational piety. The same absence helped create the more variegated and permissive Boston that could nurture Benjamin Franklin, a figure hard to imagine under the government of John Winthrop.

Because Mather often used Doing Good to countermand his anger, the benevolent directives of *Bonifacius* are perversely but inevitably encompassed by resentment. Quoting an unnamed writer, possibly himself, Mather remarks: "There is not any revenge more heroic, than that which torments envy by doing of good." The chapter-length Preface and Conclusion that bracket the book similarly twist Arndt's "heroic meekness," born in mystical identification with Christ, into Matherean "magnanimous *courage,*" born in anticipation of abuse. The Preface hammers at the masochistic precept that "a man of *good merit,* is a kind of *public enemy,*" and sets forth the dismal rewards of Doing Good in paragraphs successively headlined "MISCONSTRUCTION," "DISCOURAGE-MENTS," "INGRATITUDE," "ENVY," and "DERISION." Mather's warnings echo not the incomparable Francke but the smutty serenaders stealing clubs from his woodpile, Joseph Dudley guffawing over Kate Maccarty—"INDEED, FATHER, IF I SHOULD SAY I DID SEE HER, I SHOULD TELL A GREAT LIE"—and, behind them, jeers about his knocking off invisible chains, the humiliations of the stammerer, cuffs to the pious child who rebuked his playmates:

> *Essays to do good* shall be derided, with all the *art* and *wit,* that [the devil] can inspire in his *Janizaries.* . . . Exquisite *profaneness* and *buffoonery* shall try their skill to laugh people out of them. The men who abound in them shall be exposed on the *stage; libels,* and *lampoons,* and *satires,* the most poignant that ever were invented, shall be darted at them; and *pamphlets* full of lying stories, be scattered, with a design to make them *ridiculous.*

Gloating for pages about the "hopes of disaffected men, to see you *come to nothing*," Mather fixed in *Bonifacius* the myth of himself that would rule much of his later life, an elaborated version of his earlier inability to *"do enough"*: Do Good, Be Spurned, Do More Good.

Besides its value for Mather in managing his rage, Doing Good also reduced his guilt over his ambitiousness. The two, he had always understood, were most intimately related, his anger swelling whenever in his hunger for applause he was served with scorn. Although he published *Bonifacius* anonymously, he confessed to unashamed pride in it: "'Tis a vanity in writers, to compliment the readers, with a, 'Sorry 'tis no better.' Instead of *that,* I freely tell my readers: I have written what is not unworthy of their perusal. If I did not think so, truly, I would not publish it." The statement makes a notable and surprising contrast to his many earlier stratagems for subtly denying-claiming authorship; similar statements appear in several of his other works in this period, on whose title pages he boldly identified himself as "Cotton Mather, D.D." Clearly what changed his view of his writing was the feeling that Doing Good provided a plausible rationale for his ambition. "I will venture to say," he wrote in *Bonifacius,* "the book is full of *reasonable* and *serviceable* things; and it would be well for us, if such things were hearkened to; and I have *done well* to offer them."

Brazened by Doing Good, Mather also included in *Bonifacius* an advertisement, more than four pages long, for "Biblia Americana." He defended the self-endorsement by invoking his newfound rationale: "To bestow the censure of *pride* and *vanity,* on the proposing of such a work for publication, would be therewith to reproach all attempts in such a way to serve the public." Not only did he intend Doing Good, but also, he added frankly, he had labored on the book fifteen years, and "It is a *lawful* and a *modest* thing, for a man to desire, that so much of a short life, as has been spent in such a preparation, should not be *spent in vain.*" That the gigantic effort might be wasted, it should be added, had already shown itself a grim possibility. During an illness four years earlier, in 1706, he had put a climactic spurt of effort into the work, fearing he might die before he could complete it. The intense application only worsened his health, but enabled him by May of that year to thank God for having "so happily finished my great Work"—which he had not. In the fall he sent to England an advertisement for the book entitled "An American Offer to serve the Great Interests of Learning and Religion in Europe." But this seems never to have been published, or at least not to have won subscribers. He kept adding illustrations, and included the new advertisement in *Bonifacius* in hopes of moving "some generous minds, to forward an undertaking so confessedly worthy to be prosecuted."

Mather's advertisement states that two folio volumes are now ready for publication, designed for "all impartial Christians, of whatever denomination or subdivision in Christianity." To such readers he promises a stupendous feast. Among its themselves-gorging main courses, as described in the advertisement, are his arrangement of Scripture in the order of events, "which exhibition alone, will do the service of a valuable commentary"; the amendment and refinement of existing translations; the rescue from misinterpretation of the laws of Israel, with a history of the city of Jerusalem from the days of Melchisedec to the present; the reconciling of apparent contradictions in Scripture; the linking of Old Testament types with their New Testament antitypes; and an "elaborate and entertaining" history of the Jewish people in every place from the birth of Christ to the present.

Among his other choice offerings, Mather also promises to have applied recent works of travelers to explaining biblical geography, including the location of Paradise and the peoples of the whole earth; recent historical knowledge to clarifying scriptural texts concerning ancient idolatry, agriculture, architecture, and warfare; talmudic and other Jewish writings to demonstrating the truth of Christianity; the most recent scientific knowledge to understanding the Creation, the Flood, and the Conflagration, as well as the plants, animals, diseases, astronomical events, and powers of the invisible world mentioned in Scripture; and all of history to illustrating the fulfillment of biblical prophecy. Having also heavily seasoned the work with characteristic and intriguing lore about Indians, angels, medicine, classical poetry, and much else, he promises the treats of "many thousands of curious notes, found scattered and shining, in the writings both of the *ancients* and the *moderns,* laid here together in a grateful amassment."

After advertising "Biblia Americana" through *Bonifacius,* however, Mather continued collecting material. In the year 1711 alone he gathered more than a thousand illustrations, adding them to those which in the completed work range from a brief paragraph to thirty or forty double-columned large folio pages. Fattening apace, the omnivorous work was on its way to becoming one of the *"Libri Elephantini,"* as he called books that require *"twelve hundred and sixty oxhides for a covering."*

*

Nammatchekodtantamooonganunnonash. Christianizing the Indians of New England—in whose language this transliterated word, Mather scoffed, means "lusts"—was for him a major goal of the broader attempt to spread the Reformation, thus a major component of Doing Good. "The Greatest Service that can be done to Mankind," he wrote, "is to introduce *Pure Christianity* every where." His wish to forward this service among the Indians in his region took new energy from his admiration of Pietist missions in far-off places like India, and from increased efforts of other religious groups which made those of Dissenters seem halfhearted: "The *Mahometans* out-do us; The *Quakers* out-do us; The *Socinians* out-do us; The *Papists* make us Ashamed.. . . . They will bear the Loathsome and Irksome Wigwams of the Indians in an howling Wilderness, if they may but *Win* over the Savages to their Superstitions."

But in fact some progress, from Mather's viewpoint, had been made in converting local Indians to New England Protestantism. In a five-page "Appendix" to *Bonifacius* he described the current state of missionary efforts in Massachusetts. War over the last fifty years had desolated at a stroke "whole nations" of New England Indians, greatly reducing their number. The Indians to the east were being deluded by the Catholic French, who taught them that Christ "was a *Frenchman,* and that the *English* murdered Him." On the other hand, most of the Indians currently under English influence had to some degree been christianized. By Mather's count, Martha's Vineyard had ten Christian congregations, Nantucket at least three; the mainland had between twenty and thirty, with about three thousand Indians under Christian instruction by ten English preachers and twenty to thirty Indian teachers. Worship in the Indians' churches, moreover, clung more closely to the religion of the first settlers than in some present Congregational churches—marked by pertinent prayers, orthodox sermons, and particularly pleasing psalmody, "with a melody outdoing many of the English." The present aims of the missionary work, Mather concluded, should be to preserve the Christianity already developed among the Indians, progress in anglicizing them, and rid them of the drunkenness which threatened their christianization. But in practice, he concluded, these aims are "encumbered with difficulties, beyond what can be by most men in the bare *theory* imagined."

In converting the Indians of New England, Mather and others hoped not only to spread the Reformation, but also to pacify a fierce and proud enemy. On this point—having passed his entire life close by recurrent and murderous Indian fighting, in which he lost a relative—he discarded his role of peacemaker. While he embraced Christian Indians as brethren in Christ he damned infidel Indians as "Ravenous howling *Wolves,*" at once brutal, infantile, and diabolic. He exhorted some troops in 1689 to literally exterminate them: "*Turn not back* till they are *consumed: Wound* them that they shall not be *able to Arise;* Tho' they *Cry;* Let there be none to *Save* them; But *Beat* them small as the *Dust before the Wind,* and *Cast them out,* as the *Dirt in the Streets.*" He also ridiculed unconverted Indians as bestially ignorant: having never seen a ship until the arrival of Europeans, although they dwelt amidst superlative ship timber; using stone implements, in an iron-rich country; their habitations a few poles stuck in the earth, their medicine a heated cave for sweats. Mocking the Indians' sesquipedalian-sounding language, he proposed calling the bloodiest of them by one of their own "*Indian* Long-winded words," and devised the macaronic name "*Bombardo-gladio-funhast-flammi-loquentes.*" Because he also considered Indians "lazy drones" and "impudent liars" lacking in all family government, he also feared their effect on white neighbors and captives, some of whom showed a propensity to join Indian society.

More than that, unconverted Indians were to Mather, and to many others, children of the devil. Early travelers to America had observed again and again that the Indians' religion consisted in worshiping the devil as God. Mather often speaks of Indian powwows raising devils in the shape of bears, or practicing "Diabolical *Charms*" to keep English dogs from attacking them, or fashioning arrowhead-shaped pieces of leather to be taken up by some demon and conveyed into the bodies of persons to be afflicted. Many believed that as the devil was "God's ape" and as, in Joseph Mede's view, America was uniquely the land of the devil, so the Indians were a satanic parody of the Puritans, the Chosen People of the devil as the Israelites, and then the Puritans, were the Chosen People of God. The Rev. John Higginson speculated to Mather that Indians who settled around Mexico were conducted there by the devil "very strangely Emulating what the Blessed God gave to *Israel* in the Wilderness." Mather even considered the possibility that the Salem outbreak might in part have arisen from the black arts of Indian sagamores, well known to be "horrid *Sorcerers,* and hellish *Conjurers,* and such as conversed with *Daemons.*"

In hopes of redeeming and quelling the natives of New England Mather threw himself into the missionary work, as into everything else, energetically. In 1698 he had been appointed a commissioner of the oldest Protestant missionary organization, the New England Company, founded by act of Parliament in 1649 to convert the New England Indians to Christianity. The Company invested funds and from the interest sent money to the commissioners, who included Increase Mather and Samuel Sewall. The commissioners then disbursed salaries to itinerant missionaries, and funds to Indian preachers and to settlers who provided allied charitable and educational services. Mather attended the commissioners' meetings, held at their homes or at the Town House, and became the New England Company's chief informant on the missionary work, sending them such tokens of progress as a poem in Latin and Greek by a "pregnant Indian youth" and long epistolary reports. These were greatly appreciated and commended in London (in further contrast to his reception at home), where his chief correspondent was Sir William Ashurst (Sir Henry's younger brother), a former Lord Mayor of London who was governor of the company from 1696 to 1720.

Mather's involvement in the Company intensified just as his own *Bonifacius* was published and just as a complex and much debated problem for the Company also came to the fore again. This was whether to convert the Indians in their own tongues or to anglicize them first and pursue their conversion in English. The question also bore on the huge project of reprinting John Eliot's famous Indian Bible. Written in a transliterated version of the Natick dialect, and first published in 1663, two hundred leatherbound copies were immediately circulated for the Indians' use. In 1708, the New England Company undertook to reissue Eliot's Bible, but its strange-looking words and its length made the presswork painfully vexing, slow, and expensive. In July 1709, a fire in Samuel Sewall's bedroom also destroyed the printing paper. Mather seems to have doubted the usefulness of the project but hesitated to publicize his opinions, perhaps because of his respect for Eliot. Samuel Sewall was probably speaking for Mather when he relayed to Sir William Ashurst in 1710 the objections of some commissioners: that Indian teachers complain of the absence of Indian terms for Christian concepts; that different tribes have different dialects; that many Indians find Eliot's written approximations of their speech unintelligible. Moreover, Sewall said, if the Indians retained their language they would retain with it "a Tincture of other Savage Inclinations, which do but ill suit, either with the Honor, or with the design of Christianity," whereas the expense of reprinting Eliot's Bible might go far toward teaching the Indians English. Writing to Ashurst himself, Mather observed that most commissioners opposed the reprinting but that to anglicize the Indians "is much more easy to be talked of than to be accomplished." In any event he urged that the presswork could be done more cheaply in London than in Boston, where he estimated it would take more than seven years. But no London printers knew the language, and in fact the reprint was doomed never to appear.

Mather also personally attended several communities of christianized Indians. In July 1712, he and other commissioners visited the languishing settlement at Natick, reduced, largely by long years of war, to scarce thirty families. The commissioners hoped to restore the population by inducing neighboring Indians to move in with them. Mather preached at the Indian meetinghouse (in a pulpit without Bible, cushion, or hourglass), talked with the Indians about their political affairs, heard an Indian minister perform religious exercises in an Indian language, and received "handsome Returns of Thanks." Desiring to bring the Indians into compact, English-style communities, he greatly approved the purchase by the Company in 1713 of Martha's Vineyard, in an effort to consolidate local christianized Indians. His manner with such Indians was paternalistic, but wholly without the hollering vengefulness he directed at pagan Indians. He told some Indians who were being settled at Gay Head, for instance, that "tho' we would have you own your dependence on the good and great protectors you have in London, who have bought this land for your benefit, yet we shall use all the care of kind fathers to make your condition comfortable." While oblivious to the cost, in human agony, of the Indians' depletion and resettlement, Mather recognized that the first Puritans had settled on Indian territory, and wished the Indians' rights to their little remaining land be respected. Thus he urged that "the *Reliques* of the *Aboriginal Natives* here, upon whose Land we were Entered, might have an Everlasting and Unalienable Claim unto some Little Scraps of a Vast Country, once entirely Possessed by their Ancestors."

Mather and the commissioners hoped not to christianize the Indians of New England but, more accurately, to Puritanize them. They accordingly distrusted the Anglican missionary efforts of the rival Society for the Propagation of the Gospel in Foreign Parts. Chartered in 1701 and composed of prominent prelates and politicans, the SPG had been organized by the Bishop of London to study the Church of England's status in the colonies. Mutual abhorrence of the work of Jesuit missionaries to some degree enforced cooperation between the SPG and the New England Company. Indeed, Ashurst laid before some bishops in the Society Mather's *Letter; About the Present State of Christianity among the Christianized Indians* (1705), as proof that "our ministers (tho' not Episcopal) are Capable of Doing Good." The bishops were impressed by Mather's description of the purity of Congregational worship in some Indian churches, so much so that the Archbishop of Canterbury himself ordered the pamphlet to be presented at a meeting of the SPG. The Society became curious about the New England Company's methods, asked to inspect its charter, and requested from Ashurst an account of its funding operations, assuring him they had "no sinister Ends in this Inquiry."

Mather generally approved this ecumenical cooperation with the SPG. But still apprehensive about the possible establishment of an American episcopate, he also deplored the presence of High Churchmen in the Society, and suspected SPG missionaries of trying to convert not Indians but Congregationalists. A rather ambidexter letter by him in 1706, seemingly intended for the SPG, was withheld from the Society because of what his English correspondent called its "hard Expressions." He began by praising the "worthy Persons, who compose the Society," but added his hope that they would shun High Churchmen—"highflyers," as he barbedly called them, "who may be crept in." He also criticized the Society for sending missionaries to towns that had been well instructed in Christianity for generations, on the pretext of gospelizing a few scandalous families. The missionaries were trying, he suggested, to subvert "the most instructed Christians in the World," persons "not yet so illuminated" as to demand Episcopal ordination and Church of England ceremonies. If they kept trying to undermine Congregationalist strongholds, he said, the "noble Society for the Propagation of Religion in America, will greatly wound Religion, and their own Reputation also." His distrust of the SPG grew steadily, so that by 1716 he was referring to it as the "Society for the Molestation of the Gospel in foreign Parts."

Mather received no salary as a commissioner, but the Company in 1709 awarded him £25 in consideration of his "great Services in promoting the work of Converting the Indians by his writings and other ways." Mather did increase his value to the Company by publishing virtually a title a year relating to Indian affairs. These include *An Epistle to the Christian Indians* (1700; Indian title, *Wussukwhonk En Christianeue asuh peantamwae Indianog*), offering in Indian and English a compressed description of the whole of Congregational theology and church government; *A Monitory, and Hortatory Letter, To those English, who debauch the Indians* (1700), denouncing the sale of strong drink to the Indians, which makes them unemployable, destructive, and sotted beyond christianizing; *Hatchets to Hew Down the Tree of Sin* (1705), containing an English-Indian digest of Massachusetts laws against buggery, incest, and other crimes; and *Another Tongue brought in* (1707), providing a quadrilingual catechism in Iroquois, Latin, English, and Dutch for use by traders in beaver skins among the Iroquois, to counter Catholic missionary efforts among them.

Writing from a nonmissionary viewpoint, Mather also published many accounts of Indian fighting and captivity. They include one of his most vividly written works, *Decennium Luctuosum* (1699), recounting the decade of Indian warfare between 1688 and 1698. As history the book is notable for its many comments on historical theory and on the style and veracity of other historians, and for its indefatigably gathered and carefully sifted information. Yet Mather compared it to *The Iliad,* for in exultantly describing the destruction of the "Rapacious Wolves" he saw himself as genuinely an epical writer, narrating the heroic origins of an emergent civilization, occupying in early America something of Homer's position in ancient Greece. Intent as always on holding as well as informing his readers, he managed by many formal inventions and witty transitions to accommodate his digressive and fanciful imagination, so as to include every last bloody butchery or hair-raising escape, and many "charming and useful Entertainments." To an unusual degree among his works the book abounds in alliteration, foreshadowing, metaphor, and other purely literary devices, in a style at once erudite, pious, and racy. For instance, in telling how the celebrated Hannah Dustan of Haverhill rose in the dead of night and, with a nurse and a young boy, hatcheted her Indian captors to death, skinning ten scalps, he effectively used syntax and sentence rhythm to convey staggering:

> they struck such Home Blows, upon the Heads of their *Sleeping Oppressors,* that e're they could any of them Struggle into any Effectual Resistance, *at the Feet of* those poor Prisoners, *they bowed, they fell, they lay down; at their feet they bowed, they fell; where they bowed, there they fell down Dead.*

Mather also reproduced much amusing dialogue, most delectably a remark made to him by a Quaker, who rudely accused him of doing all the talking: *"Thou art a Monster, all Mouth, and no Ears."*

*

A final, outstandingly personal and consequential plan for Doing Good Mather proposed in his diary in July 1711: "There is one good Interest, which I have never yet served, and yet I am capable of doing some small Service for it." Having always believed that Christ and God were glorified in the progress of human knowledge resulting from the study of nature, he now decided to make a "valuable Collection of many Curiosities, which this Country has afforded; and present it unto the Royal Society." In thus promoting still another good cause, he sent to London in batches of four to a dozen over the next twelve years, some eighty-two scientific dispatches.

Founded around 1660, the Royal Society took as one of its main purposes the accurate collection, classification, and interpretation of scientific data. It kept an enormous correspondence with *virtuosi* all over the world (of whom only a small number were elected Fellows), carried without charge by ships of the East India and other English trading companies, and in packets of the Secretary of State. In relation to himself, Mather regarded the Society's work with mingled hope of joining a superior world aloof from the mundane bickering and ignorance of common humanity, desire to Do Good, revenge toward his enemies in Boston, and admiration for new learning:

> how worthy it [the Society's undertaking] is to be pursued by gentlemen who would *show themselves men;* how useful it has already been to mankind, and capable of being yet more applied unto the *best of purposes;* a tendency it has to refine and sweeten the minds of men, and reconcile them unto *just regards* for *true merits* in one another; with an extirpation of that noxious clamor-wort, the *party-spirit;* and, finally, how generously the more polite literators of the world go on in it, with a decent contempt on the banters of the *brutish among the people. . . .*

His communications to the Society, entitled "Curiosa Americana," animatedly project this Matherean mixture of snobbery, altruism, resentment, and inquisitiveness.

In addition to being scientific communications, the Curiosa are literary letters, written, Mather said, with "my most exquisite Contrivance," and containing some of his most polished and shapely prose. They radiate with greater liveliness than perhaps any of his other works the personality that many contemporaries found gracious and entertaining. On one letter he sketched diagrams of the planetary motions, doodling into the the sun half-moon eyes and a large smile. His delight in writing to the ostensibly more receptive world outside Boston registers also in the playful tone of the letters, particularly their elaborately turned salutations and closings, which pun on the subject of the dispatch. For instance, a later letter on "Uncommon Dentition"—about a Harvard student whose gums presented not teeth but a *"White, Sharp, continued Edge"*—ends with the flourish: "nothing, that ever my *Teeth* ever had under the Mastication can be so grateful to me, as the Instructive Things, which you can and will give me to feed upon. I beseech you, Let there be therein a *Continual Feast* allow'd unto, Sir. . . ." Aware of his self-delighted difficulty in settling down to the subject, he asked one correspondent at the Society to abide his "little excursions" as "one of those natural weaknesses which all men of breeding indulge in one another."

The weakness was as much cultural, however, as personal. Mather's evident discomfort in addressing sophisticated, cosmopolitan men, members of the Commonwealth of Learning to which he aspired but felt inadequate, arose from a sense of living, as he wrote, "in an infant country entirely destitute of philosophers." For all his exuberance he freely and frequently acknowledged how the New World lagged behind the Old in knowledge, and often seems to say that he is only telling the English virtuosi what they already know: "These Things are so much better known to you," he writes in a letter on rainbows, "that I can make no Apology for the *Little Touch* I now give upon them, Except it should be this; I was willing to have you think, that your *American* Friends also are not utterly unacquainted with them." The Curiosa exude the provincial strangulation of the country fop, of someone self-consciously addressing the learned world without being certain what it is.

In terms of the Society's own interests, Mather's justification for addressing it at all was the hope of communicating "all New and Rare Occurrences of Nature, in these parts of the World." The Curiosa, that is, contain an embryonic element of nationalism. Mather often reminds the Society that his subjects are *American* curiosities: a black snake that fell from the sky, in Lynn; a tree limb found seventeen feet underground, in Springfield; a huge balancing rock that teeters during storms, in Gloucester. Far more descriptive than explanatory, the letters make no larger claim than to add to the Society's worldwide collection of natural history some remarkable specimens from America, to be deciphered by virtuosi abroad and by them fitted into larger schemes of natural philosophy. In choosing the humble informant's role, Mather for a change realistically assessed his abilities and limitations, contributing useful data to major European scientific debates that lay beyond his competence and also his access. Just the same, probably no other colonial American writer was as aware of physically inhabiting the New World as Mather, and as preoccupied with seeing how it differed from the Old World. Feeling both challenged to report the uniqueness of his country and pained by the relative crudeness of its intellectual life, he wrote invariably as "your American Friend"—a condition of which he was at once proud and embarrassed.

Mather collected his scientific lore widely. Some came from his own observation, such as the egg grown inside another egg which he had held in his own hand (an example of "monstrous impregnation"). Several of his own earlier writings supplied other curiosa, beginning with a collection of natural oddities he had made in Latin as a youth. He also took materials from his father's *Illustrious Providences,* revealingly. For minus the lightened style, Mather's Curiosa closely resemble the remarkable providences he and his father had always collected. Providences display the wonders of God in history, declaring His judgments and will; Curiosa display the wonders of God in nature, declaring His workmanship and the operation of natural law. Mather also used his father's method of soliciting well-attested information about natural rarities from ministers and other credible persons throughout New England, for instance asking physicians for accounts of unusual cures in their practices. Once he sent the Boston physician John Perkins to investigate reports of a prodigious intestinal worm; Perkins found, even after souvenir-mongers had taken pieces away, 118 feet remaining.

Mather's favorite source was probably John Winthrop of Connecticut (1681-1747), "a Friend, who is better to me than a Brother." His affection for this younger man sprang from his veneration toward the three previous generations of prominent Winthrops, beginning with the John Winthrop who led the great migration of 1630 to New England. The next two generations combined public service and scientific curiosity to become, Mather wrote, "a Family sent into the world on purpose to help and heal its Maladies." The library of the second John Winthrop (1606–1676)—the first governor of Connecticut—contained the poems of John Donne and a huge collection of alchemical works; he was also the first colonial Fellow of the Royal Society, in fact a charter member of the Society itself. The third generation of Winthrops was represented by Wait-Still Winthrop (1642–1717), Chief Justice of Massachusetts and, Mather called him, a "Master of Medicines." These he gave free to multitudes of poor people, including a remedy composed of nitre and antimony, invented by his father, called Rubila. Mather's friend John Winthrop was Wait-Still's son. Together with their joint sense of prominent family descent and mutual scientific interest, they commiserated on a feeling of being more refined and intelligent than their neighbors, and mistreated by them.

Mather frequently praised the younger Winthrop as a Christian philosopher and gentleman, but felt that he failed to live up to his possibilities and heritage. Winthrop's correspondence does leave an impression of self-pampering shallowness: one letter speaks of his distaste for shopping in Boston—"Everything very ordinary . . . . slimsy gaudy things"—but of finding at one store an attractive camblet, "the genteelest thing I had seen anywhere." Genteel camblet or no, Mather often asked Winthrop to use his "philosophical Genius and Gentlemanly Leisure" to provide material for him to send to the Royal Society, such as a description of the color, horns, and other features of the moose, and an account of a remarkably violent storm that buried sheep under sixteen-foot-high snowbanks. With Mather's request for material on the water-dove he had limited success; as he told Mather, he was going to send a water-dove itself but a cat got into his study and tore it to pieces.

Mather's letters to the Royal Society encompass virtually all the sciences of his time, including astronomy, botany, zoology, geology, and meteorology. Given his intention in youth of becoming a physician, his confessed weakness in mathematics, and his delighted fascination with the flocks of pigeons around Boston, it is not surprising that the largest number deal with medicine, the fewest with mathematical sciences, and perhaps the best-humored with ornithology. Occasionally he enclosed scientific specimens, in one instance six or seven dried plants which he had been unable to find listed in any European herbal, and presumed to name. Another time he sent as a specimen of a fossil a thickly encrusted piece-of-eight given him by Sir William Phips from his fabulous underwater horde; it had hung in Mather's library nearly thirty years. To make plain what these communications, written between 1712 and 1724, reveal about Mather's role in the development of American science, would require a separate book-length study relating them to the state of European scientific knowledge at the time. Instead, reserving a few general comments for later discussion of his last Curiosa, his first series of Curiosa shall be summarized in tabular form below as representative of the whole, followed by brief analysis of the lengthy manuscript he sent the Society in 1715.

The first series of Curiosa, just over a hundred manuscript pages, consists of thirteen letters written over two weeks in November 1712, and addressed to Dr. John Woodward and to Richard Waller. Woodward, the Society's Provincial Secretary, was an eminent geologist whose still celebrated *Essay Toward a Natural History of the Earth* (1695) called attention to the existence of strata in the earth's crust; Waller, Secretary of the Society for more than twenty-five years, was a businessman who wrote on physiology, zoology, and linguistics. Each letter essentially treats a single subject, but with frequent asides. Mather also addressed a lengthy plea through Woodward to "Ingenious and opulent men" to publish his "Biblia Americana," from which he also drew the first of his Curiosa:

   1. On Giants, discussing the remains of an alleged giant unearthed

near Albany, New York, in 1705, one of whose teeth and some of whose bones Mather says he had the satisfaction of handling, including a presumed thigh bone seventeen feet long.

2. Local Flora, some used for cures, including an Indian cure for syphillis.

3. Ornithology, with a finely accurate description of a hummingbird, and the speculation that some birds may migrate to small planetary bodies surrounding the earth but too small to be observed by present telescopes.

4. Strange Antipathies, and the Force of Imagination, with cases of "Husbands who *breed* for their Wives" and of a New Englander who had a stone at the root of his tongue yet urinated in intolerable pain as if it had been in his bladder.

5. Monstrous Births, in Latin.

6. Cures Appearing in Dreams (including the warm-wool cure dreamed by Mather's deceased wife Abigail), with the suggestion that such dreams may be the work of good angels, although possibly of evil angels doing good for evil ends.

7. Tiny Wounds That Have Proved Mortal And Extremely Grievous Wounds That Have Not, including the story of a dropsiacal New England woman who vomited pieces of skin, and whose autopsy disclosed that she had "*no Bowels* at all" and "not so much as a bit of a Bladder."

8. Indian Methods of Keeping Time.

9. Rainbows, with three diagrams, citations of Descartes, Halley, and Newton, and remarks on rainbows as prognostics.

10. Apparitions, including a case Mather reports several times elsewhere concerning a man named Joseph Beacon, to whom appeared the specter of his recently murdered brother, revealing to him the murderer's identity.

11. Rattlesnakes.

12. Thunder and Earthquakes, with description of a large rock in Taunton containing allegedly prehistoric inscriptions in "unaccountable Characters."

13. Demography (essentially), speculating on the population of the world before the Flood and describing cases of extraordinary childbearing and longevity, including a woman who had thirty-nine children and a Rhode Islander aged 110 who had been married to his wife—herself more than 100—for more than eighty years, with the "further odd Circumstance of their Friendship, that they constantly Eat upon one Trencher at the Table."

Even these capsule summaries may seem to confirm the standard charge against Mather of credulity. But in what strikes a modern reader as fantastic in them, his Curiosa differ little from other contributions to the Royal

Society, which received his letters, we shall see, with enthusiasm. Besides, his Curiosa equally represent the observations and beliefs of his many informants, and obviously were generally held. Boston newspapers often printed reports about, for instance, a "Merman or Sea Monster" sighted at Brest, or a pond in Rhode Island from which at one time were taken 700,000 bass, "by a moderate Computation." Indeed, several freak events reported by Mather are rather simply explained and still occasionally occur. His communication to the Society on "A Woolen Snow," concerning the fall of quantities of wool from the sky, is no more unaccountable than the hundred and fifty fish that dropped to earth from the heavens in Australia in 1974, presumably sucked up from the sea by a waterspout created by high oceanic winds.

After sending a second series of Curiosa, in ten letters, in 1714, Mather sent the following year the manuscript of a work entitled "The Christian Virtuoso," asking that it be deposited in the Society's archives if it did not find a publisher. The work appeared in over three hundred pages in 1721 as *The Christian Philosopher*—the first general book on science to be written in America. It differs fundamentally from his "Curiosa Americana," aiming not to describe striking natural phenomena in America but to summarize significant findings of European scientists, including recent ideas about gravity and about the speed of light. With rapturous admiration for new scientific learning—"*Ideas,* like the *Sands on the Seashore,* for the vast *variety* of them!"—Mather quotes the work of such eminent figures as Flamsteed, Leeuwenhoek, Huygens, and, repeatedly, "The incomparable Sir *Isaac Newton.*" He meant literally his statement that *The Christian Philosopher* represents "A Collection of the Best Discoveries in Nature," for like "Biblia Americana" the book is an amassment of illustrations and quotations. The "very little" of his own in the work, he points out, amounts to a few curiosa and some pious "improvements" that draw from observations on comets or volcanos the proper religious significance. Indeed an important part of his purpose was to show others the spirit in which he had pursued his own "Enquiries into the Wonders of the Universe, so it is both an Instruction and a Pattern to a serious Mind." He tried to demonstrate, that is, how a Christian might come to terms with the new science itself.

Like most virtuosi in the Royal Society, Mather believed that the investigation of nature could lead only to the good of man and the greater glory of God. The two writers on whom he drew most frequently in *The Christian Philosopher* were John Ray and William Derham, the authors respectively of *The Wisdom of God Manifested in the Works of the Cre-*

ation (London, 1691) and *Physico-Theology, or a Demonstration of the Being and Attributes of God from His Works of Creation* (London, 1713). For Ray, Derham, and other so-called physico-theologians, recent scientific disclosures of the vastness of the stars or the complexity of the human body but proved the existence of divine purpose in the cosmos. Following them, Mather in *The Christian Philosopher* also delineated a minutely purposive universe, where lice exist to deter people from slovenliness, and teething is deferred to protect the nipples of wetnurses:

> How surprisingly is the *Head* and the *Neck* of the *Swine* adapted for his rooting in the *Earth!* How the Neck, Nose, Eyes and Ears of the *Mole,* adapted in the nicest manner to its way of subterraneous living! The strong Snout of the *Swine,* such that he may sufficiently thrust it into the Ground, where his Living lies, without hurting his Eyes; and of so sagacious a Scent, that we employ them to hunt for us and even his *wallowing in the Mire,* is a wise Contrivance for the Suffocation of troublesome Insects!

Imagining a Creator supercopious in benevolent ingenuity, Mather moved almost effortlessly in his thinking between theological and scientific modes of explanation.

But the very piety evident in such thinking—widespread among Christian scientists of the eighteenth century—obscured its dangerous implications, and unwittingly led Mather close to irreligion. Although the physico-theological disclosure of an intricately contrived universe was meant to provide a rational foundation for Christianity, it tended in practice to displace Christianity. In trying to prove God's existence from natural phenomena, and in using new standards of proof and debate, it quietly relegated essential Christian ideas to the background, especially losing sight of the Son. Mather shared unawares in some of this subversive shift in emphasis. The Creator he depicts in *The Christian Philosopher* no longer seems the wrathful Jehovah of the jeremiads, but rather the smiling Deity of liberal eighteenth-century Protestantism, ordering things so, that "whatever is natural is delightful, and has a tendency to Good." Only half-a-dozen pages from the end of the book, moreover, does Mather introduce a section on the Savior, by saying "the CHRIST of God must not be forgotten"—as He almost is. Indeed the clockwork universe described in *The Christian Philosopher* seems an altogether improbable setting for the great drama of Redemption:

> The Great God has contrived a mighty *Engine,* of an Extent that cannot be measured, and there is in it a Contrivance of wondrous *Motions* that can-

not be *numbered.* He is infinitely gratified with the View of this *Engine* in all its *Motions,* infinitely grateful to Him so glorious a Spectacle!

Such a predictable universe seems inconsistent with inflows of supernatural grace, much less with ghosts who reveal murderers, evil angels who foment earthquakes, and other unscheduled wonders of the invisible world.

Mather shrank, however, from fully accepting a mechanical universe. He did so at the expense of some raggedness in his thinking but in the name of his own experience. Having witnessed the invisible world himself, he announced in *The Christian Philosopher,* his belief in it was unshakable: "I do here in the first place most religiously affirm, that even my *Senses* have been convinced of such a World, by as clear, plain, full *Proofs* as ever any Man's have had of what is most obvious in the *sensible World.*" Nor was Mather prepared to give up arguing the existence of God from the potency of witches, to argue it solely from the snouts of swine. After praising the power of the mind and the inventions of the age, he ended his book by remarking that the enginelike wonders of the visible creation dwindle "compared to those that are out of sight, those that are found among the *Angels that excel in Powers.*" He made room for pneumatological phenomena in a mechanical universe by emphasizing the limitations of reason and uncertainties in the science of his time. He viewed human reason, especially in humanity's fallen state, as a blunted instrument, incapable of penetrating all of *"covered Nature"*—"Every Thing puzzles us. Even the Nature, yea, the *Extent* of an *Atom,* does to this Day, puzzle all the Philosophers in the World." Such puzzles left aspects of the universe open to nonmechanical interpretation.

One measure of Mather's resistance to a wholly mechanistic view of nature is his treatment of comets, one of several spectacular celestial and atmospheric phenomena viewed by his father, and many others, as omens. In earlier life he had had little difficulty conceiving such events as operating under natural law, but through the agency of angels or devils. More recent scientific notions evidently made it less easy for him to think so. In *The Christian Philosopher* he cited Newton's speculation that vapors from comets may fall into the earth's atmosphere by gravity and nourish vegetation. "If this be so," Mather reasoned, "the Appearance of *Comets* is not so dreadful a thing, as the *Cometomantia,* generally prevailing, has represented it." The "If" is significant, for the element of doubt allowed him to cite opposing opinions that comets may be ministers of divine justice or habitations of animals in a state of punishment, and to propose that some celestial spectacles might be prognostics, others not.

Mather also considered mechanical principles inadequate to explain large areas of biology. In pondering vital phenomena involving the pursuit of goals he continued to entertain the ancient idea of a plastic spirit—a spiritual power or life force akin to the soul, working within matter to produce the configurations of various beings. He found such vitalistic, as opposed to mechanistic, thinking necessary to understand phenomena like the regrowth of plants from parts of their stems. In a 1716 curiosa concerning generation, for instance, he speculated on the possibility of regrowing amputated limbs. In conceiving generation he accepted the contemporary theory of "animalcules," suggested by microscopic study of sperm cells: living things exist infolded as tiny seeds, invisible to the eye but containing "the whole *Bodies* of the *Animals,* even to all their *Nerves* and *Fibres*"; generation is the augmentation of the original tiny parts within the seed. He speculated that the plastic spirit which animates and directs this augmentation might be able to renew an augmented part which had been lost or removed. As always, he recognized that the notion of plastic spirit was occult; but in this case he found mechanical hypotheses equally so: "I was trying for a more mechanical Account of this matter, without flying to the *Plastic Vertue;* which if I call *unintelligible,* I must confess my Mechanism to be so too." Although drawn to the mechanical view of nature and in awe of the scientists who composed it, he thus never surrendered his belief in Spirit. "The more progress we make in *Experimental philosophy,*" he wrote later, "the oftener we shall find ourselves driven to something so much beyond *mechanical principles.*"

In conceiving of matter as energy, modern physics to a degree vindicates Mather's clinging to a vitalistic universe. Doing so, however, prevented him from fully appreciating the science of his time. His communications to the Royal Society also disclose two more of his serious limitations as a scientist. For one, he had little interest in the experimental method—that is, in the active questioning of nature under conditions defined by the experimenter—as opposed to bare observation of the phenomena nature presents. Such experiment was of the essence of the new science, distinguishing it from Aristotelianism and scholasticism. His limited mathematical knowledge also barred him from any real understanding of the advance in the exact mathematical description of nature that was one of the great achievements of science in the period. To judge Mather by such standards may however be unfair. Science was never for him an autonomous activity, but always a handmaid to religion. He fully recognized his inferiority to the great virtuosi of Europe, and always spoke of his scientific work, except in medicine, with modesty.

Leaving aside Mather's single greatest scientific accomplishment, which still lay ahead, he figures most importantly in the history of American science as a disseminator and popularizer of new scientific knowledge. From his pulpit he promoted the Copernican view of a heliocentric system and, invisible chains to the contrary, he took a rationalistic delight in exploding such popular superstitions as the theory of spontaneous generation and the cure of scrofula by the touch of a seventh son. Some more specific scientific contributions can be credited to him as well. Beginning in *Bonifacius* and continuing through "Curiosa Americana" and his later medical works, he gave pioneering attention, unappreciated at the time, to psychogenic causes of illness. His Curiosa also contain what seems to be the earliest known account of plant hybridization, confirming the then newly announced doctrine that flowering plants reproduce sexually—the basis for the Linnaean system of classifying plants. He also noted for what seems to have been the first time, the fact of dominance, later important in Mendel's theory of heredity. His profound curiosity about generation, we shall see, would lead him to major contributions to the treatment of smallpox. Finally, the observations on natural phenomena which he sent to London represented a wholly new level of performance by a colonial contributor to the Royal Society. Through the network of the Society's correspondence and publication, he not only gained a reputation in many parts of Europe for his own scientific work, but also advertised to the Old World the growing scientific community in the New.

The Royal Society rewarded Mather's efforts to Do Good. Secretary Waller reported to him in July 1713 that his first series of Curiosa "very well pleased and Entertained" the members, and that his future communications would be "extremely acceptable." Waller and Dr. Woodward also prepared some more detailed notes on their or the members' reactions, calling his account of the largeness of American wild turkeys and eagles "remarkable," and praising as seemingly new his description of the juice in the rattlesnake's gallbladder—withal indicating that the Curiosa received respectful and thoughtful attention. In his need at this time for encouragement, Mather had hinted that he would be pleased to see his work acknowledged in the Society's published *Transactions,* begun in 1665 and regularly received by the Fellows. An eight-page extract from the first series was published in the April–June 1714 *Transactions,* apparently making Mather the first New Englander since Governor John Winthrop of Connecticut to be published in that prestigious journal, which circulated throughout the world.

Seeking recognition even more blatantly, Mather upon sending his first series decided also to send a "Modest Intimation" that he would enjoy becoming a member of the Royal Society himself. The hint took the ambidexter form of an inverted confession, to Waller, of his unworthiness: "I cannot presume so much upon my own merits as to dream of being thought worthy to be admitted a member of that more than illustrious Society." He had in fact already been voted into the Society; in October 1713, he received news that at the next election "I shall be made, A FELLOW OF THE ROYAL SOCIETY." Giddy with delight in the distinction, he replied to Waller that he had resolved to send contributions annually to the Society for the rest of his life. Hereafter he often printed the designation "F.R.S." on the title pages of his works, together with his "D.D." from Glasgow. Although membership in the Society signified serious interest in science rather than technical or professional competence, the honor was genuine, for he had become only the eighth colonial elected to one of the most illustrious scientific bodies in the world.

In the "F.R.S." beside his name, Mather saw a signally surprising favor of heaven, "One that will much encourage me, and fortify me, in my Essays to do Good." It also gained him one advantage he sought from these essays. It heightened, he wrote, "the superior Circumstances, wherein my gracious Lord places me above the Contempt of envious Men." It exalted him above the other trees of the field, especially above the Governor Dudleys, the rasping serenaders, the swarmers who wanted pews for their despicable families, putting him, so he supposed, beyond their reach.

*

Despite Mather's strenuous attempts at this time to guard his wrath, it often slipped irresistibly by his watchfulness. Sometime it passed in the guise of a provocativeness which incensed his contemporaries more than any other feature of his personality. For all his geniality, many who knew him sensed in his behavior, as modern readers cannot but sense in many of his writings, something awry, a disturbing discrepancy between act and intent. This unsynchronized quality in Mather—an aggravated version of the ambidexterity earlier noticed by Robert Calef—was of course the product of his enormous strain in returning benignity for abuse, of the fact that his goodwill and good cheer were often deliberately reversed expressions of hurt pride, anger, and discouragement. This underside often seeped through—as the buoyant essays to Do Good of *Bonifacius* come encased in scornful warnings against "INGRATITUDE" and "DERI-SION"—tainting his behavior and his writing with a pervasive and provocative ambivalence.

The defining moods and gestures of Matherese—to give this ambivalence a name—are belligerent courtesy, self-flattering modesty, fretful calm, denigrating compliments, unacceptable offers. Mather came more and more to use such gallingly provocative tactics on his contemporaries, helping to explain why they often acted toward him with what he considered base ingratitude. A Scots minister named John Squire, for instance, visited New England around 1715, but refused to take communion with New England churches, and in Mather's view acted with unbecoming levity and arrogance. Squire's disrespect riled Mather the more because of his pride in his D.D. from Glasgow, and his much publicized veneration for the Church of Scotland. Although infuriated, he decided to Do some Good, and invited Squire to lodge with him, at no cost. As added inducements he promised Squire that the accommodations would be inferior to few in Boston and the library superior to any. A brotherly offer, until his final inducement, where his contempt broke through: "To which this easy Circumstance will be added; that all the while you stay, you shall not hear those Things, which we take to be your Weaknesses, uneasily insisted on." Squire was not disarmed by such palpable combinations of hospitality and condemnation: "your Civilities," he told Mather, "Savour the worse to me that they are cast so frequently in my teeth."

Squire was not alone in finding Mather's private language of self-control jolting. Modern readers still react with puzzled annoyance to the obtuseness of Matherese, the spectacle it affords of a vengeful egotist nakedly transparent, and all unknowingly, through his contrarily expressed forgiveness and charity. Benjamin Colman detected his practice of simultaneously saying and unsaying, and admonished him for it. After Mather apparently wrote to him expanding fulsomely on the subject of charity, Colman replied that he was glad for Mather's enthusiasm on this subject but cautioned him that he would not be perfect in charity himself until he displayed "as much Care not to provoke Wrath, as power afterward to despise, or triumph over, it." Colman's acute remark suggests that Matherese served more than simply Mather's anger. For Mather also felt intensely guilty about his anger: in "my Hatred and Malice towards other Men," he wrote, "I have been a Degree of a Murderer." Thus in provoking others to condemn and revile him, he evidently also sought to thrash his own hated murderousness. More than any other characteristic of

Mather's, it is this impossibly provocative fusion of the conciliator and the troublemaker, of his goodwill and his rage, that has always made him seem at once splendid and contemptible.

When not surfacing through his benevolence, Mather's anger sometimes simply took a different route around his guardedness. He had always exhorted and denounced the rising generation, but his many sermons to the young around 1710 seem to translate into dire warnings to them the pent-up hurt he felt toward Dudley, Leverett, and others. To cite only two brief instances, from sermons published in 1710 and 1712, of this redirected rage:

> [The minister] is above the reach of Hurt from your Malignity. You do but add unto his *Crown,* as often as you Express your Disaffection to him. Do, Go on to make him the Object of your Venom; Throw all the Dirt of a *Street* upon him, if you please; Do, *Go on still in your Trespasses.* You will *Wound* your selves, and none but your selves Wretches. . . .
>
> Silly Children, the Minister of God is above all your Silly Attempts. You can't hurt *him.* If the Wrath of God, had not left you bereft of your Wits, you would feel, that you hurt but *your selves.* Your Venomous *Arrows* are all Shot against a *Rock.* They'll prevail nothing against an *Iron Pillar,* and a *Brasen Wall!*

Astonishingly, on virtually the same days that Mather could subject the children in his congregation to these sniggering anathemas he could compose genteel Curiosa to the Royal Society, praising the works of human reason. More astonishing and also distressing, he could in this period at one moment praise Francke for his beneficence to poor children, and at another threaten children in his own flock, uncharacteristically, with punitive incineration:

> There are *Children,* whose Doom will be to be *Burnt to Death,* in the *Day of the Lord that shall burn like an Oven.* There are *Children,* whom God will send into *Everlasting Fire with the Devil and his Angels.* And what *Children?* Why, *Wicked* Children; The *Children* that make themselves the *Children of the Devil.* . . . Go into the *Burying-Place,* CHILDREN; you will there see *Graves* as Short as your selves. Yea, you may be at *Play* one Hour; *Dead, Dead* the Next. Little do you dream, CHILDREN, How near you may be to an *Evil Time;* Any more than the *Fish* which you sometimes Catch, are aware of their *Evil Time!*

In discharging his stifled anger at powerless objects, Mather called attention to the side of himself that was both chaotic and, in the popular mind, longest remembered.

Mather's tantrums and provocations are redeemed, if at all, by two consistent features of his personality. First, his concern for human misery, however at times enmeshed with baser feelings, was genuine, and issued in innumerable acts of kindness. Also, since adolescence he had been himself anguishedly aware of his envy and rage. With countless self-condemnings and resolves he struggled to subdue these traits in himself, of which he sternly disapproved but which nearly always mastered him. It was his destiny, his tragedy, often to end up lamenting: "I can't Sufficiently preserve that Sedate, and Serene, and Comfortable Frame of Mind which belongs unto the *Peace of God.*"

Mather's exasperating difficulty in composing himself had a further unfortunate result. He fought off his sense of rejection, we have seen, by multiplying his efforts to please and by seeking recognition outside Boston. Such comfort as he gained was bound to be imperfect and transient, for his feeling of insufficiency was ingrained, and his offerings to London or Glasgow brought with them the same personality that often antagonized his neighbors. His attempts to attain elsewhere the acceptance denied him in Boston extended a vicious cycle—Do Good, Be Spurned, Do More Good, Be More Spurned—and won him a heavy burden of further disappointment.

Some of this result can be seen by looking a little beyond the period of Mather's quarrel with Governor Dudley, to about 1715. His spat with the Scots minister John Squire already suggests how the consolation he felt in being welcomed by luminaries in the Church of Scotland throve on the distance separating him from them. Facing another visiting Scotsman in Boston, young [Patrick?] Erskine, he found himself again repulsed. Evidently hoping to demonstrate yet again his gratitude for the D.D., he invited the youth to visit him as often as possible, made him "as handsome a treat at my table as I could," and tried artfully to drop improving admonitions on him. These may have been no more artful than those he offered Squire, for Erskine, he complained, proved "unaccountably shy" of visiting him. Worse, Erskine married without consulting him and, as Mather put it, "the plot was carried on with such privacy" that he knew nothing of it for some time after it succeeded. Still worse, Erskine and his wife had their marriage performed by Benjamin Colman and joined his Brattle church.

Mather's stepped-up promotion of "Biblia Americana" abroad also begot fresh resentment. His five-page notice in *Bonifacius* apparently having failed to attract subscribers, he advertised the work again in England in 1716, this time in a sixteen-page pamphlet entitled *A New Offer To the*

Lovers of Religion and Learning. By now the ever burgeoning work had grown, by Mather's reckoning, to more than three times the size of *Magnalia Christi Americana.* The new advertisement contained a specific subscription plan: interested persons would send in their names affixed to a promise to take off a two-volume set, at a price set by the bookseller with the advice of three unexceptionable London ministers.

Yet English readers proved no hungrier for Mather's *New Offer* than young Erskine for his invitations. Baffled and hurt by the rejection, and more usually the silence, he wrote one letter after another, trying to account for the neglect of him. The English, he bitterly told one London correspondent, count New Englanders "what we really are, of too little use or worth for them to converse withal." The London booksellers, he told another correspondent, showed no interest because "*In one word, they are booksellers.*" Particularly he blamed the London Dissenting ministers, to whom he had often applied for help in publishing the work. They "do not seem to overvalue literature," he snipped, "Nor do they seem to think that it is much for their interest or honor to have any of their number do things of much consideration in the commonwealth of learning"—just what he expected, he told still another correspondent, "from men of their Narrow Spirits." Forsaken by those who should have appreciated him most, he issued an extraordinary spiteful warning to some Dissenting ministers in London that if they "cast it off," the work might be published under the auspices of "eminent Persons" in the Church of England.

The *New Offer* having failed in Scotland also, Mather tried to soothe himself by thinking that were the work not in English his admirers among the German Pietists would publish it. But from his London go-between with the Pietists, Anthony William Boehm, he got only the discouraging advice to copy out the whole of "Biblia Americana" (which might have taken years) and to lodge the transcript with an eminent London divine, for viewing by persons who might consider subsidizing its publication. Boehm also brusquely criticized the *New Offer,* pointing out to Mather that he had advised subscribers to send in their names—but had failed to tell them where or to whom!

Mather was wholly unable to accept the explanation given him by literally dozens of persons, that "Biblia Americana" was a valuable work but prohibitively costly to publish. In his mind, those who failed to confirm his worth were not simply shying from a project that could have cost little less than the reprinting of Eliot's Indian Bible but were, as many others had done, affronting a great and unselfish man. Snubbed in London, he responded as he often did in Boston, by grandiose self-promotion offered with accusative sarcasm: "I do not Expect," he told one London bookseller, "that my own having, near two hundred and forty times, entertain'd my Friends with publishing by the way of the press, Treatises and composures on various Arguments, and in various (Living as well as dead) Languages, will obtain for me with some, the Favour of being thought capable of any valuable performance." To elicit guilt and let off steam he made this harrumphing enumeration of his many works amidst his many other employments a sort of set piece, the numbers of works growing with each new cajoling letter he sent. Since the age of seventeen, he told Sir William Ashurst, he had had

> lying upon him, the ponderous Employments of the Evangelical Services, which the greatest Church in these Colonies has expected from him, and . . . he has in this while undergone the Humiliations of publishing more than Two hundred and fifty Books, of several Dimensions, on various Arguments, in Diverse Languages; yet . . . there is performed in the *Biblia Americana,* more than all that is promised in the Advertisement.

If only a few "persons of Quality" overseas favored the work, Mather felt certain, "Vast Subscriptions would soon be sent in." But they did not; the subscriptions never came. In October 1716, he wrote in his diary that the publication of "Biblia Americana" was "to be despaired of."

Mather's service to the New England Company also proved often thankless. He complained to the directors in London about the inadequacy of their remittances, which forced the commissioners to pay from their own pockets toward the salaries of ministers and schoolteachers employed in the field. President Leverett of Harvard provided a further annoyance: Dudley appointed him a magistrate to the Indians without the commissioners' concurrence and demanded that he be paid from Company funds. Finding the other commissioners sluggish as well, Mather several times offered to resign, but was kept going by the Company's gratitude for his work. When they awarded him £25 he wrote to London saying he considered himself repaid in the pleasure of serving them and wished to decline the gift, but accepted it as affording him "opportunities for continual and considerable expense of Time and Thought; and purse too (tho' that an Article not worth mentioning)"—which, translated (parentheses in Matherese often revealing-concealing the gist), means he disdained the money but needed it because the Company was forcing him to spend his own funds on its behalf. In Matherese again he begged the Company in 1712 to dismiss him because of his many other obligations, managing in the course of confessing his ineptitude to reveal himself to be invaluable:

> The uttermost that I can pretend unto, is, To give my constant Attendance at the Meetings; and a small Assistance to the Shaping of our Projections; and write Letters upon occasion to the Indian preachers and churches; or perhaps give Directions to the Instruments employ'd by your Commissioners; and receive and pursue Addresses to the Commissioners from such as please now and then, to make use of me in so befriending of them.

As always now, appreciation cooled him off and inspired higher flights of Doing Good: "The Corporation in *London,* having refused to dismiss me, (as I desired,) . . . I would more than ever set myself to serve them."

New frustrations came to Mather even from his election to the Royal Society. His first series of Curiosa, a hundred pages of manuscript, appeared in the *Transactions* as an eight-page summary. Whether the shrinkage disappointed him is unknown, but his Scots correspondent Robert Wodrow read the summary abroad and wrote him sympathetically, "It is my loss and that of many others, that we have not the full copies of your valuable letters, referred to in that short abstract." Nor do we know if Mather winced over the abstract writer's account in the *Transactions* of "Biblia Americana," which reported that Mather had described a large work in manuscript, "but does not name the Author." (Like his failure to tell readers of the *New Offer* where to send their subscriptions, the slip suggests self-sabotaging guilt over the towering ambition of the work.) Mather may not even have received a copy of the summary, for he complained to John Winthrop that "Our friends of the Royal Society do strangely neglect us (or packets miscarry). I hear of many things of mine published; but I never saw them."

Mather also discovered that his name was somehow omitted from the catalogue of the Society's Fellows. Of course he did not howl over this latest bit of ill-fated disregard, but rather made known his hurt to the Society in a promise of greater service. He would annually treat it to so many communications, he wrote to London, "that if every member of that illustrious body whose name stands in the catalogue (an honor not yet obtained for mine) will do but half as much, the stores in your collection will soon become considerable."

9

Of 15, Dead, 9

⌘

AT THE TIME of Governor Dudley's arrival, Mather had married Elizabeth Hubbard Clark, a young widow twelve years younger than himself. Her father was the Boston physician Dr. John Clark, whose father had been a physician also; on her mother's side she may have been related to an English noble family, the Saltonstalls. She had been briefly married to a Boston mariner named Richard Hubbard, with whom she had a son around 1699. Later accounts describe her as a woman of "singular *good-Humour* and incomparable Sweetness of Temper," having a "very handsome engaging *Countenance.*"

Elizabeth may have grown up in the Anglican church, for her father is known to have attended the first Church of England meeting held in New England, in 1686, under the Rev. Robert Ratcliffe. At some time, however, she heard the Mathers preach, and it was their preaching, according to Cotton, that turned her to Christ; three years after their marriage she was admitted to communion in the North Church. Indeed until her illness and death in 1713 left him more painfully isolated than ever, he entered in his diary little else about her than his efforts to assist her spiritual development and make her an asset to his ministry. He emphasized to her three points on which ministers' wives had made their names precious to posterity: constancy and fervency in their devotions; ingenuity and labor in instructing their families in piety; and compassion toward the miserable in their neighborhood. Thus he looked out for suitable books of piety for her, recommending that she attempt to draw from them matter for her private devotions, and urged her to take notes after the preacher during sermons, as he did, both for her own advantage and as an example to others. He resolved to say something instructive to her whenever she

261

came to his study, or he to her in their room, or when she brought him his "short Breakfast" and sat with him as he drank it. He also encouraged her to visit their neighbors frequently and contrive some act whereby she might say when she left, "Some Good has been done, where she was."

Mather and Elizabeth lived in the house he had inhabited for most of his first marriage, a few streets from his father's house and from the North Church. Apparently a substantial, three-story building on a plot 38' by 120', it expressed his belief that God allowed humanity a middle estate—neither so much nor so little comfort as to make people unmindful of their souls. No very exact picture of the house can be reconstructed, but it had a fence, a gate, a well, and a yard, and was sizable enough for Mather to hold large meetings in. The house also had a garden, which he tried fashioning into a "Sort of an earthly Paradise," using its trees and herbs as subjects of his devotions in the time he spent there. Among the known appurtenances inside were a stove, a *"Repeating Clock, and a very curious One,"* and "agreeable mottos" which he resolved to post in every room. Aside from a parlor apparently reserved for receiving visitors, the center of the house for Mather was his large study, containing a "very *easy Chair.*" Above the door in capital letters he posted, as a warning to tedious visitors or interrupting friends, the motto "BE SHORT"—although, his son Samuel added, "let him be ever so busy when a Friend came to see him, he threw all by."

The center of this center, something Mather had greatly desired and valued since youth, was his cherished library. At the time he married Elizabeth he owned between two and three thousand books. They stood in "Boxes," presumably stacked against the walls of his study—not only a predictably large number of religious and theological works in several languages, but also many volumes of history, classical literature, and Neoplatonic philosophy, and important scientific works by Boyle, Descartes, Gassendi and others, a testimony to his prodigious learning and curiosity. The earliest surviving volume from his collection may be Conrad Lycosthenes' *Apophthegmata* (Geneva, 1668), which he owned at the age of ten. From at least that time his library grew both gradually and through such accessive leaps as his purchase at the age of nineteen of ninety-six books from the Harvard library (offered for sale as duplicates), and his acquisition in 1709 of a group of six hundred sermons. Many books passed down in the family, and many volumes bear inscriptions of several generations of Mathers. He kept his collection current by often sending to London for recent books and journals and by managing to inspect new arrivals in America: "Seldom any *new Book* of Consequence finds the way from beyond-Sea, to these parts of *America,* but I bestow the Perusal upon it." Living near his father, who also read and acquired books voraciously, he had easy access to his father's library, so that Increase's collection "which was not much Less than Mine, was also in a manner *Mine.*"

How many books Mather accumulated in his lifetime is uncertain, but by the end of his life he probably owned the largest library in America. In 1686, when Mather was twenty-three, the English bookseller John Dunton visited him and judged his collection even at that time one of the finest private libraries he had ever seen: "as the Famous Bodleian Library at Oxford, is the Glory of that University, if not of all Europe," Dunton wrote, "so I may say, That Mr. Mather's Library is the Glory of New-England, if not of all America. I am sure it was the best sight that I had in Boston." Mather's son Samuel is said to have put the total collection— probably including the library of Increase Mather—at seven or eight thousand volumes, plus a very large holding of manuscripts passed down in the family through five generations.

Entering middle age in these years, Mather found himself the head of a large household. Both his parents were aging and ailing, Increase, we have seen, suffering various ills and fearful of diminishing mental power. Cotton rarely mentions his mother, Maria Mather, although she too had various serious ailments, being at one time so lamed by rheumatism that she could not stand for more than six weeks, and was growing infirm and feeble. As she turned seventy, in 1711, he gave thought to helping prepare her for appearing before God, and resolved to discourse with her "as prudently and as takingly as I can, on that illustrious Point." He had also brought to his marriage with Elizabeth the four children surviving of the nine he had had with his first wife—Katharine, Abigail ("Nibby"), Hannah ("Nancy"), and Increase, Jr. By 1711 he and Elizabeth had had four children more: Elizabeth (b. 13 July 1704), Samuel (b. 30 October 1706), Nathanael (b. 16 May 1709), and Jerusha (b. April 1711). Nathanael, apparently named for Mather's dead brother, however survived only six months. Elizabeth presumably also brought to the house her son by her first marriage, although Mather never mentions him. Nevertheless, as he neared fifty, Mather was perforce more a parent than ever before, the father of five daughters and two sons ranging in age from Katharine, now about twenty-two, to the newborn Jerusha, the other children being seventeen, fourteen, twelve, seven, and five years old.

Mather's household also had numerous long- and short-term servants and slaves—male and female, white, Indian, and black. He often publicly denounced what seemed to him illegal and brutal aspects of the growing colonial slave trade. In 1723, after several Boston blacks committed a series of arsons and even threatened to burn down the town, he asked Bostonians to consider whether blacks are "always treated according to the Rules of Humanity?. . . . . . Are they treated as those, that are of one Blood with us, and those that have Immortal Souls in them, and are not mere Beasts of Burden?" Unlike Samuel Sewall, however, Mather was in no sense an abolitionist, and he generally thought blacks superstitious and stupid. In his view, Christian law allowed slavery but "wonderfully Dulcifies, and Mollifies, and Moderates the Circumstances of it." He appealed rather for humane treatment of slaves, and especially for their christianizing, in the face of prevailing views that conversion would make slaves discontented or might even entitle them to liberty, Christians in theory being forbidden to keep other Christians as slaves. Mather attacked these views in *The Negro Christianized* (1706), where he reminded slaveowners that "They are *Men,* and not *Beasts,* that you have bought," and urged that far from becoming restive, christianized slaves would serve their masters more patiently and faithfully. Mather did much else toward christianizing black slaves: trying to promote the work by act of Parliament in England; publishing for householders a streamlined, three-question catechism to instruct their "poor Stupid Abject *Negro's*"; paying from his own pocket the weekly wages of a schoolmistress to teach blacks to read; and resolving to entertain the religious society of blacks of the North Church piously at his house.

In 1706 some members of his congregation spent forty or fifty pounds to buy him a young black man "of a promising Aspect and Temper." Seeing the acquisition as a "mighty Smile of Heaven upon my Family," he named the slave Onesimus, after the runaway slave in the New Testament who was converted and became virtually a son to Paul. Since for Mather and other Puritans, servants were to be treated as family members—as persons, that is, for whose salvation the householder was obliged to be deeply concerned—he labored with a combination of piety and contempt for Onesimus' conversion. Consistent with his belief that blacks did not differ from the rest of humanity in their capacity for salvation, he found Onesimus governed best by "the Principles of Reason, agreeably offered unto him," encouraged him to read and write every day, and allowed him to marry. (Whether Onesimus' wife joined the Mather household is unclear; the couple had a son, who died, however, in 1714.) He also permitted Onesimus to work outside the house and gain an independent income, charging him to keep the rules of honesty and to devote part of his income to pious purposes. For all that, Mather did not differ from most other Puritans in regarding blacks as alien and untrustworthy. He kept a "strict Eye" on Onesimus' company and activities, including "some Actions of a thievish Aspect."

Amidst his multitudinous duties and services, and despite his many upsets, Mather enacted his domestic role with great thoughtfulness and affection. He viewed parental love and responsibility as, next to devotion to God, the supreme human fact: "*Nature* knows not a greater Passion. . . . *To all men Living, their Children are as dear as their very Lives.*" He conceived child nurture as a joint venture among parents, ministers, and schoolmasters, aimed at making children gentlemanly and ladylike Christians—pious, literate, and well-mannered. In his many published works on the subject he advised that Scripture learning should begin as soon as children come out of swaddling clothes and can learn anything; later they should be made to read Scripture every day, form prayers out of what they read, and repeat sermons. When children reach a suitable age, parents should pray and weep with them, making them "*Witnesses* of the *Agonies,* with which you Address the Throne of Grace on their Behalf. *They'll never forget it!*" Mather also wished children to attain secular learning and to come to think that "to learn all the brave Things in the world, is the bravest Thing in the world." To this end he urged that they be taught to spell and read well and to keep neat writing books, entering into them profitable thoughts. To inculcate benignity in them, parents should set them doing kind services for other children and caution them to return good for evil.

To induce children to act upon such principles of reason and honor, Mather believed, parents must beget in them a high opinion of the parents' love for them. And to earn such affectionate respect from their children, parents must avoid harshness. Although Mather discounted the child's own will and counted a parent's word absolute law, he deplored all severity in child rearing: "The *slavish* way of *Education,* carried on with raving and kicking and scourging (in *Schools* as well as *Families,*) tis abominable; and a dreadful Judgment of God upon the World." He allowed for blows only in cases of very extreme misbehavior, and then not in fury or passion. As a general principle of discipline, he recommended that parents so combine pleasure and instruction that being deprived of instruction is punishment enough.

Mather conscientiously applied these principles to raising his own children, on whom he lavished attention. Except for his preaching and pastoral visits, he spent his day at home, shuttling between his family and his study, into which he often called the children to converse or to pray.

Each morning at nine (and again each evening) the family gathered for catechizing, praying, Scripture reading, and psalm singing, the children who were at school in the neighborhood coming home to take part in the devotions. He seems also to have required the children to write daily in their blank books, at a stated hour during which he gave them materials "both devotionary and scientifical." He outfitted each child with a one-shelf library taken from his own collection, adding some book to their stock each week, especially works by himself and his father. Privately he prayed constantly for their conversion and physical well-being, and tried each night to take an account of how they had spent their time during the day.

True to his own views on discipline, Mather sought to grace his instruction of his children with the same ingenuity and facetiousness for which contemporaries valued his conversation. He tried in his table talk to "Entertain" their minds and polish their manners by discoursing on novel and useful subjects. Before rising he would every day relate a story that might be helpful to "the *Olive Plants about the Table.*" Whenever coming upon one of them by-the-way he let fall some memorable and instructive sentence, a practice requiring, he found, "some Study, and Labour, and Contrivance. But who can tell, what may be the Effect of a *continual Dropping?*" Combining teaching and amusement, he similarly filled time with them on the road in his "Chariot," offered inventively pious reminders when they were at sports or games, "which the Circumstances of their play may lead them to think upon," and improved such other family activities as baking, gardening, or laying in provisions ("*Lord,*" he exclaimed when brewing, "*let us find in a glorious Christ, a provision for our thirsty Souls*"). When he gave the children money or some other gift he tendered as well some maxim which if they practiced, he told them, would be worth more to them than "the Little Thing which I now bestow."

As Mather proposed, the agreeableness of his instruction also proved useful in discipline. He tried to make his children feel privileged in being taught by him, so that the sorest punishment they could feel was "To be chased for a while out of *my Presence*"—a somewhat manipulative use of his children's dependence on his approval, reminiscent of his own childhood relation to his own withdrawn father, who spent sixteen hours a day in his study. Mather's many aggravations at this time seem to have made some difficulty for him in preventing angry outbursts against his children, and he occasionally reminded himself that upon any occasion of discipline he must "with all possible Decency govern my Passion.

My Anger shall not break out, into any froward, peevish, indecent Expressions. I will only let them see, that I don't like what I take notice of." But generally Mather was a notably mild and amiable parent. His success in reproducing his own affectionate domestic values in his children is illustrated by an episode in 1711 in which little Samuel mistreated his sister Elizabeth. Mather gave Lizzy a piece of fruit, but gave none to Sammy to punish him for "being so cross to her." The father no sooner turned his back, he discovered, "but the good-condition'd Creature fell into Tears, at this Punishment of her little Brother, and gave to him a Part of what I had bestowed upon her."

In attending to his children's material needs Mather was less successful. His wish to provide for them in case he died was quickened by uncertain health—a lingering morning cough and recurrent head and jaw pains that sometimes restricted his ministerial work, the headaches forcing him one morning to "lie down like a Stag in a Net." He treated these with various remedies and by riding horseback a few miles out of town—a practice he constantly recommended to others. Yet he realized he could leave little behind for his children's upkeep. His salary furnished no more than their subsistence and education and, unlike his father, he grumbled little over insufficient pay and cared little about financial matters. He could only hope that God would reward his service by providing for his children if he died. But the largeness of his family, and probably also the wider economic straits of Dudley's administration, sometimes left him and his children pressed. He noted in 1709 that having fallen into some wants, "I had not Clothes fit to be worn. . . . And one or two of my Children are no better accommodated." It was only in answer to prayers that in 1711 Increase, Jr., came by clothing for the winter. Nor were the hard times eased by Mather's insistence, whatever his own circumstances, on Doing Good: "Tho' I can get no better Clothes than Rags for myself," he wrote, "yet the Lord honours me, by making me the happy Instrument of clothing other people. The Poor have numberless Reliefs, out of my Purse, and by my Means from others, and the Naked are clothed."

In preparing his children for adult social life, Mather trained his daughters to be gentlewomen, his sons to be ministers. He resolved to have the girls cook at least one new thing a week, but he also had them write daily and read in one of the sciences, and he taught them shorthand and Hebrew. His pious but affable eldest daughter, Katharine ("Katy"), a "*Lamb* inexpressibly dear . . . a *Constellation* of every thing that could Endear a Daughter," became not only able with the needle and knowledgeable about the table, but also dextrous with her pen and in wax sculpturing, highly accomplished in Hebrew, and skillful in both instrumental and vocal music. To enable her to Do Good, Mather also determined on having her obtain knowledge of medicine. Proud that he had provided for her "so polite an education," he prayed to God to see her well married.

Mather's two sons, however, were turning out to have sharply differing personalities. His and Elizabeth's son Samuel early showed a bent for the Mather family's several generations of learning. By the age of six, in 1712, Sammy could read so well that Mather decided to supply him continually with Latin and English distichs to be learned by heart, with rewards for learning them. His son by his first marriage, Increase, Jr., also gave early signs of realizing the advice Mather had received from heaven that the boy would be "a Servant of my Lord Jesus Christ throughout eternal Ages." In addition to Creasy's formal schooling, Mather wrote out verses for him to memorize, hoping to improve him at once in goodness and reading, and sent him as well each day for instruction to the older Increase, the boy's grandfather. By about 1712, when he was thirteen, Creasy had grown so proficient in classical languages that Mather considered holding their "daily discourse" entirely in Latin, and planned to have Creasy turn the Greek of Posselius into Latin verse. To foster Creasy's conversion, Mather wrote down for him "certain Questions of the last Importance," and obliged him to write answers. He also rewarded the boy with money for transcribing works that might inform his mind and manners, and tried to have school themes assigned him that would promote goodness and virtue. Often he called Creasy into his study to sit with him as he read aloud various "Documents of Piety, and of Discretion," including parts of "Paterna," the autobiography he had begun writing for Creasy at his birth.

But Creasy somehow failed to feel the allure of the Mather past and of the Lord's service. Mather suspected that the boy ignored secret prayer and, calling him into his study, made him promise to desist from a prayerless life. Worried also that bad company was corrupting Creasy, he warned him to shun "vicious and wicked Lads" and urged him to spend Sabbath evenings with serious youths, reading pious works. As his own son began exhibiting the evils of the rising generation which he had often denounced from his pulpit, he prayed repeatedly to God to grant Creasy His converting influences, and often moaned into his diary: "I am full, full of Distress, concerning my little Son *Increase*. . . . . . My poor

Son *Increase!* Oh! the Distress of Mind, with which I must let fall my daily Admonitions upon him."

When Creasy reached thirteen, the time for his admission to Harvard, he failed to follow his father, grandfather, and five uncles into the school. Instead, after long deliberation, Mather decided to steer him toward the business world, and redirected Creasy's education toward secular life. Like his father, the boy had an elegant handwriting that might have suited him to work as an accountant or scribe, and he now concentrated on perfecting his writing and ciphering. Believing that Creasy had an aptitude for mathematical studies, Mather encouraged him to master geometry, trigonometry, and navigation. And to give the boy a polish that might serve him in business life, he also had Creasy trained in fencing and music. Just the same, he keenly wished him to appreciate the life of the mind, and tried to "ply him with all possible Methods for a most liberal Education in other Points [than business]; that he may be a man very useful in the World." When Creasy was fourteen, in mid-1713, Mather began seeking a businessman to whom he could be apprenticed, and by the fall seems to have located a religious merchant family to take him in.

*

The winter of 1713 brought the worst epidemic of measles in colonial American history. The disease first appeared near Newport, Rhode Island, in the summer, broke out at Harvard College in September, and by October arrived in Boston, where, Mather estimated later, it infected thousands of people and killed 160 in two months. To gird his neighbors for what might be coming, he decided to devote his public sermons and prayers to the subject of affliction. Fearing as well that his own household might share deeply in the common calamity, he undertook to make more numerous expressions of piety at home, to prepare his children for death, and to send up many supplicatory prayers himself, "that so the Wrath of Heaven may inflict no sad Thing on my Family."

In about two weeks Mather's entire family had been smitten, beginning with Creasy. Having survived choking on a pin during infancy and smallpox contracted during the epidemic of 1702, the boy fortunately recovered quickly, and Mather obliged him to write up special resolutions for his future conduct. But Creasy was no sooner well than Nibby, who had gotten smallpox in the same epidemic, lay "very sick" of measles, followed by "dear *Katy*" (although in "somewhat more favorable Circumstances"), and then by Mather's wife, Elizabeth, who had very recently given birth. Within only a few days his daughters Nancy, Lizzy, and Jerusha—aged seven, nine, and two—also took the disease, and Sammy, aged seven, as well as the Mathers' maidservant. "Help Lord," Mather wrote, "and look mercifully on my poor, sad, sinful Family, for the Sake of the Great Sacrifice!"

As such threats to the public welfare always did, the epidemic quickened Mather's desire to Do Good, and he proposed fighting it not only by prayer but also by his considerable medical knowledge. Certain that proper care might save many lives that would likely be lost through mismanagement, he considered printing a pamphlet of advice and lodging it among sick families, and inserting brief directions for treating measles in the newspaper. He clearly hoped, however, to avoid antagonizing local physicians by presuming on their expertise, and consulted beforehand with some doctors, who seem to have declined joining him in publishing the pamphlet but approved of his doing so himself. Even so, when the two-page work appeared later in the year, as the measles spread into the countryside, he specified that he intended his instructions for people unable to afford physicians, or beyond their reach. But at whatever risk of criticism from the medical profession, he hoped to distribute it widely to save lives: "Tho' doubtless my Action may expose me to some Invectives, yet my Conformity to my dear Saviour, in what He did for the sick, will be my inexpressible Consolation."

One historian of medicine has called Mather's *Letter About a Good Management under the Distemper of the Measles* (1713) "particularly because of its originality, one of the very few classics of early American medicine." Abandoning his habitual attempt to charm, Mather wrote his instructions "in the plainest manner that is possible," so that any nurse could administer them. After observing that in Europe measles usually proved a light malady, but in these parts of America "*Grievous* to most, *Mortal* to many," he described the symptoms of each stage of the disease, beginning with headache, eye pains, and dry cough, and reaching a turning point about three days after the eruption of red specks, often with such frightening but usually transient symptoms as vomiting and fainting. In mild cases he recommended allowing patients to maintain their routine until the specks appear, then to stay warm and at home, feeding sparingly on bland food. In more serious cases patients should lie warm in bed, consulting a physician if high fever persists. Aside from suggesting such remedies as teas or hot honey, the brunt of Mather's *Letter* is its reiterated caution against overtreatment, which may only worsen the disease: "*Don't kill 'em!* That is to say, With mischievous Kindness. Indeed, if we stopt here, and said no more, this were enough to save more *Lives,* than our *Wars* have destroyed." Mather's main, and important, advice was in effect to let nature take its course.

Elizabeth was the first in his family to die. Since first learning of the outbreak of the disease in Rhode Island, he had felt a "strong Distress on my Mind" that it would be calamitous to his family, and had related his premonition to friends "often, often." He was particularly apprehensive for Elizabeth because of her advanced pregnancy, as the disease often proved fatal to women who were with child. She gave birth on October 30, very easily, but somewhat prematurely—the result, Mather concluded, of her "too diligent an Attendance on her sick Family." Mather baptized the twins on November 1, naming the girl Martha, after Elizabeth's mother, and the boy Eleazer, after the biblical Martha's brother, a "priestly Name" identical with Lazarus.

Three days after the baptism Mather saw that symptoms of measles had begun appearing on Elizabeth. A few days after that she was in a "dangerous Condition," unable to rest, raising fears that she might die or become distracted. He apparently did not pray for Particular Faiths, as he had during his first wife's long illness a decade earlier. Several times in the interval he had been strongly tempted to regard powerful mental impressions as Particular Faiths from heaven, but "having been *once* buffeted in that Experience, I durst hardly any more countenance it." Despite Elizabeth's long sleeplessness, her mind had remained lucid, and he prayed with her many times, tried to offer consoling discourses, and readied her for death. It comforted her, he thought, to see that his children by his first marriage were as fond of her as her own.

On November 8, with his children lying ill and much sickness in the neighborhood, Mather preached at the North Church on the text John 18:11, The Cup which my Father has given me, shall not I drink it? Not without overtones of older, displaced bitterness he depicted Christ's submission to suffering: a man exposed to contempt for his ministry, jeered at, defiled by spit, yet patient under affliction, a pattern for all afflicted believers, "When the *Cup* appointed for you, is imposed on you, *Now* take it," he admonished his congregation. "Perhaps, 'tis the *Cup* of a *Funeral.* That which was the *Desire of thine Eyes,* and the Delight, and the Darling of thy Family, must have its *Funeral.* . . . Take it." The same day he observed, at home, "surprising Symptoms of Death" on Elizabeth, who had lain sleepless whole days and nights.

Whatever Mather's own council of patient submission, the prospect of Elizabeth's death was not easy. The marriage, despite his initial uncertainties about it, had worked out well, and he had found Elizabeth a woman of conspicuous piety, virtuous deportment, and benign temper, beloved by many. "To part with so desirable, so agreeable a Companion, a Dove from such a Nest of young ones too! Oh! the sad Cup, which my Father has appointed me!" He had prayed and cried to God often that this particular cup would pass from him, but somehow without being able to produce in himself the appropriate spiritual state. Now he saw the meaning of his deadness of heart: "My Supplications have all along had, a most unaccountable Death and Damp upon them!" Elizabeth died on the afternoon of November 9, ten days after giving birth. In the room with her body Mather again tried to persuade himself into a state of resignation in which to suffer without complaint the will of God in taking "my dear, dear, dear Friend."

The next to die, on November 14, was Mather's maidservant, as he learned on arising that morning. She had been stricken about two weeks earlier, together with his children, but her measles passed into a "malignant Fever." He found some compensation for her death in the fact that she had come to his family a "wild, vain, airy Girl" but had grown disposed to serious religion, awakened to fervent secret prayer, and at last brought into covenant and baptized, "and my poor Instructions, were the means that God blessed for such happy Purposes." With her death he resolved to intensify his own repentance for any miscarriages in his behavior toward his servants.

The twins Eleazer and Martha died next. Elizabeth's easy delivery had encouraged Mather to hope that he had been mistaken in his earlier premonition of family disaster. But only two weeks after the twins' birth, and a day after the passing of his maidservant, he found both newborns "languishing in the Arms of Death." Eleazer died first, at about midnight three days later, Martha two days after that.

The need to anticipate and bear up under the death of children had been a prominent theme of Mather's ministry. He had often reminded his congregation that at least half the children of men die before the age of twenty, and that "In the *Deaths* of your Children, Endured with a due Submission, to the *Father of Spirits,* you offer up some of your Fattest *Sacrifices.*" His own power of quietly sacrificing his most choice was called upon, for although most of his other children seem to have recovered by the time of the twins' death, his daughter Jerusha, about two and a half years old, still lay dangerously ill with a high fever. She had been named for his youngest sister, who had died in childbed of her first child at the age of twenty-six—a woman of promising intellectual ability and a "considerable Mistress" of her pen, of whom he had been greatly fond.

With the loss of Elizabeth and the twins, not to mention the deaths of five other young children during his first marriage, the "dying Circumstances" of "dear pretty Jerusha" were to Mather nearly insupportable: "I begg'd, I begg'd, that such a bitter Cup, as the Death of that lovely child, might pass from me." On the night of November 21, Jerusha asked him to pray with her, as he did with distress but without protest to God, having earlier in the day attended the funeral of his twins. She lay speechless many hours, he recorded, but finally her speech returned a little to her and she said the minute that she died *"That she would go to Jesus Christ."*

Next day, with Jerusha lying dead in the house, Mather preached to his congregation as one who had seen five deaths in his family in less than two weeks and was tomorrow, he said, "to attend the Funeral of a Child which was Two years and seven months old." His calamities had become a matter of town talk, and he was aware that the "Eyes of the People are much upon me." Eager to have at least "the Happiness to do the more Good for every Evil that befalls me," he had something to offer his listeners: although he had fervently hoped for Jerusha's recovery, he had once again found—*"Nevertheless!"*—that the God who created and loved him had strengthened him to acknowledge that love by submissive acquiescence. Thus he stood in his pulpit as a model of "ONE who *Lives* in the midst of *Deaths*," and took as his doctrine *"Dying Daily,"* whose several meanings he elucidated. To die daily means to keep a lively sense that we daily progress toward death, that every day may be our dying day; means to die to the world, mortifying ourselves so as to regard the world as a *"Despicable* Thing." In dying daily we draw out the bitterness from death itself. Determined to make his cross bear still more fruit, "tho' the cross be but a dry sort of a tree," he preached another sermon three days after Jerusha's funeral, on the doctrine that A Good Man is a Strong Man. But this day, a day, he said, "which truly may be called, a *Night,* rather than a *Day,"* he confessed with some weariness to his own need for strength. "The Poor Man, who Preaches these Things," he told his congregation, "is far from asserting his own *Claim* to all this Character; and his *Want* of it, is the bitterest *Cup* in his *Adversity.* All that he can say, is, That when you, O dear People of God, are Pressing after this Character, he hopes, you will Pray for *him,* that he may share with you, in so great a Consolation."

In December, with his household recovered, Mather began dedicating himself to new or more active exercises of devotion. He felt that the events of the last month—"a *Month* which *devoured* my Family"— obliged him to renew his practice of setting apart whole days of prayer and fasting. The unfamiliar quiet in the house owing to the removal of small children from it also allowed new exertions for his surviving children, none now under seven years old. He would labor for Creasy's conversion, and furnish each living child with a "Closet of Remedies" by which they might relieve the miserable. For himself, he prayed for divine aid in behaving with discretion and purity in his single state. Some "silly People" had already brought him " a foolish Message from a Gentlewoman," but he felt he must spend the rest of his life in widowerhood.

As Mather digested and began to ruminate on his loss, he doted particularly on the meaning of Sacrifice. Since God had lately so much called him to such a work, he desired to develop a special skill and will for it. He proposed an exercise to himself: he would look on all his enjoyments, very often look on the dearest and most valuable of them, and in looking conceive to himself a sacrificing thought. "*O my dear Saviour,*" he would think, "*If thou shalt be most glorified, by my having this taken from me, I resign it, I forego it, I am content and willing to be without it.*" Accustoming himself to Sacrifice would earn him a true share in the royal Priesthood. By accustoming himself to sacrifice, too, he would be "prepared for *all Events.*" At some moment he wrote out on the back cover of one of his notebooks the names of all the children he had fathered, drawing a line to separate the offspring he had had by his first and second wives, both now dead.

> Abigail
> Katharin[e]
> Mary
> Increase
> Abigail
> Mehetabel
> Hannah
> Increase
> Samuel
> _____
>
> Elizabeth
> Samuel
> Nathanael
> Jerusha
> Eleazer
> Martha

Beside the list he wrote down the dreadful tally:

> Of 15,
> Dead, 9
> Living, 6

As was his custom, Mather closed his diary for the year 1713 on February 11, 1714, the day before his birthday, noting that "The fifty first Year of my Age is terminated."

Mather's fifty-second year began badly. On April 4, his mother, Maria Mather, died at the age of seventy-two. He and his father preached and published complementary sermons on her death. Increase dedicated his sermon to his children, telling them they had lost a "Tender Mother" and compulsorily reminding them they "will very shortly be *Fatherless* as well as Motherless," yet composing a loving tribute to his companion of fifty-two years, a woman, he said, who "did me good and not evil all the days of her life." Cotton, in his sermon, drew for his congregation the character of an ideal mother, one with a strong natural inclination to comfort her children, pray for them in distress, teach them their catechism, groan to heaven over their spiritual estate. When such a mother sees a son now a man, and a worthy and useful and noted man, then her affection to such a son will be "very Passionate, very Rapturous, very Marvellous, nothing will be equal to the Transport of it." Then he explained that in making his ideal portrait of a mother he had had, of course, "somebody *sitting* before me for it."

Of course, too, Mather cautioned his flock that while sorrow for a mother's death is allowable, God has better comforts for His children than has the most affectionate mother in the world, God extends to His children more than maternal consolation, takes mothers away to bring His children to more entire dependence on Him alone, teaches His children not to expect comfort from the children of men, in whom there can be no comfort.

IV

SILENCE DOGOOD

(1714-1724)

‚‚◦⌒◦‚

"Mather. *What* a force. . . ."

—VALÉRY LARBAUD, quoted in William Carlos
Williams, *In the American Grain* (1925)

The diary of Cotton Mather is a treasure-trove to the abnormal psychologist. The
thing would be inconceivable if the record were not in print. What a crooked and
diseased mind lay back of those eyes that were forever spying out occasions to
magnify self! He grovels in proud self-abasement. He distorts the most obvious
reality. His mind is clogged with the strangest miscellany of truth and marvel. He
labors to acquire the possessions of a scholar, but he listens to old wives' tales with
greedy avidity. In all his mental processes the solidest fact falls into fantastic perspective.

—VERNON LOUIS PARRINGTON, *The Colonial Mind
1620–1800* (1927)

His character was now definitely formed, his mind at fourteen had reached the limit
of its growth: all else afterward was mere expansion in the sense of things observed
and memorized, a collected mass of information, but the actual capacity of his mind
was measured finally at adolescence. He was a typical wonder-child.

—KATHERINE ANNE PORTER, "Affectation of
Praehiminincies (A.D. 1663–1675)" (1934)

. . . a witches' chowder
(All my eye and Cotton Mather!)

—ROBERT FROST, "Clear and Colder" (1936)

Read (if you can) the writings of the great doctors of seventeenth-century Calvin-
ism, the heirs of Calvin and Beza, Buchanan and Knox. Their masters may have been
grim, but there is a certain heroic quality about their grimness, a literary power
about their writing, an intellectual force in their minds. The successors are also
grim, but they are grim and mean. Perkins and 'Smectymnuus' in England, Rivetus
and Voëtius in Holland, Baillie and Rutherford in Scotland, Desmarets and Jurieu in
France, Francis Turrettini in Switzerland, Cotton Mather in America—what a gallery

of intolerant bigots, narrow-minded martinets, timid conservative defenders of repellent dogmas, instant assailants of every new or liberal idea, inquisitors and witch-burners!

—H. R. TREVOR-ROPER, *The European Witch-Craze*
. . . and Other Essays (1969)

. . . twisted with subtlety, like the dark, learned, well-connected Cotton Mather. The supreme bookman: Mather wrote 450 books, all printed. It seems a slander that he could have done so much harm when all his nights and days were spent writing and looking up brilliant quotations.

Mather, the Salem witch-hanger, was a professional man of letters employed to moralize and subdue. His truer self was a power-crazed mind bent on destroying darkness with darkness, applying his cruel, high-minded obsessed intellect to the extermination of witch and neurotic. His soft bookish hands are indelibly stained with blood—a black image to set against our white busts of Washington and Lincoln. Perhaps in his cross-examinations of the harmless and foolish, Cotton Mather oddly exposed a deep, symbolic, incongruous intelligence that nearly made him immortal.

—ROBERT LOWELL, "New England—and Further"
(1977)

10

Lydia Lee George

⁓◦◦⁓

AT THE TIME of Cotton Mather's birth, his family home on Cotton's Hill overlooked an islanded peninsula on the edge of a wilderness, inhabited by about three thousand Puritans. But now, some fifty years later, Boston had about twelve thousand diverse inhabitants, and its handsome houses, public amusements, and tempting shops made it in many minds a city.

To be sure, Boston remained in ways a vulnerable place—occasionally rattled by earthquakes (one tremor shifted wall stones at Cambridge in 1705), swept by epidemic diseases, imperiled by fire. In October 1711, a drunken oakum picker accidentally ignited rubbish in the backyard of an old South End tenement, touching off the most destructive fire in the history of the colonies. Unextinguished for seven hours and visible twenty leagues at sea, the conflagration consumed whole streets of houses—including the treasured First Church and the Town House—and lay the central district of Boston in ashes. A growing and heterogeneous populace met such disasters with thoughts less of invasion, however, than of expansion. Members of the First Church erected a new and much finer meetinghouse—in brick, seventy-two feet long, its three stories surmounted by a bell tower that dominated the center of Boston. A new Town House went up, enclosing the courts and the government meeting rooms; also made of brick and more imposing than the old Town House, it quickly became Boston's showplace.

Indeed a half century after Cotton Mather's birth, Boston everywhere manifested physical growth and urbanization. Of the town's three thousand houses, about a third were now brick or stone, often distinguished by fine masonry, in part to resist fire, a hazard also reduced by a fire department of twenty men and six engines. Streets had been widened, extended, and given official names, and until it proved too expensive were effectively cleaned by carts and horses hauling off dirt and refuse at town expense. By 1720 the town had the finest highway system in the colonies, superior to that of most English cities, and a sewer system that provided the best drainage of any town in America or England.

Despite the restraining effects of war, too, Boston had become the main entrepôt in the colonies for European goods. Through it, New Hampshire lumber, Connecticut grain, and New York furs passed to Europe, England, and the West Indies, to be exchanged for wines, salt, and other foreign commodities. Boston also led all other towns in shipbuilding. Ship masts in the harbor, said one observer in 1719, "make a kind of Wood of Trees like that which we see upon the River of Thames." In 1716 a lighthouse was completed at the entrance in the harbor to facilitate navigation. A new fortification, Fort William, was built in the harbor, mounted with about a hundred pieces of ordnance. The crowded shoreline, dense with wharves, gained a spectacular addition in 1714, together with the rebuilding of the South End, by the completion of the extraordinary Long Wharf. Built the width of King Street, the wharf extended this main street of Boston into the bay for nearly a third of a mile, providing a pier at which even very large ships could unload without the help of lighters. Debarked at the Long Wharf, a visitor could proceed directly up King Street about eight hundred feet to the new Town House, at the heart of Boston.

To walk that gently arching path was to have an alluring, Fifth Avenue view of the town's vigorous commercial life. A stroller might begin by inspecting the cornucopia of goods sold from warehouses built on the Long Wharf itself—rigging and casks of nails, cider and wine, women's muffs and necklaces, gunpowder and indigo, "choice Pictures, fit for any Gentleman's Dining Room or Stair-case"—then proceed up King Street, a busy commercial thoroughfare, past the shops of the London jeweler James Boyer, or of Andrew Faneuil offering silks and French salt, or Philip Hedman vending fine black cloth and "New fashion Looking-Glasses," stopping perhaps at Selby's or Hall's Coffee House along the way, or detouring to the signs of the Bunch of Grapes, the Baker's Arms, or the "Black Boy a Grinding," until arriving at the central Town House, surrounded by a thriving merchant exchange and the Exchange Tavern, there to browse at still other retail shops selling cloth or books or prints or toys.

Social life kept pace with commercial. In their houses, furniture, tables, and dress, it was said, Bostonians lived as splendidly and showily as the most considerable tradespeople in London. Between 1700 and 1711 sixteen new booksellers opened; by 1720 the town had five busy printing presses and three newspapers. New elementary schools had been established, and under President Leverett once tottering Harvard had revived. The fifteen or twenty undergraduates of fifty years ago had multiplied by 1719 to one hundred and twenty; by the next year many of them were housed in Massachusetts Hall, a brick building a hundred feet long and forty wide. Around town at various times, one might take lessons in dancing, treble violin, and spinet from George Brownell; see "Moving Pictures" featuring animated mills and ships; attend a horse race run in Cambridge for a £20 purse; or on the Bowling Green watch a man named John Coleson baiting a bear.

Urban pleasures also brought urban problems. With its several bawdy houses, rampant public drunkenness, and increasing numbers of poor, Boston experienced much petty crime, and with that an uncustomary locking of doors and a growing constabulary. In 1711 an act was passed for suppressing robberies and assaults, punishing muggers by branding in the forehead and six months' imprisonment, with death for a second conviction. Civic violence was aggravated by Boston's ever larger number of slaves, who were sold all over town, including near the churches. Scarce a house in Boston except the very poor, it was reported, lacked black servants, and every issue of the *News-Letter* carried ads for "A Negro Man Aged about 16 years, to be Sold," "A Negro Child to be given for the Rearing," "A Negro Girl aged about Eight years, to be Sold." The slave population was not only large but also resentful, prone to theft, rape, murder, and arson. In the summer of 1723, after a few blacks had been publicly whipped for setting fires, it was rumored that blacks planned to burn down Boston itself.

Here a John Eliot in his apostolic leather girdle could only have seemed, for better or worse, preposterous, while, as one English visitor wrote in 1719, "A Gentleman from *London* would almost think himself at home in *Boston*." This Boston of wharves laden with muffs and prints, of pilastered brick houses—and of exhibitions of bearbaiting—made a fit setting for Cotton Mather's marriage to Lydia Lee George.

*

In some ways, Lydia seemed to Mather such a woman as he had not dared marry when, a dozen years earlier, he resigned young Kate Maccarty. Among many appealing elements of her past and personality, she was the daughter of the Rev. Samuel Lee, no longer a well-known figure, but one of the most intelligent and forceful men in the history of early New England: "hardly ever a more *Universally Learned* Person," Mather remarked, "trod the *American Strand*." Educated at Oxford and appointed by Cromwell to the ministry of an Independent church near London, he emigrated in 1686 to New England, settling as a minister in Bristol, Rhode Island, where his inheritance from his very wealthy father enabled him to erect a fine house.

Although Lee returned to England after the Glorious Revolution of 1689, his few years' stay in New England impressed. From America he sent home naturalistic accounts of the Indians, of rattlesnakes, and of American diseases and epidemics. Several of his sermons were published in Boston and rank among the very best American Puritan sermons by their originality, verbal artistry, and deep acquaintance with natural science. The sale of his library in Boston in 1693 occasioned the first printed sale catalogue of books in New England: about one thousand titles in sixteen double-columned pages, including "*Newtons* Astronomy." To Lydia and his three other daughters he left a rich estate of £1300 each, plus his many manuscripts on chemistry, medicine, and other subjects. Inevitably Lee's interests and accomplishments brought him in touch with the Mathers. His daughter Anne was a member of their church, and in one letter he speaks of Increase as his "*highly honoured friend*" and mentions sending two books to "your good son." Cotton took extensive notes on nine sermons preached by Lee, and wrote a Preface to Lee's *Great Day of Judgment* (1692). He also extracted much material from Lee's published and manuscript writings for "Biblia Americana," with admiring acknowledgments of their authorship.

This heritage of intellectual distinction and family wealth already recommended Lydia to Mather. But her previous marriage added the extra attraction of civic prominence and probably even greater wealth. Her deceased husband, the merchant John George, had been a leader in the growth of Boston. A town selectman in 1701 and 1713, George was placed on a committee of thirty-one chosen in 1708 to formulate a scheme for the better government of Boston; five years later he and some associates proposed to the General Court the erection of the lighthouse at the entrance to the harbor. He was also one of the original proprietors of the Long Wharf, perhaps the greatest civic project undertaken in colonial Boston. Earlier he had owned a warehouse on the Boston dock, where he sold among other wares gunpowder, grindstones, and anchors, in partnership with a man named Nathan Howell, who was also his son-in-law and co- or part-owner with him of at least three sloops. With the building of the Long Wharf, George moved his warehouse there, dispensing maritime supplies from the great wharf itself. His sizable business dealings involved him in sizable litigation: the court cases involving him occupy nearly a page and a half in the index to the Judicial Court files.

Well-to-do and socially visible, the Georges were liberal in their religion. John George was one of the original subscribers toward building a Church of England chapel in Boston in 1689, and later one of the original undertakers of Colman's Brattle church, to which he and his wife, and their son-in-law Nathan Howell, belonged. Colman's close advisory relation with Lydia is revealing of her worldliness. Not long after the founding of the church, as noted earlier, Lydia asked his advice about her manner of dress, confessing she spent too much thought on it and indulged the "vanity of Vying with others." Colman however reassured her that her dress was suitable to her plentiful estate, high birth, and prominent station: "You have been educated in the wearing rich apparel; Mr. George chooses you should continue it, it is not offensive nor grievous to sober Christians." This education cannot have been slowed by George's death in November, 1714, at the age of forty-nine. Making Lydia sole executrix of his will, he left her a great estate that included their pew in the Brattle church, a black servant and an Indian woman, and two-thirds the value of his household goods, of his part of the Long Wharf, of his warehouse, and of the stocks and profits of his partnership with Nathan Howell.

Mather waited scarcely a month after George's death before visiting this rich and distinguished widow, accompanied by his children. As Lydia's pastor, Benjamin Colman told Increase Mather that some people placed "inconvenient constructions" on the visit, presumably because of the recency of George's death. Cotton, who had grown if not warm toward Colman at least affably correct, explained that he had intended writing to Lydia instead, and was aware at the very time of the visit that "I did imprudently." His misgivings arose not only from the timing, but also, as he told Colman, from his "unrecommendable circumstances." For one thing, his financial situation was the reverse of Lydia's. During his quarrel with Dudley over the allegedly illicit trade with the French, he had been compelled to rebuke one of the traders, John Phillips, the brother of his deceased wife Abigail. In doing so he enraged his father-in-law, who, it was hinted to him, had cut him and his children from his will.

Even more than he felt unpresentable, Mather felt weary. His years of public quarreling and of isolation in Boston, the harrowing deaths in his family only a year ago, had left him worthy to be called, he said, "*Medio-*

morto, that is, Half-dead." He told Colman that although people kept suggesting that he marry, and although he was sometimes foolishly tempted, he had grown used to a mortified life and at last always came to his senses:

> It is, I confess, too natural for us foolish old men, when we have a whimsy from every quarter buzzed into our ears, to think a little, *what there may be in it.* I have, no doubt, foolishly enough been ready to fall into this weakness. But as yet my old age has not got so far but that I presently recollect, I presently am sensible of the *delusion,* presently bring all to rights, as a dying man ought to do.

Despite the sensible tone, Mather's assurances to Colman that he was too impoverished and worn out to consider marriage seem to have been in part motivated by a different concern: that Colman would resent his suit as an effort to lure Lydia from his ministry, conceivably from his affections. For Mather added in a postscript that he had told Lydia in person and in writing that Colman's "conversation would be so profitable and so comfortable there would never be the least need of any other." And he hoped, he said, "I need not ask you to continue in affording as much of it as is possible to one so very worthy of it." This curious hope sounds like jealousy expressed in Matherese. However that may be, Mather assured Colman that he had resolved to visit Lydia no more, affording neighbors no reason to suspect him "of any designs not proper for me."

But actually Mather was smitten by Lydia George, and felt not "*Medio-morto*" but rejuvenated. For a while he continued his suit eagerly but from a distance. In February or March 1715, he sought help from Mrs. Gurdon Saltonstall, the wife of the governor of Connecticut. Buoyant, he told her he had "struck for a very valuable fish" but must dangle an unknown number of months, like the whaler who knows to "let the fish run for a considerable and convenient while." While he sat it out he asked Mrs. Saltonstall to write in his favor to Lydia, promising that the best people in the country approved her entertaining his suit.

In the same confidently ebullient mood Mather sent Lydia herself a long letter of courtship. Mixing affection, formality, and banter, it was nicely composed to disclose the depth of his feeling without making her feel rushed. He addressed her as "Madam," as in recognition of her social rank and accomplishments she seems generally to have been called. Respectful also of her intelligence, clearly an important ingredient in her appeal to him, he began by offering, earnestly but good-humoredly, a sort of syllogism from whose premises her "good skill at making inferences" might draw the correct conclusions about him. If, he said, he were a person who spent his life doing good to people of all sorts, who loved his neighbors, and who prayed for those who abused him, then it could be "reasonably inferred" that someone who might come in the nearest possible relation to him would be "loved by him as much as can be wished by her." Admiring Lydia's "wisdom," he said, and feeling honored to be sometime admitted to her tea table, he wished to take no step of which she would disapprove, nor press for any public appearance she might judge unseasonable. But in the privacy of his letter he wished her to know that his regard for her qualities, and his desire to devote himself to her, were enormous:

> . . . he begs your leave that it may not be thought too soon for him to tell you, that your bright accomplishments, your shining piety, your polite education, your superiour capacity, and the most refined sense, and incomparable sweetness of temper, together with a constellation of all the perfections that he can desire to see related unto him, have made a vast impression upon him.

Ready to strike now, he also made it plain that he considered Lydia a record catch:

> If ever he should be so inexpressibly happy as to enjoy you, he could not but receive you as a wondrous gift of God unto him; a token that the unworthiest of men had yet obtained favor of the Lord. Such an idea he has conceived of you, that everything you shall be or say or do, will forever please him; and the pleasing of you will be his continual study and rapture.

In his desire to marry Lydia, he added, he had the general approbation of the public, especially the "more praying people," and he concluded by asking permission to say to her personally the same things he had written to her.

Lydia did grant Mather at least one interview alone with her, around March 21, 1715—in order, she said, that he might fully know her mind. This she did not bother to disclose in syllogisms. Regarding his suit, she said she desired to "hear no more of it," and that he would "speak and think no more of it." During their several hours of conversation she told him nothing else he wanted to hear, either. She suggested that other available persons would be more "agreeable" than herself, in whom people's prayers for him were more likely to be answered. Had he mentioned nothing of marriage, his visits, as a minister, would have been a consolation and satisfaction. But she forbid him to write her any more letters, and insisted on his making it known that, as to their rumored courtship, "there is nothing in it."

While hearing out this flat rejection, Mather tried to be, he said, "as calm, and as pertinent, and as obliging, as my dull Wits" allowed. He proposed that instead of saying "there is nothing in it," he would tell people that his suit was a matter which "Madam is not at present disposed to hear of." Lydia made the obvious but discouraging reply: people would say, "why does she entertain him? if she have no purpose hereafter to allow of his Intentions?" No, she was firm on it, she wanted him to discontinue. He said at last that, as a testimony of his esteem for her, he would entirely sacrifice his satisfaction to hers. She answered, "*Say, and Hold.*"

Rejection always unstabilized Mather, but Lydia's made him writhe. He blamed himself for having blunderingly antagonized her: "I have hitherto done just nothing that is Right. And it is a killing thing to me, to think, that I have been led into Steps, that have been so very offensive, and have occasion'd so much Trouble, to a person for whom I must always have so great a veneration." A relative of Lydia's suggested that he try to see her one more time, but he feared reviving the gossip which had helped alienate Lydia from him. The prospect of receiving further "wounds from an Hand, I so much admire" also worried him: "My tender Spirit and Health will suffer so much, and I shall be so unhinged for my Employments." And would persistence help? Lydia had made known unambiguously, bluntly, dismally, what she wanted: "that I would come no more." Brooding on her charge to him—"*Say, and Hold*"—he reaffirmed his decision to respect her wishes, and to stay away, "tho, the Earth could not afford me a greater pleasure, than her most agreeable Conversation."

But only for a while. For by this time Mather was deeply, romantically in love with Lydia. Although his first two wives, Abigail Phillips and Elizabeth Clark, make phantom figures in his diaries, little mentioned until their deaths, it is clear that in marrying them he sought irreproachably pious women whom he might bring to Christ and who would honor the ministry. But Lydia appealed to his restrained or disguised sensuality, worldliness, and ambition. His diaries speak little of wishing to aid her salvation and much of her endearments and station, little of his prayers but much of his fondness. Unable now to stay away, he decided to interpret Lydia's prohibitions against his visits as temporary, and reached out to her through her relative Thomas Craighead, an Irish minister and physician recently arrived in New England. He asked Craighead to assure Lydia that he would honor his resolutions to "keep out of sight" until

Colman directed him to appear, although formed merely "to gratify her; whom I can undergo anything to oblige, even while I have never yet received one favorable word or Look from her." Delay he would, but he could not desist. He also asked Craighead to tell Lydia that despite her protests, "I can by no means lay aside those vast Respects but must renew my Endeavors one Day, to make her yet more sensible of them."

In the spring Mather managed to penetrate Lydia's fear of gossip and, perhaps, her reservations about him. His courtship may have been spurred by the remarriage in May of his seventy-six-year-old father—"The marvellous old man," he noted two years earlier, "continues to do notable things"—who married Ann Lake Cotton, the fifty-two-year-old widow of his nephew. By what means Cotton Mather forwarded his own suit is unknown; the surviving evidence consists of several undated drafts of letters and notes, apparently written in April and May, indicating both progress and delight. One scrap reads: "I was never got so far in it, as I now with unspeakable Joy find myself. And now, my Lovely Creature, Do you go study my Lesson; and get beyond me." The draft of another letter, playfully addressed to "my *Mabel*," again hints at Lydia's attachment to Colman, and Mather's view of him as a rival for her attention; it reassures her that "The only Damage you are Like to suffer by me, is, that I am Like to take you from the ministry of so true a *Chrysostom*," and promises to repair the damage by procuring "your Enjoyment of as much of him, as I can help you to." Although the scraps also contain routine admonitions that Lydia not set her love for him above love for God, they generally read less like communications from the minister of the North Church than like *billets-doux:* "My—(Inexpressible!) I am afraid you been't well, because my head has ached pretty much this afternoon. The pain of my heart will be much greater than that of my head if it be really so"—signed, "one who loves you inexpressibly."

On June 24, Lydia Lee George and Cotton Mather put their signatures to a prenuptial contract. Many colonies permitted such agreements, by which women might preserve their property rights after marriage; Increase Mather and his new wife had legally bound themselves to have no say in each other's estates. The contract between the wealthy Lydia and the penurious Cotton, however, protected Lydia alone. Her desire for such an agreement can be variously interpreted: fear of being exploited as a rich widow; distrust of Mather's financial sense; the desire to be in control. Whatever its impetus, the contract stipulated that because Lydia was "vested in her own right with some Considerable Estate," it was not unreasonable that she retain power to manage it "according to her own

mind and Will." Mather agreed to give her sole and complete management of the property she owned and its income, to:

> Impower and employ as she shall think fit All the Lands Tenements mon-
> ey goods Chatells or other Estate whatsoever which of right is belonging
> appertaining or payable unto her, and to take Receive and dispose of her
> own use all the Issues profits benefits and Incomes thence to be made. . . .

More specifically, Lydia's control over her estate was understood to exist
"without any Let hindrance or denial of the sd Cotton Mather." Mather
bound himself to the agreement under a huge penalty of two thousand
pounds.

Ten days later, on July 5, Mather and Lydia were married, by Increase
Mather. Cotton spent the following night in private devotions, making
"New Espousals to HIM," thanking God for affording him such a consort.
On the Sabbath he preached at the Brattle church—once the site of his
sorest anger, now of his greatest joy—"which I am robbing of an invaluable treasure and beauty." He chose a text from I Sam., concerning "the
dark Hours of a *sorrowful Spirit*" who poured out petitions to God in his
darkness and was answered.

It seemed that way. "Perhaps the married State," Mather wrote a
month after the wedding, "never Exhibited an Example of a Greater Harmony, than what is between me, and the admirable Companion, which
Heaven has bestowed upon me." His pleasure with Lydia ended the long
period of cheerless mortification and angry gloom brought on by his
quarrels with Governor Dudley, his fears of an Anglican Harvard, satiric
verses on his "Diploma," the losses of his children and of Elizabeth, a
six-year rut of endless misconstructions transformed into Goods Devised,
endless celebrations of the *"Heavenly Skill of Sacrificing."* Now reaping
instead, his life renewed, he filled his letters and diaries for the next
eighteen months with superlative praises for the "best of women in the
American World," the "greatest of all my Temporal Blessings," the "Collection of a Thousand Lovelinesses!"

No portrait of Lydia has come down, but Mather found her, among her
other attractions, beautiful. Doting on her charming physical presence,
he again and again was forced to remind himself that her "Beauty lies in
her having so much of His Image upon her," to caution himself that "in
the midst of the Admirations wherewith I Look upon her, I must presently
think, She is nothing but what God makes her to be." Argue himself as he
would, delight in Lydia's creatureliness tinged even their mutual devotions with carnality. When they often prayed together in his study with

tears and moans, he found himself inspired: "The Company of my Excellent Consort with me, had its Influence, to make the Services of the Day
go on with the more Soaring Devotions. I took her with me into my
Library; where we together poured out our Souls, and our prayers, and
our Tears before the Lord; and also blessed Him for one another."

Whatever subtle sensuality lay in such soaring devotions together,
Mather of course took seriously the challenge of refining Lydia's religious
life. He wished, he said, to help her toward "those Attainments in the
royal Priesthood, wherein the Life of my own Spirit lies." To this end he
resolved to convey to her the main thoughts in his reading of the Pietist
John Arndt, and to encourage her visits to the poor in the neighborhood.
His success is uncertain, for no record exists of her being admitted to the
North Church, and she evidently missed Colman's ministry; an unaddressed letter by Mather, quite certainly to Colman, remarks that Lydia
"Laments it as the principal Calamity of our End of the Town, that she
sees you so seldom." Just the same, Mather found to his delight that her
refinements of education, birth, and station were matched by superior
spiritual capacities: "oh! how happy am I," he wrote, "in the Conversion
of so fine a Soul, and one so capable of rising and soaring to the higher
Flights of Piety!" Lydia could do nothing wrong.

Mather's removal to a handsome new house sharpened his feeling of
unaccustomed pleasure and good fortune. The house had been rented for
him by his congregation before his marriage, late in January 1715; he
probably proposed their doing so, perhaps to make his prospects seem
more appealing to Lydia. Although the congregation rented the house
only "until some further provision be made for him," he apparently lived
there the rest of his life, the church supplying his rent and repairs. Confusions in the surviving records make it difficult to locate the house certainly, but it seems to have stood on Ship Street in the North End, close
beside the wharves and harbor.

Mather now lived in what seems to have been an unusually fine wood-
en building, much more ample and comfortable than his first two homes,
befitting Lydia's rank. Three and perhaps four stories high, it contained
both a little and great parlor, a great chamber, and several garrets and
cellars, with adjoining yards, gardens, and pastureland. The size may be
estimated from Mather's having convened a church council in his "spa-
cious Hall," and gathered a local "Society of Pious Children" in his "ca-
pacious Library, which is three Stories above my Study." In the garden he
strolled and meditated, enjoying the springtime arrival of the "glories of
Nature." He walked too among the vessels wharved just below the house,

talking to the seafaring people and giving them books of piety. Whether to manage this large house Lydia brought with her the servants willed her by her deceased husband is unknown; Mather took along his servant Onesimus, but Onesimus began to prove "wicked, and grows useless, Froward, Immorigerous [rebellious]." Around 1716 Mather allowed him to purchase his release, by putting up money toward buying a black youth to serve in his stead—probably the "little Boy" Mather acquired in November 1716, whom he named Obadiah. Onesimus continued to help around the house, however, and in addition to Obadiah and very likely other servants, domestic chores were shared for a while by a Spanish Indian girl.

Altogether, in his new habitation Mather felt as happy as he believed the world could make him, and he often exclaimed cheerfully over the welcome, surprising reversal of his fortunes: "A most wonderful Prosperity! A valuable Consort! A Comfortable Dwelling! A kind Neighbourhood! . . . Blessings without Number."

*

To Mather's great content and gratification, Lydia quickly formed an affectionate relationship with his six surviving children. He found them willing to obey her directions and follow her example, taking "unspeakable Delight, in the Incomparable Mother, which God had bestow'd upon them." Once when Lydia left on a trip, Mather described for her in a letter the lamentations "among all your Children, when that word Mother not come home, was heard among us . . . . We are not sensible that the sun shines into any Room in the House, nor that our Chocolate has any Sugar in it." (As a chirpy token of his own lovelorn condition "while the best Creature I ever saw is out of my sight," he began growing a beard.) His daughter Abigail may not have moved with him into the new house, for a month after her father's marriage she herself married an attorney named Daniel Willard. (A year later the couple presented Mather his first grandchild, a girl.) Lydia also had a daughter, Katharin, who had been married to John George's partner Nathan Howell. After his death she married the young merchant Samuel Sewall, the judge's nephew; the couple may have lived a while with the Mathers.

Samuel, about eight and a half years old at the time of Mather's remarriage, showed a dismaying appetite for diversion. Mather often pondered what to do to raise his mind "above the debasing Meannesses of Play," and among other things composed and had him turn into Latin some sentences about the right uses of play. To nourish the boy's conversion he also considered having him keep sermon notebooks, as he had done, and offered Sammy his library for holding religious exercises with a "Society of sober and pious Lads." Like his father too, Sammy retained in his personality something sportive, but by the age of twelve or thirteen had begun exhibiting his father's learning, literary tastes, and piety as well. Able by then to converse with Mather in Latin, he kept a commonplace book of "Quotidiana," the entries indicating a bent at once scientific, literary, and filiopietistic—material from Grew's *Cosmologia Sacra* (1701) and from Bayle on comets, but also excerpts from Boileau on style, verse quotations from Dryden and Pope, and illustrations from "Biblia Americana." By the summer of 1719 the "very promising little Spark," as Mather delightedly thought him, was ready for entrance to Harvard.

Sammy's admission forced Mather to palliate his bitter relation to John Leverett, still the college president. He wrote to Leverett in July 1719, recommending Sammy's qualities and asking Leverett's care for him as president, tutor, and surrogate father. Sammy, he said, was of a "capacity good enough . . . is of a temper singularly sweet and sociable, is of unspotted morals, not without a tincture and a tendency of the more vital piety, has the manly prudence and reserve in which his years are somewhat anticipated." With that he left Sammy to Leverett's "wise, and kind, and paternal tuition"—as he brought himself to describe the man he still considered unworthy of the presidency, and privately detested. With his habitually elaborate paternal care, he also wrote out for Sammy an essay-length set of "Directions for a SON going to the College," advising him to read Scripture daily, peruse books of piety (including *Magnalia Christi Americana,* especially for the "lives of the excellent persons in it"), and fix his mind on the fact that the chief end of his life was to serve God. For Sammy's success in his studies, Mather advised above all that he shun "profane and vicious persons, as you would the pestilence."

One dark intrusion on Mather's new happiness came from his daughter Katharine. Not only had he always owned a special fondness for daughters: "The Tenderness of one for the dearest *Lamb* in the World," he wrote, "could not be represented in a more lively Expression of it than this; *It was unto him as a Daughter.*" But he had also given special care to politely educating and cultivating this "*Lamb* inexpressibly dear to him," so that Katy could make waxworks, play musical instruments and sing, compose pious verses, and read Latin and Hebrew fluently. A remarkable example of youthful piety also, and very much a child of Cotton Mather, without being crabbed or morose she delighted in religious retirements, experienced conversion, and wrote on one occasion, "I take an unspeakable pleasure in all manner of *Beneficence*. If I can see *Opportunities* to *Do Good,* I need no *Arguments* to move me to it." Seemingly a sweet and brave girl she apparently got along well with her new stepmother, whom she would not call "mother-in-law" because Lydia acted toward her like a real mother.

But about a year and a half after Mather's marriage, Katharine became the tenth of his fifteen children to die. Like her siblings she had been infected during the 1713 measles epidemic; she survived, but to a residue of the infection was attributed her falling ill in April 1716, the beginning of an eight-month decline that ended with her death in December, of what was described as consumption. As Mather again set before himself the sacrifice he must be prepared to make, he traced her deterioration in his diary, punctuating the otherwise blissful account of his new marriage with cries of "Ah! My dying Daughter! My dear dying Daughter!" As Katy lingered, wasted by consumption and given up by the physicians, he tried to treat her by a root grown in Lebanon, Connecticut, and sent him by his friend John Winthrop; known as Culvers Root, it was to be dried, pulverized, and mixed with honey into hazelnut-sized pills. But by November Katharine could not attend family prayers, and Mather prayed with her daily in her room. In December she expressed doubts about her acceptability to Christ; he told her that her trial of faith was from Satan, who knew she was to go where he could not, and that "she should see herself called into a *Marvellous Light.*" He spent much time near the end sitting with her, trying "to strengthen her in her Agonies." She died on a Sabbath at three in the morning and was mourned, despite the snow and cold, at a large funeral. That she might outlive her death by doing good after it, Mather published *Victorina* (1717), a sermon on the pleasures of true piety, containing an account of her life.

Katharine's death did not diminish Mather's satisfaction in his marriage. He was pleased, too, by signs of maturity in his often errant son, Increase, Jr. Alone of Mather's children, sixteen-year-old Creasy was not at home for his father's wedding, being then in England. Mather had agreed to pay the boy's passage aboard a ship commanded by the son of the merchant John Frizzell, there to travel as a passenger but to perform and learn the duties of a sailor. Although resigned to Creasy's having chosen a life of action rather than of study, he seems to have had reservations about Creasy's entering the maritime trades, but thought it harmful to disregard the boy's actual abilities: "I have been perhaps too willing to indulge and follow the genius of a child in the choice of a business for him," he confided to Sir William Ashurst, "as knowing that if that be not very much consulted, a child will never prove considerable." As he sometimes did in other circumstances, he wrote out a letter to Frizzell, for Creasy to send and sign as if by himself. "'Tis too well known," he had Creasy explain, "that my inclination is more for business than for learning. And being inclined unto the business of the sea, my friends have a prospect of my arriving sooner to some figure on that element than on the long wharf or the dock." In the letter he had Creasy tell Frizzell that having perfected himself in the theory of navigation, he must take to sea to learn the practice. Though a novice, he hoped he would not have to "enter at the cook-room-door." Yet he promised to obey orders and apply himself to every shipboard duty of which his superiors judged him capable. He also requested a fortnight's leave, upon arriving in London, to visit his uncle Samuel in Witney.

The visit turned into a stay of several months. Samuel, about ten years younger than Cotton, was the minister of a Congregational church in Witney, near Oxford. He invited Creasy to remain with him in the belief that Increase Mather—so long and so often planning or foreseeing a return to England—was at last actually about to return, to deliver an address from the Massachusetts ministers to the new king. (The North Church voted unanimously against Increase's mission, however: "I am now like to die in New England," Increase lamented, "whereas two months ago I was like to die in England.") Samuel found Creasy troublesome. The boy arrived in Witney with debts he had somehow incurred, only ten shillings in his pocket, and but one shirt, "so bare in every respect," Samuel said, "that I was perfectly ashamed." Samuel had credit extended to Creasy at a local store so he could buy clothing, and wrote to Cotton asking him to send a remittance for his son, to be managed by someone else. "I perceive," he told his brother, "he is infected with the disease which is the blemish of the Family viz. to spend inconsiderately and take no thought about providing against future unavoidable occasions. If I can I will cure him."

But curing Creasy was not simple. His mother—Mather's first wife, Abigail—had died when he was only three, and his father's remarriage rapidly produced several other children by a stepmother. Something in Creasy had stayed restless and turbulent. Samuel found that when he took the boy on a visit to tempting London, he had to "keep a pretty strict eye over him"; he decided to keep him at Witney, lest he return to his father "with a worse Character than he had when he came." Mather wrote to Creasy sometime in the fall to reinforce his brother's admonitions, instructing him to heed Samuel's lessons and urging him to make "all the Vices of Dishonesty, Debauchery, and False-speaking . . . abominable to you."

Mather's disappointment in Creasy's erratic behavior was tempered, however, by recognition and respectful love of his spiritedness and lack of malice. Thus he was wracked to learn in April that Creasy had been stricken with rheumatism and had lost the use of his limbs: "Oh! The Anguish with which I am to cry unto God, that He would yet be gracious to this poor Child, and make him a new Creature, and an useful Man, and return him to me! Oh! the Resignation to which I am called on this Occasion!"

For once, Mather was spared very protracted anguish about his children. The letter from Samuel informing him of Creasy's illness was apparently long delayed, for only a month after he received it, Creasy himself returned from abroad. He returned not only, it seems, hale, but to Mather's relief also greatly changed, "much polished, much improved, better than ever disposed. . . . I am astonished at the Favors of the prayer-hearing Lord. O my Father, my Father, how good a thing it is to trust in thy fatherly Care!" To Mather's further delight, Creasy stepped immediately on his return into a "lucriferous, agreeable, and honorable" business. Its exact nature is unknown, but Mather speaks of Creasy's being fixed in "the Business of the Store-house," with an expectation of being taken into a partnership.

*

By the time Mather courted Lydia George, his violent exchange of denunciatory letters and pamphlets with Joseph Dudley lay some seven years behind, and his relation to the governor had regained something of its initial tone of barbed courtesy based on recognition of mutual usefulness. Many different considerations probably drew Mather back into Dudley's orbit. For one, Dudley had proved his staying power. Although Sir Henry Ashurst had continued in London his crusade to have Dudley removed, he found the governor a person "of such insinuation . . . that only Satan himself hath greater," and he accomplished nothing. Mather seems to have resigned himself to cooperating with Dudley to salvage what vestige of political influence remained to him. Although his relation to John Leverett's Harvard was also a "very Imperfect Sort of Thing," he served with Dudley in 1712 as part of a commission to manage a large bequest to the college. Mather cannot have found such cooperation agreeable, but it was practical. The bequest had become a matter of legal contention in England, and without the authority of Dudley and the Mathers to administer it might conceivably have been lost. Compared with Dudley's stormy first half-dozen years as governor, too, the later half-dozen were quiet; the Treaty of Utrecht in 1713 for a while ended England's warfare against France, and brought the English North American colonies an extended period of peace for the first time since 1688.

Dudley also gave Mather less reason to fear his support for the Church of England, which demonstrated itself to be nominal. Although the governor signed a petition in 1713 from the Boston Anglican chapel, endorsing a scheme to establish bishops in America, the minister of the chapel complained that Dudley in fact belonged to a Congregational church in Roxbury, where he lived, and had not taken communion at the chapel for years. Mather was conscious, in addition, of Dudley's advancing age: laid up with gout in 1715, the governor had to be carried to the Town House in a sedan chair, and borne in it up most of the stairs. Finally, amidst the new generation that had grown up since the abrogation of the old charter, Dudley cut a less anomalous and threatening figure. Time had made it less inconceivable that the government should rest in one who saw New England not as Christian Israel but as crown territory.

Nothing so nearly reconciled Mather to Dudley, however, as the death of Queen Anne in August 1714, which brought new attempts to remove the governor. The event triggered the same reaction that had first won Dudley the governorship, namely fears that if he were not appointed someone worse might be. About two months after the queen's death, Mather wrote to William Ashurst in London, saying that "of late Months" he had lived in "Good Correspondence" with Dudley, and shared the general opinion that Massachusetts would be happier in him than in some who might be "*Strangers to us; or not of our Nation.*" The reasoning was well founded, for early in 1715 the new king, George I, appointed as governor Col. Elizeus Burgess, a man who had been tried for the murders of two men, one of whom he killed in a duel, the other, an actor, at a tavern. Yet Mather's reasoning also proved unnecessary, for Burgess resigned his office and never crossed the Atlantic. For a while, Lt. Gov. William Tailer acted as governor, until the arrival, in October 1716, of Samuel Shute.

Mather was glad for the political changes initiated by the new king, coinciding with the happy first years of his marriage. He rated George's accession a "great thing," replacing the High Church climate of Anne's reign by a monarch "so little in the French interests." The new governor pleased him even more, for Samuel Shute had a distinguished military record in fighting the French and, more important to Mather, belonged to a prominent family of English Dissenters. His grandfather was the famous Presbyterian minister Joseph Caryl, author of a twelve-volume commentary on the Book of Job; his brother, Lord Barrington, led the Dissenting interest in Parliament. In Mather's mind, Shute augured a government if not on the model of John Winthrop exactly, then of William Phips, one that while serving the crown would also hearken to Boston's Congregationalist ministers. After more than fifteen years of political impotence, he saw hope of regaining his place at the governor's table.

Shute no sooner arrived in Boston than Mather decided to "improve my Acquaintance, which I am like to have with him, for all the good Purposes imaginable." He preached before the new governor on October 11, and not long after sent him a rather obsequious letter complimenting his "wisdom and goodness," his "generous concern" for the public, and the "charms of Your Excellency's Speech." While everyone would be zealous to serve Shute, he said, the governor would "never have a more hearty Servant" than himself. Faithful to his promise, he lent Shute all his support, sometimes at the cost of personal compromise. Like Dudley, Shute seems to have been wary of offending any large religious group in Boston. Thus although he apparently joined a Congregational church in 1717, the following year he headed subscriptions for a new gallery at King's Chapel, where he attended Sabbath worship. Far from damning Shute, Mather praised him for showing no "Partiality for Little Parties in Religion." He also urged that the governor's salary of £1000 be increased.

For his efforts, Mather at first enjoyed with Shute the most cordial relationship he had had with any governor since Phips. Indeed he became virtually Shute's friend, often writing to him flatteringly, advising him on public appointments, sending publications, and receiving from him "singular Testimonies of Regard." At least once Shute invited him to send a servant to his cellar to take away a gift of wine, which Mather promised to do, adding unctuously: "Your Wine is good; but the Kind Aspect of your Excellency with it, upon him to whom you send it, sublimes it into Nectar." Inclined to evaluate others in extremes of best and worst, Mather believed that even had the people of Massachusetts retained their right to elect their own governor, they would have chosen Shute: "under the Best of Governours," he wrote in 1718, "our People enjoy all the Tranquillity which can in this present Evil World be looked for."

The change of administrations also brought to prominence a protégé of Mather's, the highly capable, and satirical, Jeremiah Dummer. Born into the affluent Boston merchant class in 1681, he took a B.A. and M.A. at Harvard, then visited Europe and did graduate work in Holland, where he published several works. He returned to New England to preach, but decided to leave the ministry and also declined a professorship of philology at Harvard. Instead he went into business and returned to London, where he played cards and watched "the great female beauties" at the House of Lords ("I tho't I could have gaz'd at them for ever"). As the growing regularization of New England's ties with the mother country brought awareness of the need for constant representation at Whitehall, he was appointed agent for Massachusetts, a role he considered "a very great honour." Later he was appointed agent for Connecticut and New Hampshire as well. His access in London to such persons as Addison, Steele, and Newton gave him a voice in the appointment of colonial officials, and in delaying measures in Parliament directed against the colonies. Resourceful and effective, Dummer could have become, it was later remarked in New England, prime minister.

Dummer greatly admired Mather and felt "bless'd," he said, to have such a "Dear and Worthy Friend." He looked up to Mather as the pattern of a "useful conversation" in life, although a lofty one: "I follow halting after his footsteps tho' far behind and at a great distance." Mather's company and person not only inspired Dummer but also amused him. He enjoyed their trips to Salem—Mather, he noted, "thinks wherever he comes, that he's up to the knees in Pigs"—and shared Mather's quarters there, later sending from London some verses by Waller to be hung in a frame in their bedchamber. Mather on his side recognized Dummer's diplomatic skill and influence, dedicated to him an important but now lost work called "Religio Generosi," and used him as a go-between with London publishers. He also found Dummer exasperating, a potential Creasy who however overcame his worst propensities. He attacked in print, and urged Dummer to retract, his unorthodox views on the Sabbath. Orthodox or not, Dummer may have been the one person who could criticize Mather's writing without enraging him. Their correspondence is enlivened by much tongue-in-cheek byplay about the number of Mather's publications, which Dummer several times told him frankly was damaging to him. This Mather took with half-amused indulgence laced with subtle hurt, in one instance sending Dummer a recent work with the apology that he did not ordinarily "nauseate you, with any of my published Composures." Somewhat acid, but lively and admiring, Dummer was the sort of man Mather could not resist.

Dummer's value to Mather, and to New England, became particularly evident in the founding of Yale College. Mather's own part in creating Yale has often been interpreted as an expression of his scorn for John Leverett, and toward Harvard under his presidency. But nothing in Mather's work for Yale suggests a motive beyond desiring to see a Congregational college in Connecticut, where he had such good friends as Governor Saltonstall and John Winthrop, and had long been concerned for the christianizing of the Mohegan Indians. It is true that Mather's name was mentioned for the rectorship of the new college, although it so appears only in private correspondence, and he may not have known of it. It is also true that at the time of his involvement with Yale, he complains in his diaries of the "Venom and Malice which the disaffected Rulers of our College, treat me withal!" But for all his disgruntlement he never cut himself off from Harvard affairs entirely (in 1714 he served once again as an Overseer), and it seems unlikely that he would have risked antagonizing Leverett at a time when Sammy was just entering Harvard under his tutelage. Besides, Colman and others also worked to promote Yale without feeling disenchanted about Harvard, and in their recruitment the two schools were too distant from each other to be competitors.

Yale College began taking shape in 1716, when the trustees of a small collegiate school at Saybrook voted to move to New Haven. The costs of raising and furnishing new buildings were great, but a benefactor was available in the person of Elihu Yale, a London diamond merchant who had been born in Boston of New Haven stock. As a young man Yale had emigrated to Madras, India, where he made a fortune. Becoming president of the East India Company, he had lived protected by several hundred guards, carried on an ostrich-fan-shaded palanquin. Yale intended bestowing a charity on some college at Oxford; but Jeremiah Dummer pointed out to the Saybrook Collegiate School that Yale was, after all, a Connecticut man by birth, and his bounty would be more suitably bestowed at home. Dummer himself solicited a gift of books for the school from Yale, part of a library of perhaps a thousand volumes which he begged or otherwise obtained from people in London: Steele sent complete sets of the *Tatler* and *Spectator*, Newton took down from his own shelves copies of his *Opticks* and his *Principia*.

Mather wrote to Yale soliciting his aid for the new school. As a member of the Church of England, Yale had doubts about supporting an "Academy of Dissenters," as he called it, the school being clearly intended to serve Congregational interests. Tactfully Mather appealed to him as a New Englander, and depicted the religious life of New England as based on "Catholic and generous principles of Christianity, and . . .

beyond the Narrow Spirit of a party." He stressed to Yale that the God who gives power to get wealth makes the wealthy no more than trustees of it, and mentioned a particular method of Doing Good:

> The Colony of *Connecticut*, having for some years had a College at *Saybrook*, without a collegiate way of living for it, have lately begun to erect a large Edifice for it in the Town of *New-Haven*. The charge of that expensive Building is not yet all paid; Nor are there yet any Funds, of Revenues, for Salaries to the Professors and Instructors of the Society

Then he proposed to Yale that for his beneficence he might have a monument that would be "much better than an *Egyptian pyramid*": the school forming at New Haven, he suggested, "might wear the Name of, YALE-COLLEGE." About five months later there arrived in Boston Yale's gift of three bales of goods to be sold for the school's benefit, plus a large box of books and a full-length portrait of the king by Kneller—the largest gift the school had ever received from a private person, worth about £800.

Mather was greatly pleased that he had been able to help the new college, but somewhat uneasy over having in effect christened it. He apologized to Governor Saltonstall for his "inexcusable presumption" in making himself "so far the God-father of the Beloved Infant, as to propose a Name for it." He did so, he explained, because he had been told that Yale might exceed his previous generosity if the school were named after him, and he asked Saltonstall to comply with his proposal. At the commencement of September 10, 1718, the trustees met in their new building in New Haven and formally gave the college Yale's name. They also wrote to Mather, effusively thanking him for his "noble and charitable regard to our infant Nursery"—regard, we shall see, that would turn to shocked regret.

∗

A simultaneous and far-reaching development in Mather's religious life shared in the harmony of his new marriage and his contentment with the new government. For twenty-five years, since the attempted union between English Presbyterians and Congregationalists, he had entertained the hope of unifying the Protestant churches. The failure of the United Brethren did not end his ecumenical enthusiasm, which now revived as an articulated vision of a pan-Christian union that would disregard variations of polity and worship and rest on a few distilled Gospel principles of vital piety. His efforts place him in the mainstream of religious revivalism reaching through the Great Awakening of the eighteenth century to such modern expressions of ecumenism as the World Council of Churches.

Around 1715 Mather exuberantly began detailing and publicizing what he called a "RELIGION OF THE EVERLASTING MAXIMS." Its first expression was *The Stone Cut out of the Mountain* (Latin title, *Lapis e Monte Excisus*; 1716), a "little Thing," he called it, "which is of greater Expectation with me, than anything that I have ever yet been concerned in." How much he expected of the work appears in his trying to have it translated into several languages, and in his hope of sending copies of it to eminent members of Parliament and to Hindus in Malabar, as well as to England, Scotland, Holland, Switzerland, France, Germany, and India. Although the diminutive work is but an octavo pamphlet of thirteen pages in English, with thirteen pages of facing Latin translation, its brevity was an achievement, the result, Mather said, "of more than a Little contemplation. St. Barnaby's Day would not be long enough to recite all the views which the author had in the composing of it." As he also observed, Luther's essays demonstrated that, if distributed far and at the right time, "Little Engines of Piety" might accomplish wonders.

In *Lapis*, Mather reduced religion to fourteen unshakable maxims on which Christians throughout the world of whatever sect, except Catholics, would agree. He made it unnecessary to list them here, for over the next year or so, as he continued vigorously to preach and promote this "Universal Religion," he reduced the number of maxims to three. These he summarized in *Malachi* (1717): belief in the Trinity, utter reliance on Christ for salvation, and love of neighbor out of respect for Christ. "*Real* and *Vital* PIETY"—the basis of Christian union—thus consists simply of "*Fearing* of God, and in *Prizing* of His CHRIST, and in *Doing of Good* unto Men." Mather conspicuously omitted matters of church organization or discipline, which he devalued to "*Lower* and *Lesser* points of Religion," subject to great diversity. No longer writing as someone committed to the Congregational ideal of church government, that is, he trumpeted a religion that could have existed had the Cambridge Platform never been drafted:

> Sirs; They are not External *Rites* and *Forms*, that will distinguish, *The People of* GOD. The *Kingdom of GOD comes not* with the *Observation* of such things as those. No; 'Tis a People found with various *Rites*, and in various *Forms. Hear this, All ye People; Give Ear, all ye Inhabitants of the World.* The PEOPLE of GOD, are All that cordially embrace our *Everlasting* MAXIMS of PIETY, and *Live unto GOD* upon them, in whatever *Subdivision* of *Christianity,* they are to be met withal.

This was a religion not for the Christian Israel of the Fathers but, as Mather said, for "millions of people in the world."

Mather's Universal Religion brought him equally far from the pneumatological realm of energumens and ringleted angels. He considered his Maxims of Piety a "*Reasonable Religion*," suitable for rationalistic, cosmopolitan persons who valued such social by-products of vital piety as fair dealing, the suppression of ill will, and helping others. Quoting Francke, he emphasized that these benevolent effects are superior to supernatural exhilaration and prophetic ability:

> To have such a *Discerning* of our selves and our Interests, as these MAX-IMS would help us to, is a more *Glorious* Thing, than to have a sight so refin'd, as to *Discern Spirits*. To have our *Evil Tempers* mended and cured by these MAXIMS, is a more *Glorious* Thing than to cast out *Evil Spirits*. To behave our selves *Wisely* as these MAXIMS teach us, from a *Foresight* of our *Eternal Judgment*, is a more *Glorious* Thing than to *Foresee* and *Fore-tel* Futurities.

In all but renouncing a thirst for the invisible world, Mather also came close to reducing the supernatural experience of grace itself to rational understanding. Noting that the many discourses concerning tests for grace sometimes leave the candidate for conversion in "as much *obscurity* and *perplexity* as before," he proposed assent to his three everlasting maxims as a "*Short* and a *Sure*" test for grace. Assent to them means that "Thou art most certainly *passed from Death to Life*. And the Experience of such Things as these, is preferable to all the *Joys of Impulse*, whereof some Enjoy the Raptures; tho' those also may be *Better than Life*." Minimizing the two essential features of Congregationalism, its view of the church and its mystical piety, Mather's Universal Religion aimed rather at quenching the fires of religious controversy, creating harmony in society, allowing scope to reason, and doing good to others out of fear of God and love to Christ.

Mather's ecumenism increasingly convinced him, also, of the need to indulge religious differences. His many calls for toleration make him seem more a figure of the Enlightenment than of the seventeenth-century, closer to Thomas Jefferson than to John Cotton: "PERSECU-TION, That *Prince of Devils* which fills the World with *Desolations*. . . . 'Tis an *Hellish Monster* which all Mankind ought with an *United Cry* to chase from off the Face of the Earth!" Mather went far himself in practicing this toleration. In a published letter to Francis De la Pillonniere, a professed Arminian who had converted to Protestantism from Catholicism, he admitted that as a Calvinist he must differ with him, yet proposed that in being animated by the same "Maxims of Piety," Arminians and Calvinists could together help create a second, "reformed Reformation," a "NEW PEOPLE of the good Men in the *several Parties.*" In an even bolder display of the Universal Religion Mather preached in 1718 at the ordination of Elisha Callender, a Baptist minister. He apologized to Callender's congregation if, as Baptists, they had received unbrotherly treatment in the past from fellow Bostonians, and he proclaimed: "*Liberty of Conscience* is the Native Right of Mankind."

Many different features of his life and time drew Mather, popularly imagined as the quintessential Puritan bigot, into the vanguard of religious toleration. An ecumenical movement, to recall, had existed within at least a sector of English Puritanism since the Elizabethan period, and was particularly marked in Richard Baxter. It intertwined with the ecumenism of the German Pietists, who praised Mather's *Lapis* for emphasizing "Substantials" rather than "Circumstantials." Although Francke produced the greatest ecumenical and missionary network since the Reformation (joining Germany, Holland, England, America, France, Italy, Switzerland, Poland, Russia, South Africa, India, and the Scandinavian countries), the immediate German Pietist influence on Mather's own ecumenism was likely Philipp Jakob Spener, who reduced the whole of Christianity simply to a confession of sin and a profession of faith in Christ.

Mather's career in Boston under Andros, Dudley, and now Shute enforced his ecumenical notions by making it impossible for him to conceive New England any longer as the redeemer of the English nation. To put the case a different way, his ecumenism celebrated the world created by the new charter. Where he once railed at the innovative Brattle church as a satanic invasion, he now proclaimed the growing cosmopolitanism of Boston as a model for a second Reformation. In fact the variety of worship in the town was increasing in proportion to the increase in the number of churches; as Mather noted in 1717, the place had become something of a sectarian melting pot, containing ten places of worship, of which seven were "Churches of the UNITED BRETHREN" divided only by differences in circumstantials. The feuding in Boston which had accompanied this transformation also fed Mather's ecumenism for, consciously at least, he came to abominate public quarrels. His ecumenism was a large-scale expression of his deep-rooted and complex desire for reconciliations of all kinds.

At various times, it needs special emphasis, Mather's religious liberalism expanded or contracted, for his disposition to embrace other sects changed with changing political, social, and personal events. Around 1715 it was also quickened by again-aroused millennial expectations, such as he had felt before in the 1690s. Eschatology and ecumenism were intimately related, for the millennium would not arrive before the achievement of Christian unity. The Universal Religion of *Lapis* and *Malachi* was both Mather's response to signs of evolving unity which he perceived and his attempt to foster them. Virtually all commentators on prophecy insisted that the exact date of the Second Coming could not be known; but 1716, the year in which Mather published *Lapis*, had become something of an exception. It was the year chosen by the most learned scholar of prophecy in the English church, Joseph Mede, as the time for Christ's return. Newton's associate, William Whiston, had also made very detailed computations and had announced in his *Essay on the Revelation of Saint John* (1706) that 1716 would see the fall of Catholicism—that is, of Antichrist. Mather respected these predictions, and had declared as early as *Bonifacius* (1710) that "M.DCC.XVI is a-coming." Again he watched for such other harbingers of the millennium as the fall of the Turkish empire, the conversion of the Jews, and great earthquakes or similar remarkable providences. He interpreted the death in 1715 of the "French *Moloch*" Louis XIV—"the Greatest *Adversary* of . . . *Christianity*, that ever was in the World!"—as a certain preliminary to the Second Coming, a shaking of the ground toward that "Stupendous *Earthquake*" that would "issue in wondrous *Glory to the God of Heaven*." Taking the adoption of the Universal Religion as itself the "greatest Sign that some of us can see of the Kingdom of God approaching," he closed his *Lapis* by making it known that "The *Great Trumpet* is now to be Blown."

One other ambitious religious undertaking by Mather at nearly this time deserves mention here, although its consequences emerged only after the early years of his marriage. His lifelong enthusiasm for psalm singing earned him a place in the history of American music. He valued psalmody because, like most Puritans, he considered it a form of prayer, but his special delight in it perhaps stemmed from his early speech problems, as many stutterers can sing without difficulty. He collected many illustrations on ancient Hebrew music into "Biblia Americana," urged singing as a daily act of devotion, and regularly sang with his family at household prayers, and by himself, especially during his many fasts, vigils, and illnesses. He also composed "Vast Numbers" of hymns, a few of which he transcribed in his diary or included in other works. Apparently he wrote and published an entire book of hymns, *Songs of the Redeemed* (1697), although no copy is known to have survived.

In 1718 Mather published an ingenious 464-page psalter, with commentary, entitled *Psalterium Americanum*. His innovative, fourfold aim he explained in a seven-page set of proposals for printing the elaborate work by subscription. He considered no current version of Psalms satisfactory because all of them sacrificed exactness to "the *Clink* of the *Rhime*." To preserve the meaning he decided to follow some "famous pieces of Poetry, which this Refining Age has been treated withal," and to produce a translation in what he called, with his habitual insensitivity to poetry, blank verse. He apparently understood by blank verse simply unrimed verse, for the translations are in unrimed iambic tetrameter and trimeter. In striving for a highly literal version, Mather had two further purposes in mind. Following a long line of Reformed thought he viewed Psalms as "the most *Prophetical Book* in the World," a forecast in Old Testament types of the religion of the New Testament. To render the Hebrew exactly was to delineate darkly the coming of Christ, and he included in *Psalterium* a very large number of glosses (mostly taken from "Biblia Americana"), interpreting the Old Testament texts as prophecies of the Redeemer. By translating literally he also hoped to undermine a recent and increasingly popular fashion in psalmody, the deliberate departures from Hebrew being made by his correspondent and "very dear Friend" Isaac Watts, whose *Psalms of David Imitated in the Language of the New Testament* (1719) later dominated colonial Protestantism. As the title suggests, Watts attempted not to translate the Psalms but to rewrite or imitate them in Christian terms, ending the divorce in Protestant worship between preaching and singing, by which churchgoers heard about Christ but sang about David. Although Mather delighted in Watts's "excellent composures" and reprinted many of them, he frowned on having a psalter "without any Air of the Old Testament in it," its typological references to Christ being shed along with the "*Jewish Dress.*" By contrast with Watts's christianized psalms, Mather's *Psalterium* transforms the Old Testament songs into a millennial saga of the coming of Christ and the conversion of the Jews, providing "*The Gospel according to* DAVID."

Mather had a musical reform in mind as well. By making his translations in "blank verse" he proposed simplifying Congregational psalmody by reducing the number of metrical patterns to be sung. (Probably to make a larger repertoire of tunes possible if desired, however, he made use of a clever typographical device, employed earlier by Richard Baxter, by which singers might elect to pronounce or omit extra bracketed syllables.) Some such reform was needed for, like many other Protestant leaders in England and America, Mather believed that over the last few generations psalmody had steadily deteriorated. In 1717 he found some members of his own family "so indifferent at Singing" that he often had to omit it from evening family worship. By 1720 many other New England ministers were complaining about the carelessness in singing and the lack of a musical standard.

To improve public singing, several churches attempted to teach their congregants to read music, sparking the angriest and longest-argued aesthetic debate in early America. In the "more polite city of Boston," Mather wrote later, note reading met with general acceptance; but "in the country, where they have more of the *rustic*, some numbers of older and angry people bore zealous testimonies against these wicked innovations, and this bringing in of popery." Some members of a congregation near Boston were so "set upon their old *howling*" that they declared for the Church of England. Contention grew so intense as to require the calling of several church councils to compose differences. What made the issue divisive was in part that the skill of reading notes could be used in singing not only the sacred but also the profane; one handwritten singing book from Westboro, Massachusetts, in 1721 contains not only devotional tunes but also "Love Triumphant" and "The Beaux Delight." The introduction of musical literacy and skill also very often pitted young against old, gifted against bumbling, town against country. Those who defended regular singing, as note reading was called, made their case in about a dozen sermons, instructional works, and pamphlets published in New England from 1720 to 1727, arguing on scriptural and other grounds for trained performance.

Often sympathetic to the young and to new ideas, especially in this period, Mather actively allied himself with the proponents of regular singing. He preached in March 1721 to a society of persons learning to sing, before a full house, where the singing, Samuel Sewall found, was "extraordinarily Excellent, such as has hardly been heard before in Boston." He also contributed to the debate a pamphlet entitled *The Accomplished Singer* (1721), in essence a lengthened reworking of the Introduction to his *Psalterium*. Here he deplored the degeneration of psalmody into "*Odd Noise*," and urged the young especially to learn to read music. Christians, he said, should "Serve our GOD with our *Best*, and *Regular Singing* must needs be *Better* than the confused Noise of a Wilderness."

In arguing for the development of musical literacy in New England, Mather sided with the future health of the arts in America. In 1721 his nephew and disciple, Thomas Walter, published in Boston *The Grounds and Rules of Musick Explained,* one of the first two American books of music instruction. Within the next half century the fateful controversy over regular singing led to the creation in New England of singing schools, then of singing masters to conduct them, and at last of native tunesmiths to compose music for them. Ultimately one recipient of Mather's multifarious energies was the Boston singing master and tunesmith William Billings, whose 1770 collection, *The New-England Psalm Singer,* was the first volume of American-composed music.

Nineteenth-century photograph of Increase Mather's house. (*Boston Public Library, Print Department.*)

Nineteenth-century drawing of the North Church. (*Boston Public Library, Print Department.*)

Old North Church.
In North Square Boston.

Samuel Sewall (1652–1730), the Mathers' close friend, by John Smibert (1688–1751). (*Museum of Fine Arts, Boston.*)

Governor Joseph Dudley (1647–1720), artist unknown. (*Massachusetts Historical Society, Boston.*)

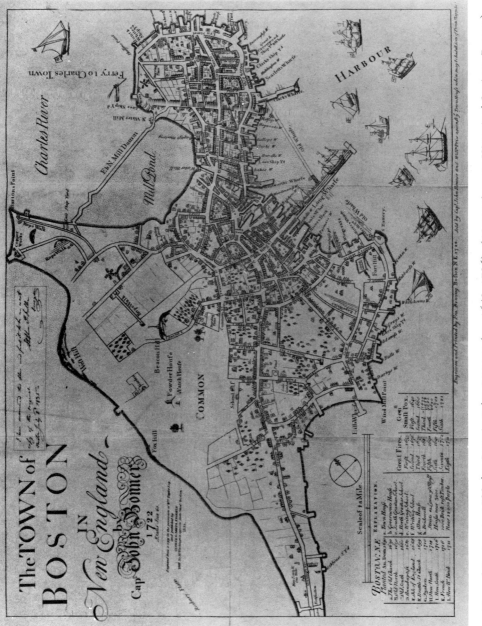

Map of Boston in 1722, by Captain John Bonner (ca. 1643–1726). (*Massachusetts Historical Society, Boston.*)

THE
New-England Courant.

From MONDAY January 29. to MONDAY February 5. 1722

Aliud est maledicere, aliud accusare. Cic.

JUDICIOUS Author observes, That there is nothing in which Men more deceive themselves than in what the World call Zeal. There are so many Passions which hide themselves under it, and so many Mischiefs arising from it, that some have gone so far as to say, it would have been for the Benefit of Mankind, if it had never been reckoned in the Catalogue of Virtues. The fatal Effects of Zeal among our Selves, has almost perswaded me to be of this Opinion. A furious pretended Zeal, which only regards Matters of Opinion, has been improv'd against my self with a Design to destroy my Reputation and Interest amongst those who are Strangers to my Person: And that this Design might be the better carried on, some Persons have been so undutiful to the Reverend Dr. *Increase Mather*, as to perswade him to prefix his Name to an Advertisement in the last Weeks *News-Letter* and *Gazette*, wherein the mildest Appellation I meet with, is that of a wicked and cursed Libeller. This Charge I now lye under from the oldest Minister in the Country, and in order to clear my self I shall first give an Account of the first Cause of the Difference between us.

The Week before the *Courant* of *Jan*. 1. came out, a Grandson of Dr. *Increase Mather* brought me the following Account of the Success of Inoculation in *London*,

A Passage in the London Mercury, Sept. 16.

' Great Numbers of Persons in the City and the Suburbs ' are under the Inoculation of the Small Pox. Among the ' rest, the eldest Son of a noble Duke in Hanover Square, ' had the Small Pox inoculated upon him.

This he said his Grandfather desir'd me to insert in my next, and affirm'd that he had transcrib'd it himself, and that it was Word for Word with the Account in the *London Mercury*. About Noon on the Day that the *Courant* came out, I saw the Four first Pages of the *London Mercury* of *Sept.* 16. and found nothing in them, but that *the eldest Son of a noble Duke in Hanover Square, had the Small Pox inoculated upon him INCOGNITO*. Here our young Spark was detected in a downright Falshood, and lost his Credit with *Couranto*; and I had great Reason too to believe that the first Part of the above Paragraph was not in the other Half-Sheet of the *Mercury*, because both Passages related to Inoculation, and might (no doubt) have been as well inserted together. The next Week I inserted a Letter in the *Courant*, which asserted, that the former Part of the Passage, viz. *Great Numbers of*

proving it. Whether he remembers it or no, his Grandson *Biles*, by his Order, desir'd me to set him down as a Customer some Time ago; but upon the Appearance of a Letter in the *Courant*, wherein a certain Clergyman was touch'd upon, he dropt it as a Subscriber, but sent his Grandson almost every Week for a considerable Time to buy them; by which Method he paid more for the Paper and was more a Supporter of it, than if his Name had been continu'd in the List. At length, being weary with sending, he became a Subscriber again, and express'd no Dislike of the Paper till after Mr. *Musgrave* had publish'd his Grandson's Letter in the *Gazette* of *Jan.* 15. So that he both had and paid me for one Paper after that which he so much dislikes. The Truth of this I am ready to declare upon Oath, against the Testimony of all the Men in the Country. And that he has been a Subscriber, and consequently a Supporter of the Paper, the following Letter under his own Hand, will sufficiently prove.

Mr. Franklin,

' I Had Thoughts of taking your *Courant* (upon Tryal) for ' a Quarter of a Year; but I shall not now. In one of ' your Courants you have said that *if the Ministers of God* ' *are for a Thing, it is a Sign it is from the Devil*, and have ' dealt very falsly about the *London Mercury*. For these and ' other Reasons, I shall NO MORE be concerned with you.
Your well wishing, but grieved Friend,
I. Mather.

In the next Place he says, *In one of his vile Courants, he insinuates, that if the Ministers of God do approve of a Thing, its a sign it is of the Devil, which is a horrid Thing to be related.*

The Words in the *Courant* are in a Dialogue (by an unknown Hand) between a Clergyman and Layman, and are exactly as follows,

Cl. But I find, all the Rakes in Town are against Inoculation, and that induces me to believe it is a right Way.

Laym. Most of the Ministers are for it, and that induces me to think it is from the D——l; for he often makes use of good Men as Instruments to obtrude his Delusions on the World.

The Doctor must know, that Satan once stood up against *Israel*, and provoked *DAVID* to number the People. *Joab*, his wicked General, was not so easily provok'd to this Evil: The King's Word was abominable to him. This is Doctrine which I have often heard from the Pulpit, and if I am condemn'd for publishing it, I may venture to say (in the Words of the Doctor's Grandson, that I have Company of which I need not be ashamed.

Again, *And altho' in one of the Courants it is declared, that the* London Mercury Sept. 16. 1721. *affirms*, That Great Numbers of Persons in the City and Suburbs are under the Inoculation of the Small Pox; *in his next Courant he asserts*, That it was some busy Inoculator, that impos'd on the Publick in saying so.

Front page of James Franklin's *New-England Courant*, with news of inoculation in London. (*American Antiquarian Society, Worcester, Mass.*)

Benjamin Colman (1673–1747), minister of the Brattle church, engraved from a painting by John Smibert (1688–1751). (*American Antiquarian Society, Worcester, Mass.*)

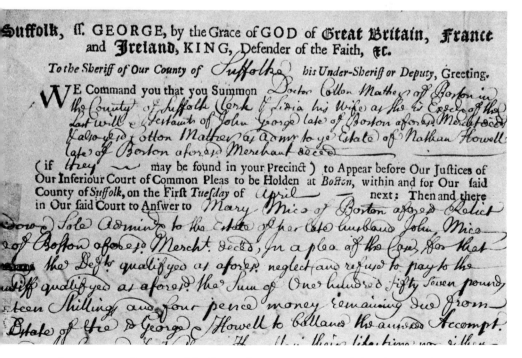

Summons to Cotton and Lydia Mather, concerning a debt of £157 14s. (*Supreme Judicial Court, Boston.*)

Richard Mather (1596–1669), Cotton Mather's paternal grandfather, by John Foster (1648–1681). (*American Antiquarian Society, Worcester, Mass.*)

Increase Mather (1639–1723), Cotton Mather's father, attributed to Jan van der Spriett (d. 1693). (*Massachusetts Historical Society, Boston.*)

Cotton Mather (1663–1728), engraved
by Peter Pelham (1697–1751). (*American Antiquarian Society, Worcester,
Mass.*)

Samuel Mather (1706–1785), Cotton
Mather's son and successor, by John
Greenwood (1727–1792). (*American
Antiquarian Society, Worcester, Mass.*)

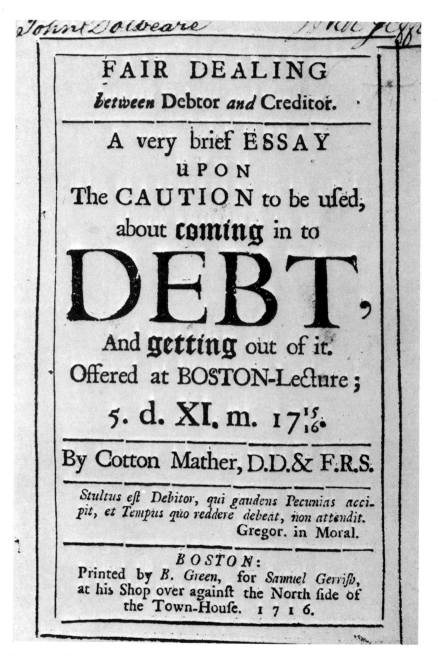

FAIR DEALING
between Debtor *and* Creditor.

A very brief ESSAY
UPON
The CAUTION to be used,
about **coming** in to

DEBT,

And **getting** out of it.
Offered at BOSTON-Lecture;
5. d. XI. m. 17¹⁵⁄₁₆.

By Cotton Mather, D.D.& F.R.S.

Stultus est Debitor, qui gaudens Pecunias acci-
pit, et Tempus quo reddere debeat, non attendit.
Gregor. in Moral.

BOSTON:
Printed by *B. Green,* for *Samuel Gerrish,*
at his Shop over against the North side of
the Town-House. 1 7 1 6.

Typical title page of a work by Cotton Mather, with his "D.D. & F.R.S."
(*American Antiquarian Society, Worcester, Mass.*)

11

Tria Carcinomata

◦◦◦

MATHER's newfound happiness was brief. By the spring of 1717, a year after Creasy's return from England, he was once again sputtering over the boy's unruliness, devoting whole days of supplication to ask an end of Creasy's "Course of Impiety." He had little belief in the proverbial minister's son, indeed considered it a "Popish and Cursed LIE, that the Children of *Ministers* do usually miscarry more than *Others.*" Yet he was beginning to admit the possibility that Creasy would in fact miscarry, that from his miraculous rescue in England he would drown again past saving.

"Suppose," Mather asked himself, "that a Child of my singular Love and Hope, should fall into Sin, and be after wondrous Means of Recovery, yet so abandoned of God, and so ensnared in Vice, that there may [be] terrible Cause to fear lest he prove a Cast-away." How in such circumstances, Mather wondered, should he act? He must be sure not to confuse his grief with his shame. He must separate his pain over Creasy's abandonment to sin, from his vexation at "missing the Reputation and Satisfaction which a Child of more honourable Behaviour might bring unto me." Preparing himself, distressed, he took the boy into his library, prayed with him, pleaded with him. By making Creasy "see and feel my Agonies for him," he did induce him to express repentance. "Methinks," he wrote cautiously, "I hear the glorious One saying to me, *Concerning thy Son I have heard thee!*"

But by November Mather heard, or felt, something else as well, a "strong Impression on my Mind, that some very trying and grievous Thing is near unto me." Such impressions had often misled him, of course, but not this one. Two days later a "thing" came to pass, not just trying and grievous, but shocking. Mather was informed or, rather, "astonished with

307

an Information," that a prostitute had named Creasy as the man who got her pregnant. A "Harlot big with a Bastard," as he put it, "accuses my poor Son *Creasy*, and lays her Belly to him." People whose judgment he trusted believed Creasy innocent, but Mather felt no less bewildered and humiliated: "Oh! Dreadful Case! Oh, Sorrow beyond any that I have met withal! what shall I do now for the foolish Youth! what for my afflicted and abased Family?"

However shaken, Mather acted with uncustomary aplomb. Illegitimacy was a common problem in early New England, and hardly a session of the Boston court failed to hear a bastardy case, usually assigning the onus and responsibility to the woman. Only two months after the charge against Creasy, for instance, a Boston court ordered a "Putative Father" to pay three shillings a week for as long as the court declared, while it imposed a fine of £3 and ten stripes at the public whipping post on his lover, a woman wonderfully named "Elinor Redhead." Mather seems to have managed to prevent Creasy's case from coming to court by keeping Creasy "confined and retired with me, until the Storm shall be blown over." With Creasy sequestered in his house, Mather plied him with directions for spending his time, assigned him sermons to read, prayed with him and Lydia in the study, meanwhile warning himself to stay calm under his provocations.

But despite Mather's concern and continuous prayers for him, Creasy, "My poor Son," was intractable. Only two weeks after the disclosure, the boy "made a worse Exhibition of himself unto me . . . than I ever yet met withal." Mather's failure to produce some lasting reform in Creasy made him feel more helpless than ever: "O my God, what shall I do? what shall I do?" Although his affection for Creasy was great, so now was his disappointment. Probably at around this time, in late 1717, he started writing a continuation of "Paterna," the exemplary autobiography he had begun writing for Creasy at the time of his birth. He addressed this second part, however, to Sammy. He also revised the first part to make it seem that it too had been written not for Creasy but for his more promising younger son, who might more usefully see in his father's life a model of constant devotion and unceasing heaven-mindedness.

Powerless to reclaim Creasy, Mather now also looked on helplessly as his blissful marriage turned riotous. Nothing of the turmoil appears in his diary for 1718, which scarcely mentions Lydia. Instead, Mather recorded the domestic events of 1718 in a separate notebook, where he explained why he omitted them from his diaries. There he wrote: "The Consort, in whom I flattered myself with the View and Hopes of an uncommon Enjoyment, has dismally confirmed it unto me, that our *Idols* must prove our *Sorrows.*''

Whatever her other attractions, Lydia hardly matched Mather's picture of an ideal Puritan wife. This person, as he depicted her in his popular conduct book, *Ornaments for the Daughters of Zion* (Cambridge, 1692), regarded her husband as a divinely appointed guide, whom she always addressed with respect, whose moments of rage she always strove to mollify with meekness, whose will she so obligingly obeyed that "If her *Abraham* give order, *Make Ready quickly three Measures of Meal* or the like, 'tis as *quickly* done." The wellborn, wealthy, and worldly Lydia, however, was no one to measure Mather's meal quickly. She was instead highly independent-minded, as well as vain, jealous, manipulative, and perhaps psychopathic. Her father, the brilliant Rev. Samuel Lee, had expected his daughters to marry into the best and most honorable families. But one of them conducted a very public quarrel with her husband; another married a Rhode Islander "supposed to be rich but deceived her"; another clandestinely married Lee's own servant, Harry. And Lydia married Cotton Mather. And Cotton Mather had heard Lee observe in one of his sermons that the Emperor Augustus called his three daughters *Tria Carcinomata*—three cancers.

Early in their marriage, Lydia had sometime exposed her "proud Passions" to Mather, but he had overcome them, he said, with mildness and patience. In 1718, however, she exploded in "prodigious Paroxysms." Scarcely able to deal with her, he found it "a Year of such Distresses with me, as I have never seen in my Life before." It was not merely that Lydia reviled him. It was that her revilings came and went. When her paroxysms exhausted themselves she once more treated him lovingly, indeed with a "Fondness, that it may be, few Wives in the World have arriv'd unto." Yet the paroxysms always returned, and as they returned they grew more frequent. At last she so outrageously insulted him that Mather believed she might be mad, "which may be somewhat Hereditary," or even possessed. Whether genetic or diabolical in origin, Lydia's outbursts revived one of his worst fears. Throughout 1718 he lived in "a continual Anguish of Expectation, that my poor Wife, by exposing her Madness, would bring a Ruin on my Ministry."

Among the objects of Lydia's "Venom" were Mather's diaries, which she seems to have inspected. Fear of her paroxysms led him to record "not one disrespectful Word of this proud Woman." To allay her suspicions about what his diaries contained he prepared a "true Account, given at the Desire of my Consort, under my hand." This weirdly pathetic document consists of seven pages of extracts from his diaries since the time of their marriage, all related to Lydia and all demonstrating that his private ruminations about her were approving and affectionate—an anthology of diary references to Lydia as his "Lovely Consort," his "Discreet Consort," his "Excellent, Religious, and Ingenious Consort," his "dear, amiable, valuable Consort." He concluded the extracts with a signed statement avowing that if his diaries for 1718 mentioned any "*uncommon Distresses*," these were to be understood as referring to some of the children, "and nothing to be misapplied unto her."

Fear of what Lydia might be capable of doing also led Mather to hide his diaries. But in her "indecent Romaging" Lydia found them, and kept them. He would, she said, "never see them any more." In the hope of getting her to give the diaries back he offered to blot out whatever she disliked. She refused. Seemingly bent on tormenting him, she offered instead the hope that she might return his diaries for the last four or five years "some time or other."

Lydia turned her wrath at Mather against his children as well. Early in their marriage he had thanked God in his diary for bestowing "an excellent Mother" on them; now he went back to this passage and added, in the margin, "*Ah! quam deceptus!*" Although pained by the "dreadful Distresses which a furious and froward Stepmother brings upon my Family," he felt obliged to encourage the "several abused Children" to obey Lydia. He called them into his study and pressed them to regard "the sad Things that are come upon them" as, like all affliction, a loud argument for turning to God. The children's problems were compounded by an economic crisis in 1719, so severe that Mather saw the possibility of a revolution. Lydia apparently refused to help out from her own estate, for the scarcities and soaring prices forced Mather to cut back on household expenses, including those of the children. Sammy was perhaps affected most, for Mather was unable to continue paying for his college education, raising the possibility that this "son of uncommon Hopes" might have to discontinue his preparation for the ministry. As if providentially, there arrived at Harvard a bequest from an English Baptist named Thomas Hollis, from the interest of which, at the suggestion of Increase Mather, a scholarship was provided for Sammy. Hollis consented, expressing regret that the grandson of Increase Mather should come under the character of the "poor in this World."

Increase himself added to his son's trials when, around the spring of 1719, his health took a sudden bad turn. Now eighty-one years old, Increase had been in uncertain health the past two years anyway, suffering

gout, losses of memory, and stomach trouble. To these were added renewed nightmares that became so severe he feared his breath might stop.
The brethren of the North Church kept a day of prayer for a successor to
him. Feeling "Broken with Age," he filled his diary with crotchety protests of "Time lost by Impertinent visitors," complaints that his sermons
"stick in the birth." In June 1719, fearful that when dying he would be
unable to speak—as his father, Richard Mather, had been—he drew up
his will. Cotton seems to have spent much time with him despite his own
difficulties, wanting his father to be "wholly out of the Pain; which my
Absence always gives him."

Mather dealt with his accumulating burdens in ways both old and
new. His love for Lydia, or at least the experience of having loved her,
lingered and craved some object. In March 1718, he made a virtually
unique entry in his diary in Greek, presumably so Lydia could not read it.
It speaks of his need to mourn bitterly his "former pollutions" and of his
belief that God does not require him "utterly to lay aside my fondness for
my lovely Consort," suggesting that he resorted to masturbation or that
despite their wrangling he maintained sexual relations with her. Apparently, however, his thoughts wandered to other women, for he also wrote,
in Greek, "I must abhor the least tho't of regard unto any other Person
but this dearly beloved of my soul." More familiar, his troubles brought
renewed demands for self-mortification and for governing his tongue,
such as he had enforced on himself at the height of his estrangement
from Governor Dudley. After barely three years of satisfaction and pleasure, he again saw himself as a Christ-like victim, and found secret pleasure in thinking of "the Gratification which is done unto Him, in the sad
Things which tear me to Pieces before him." Again he mightily inculcated on himself the need to "suppress all Ebullitions of sinful Wrath and
Rage; all wrathful and raging Expressions, and unadvised Speeches."
Again dead to the world, he decided not to have his portrait painted,
although he had sat for some drafts of it, and felt tempted to destroy his
diaries himself and to keep them no more.

Mather's distress also awakened an older form of coping. For the first
time in twenty-five years, it seems, he began communing with angels. "I
am tried unto the uttermost, in my domestic Circumstances," he wrote at
the end of January 1719, "But my dear SAVIOUR . . . admits me to such
Communion with Himself as makes me a glorious Compensation." His
diaries leave it uncertain whether angels appeared to him as palpably as
they did in 1693; the descriptions consist mostly of rapt exclamations and
statements of the incommunicability of the experiences: "unutterable!

unutterable! unutterable! . . . . . . wonderful! wonderful! Astonishing!" In March 1718, he devoted a day of fasting and prayer to angels that dazzled him by its glory: "the Flights, which I thus took among the holy ANGELS. I find my Pen unable to write the Things, and the Terms, to which my Soul mounted up as with the Wings of an Eagle." He interpreted his several amazing enjoyments during the year as God's requital for his woes, "a rich Compensation, for all the Sorrows, which are appointed for me."

*

On March 9, 1719, Mather began needing richer compensation than ever before. That day a deputy sheriff came to his house and, with Mather away, read a summons to Lydia. It directed them to appear in court to answer a claim of £157 made by Mary Mico, the widow of a Boston merchant, for supplies she had sold to Lydia's deceased former husband, John George, and his also deceased business partner and son-in-law Nathan Howell.

This ominous summons was the outcome of a seemingly benign event. In June 1716, one year after his marriage, Mather had agreed to administer the goods, rights, and credits of the estate of Nathan Howell, who had been married to Lydia's daughter. The exact value of the estate is unknown, but may be gauged from an inventory taken after perhaps £4000 in debts had been cleared. It shows a very large estate worth over £7609, consisting of warehoused goods, buildings, land, and ships, and of nearly £5000 in uncollected debts. The inventory also shows debts owing from the estate in the amount of £4157.

In taking on the administration of this estate, Mather had perforce also taken on some of the unsettled affairs of the defunct Howell-George partnership, and of the deceased John George himself, for whom Howell had been acting as an administrator. And in addition to discharging the complex accounts of what had been a large mercantile firm, he to some extent had also assumed responsibility for looking after Howell's two young children, George and Nathan, who in 1716 were about three and a half and two years old. Their father, also, had not left the world tidily. Howell, as Mather remembered him, had been a "sorry, sordid, froward and exceedingly wicked Fellow," and a spendthrift as well: "Had he lived, he had soon brought a Noble to Nine-pence."

Mather undertook this large load out of love for Lydia. He was "conquered," he explained, "by the Importunity of those unto whom it was impossible for him to deny any thing," and he hoped that what money remained after settling the estate might enable Lydia to do some "special Service for God and His Kingdom." He also felt that the payment of debts due a great number of creditors would be a justice pleasing to heaven, and he wished to do a kindness to the widow and the two young orphans, unfortunate sons of a "wretched Father." For all that, he accepted the administration knowing, as he often freely confessed, that he had no talent for business, and had made keeping out of debt "a great Point of Religion with me." Having often preached on the dangers of debt, only six months before assuming the administration he had cautioned his congregation against the risks of suretyship. Quoting Solomon's saying that *"He that is Surety for a Stranger shall be sore Broken for it"* (Prov. 11:15), he had warned that although it is a breach of charity never to stand surety, doing so demands exquisite caution: *"Think over and over again; Am I Safe? Does God call me into any Sponsorial Hazard? Do not the Circumstances of my Family forbid my coming into them? Shall I not by'nd by Repent most bitterly, and even tear my Hair for the Vexation of my coming under these Encumbrances?"* In speaking of hair-tearing vexations, Mather was more than usually prophetic.

Mather explained later that he had always protested against meddling in the administration himself, but instead, with the consent and advice of the relatives concerned, had turned it over to attorneys. At first he hired Pelatiah Whittemore and Daniel Willard, the husband of his daughter Abigail. Notices were placed in the *News-Letter* beginning in January 1717, calling on those who owed money to the estates of George and Howell to pay their debts through Willard and Whittemore, "that so the Trouble which will otherwise necessarily follow, may be prevented." The trouble, however, was not prevented, and what followed was unlikely to make Mather or his ministry popular.

Forever bent on Doing Good, and having pleaded often from his pulpit for creditors not to beleaguer debtors, Mather found himself now a large creditor, again and again hauling debtors into court. His first taste of being a financial shark seems to have come on December 14, 1716, when on his behalf as administrator of the Howell estate, a writ of attachment was issued against a Plymouth mariner named Michael Packanet, who owed the estate £9 15s. The judicial procedure began with the issuance of this writ against the defendant, who was summoned to appear later for a hearing of the case at the Court of Common Pleas. Packanet had no goods to attach so he was put into the Plymouth jail. In January, Mather took to court Nathaniel Oliver, a merchant, and Timothy Thornton, a shipwright, who owed the estate some £6000. They also were ordered to jail unless they paid the debt, part of which they managed to return as the case continued into the spring.

For Mather this was merely an initiation into years of lawsuits. In 1717 alone he pressed no fewer than twelve suits on behalf of the estate, mostly involving small sums owed by people of even smaller means. For instance, on March 3, a writ was issued against Nicholas Davison, a Newbury mariner who owed the Howell estate nearly £7. A sheriff went to his house and, unable to find him, attached two chairs and left a summons. The same day a writ went out against a Plymouth yeoman named Eliezer Dunham, who owed £4 2s 1d; the sheriff handed him a summons and attached a trunk. On March 18 a writ was issued for Benjamin James, a Marblehead fisherman who owed £5 18s for shrouds and twine. When the last two cases were heard at the Court of Common Pleas on April 2, Mather reached some unspecified agreement with Dunham, but the writ against James was dismissed as not having been served. The court heard the case against Davison on July 2, and ordered payment to Mather, plus damages and court costs.

These cases can stand as representative of the many others in which at Mather's instigation the sheriff confronted some fisherman or shipwright or blacksmith, attaching his tables or trunks or chairs for the sums he owed for cordage, cod line, or dock nails. Some cases were more complicated. At least two involved residents of Maine, one of whom both owed money to John George and had sold land to Nathan Howell and then committed acts of trespass upon it. At least one case, for £9 15s 3d, resulted in a jury trial, which found against Mather and charged him for court costs as administrator of the estate.

Other of Mather's suits did not succeed either, usually, it seems, because the debtors were impoverished mariners unable to pay. And by the end of 1717, although he had acted as administrator for eighteen months, many more debts remained outstanding. Feeling he must "hasten the Settlement of Affairs," he transferred the attorneyship from Whittemore and Willard to Samuel Sewall, the judge's nephew. Sewall ran a notice in the *News-Letter* calling on debtors to pay, so the estate could satisfy its creditors. For Nathan Howell had left creditors as well, plenty of them. By about 1719 Mather's attorneys had with "vast Fatigue, and much projection and contrivance" paid out nearly £4000, much of it in small sums, owed by the estate.

The sheriff who appeared with a summons at Mather's house on March 9, 1719, seems to have come with the first suit not by the estate, but against it. Mary Mico, the widow of a Boston merchant, charged John

George and Nathan Howell with owing some £157 for canvas, oakum, cable, and other supplies. She sued for the money, naming Lydia as executor of the estate of John George, and Mather as administrator of the estate of Nathan Howell. Unfortunately, because Mather's diaries for 1719 and 1720 have not survived, his reaction to receiving the summons is unknown. It may be estimated, however, from the sermon he delivered two days later, on Acts 19:36.: *Ye ought to do nothing Rashly.*

The manuscript probably contains more crossouts and blots than that of any other sermon Mather wrote, implying that he composed it in the very state the sermon condemns. Apoplectically he warned his congregation to beware of every form of rashness, many of which he had committed himself, especially including the undertaking of sureties:

> O *Citizen of Zion*, Engage nothing but wh[at] thou *mayst* Engage, and what thou *should*[st] perform, nothing but what is within thy *Compass*, and will not be against thy *Comfort.* . . . And there is one sort of *Rash Engagements*, which you must shun above the rest, if you would keep out of Sore Entanglements. You shall be informed what they are; prov XI. 15. *He that is Surety for a Stranger shall* [smart] *for it.* . . .

As if regarding the summons from the perspective of his betrayed passion for Lydia and his frustrated concern for Creasy, disappointments that should have schooled him in distrust, he also condemned rash marriages and rash hopes for children:

> Be sure we admit and Cherish *Rash Expectations*, when we hope to find that in *Creatures*, which they will not afford unto us. . . . Alas, how prone are we to Look for more from *Creatures*, than they will yield unto us. . . . Tis often so, that we Likewise *Expect* this and that great Consolation from such or such a particular Creature. We have a *Child* perhaps whereof we say, *This Same shall* comfort us! Anon we find so much *Vanity,* and so much *Vexation,* attending the *Creature,* that we see, *Twas Rashly done to look for Grapes from Thorns.* . . .

Badly rasped by reaching for such grapes himself, Mather concluded that human comfort is concerned in not acting from passion.

Aside from venting his angry self-reproach in public, Mather seems to have drawn up for the court hearing, in July, a document entitled "The Answer of the Administrator upon the Estate of *Nathan Howel* [sic] deceased, unto the Citation served upon him." In it he explained that much had been paid to creditors from the estate already, including a considerable part of the debt to Mico. In the process, one of the attorneys (possibly Whittemore) was "suspected of some disallowable proceedings," both attorneys had been let go, and a new, single attorney chosen. He petitioned for a postponement of the hearing until the next court session, "Long before which Time, he hopes, Everything will be done unto the just Satisfaction, not only of Mrs. *Mico* but also of the other creditors." Whether he ever presented this document is unknown, but in July the court ordered payment to the widow Mico, plus damages and court costs. After the judgment was rendered, Cotton and Lydia both appeared in court and entered into recognizance with sureties to appeal their case at the next Superior Court.

Mather began trying desperately to disentangle himself from the administration. At the end of the year he wrote to Samuel Sewall, presumably believing that as the probate judge who had granted him the administration, Sewall could release him from it. The situation was awkward for Sewall, and complicated. On the one hand, Mather was his lifelong close friend. But Sewall's nephew (confusingly also named Samuel Sewall) had married Lydia's daughter, the former wife of the deceased Nathan Howell, and the couple were now at odds with Mather over the administration. The younger Sewall had at first agreed to act as an attorney in the business himself, but had then withdrawn; or rather his wife Katharin had forbidden him to act—harboring, Mather believed, "ill intentions to plague" him, although he had married the couple himself. The younger Sewall, as the stepfather of the two Howell children, was also pressuring Mather to hasten settlement of the estate.

Judge Sewall did not reply to Mather for two months, when he apologized for his long delay and sympathized with Mather's wish to "obtain freedom from this perplexing Administration." He suggested that Mather prepare an inventory of what had been received by and paid from the estate, and of the money owing the attorneys—quickly, Sewall said, "for your sake, and for the Orphans, and my own." Although the inventory was prepared it did nothing toward releasing Mather from his administration. Sewall, either because he lacked authority to help Mather, or because of the involvement of his nephew, failed to act.

With his passion for respectability, his sense of himself as a model to his children and the community, his solemn pride in his ministry, for Mather to find himself on the wrong side of the law proved fearsomely unnerving. His liability for huge unpaid debts; the writs, the sheriffs, the courts and their threats of force; the possible, and freezingly ignominious, shadow of debtors' prison—all aroused in him a near-shattering anxiety. On the night of April 13, sometime after nine o'clock, Judge Sewall received an anonymous letter, purporting to be from a friend of Mather's, with a request to burn the letter after reading.

The author—who may well have been Mather himself, although the letter is not in his hand—drew an alarming picture of Mather's condition. Overwhelmed by the administration of the estate, he was sinking under such "heavy and many troubles" that unless help came speedily "we shall quickly lose him." So dispirited he could speak to no one and talk of nothing, he lived in a state of dread: "every one that knocks at his door surprizes him, that his heart dies within him, as he sayes, fearing there is an Arrest to be serv'd on him, or some body to dun him for a Debt." Worse, the younger Sewall has led him to think that he contemplates prosecuting him for maladministration. The writer implored Sewall not to be swayed by his nephew or his nephew's wife, but despite their interference to help rid Mather of the administration. Otherwise, he said, the result would be "the Death, or . . . some thing worse than that soon coming on that distressed tho' worthy Gentleman."

This letter also contains the one surviving clue to Lydia's apparent failure to relieve Mather by covering the debts herself. Their marriage contract, of course, forbad him any access to her wealth, under a penalty of £2000, and she may simply have wished to torment him. Or she may have run out of funds herself, although since the contract mentions that she had come into a "Considerable Estate" this seems unlikely. Sewall's anonymous correspondent, however, noted that Mather's "Terrible wife" would "have a great Estate whether there be one or no," suggesting that Lydia did not credit the inventory Mather had prepared, but believed that her deceased former husband had left funds sufficient to satisfy creditors. For whatever reason, Mather was forced to pay off the debts of the estate himself.

The seriousness of Mather's situation was deepened by the simultaneous economic crisis in Boston which had forced him to find scholarship money for Sammy. People were unable to get work, the value of bills of credit had fallen and, by one account, a "great Part of the Town can hardly get Bread to satisfie Nature." The lack of a medium of exchange forced many to labor for goods, then faced them with selling off long-held homes at half-value as creditors called in debts and demanded money. A vast number of lawsuits resulted, allowing lawyers and other court officers, it was claimed, to "grow Rich on the Ruins of their Neighbours." The April 1720 court session in one county alone issued more than a thousand writs.

Mather depicted his superlative share in this general plight in an undated "Statement" which he characterized as "*One Small Instance of the Hardships, which the Dealings of the people in the Country run into.*" After describing how he had indiscreetly allowed his name to stand as the administrator of an estate, he told of his many problems in discharging a debt of £50 owing, with interest, to someone in Hartford. The debt had been paid, but the man's attorney now demanded an additional £20 to cover the debt and interest "at the Extravagant price whereto silver is risen at this day." Mather asked the Hartford creditor to forgo this surcharge, considering the financial difficulty which the depreciation of bills of credit had brought upon everyone. He explained that he had profited nothing from handling the estate, but on the contrary had put up "*between Three and Four hundred*" pounds of his own to answer creditors, leaving him an "Empty Pocket" and nothing else in the world "but a Few Books, and a little Houshold stuff and plate, that I could call my own." Despite Mather's entreaties and the intercession of prominent people in Hartford, the creditor insisted. Indeed through his lawyer— "counting me too mean a person to receive a line from him"—he threatened Mather with either paying the twenty pounds or going to jail. Mather did pay, and from his own funds. Overcoming evil with good he refused to name the person who had thus "*extorted* from a poor Minister," but instead concluded with his hope "to meet with him in *Paradise,* who would have laid me in *Prison.*"

Certain that Sewall's nephew and Lydia's daughter, his own stepchild, wished to harm him, Mather was by the fall fixed in believing that his deliverance lay only in getting Judge Sewall to release him from the administration. In October he wrote to Paul Dudley, the son of his former foe, Joseph Dudley. "No words can express the anguish," he said, "with which this petition comes to you." Sewall, he said, had often promised to free him from the administration, and he asked Dudley to visit the judge and be resolute in making him act: "see him do what he must for my relief, even . . . before you stir out of the room." Whether Dudley went to see Sewall is unknown, but Mather's demanding request again failed. Sewall refused to act.

Apparently despairing of Sewall's help, Mather in early November petitioned a higher authority, the governor's Council. In his defense he drew up a set of "Reasons why the Administrator on the Estate of *Nathan Howel* [sic] deceased should be Released from the Bonds of Administration Humbly Offered." First, he told the Council, in letting himself be "unhappily drawn into" the business he had acted indiscreetly, harmed his ministry, and received from those who benefited from his work only "unaccountable Ingratitude." Second, he had shown himself, he admitted, to be altogether unqualified: "Were he, *Non compos mentis*, This would be thought enough to Release him; Now if there has not been enough either to *Declare* him so, or to *Render* him so; yet there is enough to represent him as Incompetent." Third, the administration having been carried on with entire fidelity, thousands of pounds in debts had been paid, large sums had been collected, and the "Trouble which remains, is very little in comparison of that which has been already waded through." Mostly, however, Mather pleaded the misery to which his rash act of compassion had reduced him: "the Sufferings of the present Administrator are so Insupportable, and he is in such peculiar circumstances, that he cannot but press for a Release from his Bonds, with an Importunity, which he hopes will move the Compassion of them who can deliver him."

Auspiciously, this time Mather had the support of the younger Sewall and his wife Katharin, who also petitioned the Council to discharge Mather and reimburse him for his expenses. Their motives were not entirely selfless, for at the same time Sewall's wife petitioned for an adjustment of a personal debt connected with the estate. Nevertheless, the Council allowed Mather £200 out of the estate for his trouble and expense in the administration, and agreed to dismiss him—"in case any proper person will undertake the same."

But no proper person did so. The new year found Mather still in charge of the estate, with large new demands being made against it. The beating in his private life apparently lamed his ministry, for when preaching on his birthday, February 12, he found that "my *locks are cut*. I performed so pitifully." What impaired his performance may have been a return of his stutter, for he added, without further explanation, "This last bout has been the most shocking that I have had this twenty years." He had been invited to preach the lecture the same week, "But I can't—I can't," and he asked another minister to substitute for him. He also wrote abroad in April to the New England Company, "so discouraged by some occurrences," he said, as to ask again to be dismissed from his work as an Indian commissioner.

Mather needed no more discouragement, but Creasy provided some. "My Miserable, miserable, miserable Son *Increase!*," he moaned on April 4. "The Wretch has brought himself under public Trouble and Infamy by bearing a Part in a Night-Riot, with some detestable Rakes in the Town. Oh! What shall I do?" While struggling to extricate himself from the administration he fumed anew over Creasy, determined that until his son showed signs of repentance he would, this time, "chase him out of my Sight; forbid him to see me." He seems to have sent Creasy for a while to Increase Mather, who also denounced the boy for having acted to "the dishonor of God and of his friends and Relations." With Creasy out of sight, Mather decided to write him a "tremendous Letter," setting his crime before his eyes and, after so much coddling, threatening that until the boy genuinely repented he would "never own him or do for him, or look on him."

As always, Mather's storming left unmoved his fixed love for Creasy. Much in his son's personality mirrored his own more amiable self, and he cherished Creasy's many virtues—"a singular sweetness of temper (which, alas, has been a snare unto him), a ripe wit, a sharp sense, the ornaments of a gentlemanly education." While offering prayers at a baptism on April 23, he found himself thinking of Creasy and, in tears, he asked God why He called the children of men: "Was it, that they might be given up to Blindness and Hardness, and Madness? Was it that they might have the Distempers of their Souls lie uncured, when one gracious Word of thine can cure them?" The answer was of course no; he would yet believe, yet see God perform wonders for his children. "Ah, poor *Increase*," he wrote. "Tho' I spake against him, yet I earnestly remember him, and my Bowels are troubled for him."

Seeking some help in reforming Creasy, Mather introduced the boy to the young minister Thomas Foxcroft. That Creasy himself desired Foxcroft's acquaintance he saw as a hopeful sign that his son might yet learn serious piety, adherence to business, and horror of evil company. He wrote to Foxcroft hoping he would allow Creasy some improving visits, promising that "when you see him, you will certainly love him."

*

Weighed down by Lydia's paroxysms, Creasy's escapades, and his creditors' demands, Mather simultaneously began paying for his friendly support of Governor Shute. The new administration created discord, and all of the governor's enemies became his.

Opposition to Shute solidified over the economic crisis in Massachusetts, although it first gathered around a related issue, the founding of a public bank. As Mather explained the issue, which originated in Dudley's administration, for several years much of the business of Massachusetts had been conducted in government bills of credit. As the province by raising taxes managed to pay off its large debt, incurred during long years of war, these bills were being retired to the public treasury and destroyed, depleting the circulating medium. Businessmen complained that the number of bills in circulation was "no more than *a sprat in a whale's belly*," and far too few for the country's commerce. To provide a medium of trade, a group of men proposed forming a private bank which would issue its own bills. This plan met with violent opposition, however, and as an alternative the Dudley government proposed issuing and lending out more bills of credit like the earlier ones. Mather had supported the private bank scheme, perhaps because its sponsors were political antagonists of Dudley. He did so without conviction, however, acknowledging both his own naiveté in finance and the sincerity of those who claimed that the government's scheme would better serve the public interest.

The change of administrations put Mather on the wrong side of the bank issue. Those who favored the private bank, once political antagonists of Dudley, now became political antagonists of Shute, who opposed the issuance of more paper bills altogether. Never more than lukewarm in his support for the private bank, Mather came around to Shute's position and was accused of having changed his views, although he insisted that "*cujus contrarium*. I have never done so, to any one man in the world." He might have escaped serious public attack except that the private bank became the nexus of wider political arguments, and those who favored it aligned themselves against Shute over many other issues as well. Preeminent in this opposition, and both supporters of the private bank, were Oliver Noyes, a wealthy real estate speculator and founder of the Brattle church; and Elisha Cooke, Jr., son of the Elisha Cooke who for years had unforgivingly denounced Increase Mather's acceptance of the new charter. The elder Cooke had died in 1715, leaving the son probably the wealthiest man in the colony. The younger Cooke also inherited his father's political following, and assembled something like a political machine in Boston, which elected to the House representatives hostile to Shute. By 1719 they found much to be hostile about. For in the economic crisis that developed, not only did money disappear from circulation, but also the value of bills of credit depreciated, trade in general declined, and inflation became severe. The crisis, we have seen, worsened Mather's own difficulties in discharging the debts of the estate, and also produced many pamphlets, much talk of reviving the private bank scheme, and bitter divisions in towns, churches, and even families.

Amid this plethora of other trials, Mather exerted himself to support Shute, on whom much of the blame was laid. On March 12, 1719, only three days after a sheriff first appeared at his door summoning him to

court, he preached a sermon before the General Assembly, recommending Shute's policies. As the grand expedient for relieving the economic
crisis he urged not the issuance of more paper bills, which Shute opposed, but public frugality—an argument that had long been used against
the private bank, and which in effect blamed the people, not the government, for the crisis. He also urged total loyalty to Shute as expressive of
loyalty to the crown. For in opposition to Shute he foresaw the possibility
in Boston of "*Raging Waves of the Sea* . . . Mutinous, and Seditious, and
Rebellious Actions." To oppose Shute, he implied, was to reawaken suspicions in London about the loyalty of New Englanders, and perhaps to
risk loss of the present charter. Shute and his allies pressed to have the
sermon printed at government expense, although Mather's vision of social convulsion made Samuel Sewall fear that the printing might itself
invite Parliament to revoke the charter. Shute tried to have the matter
voted on, but met stiff resistance and broke off the debate; the sermon
apparently was printed at government expense.

Mather had been warned from London by Jeremiah Dummer that
moves might be made there to remove Shute. In a further show of support, Mather wrote abroad to Shute's brother, Lord Barrington, praising
the governor as "generally and passionately beloved." He intended this
long, highly laudatory letter privately, no doubt to enlist Barrington's
help; but it somehow made its way into an English newspaper in May
1719 and was reprinted in Boston, bringing down on him the "fury and
outrage" of Noyes, Cooke, and their party of "venomous malcontents."
Aggravatingly, Shute seemed to take no notice of the assault; in fact
Mather was told that people in the government derided him behind his
back—a thing, he said, "I must believe with discretion." Discretion never
having been one of his strengths, least of all when he was besieged, he
spread a report that Cooke, alleged to be a heavy drinker, had been drunk
for several days. The story was challenged, forcing him to draw up a
written retraction for Cooke to use in absolving himself. But having retracted he continued referring to Shute's enemies in his correspondence
as a "party of Tipplers."

Opposition to Shute and contention in Boston came to a head in the
spring of 1720. By then many people in financial distress saw Cooke as
their spokesman against the government, while Cooke had become not
only Shute's political adversary but also personally repugnant to him,
among other reasons because of a report that in company, and too punch-
drunk to stand or walk, he had implicitly called Shute a "Blockhead." In
May, the House chose Cooke for its Speaker. Shute negatived the choice

on the ground that Cooke had ill-treated the king's governor, and directed the House to choose a different speaker. Shute also negatived the choice of two councillors, Nathaniel Byfield and John Clark, who had been staunch supporters of Cooke. The governor's negative enraged the House and begot a heated debate on questions of privilege, and of whether a governor had power to overturn a House decision. Shute reminded the representatives that Governor Dudley had also disallowed a Speaker, and had been confirmed in his right to do so in London (as Shute was later). He advised the members to choose another Speaker, and to reserve their asserted right until the matter could be laid before the king. The House refused, in reply to which Shute dissolved the session.

Apprehensive that such political chaos might endanger the charter, Mather seems to have doubted the wisdom of Shute's negative on Cooke. But he just as strongly considered Shute well disposed to New England, a mild man pricked to act intemperately by Cooke's truculence. Indeed Shute's behavior bears out the impression of him given later by Thomas Hutchinson, that he was a man of integrity but a lover of ease and lacking artfulness, anxious to avoid controversy but without skill in doing so. To defend Shute, but also in the larger hope of quieting the building uproar, Mather, it seems quite certain, produced an anonymously published pamphlet entitled *News from Robinson Cruso's Island* ([1720]). Even granting his ingrained ability to continue working amidst defeat and disappointment, his ability to do so now seems remarkable, for the tumult over Cooke occurred little more than a month after the anonymous letter to Sewall depicting his state of dread as he awaited arrest. In whatever state, he told of Robinson Crusoe coming to Boston, here called the island of "*Insania*," just when some "rash Men willing to see the Country all in Confusion" insisted on having Cooke, the ideal choice for Speaker had the intent been to spite the governor. Crusoe delivers a speech chastising Cooke's supporters for bringing chaos on the country and forcing the good-tempered Shute to act dictatorially, simply for the pleasure of illtreating him. He warns that they are again risking the charter, betraying the country under "*the Hypocritical disguise of contending for your Privileges.*"

Although the House called on Shute to punish the "authors" of the pamphlet for libeling some of its members, suspicions that Mather was the single author were apparently rife. In July appeared a rebuttal, *Reflections upon Reflections: Or, More News from Robinson Cruso's Island* (1720). Obviously with Mather in mind, the author attributed the earlier pamphlet to "one, whose *Scribendi Cacoethes* [itch for scribbling] has made him famous on both sides the *Atlantick*" and whose brain "is over-charged with so great a variety of News, that the Country feels themselves on many accounts the *worse for him.*" He dismissed Mather's suggestion that in choosing Cooke the House had led a "good Spirited" governor to act harshly, insisting that the choice of a Speaker was one of Massachusetts' valued political rights. Mather's "Learned Jargon," he said, was aimed at frightening New England out of its privileges and rendering "our selves obnoxious to the Curse of succeeding Generations."

Mather, probably hoping to disconnect his name from the Crusoe pamphlet, drew up a three-page tract entitled "A Few Remarks . . . on the Choice of A *Speaker,*" where he announced:

> To prevent such mistakes as people have run away withal, about the Authors of the Late Account of *Cruso's* Island, (and some other things,) it must be known that the publisher of that and of these Remarks, is no native of *Boston.*

This Matherese avowal of course leaves open the possibility that even though Mather was not the "publisher" of the pamphlet, he was the author. He did not publish "A Few Remarks," perhaps because it qualifies his support for Shute, representing more candidly his view that the governor had acted unwisely. This time he disguised himself not as Crusoe but, cleverly, as an anonymous member of the House who is opposed to negativing Cooke and desires to preserve the House's privileges. But this member distinguishes between the House at large and the "Shortsighted and Hot-headed Party" within it who champion Cooke fanatically, a party who "being disappointed of a private Bank, and of a Governor, whom they Expected, have all along mal-treated our present Governor, hoping to tire out his gracious patience and goodness with Bad Usages." Since Shute had laid the matter before the king, he urged the representatives to waive the controversy and go on with public affairs, warning that if Cooke's party were allowed to further embroil things, the crown would take notice of the "*ungovernable Spirit*" in Massachusetts and reconsider the charter.

Mather was also accused of persuading Shute to negative Dr. John Clark, one of the newly elected councillors. The charge discomforted Mather the more because Clark was the brother of his deceased wife Elizabeth and, as a physician, had attended her during her final illness. The Clarks, also, were now caring for Mather's daughter Liza, his dead wife's namesake and their niece. She may have been driven from Mather's house by Lydia's turn against his children, but in any case she seemed to him the "lively image" of Elizabeth, a living reminder of a happier past and of a "never-to-be-forgotten mother." Clark, believing his former brother-in-law had advised Shute against him, had publicly expressed aversion toward Mather, so Mather instead wrote to Clark's wife. He swore "as before the Glorious Lord" that he had been in no way "directly or indirectly accessory or instrumental to this negative," but on the contrary had advised Shute against it. All he had ever done, he said, had been to express his unhappiness over the misunderstanding between Shute and Clark; those who gave these innocent remarks a defamatory appearance did so to sow discord. Thanking the Clarks for their goodness to Liza, he lamented that his character lay "much at the mercy of lying and loathsome talebearers."

A new session of the House was scheduled for July. Seemingly on the chance that it might stubbornly again choose Cooke for Speaker, Mather prepared, apparently for Shute's use, a memorandum entitled "In case, the Representatives make Choice of E.C. for their Speaker." Here he disclosed to the governor his real view and suggested that, if pressed by the House, Shute should accept Cooke's nomination. He also offered Shute a face-saving but plausible rationale. Shute could claim that although the recalcitrance of the House might well be answered by prorogation, everyone knew that his chief desire "forever is, the prosperity and Tranquillity of the people." Aware of the need to resolve urgent public problems, he would therefore "suspend those Expressions which he might justly give . . . until His Majesty's pleasure be further known." Mather's coaching was unnecessary, for in its new session the House, after three votes in which Cooke led the field, chose as Speaker a representative from Salem. They also reduced Shute's salary, however, and told him plainly that "whoever was of advice to his excellency" had not consulted the king's interest or the public good.

At this point Mather might reasonably have ended his covert campaign against Shute's foes. Instead, some unnamed scurrilities against him goaded him to act with, he confessed, "perhaps too quick and Keen" resentment. Writing to several correspondents around August, he mocked Cooke and his allies as "*idiots* and *fuddlecaps* and *men that love and make a lie*," and called them "*American* (worse than *African*) monsters." His letter or letters somehow got to Cooke, who with two or three representatives, Mather said, made him "sufficiently sensible of the Resentments which they have upon it; and they want not for will or skill, to do it further unto the last Extremity." He seems upon Shute's request to have apologized for the epithets, but he continued to tell others that they were deserved. In December someone in Cooke's party published still another pamphlet, *New News from Robinson Cruso's Island* (1720), attacking Mather for slandering people privately, for caricaturing New Englanders as "*worse than the Savage Monsters of Africa*," and for stirring up old fears about the charter. The writer advised him not to meddle in state affairs, of which he knew nothing, and offered a caricature himself: Mather as Pope, "the great DON-DAGO, the *Primate wou'd be* of our Island." As Mather admitted to his friend John Winthrop, "I own myself not a match for them."

In this Mather was several ways correct. Not only was he ignorant of finance and engulfed in domestic problems, but the private bank issue and the negative on Cooke brought with them a dramatic change in political perspective. The pamphleteers spoke for a new, increasingly powerful segment of society that could consider social issues without reference to the original Puritan vision of a covenanted people, to whom the resolution of New England's problems was not moral but financial and political. They became, as Perry Miller remarked, "the first authors in New England to argue a case with hardly so much as a genuflection in the direction of religion." The language of their politics was not that of provoking evils and public fasts, but that of privilege, depreciation, and the balance of trade.

Neither upbringing nor inclination qualified Mather to discourse in this language, much less to handle its accompanying infighting and chicanery. Yet as he undertook to defend Shute he was himself drawn into the game. The charges that he self-servingly changed his views on the bank or betrayed his brother-in-law or gossiped about Cooke's tippling are only instances of repeated accusations of underhandedness and smear tactics. In 1717, a middle-aged Harvard graduate named Joseph Parsons charged him with communicating to the New South Church, to which Parsons had been proposed for the ministry, a private letter that, he said, "*utterly ruined*" him there. Mather dismissed the charge as false, but the following year he was similarly accused of having communicated to a man named Rogers a letter addressed to him from a man named Emerson, in which Emerson had used "Invectives" against Rogers. Mather flatly denied that Emerson had sent him such a letter, much less had he confided it to Rogers. Whether Mather acted treacherously in these cases is unknown, but in similar cases much condemning evidence has survived. To give only two examples, around 1720 he wrote to the merchant John Frizzell, to whom he had written before in Creasy's name. Now he fabricated an anonymous letter (like the one Samuel Sewall received describing Mather's dread), asking Frizzell to help subsidize publication of one of his works. Frizzell had been a member of his congregation, and Mather knew him well. Yet in the letter Mather introduced himself as "one that never spoke to my remembrance one word to you in all my Life." To appreciate the letter's utter deceitfulness, it must be stressed that the document is entirely in Mather's hand and that he wrote it himself:

> I have the honour of some acquaintance with Dr. Mather, the younger, a person whom you as well as I have a high value for. Among his other favors, he communicated unto me a composure of his entitled *The Work of the Day*. . . . The composure, if I have any judgment, is a most illustrious and uncommon performance: 'tis filled with rich and rare thoughts, and among the entertainments which eminent men have given us, I have not seen the thing that equals it. Let me peruse it never so often, every paragraph still appeared new to me, and I still discovered new treasures and beauties in it.

Mather went on to urge the wealthy Frizzell to help bring "this noble work of the Doctor's into the world," signing himself "Your unknown friend and servant."

The other case exposes Mather offering one opinion to a person's face and another behind his back. In the summer of 1720, the Harvard Overseers considered granting an honorary M.A. degree to Daniel Neal, a London Congregational minister who had written a two-volume *History of New-England* (London, 1720). Neal sent a copy to Mather, who returned a buttery reply. New Englanders, he said, should be grateful "that any men of worth should count such a poor, despised, maligned country as ours worthy of their cognizance." But he added that New England was never famous for gratitude to its benefactors, and warned Neal not to be surprised if his "well-penned History" failed to receive "just consideration of your merits." In actuality, Mather was enraged. Neal had given an unflattering picture of the New England ministry, and had commented of the *Magnalia* that had the author *"put his Materials a little closer together, and disposed them in another Method, his Work would have been more acceptable to this Part of the World."* Although Mather told Neal that "some of our best men are considering of the most proper way to testify their . . . thankful reception of what you have done for us," these were not remarks for which he would gladly see Harvard award an honorary M.A.

The day before a college committee concerned with awarding the degree was to meet, Mather wrote to two unnamed persons, asking them to convey his views to "your honorable President." The phrase itself was two-faced, for when writing "under the darkest concealment" to Shute, he referred to Leverett rather as "the (pretended) President." He admitted that in public he spoke "with all due tenderness of Mr. Neil's [*sic*] performance," and in fact believed he deserved some acknowledgment; but he would reveal to them thoughts which the "law of goodness will release me from uttering unto others." Concerning criticism against his *Magnalia* he was, naturally, indifferent—both to "the invectives which that poor work has undergone, and," certainly, to "the compliments (very excessive ones) which I have received from eminent persons in more than three nations upon it." But in fact Neal's history, he said, was only his own *Magnalia* annalized and denuded into a "dry political story." Neal treated Harvard as if no one educated there could write modern English; Neal took his story of the Salem witchcraft trials from "such a senseless, lying, malicious wretch as Calef"; and Neal, to "pass by a thousand other things," was simply a "very weak and shallow man." (The letter did not prevent the Overseers from awarding Neal the degree.)

In the past, Mather's resentments had found subtler outlets than overt lying, talebearing, and duplicity. This moral deterioration in Mather seems the result both of his exhausting personal problems and of his compliance with changed standards of political life in Massachusetts, whose earlier tribal solidarity was becoming fragmented by party interests, and whose members, as Mather wrote, were becoming "all generally Alienated from one another, broken into Factions, and Sacrificing all to *Cursed Animosities*." Politically and emotionally out of his depth, Mather was now simply unable to manage his rage becomingly. When his foe Oliver Noyes, a popular leader in the House, died in March 1721, of apoplexy, he exulted. "Methinks," wrote the minister of the North Church, "I see a wonderful Token for good in this Matter; And I go on with humble Supplications to the Lord."

*

Mather's ministry dealt him two final aggravations. The first was the revival of the Arian heresy in England, climaxed by the divisive Salters' Hall controversy of 1719. Arianism arose during the earliest period of Christianity from the attempt to reconcile the unity of the godhead with the distinction of personality in the Trinity. Arius, writing in the fourth century, distinguished the Father from the Son, endowing Christ with free will and a capacity for change, implicitly making Him neither divine nor eternal. As an institution Arianism formed the religion of the eastern half of the Roman Empire until late in the fourth century; as a doctrine, it figured in later Christian disputes as well. It had a revival among rationalistic theologians in eighteenth-century England, and was linked to Newtonianism, as Newton's passionate belief in One Creator similarly relegated Christ to an inferior role. Mather had preached and written against Arianism sporadically. In 1702, for instance, he argued that the doctrine of the Trinity was known only through revelation and could not be comprehended by reason, and treated rationalistic Arians as "Fools, that will believe nothing, except they can put their Hands into the Sides of it."

That Arianism might become genuinely troublesome began to strike Mather in 1711, as the doctrine began winning adherents through the writings of the rationalist William Whiston. Trained for the ministry and ordained, Whiston yet pioneered the offering of public lectures on science, and in 1703 had succeeded Newton as professor of mathematics at Cambridge. He had also come to find the doctrine of the Trinity unacceptable, announced his view in 1708, and was eventually deprived of his professorship. Mather admired Whiston as both a talented mathematician and a prolific writer on theology, had a correspondence with him (which has not survived), and often cited his scientific writings in "Biblia Americana." But Whiston's attempts to promote the Arian diminishment of Christ alarmed him. "My learned Friend *Whiston*," he wrote in 1711, "is likely to raise a prodigious Dust in the world, by reviving the *Arian* Opinions." He feared the dust raised not only in the world but also in himself, for his own strong rationalistic bent had long made him susceptible to weakenings of belief. "I am likely," he added, " to have my own Mind shock'd with more than ordinary Temptations on this Occasion." Indeed the next year he began reeling from doubts about the Trinity, his mind "hideously assaulted and harassed" by temptations to Arianism. By importuning God, however, he managed to receive a "Sweet Satisfaction . . . in His Truth, concerning Three Eternal Persons in His infinite Godhead."

Mather wrote several anti-Arian tracts over the next few years. But although thankful that Arianism had not crossed the water and contaminated New England, he looked perturbedly on its steady advance abroad, helped along by the other outstanding English Arian, Dr. Samuel Clarke, an English divine and disciple of Newton, whose *Scripture Doctrine of the Trinity* (1712) declared the Father alone supreme. By 1717 it had become evident to Mather that Arianism had slowly made its way not only into the Church of England but among the young Dissenting ministers also. A sharp turning point came in February and March 1719, when a

group of English Nonconformists—Presbyterians, Baptists, and Congregationalists—met in Salters' Hall in London. They were called to advise on
how to treat three Dissenting ministers in the west of England who were
suspected of Arianism. In the course of deciding, a suggestion was made
that the Assembly should itself declare adherence to orthodox Trinitarian
views, as laid down in the first of the Thirty-nine Articles and in the fifth
and sixth questions of the the Westminster Catechism. Failure to subscribe to such a declaration could easily be interpreted as a sign of holding Arian views. Yet the proposal split the assembly: sixty-three ministers
agreed to subscribe, fifty-three refused, on the ground that they would
not make human (that is, nonscriptural) creeds a test of soundness of
faith. Sixty ministers who wished to subscribe set up an assembly of their
own.

Mather learned of the Salters' Hall dispute just as he began litigating
the first suits against the Howell estate. However preoccupied, he was
thunderstruck. News of apparently broad inroads of Arianism, and of a
serious split among the English Dissenters, seemed to him "the most
grievous tidings that ever came over the Atlantic unto us." Blaming Whiston and Clarke as "the two grand satanic tools of this mischief," he dispatched a rush of letters pouring out dismay over the great "Schism arisen
among our United Brethren" and over the ministers who refused to subscribe. Isaac Watts assured him that the subscribing ministers themselves
believed that only a very few London Dissenters had become Arians, and
that the nonsubscribing ministers refused not because they were Arians
but because the subscription was "begun in a disorderly manner breaking
in upon other business and with much anger," and because they feared
such a subscription might be used as a religious test to exclude persons
from the ministry or from communion. Mather was apparently unconvinced, perhaps because he always suspected Watts's own religious leanings. Indeed Watts, a liberal and at times perplexed Calvinist who later
moved towards Unitarianism, admitted to Mather that he believed people
could be saved by conceiving Christ as omnipotent, omniscient, and al-
sufficient "and yet not equal with God the Father."

Mather regarded the nonsubscribers' refusal to endorse a nonscriptural statement of creed as an effort to use the ideal of Christian union to
promulgate Arianism. The Salters' Hall controversy thus exposed the ecumenical Universal Religion he had been fostering as another of his conflictedly conciliatory attempts to resolve the irreconcilable. His vision of
reasonable men of different sects united by a few maxims of vital piety
had of course been an imperfect thing. It excluded Catholics because of

their doomed role in Protestant eschatology, and Mather never meant it to encourage Congregationalists to give up their sectarian identity. His toleration, as Richard Lovelace remarks, was "most successful when it was directed toward those who did not have the drawback of being his neighbors." Mather wished to continue forwarding his "Syncretism of Piety" and to oppose religious persecution, yet to bar Arians from the Christian union for denying Eternal power and godhead to Christ, transforming the Savior into a mortal idol. He sent a barrage of letters to Dissenters abroad trying to make clear the difference between toleration and acceptance of heresy, indulgence and communion, forbearance and fellowship.

Mather also set forth his views publicly in *Some American Sentiments on the Great Controversy of the Time,* a formal epistle addressed to four London ministers and dated July 1, 1720, the same time as his defense of Shute over the negativing of Cooke. That sensitive episode, together with the recent attack on his style by Daniel Neal and the continued "unaccountable contempt" of London Dissenters toward publishing "Biblia Americana," may explain his beginning, in Matherese, with a defiant *mea culpa:*

> We should not be insensible, (having been very publicly inform'd of it) *That the Style and Manner of the* New-England *Writers does not equal that of the Europeans:* Nor should *he* who now writes, and who among them is the *least of the Ministers, and the lowest in Merit,* be without a very humble Sense of his Inability in point of *Sense,* as well as of *Style,* to offer any thing worthy of Consideration among the *Europeans.*

Having thus, as often before, defended himself against abuse in advance of receiving it, Mather attempted to square the ideal of Christian union with the exclusion of Arians from it. At the moment, he said, two truths demand realization: first, that no one is to be forced by civil penalties to a religious belief contrary to conscience; second, that all who truly live to God are united by certain maxims of piety entitling them to communion with each other. But these truths must be served cautiously, or Christianity be subverted. Concerning "the *plausible* Cry now so much in vogue, of *Nothing to be subscribed but the Express Words of Scripture,*" he observed that every heretic, even a papist, would so subscribe, and gain license to perpetrate damnable heresies under cover of orthodoxy. A meaningful union of Christian sects must include an express belief in the Trinity as a basis for communion and salvation, requiring not merely profession of belief in Scripture, but renunciation of Arianism. Otherwise many may claim communion with the pan-Christian church yet "continue under the Power of those *Heresies,* which are inconsistent with the *Life of GOD* in the Soul." Such claims, he suspected, signified "a strong and a deep *Conspiracy* in our very sinful Nation, to dethrone the Eternal SON of GOD."

Mather's professions of religious liberalism had led him into a compromised position two decades earlier, when he first endorsed the Presbyterian-Congregational union in London, then blasted the creation of the Brattle church at home. As happened then too, others now accused him of contradicting himself. They reproved his stand on Salters' Hall, he said, for "not consisting well with my zealous profession for a union on the terms of piety," a charge he thought "to be pitied rather than answered." One of his critics, the Baptist Thomas Hollis (whose bequest to Harvard was providing a scholarship to Sammy), pointed out that in demonstrating his Universal Religion, Mather had not long ago preached, surprisingly and generously, at the ordination of Thomas Callender, a Baptist minister. In his much publicized sermon Mather had denounced intolerance, yet he now called the nonsubscribers at Salters' Hall heretics. Mather must have received a misleading account of the controversy, Hollis suggested, or he would not impute damning sins to "his Brethren who Love the Lord Jesus. . . . so contrary to the Catholic charity he expressed" in his sermon. Invoking an old ghost, Hollis also complained that in alluding to a "plot" against Christianity, Mather was fomenting discord while those in England were seeking harmony. The charge that Mather overreacted to the events at Salters' Hall was probably just. Benjamin Colman wrote of a similar subscription crisis at an Irish assembly somewhat later, that he did not approve of those who declined the subscription, "yet I am far from imputing Arianism to them. I am herein water to Dr. Mathers Heat."

At the same time, Mather was setting up his ministry for serious damage. This second aggravation began in 1720 with the Rev. Peter Thacher of Weymouth. As Benjamin Colman related the precipitating events, Thacher had grown melancholy and in ill health at Weymouth, so he asked his church to dismiss him to go elsewhere. The relation between a minister and his flock being to many New Englanders, Colman remarked, "like that between husband and wife," the church refused. Yet Thacher insisted, got support from neighboring ministers, and the church released him. In Boston, Thacher was invited to preach as the colleague of the Rev. John Webb at the New North—the church that had been formed by the swarmers who had abandoned the Mathers' church.

Almost all the Boston ministers disapproved Thacher's conduct in securing his dismission from Weymouth, except the Mathers. They perhaps admired his acknowledged learning, piety, and ministerial gifts, for they are said to have advised and assisted him about his move from Weymouth, and they invited him to preach for several months with them. But Thacher encountered resistance within the New North itself. Forty or fifty congregants vehemently opposed his settlement with them, arguing that a minister ought to stay where God had appointed him, and deeming it unethical for a larger and wealthier congregation to deprive a smaller one. They felt strongly enough about Thacher's ordination to warn that if it proceeded they would swarm from the New North and form still another new congregation.

Shaken by the prospect of a third Congregational meetinghouse rising in the North End, Mather and his father "turned Cat in pan," as a contemporary put it, and became Thacher's "utter Enemies," helping him "into a Snare and there leave[ing] him." Having at first advised and assisted him, they now worked to obstruct his settlement at the New North, lest his opponents there band together as a new church, another rival to their own. They joined Colman and some other Boston ministers in arguing that a pastor should not be removed from his flock except for very weighty reasons, such as did not appear in Thacher's case, nor without a church council, which had not been called. They also urged the dissidents in the New North not to build another meetinghouse.

Despite this resistance from Mather and the others, Thacher's admirers in the New North pushed for and obtained his installation, which was a fiasco. The Mathers, by one account, persuaded other ministers not to attend the ceremony, apparently only two participated, one of whom was Thacher's uncle. Thacher and his uncle came to the church out a back gate and through alleys to escape interception by a hostile crowd determined to block the installation. When the crowd realized they had slipped by, it stomped into the gallery and, standing instead of sitting, protested the ceremony so noisily that no prayers could be conducted. In the din, a minister called for and received the consent of the brethren and of Thacher to what passed for his installation: "no Bear Garden certainly was ever like it," one contemporary said, "such Treatment and Language had they, that hardly was ever given to the vilest of men."

The end result of this row reached Mather on April 30, 1721, little more than two weeks after Creasy's "night-Riot," calling him "unto an uncommon Trial," he said, "wherein it will be found, whether I am Dead unto Creatures." Thacher's opponents in the New North had decided to withdraw and build the New Brick Church, popularly and appropriately referred to as the "*Revenge* Church of Christ." As Mather had feared, too, in order to fill their house the "enraged, violent, boisterous Men" who built the New Brick persuaded a "mighty Number" of his own flock to join them. He thus found his congregation abandoning him a second time, seduced by "the Religion of Pues which with a proud, vain, formal People seems to be now the chief Religion of the Town." Acknowledging that this new, very large, and nearby church was the finest in New England, while his own was in "crazy condition," he drafted a set of subscriptions toward building a new meetinghouse for his congregation. It grieved him too that his father took much to heart the swarming of these "foolish People from Him in His Age."

How many left Mather's ministry is unknown, but must have been substantial. "Tis incredible," he wrote on May 1, "what Numbers are swarming off." Just the same, in the customary show of fellowship he was asked several days later to preach the first sermon in the new church. In it he praised the New Brick as the most "*Beautiful House*" in the land, and at the end of the sermon he spoke directly to the many before him who had left his ministry. Although Increase, who was present, was apparently too ill to preach, he could not have surpassed his son in deploying pastoral concern for the salvation of the swarmers' souls as the vehicle for conveying squirming contempt for their treachery. Cotton offered the Judases Christ-like absolution for having crucified him and his father:

> When our dear SAVIOUR was within a Few Minutes of His Death, we read, *Many of them*, who attended on His Ministry, *Went away and walked no more with Him*. A very *Great Withdraw* from our Ministry many may think it will be a *Trouble* to us; and if we were not used unto *higher Sentiments*, than the People who offer it, it might be so. But we have *Learned CHRIST* better than that. I do assure you, *My Friends*, I hope you will find it more of a *Triumph* than of a *Trouble* to us.

Fusing his father's long-suffering manner with Matherese, he suggested that the building of the new church was timely, for he and Increase were about to die:

> 'Tis a Circumstance, that carries a Strong and a Strange *Consolation* in it; That our Claim to the *Royal Priesthood* is just finishing in this Addition to the many *Sacrifices*, which our Lives have been fill'd withal. That we have now done with a *World*, that has nothing in it worth Staying for; That we are just Entering into the *Joy of our Lord*, and are within a Few Weeks of seeing the *Best Hour* that ever we saw. . . .

Reminding the swarmed members how diligently he and Increase had labored for their salvation, he ended with lovingly regretful insinuations that little of it seemed to have done any good. Of this bravura kiss of death he observed in his diary: "with high Strains of Sacrificing, I give all the People to see, how easily and cheerfully we endure their Departure from us."

Suddenly, just two weeks later, Mather's multiplying defeats in his church, his family, and the government were for the moment swept from his mind, replaced by a public catastrophe. Unaware that it also held for him a personal triumph, he recorded on May 26: "The grievous Calamity of the *Small-Pox* has now entered the Town. The Practice of conveying and suffering the *Small-pox* by *Inoculation*, has never been used in *America*, nor indeed in our Nation. But how many Lives might be saved by it, if it were practised?"

12

The Paths of the Destroyer

〜ᵒᶜ〜

THE SMALLPOX epidemic that struck Boston in April 1721 lasted a full year
and infected half the city, yet it was not unexpected. Smallpox seemed to
break out at regular intervals, the last epidemic having come in 1702–3.
Because of the isolation of Massachusetts, the great infectious diseases
there tended to be epidemic rather than endemic. Smallpox, measles, or
diphtheria might arrive devastatingly, then disappear for years; when
enough nonimmune people accumulated, it came again.

Mather himself observed that beginning in 1630 smallpox arrived in
Boston precisely every twelve years. Betweentimes some vessel would
bring the disease, but it would not spread. Yet in the twelfth year "no
precaution would keep it off"; it would become "so raging, so reaching"
as to afflict even fetuses, who were "born full of it upon them." Somehow
for the seventh epidemic, predictable by Mather's computations in 1714,
the pattern did not hold. He speculated that the irregularity was owing to
the measles epidemic of 1713 that killed three of his children and his
wife, the "compassion of Heaven" refusing to add smallpox "unto what
we suffered the year before." Both Mathers later took credit for having
warned prophetically against the near approach of the disease. About six
months before the outbreak Increase preached a sermon predicting some
heavy judgment on Boston; a month or two later Cotton was stirred by a
heavenly afflatus to deliver a lecture on Trouble Near, in which he too
foretold "the speedy Approach of the destroying Angel."

Civic authorities seem to have been no less aware than the ministry
that an epidemic might come soon. A law passed in February 1718 required ships carrying infectious diseases to anchor near Spectacle Island
in the harbor, so that the infected persons and cargo that might transmit

336

infection could be removed to the island's public hospital. The law was tested in October 1720, when a sloop arrived from the Canary Islands bearing smallpox. Several persons were put ashore at the island's "Pest house," then allowed to continue to Boston in fresh clothing after being declared healthy. The captain of the ship, however, apparently died, and the selectmen ordered that no one who had attended him in his illness might enter Boston until judged to be uncontaminated.

It was the *Seahorse*, a ship from Salt Tortuga owned by John Frizzell, that brought the lethal epidemic of 1721. On April 15 the Council debated whether to grant the ship entry to Boston. Although the *Seahorse* seems to have stayed in the harbor, on May 8 the selectmen reported that a black man from the ship was in Boston, and stricken. They voted to have Dr. John Clark (Mather's former father-in-law) board the ship and report on its condition. A second black man, a servant in Boston (whether connected with the ship is uncertain), had also taken the disease, and to isolate him the selectmen appointed two "prudent persons" to seal off the house in which he lay, allowing no one to leave or enter without their permission. Four days later, apparently after Dr. Clark made his report, the selectmen noted that two or three other men aboard the *Seahorse* also had smallpox, and voted to ask Governor Shute to call a council, to advise about sending the ship to Spectacle Island.

The next week a group composed of justices, selectmen, Overseers of the Poor, and constables searched Boston houses. They reported finding no house contaminated but the one sequestering the black servant, who they said had almost recovered. This report, like the many later official announcements, may have been designed less to inform the public than to prevent panic, for the selectmen voted just the same to clean the streets and lanes, impressing carts to carry off dirt and requiring twenty-six free male blacks and mulattos to work six days at the task. By the last week in May there were not one or two or three infected persons, but eight, one of them in Bennett Street, at the North End.

Mather feared for his children and himself, smallpox being probably the most infectious of all diseases. His friend Dr. Zabdiel Boylston graphically described some of its hideous effects:

> Purple Spots, the bloody and parchment Pox, Hemorahages of Blood at the Mouth, Nose, Fundament, and Privities; Ravings and Deliriums; Convulsions, and other Fits; violent inflamations and Swellings in the Eyes and Throat; so that they cannot see, or scarcely breathe, or swallow any thing, to keep them from starving. Some looking as black as the Stock, others as white as a Sheet; in some, the Pock runs into Blisters, and the

Skin stripping off, leaves the Flesh raw. . . . Some have been fill'd with loathsome Ulcers; others have had deep, and fistulous Ulcers in their Bodies, or in their Limbs or Joints, with Rottenness of the Ligaments and Bones: Some who live are Cripples, others Idiots, and many blind all their Days. . . .

To such rank ravaging two of Mather's surviving children, Elizabeth and Sammy, were vulnerable, having been born since the last epidemic. They were both terrified of catching the disease. Mather called to heaven for guidance about whether to send them out of town, and for help in submitting "if these dear Children must lose their Lives." Because he would inevitably be called into the rooms of the sick, he felt his own life must also become threatened as the epidemic inevitably spread. Concerned also for the general public, he asked ministers to hold days of fasting and prayer, adapted his own sermons and prayers to the calamity, and called for aid to the "Miserables neglected and perishing in Sickness."

Mather's charitable and zealous concern for the sufferers led him to a more important resolution also. He decided to propose to the Boston physicians that they try a new method of preventing the disease. For years, beginning with his boyhood interest in medicine, his life had moved him toward this resolution. In adolescence, when acting as an amanuensis for the physician William Avery, he had communicated to Robert Boyle in London some of Avery's theories about smallpox. During the previous smallpox epidemic in 1702–3 he had pressed Boston physicians to use the more moderate methods of managing the disease favored by the famous physician Sydenham. More recently, in 1716, he had addressed to the Royal Society an essay on "Curiosities of the smallpox" in the course of which he urged Dr. John Woodward to help bring inoculation into experiment and fashion in England. "For my own part," he added, "if I should live to see the smallpox again enter into our city, I would immediately procure a consult of our physicians, to introduce a practise which may be of so very happy a tendency."

Mather now did that. He drew up an address, dated June 6, 1721, which was circulated in manuscript among local physicians, describing a *"Wonderful Practice"* lately come into use in some parts of the world. In fact, inoculation had been performed as folk medicine for centuries in Africa, India, China, and even in parts of Europe. Late in the seventeenth century, accounts of the Asiatic practice began arriving in England, and began to be studied and recommended after the operation had become popular in Turkey early in the eighteenth century. The first recorded inoculation in England had been performed only two months before

Mather's address, in April 1721, smallpox having struck London almost simultaneously with the epidemic in Boston, and probably also introduced by ships from the West Indies.

Mather based the method he recommended to the Boston physicians on two accounts published earlier in the *Transactions* of the Royal Society. The first, in 1714, had been sent from Constantinople by a physician named Emanuel Timonius, and appeared in the issue that carried the summary of Mather's *Curiosa;* the second, in 1716, had come from a Venetian named Jacob Pylarinus, who had observed the practice in Smyrna. The accounts seem to have been discussed in the Boston intellectual community after their appearance, and Mather received some confirmation of the success of inoculation from people in his neighborhood who had recently come from Constantinople. But Mather had learned about inoculation "many months" before the appearance of Timonius' account. His black servant Onesimus had described to him the use of inoculation among his people, the Guramantese, and had shown him a scar on his arm left by it. Onesimus' description, Mather told the Royal Society, was "the same that afterwards I found related unto you by your Timonius."

In his letter to the Boston physicians Mather briefly described the practice related to him by Onesimus (and afterward confirmed to him by other Africans), then in greater detail summarized the published accounts of Timonius and Pylarinus. To the Africans, Mather said, a merciful God brought an "*Infallible Preservative,*" which he tried to describe in Onesimus' own words: "People take Juice of *Small-Pox;* and cutty-skin, and putt in a Drop; then by'nd by a little *sicky, sicky;* then very few little things like *Small-Pox;* and no body die of it; and no body have *Small-Pox* any more." Mather's use of dialect here mattered, for now and later the opponents of inoculation made much of the social class and intellectual credentials of those testifying to its effectiveness. Keenly aware that Onesimus' folkish narrative would not be persuasive enough, Mather added the fuller description of "Superiour Persons in the *Levant.*"

As Mather summarized the account of Dr. Timonius, inoculation had been used in the Levant for about forty years, and having overcome irrational prejudices against it had over the last eight years proved successful on thousands of persons: not one of those inoculated died of the disease. At Constantinople the inoculation is ideally performed at the beginning of winter or spring, using as healthy a young person as can be found who is stricken with smallpox. Twelve or thirteen days into the illness, some of the youth's larger pustules are pricked with a needle, the matter being pressed out into a washed vessel and carried without delay to the inoculee in a stopped bottle, kept warm in the bosom of the messenger. The inoculation is performed in a warm room. First, several small cuts are made with a needle or lancet in the patient's arm muscles. Then on each cut is placed a drop of the matter, or "variole," which is mixed well with the flowing blood. The wound is covered by a concave object, such as a walnut shell, and bound so that the arm is not rubbed by garments. Usually, according to Timonius, ten or twenty pustules break out on the inoculee, who stays at home, keeping warm and on a light diet. The incision runs with pus several days, but in a short time the pocks dry and fall off, rarely pitting.

The method Pylarinus observed, Mather continued, differed only slightly, originating in Smyrna also as folk medicine among the "Mean, Coarse, Rude Sort of People." Pylarinus described the procedure used by a "notable *Inoculatrix*" who advised performing the inoculation only in winter. Instead of incisions she made pinpricks with a gold or iron needle in the forehead, chin, cheeks, wrists, and insteps (unnecessarily many, Pylarinus felt). The wounds often became sore and sometime produced abscesses in some "Emunctory" (a body organ that drains off useless secretions). But, like Timonius, Pylarinus affirmed that ill consequences had been rare. For himself, Mather told the physicians, he felt "very confident no Person would miscarry in it, but what *would most certainly* have miscarried upon taking the Contagion in the *Common Way.*"

How many physicians read Mather's address is unknown, as is the number of physicians then operating in Boston, but only one of them immediately responded, Dr. Zabdiel Boylston. Born in Brookline, he had been trained in medicine by his father, and ran an apothecary shop where he sold surgical instruments and a wide variety of drugs "both Galenical, and Chymical" as well as painters' colors and nostrums for growing hair. His wares do not inspire confidence, but they are deceptive. Before the smallpox epidemic he had performed some virtuoso feats of surgery. Especially interested in lithotomy, in 1707 he successfully removed an egg-sized stone from a thirteen-year-old boy whose life had been given up. In 1718, in the presence of several ministers and other spectators, he did a mastectomy on Mrs. Edward Winslow, whose life was also despaired of because of the bleeding, growth, and stench of a cancer on her left breast. Her husband waited two years to be sure the cancer did not return, then published personal testimonials to Boylston's skill in two Boston newspapers, observing that several doctors had labored unsuccessfully to relieve her "dreadful" cancer until Boylston "cut her whole Breast off" and dressed the surgery "in the space of five Minutes by the Watch of one then present," wholly curing her. Eventually becoming the first American-born physician to be celebrated in England, Boylston later lectured at the Royal College of Physicians and was received with exceptional honor at the Royal Society.

Boylston approved of Mather's versions of the Levant accounts, and believed that in giving them to the physicians Mather had acted out of compassion. Mather wrote to him on June 24, praising the "very much good which a gracious God employs you and honours you to do in a miserable world," and suggesting that if after serious deliberation Boylston thought it advisable to try the inoculation, "it may save many lives that we set a great value on." Two days later, Boylston inoculated a thirty-six-year-old black servant, a two-and-a-half-year-old black child, and his own six-year-old son Thomas. The adult became free of symptoms in two or three days, but Boylston believed he had had the pox before. The children began having complaints by the sixth day, became somewhat hot and sleepy on the seventh, showed about a hundred "kind and favourable" pocks by the ninth—and after that soon were well.

The news of Boylston's experiments and of Mather's encouragements to them scared most Bostonians. Civic authorities had made futile efforts to contain the epidemic and allay public dread, appointing more guards, moving the grammar school to the Town House after three cases broke out in School Street, publishing bromidic progress reports that understated the size and seriousness of the epidemic. ("It is a thousand pities," Boylston later remarked, "our Select-Men made so slight and trifling a Representation of the Small-Pox, that had always prov'd so fatal in *New-England*.") Many people feared that inoculation would not halt the inexorably spreading disease but spread it further. The fear was not unjustified, because if used indiscriminately inoculation could in some circumstances spread the disease and, as then practiced, could have painful and revolting side effects. A reliable account of a successful inoculation later in the year reported that the patient wished he had not been inoculated; after the eruptions began, his pupils dilated, his incisions ran, and about eighty pustules appeared on his face, others on his scrotum.

Mather found himself and Boylston becoming objects of panicky abuse: "They rave, they rail, they blaspheme; they talk not only like Idiots but also like *Franticks*." He was of course no stranger to vilification. And feeling he had acted neither self-interestedly nor conflictedly, he enjoyed despite the abuse an "unspeakable Consolation," he said, in having instructed the physicians in a method of "infallibly" saving lives. Equally confident, Boylston placed an ad in the Boston *Gazette* affirming that his three experiments had validated the accounts of Timonius and Pylarinus: their success showed that no one need fear receiving many pustules from the inoculation, being scarred in the face, or ever taking the disease again. He also served notice that in a few weeks he planned to perform further inoculations. Before doing so, however, he publicly invited the other Boston physicians to visit his patients and judge his success.

With Mather certain of his cause, and Boylston determined to proceed, the selectmen took testimony on July 21 from a Dr. Lawrence Dalhonde—a "*French* Fellow of a very vicious Character," as Mather called him, who had witnessed disastrous inoculations in Europe. He testified that in Italy twenty-five years ago he had seen thirteen soldiers inoculated, of whom three were unaffected, six made a difficult recovery but developed tumors and gangrene, and four died; in Spain an inoculated soldier became frenzied, and his autopsy disclosed infected lymph glands and ulcerated lungs. The Boston physicians found Dalhonde's testimony so convincing that instead of accepting Boylston's invitation they signed a statement asserting that inoculation tends to infuse the blood with "malignant Filth," spreads infection, kills many, and would likely have the "most dangerous Consequence" in Boston.

Three days after Dalhonde's interview, a pseudonymous correspondent to the *News-Letter* amplified the attack on Boylston. Mather, he said, out of a "Pious and Charitable design of doing good," had recommended inoculation to the local physicians, who all declined except a "certain *Cutter for the Stone*." Reckless and inept, and lacking an academic degree, Boylston tried inoculation at his home in Dock Square, the most public trading place in Boston, and during the stifling heat of summer, although the Levant relations advised attempting it only in winter and spring, with the result that his own inoculated child took a violent fever and barely escaped with his life. The writer also hinted that Boylston's acts could be construed as felonious, a "*Propagating of Infection and Criminal.*"

These charges of incompetence provoked a sharp exchange between Boylston's defenders and detractors. Benjamin Colman, for one, thought the letter grossly partial in rebuking Boylston but pardoning Mather, who "push'd on the Attempt and openly rejoic'd in it," Colman said, adding that he believed both men had hoped to do good. In the next week's *Gazette*, he joined Cotton and Increase Mather and three other ministers in expressing distress over the lampooning of Boylston as a "*Cutter for the Stone.*" By his dexterity as a surgeon, they said, Boylston had honored the country and shown compassion for many miserable people; although lacking a degree he had studied hard and observed much, and practiced long and with great success. The ministers' endorsement was answered the next week by a writer who dismissed them as "*Six Gentlemen of Piety and Learning, profoundly ignorant of the Matter.*" In recommending the "Practice of the Greek old Women," he said, they pretended to expertise on "one of the most intricate practical Cases in Physick." In defending Boylston they fancied him "some *Romantick Character*, something beyond that of candid *Sydenham*," begarlanding him with "all the fulsome common Place of *Quack Advertisements.*" In fact many readers, he said, took their endorsement for humor.

This flurry opened what became a nearly year-long war of pamphlets and letters-to-the-editor, in which the successive attacks, counterattacks, and counter-counterattacks grew ever more bitter and personal. Meanwhile the disease was becoming epidemic. On July 29 the selectmen again assessed the town and discovered 168 persons infected—a probably undervalued count, as the reassuring tone of their report suggests: "and but Eighteen by GOD's Goodness are Dead, and Several of them lost by Carelessness and not by the Distemper." Public apprehension surged with the news that parts of the Mediterranean and France were being visited with bubonic plague, which could be brought to New England atop the smallpox. One newspaper writer implied that inoculation might make people more vulnerable to plague and even breed it, because plague boils break out in emunctories, the very places where the Levant accounts said that abscesses sometime appear after inoculation. As Boston newspapers told grisly stories of the streets of Marseilles strewn with dead cats and of slaves carting off corpses, Governor Shute issued a proclamation on August 4, requiring every vessel arriving from France or the Mediterranean to undergo a forty-day quarantine before unloading.

Despite the thickening air of menace and a reprimand from the selectmen and justices, who forbad any further inoculations, Boylston inoculated seven other persons in July, and seventeen in August, of whom one died. Mather, undaunted also, prepared a short essay on the treatment of smallpox containing a notable medical point. The cause of smallpox was at the time wholly unknown. But in discussing inoculation Mather speculated that the disease might be an "*Animalculated Business*"—that is, that it might originate in tiny organisms, a suspicion which has been confirmed, he said, by viewing the pustules under a microscope. He does not make clear whether he or someone else in Boston raised or confirmed this possibility. If he came himself to the belief that smallpox was caused by a pathogenic organism, he must be credited with having stumbled unaided on the momentous germ theory of disease.

Opposition to Mather's and Boylston's further efforts now produced a permanent forum and a formidable spokesman. On August 7, 1721, appeared the first issue of *The New-England Courant*, a newspaper published by James Franklin (who had printed in 1719 Mather's *Vigilius*, a sermon on drowsy devotions), soon to be joined by his younger brother Benjamin. Its chief aim, one contributor wrote, was "to oppose the *doubtful* and *dangerous* Practice of *inoculating* the *Small Pox*," and for nearly ten months the *Courant* inveighed relentlessly against the inoculators' character, credentials, and beliefs. But the paper also set itself satirically against the college, the magistrates, the wealthy, and much of the Massachusetts establishment. More clearly than any other features of New England's life, its lively verse and prose about cuckoldry and bachelordom, its serialization of Fielding's *Jonathan Wild*, its assaults on efforts to date the Second Coming, its tone of tongue-in-cheek irreverence, giving authority to once-marginal social tendencies gathering throughout Mather's lifetime, sounded the funeral knell of the Puritan Fathers. The paper also now gave a public voice to Mather's and Boylston's main antagonist, Dr. William Douglass, whose presence in the debate highlighted the amateurism of Mather and Boylston both. A Scotsman educated at Edinburgh, Paris, and Leyden (where he studied with Boerhaave), Douglass was the one physician in Boston with an academic degree in medicine. Indeed it was he who apparently loaned Mather—a "credulous vain preacher," Douglass called him—the accounts by Timonius and Pylarinus which Mather knew, "that he might have something to send home to the Royal Society who had long neglected his communications as he complained."

Douglass first sprang on the inoculators in two anonymous pieces in the *Courant* in August. In the first, a grim satire, he told of reading at the same time a defense of inoculation and also news of an intended expedition against the eastern Indians. The two blending in his mind produced a brainstorm: fight the Indians by inoculation. He would arm some inoculators with lancets and nutshells, supply pus and "Negro Yaws" for ammunition, and award a £5 bounty for each Indian killed by inoculation, and double that for each Indian who "survives, conveys and spreads the Infection among his *Tribe*." More soberly and frontally, in his second essay he rejected inoculation as a desperate remedy more suitable for plague, dangerous in itself and useless in preventing smallpox from occurring in the common way. He also accused the inoculators of playing down the severity of the reaction, which he said included violent fevers and ulcers in the groin and other glandulous parts, with swelling and loss of the use of limbs, as in cases of venereal disease. In the spirit of the selectmen, he also claimed that the number of burials since the arrival of smallpox was no greater than the number during the same period in other years. The real danger in the epidemic, he warned, was social chaos, which might destroy commerce and frighten others out of sending provisions to Boston.

What made Douglass worth hearing was not simply his professional training but also his essential seriousness. No Neanderthal or fool, he observed the epidemic with inquisitive scientific interest, recording "intricate incidents" in hope of learning the "mazes" of smallpox. Nor did he doubt the potential value in inoculation. Rather, as a knowledgeable physician, he deplored the present methods of performing it, pointing out correctly that inoculated persons might communicate the disease if not kept in isolation until the infection ran its course; the disease might more certainly be escaped, he said, by merely moving to the country. He also thought the inoculators people with little knowledge and rash impulses, and believed the practice must be tested by other than "*Greek old Women, Madmen and Fools.*" As this crack suggests, Douglass gained added confidence in his views from his haughtiness, his medical degree and foreign birth making him feel superior to others in Boston and act toward them patronizingly. He was also somewhat avaricious. Many physicians opposed inoculation, Benjamin Colman said later, "because it would have saved the Town Thousands of pounds that is now in their pockets," and Douglass cared about making money from the many smallpox victims he treated during the epidemic. Explaining afterward to a correspondent why he had not had time to write up his medical observations, he said he found it "more natural to begin by reducing my smallpox accounts into bills and notes for the improvement of my purse." However motivated, Douglass on his own and through the *Courant* helped organize Boston against the inoculation.

*

The tense, charnal atmosphere ate at Mather's patience and energy. Day after day throughout the summer, he fulminated in his diary against the "false Reports, and blasphemous Speeches, and murderous Wishes." The situation also called to his demonology, in which such massive onslaughts against mankind as epidemics and such obstructions to human progress as attempts to impede scientific knowledge, were characteristic works of evil angels. Believing that only their unwelcome presence could explain the rage against inoculation, he saw Boston benighted by the

"Power of Darkness," "Satanic Fury" again astir, the place become "a dismal Picture and Emblem of *Hell; Fire* with *Darkness* filling of it." Only their presence could explain the "crying Wickedness of this Town, (A Town at this time strangely possessed with the Devil,) and the vile Abuse which I do myself particularly suffer from it, for nothing but my instructing our base Physicians, how to save many precious Lives." Repeatedly he applied for "uncommon Assistance" from above so that he would not act frowardly, "or fall into any of the common Iniquities, of Lying, and Railing and Malice."

Very tryingly, Mather found the festering epidemic no restraint on his wife, his errant son, or his creditors. In July Lydia took into the household a young woman related to her (her niece, it seems certain), whom Mather regarded as negligent in piety and a usurper: "my own Children must be turned and kept out of Doors, and their Place be taken by a Stranger so unacceptable to me." Creasy apparently had been sent away again for improvement, but Mather found him still impenitent, and by September seemingly again in debt: "A vile Sloth, accompanied with the Power of Satan still reigning over him, ruins him, destroys him." He decided to ask the boy to live with him once more "that I may have him under my Eye continually." Once he returned, Mather gave him reading to transcribe and extract for his commonplace books, and as ever prayed for the conversion of "my miserable Son *Increase*."

Smallpox or no, creditors to the Howell estate dunned Mather vigorously. Shortly before the epidemic, in April, he and Lydia had defaulted on a claim against both the Howell and George estates by the wealthy Boston merchant Andrew Faneuil, for nearly £120, a large amount that Faneuil had long demanded. Apparently now wholly out of funds to pay Faneuil, and still unable to win his release from the administration, Mather petitioned the court for permission to sell part of Howell's warehouse on the Long Wharf, which was granted. Although he managed thus to satisfy Faneuil's claim, he was unable to sell other property to settle other claims, seemingly because the court's decision applied only to Faneuil. And each sale had to be approved by Lydia's daughter and her husband, relatives who he believed had "laid a deep Design, assisted with crafty and cruel Adversaries, if they can, to ruin me." Having profited nothing from the estate, but being owed much by it, he was by July in "considerable *Poverty*," owning not "a Foot of Land in all the World. My Salary is not enough to support me comfortably, I meet with many Wants and Straits: in my Diet, much; in my Habit, more." The little estate he had had been sold, and the money gone to pay debts; if he put something aside for his necessities, it disappeared. He began forwarding new dunning letters to his attorneys, promising creditors he would spur their efforts to satisfy the claims.

But having borne the deaths of ten of his children already, Mather worried most that smallpox might visit his family. His first concern was for the two frightened adolescents born after the last epidemic—Elizabeth, about to turn seventeen, and Sammy, nearly fifteen. Sammy came home from the college in June, as the disease spread in the North End, and was afraid to return to Cambridge; Liza lived even "in greater Fears than he." Mather wished to have them inoculated. But he also wished to avoid further exciting the town: the "cursed Clamour of a People strangely and fiercely possessed of the Devil, will probably prevent my saving the Lives of my two Children, from the Small-pox in the Way of Transplantation." He importuned heaven for their safety, and to quicken Liza's flights to Christ gave her a book relating the death of a young Frenchwoman. Sammy, however, begged to have himself inoculated. Mather reasoned on one side that if he denied Sammy and the boy took the disease he would have to answer for it; on the other that if he agreed and the inoculation miscarried "my Condition would be insupportable." But other circumstances argued for inoculating him: ten "remarkable Experiments" had been successfully performed in the North End; Sammy's Harvard roommate and best friend had died of smallpox; Increase Mather advised that the inoculation be performed but kept secret. Deciding that "I could not answer it unto God, if I neglected it," Mather uncertainly consented.

A few days after the inoculation Sammy became "pretty full" of pocks and his fever had risen beyond expectation. Mather thought his condition "very hazardous." He believed both that Sammy had been infected before the inoculation, and that the procedure had been imperfectly performed, Sammy receiving only one incision, and that "so small as to be hardly worthy the Name of one." Again the possibility of the death of one of his children confronted him, this time the death of "so hopeful a son." He set apart August 25 as a day of prayer for Sammy, begging that he might live and fulfill his ministry. Girding himself, however, he contrasted the meaning to him of his family with the meaning of an "infinitely more desirable Christ," who would abundantly satisfy him "in the Withdraw of these and all Creatures from me." While praying in his study on August 30, mentally offering Sammy as a sacrifice to God, he decided to open his Bible at random; if the place he chanced on did not provide appropriate matter for meditation, he would turn to and meditate on the story of Jesus' miraculous cure of the son of a nobleman. To his surprise, the

Bible opened at that very place, offering to his eye the line: Go thy Way, thy Son liveth. The same evening Sammy's fever rose to a distressing degree. Apparently delirious, Sammy made a fervid request, "under an Impression of such Violence upon him, as if it came from some superior Original." He asked impassionedly to have a vein opened in him, with the result that his condition eased utterly and he smoothly recovered.

Unexpectedly, however, two of Mather's children born before the last epidemic and presumed immune had also become stricken—conceivably, but improbably, by some other disease. They were his daughter Hannah, about twenty-five years old, and his twenty-seven-year-old daughter Abigail, the wife of his attorney, Daniel Willard, and now in late pregnancy, near to giving birth. Hannah had remained unmarried, perhaps because as a child she had fallen into a fire, so seriously burning the right side of her face and her right hand and arm that her life was feared for; her face may have remained badly scarred. On September 3 the physicians announced that "poor *Nancy*, dear *Nancy*" had not many hours to live. Praying with her often to prepare her, Mather felt a "strange Light" on his mind that she would recover, a persuasion encouraged when for a few minutes she regained her senses and speech and told him that she too had received some inner assurances. Although Nancy did recover, Abigail, "Nibby"—a good and kindly woman, Mather thought her—also lay in "dying Circumstances," and in this condition gave birth to a daughter. Named "Resigned," the infant was to be baptized on September 24; but that day she died, apparently while Mather was conducting services in church, with the baptismal water standing ready. Mather had little time to grieve, for the next days occupied him with strengthening Nibby in her own death struggle. Ironically, Nibby's mother and namesake had died (of breast cancer) during the previous smallpox epidemic, her eight months of suffering initiating with a miscarriage. Nibby, fearing for the state of her soul and longing for deliverance, died a hard death between ten and eleven on the evening of September 26—the eleventh of Mather's fifteen children to die.

Now nearly sixty years old, Mather had discovered the proper, and for him the logical, response to hard deaths, not meekness so much, or submission, but, better, silence. The day before Nibby's burial he preached a sermon later published as *Silentiarius* (1721), a title rich in personal history. Having given much energetic discipline to mastering his unruly speech, or much ingenuity to denying its quirks by gorgeous fluency, he now took for his doctrine the concept that "Our GOD is never more *Praised* than by our *silence.*" Righteousness demands, he said, the recognition that whatever sad things befall us, and whatever good things, representing God's will they must be received in noiseless uncomplaint. Recognition that *"The Lord is in thy Adversity"* demands, he repeated over and again, the *"Holy silence* wherewith we are to Glorify Him." Unspeakingly we must let our feelings grow as cold as may be and bear our sad things with mortified muteness, "the *Holy silence* of those who are *Crucified unto the World."* A man hanging on a cross "has *little to say,* unto any thing that *this World* has to offer unto him," is in his silence free among the dead. For himself too, he told his congregation, he would try to hold his peace: "IT becomes *me* to do so, who have this Day, a DAUGHTER (together with *her* New-born *Daughter,*) waiting to be *Buried out of my Sight,* whom others as well as I, could not but always with much Affection *Look* upon."

*

A canvass of the town at the end of September, perhaps again understated, counted 2757 persons infected since the beginning of the epidemic, of whom 203 had died. Fear of contamination had also in effect embargoed Boston, so that with winter at hand, grain, butter, and firewood were not coming into town and sold at inflated prices. To deal with the crisis, public officials provided a ferry to Boston from the harbor for wood-vending sloopmen who feared entering the town, ordered Indian hostages suspected of being diseased moved from the Cambridge prison to Castle Island, and distributed funds from the public treasury to relieve the many otherwise able people financially reduced by the epidemic. Considering inoculation little less dangerous than the epidemic itself, a town meeting voted in November to require the immediate removal of any in town found inoculated, and the selectmen voted to require any person coming to Boston from another town seeking inoculation to be sent to the Spectacle Island hospital.

Mather and Boylston, however, persisted in administering and justifying inoculation. Boylston inoculated 31 persons in September, 18 more in October, and 103 in November, as the epidemic began reaching its worst intensity in Boston. With some 322 persons in the North Church stricken in mid-October, Mather daily visited "loathsome" sickrooms and himself fell ill of a fever brought on, he believed, "by the Poisons of infected Chambers." Although wondering "Is my Hour come?" (and adding, "Tis welcome"), he joined Boylston at the end of October in publishing a defense of inoculation in the *Gazette,* partly to repudiate false rumors,— for instance, that those inoculated stank. In their view, inoculation had succeeded beyond even their hopes. They claimed that only one inocu-lee, a Mrs. Dixwell, had died, and everyone who knew the case believed her death was not caused by inoculation. A few inoculees had erupted in more pustules than the Levant accounts mentioned, but they had under-gone little sickness; most inoculees had had few pustules, and had expe-rienced "in a manner, *Nothing.*" Some who were dying of smallpox or had seen its terrors, Mather and Boylston concluded, had begged their friends to become inoculated.

Someone tried to kill Mather about two weeks later. One person who came to Boston seeking inoculation was Mather's nephew Thomas Wal-ter, the minister at Roxbury—a supporter of the method and a leader in the regular singing movement. A few months earlier, an anti-inoculator had attacked Walter in print as an "*obscene* and *fuddling Merry-Andrew,*" depicting him and another debauched spark with some punch on a bed, together with "two Sisters of not the best Reputation in the World." Mather put the young minister up in his own "Lodging-Room," where, inocu-lated, Walter lay on November 14. Toward three o' clock in the morning, somebody threw into the room a "fired Granado." Had the ball landed on Walter's head, Mather said, its weight alone would have killed him. But the grenade was also loaded, the upper part with powder, the lower with a mix of powder and turpentine "and what else I know not." Had it exploded, Mather believed, it would probably have killed anyone in the room, and certainly have set fire to the room itself and soon destroyed the house. But the grenade, in passing through the window, struck the iron in the middle of the casement, so that when the grenade hit the floor the "fired Wild-fire" in the fuse shook out. When the grenade was examined there was found, tied around it with a string, the message: "COTTON MATHER, *You Dog, Dam you; I'l inoculate you with this, with a Pox to you.*"

The attempted assassination was much talked of in Boston and, thank-ful, Mather marked his "miraculous" deliverance by preaching on the text, This night there stood by me the Angel of the God whose I am, and whom I serve. Yet while he felt providentially rescued, the episode also confirmed with frightening lifelikeness his ancient conviction that no gifts suffice to win love, that, like Christ, those who Do Good are spurned. His execution had been sought, he wrote, for "such a Crime as this. I have communicated a never-failing and a most allowable Method, of preventing Death." As the bomb had not only terrorized Mather's fam-ily but also endangered neighboring houses, Governor Shute, upon a request by the House, made a proclamation at the college on November

16, directing the sheriffs, constables, and other officers to identify the would-be assassin, calling on other citizens to help, and promising to give a reward of £50 plus a pardon to any accomplice who came forward and confessed.

Not everyone, Mather discovered, was eager to help. Some applauded the bomb throwing and promised, he said, "that tho' the first Blow miscarried, there will quickly come another, that shall do the Business more effectually." Intent as always on returning good for evil, he prayed for the welfare of the "unknown Person, who sought my Death by the fired Granado," and now found in himself a new, unfamiliar sort of thankfulness. Although he lived daily expecting another attempt to kill him, he became filled with joy at the prospect of his approaching martyrdom. Indeed, if he caught himself asking to be spared, his mouth became strangely stopped, his heart strangely cold; but when he thought of "suffering Death for saving the Lives of dying People," he became ravished by a "Joy unspeakable and full of Glory." Experiencing the divine consolations that sometimes irradiated the minds of martyrs, which previously he knew only in his reading, he began to fear doing anything for his safety, even to long for the hour of his assassination.

Insidiously the smallpox spread outside Boston to Newport, New London, Plymouth, Salem, Ipswich, Sandwich, Roxbury, and many other New England towns. Mather and Boylston promoted the new method there also: in all about 135 inoculations were performed outside Boston, it was estimated, nearly a hundred of them by Boylston. In early December, Mather gave copies of a description of the method, perhaps in manuscript, to physicians and others "in several Parts of the Countrey." As these towns tried to stave off the disease with quarantines and fasts, the inoculations produced pamphlet controversies similar to Boston's, and other like results. Mather learned that a minister at Marblehead, for wanting to be inoculated, was "likely to be murdered by an abominable People, that will not let him save his Life."

Mather also addressed himself to the simultaneous, although worse, smallpox epidemic in populous London, and its attendant controversy. As earlier noted, inoculation in London began in April 1721, with the daughter of Lady Mary Wortley Montagu. Mather seems not to have been aware of this when, in May, he proposed the method to the Boston physicians. Reports of the Boston inoculations were printed in London newspapers, just as Boston newspapers ran accounts of the London inoculations, the English inoculators citing Mather, the English anti-inoculators citing Douglass. In November Mather wrote the first of three communications on smallpox which he sent to the Royal Society. It gives a full historical narrative of the Boston crisis from May to November, followed by a step-by-step description of the Boston method, which was quickly published in the Society's *Transactions.* Here Mather offered several revisions of the Levant accounts, which he said had understated the number of pocks that erupt on the inoculees; the Boston inoculations usually brought not ten or twenty, but in some persons hundreds of them and in others very few. While experimenting, Mather indicated, Boylston introduced some changes in the Levant method, dressing the incisions with warmed cabbage leaves instead of a concave object, and taking the variole from an inoculee instead of from a smallpox victim. In an important updated communication to the Royal Society a few months later, announcing the successful inoculation in America of, now, almost three hundred persons, Mather added several curiosa observed in Boston, such as the seeming immunity to the disease of persons who had been smitten first by plague, and the failure of pigeons to hatch during the epidemic. Boston experience also taught that in some seemingly hopeless cases, cure has been achieved by blistering the patient's wrists, ankles, or both, allowing the discharge to run until the danger is over.

Whether the accounts from Boston helped to turn English public opinion for or against the inoculation has been debated. Whether it helped or hurt, Mather's second communication was quoted extensively in, and the full text appended to, the second edition of *Mr. Maitland's Account of Inoculating the Small Pox Vindicated* (London, 1722). Dr. Charles Maitland, an eminent physician who had practiced inoculation in Turkey, had himself earlier provided support for the Boston inoculators. In August 1721, he successfully inoculated seven prisoners in Newgate (upon condition of their receiving the king's pardon) before about twenty-five physicians, surgeons, and apothecaries, news of which appeared in Boston newspapers. Maitland's lead and the example of Lady Mary Wortley Montagu did win some favor for inoculation in London. How much Mather's own communications contributed is speculative. The two facts may not be related, but five days after Mather's second communication was presented at the Royal Society, the British royal princesses submitted themselves to inoculation.

*

By about mid-December Boston had become so generally infected as to make further inoculations useless. As the epidemic peaked, the focus of controversy surrounding it shifted from the safety of inoculation to the integrity of the New England ministers who had promoted it, bringing to a near climax several decades of building discontent with the ministry. Following Mather, many other ministers had come to advocate inoculation, including Benjamin Colman, Solomon Stoddard, John Wise, and several younger divines. Increase Mather, although ill, aging, and discouraged ("I am now in my 83 year," he noted a day after his birthday, "Unprofitable"), had also often visited infected persons, prayed with sick blacks, and championed the new method. Their efforts were assailed in months of virulent newspaper articles and pamphlets, whose open contempt for the ministry seemed to Samuel Sewall "a Very great Degeneracy from Our forefathers."

The number of these attacks makes extensive summary and quotation tedious, but in essence the anti-inoculators pounded on two related indictments: that the ministers were hypocritical and authoritarian. Many turned the ministers' own weapons back upon them and blasted them for deserting orthodox religious principles. By the logic and long practice of the covenant theory and the jeremiad, disasters such as earthquakes or epidemics were to be regarded as divine judgments, to which the correct response—as indeed the ministers had always insisted—was repentance and reform. Several writers in the otherwise satirical *Courant* claimed that the epidemic was a divine judgment on the country's provoking evils of profaneness, idleness, and luxury, and, sounding for all the world like Cotton Mather, called not for inoculation but for reformation, "returning unto Him who is smiting of us, that so he may turn from the Fierceness of his Anger, and cause his Fury towards us to cease." Others protested that in taking their arguments not from Scripture but from heathens in Africa and the Levant, the ministers had "revolted from the good old way, and have set up a way that their Fathers know not of."

While some anti-inoculators tried to outflank the ministers, others centrally assaulted the ancient alliance between Moses and Aaron, questioning the ministers' qualifications for meddling in civic affairs. As the *Courant* portrayed the ministers, they had no knowledge of medicine, and rested their case for inoculation on nothing more than *ex cathedra* say-so:

> *Cl*[ergyman]. The Ministers of the Gospel, who are our Spiritual Guides, approve and recommend this Practice; and they are great and good Men, who would not impose on the World; and surely, you ought to fall in with their Opinion.

Such complaints that the ministers used the traditional respect for their office to enforce their ignorance often carried an undercurrent of class antagonism, as appears in two pamphlets by a man named John Williams. An acquaintance of the Mrs. Dixwell who was widely alleged to have died of inoculation, he seems to have run a "tobacco-cellar" where he dispensed tobacco, drugs, and free medical advice. Mather flicked him off as a "sorry *Tobacconist;* who could hardly spell a Word of *English,* (even the word *English,* from his acute Pen was *Engleche*)." But here Mather missed, and in a degree confirmed, Williams's point. For in trying to show that neither Scripture nor medical theory justified inoculation, Williams flaunted rather than hid his rudimentary knowledge and garbled reasoning. Most ministers, he wrote, are "of a contrary Party to the Bulk of the People, with respect to the public Affairs here in this Town," and he paraded illustratively as an illiterate mechanic, one of the commons whom the ministers disdain as a vulgar mob and consider stupid for lacking a Harvard degree. Tracing the history of ministerial error in New England back through inoculation and the banking crisis, he began with the Salem witchcraft trials, "when so many innocent Persons lost their Lives." Many other anti-inoculators made the same taunting connection. Douglass observed that all countries have been subject to infatuation, which in New England seems to have concentrated in some of the ministry, as shown by "The *Persecution of the Quakers* about the Year 1658, the *hanging of those suspected of Witchcraft,* about the Year 1691. . . . and *Inoculation,* or *Self-procuring the Small Pox,* in the Year 1721."

Pro-inoculation allies of the ministry returned these shafts point by point. Typical of many counterthrusts is a sixteen-page pamphlet entitled *Vindication of the Ministers of Boston* (1722), published "By Some of their PEOPLE." (Mather seems to have supplied material for this pamphlet, and may have written parts of it.) Alert to the *Courant* writers' "saucy" tactic of preaching Providence and Scripture to the ministers, they thought it "very strange and ridiculous, to see the Satyrists play the Divine." The Boston ministers, they said, were neither meddlesome in politics nor ignorant of medicine; rather they desired the good of the community, and their ranks perhaps contained men "such as the best PHYSICIANS in the Land, need not be ashamed to *advice* withal." Among such men they particularly praised "the *Learned* Dr. COTTON MATHER, *Fellow of the Royal Society,*" who scorns to "draw his GENEROUS PEN for his own *Vindication,* against the many foolish PAMPHLETS that are pointed at him; and who changes not his *Temper* for all their invidious Calumnies."

Mather needed vindicating, for those who rose up at the ministry usually marked him out as the chief ministerial spokesman for inoculation, and the most authoritarian and ignorant. The many charges of deceit made against him during his defense of Governor Shute clung and were now repeated, ranging in seriousness from the *Courant's* hits at his "Equivocations, mental Reservations, and Jesuitical Evasions" to Douglass's charges of blatant lying. At the time of the first inoculations, in May, Mather and his supporters had justified the experiments on the ground that Mather first cautiously sought the counsel of the Boston physicians, and gave them the accounts from the Levant and from his servant Onesimus. In the first months of 1722, however, Douglass reviewed these earlier events and claimed that Mather had set Boylston experimenting before the physicians had a chance to meet and that, when consulted, the physicians condemned the practice. He also charged that Mather did not send him a copy of his letter to the physicians, excluding him from the consultations. Mather's reason, he implied, was that he owned the issue of the *Transactions* which contained the original, Latin, account by Pylarinus, enabling him to see what, to win support, Mather had omitted, mistranslated, and falsified. Douglass said that Mather translated as "ill consequences," for instance, a Latin word meaning "mortal," suggesting in his translation that inoculation might have side effects where the Latin of Pylarinus indicated it might be mortal. Mather challenged Douglass to produce the volume so the accuracy of his rendering could be judged. Douglass refused, with the unpersuasive excuse that concern for the lives of his neighbors obliged him to keep the account out of circulation.

Mather's detractors often struck for his jugular, declaring their hilarity over his many publications. One after another chuckled publicly over his "innate Itch of Writing," derided his want of "Grammar Learning," mirthfully quoted him against himself, requoted Oldmixon on *Magnalia* ("so confus'd in the Form, so trivial in the Matter, and so faulty in the Expression"), flouted without naming those who "have so great an Opinion of their own Works, although there is no Beauty nor comeliness in them," took off his literary posturing: "*I am a Man of Letters . . . but all the illiterate Scribblers of the Town* (the Leather Apron Men) *are* proud and vain Fellows." Douglass aimed for an equally vulnerable place, ridiculing "Curiosa Americana" as "trivial credulous Stories"—for instance Mather's "Fancy" that pigeons in New England roosted in "some undiscover'd Satellite" of the earth—advising that instead of writing on inoculation Mather "write some Observations on a *Physical Account of a Phantom* he does not comprehend." Many others gibed at Mather's D.D. and F.R.S., for instance explaining that the University of Glasgow had "gratify'd his

Vanity" with a D.D. out of respect for New England, or that he won homage by coyly showing himself receptive to it, having, the *Courant* said, "kept an open Breast to receive *Honours of all Sorts.*" One pamphleteer, cheekily addressing himself to "the Very Reverend and Learned Dr. COTTON MATHER" (otherwise "C.M. D.D. and F.R.S."), travestied Mather's self-puffery and annoyingly advertised sonship: "*The young Gentleman* has been above Forty Years a celebrated Preacher, and has been so acknowledged by *Foreign Universities,* as no *American* ever was before him, and justly merits the Honour of being a Member of the ROYAL SOCIETY: He has a GREAT NAME in distant Lands; and *foreign Countries* have a great *Veneration* for him."

Mather's membership in the Royal Society, an important item in the squabble over his qualifications, itself came under suspicion. Doubts about it were first raised by John Checkley, an apothecary and self-proclaimed virtuoso who had studied at Oxford. Although born in Boston of old Puritan stock, Checkley was an Anglican, and he accused the New England churches of praying to the devil. He had also seen a printed list of Fellows of the Society and noticed, as Mather had noticed earlier, that it did not include Mather's name. Just before the epidemic, he wrote to the astronomer Edmund Halley at the Society, asking him to send proof, if any existed, of Mather's membership. It would be, he said, "an Act of Charity to a disturbed, persecuted . . . Son of our holy Mother Church of England," and would help him defend himself against "these Sons of Strife, Schism, and Sedition." As the inoculations began, Checkley became associated with Douglass and the anti-inoculators of the *Courant.*

Amidst the winter campaign against the ministry, and before the truth of the matter could be determined, the anti-inoculators publicly questioned the authenticity of Mather's F.R.S. In January the *Courant,* while alleging that a supposed account of successful inoculations from London had been invented by Boston inoculators, said the account was no more to be found in a certain London newspaper "than COTTON MATHER D.D. is to be found in the List of the *Royal Society.*" Douglass recommended in a pamphlet that Harvard might disown Mather, "as it seems the *Royal Society* have already done, by omitting his Name in their yearly Lists." Mather wrote to Dr. Woodward asking him to confirm his election, but for some reason received no reply; indeed it took him two full years to establish his membership. When Checkley's letter was read before the Society, in June 1721, an official explained that the membership lists excluded the names of Fellows who had not been inducted in person. Dr. Waller explained to Mather that the lists were not official rosters; rather, they were used in voting at yearly elections, and consequently they omitted the names of Fellows who could not attend the elections. To silence charges of impersonation against Mather, the Society decided to investigate the case thoroughly. But their goodwill only disclosed a real discrepancy. Somehow the minutes of the Society's meetings failed to show that any vote had ever been taken on Mather's candidacy.

Mather wrote to the Society in May 1723, saying he relied on its justice to clear him, but would instantly comply should the Fellows intend him to "lay aside my pretensions to be at all related unto that illustrious body." At the time he wrote he seems to have been unaware that, the previous month, Dr. Woodward had explained to the Society that Mather had been nominated for membership a decade ago; the nomination was to have been voted upon, but somehow the ballot was never taken. After Woodward laid out the situation, the Society voted and elected Mather a Fellow. There is no question, however, but that Mather's correspondents in the Society believed, and had led him to believe, that he had been elected a Fellow in 1713.

This onslaught of diatribe and insinuation against Mather angered his sons. Creasy, despite his own running battle with his father, exposed himself to danger, Mather recorded, "by a violent and passionate Resentment of an Indignity, which a wicked Fellow offered unto me," although no details of this incident survive. Sammy, having prospered from inoculation himself, defended his father truculently in the *Gazette*. There he charged James Franklin and his *Courant* with trying "to Vilify and Abuse the best Men we have," and threatened that "there is a Number of us who resolve, that if this wickedness be not stop'd, we will pluck up our Courage, and see what we can do in our way to stop it." Sammy's article appeared anonymously but was quickly identified as his, bringing down on him a half-dozen separate blasts. He was dubbed an "Ill-bred School-Boy," a "young scribbling Collegian," a "*Chip of the old Block* (by Direction)." One Couranteer quoted a line from his father's *Magnalia*— "Bloody fishing at *Oyster* River; and Sad work at *Groton*"—and observed that Sammy's readers would feel "*There is bloody Fishing* for Nonsense *at* Cambridge, *and sad Work at the* College." Another condemned Sammy's "poysonous and more than Humane Malice" as a lasting reproach to Harvard, but concluded: "It seems the *venomous Itch of Scribbling* is Hereditary; a Disease transmitted from the *Father to the Son*."

Although well practiced in receiving comeuppance, Mather had never before been so publicly, relentlessly, and ferociously clawed. Considering his many other nerve-fraying trials at the time and his quick temper, he acted with remarkable and uncustomary restraint. Privately he railed in his diary against the "prodigious Nonsense, and Folly, and Baseness ever now and then expressed by the People," and probably supplied some material for pamphlets and articles by his defenders. Once he also stopped James Franklin, the publisher of the *Courant,* in the street and with an "Air of great Displeasure," according to Franklin, warned him that "*many Curses*" awaited those who made it their business to traduce ministers: "*The Lord will smite thro' the Loins of them that rise up against the Levites. I would have you consider of it, I have no more to say to you.*" Otherwise Mather this time obeyed his own injunctions to beware of speaking intemperately and of spreading false reports. But the silence he imposed on himself in the insulting hullaballoo left him depressed: "By a dark and a faint Cloud striking over my Mind," he wrote on December 31, "I begin to feel some Hazards, lest my Troubles, whereof I have a greater Share than any Minister in the Country, grow too hard for me, and unfit me and unhinge me for my Services."

In this defeated mood, Mather addressed a meeting of ministers on January 16 and implied that he was considering moving his ministry from Boston. By daily pursuing his desire to Do Good, he said, he had "entirely ruined myself as to this World, and rendered it really too hot a Place for me to continue in." He and his conduct had become subjects of the "most false Representations imaginable," which he might easily have confuted but chose to bear in silence. As a result, except among a few of his "little Remnant of a Flock," his serviceableness had become crippled. "I must employ my Faculties," he told the ministers, "in projections to do good in more distant Places"; he had "there"—without saying where—"a Prospect of some Things, whereof I shall know more hereafter." Promising to cooperate with other ministers in their own designs, he announced the cessation of his: "*I have done! I have done! I have done* treating you with any more of my Proposals."

Mather's announcement of his withdrawal from public affairs, and perhaps from Boston itself, failed to convince the anti-inoculators. Even after his address, they repeatedly lambasted him for reviling the town in daily speech ("Who is it that in common Conversation makes no Bones of calling the Town a MOB?") and for claiming that the *Courant* was run by a Hell-Fire Club, referring to the notorious London clubs whose members blasphemously styled themselves God the Son or St. John the Baptist, and under such names toasted the devil. Douglass accused Mather of being the author of a scurrilous pamphlet, published around February, entitled *A Friendly Debate; or, A Dialogue Between Academicus; And Sawny &*

Mundungus, Two Eminent Physicians (1722). It does seem probable that Mather collaborated in writing this rather nasty skit, in which the pro-inoculation character Academicus defends Mather as a "Celebrated Preacher" well-read in medicine, the sense and style of whose writing "charm all Competent Judges." In addition to praising Mather, the skit ridicules Douglass as a malicious liar and the tobacconist Williams as an illiterate, turning upon them the same caricatures that had earlier been applied to Mather. Here it is Douglass who pompously swaggers, de-nouncing the other Boston physicians as *"Illiterate Numskulls . . . while, I traffic to the Metropolis of Literature, and receive ample Communica-tions from the very learned* A.S.F.R.S. & M.D." Academicus even darkly hints that Douglass and his supporters conspired in the attempted assassi-nation of Mather. Williams appears as the moronic Mundungus (a slap at the allegedly cheap quality of his tobacco), who believes that the best place to write a treatise on inoculation is a tobacco cellar; or, in his wretched spelling, that the best place to *"rigte tretes on Inokelacion is a Thobacko ciller."* The pamphlet offers as an appendix a dictionary of the *"Mundungian Language,"* and proposes designating Williams Professor of Mundungian at Harvard.

By the time this skit saw print, the epidemic was dramatically waning, nearly revealing its toll. The selectmen ascertained in February that some 5889 persons had been infected, of whom 844 had died. By early spring the surrounding controversy had degenerated into almost entirely *ad ho-minem* screeching. In its issue of March 19–26, 1722, the *Courant* com-pared Mather to a *"peevish Mongrel"* and to *"Dunghill Cocks"* and called him, among other things, a *"Baboon."* Whatever the nadir of catcalling, the most resonant and auspicious epithet appeared in the April 2 *Cou-rant*, which published the first of a series of satirical essays by James Franklin's sixteen-year-old brother, Benjamin. At an even younger age he had published and written two ballads (no copies of which survive), but these essays mark his literary debut and offer in the bud the adult Frank-lin's inimitably sly boldness. He created for his pseudonymous narrator a homely widow at whose house lodges the minister of the town, by whose assistance she promises to beautify her writings with "a Sentence or two in the learned Languages, which will not only be fashionable, and pleas-ing to those who do not understand it, but will likewise be very ornamen-tal." By nature the widow is a person of "extensive Charity, and a great Forgiver of *private* Injuries." But she is likewise endowed with "a natural Inclination to observe and reprove the Faults of others, at which I have an excellent Faculty." She is called Silence Dogood.

In that devastatingly felicitous name, Franklin summed up what Mather had become in the minds of many Bostonians, a biddyish seriocomic martyr eternally vaunting his tiresome benevolence and meekness. Although Silence Dogood did not join the *Courant's* war on the inoculators, her satires of Harvard and of New England funeral elegies also sum up the effects on Puritan Boston of a half-century of religious bickering, political melees, economic crises, crown politics, and urban growth—the outspokenness of the rambunctious young, the new spirit of amusement, the diminished force of custom, the declining authority of the ministry.

*

The selectmen found isolated smallpox cases in the spring, including two in April; one of these, a collarmaker, was buried late at night to avoid the possibility of infecting people who had recently returned to Boston, having fled town to escape the epidemic. But by mid-May, about a year after its outbreak, the epidemic was all but over. Ads in the *Courant* called to gentlemen wishing to "Recreate themselves with a Game of *Billiards*." About a hundred regular singers in the New Brick Church performed three-part singing from the gallery, a decisive innovation, in effect a concert of sacred music by trained singers separated from the congregation.

Ironically for Mather, just as the epidemic ended it meshed with his ongoing troubles over the Howell estate. Out of funds himself, we have seen, he had tried to satisfy creditors by selling off part of Howell's property on the Long Wharf, although these sales had first to be approved by the court and by Lydia's daughter, Katharin, and her husband Samuel Sewall, people who "intend my Hurt." In January he had been able to give part of George's warehouse to a creditor to pay off more than £250 owing from the estate. In May he again petitioned the court to sell some property, but Sewall and his wife, along with their two children George and Nathan Howell (and Lydia and her troublesome niece), were now at the hospital or pest house on Spectacle Island, where the selectmen had removed them on May 15. (By a different account, they were driven there by a "mobbish Crew" in Boston.) The Sewalls and two other people had become subjects of Boylston's six final inoculations, on May 11 and 12. A visitor found them supplied with nurses and necessaries, the two children, aged eight and ten, playing about without complaint, but Katharin's menstrual schedule thrown off by the inoculation, and the incisions on her and her husband running badly. Under inoculation, Sewall addressed the court clerks from Spectacle Island, saying he had been informed that

Mather had petitioned to sell some of Howell's real estate; if the court found it true that the "Bad Debts" made the estate insufficient to satisfy creditors, he said he had no objection to disposing of the property.

These final inoculations apparently stirred rumors and apprehensions in country towns that "great Numbers" in Boston were again infected, and brought some final salvos against Mather and Boylston. Boylston was brought before a town meeting, where he solemnly promised to inoculate no one else without permission from town authorities. Recalling that Mather had continued his pneumatological experiments even after the witchcraft trials ended, the *Courant* scowled that although inoculation seemed to have exited in January it had returned, "like the Infatuation Thirty Years ago, after several had fallen Victims to the mistaken Notions of Dr. M_____r and other learned Clerks concerning Witchcraft."

Impaled by the *Courant* as a pontifical bogeyman of the superstitious past, Mather had in fact spoken on behalf of the future. Inoculation was the first major achievement in preventive medicine. Credit for introducing it can be given to no single person, but Mather and Boylston made the first large-scale test of the practice, a critical event in its eventual adoption in Europe and America, and in the history of immunology. Although Douglass continued to doubt the safety of the method, with the epidemic over he conceded confidentially to Cadwallader Colden in New York that smallpox "seems to be somewhat more favourably received by inoculation than received in the natural way." Here if nowhere else Mather had been, unambidextrously, on the right side.

To say that Mather's behavior seems in retrospect heroic leaves open the question of his motives at the time. Did he blunder ahead on skimpy evidence and knowledge, as the anti-inoculators charged, propelled by arrogance about his ministerial rank, vanity about his accomplishments, pride in his family name, and contempt for the mob? Was he driven, as Perry Miller believed, by neurosis? On the contrary, Mather's every comment about smallpox in his published and unpublished works bespeaks long and much pondering of the disease, intelligent trust in Boylston's gifts, strenuous self-control in a furnace of abuse, and transcending these a desire that his neighbors live, not die. True, he was not a trained physician. But none of the English colonies had licensing authority, medical schools, or general hospitals, and many ministers practiced medicine. Indeed a professional physician such as Douglass would likely have done less than Mather, whose zealous efforts during the epidemic required as much moral enthusiasm as medical understanding, and whose science and religion nourished each other.

Of course Mather could not escape being what he was, and his daily conversation and behavior during the crisis may often have carried provocatively Matherean fire and water. By the same token, part of Mather remained genuinely nurturing and generous. Toward those who risked inoculation he felt a paternal intimacy: "being all of them indeed my *Patients*," he wrote, "I would consider them as my *Relatives*." As the disease reached unstoppably into several parts of Europe at the end of the year, he also considered sending an account of the Boston experiments to Holland: "Who can tell, but Hundreds of Thousands of Lives, may be saved by this Communication." Moreover, he consistently gave the real credit for inoculation to Boylston: "*this* is the gentleman," he wrote later. "When the rest of our doctors did rather the part of butchers or tools for the destroyer to our perishing people, and with envious and horrid insinuations infuriated the world against him, this worthy man had the courage and conscience to enter upon the practise." Boylston, Mather said generously, and "he alone, with the blessing of Heaven, saved the lives of I think several hundreds; yea, at one time he saved a whole town from a fearful desolation."

A year after the epidemic Mather sent the Royal Society a seventeen-page essay on smallpox. In its final blast at Mather, the *Courant* had gloated to think that he was sending further accounts to England, for the Royal Society, they observed, had for its secretary the eminent Dr. James Jurin, a "Man of solid Judgment" who took pride in detecting "whimsical groundless Conceits, credulous Relations, and false or trivial Reasonings." Again the *Courant* was wrong, for the Fellows devoted to Mather's essay, and his other communications, three consecutive meetings. Their interest was evidently intensified by the decimating continuance of smallpox in London, where by one count more than two thousand persons died of the disease in 1722, and more than three thousand in 1723. In his essay Mather refuted a host of religious and seemingly commonsense objections to inoculation. Written in retrospect, his arguments are better organized and more assured than in his earlier writings on the subject, based now on "*Constant Experience*"—a pounding refrain in the essay— and offered with conclusive firsthand experience of the success of inoculation "upon both *Male* and *Female*, both *Old* and *Young*, both *strong* and *weak; Whites* and *Blacks*; on *Tawnies*, on Women in *childbed* . . . on Women *with child*, at all Seasons." He also rehearsed for the Society his personal role in the epidemic, his initial appeal to the Boston physicians, the dubious satisfaction they and Douglass and Williams might derive from "seeing above a Thousand of their Neighbours within a few months killed before their eyes," the rage against himself of people who "actually *seek* the *Death* of the Friends, that only show them how to save their Lives."

But the gist of Mather's message to the Society was in his impassioned beseeching tone, a plea for the adoption of the method in England and elsewhere. In his final paragraphs he hypothetically interrogated those who vehemently opposed inoculation. Had they "no dread at all," he would ask them, "of being accessory to the *Innumerable Deaths,* which may be, in part, owing to their boisterous Opposition." Was it not bold presumption in them, he would ask, to make that a sin which God the Judge of all commanded as a duty? Was it not criminal ingratitude to the God of health to treat with neglect and contempt a method of sparing lives from so great a death, and to multiply abuses on those who thankfully and obediently embraced His blessing? He answered his questions himself, hardly sounding like a Silence Dogood:

> *We,* that cry with a loud voice to them, *Do yourselves no Harm,* and show them, How to keep themselves from *the paths of the Destroyer,* are conscious of nothing, but of a *pity for Mankind* under the *Rebukes of God;* A concern to see the *madness of the people;* A desire to have our neighbours *do well;* and a solicitude for a *Better State of the World.* And all the Obloquies, and Outrage we suffer, for our Charity, We shall entertain as *Persecutions* for A *Good Cause,* which will not want its Recompences.

13

Crackling of Thorns Under a Pot

THE TWO YEARS that followed the smallpox epidemic were the most harrowing of Mather's life. The departures from him, each more comfortless than the one before, began in the fall of 1722. On September 25, fasts were held at the Old North and the other New England churches, to evoke an effusion of God's spirit on the rising generation. Such fasts were of course frequent, but for Mather the occasion and aftermath of this one were specially ominous. Indeed giving both the morning and the afternoon sermons, he preached all day, on the text Matt. 9:18, My Daughter is even now dead. For once this was not literally his daughter nor literally a death, although it brought little less distress.

Together with its ominous occasion, soon to be explained, the fast marked the last appearance in his pulpit of Increase Mather. Now eighty-five years old and ailing, he had been treated gently or ignored by the anti-inoculators even though he too had sponsored the new method. In the wake of the epidemic he felt so debilitated by age that he had no hopes of preaching another sermon. His gouty right hand had become "*Paralitical*" and shook so that he was unable to pen a long discourse. On September 4 he wrote an attestation for his son's *Coelestinus* (1723) in which he announced that he was every hour looking and longing for heaven. Such announcements were also frequent, of course, but as he performed during the fast-day ceremonies three weeks later, one congregant observed that he prayed "so low that I could hardly hear a word; was spent." Two days after the fast he fainted, suffering what his son believed was apoplexy. He revived in a few minutes, but "it so enfeebled him," Cotton wrote, "that he never went abroad any more."

Other losses beset Mather as Increase lay dying. Unexpectedly he lost a different father on December 27, when Governor Shute boarded the *Seahorse*—the ship that had brought in smallpox—and suddenly left for England, having notified no one of his departure. Shute had become "tired and soured," Mather wrote, by opposition from a "little and wretched" but politically powerful clique, old-line frustrated supporters of the private bank who misled the House into producing votes "which any Governor must count intolerable." These votes included one to cut his annual salary by £200, but he had wrangled constantly with the House, increasingly so around 1722. Mather had counted on his cordial relation with Shute to restore his political effectiveness. Considering the accusations Shute might make against New England, perhaps again endangering the charter, he not only regretted Shute's departure but also expected "miserable changes, and very heavy chains, to be hastened upon us."

Mather quickly gained the displeasure of the interim government, under acting governor William Dummer (the brother of Jeremiah Dummer). In February 1722, near the end of the epidemic, he had preached on the text They shall go out of one Fire, and another Fire shall devour them (Ezek. 15:7). Upon Shute's departure, Mather claimed that this reference to "another Fire" ten months earlier had been a prophecy of the near dissolution of the government and of new threats against the charter by Shute's complaints in London. The *Courant* made sport of his claim and spoofed his breastbeating ("behold a more *Cruciating* fire is devouring us! Ah sinful people of *New England*"). In reply to the paper's continuing attack on the ministry, Mather began publishing in the *Boston News-Letter* a nine-part series of articles on "The State of Religion," a lengthy miscellany of pieces with extracts from his own *Advice, To the Churches of the Faithful* (1702). Either thoughtlessly or deliberately, he included extracts from this earlier work that criticized the "iniquities" of two English monarchs and that upbraided the Church of England for harboring "a Set of men, who call themselves *Protestants,* and yet Assert and Attempt an Ecclesiastical Coalescence with a *Foreign Jurisdiction.*" Outdated aspersions on former English rulers and on the English church were unlikely at this sensitive time to please authorities in London to whom Shute was addressing complaints about New England's loyalty. For his carelessness or misjudgment, Mather found the new government viewing him as "a publisher of dangerous libels," forbidding him to continue his series, and directing him to "look upon it as a piece of proper modesty, to be as little as possible in their presence."

Losing money also, Mather remained never-endingly dunned for large sums he could not pay, and in this, as in little else, now being copied by Creasy. One suit came from the Cambridge minister Nathaniel Appleton, for £264; another from Joseph Baxter of Medfield, for £318. In both cases Mather and Lydia defaulted by not appearing in court, and were ordered to pay the debts. But he seems to have successfully appealed the judgments because of irregularities in the writs, and he retaliated by later suing Baxter for £161 owing to the Howell-George estate, the sheriff attaching Baxter's house and land to the value of £200. Creasy, at last walking and talking just like his father, was bound over in March 1723 for £3 he owed to a Boston tailor named Foxley Sanderson, ordered to "not depart without license" but to answer the charge in court. As his father often did, he failed to appear, and the court ordered payment plus damages. In June Creasy was sued twice, once for £8 owing to a Boston widow and again for the same amount on a promissory note nearly two years old to Increase Gatchel, a dancing master and vendor of "Choice good Italian Fiddle-Strings." Creasy's debt to Gatchel provides at least a peep at what dismayed Mather about the boy's company. When some young men were denied admission to Gatchel's Hanover Street dancing school, they shattered all of his windows and threatened to kill him.

In these circumstances Mather awaited the loss of his father. Increase lingered helplessly, sometime judged unable to live out the week. To return now to the occasion of the September fast, Mather and many others attributed Increase's moribund state to his grief over the figurative death of the figurative daughter. The "daughter" was a minister named Timothy Cutler, who two weeks before the fast had closed his public prayers with the words "*and let all the people say, amen.*" Had Cutler been an Anglican preaching at King's Chapel his choice of words would have gone unnoticed. But he had been born in Charlestown and educated at Harvard, and was rector of Yale College; and he had publicly closed the Yale commencement by thus reciting the words of the Episcopal form of prayer. This was the death. It was as if the president of the United States at the Tomb of the Unknown Soldier on the Fourth of July had sung the *Internationale.*

Mather was aghast at the "treacherous Rector," not only as a founder of Yale but also as a minister. For the day after the infamous commencement Cutler had declared, as Samuel Sewall put it tersely, that "there was no Minister in New England." Cutler, one Yale tutor, and five neighboring Congregational ministers met with the college trustees in the Yale library. Each speaking for himself said he had come to consider his Congregational ordination invalid, and to believe that only ordination according to the Church of England practice might entitle him to administer the ordinances. Three of the defectors were ultimately dissuaded, but the trustees excused Cutler from the rectorship and he left for England to be reordained as an Anglican. One exultant Anglican contemporary, comparing Cutler's rebellion to the overthrow of Governor Andros in 1689, called it the "glorious revolution of the ecclesiastics of this country." To the Mathers it represented not merely the climax of long-mounting anti-ministerial sentiment, but also a direct threat. Cutler's passage abroad was paid by a group of Bostonians who wished him to serve as minister to a new Anglican church which they hoped to erect in Boston, a companion to the chapel that had been built under Andros. As King's Chapel stood in the South End, they proposed placing the new Anglican church in the North End—a perhaps five-minute walk from the Mathers' church.

The tumult brought Mather an offer of the rectorship of Yale. The invitation must have been tempting for, a contemporary noted, the "Contumelies and unworthy treatment he has met with in Boston would facilitate his parting with it." But probably his father's grave illness, his continuing litigation, his liking for Boston as the metropolis of America, and the reluctance of his church to release him decided him against it. While Boston newspapers reported Cutler's spectacular departure, however, he received letters from several Connecticut ministers lamenting that Yale, though newly founded, should "groan out Ichabod." The ministers confided their fear that Cutler's declaration might encourage Anglican proselytizing in Connecticut and that many students "leavened" by him might assume his principles. They sought Mather's advice on checking these threats and on handling the issue of apostolic succession. In denying the validity of their ordination, the defectors had alleged, and probably would allege again, that in the past some ministers in Connecticut had been invalidly ordained by laymen; these ministers had acted in later ordinations, presumably rendering them invalid also. The grim situation, they told Mather, demanded a stand: "we must put on our armour and fight, or else let the good old cause, for which our fathers came into this land, sink and be deserted."

Mather and the other Boston ministers had no intention of watching "the good old cause" sink. To the defenses of Boston Congregationalism which now, one Anglican said, "glutted" every town in Connecticut, Mather contributed three anonymous works. When promoting his Maxims of Universal Piety he had not envisioned an apostate like Cutler, much less his apostasy coinciding with the death of Increase Mather, and what that meant to the survival of the world of the Fathers. In his rejoinders

Mather dropped the gladsome ecumenical language of the Universal Religion, already toned-down to exclude Arians, and took up the old bludgeoning idiom of the covenanted people. Cutler and the others, he said, were "Degenerate Offspring" of their infinitely better fathers, treacherous "Sons of *New England*" who would "assist the *Common Enemy*," papistical "*Cudweeds*" who cast indignity on the "Leaders of the Flock that followed our Saviour Into this Wilderness." Especially had they betrayed their fathers, and were collaborating with Rome, in fussing over lay ordination, "that vile, senseless, wretched whimsey of an uninterrupted succession." No longer calling on Congregationalists to join godly Episcopalians at communion, he now emphasized that the New England churches had been "Planted on the very Design of withdrawing from the *Episcopal Impositions*." While he recommended patiently affording the defectors time to rethink their views, he said he saw no reason why, as they had disowned their ordination, their flocks might not disown them.

Increase reacted to these events, Mather wrote, with "too extreme a concern of his Mind." But atop his mental distress, which included delirium and bouts of forgetfulness, Increase also suffered exhausting bodily infirmities. A torturous hiccup sometime seized him for a week or two without stop, then intermitted, but returned with such violence as to corrode his diaphragm. He was also wracked by stones, which had first afflicted him at the time of his conversion, when he was fifteen. Cotton had probably witnessed the sore effects as a child, when a violent fit of stone struck his grandfather Richard Mather at Increase's house in 1699, the prelude to his death a week later. Cotton worried that he might die of the ailment himself. Increase's pain from the stone was excruciating beyond the power of fortitude to manage. Once Samuel Sewall stopped at Increase's house and heard him cry out, "Pity me! Pity me!"

Helpless to pluck out the unremitting scalding in Increase's body, Cotton tried to comfort his father spiritually. Increase was troubled by the state of his soul, and "in the Minutes of the Darkness wherein he lay thus *feeble and sore broken*," Cotton wrote, "he sometimes let fall expressions of some *Fear* lest he might after all be Deceived in his *Hope* of the *Future Blessedness*." Yet he resisted his own doubts, often calling to Christ, promising to mention His righteousness and His alone. On February 19 he told Cotton, joyfully, "*I now see, that I was deceived, when I fear'd Lest I might be deceived*." Scarce allowing Cotton to leave his room without some prayer, he also had his grandsons transcribe the account he had made in adolescence, seventy years earlier, of his conversion, and he read the relation consolingly. Whether these grandsons included Creasy is unknown, but Samuel Sewall thought it must have been "pleasant" to Increase to live to have Sammy, in the summer of 1723, graduated from Harvard.

Appropriately, Increase's final three days on earth began with a premonition. Coming out of a "Dark Minute," as Cotton recounted it, he said: "*It is now Revealed from Heaven to me, That I shall quickly, quickly, quickly be fetch'd away to Heaven, and that I shall Die in the Arms of my Son.*" After this he kept calling for Cotton, who did what he could to strengthen him. Near noon on Friday, August 23, with Increase visibly near death, Cotton said to him: "*Sir, The Messenger is now come to tell you;* This Day thou shalt be in Paradise. *Do you Believe it, Sir, and Rejoice in the Views and Hopes of it?*" Increase said "*I do! I do! I do!*" and died in his arms. The Westfield poet-minister Edward Taylor wrote that "Cutler's Cutlary gave th'killing Stob." But the autopsy performed on Increase's body revealed a polyp on his bladder and six large gravelly stones, some over an inch around. Only one of them, an observer said, "would have been Enough to have tortured a Giant to Death."

Mather had always seen his father as a celebrity, and felt proud of the honors accorded Increase at his funeral, "a Greater *Funeral*," he wrote, "than had ever been seen for any *Divine,* in *these* (and some Travellers at it, said, *in any other*) parts of the World." Increase had earned the homage, too: through his charter agency he had irrevocably transformed the life of New England, whose purity he had labored to maintain from his conspicuous pulpit for sixty years. The pallbearers thus included acting governor Dummer, John Leverett as president of Harvard, his old friend Samuel Sewall, and Benjamin Colman, aided by twelve "under bearers" from the North Church. Before the pall walked 160 students from Harvard; behind came a "vast number of Followers," in Sewall's description, including fifty ministers—a good part of the entire ministry of New England. As an also vast number of spectators looked on from the streets of Boston, the procession bore the coffin around the North Church, past Increase's house, up Hull Street, to Copp's Hill, the cemetery of the North Church. There Increase was buried in the Mather family tomb near his first wife, Maria Cotton.

Increase had drawn up a will four years earlier. His soul, he wrote, had been given to God in Christ more than sixty years ago; his goods, except his library, amounted to little. "It has been thought that I have bags by me," he explained, "which is a great mistake. I have not twenty pounds in silver, or in Bills." He specified that his black servant Spaniard should not be sold, but given his liberty and "esteemed a Free Negro." His widow

apparently received nothing, their prenuptial contract providing that neither should figure in the other's estate. To his son Samuel, preaching in
England, he left only a fourth of his library, noting that Samuel had honored his father's name but that more had been spent on Samuel's education than on the other children's, and that Samuel had gained a large
estate through marriage. Another fourth of his library he gave to his "Fatherless grandson" Mather Byles, the son of his daughter Elizabeth, requesting that Cotton see to the young orphan's education; that the boy
would not add to his son's financial burdens, he left him all his clothing
except a chamblet cloak. To his grandson Sammy he left his three folio
volumes of Piscator's *Commentary;* to Creasy, his other grandson and
namesake, he left nothing.

What little money and few goods remained Increase gave to Cotton.
This included his pendulum watch, pendulum clock, silver tankard, and
chamblet cloak, as well as all his manuscripts and half his library, desiring that the latter not be sold. Had he any great estate, he added, he
would have given the greater part to Cotton. For Cotton was, he said, "a
great comfort to me from his childhood having been a very dutiful son
and a singular blessing both to his Father's Family and flock."

Considering that Increase had at last fulfilled his lifelong threat of
abandonment, that he had reinforced through long and daily contact his
unusually potent role as his son's model, critic, confidant, and rival, and
that the two men had been for more than forty sometimes momentous
years close colleagues, links in a dynasty, Mather's feelings about his
father's death must have surged at him from every side, a swirl of competing pains. Most unfortunately, however, Mather's diaries for the period
are missing, his extant letters scarcely mention the event, and what remains of his reaction is anticlimactic and uninformative. The lost documents may conceivably have recorded his sorrow. Or Mather may have
been steeled against his father's death by repetition, Increase having in
effect been dying all his life. He may also have been distracted by his
many other problems and keeping his vow of silence. Or his feelings may
have been too deeply delicate to submit for public scrutiny, or raced so
fast as to outrun expression. For whatever reasons, his surviving remarks
about his father's death are surprisingly indirect and dispassionate.

Two days after Increase's death, as pulpits throughout New England
filled with mourning sermons, Mather again entered the North Church.
There, thirty-eight years earlier, he had heard his father preach his ordination sermon and had felt Increase's hand laid upon him, symbolically
passing on the ministerial succession. What he delivered, however, was a

formal sermon on the character of a Good Man, one who prays much, contrives good, and spreads truth—a routine sermon he might have preached on the death of any other minister. He did offer an adulatory sketch of Increase's life, and toward the end he did comment that "this House is this Day become a *Bochim;* and we are a Congregation of *Weepers.*" But he made no attempt to stand forth as an example of resignation. And he well knew that his rather tidy and low-keyed sermon could not be taken for a tribute to his father. "in this very great Auditory," he acknowledged, "there will not be One that will approve of my Performance. They will all to a Man complain, *That I have spoke too Little.*" He promised to make amends by writing his father's biography, but the intention hardly seems to justify or account for the sermon's unexpected impersonality. The 239-page biography he published the next year does give a colorfully full and historically valuable account of Increase's life (on which this biography has often drawn), and makes clear Mather's near worshipful sense of his father's greatness, and his indignation over (and identification with) his father's ill treatment by others. Yet despite its title, *Parentator* is not a life of his father but, as he refers to Increase, of "Mr. *Mather,*" a famous but misappreciated New England minister. The biography says virtually nothing of their personal bond.

Mather may have disclosed some of his feelings, indirectly, in the wholly detached sermon he preached three weeks after Increase's death, on the suggestive text God, our Father (Phil. 4:20, the same text on which Increase had preached after the death of his own father, Richard Mather). Addressing himself to all those who have lost fathers, he explored the doctrine of Adoption, by which God makes all believers His children. The intended audience and the subject themselves intimate a renewal of childlike feelings of helplessness in Mather, and need for a substitute father. He did not mention Increase, but something of the inner strain of denial perhaps shows in his opening remark that the doctrine defies expression by the "stammering Tongue of a sinful and shallow mortal." Read in this way, many of Mather's seemingly impersonal comments convey resisted feelings of vulnerability and diminishment following Increase's death, and residual resentment over his failings as a parent. As if he felt somehow safer when Increase was alive, he instructed those who found themselves fatherless to think, "I have a Father, that will provide for me, protect me, advise me, uphold me, take my part against my Enemies." His sense of capability always needing to be authenticated by the approval of Increase (and others), he also wrote as if his father's death had left hollow the meaning of his being a minister, a doctor of divinity, a

Fellow of the Royal Society: "perhaps the biggest and bravest of them appears but an Empty Title; well, But This thy Title: A Child of God! O Glorious Title! Nothing, Nothing in this World can equal it." If Mather felt littler in his father's absence, however, part of him also remembered that Increase could be present but unavailable and nearly unpleasable. In consoling other orphans for the loss of their earthly fathers, he reminded them that the Everlasting Father still lives, "A Father who give[s] me infinitely better than ever any earthly Father did. . . . A Father infinitely fuller of pity."

What few other clues to Mather's state of mind can be dug from his other works of the period point to longings for substitute, supernatural guardianship and for contact beyond the grave. In the angelological tract *Coelestinus* (1723), written during Increase's last illness, he observed that "one such significant *Friend*, as a *Good Angel* concerned for us, will signify more than . . . if all the *Friends* in the World refuse to be any further concerned for us." He seems also to have hoped for, but greatly feared, converse with Increase's ghost. Several people in his neighborhood, he said, had been visited by spirits of the dead and he may himself have been visited by the spirit of his brother Nathanael. He did not regard communications with the dead as unlawful, nor to be confused with necromancy, since the departed elect are the "Nobler Members of the *Family,* which we in a *Lower State* belong unto. And they may be thus convers'd withal." Thus in the published version of the sermon he preached immediately after Increase's death, he depicted Increase replying to a series of questions from "the *Courts of the Lord,*" that is, from heaven. Yet in some other works of this time he warned that visitations by spirits of the dead can be even more disturbing than angelic visitations. Seeing angels, he remarked in *The Lord-High-Admiral* (1723), puts people "in Frightful *Sweats;* Their *Hair* stands; their *Blood* runs cold; They are almost scared out of their *Wits.* . . . 'Tis rather more so, when the *Ghosts* of the *Dead* visit us, and show themselves unto us."

Whatever else Increase's death meant to Mather, his daily existence as he neared his sixtieth year, his way of life, would never again be the same. On December 18 his father's successor, and soon perhaps his own also, was installed at the North Church—Joshua Gee. Raised under the Mathers' ministry, Gee was respected as a learned man of powerful intellect, but also considered indolent; no Increase Mather, he never developed his potential. The carefully conducted installation was widely taken as reasserting the validity of Congregational ordination against Cutler and the other apostates. One spectator wrote that "if I had been wavering

about the validity of our ordination before, I should have been then fixed
and established by the solemnity and religious devotion visible in all
parties at the sacred action." Cotton Mather delivered the charge, Colman
and other ministers imposed hands.

On January 19, Mather entered blotchily into his assiduously kept and
usually neat church records the baptism of a man named James Cox. It
was the first baptism administered by Gee, "And indeed," Cotton wrote,
"the First, that has been administered, by any Hand, but that of *Mather*
(Father and Son,) in the old North Church, for more than half an hundred
years together."

*

Other vexations and crises left Mather little time to mourn. Within
about six weeks after Increase's death, the "miserable apostate" returned
from England, where he had been awarded the degree of S.T.D. by both
Oxford and Cambridge universities and had been ordained a priest. One
Bostonian reported that when news came that Cutler had been made
"Doc Devinity," three Boston Anglicans were "so zealous to tell doc
mather that they called him out of bed to acquaint him with it."

Shortly after arriving, Cutler preached at King's Chapel, railing against
Congregational ordination and, by one account, sparing not to "Belch it
out That we have no Ministers but two or Three." On December 29 he
presided over the first large meeting held in the new Church of England
chapel in the North End. This formidable new building, following on the
erection of Queen Anne's Chapel at Newbury in 1713 and St. Michael's at
Marblehead in 1714, made visible how substantially the Church of England had penetrated once purely Congregational territory. About seventy
feet long and built of brick, many of its features inspired by Wren's
churches in London, the chapel was originally thirty-five feet high, exclu-
sive of the wooden spire that was added later, from which were hung the
lanterns that set off Paul Revere's ride. It was not merely the outstanding
church building in the North End, but the first great Georgian church in
America.

Mather usually shrugged off the activities of Anglican ministers in
New England. When any arrived, he either made a show of welcoming
them under the Universal Maxims of Piety, scorned New Englanders who
flocked to them as "ignorant, vicious, contemptible people," or dismissed them as debauched rakes. His nonchalance could be justified by
such recent cases as that of James McSparran, a Scots Presbyterian who
had been invited to settle as pastor in Bristol, Rhode Island. Mather urged

against his settlement because of some alleged misconduct, and wrote abroad to inquire after his credentials. McSparran offered to go abroad himself to secure proof but, like Cutler, returned with Anglican ordination, and started a Church of England parish in Rhode Island. In 1721 a woman named Frances Davis testified under oath that McSparran had stayed at her parents' house and lured her to his bedroom. She said "he would have me sit on the Bed, but I said I would not, but he put his Hand round my Waste, and shoved me along, and set me down on the Bed, and then sat by Me, and pulled me down on the Bed." This "grievous wolf," as Mather called him, also tried to take off her petticoat and to feel her belly but succeeded only in clutching her leg as high as her knee. McSparran knew, the woman testified, that she resented his behavior, and told her "that if I came to Naraganset I should not come Home a Maid again." In light of such cases Mather disdained protesting the presence of Anglican ministers, reasoning that protest would induce the English Diocesan to send over abler ministers, while those already in America "have generally been such Ignorant wretches, and such debauched and finished villains, that, like the rattlesnakes in our country, they carry with them what warns and arms our people against being poisoned with them."

The mediocre success of the new chapel in the North End at first bore out Mather's strategy of allowing Church of England ministers to condemn themselves. Cutler himself estimated his listeners at about four hundred; Mather ordinarily preached to four times that number. Mather gloated over a report to him from a woman who had attended Cutler's church that "it was amazing to see, how few there, and what a sort of shabby people they were." Cutler also quarreled bitterly with his South End Anglican colleague, the lecturer at King's Chapel, the Rev. Henry Harris, who suspected that Cutler's conversion was insincere and chiefly inspired by "the prospect of a new Church in this Town." Cutler in turn blasted him as "in Lying and Villainy . . . a perfect over match for any dissenter."

But Mather soon discovered that Anglican infighting and the size of the Queen's Chapel congregation were no measures of Cutler's zeal. With something of the convert's combativeness, Cutler renounced his beginnings (Cambridge he described as a "Snotty Town of the Same Name" as English Cambridge) and saw himself as the vanguard of a thorough anglicizing of New England. Believing it would "never be well" until Harvard became "an Episcopal College," he prosecuted a claim to be admitted by right, as a "teaching elder" of Boston, to a place on the

Harvard Board of Overseers. The Overseers rejected the claim, which however created a sensation. He proseletyzed outside Boston too,—for instance, conducting Church of England services in Scituate.

Mather later felt some of the apostate's "killing Stob" himself when, in a real show of force, Cutler managed to prevent the calling of a Congregational church synod. In May 1725, Mather addressed a memorial to the General Court, in behalf of a convention of ministers. The ministers, he wrote, had observed a "great and Visible Decay of Piety" in New England, had recalled their ancestors' use of synods to "recover And Establish the Faith and order of the Gospel," and now wished to convene representatives of the several churches to consider the evils that had provoked the "Judgments of Heaven." No general synod had been held in New England for more than forty-five years, since before the loss of the charter, and behind Mather's airing of the musty covenantal idiom of the Fathers, Anglicans correctly sensed insecurity. The calling of the synod was partly meant as a display of undying tribal solidarity, to squelch enthusiasm for the further spread of the Church of England. The outspoken Anglican John Checkley, who had first questioned Mather's membership in the Royal Society, wrote that the synod was intended to halt the building of new Anglican churches, and might end in creating "something like the solemn League and Covenant, to prejudice the rising Generation against the Church."

The Council approved Mather's memorial, and sent it to the House for concurrence. But Cutler and Samuel Myles (rector of King's Chapel) addressed a vigorous counter memorial to the House and Council. Basically they charged that in calling for a synod, Mather's memorial undertook to speak for all New England, and thus treated the Church of England as if it did not exist. They also argued that because by royal authority the American colonies were annexed to the Diocese of London, it would be undutiful to the king and inconsistent with the rights of the Bishop of London to call the synod before knowing the king's pleasure. Both the Council and the House rejected this memorial as containing "indecent reflections" and "groundless insinuations." Unabashed, Cutler and Myles then complained directly to the Bishop of London, who brought the matter before the Lords Justices. Opinion in London was that, if called, the synod would reach decisions hostile to the English church, and would encourage English Dissenters to propose a synod as well, putting them in competition with the established church. The attorney general and solicitor general decided the issue on legal grounds, giving it as their opinion that synods cannot lawfully be called without royal license, and that the ministers' application through Mather to the provincial legislature was a contempt of the king. The synod never met.

Mather professed to consider Anglican fears of the proposed synod "Unaccountable!" But surely he found nothing obscure in this plain demonstration of the loosening Congregational grasp on New England's religious life, any more than in the addition soon after to Cutler's fine new church, so near his own, of a large green curtain trimmed with scarlet and white lace, and an altarpiece painted with cherubs and festoons.

While looking for Cutler to shame himself, Mather also eyed warily the complaints being made in London by the angered Governor Shute, which might risk the charter. Jeremiah Dummer wrote home that some Lords of the Regency, after hearing Shute's case against the House, declared that Massachusetts was again "dancing to the Old tune" of sedition, and under any government but Shute's mild one would be judged guilty of treason. Mather and Colman, probably to cool Shute off, tried to enlist the Boston ministers around November 1723 in composing an address to him, but it seems that the greater number of them proved unwilling.

In Boston Mather's support of Shute gained him "the utmost rage of the satanic party," he said, including "attempts made upon my very life," details of which are unknown. But at the same time he had lost favor with Shute himself. The governor's unannounced departure to make representations against Massachusetts in London had apparently left Mather uncertain whether to offer public prayers for his voyage; as the *Courant* pointed out, to pray for Shute's voyage amounted to praying for the destruction of Massachusetts. Mather thus learned that Shute had struck him from "the list of his Friends" because of a "mis-report" to him "of my being at a loss how to mention his voyage in our public prayers, immediately upon his very sudden withdraw from us." Shute probably was not pleased either by an earlier "misreport" that Mather had called his brother, Lord Barrington, an Arian (which Mather denied, saying, "I never spoke it, never wrote it, never thought it"). Obviously hoping he retained enough of Shute's esteem to persuade him not to hazard the charter, he wrote to the governor himself in early December, with somewhat timorous formality—the tone, compared with the bonhomie of his earlier letters to Shute, itself registering estrangement. He told the governor: "I cannot wish to Your Excellency the infelicity of ever being the instrument, or so much as the occasion, of bringing any hardships upon a people (be the faults of a small party among them what they will!) whose ancestors deserved and purchased all the liberties their charters have engaged unto them."

Mather's fidelity to Shute produced a new scandal, and friction between Mather and Jeremiah Dummer. The House, wanting to defend itself in London against Shute's complaints, appointed Elisha Cooke, Jr., a special agent to appear at court to explain its side of the quarrel. Cooke was of course Shute's personal and political enemy, the man he had negatived as Speaker. The choice also displeased Dummer, the regular Massachusetts agent, who disliked Cooke and his colleagues. Cooke's supporters in Boston, presumably, now undertook to discredit Dummer and Mather. Around March 1724, Mather discovered that his study had been "knavishly and c—kishly riffled," he said, and six pounds of money stolen ("enough to bear the expense of several tankards"). Also stolen was a letter to Mather from Dummer, criticizing Cooke, who was now his co-agent. Somehow the letter turned up in Cooke's hands. Copies of it were spread around Boston, with malicious comments, and with insinuations that Mather had himself released the letter and betrayed Dummer.

Mather denied this angrily. "I would much sooner have died," he said, "than have been guilty of so vile an Action, as to betray a Friend, and to his Enemies what he writes unto me." Dummer seems to have distrusted his denial, however thumping. He wrote him a rather Matherean letter, of unqualified exoneration followed by qualification. He was sure, Dummer said, that the letter came to Cooke "not with your privity"; but he added, "A little thing can't efface the remembrance of the many happy hours I have formerly pass'd in your Company. I say this in case you had inadvertantly given out my letter." As Mather put it, Dummer "rejected me as well as my Apologies" and looked on him as a "Sinner."

Mather may well have been innocent, for around the same time the study of his friend Samuel Penhallow was also rifled, and a letter to him from Mather was also shown around. Sometime later, too, Dummer had Cooke to dinner at his London apartment and asked him how he came by the letter, but Cooke refused to say. When Dummer added that he had since written only one other letter to Mather, Cooke replied with a sneer that he had that letter too at home. The espionage anyway proved unnecessary, for Cooke's agency failed. Shute successfully defended himself on points of law in official hearings, and the House was forced to accept an "explanatory charter" declaring the governor's power to negative the choice of Speaker. Having won his fight against the House, Shute, despite recurrent rumors to the contrary, never returned to New England.

As he had done when similarly under fire during Dudley's administration and the smallpox epidemic, Mather resolved once again to withdraw as far as he could from political affairs. He had become disillusioned with

Shute and Lord Barrington, his two former friends, "the Two Gentleman-Brothers (I wish I could say, on all accounts, Gentlemen,) whose odd usages of me, have made me to be . . . Ashamed of my Hope, concerning them." On April 4, shortly after the exposure of Dummer's letter, he turned down a dinner invitation from the acting governor, explaining that the government's having silenced his pen a year earlier, and his public notoriety, had forced him to retire "from the old Familiarities of the Table, as well as other Freedoms, which I once been used unto." He secluded himself not from imagined slights, he emphasized, but because of dejection born in real difficulty. His withdrawal "may be smiled at as Vapour; yet this Vapour will appear to be Reason unto one under the power of it; having at the same time a thousand other more heavy Loads upon him."

The load now included such nervewracking demands against the estate that he feared for his health and sanity. The harassments during his seven-year ordeal with the administration had been "beyond all expression miserable." But the current demands against him, for sums he really did not owe, seemed large enough to ruin him. And there seemed no possibility of avoiding the ruin. He felt bitterly deserted as well: "The Friends who might be capable of helping me, keep at a Distance from me, and appear to do little for me. The Relatives on whose Account, I have brought all this Distress upon myself, treat me like Monsters of Ingratitude." Even God seemed to have turned from him, stirring worrisome thoughts of atheism: "My continual Cries to God, all this while, seem to have no Answer, but a Growth of my Confusions . . . . . . And from the strange Dispensations that I meet withal, sometimes hideous Temptations to Infidelity are shot in upon me." The only prospect of a way out, he believed, lay in wiping himself out, "selling all my Goods to pay the Debts, and breaking up my Family." He called out to the Redeemer, "I sink, I sink; Oh! Reach out thy Hand, and save me!"

Worst of all, Mather's predicament had a revelatory effect. Like some precipitant giving body to invisible crystals in a solution, it gave shape to what had imperceptibly constituted his life, bringing before his view the hidden but all suffusing pattern of his existence. He was a man whose lot it was, he could now see, to have been denied his very self. He was a man whose unique fortune it was to be taken precisely for what he was not. To find himself near ruin for paying the debts of people who despised him was not incidental to his life but of its pervasive substance, a life that had been somehow turned inside out, where reality and appearance were perversely transposed. How much had he done for sailors, in sermons, in prayers, in books, in projections?

AND YET, there is not a Man in the world, so Reviled, so slandered, so cursed, among the *Sailors*.

How much had he done for the salvation and comfort of blacks?

AND YET, some, on purpose to affront me, call their *Negro's,* by the Name of *Cotton Mather,* that so they may with some Shadow of Truth, assert Crimes as committed by one of that Name, which the Hearers take to be *me.*

How much had he done for the profit and honor of the female sex, especially in publishing biographies of holy women?

AND YET, Where is the Man, whom the *female Sex* have spit more of their Venom at? I have cause to Question, whether there are twice Ten in the Town, but what have at some time or other spoken basely of me.

Had he not kept a catalogue of all his relatives, and each week devised some good for one or another of them?

AND YET, Where is the Man, who has been tormented with such monstrous *Relatives?* Job said, *I am a Brother to Dragons.*

Had he not written many books to advance piety and promote the Kingdom of God, more than three hundred and thirty of them?

AND YET, I have had more *Books* written against me; more Pamphlets to traduce me, and reproach me, and bely me, than any man that I know in the World.

For pages in his diary Mather extended this ranting catechism of bewildering misperceptions of his being, and bewilderingly mean rewards for his services. He had comforted his parents "AND YET" received the contrary of comfort from his children; had made "Applications without Number" for the country's interest "AND YET" been loaded with calumny and aversion; had labored for the reputation of Harvard "AND YET" it showed him more contempt than if he were "the greatest *Blockhead* that ever came from it"; had done more to vindicate the reputation of Scotland than perhaps any other Englishman "AND YET" no Englishman had been so defamed by Scots tongues and pens; had hardly ever, for fifty years, neglected to say something useful in company "AND YET" his company was as little sought as that of any minister he knew.

Near the end of his list of "Dark Dispensations" Mather returned in his diary to the most oppressive and urgent of them, the one that might ruin him:

XIII. *What has a gracious Lord given me to do,* in *Alms,* and in Disbursements on *pious Uses?* For whole Years together, *not one Day* has passed me, in which I have not been able to say, that I have done something that Way.

AND YET, tho' I am strangely provided for, yet I am a very *poor Man.* I have not a Foot of Land upon Earth. Except a *Library* and a little *Household Stuff,* I have nothing upon Earth. And this also I am now offering unto my Creditors, to satisfy for Debts, whereof I never did myself owe a Farthing. My very *Library,* the Darling of my little Enjoyments, is demanded from me. . . .

To perfect the mind-fuddling sting of these brutal paradoxes, Mather observed, even his constant preaching about affliction as God's chastisement for sin had been inverted and turned against him. People pointed at him as by far the most afflicted minister in all New England—and inferred he must consequently be the greatest sinner, "and are pretty Arbitrary in their Conjectures on my punished Miscarriages." In searching for consolation he told himself that Christ had taken possession of him, and that he had been granted a strong persuasion of a future state, to which would be postponed his receipt of "the whole Harvest of my mean Studies to glorify God."

About two weeks after Mather poured out this long entry came the moment he had dreaded all his life. The exact circumstances are unknown, but to him they seemed final. "I must either be lodg'd in the Prison," he wrote on April 2, "or forc'd into a private Withdraw." From the earliest days of his ministry he had taken notice of sorry examples of men, including his own uncle John Cotton, who through lust, avarice, or other personal weakness had disgraced their sacred vocation, and he had prayed often to be spared such a fate, the more fervently because of his honored family. But it seemed evident to him now that he had not been spared, or that others had dragged him down, and that his role as a minister was ended. Preparing to take the virtually unthinkable step, "a step which much more than all New England will ring of," he had decided to find by God's direction and by hard study the most important and affecting things to say in taking "my Farewel of the Flock withal."

The same evening, however, Mather received a "marvellous Appearance of GOD my SAVIOUR!" When feeling doomed he had often thought acrimoniously of the friends who might have eased his situation but had failed to come forward, "like Persons in a Maze and a doze." That evening, however, four leading members of his congregation, "men full of Prudence and Goodness," visited him. Awakened to the extremity of his

situation, they kindly rebuked his anxiety, and promised they would immediately undertake to extricate him, "and that without any further
Thought of mine."

*

But there was Lydia . . . and Creasy. On April 7, five days after Mather
was visited by concerned members of his flock, he wrote in his diary:
*Misera mea Conjux in Puroxysmos illos vere Satanicos, a quibus per
Annos quosdam fuerit plerumque Liberata (Vel ego Saltem Liberatus)
iam rursus delapsa*—My poor wife has now again lapsed into those truly
Satanic paroxysms from which for some years she had been for the most
part free (or at least I was free).

Exactly what set Lydia off is uncertain, but for months the household
atmosphere must have been explosively irritable. A proud woman, she
cannot have been pleased by Mather's financial condition, which apparently reduced him to accepting doles; in March he had thanked his landlord for "obliging presents for the support of my family." Nor can she
have enjoyed the notoriety. Feeling criminal, he seems to have declined
invitations to preach at other churches, and in turning down a dinner
invitation he explained that his "well-known circumstances of prosecution to *restore what I took* not away, rendered it a disgrace unto such a
table, as well as unto any pulpit, for me to make my appearance there."
The presence in the house of Lydia's niece cannot have made its mood
less touchy, for Mather thought her contemptible, "a monstrous Liar and
a very mischievous Person, and a sower of Discord, and a Monster of
Ingratitude." Lydia had already given signs of her discontent, venting an
"unreasonable and implacable Aversion" toward Hannah, the daughter
who had been severely burned during infancy, "My dear, dear *Nancy;* a
Child of so many Afflictions all her Days"; Mather weighed finding another
home for Nancy to board in. The immediate cause of Lydia's renewed
outbursts on April 7, however, may have been a fresh suit brought against
Mather. During the April court session, an executor of the estate of the
Boston merchant Joseph Buckley sued Mather and his former attorney
(and son-in-law) Daniel Willard for debts contracted in 1717, of £444. It
was probably the largest single suit Mather ever faced. He again did not
appear in court to answer and was ordered to pay £209 plus court costs.

Lydia's new paroxysms came with volcanic violence, and Mather
found them unbearable. Lydia began spewing, he wrote, *absurdissimis ac
sordidissimis mutitur Stomachationibus*—the most absurd and obscene
outbursts of splenetic anger, blowing her top. Believing that her "*Insan-*

iae" had been ordained by Christ to arouse his prayers and test his patience, he lay his troubles before God. Creasy was away again at sea, but Lydia's "horrid, froward, malicious Disposition" now also began raging over Sammy too. He prayed not only for patience but also for protection.

Virtually week by week, as happened five years earlier, Lydia's assaults alternated with wooings, but of an ardor, erotic in Mather's description of it, on the same order as her reviling. Thus two weeks after Lydia's initial paroxysms he wrote, in Latin, that not only was everything at home again calm and cheerful, but also that *fere Extatico erga me Amore, condita*—Lydia behaved with an almost frenzied show of love toward him. Only Mather's account of these episodes survives, leaving it unclear whether Lydia suffered from a clinically severe emotional disturbance or was only fed up with Mather's behavior. At his best he could act needlingly, at his worst impossibly. And his letters and diaries for the period groan with a dull self-disgust, self-deprecating remarks about his uselessness, dejected plaints that his ministry is finished. Whether he behaved at home in this black mood is unknown. But in his description of them, Lydia's ravings sometimes seem no more than extreme versions of conduct he had often received from, and often provoked in, others. Indeed his chronicle of Lydia's emotional rhythms seems loosely geared to times when a fresh lawsuit was pressed or an older one resolved.

Whatever the case, Mather found Lydia's metamorphoses unaccountable: *tam inexplicabilis est conjugis meae ad Extrema se Vertentis incertissima mutabilitas!*—how inexplicable is the unpredictable changeableness of my wife directing herself *ad extrema*. Two weeks after the house had become calm and peaceful he was again writing, *Familia mea per furentis uxoris insaniam rursus misere distracta ac turbata*—My household is again wretchedly torn asunder, and thrown into disorder through the madness of my raging wife. But, the following week, serenity again and ardor: *mea conjux in mei non tantum Amorem flagrantissimum, sed at Admirationem rapta!*—Lydia was enraptured not only with the most flagrant love for him but also with the most extreme admiration. On the downside of these swings Mather prayed for the safety of himself and his children; on the upswings he resolved to be patient, and tried to help Lydia by strewing their conversation with holy thoughts. Her ardor during her recoveries guiltily excited him. While trying to maintain her calm and to restore their marriage with soothing displays of love, he warned himself not to let his mollifying grow too intense, presumably sexual: "O! Let all possible Purity accompany it, and let me watch against all such inordinate Affection, as may grieve the holy Spirit of GOD!"

A historically fascinating, if not very revealing, glimpse of Mather's condition at this time is provided by Benjamin Franklin. Now twenty years old, the recent creator of Silence Dogood returned to Boston from his first trip to Philadelphia in late April or early May, visited Mather in his library, and later recounted their leavetaking in his *Autobiography*. Mather showed him a shortcut out of the house, through a narrow passage crossed by an overhead beam:

> We were all talking as I withdrew, he accompanying me behind, and I turning partly towards him, when he said hastily, *"Stoop, stoop!"* I did not understand him till I felt my head hit against the beam. He was a man that never missed any occasion of giving instruction, and upon this he said to me: *"You are young, and you have the world before you;* STOOP *as you go through it, and you will miss many hard thumps."*

Franklin remarked that he often thought of Mather's useful advice when he saw misfortune brought on people by their "carrying their heads too high." Mather had begun looking up himself, however. By early June, not long after Franklin's visit, he believed he saw some relief ahead: "I am not without very great Hopes, that the Designs of Satan to discompose my Family and prejudice my Ministry, are gloriously and eternally defeated."

But with July came new demands on the estate for more than four hundred pounds. "I feel the Iron . . . entering into my Soul," Mather wrote, wearing down. "I cry to my SAVIOUR, as *Peter* just ready to sink in the Waves." He managed to pay one debt, of over two hundred pounds, when members of his congregation again privately gathered money for him, which he accepted with desperate relief, "even fainting with a Sense of Gratitude." To show his profound thanks he published at his own expense a sermon on being temporally poor but spiritually rich in Christ, copies of which he gave his benefactors, writing in their names himself. He had often privately denounced many in his flock as foolish and worldly. But now he wrote an apologetic, self-pitying Preface to the work, bemoaning his unworthiness to serve people so *"fill'd with knowledge* and *full of Goodness"*; they had been to him, he professed, "what might have been more equally look'd for, if I *had been,* what I *should have been,"* and he promised to act again as their pattern. The promise soured four days after he wrote the Preface, however, when he was apparently presented with a new claim on the estate, also for more than two hundred pounds. He could meet the debt only if the creditor agreed to take his library, "which tho' so very dear to me above all temporal Possessions, I offer to Depredation." Once more, however, a few members of his congregation gave him the necessary money.

Inundated with new demands, Mather also found a change in Lydia's outbursts. They were becoming daily and more dangerous. On the last day of June, although he unfortunately provides no details, she fled from church and attempted violence on him and his household (*summas mihi meisque tentat Injurias*). In July she acted so tempestuously that he believed it necessary to banish her perfidious niece and to send ill-treated Nancy away. Otherwise wholly at a loss what to do, he turned to Christ with fearful eyes, he said, swollen with tears, praying that if the Redeemer did not snatch him from the water, *pereo, obruor, Actum est*—I perish, I am overwhelmed, it is finished. On July 31, Lydia's raging mood once more receded. Composed again, *meque summis cum Amoris Ardoribus amplexata*—she embraced her husband with the greatest heats of love.

The next five weeks heaped on Mather a new outrage, Lydia's departure . . . and then another departure, climactic and undoing. The outrage arose from the death in May of John Leverett, who had gone to bed well but in the morning, a Sabbath, was found dead. Leverett's death left open the presidency of the college, for which Mather was an obvious although now tarnished candidate. Mather had always detested Leverett, but with Sammy attending Harvard as a scholarship student had treated him cordially and requested his "wise, and kind, and paternal tuition." With Leverett gone, Mather referred to him as an *"Infamous Drone."* He did not conceal his opinion of Leverett's administration when undertaking an inquiry at the behest of the Overseers in August 1723. The date matters, for Sammy had graduated a month earlier, leaving Mather no longer dependent on "that unhappy Man, who sustained the Place of President." Leverett being no longer useful to him, he called stridently for an investigation of the state of the college on eleven counts, including whether it had not undergone a "notorious decay" of "solid learning"; whether Latin had not been discountenanced; whether the books most read by students were not "plays, novels, empty and vicious pieces of poetry"; whether the theological recitations were not cursory, the tutors uncaring, and the education in general designed to promote principles destructive of New England's religious, political, and social ideals. The Overseers investigated Leverett's administration but upheld it against Mather's indictments.

With Leverett's death Mather believed himself to be a desired successor. The stain of his many lawsuits and his now public quarrels with Lydia would seem a liability in the office, but he was told, he said, that his presidency was "most generally wished for." Benjamin Colman, himself a leading candidate for the presidency, doubted Mather's prospects. "Were the Doctors spirit of Government," he remarked, "esteemed equal to his

Literature we should go into no other name but his." But Mather's "spirit. of Government" had never been estimable, and he himself suspected that his chances were dim. Choosing to stay home from the July commencement—that "insipid, ill-contrived, anniversary Solemnity"—he restricted his hopes to praying that the presidency "not be foolishly thrown away."

But Mather learned that it had indeed, by his standards, been thrown away, and rather in his face. The presidency was offered to the Rev. Joseph Sewall, the thirty-six-year-old son of Judge Samuel Sewall. With still another Sewall uprisen to torment him, Mather wrote on August 12: "I am now informed, that yesterday the six Men, who call themselves the Corporation of the College met, and Contrary to the epidemical Expectation of the Country [i.e. that he would be selected], chose a modest young Man, of whose Piety (and little else) every one gives a laudable Character." As he often did when defeated, he turned affliction into advantage, and saw in this drubbing "unspeakable cause to admire the Compassion of Heaven." The dismissal of him was a saving joy. Actually he had dreaded "what the Generality of sober People expected and desired; the Care of the College, to be committed unto me." Actually he had always foreknown that the presidency would have earned him not prestige but sorrow: "I had a dismal Apprehension of the Distresses, which a call to *Cambridge* would bring upon me." Actually he was thankful that he had been redeemed by having been rebuffed: "the Slight and Spite of my six Friends, has produced for me an eternal Deliverance." But not even by the gratifying logic of Matherese could he hide his wrath from himself, and his tirade of self-content wound down into the recognition that he had spoken "with a little too much Alacrity." He called on God to "Help me to a wise Behaviour!"

This subsurface seething may have agitated Mather's mood the next night, August 13, and perhaps detonated Lydia's full fury. She became finally utterly disgusted and may have had some sort of breakdown, "a prodigious Return of her Pangs upon her," Mather called it, "that seemed little short of a proper Satanical Possession." His remarks on Joseph Sewall make it evident that he felt rancorous himself; yet by his understanding nothing more happened between them during the day than that he somehow, unaccountably, managed to displease her. "What was pretended as the Introduction to the present, was, that forsooth, for a Day to two, my Looks and Words were not so very kind as they had been. A mere Fancy and Whimsey!" That Mather had behaved distantly seems not unlikely, but Lydia now had no patience for being told that her feelings of rejection were imaginary: "the bare telling her so, threw her into . . .

Violences, wherein she charged me with Crimes, which obliged me to rebuke her lying Tongue, with Terms I have not been used unto." The battle seems to have raged all day, through "a thousand unrepeatable Invectives."

At midnight Mather got out of bed and retired to his study to pour out his soul to God. But Lydia would not let him escape. She arose also and, in a "horrid Rage," said she would never stay with him or live with him. In the dead of night, collecting her niece and maid, she left the house. As she had gone to lodge with a neighbor, Mather feared the scandal she might enflame by telling "numberless Lies, which a Tongue set on Fire of Hell, would make no Conscience of." He spent the rest of the night keeping a vigil with Sammy and Nancy in his library, praying and singing psalms until nearly morning, when he at last went to bed and found some rest.

Mather kept busy over the following days, yet amidst preaching on contentedness with one's condition or deciding how to handle a troublesome minister at Harwich, he brooded on the Harvard presidency and Lydia's departure. His rejection by the Corporation, as he began to assess it a bit more realistically than before, was a mixed dispensation. He would have found the work of the presidency fatiguing and troublesome ("I could never have lived a Year to an End!"). But he could no longer deny that the office might have brought him many opportunities to nourish the New England churches. Perhaps God had reserved him for other, different opportunities to do good. Mostly he worried about how his own abhorred vanity might be affected by the choice of Joseph Sewall, the "preferring of a Child before me, as my Superiour in Erudition, or in a Capacity and Vivacity to manage the Government of an Academy, or in Piety and Gravity." Although the Corporation had snubbed him for his inferior, he felt it would be "a Crime in me to be disturbed at the choice," and he prayed for help in tolerating the insult without becoming incensed and impetuous.

Mather found it even harder to comprehend Lydia's leaving him. It seemed incredible to him that the woman in whom he had invested his fullest capacity to love could value his bountiful affection not at all. Her departure stood forth as the crowning instance of his queerly inverted destiny, an "AND YET" unmatchable in its perverse betrayal. "She, whom I have perpetually studied in the most exquisite Ways, to serve, and please, and gratify, and have even undone myself to oblige her, not only does by her unaccountable Humours . . . wherein she expresses the greatest Hatred and Contempt for me, prove the most heavy Scourge to me, that ever I met withal, but also takes, various Methods, all she can to ruin my Esteem in the World, and the Success of my Ministry." The blame, he believed, was entirely hers, for he had given her no reason to mistreat him. Her behavior said as much, for her "lucid Intervals" were always "filled with Expressions of the most enamoured Fondness for me." Feeling spent and hopeless, he resolved to pray formally seven times a day (once more than usual), hoping God might grant him "comfortable Circumstances relating to the Death, which is approaching to me." Returned to celibacy after Lydia's flight, he also asked divine aid in conquering what he always knew had been excessive, and now also recognized as unworthy, desire for her: "my Consort's leaving of my Bed . . . affords me Occasions of particular Supplications, that the Holiness and Purity whereto I am so singularly called of GOD, may have its perfect Work, and that I may no longer so foolishly dote as I have done, upon a Person who treats me with such a matchless Ingratitude, and Malignity."

Two days after writing this, on the morning of August 20, as he was projecting new services for God, Mather received overwhelmingly crushing news: "my Son *Increase,* is lost, is dead is gone." He staggered under the dreadful news: "Ah! My Son *Increase!* My Son! My Son! My Head is Waters, and my Eyes are a Fountain of Tears! I am overwhelmed!"

At the time that he became the twelfth of Mather's children to die, Creasy was about twenty-five years old. Despite the young man's many failings, Mather had always cherished him, perhaps more than any of his other children. Certainly he took greater pride in Sammy, in whom, he had written, "a gracious GOD wonderfully makes up to me, what I miss of Comfort in his miserable Brother." As Creasy had not, Sammy had undergone conversion and had been admitted to the North Church; as Creasy had not, Sammy had graduated from Harvard; as Creasy particularly had not, Sammy was following his father, grandfather, and great-grandfathers into the ministry. Yet Creasy had also been his first son to survive infancy and at the time of his birth Mather had received heavenly advice that the child would be "a Servant of my Lord Jesus Christ throughout eternal Ages." When not irate with Creasy, he saw him as Sammy later described him, a boy "*well beloved* by all who knew him, for his *Superiour good Nature* and *Manners,* his *elegant Wit* and *ready Expressions.*" If Sammy perpetuated his father's learning and piety, in Creasy were much of his father's facetiousness, gentlemanly charm, and unenacted rebelliousness.

Creasy, Mather was informed, had been aboard a ship bound from Barbados to St. Peter's, Newfoundland. The ship had been out five months without arriving, and the passengers including Creasy were believed to have perished in the sea. Why Creasy undertook another voyage is unknown—on business, perhaps, or in some connection with the law-suits against him in the spring. Mather, as a preacher to a seafaring congregation, well knew that such voyages could be perilous, and regularly preached to his flock on death by water. "*Drowning,*" he wrote in one sermon, "is one of those *Accidents,* than which there is none more frequent; Thus is *the Lamp of Young men put out!* It is *at once* plung'd into the Water, and in less than three minutes perhaps it is *put out.*" How often in New England had been heard "concerning our Sons," he wrote, the words "*The Young Men are Dead.*" Mather's acquaintance with the dangers of the sea may explain why, for a month and a half before he received news of Creasy's fate, he had been having presentiments of some misfortune overtaking Creasy, which he recorded cryptically in his diary. On July 1 he had written: "Oh! what Advice from Heaven, is come to me this Day, about my poor Son *Increase!* Yea, how many Times have I been of late overwhelmed with Afflations, which tell me, that—" at which the entry breaks off. Four weeks later he recorded, again cryptically, "My Son *Increase!* my Son, my Son!"

But no afflations prepared or consoled Mather for the killing news that arrived on August 20. Added to the appalling threats of jail, the demeaning denial to him of the Harvard presidency, and Lydia's withering indifference to his love, it made a weight he felt he could withstand only with God's help: "O my God, I am oppressed; undertake for me." At the time of his drowning Creasy was unconverted, too, and Mather feared for his soul. Before leaving on his voyage, Creasy had written out and left on Mather's table an "Instrument of a Soul repenting and returning to GOD," lamenting his rejection of Christ and promising to choose only godly companions and to follow his business industriously. Mather prayed that this last-minute repentance might win Creasy his salvation: "If the Papers which he left in my Hands, were sincere and his Heart wrote with his pen, all is well! Would not my GOD have me to hope so?" Yet he had his doubts; Creasy's drowning itself suggested that God had refused him. Taking the manuscript autobiography he had begun for Creasy (but in pique rededicated to Sammy), he at some time wrote in after the account of Creasy's birth: "tho' this were a Son of Great *Hopes,* and One Son who Thousands and Thousands of *Prayers,* were Employ'd for him; Yet after all, a Sovereign GOD would not Accept of him. He was Buried in the *Atlantic* Ocean."

Three days after Mather learned about Creasy, and probably in response to the news, Lydia returned home. She returned, too, chastened and conciliatory: "my poor Wife, returning to a right Mind, came to me in my Study, entreating that there might be an eternal Oblivion of every thing that has been out of Joint, and an eternal Harmony in our future Conversation." Toward making this new start he and Lydia promised to pray oftener together than ever before, and joined in raising prayers to God, their arousing devotions being followed on Lydia's part, Mather added, by "Tokens of the greatest Inamoration." However wretched and confused she had made him by her paroxysms and her flight, he continued fixedly to love her. Through the late fall he increased his efforts to please her, especially resolving to see things her way, to improve "in Compassion to her with regard unto the Things which threaten her Comfort."

However fulsome Lydia's "Inamoration" it could not distract Mather from his bursting anguish. Nor entirely could his faith. He deeply wished to glorify God by silent acquiescence in His judgments. He even praised his Savior for enabling him to bear all the sacrifices He called him to, including the "continual Dropping which I suffer in my Family." Yet as if ambidextrously sounding out Governor Dudley or some other mortal tormentor who returned hurt for good, his praise was embittered: "I freely submit and consent unto it, that the Glorious Lord should continue the Sorrows of it upon me all the few remaining Days of my Pilgrimage, and never give me any release until I die."

Indeed what Mather's obedient resignation tried to submerge kept churning up. The Servant of Christ throughout eternal ages who had fathered a bastard and owed money to a dancing master was buried in the Atlantic Ocean. It kept returning to him: "that heavy, heavy, heavy, and amazing Heap of Distresses, which I have in the Death of my Son *Increase,* my Son, my Son!" He sought as always to make his dry cross yield fruits of righteousness. He lay plans to awaken the young to turn to God. He decided to do something toward catechizing the girls in his congregation. Yet almost daily he numbly reverted in his diary, with little further remark, to what had happened to him. "The Death of my Son *Increase,*" he wrote one day; then, on others, "Ah my Son! my Son! . . . . . . The Death of my poor son INCREASE . . . . . . the Death of my Son."

To screw his anguish tightly to the bottom, Mather remained under personal attack, even from those close to him. Constantly, indeed, each one of his troubles had driven more deeply into him the woe from another, each new difficulty with the Howell estate rendering Lydia's paroxysms the more painful, his grief over Creasy swelling his disappointment in being passed over for Joseph Sewall. Now, despite the "heavy Calami-

ties upon me," some denounced his ministry, taking "all possible Pains
. . . to fix a vile Character on me among the People of God," depicting
him as "a Person from whose Hands the Bread of Life is by no means to
be received." Yet under the shadow of whatever notoriety he noticed that
when he once more mounted his pulpit on August 30, to offer himself as
an example of forbearance under affliction, unusually many young people came to hear him, from several parts of Boston, including some who
had earlier swarmed from his ministry. Preaching on early piety, a favorite
theme, he told them that "upon Computation" more than half the children born die before the age of seventeen. That the young should cry for
the safety of their own souls and live as if they were about to die, were
lessons born in dumb departedness, "the *Loud Voice* from the Mouths of
Some, who have gone down to the *Place of Silence!—The Young Persons,*
who have been *in the Morning like the Flowers of the Field,* but have been
cut down before the Evening."

Within the week after he preached this sermon, Mather twice received
news that was astonishing. The first arrived on September 5. "We are
surprised with very probable Advice," Mather wrote, "that my poor Son
Increase is yet living." The ship on which Creasy had been voyaging had
lost all its masts, but after a "long, long, sad Passage" it had landed in
Newfoundland. After his dismal fears, tempting him to atheism, that God
had chosen not to requite his acts of good, the news was doubly joyous:
"O the astonishing Dispensations of Heaven! must it always be so, that I
must see a Sentence of Death upon good Things; and then will the GOD
of Patience and of Consolation, give me to see some Comfort in them!"
Spared, Creasy might yet be converted, although after his many disappointments Mather still felt cautious about reforming him. "If it be so,
Oh! may the Distresses of the poor Prodigal bring him home to GOD. Oh!
may I yet see strange Answers and Effects of the Prayers that have been
employ'd for him!"

There was need in fact for caution about "my Son that was dead and is
alive." The second astonishing news arrived two days later, when Mather
learned that the God of Patience and of Consolation had not chosen to
requite him. "'T was another Vessel," he wrote. The previous report had
been misleading. It had concerned a different ship: "the good News of
poor *Creasy's* being rescued and revived from Death, is all come to nothing." Creasy, it was now certain, was dead. "*Lord,*" Mather called once
more, "*Thou hast lifted me up, and cast me down.* Oh! Let there not be
thy *Indignation* and *Wrath,* in what is done unto me!"

*

Two months later, in November, the cruel plot of Creasy's fate was played out again for Mather with different actors. Joseph Sewall having declined the Harvard presidency, the office was again open, and the Corporation passed over Mather a second time. The rebuke touched on old resentment toward Benjamin Colman, a member of the Corporation, going back to the opening of the Brattle church, unhealed by twenty years of friendship, and likely compounded by Lydia's ties to Colman's ministry.

On November 6, Mather dispatched a vicious letter blaming Colman personally for having denied him the presidency. In surpassing Matherese, he first thanked Colman for considering him qualified on account of his "Biblia Americana"—"for I know you can't on any other account"—then offered his concurrence in Colman's defeat of his hopes: "I do with the greatest acquiescence and gratitude approve the declaration of your sentiments to all the country, that I am on other accounts utterly disqualified. Yea, for erudition too, as well as capacity and activity for management." What evidence remains of Colman's part in choosing the president makes Mather's high dudgeon seem irrational; at most Colman may have reported to others the view of the Corporation (of which he was only one member) that while they respected Mather's learning they doubted his ability to govern Harvard because of his temper. But Mather could see the situation only as another "AND YET," and he concluded with hearty thanks for being spurned: "I do with all possible sincerity thank you for the inexpressible ease you have given to, Sir. . . . "

On November 18 the Corporation chose for president Colman himself. "I rejoice, I rejoice, I feel a secret Joy in it," Mather wrote in his diary, "that I am thus conformed unto Him who was despised and rejected of Men." The Corporation of the "miserable College" having again treated him with their customary malignity, he felt he could easily "throw Confusion upon the Men, who would make me low in the Eyes of all the Country," but instead he looked to God for help in bearing his condition with "Prudence, and Patience, and Silence." In fact, Colman had been away from academic studies for thirty years and saw in the presidency a financial loss to himself. He declined the post, which went to the Rev. Benjamin Wadsworth, for whose encouragement the House voted £1000 of public funds toward building a handsome presidential residence.

For all the many strains in their long acquaintance, Mather genuinely liked Colman, and the following year praised in print Colman's *"pious, and acute, and cogent Pen."* His nasty letter was probably a by-product of his distraught state. For as December drew on there remained the "dreadful Sacrifice," the thing he returned to, "the grievous Calamity befalling me in the Death of my poor Son *Increase.*" As he seems to have done after his father's departure, he seems after Creasy's death also to have thought of his ghost returning. In a sermon on the death of a seventeen-year-old girl he remarked that we know little of the condition of departed souls, of what vehicles they use, "and how much of what they had in *this World;* they carry away out of the *Shipwreck* with them."

As the event receded what stood out for Mather was the demand to draw from it services to God, so that "the Child, who did so little Good, but much ill, in all the Days of his Life, may do some good at his Death." One result was *The Words of Understanding* (1724), a set of savagely mournful sermons that betray his unwillingness, despite all his calls for resignation, to subdue his will. Introducing the book as the work of Creasy's *"Afflicted* FATHER, *upon his Extinction in the* Atlantic *Ocean,"* he in one place used the sudden premature deaths of "lovely *Young People"* to emphasize the need for early piety, and imagined for himself and his readers Creasy's drowning:

> Perhaps, by perishing in the *Water,* on which they were *doing Business,* they have been extinguished!—And by being Lost, none can say how, or when, or where, *at Sea,* their *Light put out in obscure Darkness.* . . . TO see a *sparkling Youth* pass through a curious and polite Cultivation; Brilliant, with a ready Wit, a singular sweetness of Temper, and many Circumstances inviting us to look for *something* from him;—And,—*All at once extinguished.*

The entire work resounds with muffled rage at past tormentors, at Shute, at Harvard, at his father, at spouses who although not so criminal as adulterers yet "carry it so Basely, so Bitterly, so Frowardly, to their *Mates,* that they deserve to have the *Doves of the Valleys pluck out their Eyes."* Identifying himself and Creasy with Christ as doomed Sons, Mather also summed up what he had learned from life, that man is born for troubles without number or evasion:

> When we are wading thro' some grievous and some tedious Trouble, we are prone to flatter our selves, *Well, this is the last! If I were once got well out of this Trouble, all would be well.* 'Tis a great mistake. There will soon come *another Trouble* in the room of that which is gone. Men are *Fools,* if they think, their *mirth* can last any longer, than *Sparks,* or than the *Crackling of thorns under a Pot.* . . .

Late in December, Mather's cruciating fire crackled once more. Sammy had begun preaching, and now hoped to improve his training—by sailing the Atlantic to London. In part Mather wished to keep Sammy at home simply because he valued the young man's conversation and cultivation as his greatest relief. But it might also happen to Sammy. *"Lord,"* Mather wrote, *"what Sacrifices dost thou call me to! My Son, my only Son, Samuel,* whom I have at home with me." Sammy was passionately set upon the voyage, and Mather believed a refusal might lead him to "grievous Temptations." Besides, clearly becoming a Mather himself, Sammy had been experiencing a "strange Persuasion" that he would prosper in England. Full of distress all over again and fatalistic, Mather threw himself on God's will: *"I sacrifice him, O my GOD and SAVIOUR, I sacrifice him to thy Holy Pleasure!"*

As had not happened often to Mather, this proved a prayer-hearing God. Mather allowed Sammy to make the voyage. But God, he found, disposed him to persuade Sammy not to make it by way of the West Indies, rather aboard a ship bound more directly to London. Somehow the ship's departure was aborted, however. And in January, after this defeat of his intentions, Sammy gave up the idea of sailing abroad altogether. Unspurned for once by reality, Mather had been allowed to fortify himself against loss without having to bear it. "I have . . . had an Opportunity to make a Sacrifice of my only Son; and yet," he wrote thankfully, "without the actual Accomplishment thereof, to receive him again as from the Dead."

V

COTTON MATHER

(1724–1728)

~~~∞~~~

An Inventory of the Estate of Dr Cotton Mather late Deced taken by us the Subscribers July 23d 1728 as it was shew'd to us by his widow Mrs. Lydia Mather & the Children

12 Flag Chairs 24/ 8 Leather Chairs 2 of 'em high backt 24/	£ 2. 8.
17 Low Turkey work Chairs some defective @6/	5. 2.
10 Turkey work Chairs 5 broke	2.
2 Broken Cane Chairs 10/ & a Cane Couch 44/ 14 Cane Chairs	
@14/£9.16.	12.10.
1 Feather Bed No. 1. 65 at 2/3	7. 6. 3.
1 Ditto 2. 47 2/6	5.17. 6.
1 Do. 3. 57 2/4	6.13.
3 Bolsters & 5 Pillows 44 2/3 £5 4d 3 Old Ruggs 10/	5.10.1½.
1 Old Quilt and 2 Blanketts 30/ 4 Old Bedsteads 50/	4.
2 Old Oval Tables and a broken Stone Table	1. 6.
2 Old Chest of Draws Table & dressing box	3.
A Japan Looking Glass 50/ 2 Ditto black frames £4	6.10
1 pr. Old China Curtains & Vallens lased, bedstead & Curtain Rods .	5.
1 pr. of Red Curtains Mothcaten	1.
4 pr. brass Andirons 2 pr. of Iron Dogs, other broken Dogs	4.
1 pr. brass fire Shovel & Tongs, and an old warming pan	1. 1.
114 Pewter Viz. 18 Dishes, a pasty-plate, pye plate, cheese plate	
broken pewter	11. 8.
1½ doz. Pewter Plates 34/ Knives & forks 10/	2. 4.
2 brass Skillets, 1 Saucepan, 2 Candlesticks skimer, frying pan trennel	
spit	2.
1 brass Kettle 33 £4. 19/ One Copper 35 £7	11.19.
17 Iron 8/ Belmettle Mortar 15/	1. 3.
1 Old Standing Candlestick 10/ a Cross cut Saw 30/ Lumber 20/ . .	3.
1 Bed & Bolster 75 @ 2/6	9. 7. 6.
147 oz. of Silver Plate @ 16/6 Viz. One Tankard, 2 Servers, 1 pair	
Candlesticks Snuffers & Standish, & Tea Pott Several Broken	
Spoons, one Spout Cup, 1 Sugar dish, 2 Porringers	121. 5. 6.
	235.10. 10.
500 Acres of wast Land Scituate in the County of Hampshire as appears	
to us by Deed Cost	36.

John Barnard
John Goldthwait
Graffton Feveryear

Suffolks: By the Honble. Samuel Sewall Esq Judge of Pro:&c

Nathaniel Goodwin Adminr: presented the foregoing and made Oath that it contains a true and perfect Inventory of the Estate of the Rev. Dr. Cotton Mather aforesaid deceased so far as hath come to his knowledge and that if more hereafter appear he will Cause it to be added. The subscribing apprizers were at the same time sworn as the Law Directs.

Boston August 5th 1728.

Exam per *John Boydell Reg*

Samuel Sewall

14

As Merry as One Bound for Heaven

⌒◦⌒

A COUGH, a "grievous Breast-beater," accompanied by fever and a suffocating asthma, confined Mather to his house for about five weeks at the end of 1724 and early in 1725. His diaries after this "winter of much feebleness," if he kept any, are missing. Information about his daily round during the last three years of his life is therefore scant, but his correspondence and the remarks of others indicate that he remained in fairly good health through most of 1725 and 1726, then in the spring of 1727 underwent the first of three increasingly serious bouts of illness.

Seemingly drained by his illness in 1724–25, and by Creasy's death and the double loss of the Harvard presidency, Mather again withdrew from government affairs. Jeremiah Dummer applauded his "noble Resolution" to quit politics and "Solace your self in your Study and the business of your Divine Profession." Mather might well have retired from New England's political life, for although turbulent throughout his lifetime it had become relatively quiet. The Indian war ended with a peace treaty in December 1725, and while Samuel Shute remained in England, William Dummer administered the government without serious conflict. Mather's private life, as far as is known, had eased as well. In October 1724, Joseph Tallcott of Hartford brought an action against the Howell estate and was awarded £71 plus costs of the suit. But this may well have been the final demand against the estate; no further suits appear in the court records. Nor apparently did Lydia's return home after Creasy's death produce new domestic warfare. Here the lack of Mather's diaries is specially tantalizing, but the surviving bits of evidence about his marriage suggest reconciliation, however arrived at.

Sixty-two years old in 1725, Mather was, by his own standards and those of the time, an old man. In *A Good Old Age* (1726) he observed that scarce three persons in a hundred live to seventy, and he commended the work to those "whose Arrival to, or near, SIXTY, ranks them among, The AGED." He had not expected to live so long. Once he had fancied that he would die when he had written 365 works. But when he looked at his catalogue in 1726 he found he had written more than 369—not to mention the "much more bulky and weighty and wealthy" works that remained unpublished—so that "I know not the death of my death."

Despite Mather's filiopietism, his view of old age was unsentimental. He cited approvingly the Oriental maxim "that *old age is to be reckoned no part of life.*" In "Biblia Americana" he drew an ugly picture of the stage: the mercurial spirit of youth exhausted, the mouth disabled for singing, teeth unable to chew, stomach squeamish, arms trembling, thighs shrunk, the aged person grown headachy, gray, deaf, fearful of stumbling—*"Clouds* of Ignorance, prejudice, and mistake, then impair the *understanding;* the *Memory* becomes feeble and faithless; the *Imagination* grows conceited . . . *Suspicious* of Evil, but *Lothe to Believe any Good."* The condition, Mather felt, was however lamentable also incurable, thus futile and graceless to protest. To those liable to such follies of old age as hoarding, trying to act young, or refusing to retire, his advice was severe: "Good Sir, Be so Wise, as to *Disappear* of your own Accord as soon and as far as you lawfully may."

Some of these, and other, effects of age now wore on Mather himself. Grateful for having escaped the stone, he offered special thanks on his sixty-first birthday for arriving at "this great Age, free from the grievous Diseases, which carry Horror with them." On the other hand, he had begun wearing spectacles, perhaps the ones Thomas Hollis had taken from his own nose and sent him in friendship. In his enthusiasm for material progress and for alleviating human misery, he regarded spectacles as a wonderful invention. "We that are *Old People,*" he wrote, "are marvelously Blessed of GOD, by the *Use of Glasses,* which preserves the power of *Reading* with us. Inexcusable has been the Ingratitude of Mankind, shamefully to bury in Oblivion the Name of the *Benefactor* that was the *First Inventor of Spectacles;* when there stand on Record so many Execrable *Oppressors* and *Murderers* of Mankind, under the Name of *Conquerors."* Nostalgia set in also. In 1724 Mather published his first public sermon, which he had preached to a religious society when just sixteen years old. Several times he wrote to friends with whom he had not corresponded in years, inquiring whether one or another mutual acquaintance "be yet sojourning in this Land of the Dying."

But above all, old age meant to Mather uniquely a time for productivity, Fructuosus. His recovery from the long illness at the end of 1724 brought a swell of initiative. "The very little Time that remains of my Pilgrimage thro' this evil World, must be carried on with new Measures. No Time is to be lost. I must be at Work for my Glorious Lord continually and assiduously, and more than ever." Making one final attempt to "*do enough,*" he expended in his final years a torrential energy, reading and writing, his son Samuel said, "as if he had but newly taken a *Pen* or *Book* into his Hand."

Except his withdrawal from political life, scarcely one of Mather's many interests failed of embodiment in some publication or activity in the final three or four years of his life. He continued adding illustrations to his never-to-be-published "Biblia Americana." As a Protestant statesman, always watchful for the fate of international Protestantism, he was shocked by new edicts against French Protestants and by a similar revival of persecutions in Poland, Hungary, and Germany, prompting him to call attention to the Protestants languishing overseas in dungeons or executed, in such works as *Une Grande Voix du Ciel a la France* (1725) and *Suspiria Vinctorum* (1726). Still also alarmed about Arianism, he continued writing to England denouncing its spread. Most of his colleagues in the German Pietist movement had died, but he received accounts from Pietist missionaries in the East Indies, and the expectation of answers from him. His correspondence remained demandingly huge: letters, as always, from Scotland, even longer and more frequent than before; from sympathizers or those in distress, people of no repute who sought his counsel from afar; from his old and dear friend John Winthrop, whom he pressed to move to Boston from New London, Winthrop himself now being hauled to court over the administration of an estate.

Mather also continued serving as a commissioner for the New England Company, and continued to find the "Languid Aspect" of the work discouraging. Yet he believed Christianity had become fairly widespread among the Indians, and rated the success of their conversion "one of New England's peculiar glories." To promote further progress, he urged reinstituting the practice of appointing "*A visitor of all the Indian villages,*" who would return from his visits with suggestions to the commissioners for redress and reform. Until the last year or two of his life he strove to get others' accounts of missionary work printed, although his own last lengthy writing on the subject was a discourse delivered before the commissioners at Samuel Sewall's house, published in 1721 as *India Christiana*—notable for its speculations on how the Indians came to America, a subject of popular controversy well into the eighteenth century. (He inclined to the view that the Indians were Asiatic in origin, and that Asia and America had once been contiguous.) He also published a *Proposal for an Evangelical Treasury* (1725), urging that a fund for missionary endeavors be collected from donations in the churches.

In his final years Mather turned over the keeping of the North Church records to Joshua Gee, but otherwise he does not seem to have restricted his ministerial duties. The astonishing thirty-nine titles he published between 1725 and 1727 include works on every major theme of his ministry: baptism (*Baptismal Piety*), marriage (*Mystical Marriage*), grace (*Signatus*), dishonest gain (*The Balance of the Sanctuary*), charity (*Some Seasonable Advice unto the Poor*), catechizing (*Instructor*). Mather's age and celebrity now ranked him as the foremost minister in New England, and his name routinely headed lists of signatories to ministerial petitions and addresses. He still personally presided over many church councils, sometime writing up the council decisions himself. For the last times now, he preached and published sermons on such traditional occasions as a royal accession (*Christian Loyalty*, 1727) and, for more than the tenth time, capital executions. Having no reason to be fond of pirates (they immediately forced their captives, he heard, "*To curse Dr. M_____*"), he preached in July 1726 on the execution of the villainous William Fly, who with several crew members had taken over a ship after throwing the captain and mate overboard, and set out pirating. His undiminished narrative ability appears in his compelling relation of the pirates' capture and of the obdurate Fly being led to the gallows—cursing, blaspheming, but holding a nosegay, settling the noose on his own neck (with an aside to the hangman that he did not know his trade), smiling until at the entrance to Boston Harbor his corpse dangled from chains.

On one grimly customary event Mather was called to preach, mercifully, for the last time. On August 7, 1726, midway through his sixty-third year, his twenty-two-year-old daughter Elizabeth died. She had survived the 1721 smallpox epidemic although non-immune, and in 1724, about a month before the news of Creasy's death, Mather had performed her marriage to a shipmaster named Edward Cooper. Now for the last time he dramatized the need for early piety to young members of his congregation by using as an example the death of his own child, "a *Young Person, of a Polite Education, in the Fresh Bloom of Youth* . . . just Entering into the World, in Comfortable Circumstances." As for himself, the "Poor Old *Sacrificer*," Elizabeth had been one of his three remaining children. He had been called on, he explained, for "the *Thirteenth* (and not the

Least!) *Sacrifice* of this One Sort, *the Amputation and Resignation of a Desirable Offspring.*" Of fifteen, only Sammy and Nancy were left.

*

Mather earnestly wished to leave some personal legacy to the New England churches and ministry, and did so in two of his most important and lengthiest late works. Although the apostate Cutler continued challenging the Congregational establishment, Mather looked hopefully on the rising generation of ministers who were about to replace his father and himself, "*Excellent Young Men*," he thought them, "who Study and Resolve their Duty, and are the *Rain-bows* of our Churches." He was not mistaken, for they included one of the most profound thinkers in American history, the grandson of his old rival Solomon Stoddard, young Jonathan Edwards, who was ordained pastor at Northampton early in 1727. Among this new generation Mather felt closest to Thomas Prince, an older member although twenty-five years his junior. In 1718 he had encouraged Prince's settlement at the Old South church, apparently unfazed that Prince had recently returned from England wearing, Samuel Sewall as usual noticed, a wig and russet coat. By 1726 Prince had come to be, Mather wrote, "as Cordial and Constant a Friend unto me, as any I have in the world." In his last few years he put Prince to many tasks, asking him to enlist subscribers to his works, to teach and care for his orphaned nephew Mather Byles, to get material for his communications to the Royal Society, and to read and comment on his manuscripts.

Mather's successors also included Samuel, whose carefully nurtured career now was blossoming. Sammy's earliest sermons, preached when he was seventeen, won "uncommon acceptance," Mather wrote, and he was praised for "an early piety, for a manly discretion, for some erudition, and none of the worst tempers." When attending the Yale commencement in 1724, while not yet eighteen, he was awarded an honorary M.A. degree (probably in gratitude to his father). Sammy's swift success greatly pleased Mather, but also made him wary. Lest the boy become prideful he resolved to inculcate in him "the profoundest Humility, that he may express a due Gratitude unto the glorious Lord who so remarkably smiles upon him; and a Conduct so full of Wisdom, that he may not make them ashamed who have promoted him, and that he may not fail the just Expectation of the World concerning him." However cautious, Mather felt by the fall of 1724 that Sammy had advanced far enough to be shown unto Israel, as after many delays he had been a half-century before. On October 25, still short of eighteen, Sammy preached on a text recommended to him by Mather, He is my Father's God and I will exalt Him (Exod. 15: 2). He spoke now from the place where two generations of Mathers had garnered much of whatever respect they could claim in the world, the North Church—"in the Pulpit," Mather wrote, "where his Father and Grandfather before him, have served our Glorious Lord."

Mather viewed Sammy and the other young ministers as the hopes of the New England churches, and in a spirit at once of apostolic continuity, professional friendship, and paternal care he reached out to them as "My YOUNGER BRETHREN in the Evangelical MINISTRY." As a legacy to these young colleagues he prepared several works on the ministry, whose substance is comprehended in his book-length manual for ministers, *Manuductio ad Ministerium* (1726). Addressing himself to *"My Son"*—a hypothetical ministerial candidate, but suggesting some surrogate for Creasy—he here summarized his long professional experience. The tone of the book, except at the beginning and end, is urbane and convivial, and thus emblematic of the ideal of the ministry it promulgates, an ideal derived from humanist scholarship and Reformed doctrine but also from Pietist activism and personal practice.

Mather equated the function of the minister with the chief end of life itself, namely the service of God. But he defined this service broadly to include "Whatever contributes unto the *Welfare* of *Mankind,* and such a *Relief* of their Miseries, as may give the Children of Men better *Opportunities* to *Glorify* Him." He envisioned ministers such as he had striven to become himself, not only thunderous preachers winning souls to Christ from their pulpits, but also humane, liberal, and erudite gentlemen sensible of the large human good to be achieved by scientific advancement, capable of moving people to pious ends by entertaining conversation, and aware that true piety is not limited to one sect. The training he proposed thus consists not only of Scripture reading and fervent private devotions, but also of acquiring a high gloss of civility, the "Pursuit of that *Learning,* and those *Ingenuous* and *Mollifying Arts,* which may distinguish you from the more *Uncultivated* Part of Mankind." As a guide to behavior in society he recommended "Wise Observation of what you see passes in the Conversation of Politer People." He also recommended the active study of science, and acquaintance with (but not absorption in) poetry and music, including, for ministers so disposed, the refreshment of learning to play well on some musical instrument.

Mather equally emphasized urbane polish in theological study and preaching, to make the minister "a *Skilful Artist* for the Work of your GOD." Nearly as much a writer as a preacher himself, he not surprisingly paid much attention in his manual to the writing of sermons and to literary style. Resentful to the end of his life over criticisms of his prose, he also gave space to defending his "Massy *Way of Writing*," however fallen out of taste and derided by a "Lazy, Ignorant, Conceited Set of Authors." "The Writer pretends not unto *Reading*," as he explained his stylistic practice, "yet he could not have writ as he does if he had not *Read* very much in his Time; and his Composures are not only a *Cloth of Gold*, but also stuck with as many *Jewels*, as the Gown of a Russian Embassador." Such a style would come back in use when a better taste returned, he predicted, and meanwhile he asked for the same indulgence in style as in modalities of religion. "Every Man will have his own *Style*, which will distinguish him as much as his *Gate*," and people ought to "handsomely *indulge* one another in this, as *Gentlemen* do in other Matters." Still irate after twenty years over Oldmixon's twitting, he cursed for one last time that writer's *English Empire in America* as "the most foolish and faithless Performance in this Kind, that ever Mankind was abused withal."

Mather did not forget other abusers either. In addressing his "sons" he also imparted to them the less palatable experience he had gained from Calef onward, so that for all its amiable liberality *Manuductio*, like *Bonifacius*, begins and ends in gall. The twenty-page Latin Preface reeks of his rejection for the Harvard presidency and of compensatory triumph in his honorary D.D. years earlier, spitefully dedicating the work to studious youths in academies, "Principally in that of Glasgow; Next, to those in New England." "I know how meanly I am furnished," Mather told them, "and all New-England know it, and deem me utterly incapable of addressing Persons of Academical Education; and they rightly judge as I do." The personal recommendations in the equally rancid concluding section range from simple cynicism:

> One must not *Spend all he hath;* nor *Do all he can;* nor *Tell all he knows;* nor *Believe all he hears.*

to a sort of ecclesiastical Machiavellianism:

> [Influential persons] will soon fall out with you, if you don't keep Touch with them, in all their Designs; and when you cease to be their *Tool,* they will most *Forgetfully* and *Ungratefully* abandon you.

to near paranoia:

> Let them that hav abused you, *know nothing* that you *know any thing* of the matter. For such is the *Baseness* of many People, that (measuring *you* by themselves) they will *hate* you, because you *know* that they have *hurt*

you; and they will persist in their *Hatred,* which they must Justify, because
they imagine, that you *can't Forgive them.*

Growing however old, Mather thus composed his legacy to the future
ministers of New England in spunkiest Matherean counterpoint, My Sons
You Are the Hopes of Our Flocks piped against They Don't Have Cotton
Mather to Kick Around Any More.

To the churches, as distinct from the ministry, Mather bequeathed a
book-length account of their principles and practices, *Ratio Disciplinae*
(1726). The work had a rocky history, for Mather originally wrote it in
1701, but its publication and later revision were several times delayed. In
1726, greatly revised, it was again ready for publication, but this time two-
thirds of the manuscript blew away, it seemed irretrievably; some of the
pages, however, were picked up by strangers, others found in a garden,
others in a woodpile. That was fortunate, because *Ratio Disciplinae* contains much of what is known specifically today about New England's manner of worship—the gathering of a church, marriage and ordination ceremonies, administration of baptism and communion, and much else.
Mather believed the work would "prove one of the usefullest things that
ever were offered unto the churches," a substitute for an updated platform of church discipline, such as might have been written by the proposed church synod of 1725, which the government had refused to convene. He also intended the book for readers abroad, to show "unto the
Churches in the *other Hemisphere,* the Relation of what is practised in
these Regions of *America.*" *Ratio* belongs with such early American classics as Crèvecoeur's *Letters from an American Farmer* (1782) in demonstrating to Europeans basic differences between the New World and the
Old.

Mather devoted most of the book to straightforward descriptions of
specific church practices, inviting consultation rather than summary here.
This historically valuable information also serves to illustrate, however,
an ambidexter point. On one hand Mather repeatedly emphasizes that the
New England churches are Congregational (thus uniquely close to the
form of the primitive church), and demonstrates their orthodoxy by citing
matching practices recommended by the church Fathers and by continen-
tal Reformers. But he equally emphasizes that the New England churches
are not fractiously individualistic, and demonstrates their spirit of tolerant
cooperation by stressing their use of church councils and the variety that
prevails among them in the practice of circumstantials. The churches
have made Franckean Piety the only basis for admission: "A Charitable
Consideration of nothing but PIETY in admitting to Evangelical Privi-

leges, is a Glory that the Churches of *New-England,* would lay claim unto." Thus although Congregational, the New England churches have from the beginning renounced the idea of independency: "Every *particular Church* is to consider it self as a part of the *Catholic,* and owes a Duty to the *whole Visible Church* of our Lord in the World."

Of course Mather had long tried unsteadily to maintain this equilibrium between seeing New England as a pristine Wilderness Zion and as but one outpost of International Protestantism, tilting one way or another according to the deeds of government in Boston and London, his own treatment at home and abroad, activities of the Church of England, among other things. But *Ratio Disciplinae* indicates that at the end of his life he believed that the founders' ideal had failed. A person "must not be called, A *Calumniator,*" he writes, who frankly informs Europeans "That they will not find *New-England* a New Jerusalem." Most New Englanders are sober and well acquainted with religion, but worldliness and apostasy are growing. As to the country's looked-for role as a beacon in the coming worldwide reformation, "some of their *Seers* have not been without melancholy Apprehensions, lest *New England* have now done the most that it was intended for." These words—unchanged from Mather's first drafting of the work in 1701—suggest that he and his father had seen too much of life in New England to believe that it could ever be perfect or exemplary there, and that to them the City upon a Hill remained in the realm of what-might-have-been.

On balance, what Mather lost in exclusivism he gained in liberality. At the end of his life he returned to his ecumenism, and extended it to include Quakers, whom he had always regarded as not less subversive of Christianity than Catholics. In his remarkable *Vital Christianity* (1725)— significantly, published in Philadelphia—he declared that he "*unspeakably* abhors *and* laments *the abominable* Persecution *which you have suffered in former Days.*" Now viewing virtually all Christians as one, he owned a unity with Quakers in sharing a "Christ within" (construed as taking Christ for a pattern of holiness), and on this principle he embraced Quakers as fellow Christians, "our beloved *Friends.*"

*

Age did not dampen Mather's enthusiasm for science. Partly because of his constant encouragement of scientific study he could now look out on a much enlarged Boston scientific community. Several Bostonians were sending specimens and observations to the Royal Society, and the *Boston News-Letter* invited local scientific contributions so that it might some degree serve for the "*Philosophical Transactions* of *New England.*" Continuing his encouragement, Mather took up Dr. Jurin's suggestion that he interest his friends in meteorology, and presented a Boston tradesman named Grafton Feveryear with a barometer—evidently the first used for meteorological observation by New Englanders, the results of which were forwarded to the Society in 1727. As always he particularly fostered the young, especially Sammy's contemporary Isaac Greenwood, a Harvard graduate and member of his church whom, like several other young men in his last years, he decided to treat "as a sort of a Son." Bearing a letter of recommendation to the Royal Society from Mather, Greenwood went to London, where he spoke with Newton and became an assistant to Dr. Jean Théophile Desaguliers, curator of experiments at the Society and inventor of the planetarium. He brought back with him to Boston apparatus for scientific demonstrations and, in January 1727, launched a series of sixteen public lectures on science, the first of their kind in New England. The same year the Harvard Corporation appointed him to a new professorship of mathematics and natural philosophy, making Mather's protégé probably the first American to earn his living by science.

Mather was disappointed, however, in his own relation to the Royal Society during his final years. He continued sending communications, but often complained privately about the Society's failure to publish more of them or to send copies of what it had published already. Sometimes the Society replied tardily or not at all, which he feared meant either indifference or lost mail. The second fear was not fanciful, for his entire series of Curiosa for 1720—twelve letters on the whale, the Mississippi River, the quadrature of the circle, and other subjects—seems to have disappeared after being delivered to Isaac Newton as president of the Society. Despite concern over his packets miscarrying, and some resentment, he sent seven letters in 1723 and a final collection of ten letters in 1724, none of which was published, however, in the *Transactions*.

In sending his 1724 series, Mather explained that the reason he did not send Curiosa as often as he wished was partly that he had been writing, and had now completed, a large new medical work he might soon try to publish in New England. His preoccupation is understandable, for except his defense of inoculation, *The Angel of Bethesda* is his single most important achievement in science—the only comprehensive American medical work of the entire colonial period, filling in its modern edition some 322 large pages. Mather first mentions it in the "catalogue of desirables" that concludes *Bonifacius* (1710), so that the book may well have been the off-and-on labor of fourteen years. His threefold purpose was religious, medical, and in a broad sense scientific. He wished to supply for those in ill health, ingenious pious "improvements" of their condition. ("Let thy Odious *Breath*," he advised victims of scurvy, "cause thee to think, *in Speaking, how much has my Throat been like an Open Sepulchre!*") He also wanted to offer general and specific rules for preserving health: temperate diet, no tobacco, wholesome exercise, refreshment by toast and tea (which he relished himself and specially recommended to ministers after preaching). But mostly he tried to provide a popular pharmacopeia or colonial Dr. Spock, a *"Family-physician"* by whose scores of remedies families might "Save *Life,* and *Health,* and *Money.*" Accordingly the work emits a warm charity, sympathy for human suffering, and particular care for the poor.

Mather classified his remedies according to diseases as they were identified in his time, ranging from smallpox to stinking feet ("Be not slovenly, wear Socks, often shifting 'em"). He treated as illnesses conditions that would now be viewed as symptoms, such as headaches, and presented as single diseases such conglomerates as "fevers"—confusions of a sort which lingered in medical thought into the nineteenth century. Eclectic in medical theory as elsewhere, he borrowed from the published medical works of competing schools: the Galenical school of botanical remedies as well as the school of chemical remedies, even to a less extent from the occult school. The book quotes more than two hundred and fifty medical writers, and repeats several remedies verbatim from Robert Boyle's *Medicinal Experiments* (London, 1688), a collection in part intended to supply cheap prescriptions for poor people in America. Mather did not simply list prescriptions, however. Instead he related them in a perky conversational style invigorated by questions, interjections, and sallies of erudition, dividing the work into sixty-six sections called, with his usual formal wit, Capsulas.

Some of Mather's remedies remain of value, such as the use of citrus juice to treat scurvy. But many others must strike modern readers as weird: a wolfskin girdle for epilepsy; a needle first thrust into a centipede for treating toothache; a dead hand applied to wens and tumors "till the Patient feel the *Damp* sensibly Strike into him"; a clyster made of fresh butter in which have been fried the parings of stone-horse hooves. Many of these are folk remedies, and Mather so represented them, noting that "some have said" they work without vouching for their efficacy himself. But some of his other, equally weird remedies are based on contemporary medical theory. One large group, including many remedies taken from

Boyle, derive from a theory of repellency, by which it was believed that some illnesses could be expelled by repulsive substances, including vermin, pig dung, and human excrement. Discreetly apologizing that "Tis hardly *Good Manners* to write so much about it," Mather yet offered cow's urine as a remedy for asthma, "powdered *Mouse-dung*" when other means fail to relieve ischury, and boy's urine as a gargle for sore throat ("Some fancy, a Mixture from diverse Lads").

The Angel of Bethesda also contains Mather's maturest reflections on several medical ideas he had long contemplated. He devoted the longest Capsula to the symptoms and treatment of smallpox. The Capsula entitled "Ephphatha. or, Some Advice to Stammerers"—another backward glance of his last years—represents the first treatise on stuttering written in America. The seventh Capsula, "*Conjecturalies.* or, Some Touches upon, A *New Theory* of many *Diseases,*" expands his earlier speculations on the germ theory of disease. Mather now proposed that the "Invisible *Velites*" or their eggs might "insinuate themselves by the *Air*" and infiltrate bodily juices; being numerous and perhaps of different sorts, they might be responsible not only for smallpox but also for such such other varying diseases as syphillis, consumption, measles, and agricultural blight. Also merging and refining his earlier brief writings on psychogenic illnesses, he tried to show that many diseases arise from or are exacerbated by distress. He treated specific emotional and mental ills as well, to some of which he may have become sensitized by his father and Lydia, including nightmares, melancholia, and insanity. He urged understanding treatment of disturbed persons: "*We that are Strong must bear the Infirmities of the Weak;* and with a patient, prudent, Manly Generosity, pity them, and Humor them like *Children,* and give none but *Good Looks* and *good Words* unto them. . . . Tis not *They* that Speak; Tis their *Distemper!*" How many of these conjectures and conclusions Mather arrived at himself is arguable. He derived many of his comments on the germ theory, for instance, from Benjamin Marten's *A New Theory of Consumption* (London, 1720). Whatever their originality, however, Mather's remarks at least speak for his humane open-mindedness, and his prescient ability to select from contemporary science ideas of lasting importance.

In the most imaginative Capsula of *The Angel of Bethesda,* Mather consolidated several of these ideas in the single master concept of a "*Nishmath-Chajim.* The Probable SEAT of all Diseases, and a General CURE for them." The Nishmath-Chajim is his fullest elaboration, after years of pondering the notion, of the plastic spirit, an attempt to harmonize his scientific and religious ideas, his understanding of matter and of spirit, his natural philosophy and pneumatology, his vitalistic and mechanistic views of the universe—Mather's own unified field theory. In conceiving the Nishmath-Chajim he drew particularly on the notion of an Archeus propounded by the devout Swiss physician Jean Baptiste van Helmont, whose works he had known since youth. As defined in Van Helmont's huge folio *Oriatrike or, Physick Refined* (London, 1662), the Archeus is the inner "air" in every material object which determines its development, a soullike entity responsible for all change and coming-into-being in the thing, the governor of generation, the "chief Workman, containing the fruitfulness of generations and Seeds, as it were the internal efficient cause." Mather's Nishmath-Chajim is the body's Archeus, its own unique plastic spirit, a set of biological signals directing its activities without its volition. It is that by which the body "knows" to digest, "the *Spirit*, whose *Way we know not, for shaping the Bones,* and other Parts, *in the Womb of her that is with Child.*" Neither pure matter nor pure spirit, it may be "of a *Middle Nature,* between the *Rational Soul* and the *Corporeal Mass,*" a superfine matter whose particles, cohering by some unknown principle, may be finer than those of light. Most important, it may be through the Nishmath-Chajim that body and soul interact: "It wonderfully receives also *Impressions* from *Both* of them. And perhaps it is the *Vital Tie* between them."

Mather saw this vitalistic Nishmath-Chajim as the possible link between a diverse host of unexplained natural and pneumatological phenomena—muscular motion, digestion, psychogenic illness, nidification (the instinct in birds to build nests), and the waxing of the human body from the original infolded animalcule, as well as witchcraft, ghosts, and teleportation. Because the Nishmath-Chajim connects body and soul, and is affected by mental tranquillity, Mather following Helmont urged attending it in the treatment of disease: the physician who can find a way to "Brighten, and Strengthen, and Comfort, the *Nishmath-Chajim,* will be the most Successful Physician in the World." Having never wholly abandoned his pneumatology (he thought recently that Satan "obtained a permission" to scatter the pages of his *Ratio Disciplinae*) he believed that a fuller understanding of the Nishmath-Chajim might explain "Indisputable and Indubitable Occurrences of *Witchcrafts* (and *Possessions*)." The Nishmath-Chajim might also account for apparitions of the dead, for Mather considered it probable that upon the body's death "the *Nishmath-Chajim* goes away, as a Vehicle to the *Rational Soul;* and continues unto it an Instrument of many Operations," a ghost thus being a soul inhabiting a Nishmath-Chajim. Similarly he attributed to it cases in which dying persons who strongly desired to visit some distant place had been seen at the place and could describe it. He also speculated that in conjunction with the concept of indestructible animalcules, the Nishmath-Chajim could help explain the ultimate Resurrection of the Dead.

While writing *The Angel of Bethesda* Mather surmised that booksellers would demand a sale of forty or fifty pounds before risking publication. Even before completing the "large Work" he despaired of "my *Angel's* becoming visible" otherwise than in manuscript. Although he determined to "apply myself both to Heaven and Earth, to bring on the Publication" his applications failed, as did those of Samuel, who noted that it had cost his father "many Years study," and in 1739 even advertised for subscribers to bring it into print. The work was not published, however, until the twentieth century.

*

Despite this uncommonly ample late harvest, Mather's health was failing. In the last year of his life, 1727, he suffered three periods of serious illness. In April several ministers met at Joshua Gee's house to pray for his recovery; in June and July he was ill again, *"Chastened sore,* but . . . *not given over to Death";* ill again in October, he characterized himself as "*a Dying Man,* and one that sees himself going out of the World." Although weak, he carried on, preaching, occasionally serving on a committee or at an ordination, holding a church council at his home. He also sat for the well-known portrait of him by Peter Pelham, a 30" x 25" oval painted on canvas. It shows nothing of ill health, and may not be a close likeness, although persons who knew Samuel well when he was older said the portrait much resembled Mather's son. Pelham later prepared and sold a print based on the portrait, the first mezzotint known to have been made in the New World. Mather seems to have been the first American whose portrait others wanted and bought for their homes.

Lacking Mather's diaries, his general mood in the last year or two of his life can only be glimpsed in other sources. His last works and few last letters touch many moods. Some are sombrous, for he no more sentimentalized the dying than he did the elderly:

> They may *Chatter like a Bird* which a violent Hand is pulling out of its Nest; *I shall behold Man no more with the Inhabitants of the World. My Age is departed; My Life is cut off like the Thread of the Weaver. I feel Death like a Lion breaking all my Bonds.* They have no Prospect of any other, but that within a few Days or Hours, they shall have their *Life smitten down to the Ground, and go to dwell in Darkness. . . .*

Yet at other times near the end Mather seems if somber also unsubdued, as in his *Manuductio* and in a letter he wrote one year before his death to Thomas Prince. It concerns the Rev. Nathaniel Clap of Newport, members of whose congregation charged him with neglecting his ministry. Apparently, some Boston ministers asked Mather to write a letter of reproof to Clap, as he did. When he learned that another letter was substituted for it, his old touchy petulance flashed out:

> *I very well understand* the meaning of the indecency and indignity I am treated withal. To order me to draw up letters, and make me lose my time, which grows more and more precious to me . . . and then turn 'em upon me again and substitute instead of them, that which can be of *no other use* but only to render *them useless*—I say, *I very well understand it*. . . .

Assuring Prince that he would remain patient and easy, he added that he would also "look on myself as excused for the time to come from the labors of your clerkship."

Mather's dominant mood, however, seems to have been an agitated exaltation, varying in pitch from lyric joy to hectic merriment. As a Puritan, he believed and often emphasized that the true Christian dies joyously. He had witnessed such victorious deaths many times himself. In 1716, for instance, when "my dear, good, wise, and lovely *Katy*" was told that she was dying, she replied, *"Oh! I could even Sing for Joy, at what you tell me."* So despite his grim imaginings of illness and decay, Mather was moved himself to Whitmanesque carolings of death as liberation and ease:

> In *Death,* what shall we have to be *afraid* of! *Death,* which will be a *Mercy stroke* to finish the uneasy things wherein we *Die daily* and release us from all the Pain, and Grief, and Care, and the Daughters of *Heth,* which made us to say, *What Good shall my Life do unto me!* . . . . The *Angel of Death* coming with a Commission to strike us and kill us, yet says unto us, *I shall do you no hurt. Ben't scared; I won't hurt you!* That which has the Aspect of the *Worst,* as well as the *last Enemy,* becomes a *good Friend* unto us. In the most gloomy *Darkness* of the *Valley,* we may Sing. . . .

Mather's readiness to rejoice at death may account for the heightened lyricism of many of his final works, as expressed in such poetically exotic Hebrew titles as *El-Shaddai* (1725), *Zalmonah* (1725), *Hatzar-Maveth* (1726), and *Hor-Hagidgad* (1727). His late works also cultivate many striking figures of speech (for instance comparing Christ, surprisingly, to the Old Testament brazen serpent) and are pervaded by interacting complex images of trees, birds, and, particularly, singing. When he sat alone during his long illness of 1724–25, unable to read or write, he often composed and sang hymns pertinent to his condition, remarking that a soul in which piety flourishes "can *sing* in the *Valley of the Shadow of Death*. . . . triumphing over the *Fear of Death,* and beginning to *sing the Songs of the Lord,* even in a *strange Land;* the *Songs,* which none but those *chief Musicians,* the *Redeemed from the Earth,* are skilful at." He wrote several poems in his last few years as well. Six of them he included in *Agricola* (1727) as "The *Plain* SONGS OF THE Pious HUSBAND-MAN"; he seems also to have sent his friend Thomas Hollis a poem on spectacles.

At times Mather's lyric joy in the prospect of death was transposed into a feverish levity. Such is the mood of a strange madcap letter he hurriedly wrote to Prince on a cold day in January 1726, dated "Madding Day" and beginning, "If you ask, *What I do?*—Alas, methinks; my name is *Do Little."* Lopsidedly written, words crowded at the bottom or crosswise in the margin, the letter acknowledges pain ("I want Strength. My Side Aches with This!") and ends by quoting the Protestant martyr Mrs. Askew (whose name also puns on the askew script): "I am, your Brother, *As Merry as one bound for Heaven."* Still more hectic is the unfinished poem Mather handwrote in 1727 across the title page and inside the covers of a published poem entitled *A Monumental Gratitude* (New London, 1727). The published poem narrates the fate of some Yale students caught in but delivered from a storm on Long Island Sound. Mather wrote across the bottom of its title page:

> Poor Lads! the Storm has whirld your Brains around;
> And all the *Sense* is ship-wrack'd in the SOUND.

There is no knowing whether to take this as literary criticism, a swipe at Yale, self-pity, or all three. Even more bizarre, considering the occasion of the poem (with its overtones of Creasy's drowning), are the mock-heroic verses Mather wrote inside. Suited for no place so much as the *Courant,* they render as a miniature comic apocalypse a rowdy holiday feast of pigeon pie:

> Hark, Stygian Muse; the Noise and discord dire,
> Of Heated Ovens, and of Crackling Fire,
> While Smoke, and Soot, and falling Sticks of Wood,
> And Scattering Coal, and foaming Pidgeons Blood,
> With hideous Riot all deform the Floor,
> Rage, fury, firebrands, bellowing Outrage, roar,
> Reason and Sense avaunt, the py appears,

And charms at once Touch, Eyes, Nose, Mouth, and Ears.
Fall on, Huzza! Break down the Bulwarks Strong
Let Gravy gush and pidgeons Sprawl along.
Salt, pepper, Butter, Marrow, Flesh and Bones,
Mix in the Mouth while Spoons encounter Spoons
Forks rush at Forks, and plates on plates resound,
Knives Knives repel, and crust recrackles round,
War, tumult, Havock, Sputt'ring, Out-cries, Threats. . . .

And so on through about another eight lines. Mather probably wrote the verses when seriously ill, but their unexpected and mysterious death-bound merriment eludes explanation. Perhaps, like some Puritan King Lear, he returned at the worst to laughter.

Having spent much of his life preparing his soul for death, Mather also lived now in a mood of expectancy. A little before dying, he wrote, an old man "Realizes the *Invisible World* more than formerly. *Invisibles* become to him the **greatest Realities.**" When seriously ill in the summer of 1727 he had come close to knowing what would be revealed to the elect at death. He had visited then "the very *Gate* of the *Invisible World,* and had Opportunity to look a little way into the *Paradise* of GOD." What he expected to find in his afterlife he recorded in an unpublished treatise entitled "Tri-Paradisus." Apart from its eschatological interest, this lengthy work is biographically among the most revealing documents that remain from Mather's last years. For although grounded in Scripture, it amounts to an elaborate fantasy of the journey of his own soul after death and for the duration of time.

The three paradises of Mather's title refer respectively to Eden; to the place of departed souls; and to the New Heaven and New Earth to be built after the Second Coming. The first section, drawn largely from "Biblia Americana" and based on writings of Lydia's father, Samuel Lee, is an erudite exercise in scriptural geography, identifying biblical Eden with the whole of Mesopotamia between the Tigris and Euphrates rivers. This part of the work Mather seems to have written in 1712. The descriptions of the other two paradises he seems to have written in 1726, at a time when he believed himself to be hastening to them. His manner throughout the work is tentative and guarded. Praying to be free from error he reckons with what "seems" to be the dark meaning of Scripture, extrapolating the nature of the place of departed souls typologically from the Old Testament depiction of the Jewish Temple of Solomon, and the nature of the New Heaven from the biblical description of Babylon, of which it is the reverse image.

Following Scripture, Mather envisioned the future history of his liberated soul in two epochs, divided by the Second Coming. First, stripped of mortal bodies at death, the *"unsheathed"* souls of the elect shall go to the Heavenly Paradise, seemingly "an *Apartment* of the *Heavenly World,"* distinct from the superior part of Heaven where resides Christ. There the saved soul, *"Escaped as a Bird out of the Snare of the Fowlers,"* perhaps clothed in luminous garments, may see Christ, perhaps at His occasional visits to Paradise, perhaps by the soul's own raised visionary contemplations. In this paradise the departed spirit shall be inconceivably happy, delivered from disease and enemies and sin, transported by its sublimely glad worship of God. There it shall live in joyful hope of its perfected blessedness after the Resurrection, when the elect shall be gathered together and reunited with their bodies.

The second epoch of the soul, Mather believed, shall follow the final Conflagration and the creation of the New Heaven and New Earth darkly shadowed forth in Apocalypse. The wicked having been destroyed, and Satan and his minions imprisoned in places of torment, God shall translate some of the elect souls to the Heavenly City itself, the final dwelling of the Raised Saints, the New Jerusalem. Built by Christ, made of purest matter or perhaps ethereal, peopled with the elect of both sexes and all nations, here the *"Changed Ones"* shall continue as distinct individual beings, even in becoming one with God and penetrated by Him. Receiving the consummate blessedness of which their earthly grace was the token, they shall be able to see Christ and God in Him. Their bodies, material but highly spiritualized, shall be incorruptible, errorless, without deformity, of luminous beauty and brightness, able to move and fly as angels, many of whose former functions they shall assume. Indeed here they shall meet and become intimate with the angels who guarded them in life. To their enormously illuminated understandings, all shall be unriddled; they shall comprehend the obscure places of Scripture, the workings of Providence, the nature of matter. However these elect have been scorned on earth, here Christ shall open His *"Book of Remembrance"* and assign them the *"Degrees of Glory"* to which they are truly entitled.

Personal disasters had often set Mather speculating on the apocalyptic event that divides these two epochs, the Second Coming—the crowning event of human history. In several earlier publications he had projected personal anger into visions of a world consumed, and hopes for personal vindication into sights of Christ returned to punish the wicked and avenge the virtuous. Now, in "Tri-Paradisus," he drew on Isaiah, Ezekiel, and other texts to compose another such disguised malediction, imagining the destruction of a world whose ordeals and traps, at least, he had grown to hate, "a World," he said, "which is not a *Paradise* (nor is Like to afford one) but is an horrid and howling Wilderness; A Land of Pits and of Droughts, and fiery flying Serpents." As Mather envisioned it, Christ's Coming and the attendant conflagration would be heralded by volcanic eruptions and earthquakes. The onset would be sudden: men of business would be busy, the wicked plying their wickedness, the sensuous wallowing. Perhaps first over Italy, seat of the papacy, a sudden light would appear in the heavens.

Then tormenting heat will blast the devils from their high places in the atmosphere. Audible above the thunderclaps reechoing from earth's caverns, the voice of Christ will call the dead to rise from their graves:

> "*COME FORTH, my people, out of the Chambers, where I have hid you. Let my Dead Ones, Live Again.*"

The luminous risen spirits of the Chosen, ascending "as with the Wings of Eagles," will join the flocking squads of angels now visibly accompanying Christ downward to earth. People below, running to and fro, hiding from the fire and falling edifices, will wring their hands, howling one at another in anguish "beyond that of a *Travailing Woman*," as toppling nature turns dark and turns light:

> . . . there will be a *Great Earthquake;* the *Sun* will appear *as black as a Sackcloth of Hair,* by reason of the outshining Lustre in the *Chariots* of God; and the *Moon become as Blood* by reason of the Vapour wherewith our Air will be thickened; the *Stars of Heaven* will appear as if they were *falling to the Earth,* by reason of the Vibrations in the Atmosphere: The *Heaven will depart as a Scrowl when it is rolled together.*

As Christ's voice louder than a million thunderclaps calls "STRIKE!" thunderbolts plentiful as hailstones, "All-Scorching Sheets of Liquid *Fire*" will devour "*His Enemies.*" The veins of sulphur saturating the earth will immediately take fire, "Ten Thousand *Volcano's* will burst out, and throw up Flames and Vapors and Cinders, with a Rage and a Roar, that will reach unto the Heavens." The ground opening up in thousands of places will overturn mountains and swallow cities until the blazing earth itself is consumed.

Mather's vision of the Second Coming represents a drastic change of views in his final years, partly as a result of reading William Burnet's *Essay on Scripture-prophecy* (1724), which he deemed the "most penetrating, Judicious, Decisive Essay, that has ever yet been made upon that noble Subject." First he had become convinced that the conflagration of the earth would be literal, not allegorical as some commentators held, nor limited to the burning of Jerusalem. He had also come to believe that the Second Coming would be personal, an actual return of Christ to earth, a subject on which he had previously had a "thousand hesitations." He also no longer believed that the conversion of the Jews must take place before or during the Second Coming, as many others believed (including his father) and as many passages in Scripture seemed to suggest. With "a most Humble, and even Trembling, Heart and Hand," as he wrote in "Tri-Paradisus," he had come to consider this view both unscriptural and irrational, among other reasons because it seemed to him impossible that anyone could be converted amidst the flames. What the prophecy meant, he now thought, was that the Jews would be converted after Christ's Coming; or, since many Jews had been converted in early Christian times, the prophesied event may have already taken place.

Mather now believed, in fact, that there remained no signs to be looked for, that all the foretold preliminaries of the Second Coming had already occurred. Although he had once accepted the probability of Whiston's date of 1716, he otherwise frowned on commentators who brought prophetical study into disrepute by trying to fix the day and time of Christ's return too precisely. But feeling near the end himself, he was now convinced that the end of time was imminent. He had reached this conclusion by the summer of 1724, but feared publicizing it lest he seem "a vain Dreamer . . . a Man in the Falling Sickness, seized with I know not what kind of Enthusiasm." But reluctance faded in the last year or two of his life, when he at least alluded to the nearness of the Second Coming in the Latin Preface to his *Manuductio,* in such sermons as *Terra Beata* (1726) and *Fasciculus Viventium* (1726), and in a Latin commentary, *Diluvium Ignis* (1726).

Mather does not seem to have fully divulged his view publicly, however, until August 1727, when he preached on the accession of the new king, George II. He may have been encouraged to declare himself by front-page newspaper accounts, early in the year, of earthquakes in Italy. The *Gazette* reported on its front page that in Palermo an earthquake lasting twenty-five minutes had ruined most of the churches and a quarter of the houses, under which were buried more than fifteen-thousand persons; in Sicily people ran from their homes and gathered prostrate on the ground in the squares, "shedding Floods of Tears, smiting their Breasts, and saying over their Rosary with the most fervent Devotion." Whether or not inspired by this news, Mather thundered to his flock stupendous tidings:

... it may NOW, most awfully be said, *His Wrath will QUICKLY Flame!*—
we NOW know of nothing that remains to go before the Fulfillment of that
Word, *The Son of Man shall come in the Clouds of Heaven:* At which there
comes a tremendous CONFLAGRATION on a World horribly *Ripened* for
it: and as *Thoughtless* of it!

This was on August 20, 1727, six months before his death.

*

It began, the earthquake, on October 29—a Sabbath, between half-
past ten and ten forty-five at night. The sky, many remembered, had never
been more fair, the air never more serene, the stars never more glittering.
To Mather it became audible as a "horrid rumbling like the Noise of
many Coaches together, driving on the paved Stones with the utmost
Rapidity." Others heard a crashing noise, or violent thunderclap, or a
great fired chimney's bellowing "but inconceivably more fierce and terrible."

Movables clattered as the earth, in the largest quake in New England's
history, began tremblingly reeling. Cups and mugs tumbled off the man-
tel, windows and doors flew open; the kitchen in Judge Sewall's house
"Rocked like a Cradle." Houses cracked as if collapsing. Many wakened
people fled to the streets, fearful they would be buried in rubble. The
booming was not bounded by Boston. The splitting earth upthrew cart-
loads of sulfurous sand and ashes at Newbury, about forty miles northeast.
A bell tolled in Guilford, Connecticut, a hundred and sixty miles away.
Ships along the coast shook. The initial shock lasted only two or three
minutes, but until early morning could be felt the roll of aftershocks and
distant rumbles. Their possible meaning was obvious. Many persons in
Methuen, according to the local minister, feared "that it was the Great
Day of the Son of man's appearing in the clouds of heaven." Bostonians
assembled in the churches throughout the night and day, the *Gazette*
reported, in a state of "great and Just Terror and Dread."

Mather may have been feeble at the time of the quake, for two weeks
earlier he had addressed his congregation as *"One coming to you from
the Dead."* But having also recently warned of an imminent tremendous
conflagration, he felt that if ever he had preached a seasonable word he
must do so now. The Lord had spoken, and he must "render the Voice of
the Glorious GOD in the EARTHQUAKE, while it was yet scarce over,
Articulate and Intelligible unto the Hearers." The morning following the
quake he hurriedly put together what he called a speech rather than a

sermon, on Mic. 6:9—The Voice of the Lord, crieth unto the City. The bells of the North Church rang, and services were held at eleven o'clock in the morning, lasting until two in the afternoon.

Mather spoke now to a full meetinghouse. Nothing is known of his thoughts and his physical condition as he delivered the speech, but he perhaps felt very near death. For although he dealt with the earthquake, his startlingly oral depiction of a vindictive God speaking in fire and convulsion put before his listeners a lifetime of undernourishment and ill reward, its straining vatic energy a personal cry for last-minute retribution. Now no ambidexter tongue-tied jest for some Oldmixon, he commanded his congregation to listen to what he said: "O People *Trembling* before the Lord; *Hear now my SPEECH, and hearken to all my Words. For Indeed, I may declare unto you, The opening of my Lips will be of Right Things.*" They had now heard unmistakably, he said, the voice of the Lord roaring out of Zion: "Who is here of you, among them who felt the *Earth trembling* under them, that said not upon it, *When I heard, my Lips quivered at the Voice.*" They had all heard his copious Voice before but had not attended "the *Sound that went out of His Mouth.*" But now at last they could not ignore the Voice: "I see none *Asleep* at this Time. 'Tis a Congregation of *Hearers,* that I am this Time speaking to. . . . Now, Sirs, you have an *Earthquake* to give you a push." The time called for reformation, "particularly, for the stopping of that *Language of Fiends,* heard so often in our Streets, from the *Tongues that are set on Fire of Hell.*" The rest of what he knew Mather had come to warily, but now, following the quake, it was *"like a Fire in my Bones."* Even so, he divulged it cautiously: "If I should make the Cry, FIRE, FIRE! *The Fire of GOD will sooner than is generally thought for, fall upon a wretched World* . . . I should be as much *mocked,* and as little *minded,* as *Lot* was in the *Morning* of the Day when he went out of *Sodom.*" He might again be mocked, he said, but he believed that the universal conflagration and Christ's "Literal, Personal, Visible *Coming*" were at hand, and that all the promised signs "have been *given;* and are *passed,* and *over.*"

Mather's warning was not easily mocked, for widespread earth tremors continued through November. In December, news also arrived of earthquakes in such improbably remote places as the West Indies, where it was said that mountains shook and that the streets rose and fell like waves of the sea. Coupled with reports of quakes in England, Sicily, and elsewhere in Europe earlier in the year, these unsettling accounts inspired a substantial rise in admissions in many New England churches. Mather's own church admitted seventy-one persons in 1727, the largest number of his entire ministry. (The previous largest number was fifty-five, in 1691, just before the witchcraft crisis.) The converts included, on November 19, his sole surviving daughter, Nancy, for whose conversion he had long prayed.

Hoping to prolong the mood of reformation, Mather sent to Governor Dummer on December 9 a memorial he had prepared, calling for a province-wide Day of Humiliation and Supplication, that "we may be found religiously preparing for the things which may be coming." In further preparation he preached again on the earthquakes on December 14, warning once more that those who denied God would soon be consumed: "I again, and again, declare it unto you; *The Coming of the Son of Man in the Clouds of Heaven,* 'tis what we know of Nothing to Retard it or Protract it."

On December 24, with the shocks continuing, Mather preached for the last time. Speaking to his flock on the death of the Rev. Peter Thacher, he selected the text, Come my People, Enter thou into thy Chambers (Isa. 26:20). He did not threaten or warn. Instead he offered a comforting certainty, that the troubled body which goes to the cold chamber where the sun shines not, shall be reborn at rest in paradise, envisioning God. Beginning in late December, other ministers, including his son Samuel, took his place in his pulpit.

Conclusion: Copp's Hill

⟡

A *Post* set out; made the best of his Way; and in a few Hours Reached the Stage Intended. I'll tell it yet again: A *Ship* Weigh'd, and under full Sail, right before a Wind, run after the Rate of Twenty Leagues a Watch, and Anon Bore in with the Harbour . . . once more. An *Eagle* Hungry for a Prey, saw it, and with a *Nimble Wing* Seiz'd the *Prey.* This is the Short and the Long of the *Story.* Sirs, I have told you the *Story* of *Life.* This is the *Story.* In the V Chapter of *Genesis,* you have the *Story* told, Nine times over, so; *The Man was Born, he had an House, and he Died.* That's All!

—*A New Year Well-begun* (1719)

COTTON MATHER's final illness kept him at home for the last five or six weeks of his life. Certain he was dying, he wished to live only long enough to force his will into entire resignation to the will of God; after that, he told his successor Joshua Gee, "*then farewell all friends below; I shall* have nothing more to do *here.*" One other task remained to him, however. In his last affliction too he wished his own condition to instruct others, this time in the skill of dying. The many persons who visited him and recorded his final statements understood his behavior as the final demonstration of the Christian connoisseurship he had practiced all his life, a consummate example of meeting the King of Terrors with divine calm. Throughout his last illness and in his last days and hours, Benjamin Colman observed, "abundant gracious *Words* . . . flow'd from Him to every one that came about him," making "one of the brightest Accounts we yet ever had of *Grace and Peace,* and living Comforts in dying Moments."

But to Mather resignation had never come easily. Unlike his father, he had never been greedy to depart but, however beset, had found much of his life savory and devoured it, a voluptuary of time. Many comments

420

ascribed to him at the end (some smacking of deathbed hagiography) suggest a longing to linger. Often, Samuel reported, he quoted the text Thou that hast showed me great and sore Troubles, shalt quicken me again (Ps. 71:20), sometime applying it to the possibility of recovering his strength—but adding that he would be content to have the promise fulfilled at the Resurrection. Or he spoke of wishing to live at least long enough to complete some unfinished writings. And there was Lydia, she who had left him, still a "very valuable fish," he had called her in their courtship. Reminding her of their ardent devotions, he said, *"You and I must never any more retire and pray together, as we used to do."* But he told her to think, when praying by herself, that he at that moment would be singing hallelujahs before the same throne of grace, and he added: *"I'll meet you there as often as you please."*

With a boom "like a great Gun," the earth again shook and rumbled on January 14, a Sabbath, preluding not the vindication Mather predicted but a kind of vindication nevertheless, terrible in form. The next day two brothers, skating at the bottom of Boston Common, fell through the ice and drowned. They were young George and Nathan Howell, the two children of Lydia's daughter, offspring of the "monsters of ingratitude" who Mather believed had designed his ruin. They had been unfortunate sons of a "wretched Father," he wrote when taking on the administration of their father's estate, and he had resolved to extend over them "the Eye of my Care."

At daybreak two Sabbaths later the earth trembled again for a minute. Houses vibrated, rattling glassware and pewter on the shelves. Shocks followed over the next two days—the worst since the first quake in October, again sending people in great consternation into the streets. (Astonishingly, the tremors would continue into September.) The same day, January 28, the brethren of the North Church agreed to call a day of supplication, beseeching God to prolong the life of "Our Reverend and Dear Pastor." God, they said, "has greatly endeared him to us, and threatens his Removal from us by Death, which we would deprecate as a most awful Frown of Heaven."

Saturday, February 10, onlookers judged Mather to be in his worst agonies. In his last illness as before, he prayed to be spared from the torturous stones that had made his father cry for pity. Apparently he was, for Samuel described his condition as "a hard *Cough* and a suffocating *Asthma* with a *Fever*." He even managed to say, with a "sort of triumph in his air and accent," as Gee recorded his words, "And is this dying! This all! is this what I feared when I prayed against a hard death! Is it no more than this! O I can bear this! I can bear it, I can bear it!"

Sunday, as he had done throughout his last days, Mather dispensed blessings and charges to his visitors, according to their character and relation. The surviving accounts do not mention Nancy's presence. But Mather assured Sammy that he knew that his soul was in a state of grace. Instructing his son how to dispose of his private affairs and papers, he also blessed him on bended knee, saying:

> You have been *a dear Son and a pleasant Child* unto me, and I wish you as *many* Blessings as you have done me *Services* which are very many. I wish and Pray the God of ABRAHAM, ISAAC, and JACOB may be yours and His Blessing rest upon you. I wish that, as you have a Prospect of being serviceable in the World, you may be great and considerable, as the Patriarchs were, by introducing a CHRIST into the World.

When Sammy asked him what sentence or word he would have him consider constantly, Mather said, "Remember only that one word *Fructuosus.*" Although he had confided to Gee that his final views of Christ, God, and Heaven had been neither so many nor so lasting as in some former illnesses, when a friend asked what sight he now had of the invisible world he answered, *"All glorious."* Indeed he seems to have felt relief. According to Samuel, when Lydia tried to wipe his eye he said, *"I am going where all* Tears *shall be* wiped *from my Eyes."*

Monday was Cotton Mather's sixty-fifth birthday. Praying as usual with his family in the morning, he told them he had expected to die the day before, but would wait his appointed time patiently. Whether buoyed by his birthday or enacting his exemplary part to the end, he seemed to others in good spirits. A visiting minister was surprised to find him sitting up in bed with his glasses on, reading, and asked whether he was reading his name written in the Book of the Lamb; he replied, *"Yes I have found it,"* and turned down the leaf. When Lydia remarked that he was smiling at her pleasantly while she, at his bedside, was in tears, he said, *"Why should not I smile, when every thing looks smiling upon me."* A few hours before his death, which occurred on Tuesday morning, February 13, between eight and nine o' clock, he called for Gee to pray with him and said to him after the prayer, *"Now I have nothing more to do here. . . . My will is now entirely resigned to the will of* GOD." Someone observed to him that God had heard his prayers for an easy death. He answered, his last word was, *"Grace!"*

*

By custom, Mather's body lay awaiting burial for nearly a week. Meanwhile, Boston newspapers printed laudatory accounts of his life and death, and Benjamin Colman, Thomas Prince, and other ministers preached eulogistic sermons about him, assessing the human meaning of his life, and its importance to his flock and his colleagues, to Boston, to New England, and to America itself. Many of the sermons have the apologetic air, common to later accounts of Mather, of trying to do justice in limited space to someone gargantuan and perplexing. But all agree that Mather had been an uncommon person, a presence.

It was of course as a minister that Mather's colleagues most extolled him. He had been "the *first Minister in the Town*," as Colman called him, "the first in Age, in Gifts and in Grace. . . . the *first* in the whole *Province* and *Provinces* of *New England,* for universal Literature, and extensive Services." Since his youth he had given an illustrious public example of heaven-minded piety, having lived, said Thomas Prince, "in an eminent manner in the Mount with GOD." His eulogists recalled the untiring earnestness he gave, after much study and writing, to composing and delivering his thousands of sermons. Many recalled how he had zealously awakened the impenitent, heartened the discouraged, pleaded with all to come to Christ. "No more will he here *weep* over perishing Souls in *Prayer;* no more scatter the *thunders and lightnings* of God in flaming *Sermons*," Colman lamented, "No more is he to *weary* and spend himself, as we have often seen him wearied and *spent* for your Souls; never weary of his work, but often wearied in it." They recalled as well his indefatigable pastoral visits and innumerable consolatory personal calls on the afflicted or bereaved, the tempted and wounded. Nor had his concern been only for the North Church, but for the welfare and the civil and religious liberties of Protestants everywhere.

The ministers who praised Mather recognized themselves also as his beneficiaries. He had been a minister when the eldest of them were children, and before most of them were born, then had supervised their training, performed at their ordinations, obtained jobs for them, presided resourcefully over their councils. Gee recalled Mather's indulgent help in his own youthful ministerial studies, how he "bore with my infirmities; and helped me under difficulties: He quickened me to my work; and showed me an example: He instructed, admonished, and exhorted me as a father; while by his condescending goodness he raised me to the level of a friend and a brother."

Especially Mather's eulogists remembered him as the most learned man and the most voluminous writer New England had ever produced—the 388 works he published, the huge works he left unpublished, his devotion to science, his quick apprehension, tenacious memory, and ready invention. "He was a wonderful *Improver of Time*," Thomas Prince said, "and 'tis almost amazing how much He had read and studied—How much He has wrote and published—How much He corresponded abroad; not only with the several Provinces in the *British America*, but also with *England, Scotland, Ireland, Holland, Germany,* and even the *Eastern* as well as the *Western Indies*." Among Mather's works illustrative of his love for the church and its people, Prince singled out *Magnalia Christi Americana* "for the noble Care He has taken to preserve the *Memory* of the great and excellent Fathers of these religious Plantations, that was just a sinking into Oblivion." He also called attention to the ill-fated "Biblia Americana," an "extraordinary Work, that his Heart had been set on from his early Days, and has taken Him up almost *Fifty Years* to compose."

But not even Mather's lively and curious writings, the ministers agreed, conveyed the rich zest of his personality. Only those who had conversed with him knew its tang. Sought and welcome for his instructive and engaging talk, he rewarded all who came to him, the greatest man or meanest child, with some pertinent saying, some agreeable quotation graced with his own improvements, some anecdote fetched from his incomparable knowledge of the New England past, now irrecoverably lost with him. "How easy and natural did his vast Learning appear in every Company," Prince recalled, "How agreeably temper'd with a various mixture of Wit and Cheerfulness? The most knowing cou'd scarce ever leave him without knowing more, the most ungracious without some Impressions of Goodness, or any without a grateful Pleasure."

Among Mather's more general personal qualities his eulogists emphasized his passionate stamina and courteous charity, as well as his parental affection and power of resignation. "He seem'd to have," Prince remarked, "an inexhaustible Source of *divine Flame and Vigour*......Tho' fatigued in Body, never tired in Mind." Much of this energy he gave to endless projections to Do Good, abounding in generosity to the poor. Samuel praised his loving qualities as a father:

> ... how *kind,* how *loving,* nay how *fond:* We went into his *Presence* with *Delight* and never *left* it without *Regret;* His Company was so entertainingly *pleasant* and *profitable;* his *Temper* so free and open, and his *Concern* for us, for our *external,* but much more for our *interior* Welfare, so very great; and, in a Word, *his Carriage* towards us so *all-Christian,* and all Gentlemanly, that in our Opinion, it rendered him *the Delight of Mankind.*

Without mentioning Mather's torments under injury to his reputation and in the deaths of thirteen of his children, several eulogists remembered how as a testimony of faith he had suffered his awesome bereavements in silence. "Scarce any on Earth," Prince said, "have gone thro' such a great Variety and constant Succession of extraordinary *Trials.*"

It was of course not the role of Colman and the others to enlarge on Mather's many and much discussed faults. These his inner fears and historical circumstances make comprehensible but no less disfiguring. His submissiveness that would not grasp that at Salem people were being legally murdered; his meddlesome ambitiousness that stooped or strutted for petty advancement; his guile that wrote self-promoting letters under others' names; his vanity that scented out lurking slurs yet sensed no provocations in himself; his rashness that tendered spite as amity; his envy that sneered at what it could not get. Of this and what else in Mather was odious his eulogists said nothing. "Love to *Christ* and his *Servant* commands me," Colman explained, "to draw a *Veil* over every *Failing:* for *who* is without them?"

Among Mather's eulogists, Samuel probably came closest to identifying the overall achievement on which his father's future reputation might solidly rest. Might solidly: for in the popular panorama of the American past Mather still stands, like some limping Vulcan, in the mists of the country's history, from which only later emerge the more real and substantial figures of Franklin, Jefferson, and Washington. In a country that endorses democratic tolerance, reasonableness, individuality, and downrightness, this nebulous mythological Mather serves to symbolize what American character is not, or should not be—bigoted, superstitious, authoritarian, and devious. In its elements the conception is simplistic and inaccurate, while *in toto* one must look to cultural psychologists and historians of ideas to account for its gross distortion of so complex a man into a national gargoyle. Yet Sammy, in estimating his father's stature, provided part of an explanation: "*he alone* was able to support the Character of *this* Country abroad, and was had in great Esteem thro' many Nations in EUROPE."

Mather looms disfigured but large, that is, in part because he stands alone. Many of the beliefs attached to his name and scorned were after all shared by thousands of other settlers whose names few remember. But no other person born in America between the time of Columbus and of Franklin strove to make himself so conspicuous—strove, more accurately, to become conspicuous as an American. For he looked out eagerly from the New World on major intellectual developments abroad, aspiring to contribute to them by capitalizing on the limitations of provincial life. Unlike his father, who was also born in America and who won lesser (ultimately) fame, he did not hanker to live and die in England. The titles of some of his major works—"Biblia Americana," *Magnalia Christi Americana*, "Curiosa Americana," *Psalterium Americanum*—announce his affection for the place and his hope of putting America on the cultural map.

To speak very generally now, but with no intent of putting Mather in a nutshell: he was the first person to write at length about the New World having never seen the Old. Much of his career illustrates, for the first time, the costs and gains to America's intellectual and artistic life of its divorce from Europe. These costs and gains have been one and the same—a lack of standards or a freedom to create (depending on how it is viewed) which has often inspired works tainted by provincial crabbedness, eccentricity, and overreaching, but also often distinguished by their close kin, pungency, innovation, and grandeur. Some or all of these qualities impart the feel of the New World to work by many later Americans who have accepted or declared, and deeply explored, their isolation from the European mainstream—Herman Melville, Emily Dickinson, Walt Whitman, Charles Ives, Gertrude Stein, Frank Lloyd Wright, Jackson Pollock. The list might be extended (and challenged), and to be sure Mather was far more an artist of sorts than an artist. In his curiousness, epic reach, and quirkily ingenious individualism he was nevertheless the first unmistakably American figure in the nation's history.

*

Mather was buried on February 19, 1728, a cold and cloudy morning. The large number of people who gathered for the event from Boston and other towns made, said one contemporary, a "Vast Concourse Exceeding long Procession and numberless Spectators. Every heart Sad."

Taken from Mather's house on Ship Street near the wharves and harbor, his corpse was borne up Fleet Street past the Old North Church, where it was met by Joshua Gee, in deep mourning, and by the three deacons and the brethren of the church, who as a mark of special respect proceeded to walk before the coffin instead of behind it. Following the identical route that had been taken for the funeral of Increase Mather five years earlier, the procession moved along Hull Street toward the burial ground. On the uphill journey, Colman, Prince, and another Boston minister held down the funeral pall; some brethren took turns at bearing the coffin underneath, behind which walked Mather's family, in mourning, then Lieutenant Governor Dummer, the Council and House of Representatives, followed by a large train of ministers, justices, merchants, scholars, and other principal citizens, both men and women, including Samuel Sewall riding in a coach. "The Streets were crowded with People," the *Weekly Journal* reported, "and the Windows fill'd with Sorrowful Spectators all the way to the Burying Place."

The procession ended on Copp's Hill, the cemetery of the Old North. The level plain atop the hill had been, and probably still was, the site of a windmill. Although only about fifty feet high, Copp's Hill was one of the most commanding spots in Boston, affording a view of Charlestown and of a large part of Boston Harbor. Mather was interred in the large family tomb—the *"Cave of the Treasure,"* he had called it—together with his father and other members of the family. "It look'd very Sad," one observer said, "almost as if it were the funeral of the Country."

Immediately after Mather's death his pulpit was filled by the united ministers of Boston preaching a course of sermons. The North Church voted to continue Mather's salary (presumably to Lydia) as long as these sermons lasted, which was about a week; after that, the church voted £100 to Lydia out of its treasury, at the rate of £5 a month, until the end of 1729—five years before her death. Samuel prepared some of Mather's last works for posthumous publication and also began writing a brief but valuable biography of his father, containing a fresh advertisement to publish "Biblia Americana." Meanwhile his funeral sermon on his father, *The Departure and Character of Elijah* (1728), became the first of his own published works. In January 1732, after a probationary period, he was chosen pastor of the North Church, as the colleague of Joshua Gee; because of contention in the church he stayed only nine years, but remained in the ministry until his death in 1785. In 1762 he learned that his son Increase, also nicknamed Creasy, had fallen mortally ill of a fever in Havannah, only to learn that Creasy was in fact aboard a ship homeward bound . . . only to learn soon after that Creasy had indeed died. After divine services on August 15, 1776, he read to his congregation the Declaration of Independence and urged compliance with it.

Cotton Mather died intestate. The fact is surprising, for he had always been concerned about the plight of orphans and had often called on parents to provide for their children against their deaths: "Make a *Testamentary Provision* for them. Let your *Wills* be made, and in a Good order always Lying by you." Since he left no will, the power of examining and administering his estate fell to Samuel Sewall as probate judge. Sewall called on Lydia to appear in court, but she declined to act as administrator. Samuel petitioned to so act, but for some reason his petition was withdrawn. Sewall then assigned the power of administration to a Boston shopkeeper named Nathaniel Goodwin, who prepared an inventory in July 1728 as Mather's effects were shown to him and others by Lydia and the children. One of Mather's creditors charged that the inventory fraudulently omitted items of great value in order to avoid paying debts. He probably referred to Mather's library, his most valuable property, which does not appear in the inventory and which by some means or other descended to Samuel. Otherwise the only striking item on the inventory is five hundred acres of wasteland in Granville, Massachusetts, valued at only £36, to which Samuel also later laid claim. After some legal wrangling the estate was valued at £245, 5s, 10d of which the judge gave a third to Lydia, a third to Samuel, and divided the other third among the children of Mather's deceased daughter Abigail, and his one other surviving child, Nancy—the hapless daughter who had been burned in childhood, later caught smallpox and was put upon by Lydia, and afterward appears on the surviving records as "Hannah Mather, Spinster." Samuel and Lydia, however, signed over their shares in the estate to Nancy as well, for £30 and for what the quitclaim calls, without explanation, "diverse other good Causes."

But there was little to sign over. However luxuriantly he lived in heaven, Mather had not lived affluently on earth, and had lost much. What he left behind, as set down in the inventory of his estate, was dingy and mean: pie plates, lumber, a crosscut saw, three old rugs, four old bedsteads, two old oval tables, two old chests of drawers, old china curtains, old quilt, old warming pan, old standing candlestick, red curtains motheaten, broken stone table, broken fireplace dogs, broken chairs, broken pewter, broken spoons.

Documentation

IN REPRODUCING printed and manuscript primary sources I have retained the capitals, punctuation, and italics of the originals. But I have modernized spellings, lowered superscript letters, and expanded abbreviations. Legal documents, titles of works, and most quotations of verse, however, appear exactly as in the originals, with a very few deviations mentioned in the notes. In his preaching and writing, Mather apparently used several versions of the Bible, which sometimes makes his citation of texts seem erratic. For the sake of consistency in the text of the book, I have styled biblical citations in the modern fashion (e.g. Phil. 4:20), keyed to the King James version. But in the documentation I have reproduced Mather's own citations. I have reproduced dates according to the modern calendar, although Mather and his contemporaries used the Julian calendar, which began the year on March 25. Thus where Mather dated a letter "12 month 1682" I have used the modern date, February 1683.

I have indicated internal omissions from quoted material by an ellipse. But except for indented quotes, I have not included an ellipse for matter omitted from the end of a quotation. I am keenly aware of the possibilities this affords for misrepresentation, but I believe that in no case in the text does the lack of a final ellipse distort the meaning of the quotation. Where an omission has run over into the following paragraph of the source, I have indicated the gap by a double ellipse (six dots).

In the documentation below, I have used the first three words of each paragraph in the text, printed in bold face, to locate and group references in that paragraph. The references appear serially in the order of their appearance in the text. Individual references are separated by a semicolon. I trust these entries are full and clear, but their large number has made it unwieldy to group them in smaller clusters, or to document every tittle of information. Works specified in the text by date are not further documented in the notes, except in the case of *Magnalia Christi Americana*. Unless otherwise noted, all places of publication are Boston.

In the documentation I have used the following abbreviations:

A: "The Autobiography of Increase Mather," ed. Michael G. Hall, *Proceedings of the American Antiquarian Society*, LXXI (1961), 271–360.

AAS: American Antiquarian Society, Worcester, Mass.

BA: Cotton Mather's manuscript "Biblia Americana," in MAP (below), Reels 10–13; quotations identified by biblical book, chapter, and verse.

BG: *The Boston Gazette.*

BNL: *The Boston News-Letter.*

BPL: Boston Public Library, Boston, Mass.

CM: Cotton Mather.

CMHS: *Collections of the Massachusetts Historical Society.*

DI and DII: *Diary of Cotton Mather,* ed. Worthington Chauncey Ford, *Collections of the Massachusetts Historical Society,* 7th ser., VII–VIII [1912].

DIII: *The Diary of Cotton Mather, D.D., F.R.S. for the Year 1712,* ed. William R. Manierre II (Charlottesville, Va., 1964).

ERB: Extended Record Books, Clerk's Office for Suffolk County of the Supreme Judicial Court, Boston, Mass.

H: *Cotton Mather: A Bibliography of His Works,* ed. Thomas J. Holmes, 3 vols. (1940; rpt. Newton, Mass., 1974).

HCR: *Harvard College Records,* in *Publications of the Colonial Society of Massachusetts,* XV–XVI (I and II; 1925), XXXI (III; 1935), XLIX–L (IV and V: 1975).

HL: Henry E. Huntington Library, San Marino, Calif.

IM: Increase Mather.

IMD: Increase Mather, manuscript diaries, American Antiquarian Society. My deep thanks to Professor Michael G. Hall for allowing me to quote from his painstaking transcript of the diaries.

M: *Collections of the Massachusetts Historical Society,* 4th ser., VIII (1868; "The Mather Papers").

MAP: *The Mather Papers,* Part I (Cambridge, Mass., 1970; microfilm). References are identified in the notes by reel and frame numbers.

MCA: Cotton Mather, *Magnalia Christi Americana* (London, 1702). References are identified in the notes by book and page number.

MHS: Massachusetts Historical Society, Boston, Mass.

NEC: *The New-England Courant.*

NEHGR: *New England Historical and Genealogical Register.*

P: Cotton Mather, *Parentator. Memoirs of . . . Dr. Increase Mather* (1724).

PA: Cotton Mather, *Paterna: The Autobiography of Cotton Mather,* ed. Ronald A. Bosco (Delmar, N.Y., 1976).

PAAS: *Proceedings of the American Antiquarian Society.*

PCSM: *Publications of the Colonial Society of Massachusetts.*

PMHS: *Proceedings of the Massachusetts Historical Society.*

R2C: Manuscript records of the Second Church, Massachusetts Historical Society.

RS: The Royal Society, London.

SF: Suffolk Files, Supreme Judicial Court, Boston, Mass.

SLCM: *Selected Letters of Cotton Mather,* ed. Kenneth Silverman (Baton Rouge, 1971). Citations of this volume give the page number only; full bibliographical information appears on the cited page in the volume itself.

SML: Samuel Mather, *The Life of the Very Reverend and Learned Cotton Mather, D.D. & F.R.S.* (1729).

SPG: Society for the Propagation of the Gospel.

SSD: *The Diary of Samuel Sewall 1674–1729,* ed. M. Halsey Thomas, 2 vols. (New York, 1973).

SVW: *Salem-Village Witchcraft,* ed. Paul Boyer and Stephen Nissenbaum (Belmont, Calif., 1972).

SWP: *The Salem Witchcraft Papers,* ed. Paul Boyer and Stephen Nissenbaum, 3 vols. (New York, 1977).

W: Winthrop Papers, Massachusetts Historical Society (microfilm).

1. *Quantum Nomen! Quanta Nomina!*

Both his grandfathers: quote from MCA, III, 125; other information from B. R. Burg, *Richard Mather of Dorchester* (n.pl., 1976). **Cotton Mather's maternal:** John Cotton, "Gods Promise to His Plantation," in *Literature in America: The Founding of a Nation*, ed. Kenneth Silverman (New York, 1971), p. 36. Other information from A. W. M'Clure, *The Life of John Cotton* (Boston, 1846) and Larzer Ziff, *The Career of John Cotton* (Princeton, 1962). **Except for uncertain:** A, pp. 279, 280. **Increase improved his:** A, pp. 282, 285, 286. **Returned from England:** A, p. 286. **The first eight:** Walter Muir Whitehill, *Boston: A Topographical History* (Cambridge, Mass., 1959), pp. 6-7; Justin Winsor, *et al.*, *The Memorial History of Boston*, II (Boston, 1882-83), 496. **Although settled only:** "Copy of a Curious Paper," CMHS, 1st ser., IV (1795), 217; Whitehill, *Boston*, p. ii; *A Report of the Record Commissioners . . . Containing the Boston Records from 1660 to 1701* (Boston, 1881), pp. 65, 71. **The Mathers' house:** Arthur B. Ellis, *History of the First Church in Boston, 1630-1880* (Boston, 1881), pp. 42-43; Kate M. Cone, "Cotton Mather's Birthplace," *Genealogical Quarterly Magazine*, III (1902), 55-64; Chandler Robbins, *A History of the Second Church, or Old North, in Boston* (Boston, 1852), p. 216; IM, *A Sermon Concerning Obedience & Resignation* (1714), p. 39. **Virtually nothing is:** IMD, 1 Dec 1664, 27 Oct 1664, 28 Jun 1665, 25 Aug 1665. **These and Increase's:** A, p. 314; PA, p. 6; IM, *Pray for the Rising Generation* (Cambridge, Mass., 1678), p. 20. **While such nurture:** IM, *Sermon Concerning Obedience*, sig. A3; A, p. 352; P, p. 182; Benjamin Colman, *The Prophet's Death* (1723), p. 33. **Yet Increase Mather's:** P, p. 40; CM, *Early Religion Urged* (1694), pp. 83-84. **On larger, impersonal:** A, p. 284; M, pp. 96, 156. **But Increase's inwardness:** P, pp. 79, 66; A, pp. 297, 318; Colman, *Prophet's Death*, p. 36. **The years of:** R2C, p. 1; A, p. 287. **The brethren of:** IMD, 10, 11, 16, 19 Apr 1664 and 29 Jul 1664; P, p. 26. **Immediately Increase regretted:** IMD, 14 May 1664, 21-22 Jun 1664, 17 and 29 Feb 1664, 1 Mar 1664, 20 Aug 1664, 8 Sep 1664; P, p. 34; IMD, 2 Jun 1666. **What must have:** A, p. 359; CM, *Maternal Consolations* (1714), *passim*. **But these eulogies:** IMD, 4 May 1663, 28-29 Jun 1663. The speakers in these exchanges appear in IM's diaries as "C" and "M"—undoubtedly "Crescentius" and "Maria." See also IMD, 8 Apr 1664. **In the fall:** A, p. 287; IM, *The Life and Death of . . . Mr. Richard Mather*, in *Collections of the Dorchester Antiquarian Society*, no. 3 (1850), pp. 86, 77; A, pp. 288, 291; P, p. 68. **The possibility of:** A, pp. 291, 293. **During this period:** Annie Haven Thwing, *The Crooked & Narrow Streets of the Town of Boston 1630-1822* (Boston, 1920), p. 52; Robbins, *History of the Second Church*, p. 216. **Cotton later called:** DII, p. 723; Winsor, *Memorial History*, q. I, 548; Peveril Meigs, "Energy in Early Boston," NEHGR, CIV (1950), 83-90; John Bonner, *The Town of Boston in New England* (map, 1722); *Report of the Record Commissioners*, p. 154; *Boston in 1682 and 1699*, ed. George Parker Winship (Providence, 1905), p. 39. Cone, "Cotton Mather's Birthplace," dates the move in 1669, but this seems erroneous. CM remarks that the family lived in the new house for five years, and IM is known to have moved out of it in 1676. **By moving near:** A, pp. 297-98. **Not surprisingly, Cotton's:** PA, pp. 6-7. **In study and:** CM, *Corderius Americanus* (1708), p. 32; PA, p. 7 **By 1674 Cotton:** PA, p. 7; HCR, III, 329; CM, *The Angel of Bethesda*, ed. Gordon W. Jones (Barre, Mass., 1972), p. 231; A, p. 301. **Just when and:** *An Analysis of Stuttering*, ed. L. L. Emerick and C. E. Hamre (Danville, Ill., 1972), p. 12; *Stuttering: A Second Symposium*, ed. Jon Eisenson (New York, 1975), p. 55; SML, p. 26. **In explaining the:** Emerick and Hamre, *Analysis of Stuttering*, p. 128 *et passim*; Eisenson, *Stuttering*, p. 47. **Whether Cotton Mather's:** *Angel of Bethesda*, pp. 230, 226. **Christ was not:** *Angel of Bethesda*, pp. 226, 230-31. **Other**

problems than: Hamilton Vaughan Bail, *Views of Harvard: A Pictorial Record to 1860* (Cambridge, Mass., 1949), pp. 1-25; HCR, I, 1xvii ff. **No ampler facilities:** John Maynard Hoffmann, "Commonwealth College: The Governance of Harvard in the Puritan Period," Diss. Harvard (1972), p. 70; John Langdon Sibley, "Catalogues of Harvard University," PMHS (1864-65), p. 23 (IM's class of 1656 had eight students); *Robert Boyle: The Works,* ed. Thomas Birch (Hildesheim, 1965), VI, 653. **But in the:** SML, p. 4; [fragments of IM's diaries], PMHS, III (1855-58), 317. I see no reason to connect these threats by his fellow students, or general conditions at Harvard during Hoar's administration, with the "onset" of CM's stutter, as David Levin implicitly does in his *Cotton Mather: The Young Life of the Lord's Remembrancer 1663-1703* (Cambridge, Mass., 1978). Very little is known concretely about Hoar's administration, and even far less about CM's years at Harvard. Authorities on stuttering agree that it is extremely unusual for some particular, traumatic event to precipitate the impediment. For other arguments against making the connection see Hoffmann, above, esp. p. 308, n. 62. **President Hoar fared:** *Records of the Governor and Company of the Massachusetts Bay in New England,* ed. Nathaniel B. Shurtleff (Boston, 1853-54), V, 20; [fragments of IM's diaries], pp. 317, 319. **The change in:** [fragments of IM's diaries], p. 318; "Diary of Increase Mather," PMHS, 2nd ser., XIII (1899-1900), 346, 348, 349, 351; [fragments of IM's diaries], p. 319. **The demoralized atmosphere:** A, p. 302; Thomas Hutchinson, *The History of the Colony and Province of Massachusetts-Bay,* ed. Lawrence Shaw Mayo (Cambridge, Mass., 1936), I, 260; John Gorham Palfrey, *History of New England* (Boston, 1875, 1890), III, 215. **While Cotton was:** P, p. 77; Joseph B. Felt, *The Ecclesiastical History of New England* (Boston, 1855), II, 638; MCA, III, 199. **The war hardly:** A, pp. 302-3; MS letter, IM to John Cotton, 13 Dec 1676, AAS. **Increase frequently suffered:** IM to John Cotton, 13 Dec 1676. **Cotton Mather saw:** IM to John Cotton, 13 Dec 1676; A, p. 303. **Increase lost by:** IM to John Cotton, 13 Dec 1676; *Records of the Suffolk County Court 1671-1680,* PCSM, XXIX–XXX (1933), 782; "Diary of John Hull," *Transactions and Collections of the American Antiquarian Society,* III (1857), 242. **After the fire:** A, p. 303; Robbins, *History of the Second Church,* pp. 23, 216. **No record remains:** Josiah Quincy, *The History of Harvard University* (Boston, 1860), I, 591; HCR, III, 333. **Cotton later wrote:** PA, pp. 7-8; M, p. 9; Julius Herbert Tuttle, "The Libraries of the Mathers," PAAS, NS XX (1910), 348-49. **Cotton usually took:** PA, pp. 7-8; I. Bernard Cohen, *Some Early Tools of American Science* (Cambridge, Mass., 1950), p. 27; PA, p. 10. **Cotton came down:** CM, *Angel of Bethesda,* p. 50; PA, p. 8; SLCM, pp. 6-7. CM's 1677 sermon notebooks show him to have been in Boston virtually every week. **For whatever reasons:** PA, p. 10. **During his last:** R2C; PA, p. 10. **At the Commencement:** SML, p. 5

2. The Solemnest Work in the World

The ministry, for: PA, p. 15. **In his sixteenth:** R2C, p. 8; CM, *Religious Societies* (1724); SML, p. 27; R2C, 27 Sep 1680; MS letter, Samuel Bache to CM, 28 Feb 1682, BPL; M, pp. 624, 352, 606; DI, p. 34. **But that Cotton:** PA, pp. 15, 17; IMD, 6 Sep 1680; Chandler Robbins, *A History of the Second Church, or Old North, in Boston* (Boston, 1852), p. 216; A, p. 310; IMD, 11 May 1683. **Cotton feared being:** CM, *Addresses to Old Men, and Young Men, and Little Children* (1690), p. 105; MAP, Reel 3C, fr. 0454; DI, pp. 36, 20. **Increase's grave illnesses:** MAP, Reel 7, fr. 0012; MAP, Reel 3C; DI, p. 22; MS letter, CM to Richard Chiswell, 27 Nov 1683, Bodleian Library; DI, p. 63. **Cotton was correct:** R2C, 23 Feb 1681, 8 Jan 1683. **How intently the:** IMD, 8 Sep 1681; Massachusetts Archives, XI, 15. **Yet Increase did:** IM, *Practical Truths* (1682), Preface; SML, p. 27; A, p. 310. **Cotton also received:** M, pp. 611, 607; DI, p. 53; PA, p. 19. **Yet Increase seems:** PA, p. 19. **Cotton spent much:** DI, p. 9. **To discern whether:** PA, p. 19; CM, *Religious Societies,* p. 11; DI, pp. 79, 32; MAP, Reel 3C, fr. 0537. **Cotton also felt:** DI, p. 15; P, p. 27; DI, pp. 36, 93, 16. As his own son, Samuel, later wrote of CM, "while he was yet young he bid fair to be *great* for he *believed* he should be so: he *expected* it" (SML, p. 6). **The stains on:** DI, pp. 21, 5, 11, 34, 17, 39. **But having identified:** DI, pp. 28, 69. **This certainty that:** DI, pp. 6, 22, 91. **However brokenhearted, Cotton:** DI, p. 8; PA, p. 43. **Cycles of assurance:** DI, p. 35; PA, p. 44. **Such high attainments:** PA, p. 201; MAP, Reel 3D, fr. 0038; PA, p. 38. **Some means of:** CM, *The Retired Christian* (1703), p. 2; DI, p. 58. Until around the fall of 1683, CM apparently kept a diary similar to his father's, telegraphically brief entries on the day's activities, especially his reading. He found this a waste of time, however, and apparently burned the diary. The earlier years of his surviving diaries also are a revised version of some *ur-*Diary, a record of his spiritual struggle intended for profitable reading by his children and others in the future. **As if he:** DI, pp. 41, 37, 72; PA, p. 65; DI, pp. 29, 71; PA, pp. 41, 67; DI, p. 94. **Not even this:** DI, p. 62; PA, p. 50; DI, pp. 81–84; PA, p. 50. **As Cotton noted:** DI, pp. 37, 80, 81. **"Give my Stammering:** CM, *Religious Societies,* p. 18; Carol Gay, "The Fettered Tongue: A Study of the Speech Defect of Cotton Mather," *American Literature,* XLVI (1975), 451–64; IMD, 6 Sep 1680. **During the first:** DI, pp. 2, 49, 50. **Cotton tried as:** DI, p. 49; MAP, Reel 3C, fr. 0426. **In seeking the:** DI, pp. 16, 70; MAP, Reel 3C, fr. 0426; DI, p. 55. **In fact, Cotton:** CM, *The Angel of Bethesda,* ed. Gordon W. Jones (Barre, Mass., 1972), p. 228; MAP, Reel 3C, fr. 0326; DI, p. 67. There seems little doubt that CM's stutter was largely the product of his anger. One authority writes that where anger is inhibited by parental and cultural disapproval, fear and anxiety become attached to it, and to the child's feelings, thoughts, and words at the time he or she feels angry. Among other evidence of the child's distress is stuttering, "the inhibition of speaking for fear of revealing anger and its several associates." *Stuttering: A Second Symposium,* ed. Jon Eisenson (New York, 1975), p. 438. **Cotton seems to:** DI, p. 77; SML, p. 20; DI, p. 93; SLCM, p. 6. **Meanwhile, Cotton had:** PA, p. 54; DI, pp. 92, 132. **Cotton's deliberateness and:** Massachusetts Archives, X, 196. Among CM's adolescent draftings of other public documents see also Massachusetts Archives, XI, 8a and 21a. **And beginning in:** DI, p. 284; CM, *Angel of Bethesda,* p. 228. I do not intend the foregoing discussion as an Ephphatha, magically unlocking the secret of CM's personality and works. Both were obviously the sum of much more than his stutter, whose own origin is anyway obscure. Yet I do believe that his feelings about his stutter and his efforts to control it influenced many of his later non-speaking activities, and help explain many features of his writing—its voluminousness, repetitiousness, frequent long-windedness, and pervasive oral imagery—as well as his acute sensitivity to criticism of his style. Needless to say, these too were not the product of his stutter alone. In his book *Stuttering: A Psychodynamic Approach to its Understanding and Treatment* (New York, 1954), Dominick A. Barbara describes the working in some stutterers of what he calls the "*Demosthenes complex.*" His elaborate discussion defies brief summary, but is virtually a blueprint of CM's adult personality, and applicable to his written work as well. Such stutterers, Barbara explains, are often the children of persons who stress intellectual values and social prominence. Speech begins to dominate their lives, and they feel compelled to excel in something they feel is most lacking in themselves. "Through words," Barbara writes, such a stutterer "feels he can either triumph or succumb in relation to the world about him. Whenever he expresses himself, he should be able to hold the absolute attention of others and to keep his listeners in a constant state of enthusiasm and enlightenment. With words he should be powerful enough 'to build or destroy empires.' His speech becomes filled with feelings of utter perfection, boundless ambition, and rage at the slightest awareness of shortcomings or realistic inconsistencies in himself." In addition to being the wittiest and most intelligent, he must also remain honest, considerate, unselfish, and above all uncomplaining. Yet, understandably, he carries a hidden grudge, in believing he has been humiliated and shamed since childhood because of his affliction. And he uses these early hurts "to feel justified in humiliating, hurting, and vindictively triumphing over others in a compulsively indiscriminate manner" (pp. 103, 110). I believe this goes far in explaining CM's later strong feelings of envy, jealousy, and resentment toward others. **Some connection between:** Thomas Prince, *The Departure of ELIJAH lamented* (1728), p. 24. **Cotton's stutter may:** CM, *Angel of Bethesda,* p. 228; M, p. 379. **Cotton's affections and:** PA, p. 17. **Cotton says virtually:** the volume of John Cotton's sermons is at AAS, among the Cotton Family Papers; MCA, IV, 211; MS letter, Nathanael Mather to John Cotton, [ca. Jul 1685], MHS. **Among his numerous:** Josiah Cotton, MS account of Cotton family, Houghton Library, Harvard University; Josiah Cotton MS journal, MHS; SSD, I, 379, n. 14. **But the many:** Josiah Cotton, MS account; M, p. 251 *et passim;* SLCM, p. 19; M, p. 246; SF #1915 (23 [Jul?]) 1679). **From Boston Cotton:** SLCM, p. 6. **Within his family:** Theodore Hornberger, "Puritanism and Science: The Relationship Revealed in the Writings of John Cotton," *New England Quarterly,* X (1937), q. p. 513; MCA, IV, 211; MS letter, Nathanael Mather to John Cotton; Michael G. Hall, "The Introduction of Modern Science into 17th-Century New England: Increase Mather," *Ithaca 26 VIII 1962-2 IX 1962* (Paris, 1964), pp. 261–64; IM to John Richards, 10 Nov 1682, W, Reel 12. **The Cotton and:** M, p. 63; A, p. 307; Raymond Phineas Stearns, *Science in the British Colonies of America* (Urbana, Ill., 1970), pp. 150 ff.; IMD, 23 Jul 1683. **Cotton later described:** P, p. 86; Massachusetts Archives, LVIII, 133; Stearns, *Science in the British Colonies,* p. 156. **Although far older:** MS letter, Avery to CM, 10 Nov 1683, BPL; on Avery, see notes at Countway Library of Medicine, Harvard Medical School; George L. Kittredge, "Letters of Samuel Lee and Samuel Sewall Relating to New England and the Indians," PCSM, XIV (1913), 164; MS letter, Boyle to Avery, 6 Oct 1685, MHS; MS letter, Avery to Boyle [in CM's hand], [no day] Jul 1683, MHS. **Cotton also took:** M, p. 638; CM, *Elegy on . . . Collins,* p. 5; MAP, Reel 7, fr. 0011. **The beginning of:** R2C, 31 Jul 1684; A, p. 310. **But Increase still:** MAP, Reel 3C, fr. 0596–97; DI, p. 93. **Cotton's ordination was:** DI, p. 97, PA, p. 76. **On the morning:** PA, p. 76; DI, p. 98. **In this state:** DI, p. 98; DII, p. 415. **Cotton began the:** DI, p. 98. **Having spoken three:** MAP, Reel 3D, fr. 0042–48. **Cotton's ordination as:** CM, *Ratio Disciplinae* (1726), pp. 10 ff. **Now Increase and:** DI, p. 99. **The minister chosen:** MCA, III, 186; DI, p. 99. **Elevated into partnership:** MAP, Reel 3D, fr. 0047–48; SSD, I, 63. **Within about a:** DI, pp. 102–3; R2C, Oct and Nov 1685; DI, p. 114; SLCM, p. 17; A, p. 313; Kenneth Ballard Murdock, *Increase Mather: The Foremost American Puritan* (Cambridge, Mass., 1926), pp. 178–79. **Cotton preached extensively:** DI, pp. 109, 122; CM, *The Call of the Gospel (1686),* p. 51; SSD, I, 99; CM, MS sermon notebooks, HL, 11 Mar 1686. **Morgan perhaps sensed:** CM, *Call of the Gospel,* pp. 124 *et passim.* **Cotton's concern for:** DI, pp. 122–23, 132. **While pleased by:** MAP, Reel 3D, fr. 0047; M, p. 514; SSD, I, 94–95. **If Cotton's plush:** MAP, Reel 3D, fr. 0340; MAP, Reel 7, fr. 0477; DI, p. 90; IM, *A Sermon Occasioned by the Execution* (1686), sig. A3. **Especially Cotton feared:** DI, p. 126; Deloraine Pendre Corey, *The History of Malden* (Malden, Mass., 1899), pp. 266 ff.; DI, p. 125. **Cotton completed his:** DI, pp. 104, 107, 124. **Around his birthday:** DI, p. 121; *Genealogies and Estates of Charlestown . . . 1629–1818,* ed. Thomas Wyman (Boston, 1879), II, 740–41; Middlesex County Registry of Deeds, VIII: 501–2, IX:237, X:5; CM, MS sermon notebooks, HL, 30 May 1686. **Despite mounting spiritual:** PA, p. 89; DI,

p. 127. **The wedding, Cotton:** PA, p. 89; DI, pp. 127, 129. **From the first:** DI, pp. 131, 127, 133; MAP, Reel 4A, fr. 0021; DI, p. 131. **Yet as happened:** CM, MS sermon notebooks, HL, 30 May 1686; MAP, Reel 4A, fr. 0044; MS sermon notebooks, HL, 23 May 1686; MAP, Reel 4A, fr. 0049 and 0030. **A year before:** MCA, IV, 206. **It was about:** DI, p. 129.

3. The Glorious Revolution

The mentality of: "Diary of John Hull," *Transactions and Collections of the American Antiquarian Society,* III (1857), 236-37; John Gorham Palfrey, *History of New England* (Boston, 1875, 1890), II, 465 ff. and III, 88 ff. **The elements in:** IM, *Remarkable Providences* (1684; rpt. London, 1890), p. 228; "Diary of Increase Mather," PMHS, 2nd ser., XIII (1899-1900), 407; George J. Lankevich, *Boston: A Chronological & Documentary History* (Dobbs Ferry, N.Y., 1974), p. 11; "Diary of John Hull," *passim;* Peter Gregg Slater, *Children in the New England Mind in Death and in Life* (Hamden, Conn., 1977), p. 16; Lankevich, *Boston,* p. 11; SLCM, p. 7. **The Puritans' habit:** CM, *The Terror of the Lord* (1727), Appendix, p. 4; IM, *Heaven's Alarm to the World* (1682), p. 28; Williston Walker, *The Creeds and Platforms of Congregationalism* (1893; rpt. Philadelphia and Boston, 1969), q. pp. 410-11; M, p. 594. I am aware of the large body of recent scholarship that hears in these groanings a "myth" of decline. It argues that later generations of Puritans felt an exaggerated reverence for their forebears, and demanded more of themselves than did the earlier generations; they perceived a decline, the argument runs, only from the viewpoint of these unrealistic demands. I consider this interpretation wrong, but the question is too complex to discuss here. Generally, it seems to me that most scholars who speak of a myth of decline fail to make clear the standards by which the intensity and authenticity of religious experience may be judged. What the second and third generations of Puritans considered a decline embraced the social as well as the strictly religious; indeed the two were never for the Puritans separable. And the social decline was unmistakably real. **Among the chief:** Walker, *Creeds and Platforms,* p. 264 f. **Christian Israel felt:** "Diary of John Hull," p. 232; Carl Bridenbaugh, *Cities in the Wilderness* (New York, 1938), p. 72; SSD, I, 9, 4, 83; *A Report of the Record Commissioners . . . Containing the Boston Records from 1660 to 1701* (Boston, 1881), p. 139; Hamilton Andrews Hill, *History of the Old South Church* (Boston, 1890), q. p. 193; "Diary of Lawrence Hammond," PMHS, 2nd ser., VII (1891-92), 169. **The courts and:** *Records of the Governor and Company of the Massachusetts Bay in New England,* ed. Nathaniel B. Shurtleff (Boston, 1853-54), V, 59; IM, *A Call from Heaven* (1685), pp. 77, 39; Massachusetts Archives, X, 196. **But however alarming:** *Records of the Governor and Company,* IV, pt. 2, p. 166. **The royal commissioners:** *The Glorious Revolution in America,* ed. Michael G. Hall *et al.* (Chapel Hill, N.C., 1964), p. 10. **In their own:** Palfrey, *History of New England,* III, 39; *Records of the Governor and Company,* IV, pt. 2, p. 216. **Domestic and international:** David S. Lovejoy, *The Glorious Revolution in America* (New York, 1972), ch. 7 *passim; Records of the Governor and Company,* V, 495. **In the public:** MS letter, Nathanael Mather to John Cotton [*ca.* Jul 1685], MHS; IMD, 21 Jan 1684; Lovejoy, *Glorious Revolution,* pp. 154-55. **That New England's:** A, p. 313. **The following Monday:** SSD, I, 113-15. **Until the arrival:** *John Dunton's Letters from New-England* (Boston, 1867), p. 137; SSD, I, 116. **The full meaning:** SSD, I, 128. **Andros's seeming appeasement:** SSD, I, 135; Hill, *History of the Old South,* p. 267; SSD, I, 136. **The new government:** Lovejoy, *Glorious Revolution,* ch. 10; SSD, I, 143; *The Andros Tracts* (Boston, 1868), III, 124; Palfrey, *History of New England,* III, 554. **A possible means:** SSD, I, 140; A, p. 320; *Andros Tracts,* III, 124;

M, pp. 105, 102; A, p. 309; MAP, Reel 4A, fr. 0380. **Increase now openly:** MAP, Reel 4A, fr. 0412; A, p. 322. **About ten o'clock:** this and the next paragraph from A, pp. 322-23. **While Increase was:** this and the next paragraph from DI, pp. xxi-xxii (misdated 1691). **Other fragmentary evidence:** MAP, Reel 3B, fr. 063 [*sic*]; M, p. 388; SLCM, p. 13; DI, pp. 80, 93; MAP, Reel 3D, fr. 0106. Like others, however, CM was at first wary of Andros but not alarmed by his behavior. See SLCM, p. 19. **Exactly how soon:** Thomas Hutchinson, *The History of the Colony and Province of Massachusetts-Bay,* ed. Lawrence Shaw Mayo (Cambridge, Mass., 1936), I, 316n. **Andros had cause:** A, p. 331 (on the lost letters, see IM to John Richards, 17 Oct 1688, W, Reel 13); M, p. 531. **One month into:** *Andros Tracts,* II, 211; *Calendar of State Papers, Colonial Series, America and West Indies* (London, 1896-1937), XIII, 165; *Andros Tracts,* II, 211-12. On the authorship of *Brief Discourse,* see DI, pp. 133-34. **The Mathers' longtime:** *Andros Tracts,* II, 212; PA, p. 96. **The new threat:** Hutchinson, *History,* I, 317; Samuel G. Drake, *The History and Antiquities of Boston* (Boston, 1856), p. 481 f. **What remains of:** MAP, Reel 8, fr. 0069-71. **Four days later:** *Edward Randolph . . . 1678-1700* (1898-1909; rpt. New York, 1967), VI, 313; *Publications of the Prince Society,* XXX (1909), 291. **Whatever Cotton Mather's:** Lovejoy, *Glorious Revolution,* p. 240; Hall *et al., Glorious Revolution,* p. 50. **Cotton Mather spent:** in considering the authorship of the anonymous "Declaration," it should be remembered that the other Boston ministers were also present in the Council chamber. Randolph later said that these ministers, as a group, wrote some of the rebels' "printed papers," suggesting that the "Declaration" was the work of a committee (*Calendar of State Papers,* XIII, 47). Moreover, while no handwritten copy of the "Declaration" has survived, a related "Memoriall to explaine . . . the Declaration" does exist (MHS, Misc. Bound), written as an appendix to the "Declaration," and it is not in CM's hand. For these and other reasons, and lacking any evidence of Mather's authorship, I cannot accept Prof. David Levin's assumption that Mather wrote the "Declaration." See his *Cotton Mather: The Young Life of the Lord's Remembrancer 1663-1703* (Cambridge, Mass., 1978), p. 165. Lovejoy, above, makes no attempt to assign authorship to the document, wisely I believe. On the importance of the "Declaration" as a political document, see Theodore B. Lewis, "A Revolutionary Tradition, 1689-1774," *New England Quarterly,* XLVI (1973), 424-38. **All that can:** CM, *Decennium Luctuosum* (1699), pp. 27-28. **Whether Cotton Mather:** SML, pp. 42-43. **Cotton Mather seems:** *Calendar of State Papers,* XIII, pp. 47, 93; *Edward Randolph . . . 1678-1700,* VI, 313. **By then apparently:** Drake, *History and Antiquities,* p. 484; MCA, II, 45. **Having filled his:** Albert Matthews, "Notes on the Massachusetts Royal Commissions 1681-1775," PCSM, XVII (1915), 17. **Cotton Mather preached:** *The Wall and the Garden: Selected Massachusetts Election Sermons 1670-1775,* ed. A. W. Plumstead (Minneapolis, 1968), p. 135n; CM, *The Way to Prosperity* (1690), p. 30; SML, pp. 43-44; *Calendar of State Papers,* XIII, 95. On the debate over resumption of the charter and CM's position in it, see Richard R. Johnson, *Adjustment to Empire: The New England Colonies, 1675-1715* ([New Brunswick, N.J.,] 1981), pp. 94-106. **Whatever his doubts:** CM, *The Wonderful Works of God Commemorated* (1690), p. 43; Massachusetts Archives, XI, 45a. **Cotton Mather remained:** *Calendar of State Papers,* XIII, 384: M, p. 485; *Calendar of State Papers,* XIII, 165; MS letter, Myles to Board of Trade, 12 Dec. 1690, Phips Papers, MHS. **In July the:** *Calendar of State Papers,* XIII, 120, 111; CM, *The Present State of New-England* (1690), p. 28; SSD, I, 251-52; "Journal of Dr. Benjamin Bullivant," PMHS, 1st ser., XVI (1878), 105. **To eliminate France:** SLCM, p. 27; CM, *Present State of New-England,* p. 38. **The expedition was:** Palfrey, *History of New England,* IV, 51 ff.; SSD, I, 260; *Calendar of State Papers,* XIII, 369; *Publick Occurrences* (1690). **In this edgy:** Victor Hugo

Paltsits, "New Light on 'Publick Occurrences,'" PAAS, NS LIX (1949), 75–88. **Cotton Mather found:** SLCM, pp. 27–28. **Although this contrast:** PA, p. 92; CM, *Right Thoughts in Sad Hours* (London, 1689; text quotes Dunstable edition, 1811), pp. 21–22, 51. **In October 1689:** M, p. 672; MCA, IV, 211, 221–22. **Never able to:** CM, *Little Flocks Guarded* (1691), p. 7; CM bought the new house on 25 Jul 1688 (see Thwing card catalogue at MHS and Suffolk Deeds 17.1); the sermons survive as a bound manuscript of around two hundred very closely written pages in double columns, in MAP, Reel 7, fr. 0895 ff.; MS letter, IM to Richards, 4 Jun 1690 and 4 Jul 1691, W, Reel 13; DI, p. 147. **Much of this:** SLCM, pp. 25–26. **While awaiting his:** A, p. 338; DI, p. 113; Drake, *History and Antiquities,* p. 458n.; SLCM, p. 29. **The rumors came:** SSD, I, 291; DI, pp. 147–48. **Increase's four years:** MS sermon notes 1690–1694/5, AAS (in "Boston, Mass. Church Records"); A, p. 347; MAP, Reel 4B, fr. 0047 ff. **If the Mathers:** MS letter, Josh[ua?] Brodbent to Francis Nicholson, 21 Jun 1692, Phips Papers, II, MHS; DI, p. 148. **Cotton Mather also:** A, pp. 335–36; P, p. 143. **Opposition to the:** MAP, Reel 4B, fr. 0120; CM, *Optanda* (1692), p. 86. **Cotton also wrote:** CM, "Political Fables," in *Cotton Mather: Selections,* ed. Kenneth B. Murdock (New York, 1926), pp. 364, 367. **The charter's full:** MAP, Reel 4B, fr. 0051.

4. Letters of Thanks from Hell

To Cotton Mather: quotations in this and the next six paragraphs are all from CM, *Memorable Providences, Relating to Witchcrafts and Possessions* (1689), in *Narratives of the Witchcraft Cases 1648–1706,* ed. George Lincoln Burr (New York, 1914), pp. 93–143. **Mather's experience with:** CM, *Memorable Providences,* p. 123; R2C, 25 Jan 1691; MS letter, Sir Henry Ashurst to CM, 28 Dec 1691, AAS. The historian Thomas Hutchinson later wrote of the Goodwin case contemptuously, but he also remarked that he knew one of the Goodwin children, probably Martha, when she was an adult, and that she "had the character of a very sober, virtuous woman, and never made any acknowledgment of fraud in this transaction." Samuel G. Drake, *The History and Antiquities of Boston* (Boston, 1856), q. p. 496n. **The book had:** John Hale, *A Modest Enquiry Into the Nature of Witchcraft* (1702), in Burr, *Narratives,* pp. 413–14. **The linking of:** MS letter, Josh[ua?] Brodbent to Francis Nicholson, 21 Jun 1692, Phips Papers, II, MHS; Robert Calef, *More Wonders of the Invisible World* (1700; the text follows the 1861 Salem edition, published as *Salem Witchcraft*), p. 357. **Even ignoring Calef's:** CM, *Little Flocks Guarded* (1691), p. 9; CM, *Addresses to Old Men, and Young Men, and Little Children* (1690), p. 48; CM, *The Present State of New-England* (1690), p. 38; CM, *Fair Weather* (1692), p. 50. **Yet in preaching:** MAP, Reel 4A, fr. 0441; Willard sermons in Edward Bromfield's MS notes of sermons, MHS; MAP, Reels 3C and 3D. IM was widely read in pneumatology and fascinated by the invisible world. In England as a young man he spoke with a jailed witch, who confessed to him that every night for years the devil "had the use of her body." Edward Taylor Commonplace Book, MHS. **More important, if:** *The New York Times,* 23 Mar 1981, p. B6; H. R. Trevor-Roper, *The European Witch-Craze of the Sixteenth and Seventeenth Centuries and Other Essays* (New York, 1969), pp. 156–57; Frederick G. Drake, "Witchcraft in the American Colonies, 1647–62," *American Quarterly,* XX (1968), 697; "Diary of Noahdiah Russell," NEHGR, VII (1853), 59; IM, *Remarkable Providences,* in Burr, *Narratives,* pp. 37–38; CM, *Memorable Providences,* Burr, *Narratives,* pp. 131–34. **It must also:** sociologically, according to Keith Thomas, most witchcraft cases express "an unresolved conflict between the neighbourly conduct required by the ethical code of the old village community, and the increasingly individualistic forms of behaviour which accompanied the economic changes of the sixteenth and seventeenth centuries." Thomas, *Religion and the Decline of Magic* (New York, 1971), p. 561. That was true of Salem, where charges of witchcraft expressed antagonism between the village and the growingly commercial town. See Paul Boyer and Stephen Nissenbaum, *Salem Possessed: The Social Origins of Witchcraft* (Cambridge, Mass., 1974). **To us, the:** Gananath Obeyesekere, "The Idiom of Demonic Possession," *Social Science and Medicine,* IV (1970), 97–111; CM, *Memorable Providences,* Burr, *Narratives,* p. 121. **When read in:** CM, *Memorable Providences,* Burr, *Narratives,* pp. 109, 125, 119. **Mather and his:** CM, "A Discourse on Witchcraft," in *Memorable Providences Relating to Witchcrafts and Possessions* (1689), p. 4. CM's definition is close to perhaps the best-known definition of witchcraft at the time, that in Joseph Glanvill's *Saducismus Triumphatus* (3rd ed. 1689; rpt. Gainesville, Fla., 1966). Glanvill calls a witch one who *"can do or seems to do strange things, beyond the known Power of Art and ordinary Nature, by vertue of a Confedercy [sic] with Evil Spirits"* (p. 269). **Mather held the:** CM, "A Discourse on the Power and Malice of the Devils," in *Memorable Providences* (1689), pp. 2, 10, 4; CM, "A Discourse on Witchcraft," p. 6. **In their physical:** CM, "Discourse on . . . Devils," p. 2; Wallace Notestein, *A History of Witchcraft in England* (1911; rpt. New York, 1968), p. 286. **Mather's view of:** Moody E. Prior, "Joseph Glanvill, Witchcraft, and Seventeenth-Century Science," *Modern Philology,* XXI (1932–33), q. pp. 178–79; CM, "Discourse on Witchcraft," p. 16; CM, *Memorable Providences,* Burr, *Narratives,* p. 98. **Mather also longed:** CM, *Memorable Providences,* Burr, *Narratives,* p. 98; DI, p. 23; MS sermon notebooks, HL, 23 May 1686; CM, *Memorable Providences,* Burr, *Narratives,* p. 120. **Mather's determined defense:** Prior, "Joseph Glanvill," pp. 170–93; Glanvill, *Saducismus,* Introduction. Glanvill and IM corresponded. **In the style:** CM, *Brontologia Sacra* (London, 1695), in MCA, VI, 16–17, 20; CM, "Another Brand Pluckt out of the Burning," in Burr, *Narratives,* p. 313; CM, *The Wonders of the Invisible World* (1693; London, 1862), p. 52. **Cotton Mather's concern:** CM, "Discourse on Witchcraft," p. 25; "Mather-Calef Paper on Witchcraft," PMHS, XLVII (1913–14), 258; CM, *Memorable Providences,* Burr, *Narratives,* p. 102. Like other ministers, CM often denounced the widespread dabbling in amulets, fortune-telling, astrology, and other magical practices, inveighing against them not only as a form of non-institutional popular religion, but also because he believed in magic and feared its potency. In BA, he transcribed a magical practice in Latin and Hebrew so that "Ordinary Readers" would not be tempted to test it "and give the *Devil* a command over themselves" (section headed "Psalms Psalms"). CM often flirted with magic himself, especially sortilege. In the "Mather-Calef Paper" he claims to have personal knowledge of someone who could find missing objects by muttering a charm. See also Jon Butler, "Magic, Astrology, and the Early American Religious Heritage, 1600–1760," *American Historical Review,* LXXXIV (1979), 317–46. **The Goodwin case:** CM, "Discourse on Witchcraft," p. 29. **The surest test:** CM, *Wonders of the Invisible World,* q. p. 32; CM, "Discourse on Witchcraft," p. 9. **Pretrial examinations were:** SVW, pp. 5, 8, 10, 9. **A jury found:** SVW, pp. 10, 16; "Sundry Documents Relating to Witchcraft in Massachusetts," NEHGR, LXX (1916), 65–66; Deodat Lawson, *A Brief and True Narrative* (1692), in Burr, *Narratives,* p. 159; SVW, p. 16. **By April 11:** SVW, pp. 99, 120. **As these events:** DI, pp. 147, 152; SLCM, p. 35. Judging by the unusual gaps, brief entries, and messy script of CM's sermon notebooks in this period, he seems to have been ill much of March, April, and May 1692. See MAP, Reel 4B. **However ill, Cotton:** SLCM, pp. 35–40. **Much as he:** SWP, III, 749; George Lyman Kittredge, "Notes on Witchcraft," PAAS, NS XVIII (1906–7), 197–98; SLCM, p. 36. CM believed that devils could produce whatever shapes they pleased. In BA (I Sam. 27, 28) he argues that such biblical apparitions as the specter of Samuel that appeared to Saul were probably "*Cacodaemons,* which feigned themselves to be the *Spirits* of men departed." While the devil cannot use a departed soul for his purpose, CM explains, he can feign its likeness, having power to assume an innocent shape. By witches, it might be added, CM understood both men and women. See BA, Exod. 22. **Such further evidence:** SLCM, pp. 39, 37–38. **On the ultimate:** DI, p. 149; SLCM, p. 40. **By the standards:** SVW, pp. 45, 47, 51. **Bishop's execution alarmed:** italics reversed in quotations in this and the next paragraph. **Had this document:** Robert Calef, *More Wonders* (Salem ed.), p. 362. **Calef's very astute:** on Richards's close ties to the Mathers, see "Richards, John" Thwing card catalogue, MHS; MS document, "Cotton Mather, subscribers to salary," Curwen Papers, AAS; M, p. 494; John Richards Treasurer's Accounts 1669–1693, Pusey Library, Harvard University; SLCM, pp. 46–50. On CM's ties to the others see, *inter alia,* CM, *Memorable Providences,* Burr, *Narratives,* p. 94; SLCM, M, SSD, DI and DII. **And, in particular:** John L. Sibley, *Biographical Sketches of Graduates of Harvard University* (Cambridge, Mass., 1873–1975), I, q. 200; *Records of the First Church in Dorchester* (Boston, 1891), pp. 41, 93; inscribed copy at MHS; SLCM, p. 43. CM may have composed the very lengthy, adulatory epitaph on Stoughton's tombstone. See *History of the Town of Dorchester, Massachusetts* (Boston, 1859), p. 277. **Cotton Mather's relation:** DI, p. 148; CM, *Optanda* (1692), pp. 86, 14, 68. **The "ambidexterity" of:** DI, p. 151; SLCM, pp. 40, 37. Stoughton aside, the judges' behavior should not be too quickly dismissed as irrational. Some judges tried to square their legal principles with the facts of the case viewed in light of recent scientific knowledge. See for instance Burr, *Narratives,* pp. 171–72. **Indeed, Cotton Mather:** SLCM, p. 37; DI, p. 150 (the revision appears in the MS diary, MAP, Reel 1); SLCM, p. 37. **The court turned:** Brodbent to Nicholson; SVW, p. 13 ff. **Despite the cautions:** SVW, p. 121; SWP, I, pp. 376, 375, 374; Calef, *More Wonders,* Burr, *Narratives,* p. 358. **Considering Cotton Mather's:** SLCM, p. 40. **The confession of:** "Letter of Thomas Brattle," in Burr, *Narratives,* pp. 180–81; Calef, *More Wonders,* Burr, *Narratives,* p. 375; SWP, II, 689. **Cotton Mather may:** CM, *Wonders of the Invisible World,* pp. 102–3; SWP, III, 882. **Virtually all the:** SWP, II, 527–28 *et passim.* **But the most:** SWP, II, 522; SWP, I, 66; SWP, II, 647–48; SWP, III, 769. **To Cotton Mather:** see Norman Cohn, *Europe's Inner Demons* (New York, 1975), esp. p. 262. **On August 4:** SLCM, p. 40; "Diary of Lawrence Hammond," PMHS, 2nd ser., VII (1891–92), 163; CM, *Wonders of the Invisible World,* p. 38. **Like other Puritan:** quotations in this and the next two paragraphs are from the sermon as printed in CM, *Wonders of the Invisible World,* pp. 38–107. **Knowing his time:** *The Works of the Pious and Profoundly-Learned Joseph Mede, B.D.* (3rd ed., London, 1672), p. 800. Mede seems to apply his theory to Mexico and South America, but it became extended, perhaps by the Puritans, to North America as well. Many in England saw America as uniquely prone to pneumatological wonders. Richard Baxter, for instance, reported the view "That in *America,* it is a common thing to see Spirits appear to Men in various Shapes day and night." *The Certainty of the Worlds of Spirits* (London, 1691), p. 107. For CM's other versions of Mede's views see his *Souldiers Counselled and Comforted* (1689) and his French Preface to Ezekiel Carré's *Enchantillon* (1690). **Mather's sermon indicates:** CM's bafflement also appears in his letter to the witchcraft judge John Foster on August 17, in which he offers the judges, in about equal measure, encouragement, caution, and perplexity, and rightly concludes, "Sir, you see the incoherency of my thoughts" (SLCM, p. 43). **For the first:** DI, pp. 151–52. **The two surviving:** SSD, I, 294; Calef, *More Wonders,* Burr, *Narratives,* pp. 360–61. **Both these accounts:** SWP, I, 132, and II, 617; SLCM, p. 43; SVW, p. 75; CM, *Wonders of the Invisible World,* p. 159; SLCM, p. 40. **With apparently hundreds:** H, III, 1261, n. 12; *Calendar of State Papers, Colonial*

440 DOCUMENTATION FOR PAGES 111–127

Series, America and West Indies (London, 1896–1937), XIV, 63; Hamilton Andrews Hill, *History of the Old South Church* (Boston, 1890), pp. 286 ff.; P, p. 167. **Accustomed to putting:** SLCM, pp. 43–44. **While Cotton Mather:** Calef, *More Wonders,* Burr, *Narratives,* p. 367. **The next day:** "Letters of Cotton Mather," NEHGR, XXIV (1870), 107–8. **The same day:** "Diary of Lawrence Hammond," p. 164; SVW, p. 121. **Advice came to:** I have followed the text of *Cases* included in the London 1862 edition of CM's *Wonders of the Invisible World.* **The one was:** SLCM, pp. 45–46. **Around mid-October, just:** all quotations from *Wonders of the Invisible World* in this and the following four paragraphs are from the London 1862 edition. **Although the book:** on English notices, see George H. Moore, "Notes on the Bibliography of Witchcraft in Massachusetts," PAAS, NS V (1887–88), 259 ff. **These insistent disclosures:** on Baxter, see Drake, *History and Antiquities,* p. 496n.; DI, pp. 153–54. **Cotton Mather's book:** DI, p. 153. **But Cotton Mather:** PA, p. 131. **Cotton Mather did:** DI, p. 154. **About ten days:** SSD, I, 299; SVW, p. 121. **Despite the suspension:** DI, p. 156; SLCM, p. 47. **Because of Increase's:** SLCM, pp. 46–47; R2C; DI, p. 162. **About three years:** R2C; on the significance of CM's *Companion,* see E. Brooks Holifield, "The Renaissance of Sacramental Piety in Colonial New England," *William and Mary Quarterly,* 3rd ser., XXIX (1972), 33–48. **The crux of:** "The Commonplace Book of Joseph Green (1675–1715)," ed. Samuel E. Morison, PCSM, XXXIV (1943), 240. **The acceptance of:** SVW, pp. 121–22. **On November 29:** the account of Mercy Short's case in this and the following paragraphs is drawn from CM, "A Brand Pluck'd out of the Burning," Burr, *Narratives,* pp. 259–87. **These and many:** CM, *Wonders of the Invisible World,* p. 161. **The notion of:** William B. Hunter, Jr., "The Seventeenth Century Doctrine of Plastic Nature," *Harvard Theological Review,* XLIII (1950), 197–213. **Just as important:** DI, pp. 156, 152; SLCM, p. 42. **On March 28:** DI, pp. 163–64. In a footnote, the editor of CM's *Diary* incorrectly identifies this infant as "Joseph." His error represents a misreading of CM's handwriting. In the list of his children that CM drew up on the back of one of his notebooks in late 1713 or early 1714 (MAP, Reel 2, fr. 0061), the infant is plainly listed as "Increase." The editor also wrongly attributed to CM a child named William, based on a like misreading of the handwritten name "Katharin" in this list. **Mather may have:** DI, p. 164. **Mercy's "Wonderful Spirit":** for Mercy's admission, see R2C, 21 Jan 1694. **Such good angels:** Calef, *More Wonders,* Burr, *Narratives,* p. 346. **Mather began longing:** PA, p. 110; DI, p. 163. **Mather's prayers for:** CM, *The Way to Excel* (1697), p. 6; CM, *Meat Out of the Eater* (1703), p. 88; MAP, Reel 7, fr. 0297. **While Mather's views:** IM, *Angelographia* (1696), p. 65; *The Practical Works of Richard Baxter* (London, 1845), I, 625; Jacques Guillet *et al., Discernment of Spirits* (Collegeville, Minn., 1970; my thanks to Mr. Jeff Donnelly for introducing me to the subject of spiritual discernment); Richard Baxter, *The Certainty of the Worlds of Spirits,* p. 222. **However it risked:** DI, pp. 166–67; PA, p. 111. **Mather made another:** DI, pp. 171–72; **As if in:** DI, pp. 172–73; CM, "Another Brand Pluckt out of the Burning," Burr, *Narratives,* pp. 308–23 (from which also the quotes in the next paragraph). **In its other:** DI, p. 175. **It was probably:** this and the next four paragraphs from DI, pp. 86–87. On the question of dating this visitation see my "Note on the Date of Cotton Mather's Visitation by an Angel," *Early American Literature,* XV (1980), 82–86, and compare David Levin, "When Did Cotton Mather See the Angel?" *ibid.,* pp. 271–75. Some further supporting evidence for dating the visitation around September 1693 is the sermon CM preached on 3 Sep 1693, in which he remarked suggestively that "Of the beings of spirits there is manifest demonstration as Good Angels appearing to some" (MS sermon notes, 1690–94/5, AAS, identified as "Boston, Mass. Church Records"). For the translation of CM's Latin here I have followed that given in DI, with some revisions by Professor Robert Raymo. Here and elsewhere I have also reproduced the Latin entries in CM's diaries as transcribed by their editor, although the transcriptions would seem in a few places to be inaccurate. **However extraordinary, Cotton:** *Hallucinations: Behaviour, Experience, and Theory,* ed. R. K. Siegel and L. J. West (New York, 1975), *passim;* BA Cor. I. 10. **As a Puritan:** A, p. 345; MAP, Reel 4B, fr. 0362 ff. Hallucinatory experiences occurred often enough among Puritans to create notice but not wonderment. Several are recorded in the diary of the Harvard tutor Noahdiah Russell, NEHGR, VII (1853), 53–59. **Like the demons:** one authority remarks that the voices in the auditory hallucinations of schizophrenic persons are "fused with the patient's image of self" and "speak the patient's own thoughts." *Hallucinations,* ed. Louis Jolyon West (New York and London, 1962), p. 169; DI, p. 16. **Mather's need at:** CM, "Another Brand," Burr, *Narratives,* p. 321. **As Mather usually:** CM, *The Day, & the Work of the Day* (1693), p. 65; CM, *The Short History of New-England* (1694), p. 32; DI, p. 175; CM, "Another Brand," Burr, *Narratives,* p. 320; CM, *Meat Out of the Eater,* p. 35. For CM's further references to good and evil angels at this time see his *Warnings from the Dead* (1693) and the MS sermon notes, 1690-94/5, at AAS. **Mather's most vigorous:** a "Robert Calef of Boston Dyer" appears in an anonymous MS account book, 1702–1715, MHS (Ms-L); Calef, *More Wonders,* Salem ed., pp. 359, 113; Burr, *Narratives,* p. 326. **On September 13:** Calef, *More Wonders,* Burr, *Narratives,* pp. 324–26. **This "lying Libel":** DI, pp. 172–73; Calef, *More Wonders,* Burr, *Narratives,* p. 329. **Instead Mather indignantly:** this and the next paragraph from Calef, *More Wonders,* Burr, *Narratives,* pp. 333–39. **Mather and Calef:** Calef, *More Wonders,* Salem ed., pp. 116–17, 90. **Calef kept needling:** quotations in this and the next two paragraphs from the "Mather-Calef Paper." **The good angels:** "Records of the Cambridge Association," PMHS, XVII (1879–80), 271. **The counterdescent of:** R2C; MAP, Reel 4B, fr. 0249; P, p. 194. CM's nephew, Mather Byles, later recalled this rise in admissions as "a great Revival of the Work of God . . . at the Old No. Church." *Savage Papers,* PMHS, XLIV (1910–11), 685. **Both Mathers regarded:** *Savage Papers,* pp. 685–86. This episode and the one recounted in the next paragraph cannot be dated certainly, but both seem to have occurred in the fall of 1694. **A second young:** "Mather-Calef Paper," pp. 266–67. **However cautious about:** this and the last two paragraphs from PA, pp. 120–26.

5. The Parter's Portion

Six months into: MCA, II, 67; oath of Joseph Short and John Hams, 25 Mar 1693, Phips Papers, III, MHS; deposition of William Hill and Henry Francklyn, 17 Jul 1694, Phips Papers, V, MHS. **The governor treated:** unsigned, unaddressed "Letter from New England," 1 Nov 1694, Phips Papers, IV, MHS; SSD, I, 323 and n. **The unreliability of:** MS diary of Thomas Marshall, 1689–1711, MHS; CM, *To His Excellency Richard, Earl of Bellomont* (1699); DI, p. 302. **Cotton Mather's hope:** "Earl of Bellomont," NEHGR, XIX (1865), 236. **The succession of:** CM, *A Pillar of Gratitude* (1700), pp. 32–33; on the adaptation of New England to English political standards after the loss of the charter see Richard R. Johnson, *Adjustment to Empire: The New England Colonies 1675–1715* ([New Brunswick, N.J.], 1981), ch. V. **In this spirit:** the *Heads of Agreement* is reprinted in Williston Walker, *The Creeds and Platforms of Congregationalism* (1893; rpt. Philadelphia, 1960), pp. 455–62; CM, *A Letter of Advice to the . . . Non-conformists* (London, 1700), pp. 1–2. In England the union was short-lived, for the United Brethren fell apart within a few years in theological controversy. **Mather moved even:** DI, p. 149. On the growth of toleration, see G. R. Cragg, *From Puritanism to the Age of Reason* (Cambridge, England, 1950), ch. IX. **To show himself:** MS "Ratio Disciplinae," MAP, Reel 5, fr. 0130; CM, *Blessed Unions* (1692), pp. 76, 75. Becoming something of a spiritual statesman, CM also wrote at this time many works calling attention to distant religious persecution and assaying the current conditions of global Protestantism. See for instance *A Pastoral Letter to the English Captives, in Africa* (1698), *A Letter Concerning . . . Our Protestant Brethren, on Board the French Kings Galleyes* (1701), and *American Tears upon the Ruines of the Greek Churches* (1701). **While opening Christian:** on IM's opposition, see Niel Caplan, "Some Unpublished Letters of Benjamin Colman, 1717–1725," PMHS, LXXVII (1965), 116. **Yet in an:** MAP, Reel 8, fr. 0488–89; MS letter, CM to brethren of Marlborough church, 28 May 1702, Marlborough Public Library; SVW, p. 308. **In the same:** Walker, *Creeds and Platforms,* p. 469; "Records of the Cambridge Association," PMHS, XVII (1879–80), 254–81. **Mather also wished:** on May see also DI, pp. 313–15, 318, 323–24. **A more dolorous:** SSD, I, 378 and n. (the same shipbuilder called the charge "a Base piece of villainy that the man was no more Guilty of . . . than you or I was," *ibid.*); DI, p. 236 (on CM's agreement with the condemnation, see SSD, I, 379, where "Mr. Mather" probably refers to CM, as opposed to his father, "Dr." Mather); MS letter, John Cotton to Rowland Cotton, 1 Feb 1698, MHS; MS letter, John Cotton to Joanna Cotton, 6 Jul 1698, MHS; DI, p. 277. **In or out:** of CM's many writings on reform in this period (which make a valuable digest of his social views), see for instance *A Good Master Well Served* (1696), *A Family Well-Ordered* (1699), *The Young Man's Preservative* (1701), *A Christian at his Calling* (1701), *A Cloud of Witnesses* (1701?), *Methods and Motives for Societies to Suppress Disorders* (1703), and *The Day Which the LORD hath made* (1707). **Mather did not:** Richard F. Lovelace, *The American Pietism of Cotton Mather* (Grand Rapids, 1979), pp. 258–59; Robert Middlekauff, *The Mathers* (New York, 1971), p. 215. **It is more:** Henry Latimer Seaver, "Hair and Holiness," PMHS, LXVIII (1944–47), q. p. 16; SSD, I, 276. **In another dozen:** "Letter of Reverend Benjamin Colman," PCSM, VIII (1906), 247, 249. **This genial advice:** John L. Sibley, *Biographical Sketches of Graduates of Harvard University* (Cambridge, Mass., 1873–1975), IV, 122–23; Ebenezer Turell, *The Life and Character of the Reverend Benjamin Colman, D.D.* (1749; rpt. Delmar, N.Y., 1972), pp. 231, 5. **A Presbyterian Board:** "Memoirs of Rev. Benjamin Colman," NEHGR, III (1849), 112n. *et passim.* On ministerial identity, see David D. Hall, *The Faithful Shepherd* (Chapel Hill, 1972), pp. 223, 272. **The organizers of:** Henry Wilder Foote, *Annals of King's Chapel* (Boston, 1882), I, 89–93; Marian Card Donnelly, "New England Meetinghouses in the Seventeenth Century," *Old-Time New England,* XLVII (1957), 91. **In December, shortly:** on the change in psalmody, see *Records of the Church in Brattle Square* (Boston, 1902), p. 5; typed transcript of MS letter, Henry Newman to the Bishop of London, 26 Feb 1726, MHS. **In fact the:** DI, pp. 325–26. **As a first:** DI, p. 326; "Memoir of Rev. Benjamin Colman," p. 117; SSD, I, 419; MS letter, IM and James Allen to Benjamin Colman (but in CM's hand), 28 Dec 1699, MHS; DI, pp. 329–30. **With Sewall and:** SSD, I, 421; DI, p. 332; R2C; SSD, I, 422. **But the darkness:** DI, p. 333. **By coincidence, Increase's:** M, pp. 83–84; IM, *A Call from Heaven* (1685), p. 119. **Now, atop the:** DI, pp. 364, 358, 384–88. **Caught in the:** Bartholomew Green, *The Printer's Advertisement* (1700). **The publication of:** DI, p. 378. **All of the:** *The Letter-Book of Samuel Sewall,* CMHS, 6th ser., I (1886), 255. **Indeed Colman and:** Caplan, "Some Unpublished Letters," q. p. 104; on IM's opposition to the proposal, see Middlekauff, *The Mathers,* p. 225. **Mather proposed the:** "Records of the Cambridge Association," p. 270; IM, MS sermon (partly in CM's hand), 10 Jul 1679, Dreer Collection, Historical Society of Pennsylvania; MS "proposals Concerning the Recording of Illustrious providences," 12 May 1681, BPL; MCA, VI, 2. **Mather having begun:** Chester N.

Greenough, "A Letter Relating to the Publication of Cotton Mather's Magnalia," PCSM, XXVI (1927), 297–312; DI, pp. 400, 427 *et passim.* **As published in:** Samuel Stone to Wait Winthrop, 9 Jun 1696, W, Reel 14. CM's friend Nicholas Noyes of Salem also apparently donated much material. **What unifies this:** MCA, III, 13; Sacvan Bercovitch, "Cotton Mather," in *Major Writers of Early American Literature,* ed. Everett Emerson (Madison, 1972), p. 138, and see also Bercovitch's analysis of CM's life of Winthrop in *The Puritan Origins of the American Self* (New Haven and London, 1975); MCA, III, 11. **Typical of Mather's:** MCA, III, 176, 179, 180. **Virtually the whole:** MCA, "General Introduction"; MCA, III, 11–12, 74. See also the important article by Peter H. Smith, "Politics and Sainthood: Biography by Cotton Mather," *William and Mary Quarterly,* 3rd ser., XX (1963), 186 206. **Indeed Mather recreates:** MCA, III, 12, and "General Introduction." **Although Mather set:** MCA, "General Introduction." **Perhaps no feature:** Cyrus H. Karraker, "The Treasure Expedition of Captain William Phips to the Bahama Banks," *New England Quarterly,* V (1932), q. pp. 736, 740. **Yet Mather gave:** MCA, II, 66. **Mather had a:** MCA, II, 39–40. **Although Magnalia places:** MCA, II, 38, 68, 39, 42. **Like John Eliot:** MCA, II, 38–39, 41; Robert H. George, "The Treasure Trove of William Phips," *New England Quarterly,* VI (1933), 294–318. **The disparate voices:** MCA, III, 180. **For all its:** CM speaks of "Massy" writing in his *Manuductio ad Ministerium* (1726), p. 45; MCA, I, 31. **For all its:** DI, pp. 230, 169. **In several ways:** SML, "Preface," p. 3, italics reversed; DI, pp. 230–31. **Mather began the:** BA, Ps. CIV; the index appears in MAP, Reel 2; DI, pp. 170, 231. **Later chapters will:** Theodore Hornberger, "Cotton Mather's Annotations on the First Chapter of Genesis," *University of Texas Publications,* no. 3826 (1938), pp. 112–22. **"Let it not:** on Boyle and the corpuscular theory, see E. J. Dijksterhuis, *The Mechanization of the World Picture* (Oxford, 1961), pp. 40 ff. As early as 1689 CM declared corpuscularianism the "only right" philosophy. See *Early Piety, Exemplified* (1689), in MCA, IV, 211. **In many sermons:** CM, MS sermon on Eph. I. 2. (17? May 1702), Yale University Library; *Winter-Meditations* (1693), pp. 19–20.

6. Particular Faiths

Until May, 1702: DI, pp. 430, 449. **Cotton Mather's bodings:** DI, pp. 222, 264. **Such revelations would:** DI, pp. 198, 191; CM, *The Retired Christian* (1703), p. 32; CM, *The Faith of the Fathers* (1699), p. 3; DI, pp. 261–62. **Like many others:** Robert Middlekauff, *The Mathers* (New York, 1971), ch. 18; CM, *Things to be Look'd for* (1691), p. 46. **At this time:** "Problema Theologicum," MAP, Reel 7, fr. 0492–0539; IM's eschatological sermons are preserved in CM's sermon notebooks, MAP, Reel 4B, esp. fr. 0246–49; *Tulley's Almanack* (1699), n.p.; CM, *Things for a Distress'd People to think upon* (1696), p. 34. **Together with hints:** DI, pp. 316, 195; PA, p. 143; DI, p. 368. **If the caliber:** DI, pp. 204, 422. **With these many:** DI, pp. 188, 193, 206, 311. In 1701 CM published a now lost work entitled *The Good Linguist, or, Directions to avoid the Sins of the Tongue.* In part he wrote the work, he explained, in gratitude for "the wonderful Work of God, in restoring, and enlarging of my once-fettered *Speech*" (DI, p. 348). **One sort of:** *Retired Christian,* p. 27; PA, p. 102; CM, *Christianus per Ignem* (1702), p. 47. **Most of Mather's:** DI, pp. 185, 217, 282–83, 376. **Only two months:** DI, pp. 380, 382. **Mather's longing for:** DI, p. 307; PA, pp. 157–58. **The Christ-like birth:** DI, p. 336; R2C; MS letter, IM to [probably his brother Nathaniel], 4 Sep 1699, MHS; CM, *Parental Wishes and Charges* (1705); PA, *passim.* **Increase, Jr., became:** DI, pp. 336, 340, 345, 348. **Under the Phips:** HCR, IV, 174. **For years after:** DI, p. 305; Massachusetts Archives, LVIII, 187; DI, p. 308. **This time Mather's:** DI, pp. 308–9, 327–28. **The test**

of: DI, pp. 354–55. **But it, Mather:** DI, p. 356. **But by next:** HCR, IV, 173; John Maynard Hoffmann, "Commonwealth College: The Governance of Harvard in the Puritan Period," Diss. Harvard (1972), pp. 418 ff.; *The Acts and Resolves, Public and Private, of the Province of the Massachusetts Bay* (Boston, 1869–1922), VII, 255. **Perhaps because there:** DI, p. 360; HCR, IV, 146; *Acts and Resolves*, VII, 271–72; DI, p. 400; P, p. 175. **Both Mathers felt:** A, p. 352. **Abigail Mather had:** DI, p. 437; R2C, 25 Aug 1689; DI, pp. 405, 452. **A week after:** with the exception noted in the next entry, the account in this and the following five paragraphs is based on DI, pp. 405, 430–49. **By October, after:** CM's later remark about Abigail's prophetic dream appears in SLCM, p. 116. **Pleased with seeing:** DI, p. 445; *A Report of the Record Commissioners of the City of Boston . . . 1701 to 1715* (Boston, 1884), pp. 23 ff.; Ernest Caulfield, "Some Common Diseases of Colonial Children," PCSM, XXXV (1951), 24–25. **Within a month:** DI, pp. 449, 447. **Always busy, Mather:** DI, p. 446; CM, MS sermon on Eph. I. 14., 1 Nov 1702, Houghton Library, Harvard University; DI, p. 447; CM, *Wholesome Words* (1702?; rpt. 1713), pp. 4, 23. **Whatever Mather's fears:** DI, pp. 447, 452, 448. **Abigail lingered in:** DI, pp. 448–49. **Mather took pride:** DI, pp. 449–50; MAP, Reel 8, fr. 0218. **While stressing such:** MAP, Reel 8, fr. 0221; CM, *Meat out of the Eater* (1703), Preface to final sermon. **As the year:** quotations in this and the next two paragraphs from DI, pp. 448–57. **To the extent:** DI, p. 451; MAP, Reel 8, fr. 0219. **Or, Mather speculated:** DI, pp. 453–54. **Yet Mather's puzzling:** DI, p. 454. **Only two months:** DI, p. 457. **Mather never names:** DI, pp. 457–58. On the Maccartys see "Cotton Mather and Miss Maccarty," PMHS, XLVIII (1914–15), 135–38; Middlesex County Registry of Deeds, 19: 397; "The King's Arms Tavern in Boston," NEHGR, XXXIV (1880), 44. **As Mather pondered:** this and the next two paragraphs based on DI, pp. 457–59, 466–83. **Mather's heavenly messages:** DI, p. 457; MS letter, [Elizabeth Maccarty] to CM, 3 Jun 1703, transcribed in CM's hand on *verso* of her letter to him on 7 Jun 1703, MHS. **Susceptible to flattery:** Elizabeth Maccarty to CM, 7 Jun 1703. **Mather felt that:** this and the next four paragraphs based on DI, pp. 488–95.

7. Joseph Dudley

As the new: IMD, 1704 *passim;* on the gloves, see the MS letter, IM to unaddressed, 4 Dec 1704, MHS; IMD, 1 Jan 1704. **Increase conspired in:** IM, *Soul-Saving Gospel Truths* (1703), pp. 3, 6; IM, *Meditations on the Glory of the Lord Jesus Christ* (1705), p. viii; IM, *An Earnest Exhortation to the Children* (1711), "To the Reader"; A, p. 353. **The congregation Mather:** R2C, *passim*. IM speaks in 1714 of preaching to two thousand persons. See the typescript of his letter to William Ashurst, 22 Jun 1714, MHS. CM noted on one occasion that of the persons recommended by the congregation that day for particular prayers, some ninety were then abroad at sea. See CM, *The Bostonian Ebenezer* (1698), p. 77; on the widows, see *ibid.,* p. 9. The Mathers' salaries and the distribution of church donations are recorded in the MS Treasurer's Account Book in vol. 1A of R2C. Gifts of money to the Mathers appear in many different sources, for instance the will of John Richards (Suffolk Probate #2140) and SSD, II, 676. Richards left CM and IM £20 each. **Mather approached his:** DI, p. 319; on the number of sermons CM preached each year, see his annual lists in DI and DII; DI, p. 100; PA, p. 219. **Differing considerations dictated:** DII, p. 241; CM, *Brontologia Sacra* (London, 1695), Preface; CM, *Man Eating the Food of Angels* (1710), Preface. **Mather devoted equally:** on the length of CM's sermons, see for instance DII, p. 237, and CM, *Ratio Disciplinae* (1726), pp. 57 ff.; M, p. 34; CM's views on delivering sermons appear in his *Manuductio ad Ministerium* (1726), pp. 103–7, and PA, p. 77; DI, p. 531. **However demanding, preaching:**

CM, MS list of marriages, 1709, Dartmouth College Library; on CM's connection to religious societies, see PA, p. 224; on his deathbed witness, see his *Thoughts of a Dying Man* (1697), p. 4; on his nearly four hundred prayers, see DIII, p. 85. **Some at least:** MS letter, Elizabeth Atwood to CM, 2 Jul 1720, AAS; MS letter, Edward Goddard to CM, 19 Feb 1727[8?], AAS; DII, pp. 98–99. **But no aspect:** I here accept the number of CM's publications as thoughtfully computed in George Selement, "Publication and the Puritan Minister," *William and Mary Quarterly*, 3rd ser., XXXVII (1980), 219–41. Selement omits from his count reprints under new titles, fragmentary pieces, postscripts to other works, etc., and notes that if such materials were included, the number of CM's publications would reach 468. On CM's plan to bring forth one title a month, see DII, p. 462. In 1713, CM also published an *A, B, C of Religion*. **One reason Mather:** DI, pp. 539, 518, 548; CM, *The Nets of Salvation* (1704), p. 48; DI, p. 520; DII, pp. 14, 28; DI, p. 568. **The sheer number:** CM, MS sermon on Eph. I. 3., 23 Mar 1702, New York Public Library. CM's other MS sermons on Ephesians in this series are deposited at the Historical Society of Pennsylvania, and at the libraries of Yale University, the University of Virginia, Brown University, and Harvard University. CM's "Quotidiana" appears in MAP, Reel 7. **Mather also maintained:** DIII, p. 124; DII, pp. 74, 227, 212. **Mather alternately gloried:** DIII, p. 108; DI, p. 228; CM, *Winter-Meditations* (1693), Introduction; DI, p. 340; IM, *An Earnest Exhortation*, "To the Reader"; CM, *Utilia* (1716), Preface. IM often made public his dislike for elaborately learned prose. See, for instance, his *Practical Truths* (1704) and especially his Preface to Joseph Capen's funeral sermon on Joseph Green, published in Boston in 1717. That CM took his father's stylistic criticisms personally is suggested by his having declined contributing a preface to a funeral sermon in 1717, in part because he was "warned . . . in a very odd preface to a funeral sermon on Mr. Green, by a javelin thrown, as it was thought, with a particular aim at me" (SLCM, p. 250). IM in his Preface had attacked the preacher "*whose design is to set forth himself, to show his Wit and Learning, that would lace his Discourse with fine florid Phrases,*" etc. **In a variant:** MCA, II, 63; DI, p. 335. **Whatever his misgivings:** CM mentions the bishop in his *Grace Triumphant* (1700), "To the Reader"; DI, pp. 593, 545–47; DII, p. 162. **Unlike his father:** Benjamin Colman, *The Holy Walk and Glorious Translation of Blessed Enoch* (1728), p. 24; Thomas Prince, *The Departure of Elijah Lamented* (1728), p. 20. **Both Mathers had:** M, p. 482; Everett Kimball, *The Public Life of Joseph Dudley* (London, 1911), ch. I, *passim;* IM to Joseph Dudley, 20 Jan 1708, CMHS, 1st ser., III (1794), p. 128. **With the appointment:** John Gorham Palfrey, *History of New England* (Boston, 1875, 1890), III, q. 526n.; Kimball, *Public Life*, q. p. 14. **Particularly because of:** Kimball, *Public Life*, q. p. 52; Dudley to CM, 5 Jun 1689, CMHS, 6th ser., III (1899), 503; *Calendar of State Papers, Colonial Series, America and West Indies* (London, 1896–1937), XIII, 111, 120; Kimball, *Public Life*, p. 53. **Dudley's political career:** Kimball, *Public Life*, p. 67; on the scientific activities of Dudley and his son Paul, see Raymond Phineas Stearns, *Science in the British Colonies of America* (Urbana, Ill., 1970), pp. 455–72; on Dudley's activities in London, see the correspondence in CMHS, 6th ser., III (1899), 513 ff., where the quoted phrases appear on pp. 529 and 514. **Dudley began determinedly:** MS letter, Joseph Dudley to William Blathwayt, 29 Jul 1701, MHS; Sir Henry Ashurst to Wait Winthrop, 10 Jul 1701, CMHS, 6th ser., V (1892), 91; MS letter, Joseph Dudley to William Blathwayt, 22 Jul 1701, MHS; MS letter, John Quick and other London Presbyterian ministers to IM, 28 Jul 1701, HL. **Dudley also sought:** MS letter, Jacob Melyen to Abraham Gouvernour, 25 Jun 1692, Melyen Letterbook, AAS; Ashurst q. in Richard R. Johnson, *Adjustment to Empire: The New England Colonies 1675-1715* ([New Brunswick, N.J.], 1981), p. 336; MS letter, Joseph Dudley to CM, 10 May 1701, AAS.

Mather of course: SLCM, p. 65. **Like his defense:** Thomas Hutchinson, *The History of the Colony and Province of Massachusetts-Bay,* ed. Lawrence Shaw Mayo (Cambridge, Mass., 1936), II, q. 92n.; MS extract of unaddressed letter from John Leverett, 28 Oct 1701, in MS "Extract of Severall Letters from New England," HL. **However recent or:** Palfrey, *History of New England,* IV, 246n.; SSD, I, 469–70. **Five days later:** DI, pp. 464–65. **From the beginning:** William Pencak, *War, Politics & Revolution in Provincial Massachusetts* (Boston, 1981), pp. 45–46; Kimball, *Public Life,* p. 90; Philip S. Haffenden, *New England in the English Nation 1689–1713* (Oxford, 1974), pp. 123, 184; Hutchinson, *History of the Colony and Province,* II, q. p. 101; Palfrey, *History of New England,* IV, q. 253. **Dudley offended others:** George Keith, *The Doctrine of the Holy Apostles & Prophets* (1702); petition to the Archbishop of Canterbury, 23 Dec 1702, *The American Papers of the Society for the Propagation of the Gospel* (World Microfilms, 1974), Reel 12; Henry Wilder Foote, *Annals of King's Chapel* (Boston, 1882), I, 226. **Dudley's patronage encouraged:** Christopher Bridge to SPG, 19 Nov 1702, *American Papers,* Reel 12; John Chamberlayne to Joseph Dudley, ca. 1705, *American Papers,* Reel 12; Foote, *Annals,* I, 176. *Quid pro quo:* John Chamberlayne to Joseph Dudley, 10 Apr 1703, CMHS, 6th ser., III (1899), 537; SSD, I, 502, 475. Dudley's large bills for silver, wigs, and other such items survive at the Massachusetts State House, Boston. **At first the:** IMD, 1 Jul 1702; IM to William Blathwayt, 6 Mar 1705, HCR, IV, 209. Christopher Bridge, one of the ministers at King's Chapel, wrote home: "you cannot think how very industrious both the Mathers have been in opposing this design [of opening chapels outside Boston]. They have preached and prayed against it, and have treated [severely?] with many of them that come to hear me" (to SPG, 19 Nov 1702). **By contrast, Cotton:** CM, *The Pourtraiture of a Good Man* (1702), pp. 21–22; Palfrey, *History of New England,* IV, 248. **Mather and Dudley:** MS letter, Joseph Dudley to CM, 25 Dec 1706, AAS; MS letter, Joseph Dudley [unaddressed but certainly to CM], 16 Jan 1706, MHS. **While playing now-you-see-it-now-you-don't:** SLCM, p. 70; on the rumored plot, see MS deposition of Joshua Gee, 21 Sep 1702, BPL; Ashurst letters in CMHS, 6th ser., III (1899), 324 ff. **Mather's main choice:** DIII, p. 72; SLCM, pp. 68, 70, 71. **This hint of:** on the Deerfield massacre, see SSD, I, 498 and n.; on the costs of the war, see *Commonwealth History of Massachusetts,* ed. Albert Bushnell Hart *et al.* (1928; rpt. New York, 1966), II, 75 ff. **That Dudley's handling:** on Dudley's wartime efforts see the correspondence in CMHS, 6th ser., III (1899), *passim;* on the new fortifications see Massachusetts Archives, 244. **Nevertheless, in the:** DI, p. 565; Palfrey, *History of New England,* IV, q. 302. **Mather and Sir:** SLCM, p. 73; John Winthrop to Fitz-John Winthrop, [no day] Jul 1707, CMHS, 6th ser., III (1899), 388. **The new accusations:** SSD, I, 576; Palfrey, *History of New England,* IV, q. 303. **Dudley's remarkable comeback:** SLCM, pp. 75–76. **The justness of:** Kimball, *Public Life,* p. 187; SSD, I, 578, 587; John Chamberlayne to Joseph Dudley, 16 Dec 1702, CMHS, 6th ser., III (1899), 534. **In the added:** SLCM, p. 105; SSD, I, 573. CM himself had been nominated for college president by the House in 1703, but the Overseers replied that they could not accept a president "Named by that House." See *Calendar of State Papers,* XXI, 256. Most writers on CM have assumed that at the time Leverett was chosen he wished the presidency for himself. But no evidence exists that at this time he, any more than his father, desired to trade Boston for Cambridge. **But the man:** MS letter, CM to unaddressed, 7 Oct 1707, Pusey Library, Harvard University. **In behalf of:** Hoffmann, "Commonwealth College," q. p. 461. Leverett in fact is viewed as a rather conservative man concerned with reviving disused academic traditions, in Arthur D. Kaledin, "The Mind of John Leverett," Diss. Harvard (1965). **Yet Mather's view:** MS letter (typed transcript), Henry Newman to _____ Taylor, 29 Mar 1714, MHS; on Leverett's connection to the SPG see

American Papers, Reel 12; Henry Ashurst to Gurdon Saltonstall, 27 Jun 1709, CMHS, 6th ser., V (1892), 196; Henry Ashurst to IM, 10 Oct 1709, CMHS, 6th ser., V (1892), 199. **In one of:** *The Acts and Resolves, Public and Private, of the Province of the Massachusetts Bay* (Boston, 1869–1922), VIII, 796; photostated MS letter, CM to unaddressed, 7 Oct 1707, MHS. **However Dudley obtained:** Leo M. Kaiser, " 'We Are All Filled with the Greatest Hope . . . ' An Installation Speech of Governor Joseph Dudley," *Harvard Library Bulletin,* XXVII (1979), 443–44. **For Mather, who:** the account of CM's letter in this and the next two paragraphs is drawn from SLCM, pp. 77–82. **Taken aback by:** Joseph Dudley to CM, 3 Feb 1708, CMHS, 1st ser., III (1794), 135–37; SSD, I, 586–87. **Dudley's stiff personal:** I have followed the text of Dudley's *Modest Inquiry* in CMHS, 5th ser., VI (1879), 65–95. **Later generations can:** CM's superb bibliographer, Thomas J. Holmes, accepted the whole of the *Deplorable State* as his, but large portions of it seem to me both not high-toned enough and overly factual to be by him; DII, p. 15; SSD, II, 627, 663. IM may have been among the North End ministers who dined with Dudley, for he wrote later in the year that he had no personal quarrel with the governor. "He treats me with all Respect, calling me his Spiritual Father" (HCR, IV, 229). IM seems to have remained amicable with Leverett as well. **For Mather, the:** DII, p. 146. **Pranks had often:** PA, p. 183; DII, p. 139; DIII, p. 59; DII, pp. 216–17. **Abuse issued from:** John Winthrop to CM, *ca.* 1725, CMHS, 6th ser., V (1892), 428; SLCM, p. 32. **Mather of course:** SLCM, p. 72; DII, p. 105; Register of Diplomas and MS Faculty Minutes (GUA 21320, 26632), University of Glasgow (for this information I am indebted to my fine graduate student Patricia Thompson; the degree was sent to CM together with letters from the Principal of the school and the Dean of Faculty); HCR, IV, 244; MS letter, CM to Principal John Stirling, *ca.* 1712 (beginning "Most Reverend Sir. Every opportunity of addressing you"), National Library of Scotland; for one such letter of congratulations see the MS letter, Thomas Reynolds to CM, 19 Jun 1711, MHS. **Inwardly Mather always:** DII, pp. 63–64, 77. **But however guilty:** CM, *To the . . . Professors, of the Renowned University of Glasgow* (1710); MS letter, CM to Principal John Stirling, 21 Aug 1713, National Library of Scotland; *The Correspondence of the Rev. Robert Wodrow,* ed. Thomas M'Crie (Edinburgh, 1843), II, 504. **However honored abroad:** *Letter-Book of Samuel Sewall,* CMHS, 6th ser., I (1886), 407; SSD, II, 645–46; the jury message was apparently printed in BNL, 18 Dec 1710, but unfortunately no copy of this issue has survived. See Sewall's *Letter-Book,* p. 408. Unfortunately also, I am unable to identify "Facetious George" in the verses, although the name may refer to John George, the husband of the woman who later became CM's third wife. **The question of:** CM's letter appears in HCR, IV, 244; MS diary of John Leverett, 16 May 1712 and Jun 1712, Pusey Library, Harvard University. **The addition did:** DIII, pp. 44, 32. **Within a year:** A, p. 359; DII, pp. 195, 213. **Publicly forbearing, Mather:** DII, p. 194; "Autobiography of the Rev. John Barnard," CMHS, 3rd ser., V (1836), 214–15. IM's instincts may have been sound, for Barnard later donated money to the new Anglican chapel in Marblehead. See Thomas C. Barrow, "Church Politics in Marblehead, 1715," *Essex Institute Historical Collections,* XCVIII (1962), 121–27. **At Webb's ordination:** SSD, II, 772.

8. *Bonifacius*

"The Minister's *Tongue*": BA, James III.1; SSD, I, 455. **With unrelenting, sometimes:** DIII, p. 39; DII, p. 204; DI, p. 333; CM, *Golden Curb for the Mouth* (1707; rpt. 1709, which text I have followed); CM, *The Sad Effects of Sin* (1713), pp. 49–50; CM, *Faithful Warnings* (1704). p. 33. **In whole works:** CM, *The Right Way to Shake off a Viper* (London, 1711; rpt. Boston, 1720, which text I have followed), pp. 48, 15;

SML, p. 65; DIII, p. 67. **In his mighty:** for CM's notes in 1684 on one sermon by IM concerning Doing Good, see MAP, Reel 3C, fr. 0533; CM, undated MS sermon on Col. IV. 5., *ca.* 1685, Brown University Library; PA, p. 217. **Yet Mather's acts:** DII, pp. 26, 126, CM, *Desiderius* (1719), p. 7; MAP, Reel 8, fr. 0146. **How fully Mather:** CM, *The Minister* (1722), p. 14; DII, pp. 41–42, 263. **Mather's numberless acts:** DI, p. 518; DII for 1711, pp. 93, 148, 151 *et passim; A Report of the Record Commissioners of the City of Boston . . . 1701 to 1715* (Boston, 1884), p. 102; PA, p. 229. **Mather's program for:** DII, p. 23. The discussion of Pietism which follows is indebted to Dale W. Brown, *Understanding Pietism* (Grand Rapids, Mich., 1978); F. Ernest Stoeffler, *German Pietism During the Eighteenth Century* (Leiden, 1973); F. Ernest Stoeffler, *The Rise of Evangelical Pietism* (Leiden, 1971). **Some more personal:** CM, *The Echo's of Devotion* (1716), p. 11; John Arndt, *True Christianity,* trans. William Boehm (Boston, 1809), pp. xiii, 462, 247. When CM first read Arndt is uncertain. Anthony Boehm sent him an English translation of *True Christianity* in 1716. See MS letter, Boehm to CM, 28 May 1716, AAS. But CM mentions the work as early as *Nuncia Bona,* below. **One other side:** CM, *Man Eating the Food of Angels* (1710), p. 63; Kuno Francke, "The Beginning of Cotton Mather's Correspondence with August Hermann Francke," *Philological Quarterly,* V (1926), 193–95. **Mather publicized Francke's:** I have followed the text of *Nuncia Bona* in Kuno Francke, "Further Documents Concerning Cotton Mather and August Hermann Francke," *Americana Germanica,* I (New York, 1897), 54–66. **The impact of:** on Pietist references to *Bonifacius,* see the MS letter, Anthony Boehm to CM, 19 Mar 1717, AAS, wherein Boehm notes that to make CM's work known in Germany he has inserted a passage from *Bonifacius* in some historical collections printed at Halle in High Dutch. In discussing *Bonifacius* I have followed the edition by David Levin (Cambridge, Mass., 1966). **In recognizing the:** on CM's place in the history of American philanthropy, see Robert H. Bremner, *American Philanthropy* (Chicago, 1960), pp. 12–14; *The Complete Works of Benjamin Franklin,* ed. John Bigelow, VIII (New York, 1888), 484. **Besides its value:** for other works of the period in which CM explains the propriety of flaunting one's authorship, see the prefaces to *Christianity Demonstrated* (1710) and *Memorials of Early Piety* (1711). **Brazened by Doing:** DI, pp. 563–64, 570. **After advertising "Biblia:** DII, p. 162; SLCM, p. 176. **Namma [etc.]. Christianizing the:** MCA, III, 193; CM, *Another Tongue brought in* (1707), p. 2; CM, *The Nets of Salvation* (1704), p. 35. **In converting the:** CM, *Souldiers Counselled and Comforted* (1689), p. 28; MCA, III, 191–92; CM, *Decennium Luctuosum* (1699), p. 154; CM, *The Way to Prosperity* (1690), in *The Wall and the Garden: Selected Massachusetts Election Sermons 1670–1775,* ed. A.W. Plumstead (Minneapolis, 1968), p. 133. **More than that:** CM, *Memorable Providences* (1689), in *Narratives of the Witchcraft Cases 1648–1706,* ed. George Lincoln Burr (New York, 1914), p. 99; CM, *Souldiers Counselled and Comforted,* p. 31; BA, II Kings 1; *The Works of The Pious and Profoundly-Learned Joseph Mede, B.D.* (3rd ed. London, 1672), p. 800; Higginson quoted in CM, *Wonders of the Invisible World* (1693; London, 1862), p. 160; CM, *Decennium Luctuosum,* p. 103. **In hopes of:** on the New England Company, see William Kellaway, *The New England Company 1649–1776* (New York, 1962), and Frederick L. Weis, "The New England Company of 1649 and its Missionary Enterprises," PCSM, XXXVIII (1959), 134–218; on the choice of CM as a commissioner, see *Letterbook, 1688–1761, of the Company for the Propagation of the Gospel in New England,* ed. Vesta Lee Gordon, University of Virginia Library Microfilm Publications #8 (Charlottesville, 1969), p. 25; on the Indian youth, see MS letter, CM to William Ashurst, 7 Sep 1714, HL. **Mather's involvement in:** SSD, II, 621–22; *Letter-Book of Samuel Sewall,* CMHS, 6th ser., I (1886), 400–3 (Sewall's note to this letter seems to identify these views as CM's);

SLCM, p. 27; on the difficulties of the London printers, see *Letterbook . . . of the Company,* p. 126. **Mather also personally:** SLCM, p. 127; DIII, p. 54; MS letter, CM to William Ashurst, 7 Apr 1713; HL; SLCM, p. 152; CM, *Just Commemorations* (1715), p. 56. **Mather and the:** *Letterbook . . . of the Company,* pp. 71-72; *SPG Minute Books,* Lambeth Palace Library (microfilm edition, 1974), 19 Oct 1705; John Chamberlayne to William Ashurst, 23 Jan 1706, in *The American Papers of the Society for the Propagation of the Gospel* (World Microfilms, 1974), Reel 12. **Mather generally approved:** MS letter, Thomas Reynolds to CM, 9 Jun 1711 (but containing CM's letter of 1706), MHS; DII, p. 416. **Mather received no:** William Ashurst to Samuel Sewall, 3 May 1709, *American Papers,* Reel 12. **Writing from a:** CM speaks of his design for the work in DI, p. 271. **A final, outstandingly:** DII, p. 85-86. **Founded around 1660:** on the Royal Society, see Dorothy Stimson, *Scientists and Amateurs: A History of the Royal Society* (New York, 1948), and Raymond Phineas Stearns, "Colonial Fellows of the Royal Society of London, 1661-1788," *William and Mary Quarterly,* 3rd ser., III (1946), 208-68; SLCM, p. 175. **In addition to:** DII, p. 266; the drawings appear in CM's MS communication to Richard Waller, 25 Nov 1712, RS; MS communication ("Uncommon Dentition"), CM to Dr. John Woodward (but not in CM's hand), 30 Sep [1724], RS; SLCM, pp. 119-20. On dates and other bibliographical issues concerning "Curiosa Americana" I have followed George Lyman Kittredge, "Cotton Mather's Communications to the Royal Society," PAAS, NS XXVI (1916), 18-57. **The weakness was:** SLCM, p. 135; CM to Waller, 25 Nov 1712. **In terms of:** MS draft communication ("A Triton"), CM to Dr. John Woodward, 5 Jul 1716, MHS: Kittredge, "Cotton Mather's Communications," *passim.* **Mather collected his:** Kittredge, "Cotton Mather's Communications," *passim.* **Mather's favorite source:** M, pp. 442, 421; CM, *Hades Look'd into* (1717), p. 40; on rubila, see IM to John Winthrop, 23 Jun 1718, W, Reel 19, and Winthrop Commonplace Book, W, Reel 39. A large part of the second John Winthrop's library survives at the New York Academy of Medicine. See Ronald Sterne Wilkinson, "The Alchemical Library of John Winthrop, Jr., (1606-1676), and his Descendants in Colonial America," *Ambix,* II (1963), 33-51. **Mather frequently praised:** John Winthrop to Fitz-John Winthrop, CMHS, 6th ser., III (1899), 333-34; M, pp. 427, 417; SLCM, pp. 245-48; MS letter, John Winthrop to CM, 29 Dec 1719, MHS. **Mather's letters to:** on the plants, see CM's letters to the naturalist James Petiver, SLCM, pp. 216-19, and Raymond Phineas Stearns, "James Petiver Promoter of Natural Science, c. 1663-1718," PAAS, NS LXII (1952), 243-365; on the piece-of-eight, see MS draft communication ("A Singular Lime-stone"), CM to Dr. John Woodward, 24 Sep 1716, RS. **The first series:** in the account of the first series I have followed the MS versions at RS; on the reported merman, see NEC, 16-23 Apr 1726; on the bass, see BG, 17-24 Feb 1724; on the waterspout, see *The New York Times,* 11 July 1979, p. A18. **But the very:** on the tendency of natural religion to displace Christianity, see John Dillenberger, "The Apologetic Defence of Christianity," in *Science and Religious Belief,* ed. C.A. Russell (London, 1973), pp. 170-94, and John Redwood, *Reason, Ridicule and Religion* (London, 1976). **Mather shrank, however:** the final quotation is from CM, *Utilia* (1716), p. 272. **Mather also considered:** MS draft communication ("Monstrous Impregnations"), CM to Dr. John Woodward, 2 Jul 1716, MHS; MAP, Reel 7, fr. 0564. See also Lester S. King, "Basic Concepts of Early 18th-Century Animism," *American Journal of Psychiatry,* CXXIV (1967), 797-802. **In conceiving of:** on the New Science and the experimental method, see Richard S. Westfall, *The Construction of Modern Science* (Cambridge, England, 1977), esp. pp. 115 ff. **Leaving aside Mather's:** on CM's Copernican views, see SSD, II, 779; on spontaneous generation, see *Christian Philosopher,* p. 145; on scrofula, see MS letter, CM to Jos[eph] Web [undated, but beginning "Sir, At your desire"], AAS; on hybridization, see SLCM, p. 218; on dominance, see I. Bernard Cohen, "Ethan Allen Hitchcock," PAAS, NS LXI (1951), 30; for a thoughtful assessment of CM's achievements, see Raymond Phineas Stearns, *Science in the British Colonies of America* (Urbana, Ill., 1970), pp. 403–26. **The Royal Society:** Stearns, *Science in the British Colonies,* q.p. 407; MS "Notes from Dr. Woodward," 1714, W, Reel 18; CM's hint appears at the close of his MS communication to Richard Waller, 25 Nov 1712, RS. **Seeking recognition even:** DIII, p. 93; Stearns, *Science in the British Colonies,* q. pp. 405–6; DII, p. 246; MS communication (identified as "Separate Letter"), CM to [probably Richard Waller], [*ca.* Nov 1713], MHS. **In the "F.R.S.":** DII, p. 246. **The defining moods:** DII, p. 423–24. **Squire was not:** MS letter, Benjamin Colman to CM, 25 Dec 1711, AAS: DII, p. 235. **When not surfacing:** CM, *Man Eating the Food of Angels* (1710), p. 41; CM, *The Wayes and Joyes of Early Piety* (1712), p. 43; CM, *Perswasions from the Terror of the Lord* (1711), pp. 34, 35. **Mather's tantrums and:** DIII, p. 39. **Some of this:** SLCM, p. 231; Niel Caplan, "Some Unpublished Letters of Benjamin Colman, 1717–1725," PMHS, LXXVII (1965), 106–7. **Mather's stepped-up promotion:** on the size of "Biblia Americana," see DII, p. 416. **Yet English readers:** SLCM, pp. 170, 190; MS draft letter, CM to Anthony Boehm, 6 Aug 1716, AAS; DII, p. 312. **The *New Offer: The Correspondence of the Rev. Robert Wodrow,* ed. Thomas M'Crie (Edinburgh, 1842), I, 628; DII, p. 332; MS letter, Anthony Boehm to CM, 19 Mar 1717, AAS. Boehm indicates that CM had at this point deposited the manuscript at Harvard. **Mather was wholly:** MS draft letter, CM to Thomas Reinolds, [*ca.* 1715, beginning "Reverend and very dear, Sr. The Generous Friendship"], AAS; MS letter, CM to William Ashurst, 18 Oct 1715, HL; DII, p. 376. **Mather's service to:** SLCM, p. 146; on Leverett, see MS letter, IM to William Ashurst, 22 Dec 1712, HL; on the commissioners' sluggishness, see DIII, p. 65; on the award, see *Some Correspondence between . . . the New England Company and . . . America,* ed. John W. Ford (London, 1896), p. 89; MS letter, CM to William Ashurst, 10 Dec 1712, HL; DII, p. 252. **New frustrations came:** *Correspondence of . . . Wodrow,* II, 361; *Philosophical Transactions of the Royal Society,* #339 (Apr–Jun 1714), p. 64; SLCM, p. 129. **Mather also discovered:** SLCM, p. 219.

9. Of 15, Dead, 9

At the time: Isaac J. Greenwood, "A Review of William Clarke's Genealogical Statement," NEHGR, XXXIII (1879), 226–29; James Savage, *A Genealogical Dictionary of the First Settlers of New England* (Boston, 1860–62), II, 485; SML, p. 13. **Elizabeth may have:** Henry Wilder Foote, *Annals of King's Chapel* (Boston, 1882), I, 46–48; CM, *The Religion of the Cross* (1714), pp. 44–45; R2C, 24 Feb 1706; DII, pp. 185–86, 132. 210; DIII, pp. 7, 81. **Mather and Elizabeth:** on CM's house, see Suffolk Deeds 33. 131, quoted in Thwing Card Catalogue, MHS. See also DII, pp. 239, 54; DI, p. 428; DIII, p. 72; CM, *Christianus per Ignem* (1702), p. 195; SML, pp. 98, 22. CM seems also to have owned a farm at this time, which he leased out. See the appendix to the MS lease of 26 Jul 1705, Williams College Library. **The center of:** CM describes his library in PA, p. 42, and DI, p. 447; on the volumes CM owned, see Julius Herbert Tuttle, "The Libraries of the Mathers," PAAS, NS XX (1909–10), 268–356; on the large accessions, see Clarence S. Brigham, "Harvard College Library Duplicates, 1682," PCSM, XVIII (1917), 407–17, and DII, p. 2; DI, p. 548; PA, p. 42. **How many books:** *John Dunton's Letters from New-England* (Boston, 1867), p. 75 and n. **Entering middle age:** IMD, 1710 *passim;* DII, pp. 204, 51. On the birth dates of CM's children, see Horace E. Mather, *Lineage of Rev. Richard Mather* (Hartford, 1890); MS list of marriages (in CM's hand), 1704, University of Virginia Library (Elizabeth); *A Report of the Record Commissioners . . .*

Containing Boston births from A.D. 1700 to A.D. 1800 (Boston, 1894), p. 46 (Samuel); DII, pp. 8, 20 (Nathanael); DII, p. 57 (Jerusha). **Mather's household also:** DII, p. 687; CM, *The Negro Christianized* (1706), p. 26; DI, p. 570; CM, *Grata Brevitas* (1712), p, 8; PA, p. 221; DII, p. 364. In his lifetime CM owned at least three and probably more black slaves. His church records suggest that his congregation contained thirty or forty blacks, whom he often addressed in sermons. The subject of CM and slavery deserves book-length treatment, but for a useful brief study, see Daniel K. Richter, "'It Is God Who Has Caused Them To Be Servants': Cotton Mather and Afro-American Slavery in New England," *Bulletin of the Congregational Library*, XXX (1979), 4–13. **In 1706 some:** DI, p. 579; DII, pp. 222, 271, 282; DIII, p. 83; DII, p. 139. **Amidst his multitudinous:** CM, *Orphanotrophium* (1711), p. 20; CM, *The Man of God Furnished* (1708), pp. 138–39; DI, p. 536. **To induce children:** DI, p. 536. **Mather conscientiously applied:** DII, p. 21; DIII, p. 14; DII, p. 149; DIII, p. 91; DII, p. 53. **True to his:** DIII, p. 105; DI, p. 535; DII, pp. 113, 144, 198; DIII, p. 85. **As Mather proposed:** DI, p. 536; DII, pp. 127, 44. **In attending to:** DII, p. 140; DIII, p. 33; DII, pp. 245, 4, 134. **In preparing his:** DII, pp. 51, 153, 111–12; CM, *Victorina* (1717), sig. A2 *et passim;* DII, p. 78. **Mather's two sons:** DIII, p. 89; DI, p. 583; DIII, pp. 41, 72; DII, p. 106; DIII, p. 45; DII, pp. 161, 151; DIII, p. 9. **But Creasy somehow:** DIII, p. 110; DI, p. 203; DII, pp. 76, 92, 212. **When Creasy reached:** DII, p. 204; samples of Creasy's handwriting survive in the Mellen Chamberlain Autograph Collection, MHS: DII, pp. 278, 239, 225. **The winter of:** Ernest Caulfield, "Some Common Diseases of Colonial Children," PCSM, XXXV (1951), 5–6; CM, *A perfect Recovery* (1714), p. 47; DII, p. 248. **In about two:** DII, pp. 249–52. **As such threats:** DII, pp. 252, 272. **One historian of:** Caulfield, "Some Common Diseases," p. 8. **Elizabeth was the:** DII, pp. 254, 250–51. **Three days after:** DII, pp. 252–53; DI, p. 568; DII, p. 255. **On November 8:** CM, *The Will of a Father submitted to* (1713), pp. 28, 31; DII, p. 254. **Whatever Mather's own:** CM, *The Religion of the Cross* (1714), *passim;* DII, pp. 254–55. **The next to:** DII, pp. 257–58. **The twins Eleazer:** DII, pp. 258, 260. **The need to:** CM, *Orphanotrophium,* p. 12; on the older Jerusha, see CM, *Memorials of Early Piety* (1711), and DII, p. 38; DII, pp. 258, 256, 261. **Next day, with:** CM, *The Best Way of Living* (1713), p. 23; DII, pp. 263, 259, 261; CM, *The Best Way,* sig. A3 *et passim;* SLCM, p. 145; CM, *Hezekiah* (1713), pp. 1, 35. **In December, with:** DII, pp. 266, 270, 273. **As Mather digested:** DII, p. 266; MAP, Reel 2, fr. 0061; DII, p. 283. **Mather's fifty-second year:** IM, *A Sermon Concerning Obedience & Resignation* (1714), sig. A2; A, p. 359; CM, *Maternal Consolations* (1714), pp. 5–6, 40.

10. Lydia Lee George

To be sure: The description of Boston in this and the six following paragraphs draws on a very wide variety of sources, of which only the more substantial can be cited. On the quake, see BNL, 18–25 Jun 1705; many accounts of the 1711 fire survive, but see esp. BNL, 1–8 Oct 1711, and CM, *Advice from Taberah* (1711); on the new First Church building and the new Town House, see esp. Walter Muir Whitehill, *Boston: A Topographical History* (Cambridge, Mass., 1959), pp. 26–27. **Indeed a half:** Carl Bridenbaugh, *Cities in the Wilderness* (New York, 1938), pp. 146, 155–65; on the fire department, see *A Report of the Record Commissioners . . . 1716 to 1736* (Boston, 1885), p. 279. **Despite the restraining:** the quotation and most of the details are drawn from Daniel Neal, *The History of New-England* (London, 1720), II, 587 *et passim.* **To walk that:** details gleaned from advertisements in various Boston newspapers, esp. BG, 4–11 Apr 1720 ("choice Pictures"); NEC, 31 Dec–7 Jan 1723 (Boyer); BG, 8–15 Feb 1720 (Faneuil); BG, 12–19 Jul 1725 (Hedman); BG 29 May–5 Jun 1727 ("Black Boy"). **Social life kept:** Neal, *History of New-England,* II, 587, 591; Bridenbaugh, *Cities in the Wilderness,* pp. 291–92; on Harvard enrollment, see Niel Caplan, "Some Unpublished Letters of Benjamin Colman, 1717–1725," PMHS, LXXVII (1965), 111; BNL, 2–9 Mar 1713 (Brownell); BNL, 7–14 Mar 1715 (moving pictures); BNL, 22–29 Aug 1715 (horse race); BG, 23–30 May 1726 (bear). **Urban pleasures also:** on the growth of crime, see CM, *A Flying Roll* (1713); on the 1711 statute, see *The Acts and Resolves, Public and Private, of the Province of the Massachusetts Bay* (Boston, 1869–1922), I, 673–74; on the report of slaves, see Caplan, "Some Unpublished Letters," p. 131, and Robert C. Twombly and Robert H. Moore, "Black Puritan: The Negro in Seventeenth-Century Massachusetts," *William and Mary Quarterly,* 3rd ser., XXIV (1967), 224–42; BNL, 17–24 Dec 1711, 26 Nov–3 Dec 1711, 20–27 Apr 1713; Caplan, "Some Unpublished Letters," p. 131; SLCM, p. 368. **Here a John:** Neal, *History of New-England,* II, 590. **In some ways:** MCA, III, 223; PCSM, XXXIII (1940), xiii; Wilfred H. Munro, *The History of Bristol, R.I.* (Providence, 1880), pp. 131–33. **Although Lee returned:** "Letters of Samuel Lee and Samuel Sewall Relating to New England and the Indians," PCSM, XIV (1913), 142–86; Samuel A. Green, "An Early Book-catalogue printed in Boston," PMHS, 2nd ser., X (1895–96), 540–45; "Dr. Stiles's account of Rev. Samuel Lee," PMHS (1864–65), pp. 219–20; Samuel Lee to IM, 25 Aug 1687, in M, pp. 540–42; CM's sermon notebooks, MAP, Reel 4A, Jul 1686–May 1687. **This heritage of:** "The Story of Boston Light," *Bostonian Society Publications,* VII (1910), 64–65 and n.; Long Wharf Corporation Documents 1713–1729, BPL; advertisements for John George, BNL, 18–25 Aug 1707 and 16–23 Mar 1713; on George's sloops, see Massachusetts Archives, VII: 370, 396, 482. **Well-to-do and socially:** Henry Wilder Foote, *Annals of King's Chapel* (Boston, 1882), I, 137; "A List of all the Stated Communicants," in *Records of the Church in Brattle Square, Boston,* (Boston, 1902), n.p.; "Letter of Reverend Benjamin Colman," PCSM, VIII (1906), pp. 248–49; Suffolk Probate #3629 (27 Nov 1714). **Mather waited scarcely:** SLCM, pp. 166–67; DI, pp. 581–82. **Even more than:** SLCM, pp. 166–68. **But actually Mather:** SLCM, pp. 173–74. **In the same:** SLCM, pp. 171–73. **Lydia did grant:** this and the next three paragraphs from DII, pp. 305–8. **In the spring:** SLCM, p. 131; *Boston Marriages 1700–1751* (Boston, 1898), 26 May 1715; Kenneth Ballard Murdock, *Increase Mather* (Cambridge, Mass., 1926), p. 385; MAP, Reel 6, fr. 0112, 0114; SLCM, p. 174. **On June 24:** "Will of Increase Mather," NEHGR, V (1851), 445–47; Suffolk Deeds 35. 34 (24 June 1715). **Ten days later:** CM, MS "Extract of passages in my Diaries," Houghton Library, Harvard University; SLCM, p. 183. CM's wedding sermon was printed as "Shemajah" in his *Utilia* (1716). For identification of the connection of the sermon with his marriage, see MS letter, CM to Elizabeth Clark, 13 Oct 1718, AAS. **It seemed that:** CM, MS "Extract of passages"; CM, *The Sacrificer* (1714), p. 45; DII, pp. 325, 392; MS "Extract of passages." **No portrait of:** CM, MS "Extract of passages." **Whatever subtle sensuality:** DII, pp. 481, 335–36, 340; MAP, Reel 16, fr. 0658; DII, p. 346. **Mather's removal to:** MS Second Church Treasurer's Accounts, MHS; Chandler Robbins, *A History of the Second Church* (Boston, 1852), p. 298. Surviving evidence about the house conflicts. Samuel Sewall described it as "the house that was Mr. Kellond's" (SSD, II, 794), but the Second Church account says that it belonged to Thomas Hutchinson. It seems probable that Kellond owned the house but conveyed it to Hutchinson, and that it was known locally by the names of both former owners. See also Thwing Catalogue of Suffolk Deeds, MHS (14 May 1713). The house and land CM had bought in 1688 he put up for sale around 1717. See SLCM, p. 249. **Mather now lived:** Abbott Lowell Cummings, "The Foster-Hutchinson House," *Old-Time New England,* LIV (1964), pp. 61 ff.; DII, pp. 770, 577, 619, 458, 363 and n., 384, 477, 549. **Altogether, in his:** DII, p. 360. **To**

Mather's great: CM, MS "Extract of passages"; SLCM, p. 184; *Boston Marriages,* 28 Aug 1716; CM, *The Tribe of Asher* (1717), title page. **Samuel, about eight:** DII, pp. 459, 353, 565, 499, 554; Samuel's "Quotidiana" are preserved at AAS; MS draft letter, CM to Jeremiah Dummer, 13 Jul 1720, AAS. **Sammy's admission forced:** SLCM, p. 294; "A Mather Manuscript in the Congregational Library," *Bulletin of the American Congregational Association,* III (1952), 16-17. **One dark intrusion:** CM, *Bethiah* (1722), p. 4; SML, p. 14; CM, *Victorina* (1717), sig. A2, pp. 66, 80. **But about a:** DII, p. 370; on Culver's Root, see SLCM, pp. 220, 224, and Winthrop Commonplace Book, W, Reel 39; CM, *Victorina,* p. 79; DII, p. 388; SSD, II, 840. **Katharine's death did:** SLCM, pp. 179, 169. **The visit turned:** Thomas J. Holmes, "Samuel Mather of Witney, 1674-1733," PCSM, XXVI (1926), 312-22; A, p. 360; DII, pp. 322-23. **But curing Creasy:** DII, pp. 322-23. **Mather's disappointment in:** DII, p. 347. **For once, Mather:** DII, p. 352; SLCM, p. 207; DII, p. 354. **By the time:** Sir Henry Ashurst to Wait Winthrop, 24 Aug 1708, CMHS, 6th ser., V (1892), 173; DIII, p.81; Alan Simpson, "A Candle in a Corner: How Harvard College Got the Hopkins Legacy," PCSM, XLIII (1966), 304-24. **Dudley also gave:** Foote, *Annals of King's Chapel,* p. 224; on Dudley's alleged Congregationalism, see CMHS, 1st ser., VII (1801), 216-17; SSD, II, 792. **Nothing so nearly:** DII, pp. 292-93; Albert Matthews, "Colonel Elizeus Burges," PCSM, XIV (1913), 360-72. **Mather was glad:** SLCM, p. 168; on Shute, see DNB. **Shute no sooner:** DII, p. 375; MS draft letter, CM to [Samuel Shute], [undated, beginning "Sr, The God of Heaven"], AAS; on Shute's membership in a Congregational church, see HCR, IV, 265 (the pronouns are confused, but "He" seems to refer to Shute); on Shute and King's Chapel, see Foote, *Annals of King's Chapel,* pp. 267-68; CM, *A Speech Made unto His Excellency* (1717), p. 2; SLCM, p. 244. **For his efforts:** DIII, p. 380; MS draft letter, CM to Samuel Shute, [16?] Oct 1719, AAS; MS draft letter, CM to John Shute Barrington, [undated but *ca.* Oct 1716, beginning "Sr, An *American* Composure"], AAS; MS draft letter, CM to Thomas Bradbury, 13 Oct 1718, AAS. **The change of:** on Dummer generally, see Charles L. Sanford, "The Days of Jeremy Dummer, Colonial Agent," Diss. Harvard, 1952; on the "female beauties," see MS Memoranda of Jeremy Dummer, 1709-11, MHS; on Dummer as prime minister, see "A Sketch of Eminent Men in New-England," CMHS, 1st ser., X (1809), 155. **Dummer greatly admired:** MS Memoranda; on the pigs, see Sanford, "The Days of Jeremy Dummer," q. p. 90; on Waller, see MS letter, Jeremiah Dummer to Stephen Sewall, 23 Jan 1712, AAS; on "Religio Generosi," see MS draft letter, CM to "J.[eremiah] D.[ummer] Esq.," 7 Sep 1719, AAS; CM's attack on Dummer appears in *The Day which the Lord hath made* (1703); DII, p. 414. **Dummer's value to:** mention of CM for rector appears in a letter from Rev. James Noyes (a Yale trustee) in 1717, cited in Sanford, "The Days of Jeremy Dummer," p. 239; DII, p. 474; HCR, II, 424. **Yale College began:** Franklin B. Dexter, "The Founding of Yale College," *New Haven Historical Society Papers,* III (1882), 1-31; Franklin B. Dexter, "Governor Elihu Yale," *ibid.,* pp. 227-48; Sanford, "The Days of Jeremy Dummer," p. 237. **Mather wrote to:** Yale's comment q. in Dexter, "Governor Elihu Yale," p. 244; MS draft letter, CM to Elihu Yale, 14 Jan 1718, AAS; Dexter, "Governor Elihu Yale," pp. 242-43. **Mather was greatly:** MS draft letter, CM to Gurdon Saltonstall, 25 Jun 1718, AAS; MS letter, Yale trustees to CM, *ca.* Sep 1718, Yale University Library. **A simultaneous and:** on the development of CM's ecumenism, see Richard F. Lovelace, *The American Pietism of Cotton Mather* (Grand Rapids, Mich., 1979), pp. 251-81. **Around 1715 Mather:** CM, *Malachi* (1717), p. 36; DII, p. 416; the list of places to which CM intended sending the work is compiled from various mentions of *Lapis* in DII, SLCM, and *India Christiana* (1721); SLCM, p. 205; MS fragmentary draft letter, CM to Anthony Boehm, [undated but *ca.* 1716, beginning "there is none that has more"], AAS. **In *Lapis,***

Mather: all quotations from *Malachi,* except the last, which appears in SLCM, p. 205. How far CM had drifted from the older Congregational view of church government appears in his blasts at the publication in Boston of an edition of *The Churches Quarrel Espoused,* by the Ipswich minister John Wise. Here and in his later *Vindication of the Government of New-England Churches* (1717) Wise attacked as a departure from Congregationalism the movement to develop formal clerical associations. For CM's furious response, see SLCM, p. 185. **Mather's Universal Religion:** all quotes from *Malachi.* **Mather's ecumenism increasingly:** *Malachi,* p. 69; CM, "To my much Honoured Mr. *Francis De la Pillonniere,"* in *The Occasional Paper* (London), III (1718), 25–29; CM, *Brethren dwelling together in Unity* (1718), p. 37. **Many different features:** on the Pietists' praise, see MS letter, Anthony Boehm to CM, [undated but *ca.* 1716, beginning "Reverend Sir. It was in the Month"], AAS. Boehm added that some persons to whom he gave copies of *Lapis* called it "a Compendium of Mystical and Universal Divinity." CM entitled one of his own works *Pia Desideria* (1722), after a famous work of Spener's. **Mather's career in:** CM, *Zelotes* (1717), pp. 41–42. **At various times:** on Whiston, see Margaret C. Jacob, *The Newtonians and the English Revolution 1689–1720,* (Ithaca, N.Y., 1976), pp. 130–34; on Louis XIV, see CM, *Shaking Dispensations* (1715), pp. 42, 45; on the "greatest Sign," see MS draft letter, CM to Henry Walrond, 11 Jan 1718, AAS. **One other ambitious:** DII, p. 786; H, III, 1008. Both of CM's grandfathers had been involved in the production of *The Bay Psalm Book* (1640), and his grandfather John Cotton had written a treatise on psalmody, *Singing of Psalmes A Gospel-Ordinance* (London, 1650). **In 1718 Mather:** CM, *Proposals for Printing by Subscription* (1718); SLCM, pp. 311, 188; CM, *The Accomplished Singer* (1721), p. 15. For an expanded study of CM's *Psalterium,* see my article "Cotton Mather and the Reform of Puritan Psalmody," *Seventeenth-Century News,* XXXIV (1976), 53–57. **Mather had a:** Richard Baxter, *Paraphrase on the Psalms of David in Metre* (London, 1692); DII, p. 437. **To improve public:** SLCM, pp. 376, 388; Ebenezer Parkman, MS singing book, dated Jul 1721, MHS. **Often sympathetic to:** DII, p. 608; SSD, II, 976. David P. McKay has published a sermon on psalm singing allegedly preached by CM on 18 Apr 1721, as "Cotton Mather's Unpublished Singing Sermon," *New England Quarterly,* XLVIII (1975), 410–22. The manuscript does contain CM's name at the end, but seemingly not his signature. I cannot accept the sermon as his, first because the manuscript is not in his hand, second because the sermon emphasizes the musical and aesthetic side of singing whereas CM paid these lip service while emphasizing the exegetical and devotional aspects. Most important, CM's sermon list for 1721 (DII, pp. 677–81) shows that he preached on April 16 and 20, but not on April 18.

11. *Tria Carcinomata*

Mather's newfound happiness: DII, p. 480; CM, *Help for Distressed Parents* (1695), p. 13. **"Suppose," Mather asked:** DII, pp. 465–66. **But by November:** DII, p. 484. **However shaken, Mather:** MS Book of Sessions, 1712–1719, Suffolk County Supreme Court, Boston (17 Jan 1718 and p. 201); DII, p. 485. **But despite Mather's:** DII, p. 489; PA, p. xvii. **Powerless to reclaim:** DII, p. 583. **Whatever her other:** on Lee's daughters, see "Dr. Stiles's account of Rev. Samuel Lee," PMHS (1864–65), 219–20, and "Genealogical Gleanings in England," NEHGR, XLIV (1890), 393–94; on Augustus, see MAP, Reel 4C, fr. 0299. **Early in their:** DII, pp. 583–86. **Among the objects:** DII, p. 584; CM, MS "Extract of passages in my Diaries," Houghton Library, Harvard University. **Fear of what:** DII, pp. 584–85.

Lydia turned her: DII, pp. 338, 590–91; on the possibility of revolution, see CM, *Concio ad Populum* (1719), p. 25; SLCM, p. 317; HCR, IV, 302–3. **Increase himself added:** IMD for 1717, *passim;* R2C, 13 Oct 1717; "Earliest Wills on Record in Suffolk County, Ms.," NEHGR, V (1851), 445–47; DII, p. 512. IM showed CM the provisions of his will more than a year before drawing it up. See DII, p. 505. **Mather dealt with:** DII, pp. 523, 533, 557, 514. **Mather's distress also:** DII, pp. 589, 571, 578, 521, 579. **On March 9:** SF #13120 (24 Mar 1719). The following account of CM's legal difficulties appeared previously as my article "Cotton Mather and the Howell Estate," *Boston Bar Journal,* XXVI (1982), 5–13. **This ominous summons:** Samuel Sewall, MS Probate Records, MHS (the administration appears as "Nota" written in the margin of a grant of administration to Ebenezer Withrington on 29 Mar 1716); SF #15183 (25 May 1721). **In taking on:** DII, p. 410; SSD, II, 817n.; DII, p. 349. **Mather undertook this:** CM, "The Answer of the Administrator of the Estate of Nathan Howel deceased, unto the Citation served upon him," MS document reproduced in sale catalogue of Charles Hamilton Galleries Inc., New York, XC (4 Sep 1975), 46; DII, pp. 386, 444, 136; CM, *Fair Dealing* (1716), p. 12. **Mather explained later:** CM, "The Answer"; BNL, 31 Dec–7 Jan 1716/17. **Forever bent on:** SF #11222 (14 Dec 1716); Mather v. Oliver &c., ERB (1 Jan 1717); SF #11386 (19 Feb 1717). Packanet was apparently released when he promised to pay off the debt to CM at the rate of forty shillings a month. **For Mather this:** SF #11588 [*sic*] (5 Mar 1717); SF #11453 (5 Mar 1717); SF #11454 (18 Mar 1717); Mather v. Dunham and Mather v. James, ERB (2 Apr 1717); Mather v. Davison, ERB (2 Jul 1717). **These cases can:** Mather v. Morrell, ERB (1 Apr 1718); *York Deeds* (Portland, Maine, 1894), X, fol. 22; *Province and Court Records of Maine* (Portland, Maine, 1964), V, 106; Mather v. Marshall, ERB (2 Apr 1717). **Other of Mather's:** DII, p. 494; MS draft letter, CM to Pelatiah Whittemore, 11 Dec 1717, AAS; BNL, 9–16 Dec 1717; CM, "The Answer." **The sheriff who:** SF #13120 (24 Mar 1719). **The manuscript probably:** MAP, Reel 8, fr. 0135, 0138. Several of CM's published sermons in this period also refer to his marital and financial difficulties. See for instance *Febrifugium. An Essay for the Cure of Ungoverned Anger* (1717) and *A Glorious Espousal* (1719). In the latter, CM speaks of "the *Curse,* which every *Marriage* in *this World,* is likely to be more or less Encumbered and Embittered withal!" **Aside from venting:** see "The Answer"; Mico v. Mather, ERB (7 Jul 1719). **Mather began trying:** "Supposed Letter from Rev. Cotton Mather, D.D.," CMHS, 4th ser., II (1854), 122–29. **Judge Sewall did:** *Letter-Book of Samuel Sewall,* CMHS, 6th ser. (1886–88), II, 111. **With his passion:** this and the next paragraph drawn from the "Supposed Letter." **The seriousness of:** [John Colman], *The Distressed State of the Town of Boston* (1720), p. 2 *et passim.* **Mather depicted his:** M, pp. 460–62. The editors assigned this undated document the date 1725, but its content makes a date of 1720 far more probable. **Certain that Sewall's:** DII, p. 630; SLCM, pp. 326–27. **Apparently despairing of:** MAP, Reel 6, fr. 642-43 [*sic*]. **Auspiciously, this time:** MS "Petition of Dr. Cotton Mather," 8 Nov 1720, Council Records, Massachusetts State House, Boston. **But no proper:** SLCM, pp. 333, 336. **Mather needed no:** DII, pp. 611–12; IMD, 14 Apr 1721. CM does not say what happened during this "Night-Riot." But documents do survive of a riotous episode apparently two weeks later, which may by some confusion of dates be the same episode. On the streets of Boston on the evening of April 20, three young male servants cursed, swore, broke windows, threatened to break down doors, and offered "affronts and abuses" to women, for which the court offered them the choice of a fine or a public whipping. See MS Sessions Minutes (1719–1728), Suffolk County Supreme Judicial Court, Boston, pp. 85 ff. That Creasy may have been involved with this group is suggested by the fact that one of the young men was a servant to Foxley Sanderson, to whom Creasy owed money. See documents related to Creasy in Mellen Chamberlain Autograph Collection, MHS. **As always, Mather's:** SLCM, p. 337; DII, pp. 614–15. **Seeking some help:** SLCM, p. 337. **Opposition to Shute:** SLCM, p. 156. **The change of:** SLCM, p. 223. **Amid this plethora:** CM, *Concio ad Populum*, p. 25. **Mather had been:** H, II, 537–40; "Dr. Mather's Letter to Lord Barrington," CMHS, I (1792), 105–6; SLCM, pp. 291, 292; for Cooke's alleged drunkenness and the retraction, see SLCM, pp. 295–96, and the undated draft memorandum in CM's hand beginning "Desirous forever to preserve the most unspotted care," AAS; for the "party of Tipplers," see MS draft letter, CM to William Ashurst, 10 Sep 1719, AAS. **Opposition to Shute:** John L. Sibley, *Biographical Sketches of Graduates of Harvard University* (Cambridge, Mass., 1873–1975), IV, 351–52. **Apprehensive that such:** Thomas Hutchinson, *The History of the Colony and Province of Massachusetts-Bay*, ed. Lawrence Shaw Mayo (Cambridge, Mass., 1936), II, 218. **Although the House:** Hutchinson, *History of the Colony*, II, 185; text of *Reflections upon Reflections* in *Colonial Currency Reprints*, ed. Andrew McFarland Davis (1911; rpt. New York, 1971), II, 118. **Mather, probably hoping:** CM, undated MS draft document, beginning "An Extract of a passage in *Eachards*," AAS. **Mather was also:** SLCM, pp. 319, 304–5. **A new session:** CM, undated MS draft document, beginning "In case the Representatives," AAS; Hutchinson, *History of the Colony*, II, q. 179. **At this point:** SLCM, pp. 334–35; MS draft letter, CM to Samuel Penhallow, 21 Nov 1720, AAS; SLCM, p. 335. **In this Mather:** Perry Miller, *The New England Mind: From Colony to Province* (Cambridge, Mass., 1953), p. 310. **Neither upbringing nor:** SLCM, p. 229; MS draft letter, CM to Samuel Penhallow, 8 Sep 1718, AAS; SLCM, pp. 327–28. **The other case:** SLCM, p. 312; Daniel Neal, *The History of New-England* (London, 1720), II, viii. **The day before:** SLCM, pp. 313–15, 269. **In the past:** CM, *A Voice from Heaven* (1719), p. 13; DII, p. 607. **Mather's ministry dealt:** CM, MS sermon on Eph I. 13. (20 Sep 1702), University of Virginia Library. **That Arianism might:** I. Bernard Cohen, "Introduction" to William Whiston, *Astronomical Lectures* (1728; rpt. New York, 1972), p. v ff.; DII, p. 106; DIII, p. 48. On Arianism in general, see Ronald N. Stromberg, *Religious Liberalism in Eighteenth-Century England* (Oxford, 1954). **Mather wrote several:** on the advance of Arianism, see MS letter, CM to John Stirling, 10 Dec 1717, National Library of Scotland; on Salters' Hall, see Henry W. Clark, *History of English Nonconformity* (1911–13; rpt. New York, 1965), II, 193–95. **Mather learned of:** SLCM, p. 289; MS draft letter, CM to Isaac Watts, 7 Sep 1719, AAS; MS letter, Isaac Watts to CM, 11 Feb 1720, MHS. **Mather regarded the:** Richard F. Lovelace, *The American Pietism of Cotton Mather* (Grand Rapids, Mich., 1979), p. 273. **Mather also set:** SLCM, p. 273; *Some American Sentiments* in *Three Letters from New-England* (London, 1721), pp. 7–27. **Mather's professions of:** SLCM, p. 303; HCR, IV, 349; Niel Caplan, "Some Unpublished Letters of Benjamin Colman, 1717–1725," PMHS, LXXVII (1965), 128. **At the same:** Caplan, "Some Unpublished Letters," p. 119. **Almost all the:** Hamilton Andrews Hill, *History of the Old South Church* (Boston, 1890), I, 400. **Shaken by the:** Thomas Lechmere to John Winthrop, Jr., 18 Jan 1720 and 14 Mar 1720, W, Reel 19; CM *et al.*, *An Account of the Reasons* (1720). **Despite this resistance:** SSD, II, 940n.; Sibley, *Biographical Sketches*, IV, 306; Lechmere to Winthrop, 14 Mar 1720. **The end result:** DII, p. 615; Samuel G. Drake, *The History and Antiquities of Boston* (Boston, 1856), p. 558n.; DII, p. 615; CM, MS draft document, undated but beginning "Considering the crazy condition of the Old N.M.," AAS; DII, p. 617. **How many left:** DII, p. 616; CM, *A Vision in the Temple* (1721), pp. 37, 42–43; DII, p. 617. **Suddenly, just two:** DII, pp. 620–21.

12. The Paths of the Destroyer

Mather himself observed: SLCM, p. 213; P, p. 198; DII, p. 487. **Civic authorities seem:** *The Acts and Resolves, Public and Private, of the Province of the Massachusetts Bay* (Boston, 1869-1922), II, 91; *A Report of the Record Commissioners of the City of Boston . . . 1716 to 1736* (Boston, 1885), p. 76; *Acts and Resolves,* X, 28. **It was the:** SSD, II, 979; *Report of the Record Commissioners . . . 1716 to 1736,* p. 81; *A Report of the Record Commissioners of the City of Boston . . . from 1700 to 1728* (Boston, 1883), p. 154. **The next week:** BNL, 15-22 May 1721; *Report of the Record Commissioners . . . 1716 to 1736,* p. 82. **Mather feared for:** Zabdiel Boylston, *Historical Account of the Small-pox Inoculated* (1726; rpt. Boston, 1730), p. 38; DII, pp. 622, 621, 623, 628. **Mather's charitable and.** *Robert Doyle. The Works,* ed. Thomas Birch (1722; rpt. Hildesheim, 1965), VI, 610-11; DII, p. 388; SLCM, p. 214. **Mather now did:** on the June 6 address and CM's other unpublished writings during the smallpox epidemic, I have followed the exhaustive and dependable account of their dates and content in George Lyman Kittredge, "Some Lost Works of Cotton Mather," PMHS, 2nd ser., XLV (1911-12), 418-79; Otho T. Beall, Jr., and Richard H. Shryock, "Cotton Mather: First Significant Figure in American Medicine," PAAS, LXIII (1953), 137-38; John B. Blake, "The Inoculation Controversy in Boston: 1721-1722," *New England Quarterly,* XXV (1952), 489. **Mather based the:** on discussion of inoculation in Boston, see Niel Caplan, "Some Unpublished Letters of Benjamin Colman, 1717-1725," PMHS, LXXVII (1965), 124; SLCM, p. 214. **In his letter:** accepting the history of the June 6 address given in Kittredge, "Some Lost Works," I have followed the text in CM, *The Angel of Bethesda,* ed. Gordon W. Jones (Barre, Mass., 1972), pp. 107-12. **How many physicians:** BNL, 23-30 Mar 1713, 5-12 Mar 1711, 3-10 Mar 1707, 28 Nov-5 Dec 1720; BG, 21-28 Nov 1720; Raymond Phineas Stearns, *Science in the British Colonies of America* (Urbana, Ill., 1970), pp. 435-42. **Boylston approved of:** *Massachusetts Magazine,* I (1789), 778; Boylston, *Historical Account,* p. 2. **The news of:** Boylston, *Historical Account,* p. 53; Thomas Robie, MS Smallpox Journal, 1721-22, MHS. **Mather found himself:** DII, pp. 631-32; BG, 10-17 Jul 1721. **With Mather certain:** CM's characterization of Dalhonde appears in his MS "Case of the Small-pox Inoculated, further cleared," 21 May 1723, RS; Dalhonde's testimony appears in the appendix to Boylston's "Historical Account." **Three days after:** BNL, 17-24 Jul 1721. **These charges of:** MS letter, Benjamin Colman to unaddressed, 25 Jul 1721, Francis A. Countway Library, Harvard Medical School; BG, 27-31 Jul 1721; NEC, 7 Aug 1721. **This flurry opened:** BNL, 24-31 Jul 1721; NEC, 7-14 Aug 1721; BNL, 7-14 Aug 1721. **Despite the thickening:** Boylston, "Historical Account." Again following Kittredge, I have quoted the text of this essay in *The Angel of Bethesda,* p. 94. **Opposition to Mather's:** NEC, 14-21 Aug 1721; on Douglass, see Stearns, *Science in the British Colonies;* for Douglass's remark on CM, see "Letters from Dr. William Douglass to Cadwallader Colden of New York," CMHS, 4th ser., II (1854), 169. **Douglass first sprang:** NEC, 7-14 Aug 1721, 14-21 Aug 1721. **What made Douglass:** "Letters from Dr. William Douglass," pp. 166, 170; William Douglass, *Inoculation of the Small Pox as Practised in Boston* (1722), p. 20; Caplan, "Some Unpublished Letters," p. 124; "Letters from Dr. William Douglass," p. 171. **The tense, charnal:** DII, pp. 641, 635, 634, 636-37. **Very tryingly, Mather:** DII, p. 634; Creasy had signed a promissory note for £3 15s on 9 Sep 1721 to the dancing master Increase Gatchell (see SF #16999, 17 Jun 1723); DII, pp. 647, 669, 674. **Smallpox or no:** Faneuil v. Mather, ERB (4 Apr 1721); SF #15183 (25 May 1721) and documents attached to SF #15308 (17 Apr 1721); the allowance of CM's petition appears in the MS records and Minute Books of the Superior Court of Judicature, 1702-27, Supreme Judicial

Court, Boston (25 May 1721); DII, p. 630; SLCM, p. 345. **But having borne:** DII, pp. 626, 632, 628, 635, 638. **A few days:** DII, pp. 639-43. **Unexpectedly, however, two:** DII, pp. 643-44, 648-49. **A canvass of:** NEC and BNL, 2-9 Oct 1721; Thomas Lechmere to John Winthrop, Jr., 2 Oct 1721, W, Reel 19; *Report of the Record Commissioners . . . 1716 to 1736,* p. 89; *Report of the Record Commissioners . . . 1700 to 1728,* p. 159. **Mather and Boylston:** Boylston, *Historical Account,* p. 50; DI, pp. 683, 650, 654; BG, 23-30 Oct 1721 (for the identification of this as CM's, see H, I, 357). **Someone tried to:** NEC, 14-21 Aug 1721; DII, pp. 657-58. This episode was much talked of and distorted, so that to prevent misrepresentation, CM gave the NEC his own account, which the newspaper published. It closely resembles the account in DII, except that in NEC the message fixed to the shell reads: "*Cotton Mather*—I was once of your Meeting; But the cursed Lye you told of—you know who, made me leave you, you Dog. And Damn you, I'll Inoculate you with this, with a Pox to you" (NEC, 13-20 Nov 1721). **The attempted assassination:** SLCM, pp. 345-46; DII, p. 659; General Court Records, Massachusetts State House (15 Nov 1721), and BNL, 13-20 Nov 1721. **Not everyone, Mather:** DII, pp. 659-60, 663. **Insidiously the smallpox:** on inoculations outside Boston, see Stearns, *Science in the British Colonies,* p. 444; DII, pp. 662, 670. **Mather also addressed:** that CM was unaware of the April inoculation in London is suggested by his remark on August 17 that he hoped the method "may be introduced into the English nation" (DII, p. 638); CM [but published as "*Communicated by* Henry Newman"], "*The way of proceeding in the* Small Pox inoculated," *Philosophical Transactions of the Royal Society,* XXXII (1722), 33-35; CM, MS communication headed "Dr Mather of New-England" (but not in CM's hand), 10 Mar 1722, The British Library, identified by Kittredge, "Some Lost Works," as "Curiosa Variolarum." **Whether the accounts:** on the debate, see Genevieve Miller, "Smallpox Inoculation in England and America: A Reappraisal," *William and Mary Quarterly,* 3rd ser., XIII (1956), 476-92. **By about mid-December:** for works by other ministers, see for instance Benjamin Colman, *Some Observations on the New Method of . . . Inoculating* (1721); IMD, 22 Jun 1721; MS letter, Samuel Sewall to Benjamin Colman, 12 Sep 1721, MHS. **The number of:** NEC, 30 Oct-6 Nov 1721; John Williams, *Several Arguments, Proving, That Inoculating the Small Pox Is not contained in the Law of Physick* (1721), p. 14. In this and the following paragraphs I have tried to convey the main themes of the debate, especially as they concerned CM, rather than to capture its escalating effect of attack and rejoinder. As a result the summaries of various arguments are not chronological, and some later works may in the accounting precede earlier ones. **While some anti-inoculators:** NEC, 1-8 Jan 1722; on Williams, see Kittredge, "Some Lost Works," pp. 471-72; John Williams, *An Answer To a Late Pamphlet* (1722), pp. 9, 4; Douglass, *Inoculation of the Small Pox,* sig. A2. **Pro-inoculation allies of:** on CM's part in writing this pamphlet, see Kittredge, "Some Lost Works," pp. 428, 467, and DII, p. 672. **Mather needed vindicating:** NEC, 30 Oct-6 Nov 1721; Douglass, *Inoculation of the Small Pox,* and *Postscript to Abuses, &c. Obviated* (1722), p. 4. **Mather's detractors often:** on the itch, see Douglass, *Postscript to Abuses,* p. 6; on CM's grammar and his opinion of his works, see Williams, *Several Arguments,* pp. 14, 15; on quoting CM against himself, see NEC, 15-22 Jan 1722; on Oldmixon and on CM's posturing, see [Anon.], *A Friendly Debate; or, A Dialogue between Rusticus and Academicus* (1722), pp. 6, 1; on "Curiosa," see Douglass, *Inoculation of the Small Pox,* p. 20, and Introduction, and his *The Abuses and Scandals of some late Pamphlets* (1722), p. 6; on the D.D., see Douglass, *The Abuses and Scandals,* Introduction, and NEC, 15-22 Jan 1722. **Mather's membership in:** on Checkley, see George L. Kittredge, "Further Notes on Cotton Mather and the Royal Society," PCSM, XIV (1913), 281-92; MS letter, John

Checkley to Edmund Halley, 26 Apr 1721, BPL. **Amidst the winter:** NEC, 15–22 Jan 1722; Douglass, *The Abuses and Scandals,* Introduction; on CM's membership in the Royal Society, see Kittredge, "Further Notes," and Stearns, *Science in the British Colonies,* pp. 110–11 and 111, n. 65. **Mather wrote to:** SLCM, p. 360; Raymond Phineas Stearns, "Colonial Fellows of the Royal Society, 1661–1788," *William and Mary Quarterly,* 3rd ser., III (1946), 228–29. **This onslaught of:** DII, p. 664; BG, 8–15 Jan 1722; NEC, 15–22 Jan 1722; MCA, VII, 86. **Although well practiced:** DII, p. 622; NEC, 27 Nov–4 Dec 1721; DII, p. 667. **In this defeated:** DII, pp. 670–71. **Mather's announcement of:** NEC, 15–22 Jan 1722 and 5–12 Feb 1722. **By the time:** selectmen's figures in NEC, 19–26 Feb 1722; the quotations from Silence Dogood appear in NEC, 26 Mar–2 Apr 1722 and 9–16 Apr 1722. **The selectmen found:** BG, 14–21 May 1722; *Report of the Record Commissioners . . . 1716 to 1736,* p. 96; NEC, 16–23 Apr 1722 and 28 May–4 Jun 1722. **Ironically for Mather:** DII, p. 669; Writ of Execution, 23 Oct 172[1?], with note by Edward Winslow dated 1 Jan 1722, State Records Center, Grafton, Mass. (the exact dates and details of this transaction are obscure: the date on the writ is torn, and the date on the note could represent 1722/3); CM's petition appears in SF #16015 (May 1722), which also contains Sewall's reply from Spectacle Island, dated 11 Jun 1722; on the selectmen, see *Report of the Record Commissioners . . . 1716 to 1736,* p. 97; on the "mobbish Crew," see MS letter, Thomas Robie [to John Higginson], 18 May 1722, AAS; on the condition of the Sewalls, see Robie, Smallpox Journal. **These final inoculations:** NEC and BG, 14–21 May 1722. **Impaled by the:** "Letters from Dr. William Douglass," p. 170. **To say that:** for a judicious assessment of CM's part in the inoculation controversy, see Beall and Shryock, "Cotton Mather." **Of course Mather:** DII, pp. 664–65; SLCM, p. 402. **A year after:** NEC, 14–21 May 1722; Stearns, *Science in the British Colonies,* p. 411; NEC, 13–20 Apr 1724; CM, MS communication ("The Case of the Small-pox Inoculated, further cleared"), 21 May 1723, RS (not in CM's hand, but signed by him).

13. Crackling of Thorns Under a Pot

The two years: Hamilton Andrews Hill, *History of the Old South Church* (Boston, 1890), I, 409. **Together with its:** IM, *A Dying Legacy of a Minister* (1722), p. 2; SSD, II, 996; P, p. 201. **Other losses beset:** SSD, II, 1001; SLCM, pp. 356, 375; William Pencak, *War, Politics & Revolution in Provincial Massachusetts* (Boston, 1981), p. 71. **Mather quickly gained:** SSD, II, 992; on CM's claims of foresight, see SLCM, pp. 375–76; NEC, 7–14 Jan 1723; BNL, 15–21 Mar 1723; SLCM, p. 384. **Losing money also:** Appleton v. Mather, ERB (3 Jul 1722); Baxter v. Dr. Mather, ERB (2 Oct 1722); on the irregularities, see Appleton v. Mather, ERB (2 Oct 1722), and Dr. Mather v. Baxter, ERB (1 Oct 1723); on CM's countersuit, see SF #17269 (10 Sep 1723); on Creasy and Sanderson, see SF #16702 (18 Mar 1723) and Writ of Execution, 9 May 1723, State Records Center, Grafton, Mass.; on Creasy's suits in June, see SF #16980 (17 Jun 1723) and SF #16999 (17 Jun 1723); on Gatchel, see NEC, 25 May-1 Jun 1724 and 4-11 Mar 1723. **In these circumstances:** Kenneth B. Murdock, "Cotton Mather and the Rectorship of Yale College," PCSM, XXVI (1927), 397; P, p. 201; "Original Paper Respecting the Episcopal Controversy in Connecticut, MDCCXXII," CMHS, 2nd ser., IV (1816), 298. **Mather was aghast:** SLCM, p. 356; SSD, II, 996; BG, 8–15 Oct 1722; "Original Paper," p. 299; on the "glorious revolution," see Carl Bridenbaugh, *Mitre and Sceptre: Transatlantic Faiths, Ideas, Personalities, and Politics 1689–1775* (New York, 1962), q. p. 68; Henry Wilder Foote, *Annals of King's Chapel* (Boston, 1882), I, 316. **The tumult brought:** Murdock, "Cotton Mather and the Rectorship," q. p. 395; "Original Paper," p. 297;

"Some Original Papers Respecting the Episcopal Controversy in Connecticut, MDCCXXII," CMHS, 2nd ser., II (1814), 130. **Mather and the:** Bridenbaugh, *Mitre and Sceptre,* q. p. 70; [CM], undated MS document, *ca.* Nov 1722, entitled "A Faithful Relation, of a Late Occurence in the Churches of *New England,"* MHS; "Some Original Papers," pp. 133–36; CM, *Some Seasonable Enquiries* (1723), p. 12. The MS "Faithful Relation" appears to be in the hand of Samuel Mather, but contains interpolations in CM's hand, thus my attribution of it to him. Many key words and phrases in the essay also appear in "The sentiments of several ministers" (in "Some Original Papers"), which is known to be by CM. **Increase reacted to:** P, pp. 201, 207, 66; SSD, II, 1007. **Helpless to pluck:** P, p. 207; DII, p. 686; P, p. 13; *Letter-Book of Samuel Sewall,* CMHS, 6th ser. (1886–88), II, 151. **Appropriately, Increase's final:** P, p. 210; Edward Taylor, "A funerall Teare . . . upon . . . Dr. Increase Mather," *Edward Taylor's Minor Poetry,* ed. Thomas M. and Virginia L. Davis (Boston, 1981), p. 247; P, p. 210; MS letter, William Waldron to Richard Waldron, 26 Aug 1723, MHS. **Mather had always:** P, p. 211; SSD, II, 1008; "Diary of Jeremiah Bumstead of Boston, 1722–1727," NEHGR, XV (1861), 199. **Increase had drawn:** this and the next paragraph from "Earliest Wills on Record in Suffolk County, Ms.," NEHGR, V (1851), 445–47. **Two days after:** CM, *A Father Departing* (1723), pp. 23–24, 28–29. **Mather may have:** CM, MS sermon on Phil. IV. 20., 15 Sep 1723, New York Public Library. **What few other:** on neighborhood visitations and Nathanael, see MAP, Reel 7, fr. 0557–58, 0583; on the "Courts," see CM, *A Father Departing,* p. 31. **Whatever else Increase's:** Chandler Robbins, *A History of the Second Church* (Boston, 1852), pp. 115, 312–13. **On January 19:** R2C, 19 Jan 1724. **Other vexations and:** SLCM, p. 390; Abraham English Brown, "The Builder of the Old South Meeting House," *New England Magazine,* NS XIII (1895), 397. **Shortly after arriving:** MS letter, William Waldron to Richard Waldron, 9 Oct 1723, MHS; Suzanne Foley, "Christ Church, Boston," *Old-Time New England,* LI (1961), 67–85. **Mather usually shrugged:** SLCM, p. 387; on McSparran, see Wilfred H. Munro, *The History of Bristol, R.I.* (Providence, 1880), pp. 135–40; for CM's inquiry, see *Letter-Book of Samuel Sewall,* II, 118–20; Rena Vassar, "Testimony of Frances Davis," *William and Mary Quarterly,* XXXIV (1977), 475; SLCM, pp. 344, 375. **The mediocre success:** Foote, *Annals of King's Chapel,* I, 325; DII, p. 806n.; Murdock, "Cotton Mather and the Rectorship," p. 395n.; MS letter, Timothy Cutler to unaddressed, 2 Apr 1725, BPL. **But Mather soon:** Cutler to unaddressed, 2 Apr 1725; Bridenbaugh, *Mitre and Sceptre,* p. 73; BG, 26 Jul–2 Aug 1725. **Mather later felt:** *The Acts and Resolves, Public and Private, of the Province of the Massachusetts Bay* (Boston, 1869–1922), X, 628; MS letter, John Checkley to "Doctor Bennet," 15 Jun 1725, BPL. **The Council approved:** MS "Memorial of Dr. Timothy Cutler and Mr. Samuel Myles," 23 Jun 1725, MHS; John Gorham Palfrey, *History of New England* (Boston, 1875, 1890), IV, 454–55. **Mather professed to:** CM, *Ratio Disciplinae* (1726), p. 174; Foley, "Christ Church," p.75. **While looking for:** MS letter, Jeremiah Dummer to Timothy Woodbridge, 10 Sep 1723, MHS. Apparently CM and Colman were able to get an address signed by ministers in Essex County, however. See MS letter, William Waldron to Richard Waldron, 2 Dec 1723, MHS. **In Boston Mather's:** SLCM, p. 376; NEC, 7–14 Jan 1723; SLCM, pp. 354, 378. **Mather's fidelity to:** SLCM, p.385. **Mather denied this:** DII, p. 794; MS letter, Jeremiah Dummer to CM, 22 Aug 1726, AAS; MS draft letter, CM to unaddressed, undated [*ca.* 1725, and beginning "I had for many years, the Happiness of a Correspondence"], AAS. **Mather may well:** SLCM, p. 385; MS letter, Jeremiah Dummer to CM, 15 Mar 1726, MHS; for the explanatory charter, see *Acts and Resolves,* I, 21–23. **As he had:** DII, pp. 800, 792–94. **The load now:** DII, pp. 703–4. **Worst of all:** this and the next paragraph from DII, pp. 705–8. CM may well have sold off at this time some of his beloved books. Thomas Prince recorded that in 1724 he bought the six-volume *Biblia Polyglotta* (London, 1657) from a Boston bookseller, who had bought them from CM (who had a second copy). "Harvard Text-Books and Reference Books of the Seventeenth Century," PCSM, XXVIII (1935), 393. **About two weeks:** DII, p.713; SLCM, p. 383; DII, p.712. **The same evening:** DII, pp. 713-14. **But there was:** DII, p. 715. **Exactly what set:** SLCM, pp. 379, 384; DII, pp. 709, 712; Checkley v. Dr. Mather and Willard, ERB (7 Apr 1724). Lydia's reasons for particularly abusing "Nancy" (Hannah) are unclear. Of all CM's children she makes the most puzzling figure in his diary. He often speaks of her as a child particularly afflicted, but without specifying what her afflictions were. Intriguingly, within days or weeks after he mentions sending her to board elsewhere, a "Hannah Mather" at nearby Roxbury (where CM had some close relatives, the Walter family) gave birth to an illegitimate child. She was ordered to pay a fine of three pounds or to suffer ten stripes at the public whipping post. See MS Sessions Minutes, 1719-1728, Suffolk County Supreme Court, Boston. Whether this was CM's daughter I have been unable to determine. **Lydia's new paroxysms:** DII, pp. 715, 717. **Virtually week by:** DII, p. 719. **Whatever the case:** DII, pp. 719, 723, 725, 727. **A historically fascinating:** *The Complete Works of Benjamin Franklin,* ed. John Bigelow, VIII (New York, 1888), 484-85; DII, p. 731. **But with July:** DII, pp. 739, 745; CM, *The True Riches* (1724); DII, p. 745. CM mentions the first debt in his diary on 6 Jul 1724, the second on 31 Jul. The language he uses in describing them is so similar that it is possible, but I believe unlikely, that the two entries describe a single demand against the estate. **Inundated with new:** DII, pp. 735, 744-45. **The next five:** Leverett's death is noted in"Diary of Jeremiah Bumstead," p. 201; for CM's conflicting characterizations of Leverett, see SLCM, p. 294, and HCR, V, 566; for the "unhappy Man," see DII, p.723; for CM's report on Harvard, see Josiah Quincy, *The History of Harvard University* (Boston, 1860), I, 558-60; for the Overseers' investigation, see John Maynard Hoffmann, "Commonwealth College: The Governance of Harvard in the Puritan Period," Diss. Harvard, 1972, p. 588. **With Leverett's death:** DII, p. 723; Niel Caplan, "Some Unpublished Letters of Benjamin Colman, 1717-1725," PMHS, LXXVII (1965), 133-34; DII, p. 736. **But Mather learned:** this and the next four paragraphs from DII, pp. 748-53. **At the time:** DII, p. 701; Sammy's admission appears in R2C, 22 Dec 1722; SML, p. 14. Like his father, Creasy had a fine handwriting, good enough for him to make something of a living as a "writer," as he is designated in SF #16702 (18 Mar 1723)—presumably a scribe or amanuensis. **Creasy, Mather was:** DII, p. 753; CM, *Things that Young People should Think upon* (1700), pp. 8, 6; DII, pp. 736, 744. **But no afflations:** DII, p. 753; Creasy's "Instrument" appears in CM, *The Words of Understanding* (1724), pp. 98-105; PA, p. 158. **Three days after:** with one exception, this and the next five paragraphs are drawn from DII, pp. 755-68. The sermon on August 30, however, appears in *The Words of Understanding,* pp. 9, 33. **On November 6:** SLCM, p. 401. Writing to Robert Wodrow, Colman mentioned CM's "hard Letter" to him and remarked that the choice of Mather "could not be obtained of the Electo[rs]." Caplan, "Some Unpublished Letters," p. 136. **On November 18:** DII, pp. 774-75; on Colman's disrelish for the presidency, see Caplan, "Some Letters"; HCR, II, cxv. **For all the:** CM, attestation in Azariah Mather, *Sabbath-Day's Rest* (1725), p. 3; DII, pp. 764, 776; CM, *Light in Darkness* (1724), p. 3. **As the event:** DII, p. 776. **Late in December:** DII, pp. 777-78. This passage in CM's diary contains the inexplicable comment, "If this Child [Samuel], must after his two Brothers, be Buried in the *Atlantic Ocean.*" As far as is known, Creasy was the only one of CM's children to have drowned. The entry seems a slip. **As had not:** DII, p. 779.

14. As Merry as One Bound for Heaven

A cough, a: DII, p. 775; SLCM, p. 404; *Letter-Book of Samuel Sewall,* CMHS, 6th ser. (1886–88), II, 223. **Seemingly drained by:** MS letter, Jeremiah Dummer to CM, 22 Aug 1726, AAS; SML, p. 139; Tallcott v. Dr. Mather, ERB (5 Oct 1724). **Sixty-two years old:** SLCM, p. 413. **Despite Mather's filiopietism:** SLCM, p. 413; BA, Eccl. XII. 2.; CM, *A Good Old Age* (1726), p. 28. **Some of these:** DII, p. 696; MS letter, Thomas Hollis to Samuel Mather, 27 Jul 1727, MHS; CM, *A Good Old Age,* p. 21; CM's first public sermon appears in his *Religious Societies* (1724); "Presentation Copy of the Rev. Cotton Mather's Ratio Disciplinae," NEHGR, XXXI (1877), 222. **But above all:** DII, p. 778; SML, p. 139. **Except his withdrawal:** on "Biblia Americana," see SLCM, p. 414; on Arianism, see SLCM, p. 408; on Pietist missionaries, see Henry Newman to Benjamin Colman, 30 Jul 1726, MHS (typed transcript); on Winthrop, see Winthrop to CM, undated [*ca.* 1726], CMHS, 6th ser., V (1892), 423 ff. **Mather also continued:** DII, p. 803; SLCM, p. 381. **In his final:** for the petitions, addresses, and decisions of church councils, see for instance CM *et al., A Serious Address To those Who unnecessarily frequent The Tavern* (1726), and MS letter, CM to brethren of the church at Lynn, 25 Feb 1727, Essex Institute; on the pirates, see DII, p. 729, and CM, *The Vial poured out upon the Sea* (1726). **On one grimly:** on Elizabeth's marriage, see Thwing Card Catalogue, MHS, and H, II, 809; CM, *Pietas Matutina* (1726), p. 39, and "The Occasion" (italics reversed). **Mather earnestly wished:** for Cutler's petition, see MS records of King's Chapel, vol. 8, MHS; on the *"Excellent Young Men,"* see CM, *The Minister* (1722), p. 45; on Prince, see SSD, II, 858, and DII, p. 812, as well as DII and SLCM, *passim.* **Mather's successors also:** SLCM, p. 391; DII, pp. 762–63, 769–70. **Mather viewed Sammy:** CM, *Hor-Hagidgad* (1727), p. 1. **Mather did not:** I have followed the translation of CM's Latin Preface to *Manuductio* in *Dr. Cotton Mather's Student and Preacher* (London, 1789), pp. 2–59. **To the churches:** SLCM, p. 411. The 1701 version appears in MAP, Reel 5. On *Ratio* as a substitute for a new church platform, see this version, p. 174. **Age did not:** BNL, 18 Feb–7 Mar 1723 (CM probably contributed the article on a fever cure in the issue of 22–29 Aug 1723); on Feveryear, see Raymond Phineas Stearns, *Science in the British Colonies of America* (Urbana, Ill., 1970), p. 448; on Greenwood, see DII, p. 741, and Stearns, *Science in the British Colonies,* pp. 446–55, also SLCM, pp. 388–89, and I. Bernard Cohen, *Some Early Tools of American Science* (Cambridge, Mass., 1977), pp. 31–33. **Mather was disappointed:** some of CM's complaints appear in his MS letter to John Winthrop, 10 Jan 1723, MHS; on the "Curiosa Americana" of 1720, 1723, and 1724, see George Lyman Kittredge, "Cotton Mather's Communications to the Royal Society," PAAS, NS XXVI (1916), 45–57. **In sending his:** SLCM, p. 400. In quoting from *The Angel of Bethesda* here and in the next paragraphs, I follow the edition of Gordon W. Jones (Barre, Mass., 1972), and draw some points of interpretation from his excellent introduction, pp. xi–xl. *The Angel of:* on the historical significance of "Ephphatha," see Ernest G. Bormann, "Ephphatha, or, Some Advice to Stammerers," *Journal of Speech and Hearing Research,"* XII (1969), 453–61. **In the most:** on CM's early interest in van Helmont, see M, p. 673. CM thought highly enough of the concept of the "Nishmath-Chajim" to print this Capsula separately as a short work also entitled *The Angel of Bethesda* (New London, 1722), and to have included it again in his unpublished "Tri-Paradisus." **Mather saw this:** for CM's remark on *Ratio,* see SLCM, p. 411. **While writing *The:*** SLCM, p. 336; DII, p. 699; SLCM, p. 72; H, II, 739. **Despite this uncommonly:** SSD, II, 1052; CM, *Restitutus* (1727), pp. 22–23; CM, *The Balance of the Sanctuary* (1727), p. 24; on CM's occasional committee work and the like during his last year, see for instance Hamilton Andrews Hill, *History of the Old South*

Church (Boston, 1890), I, 421; *Boston Prints and Printmakers 1670-1775,* PCSM, XLVI (1973), 134 ff.; Frederick L. Weis, "Checklist of Portraits in the Library of the American Antiquarian Society," PAAS, NS LVI (1946), 89-90. **Lacking Mather's diaries:** CM, *Restitutus,* pp. 8-9; SLCM, p. 415. **Mather's dominant mood:** DII, p. 373; Katy's deathbed remark appears in CM's unpublished "Tri-Paradisus," MAP, Reel 7, fr. 0579; CM, *Hatzar-Maveth* (1726), pp. 13-14; the brazen serpent comparison appears in *Zalmonah* (1725); DII, pp. 785-86; MS letter, Thomas Hollis to Samuel Mather, 27 Jul 1727, MHS. **At times Mather's:** MS letter, CM to Thomas Prince, 31 Jan 1726, MHS; CM's verses appear in a privately owned copy of *Monumental Gratitude,* reproduced in facsimile in *Photostat Americana.* **Having spent much:** CM, *A Year and a Life Well Concluded* (1720), pp. 7-8; CM, *Restitutus,* p. 23. **The three paradises:** on the dates of composition, see DIII, p. 91, and DII, p. 811; the text of "Tri-Paradisus" appears in MAP, Reel 7. **Mather's vision of:** DII, p. 805n.; SLCM, p. 377; CM's earlier views on the Second Coming appear in his unpublished "Problema Theologicum," MAP, Reel 7. **Mather now believed:** translation of CM's Latin Preface to *Manuductio,* in *Dr. Cotton Mather's Student,* p. 9. **Mather does not:** BG, 26 Dec-2 Jan 1726/7 and 5-12 Jun 1727; CM, *Christian Loyalty* (1727), pp. 21-22. **It began, the:** CM, *The Terror of the Lord* (1727), p. 1; Arthur B. Ellis, *History of the First Church in Boston, 1630-1880* (Boston, 1881), q. p. 198. **Movables clattered as:** William T. Youngs, Jr., *God's Messengers: Religious Leadership in Colonial New England, 1700-1750* (Baltimore, 1976), p. 111 (cups and mugs, "the Great Day"); SSD, II, 1055; CM, *The Terror of the Lord,* p. 2 (ships); *Philosophical Transactions of the Royal Society,* #409 (1729), p. 125 (Newbury); BG, 6-13 Nov 1727 (Guilford); BG, 30 Oct-6 Nov 1727. **Mather may have:** CM, *Juga Jucunda* (1727), p. 1; on the length of the services and the size of the gathering, see BNL, 26 Oct-3 Nov 1727, and CM, *The Terror of the Lord,* pp. 1-2. **Mather spoke now:** CM, *The Terror of the Lord,* pp. 14, 6, 13, 19, 25, 27-28. **Mather's warning was:** Samuel G. Drake, *The History and Antiquities of Boston* (Boston, 1856), p. 577; on the rise in admissions, see Youngs, *God's Messengers,* p. 111, and R2C. **Hoping to prolong:** SLCM, p. 418; CM, *Boanerges* (1727), p. 43. **On December 24:** CM, *The Comfortable Chambers* (1728); MS Treasurer's Accounts of the Second Church, MHS.

Conclusion: Copp's Hill

Cotton Mather's final: SML, p. 153; Joshua Gee, *Israel's Mourning for Aaron's Death* (1728), p. 27; Benjamin Colman, *The Holy Walk and Glorious Translation of Blessed Enoch* (1728), p. 27. **But to Mather:** Samuel Mather, *The Departure and Character of Elijah Considered and Improved* (1728), p. 14; Gee, *Israel's Mourning,* p. 29. **With a boom:** *New-England Weekly Journal,* 12 Feb 1728 and 15 Jan 1728; DII, p. 444. **At daybreak two:** *New-England Weekly Journal,* 12 Feb 1728; on the ultimate duration of the quakes, see *Philosophical Transactions of the Royal Society,* #409 (1729), p. 127; R2C. **Saturday, February 10:** SML, p. 159; Gee, *Israel's Mourning,* p. 30. **Sunday, as he:** SML, pp. 154, 156; Gee, *Israel's Mourning,* p. 25; Samuel Mather, *Departure and Character,* pp. 14-15. **Monday was Cotton:** Samuel Mather, *Departure and Character,* pp. 15-16; Gee, *Israel's Mourning,* pp. 29, 27. **It was of:** all quotations in this and the following six paragraphs drawn from Thomas Prince, *The Departure of Elijah lamented* (1728), and from the above sermons by Gee, Colman, and Samuel Mather. **Mather was buried:** MS diary of Benjamin Walker, 1726-42, MHS; "The Diary of Ebenezer Parkman 1719-1728," PAAS, LXXI (1961), 211. **Taken from Mather's:** MS diary of Benjamin Walker; SSD, II, 1959-60; *New-England Weekly Journal,* 26 Feb 1728. **The procession ended:** Nathaniel B.

Shurtleff, *A Topographical and Historical Description of Boston* (Boston, 1871), p. 159; P, p. 211; "Diary of Ebenezer Parkman," p. 211. **Immediately after Mather's:** R2C, 13 Mar 1728; MS Treasurer's Accounts of the Second Church, MHS; R2C, 28 Jan 1732; MS letter, Samuel Mather to Samuel Mather, Jr., 18 Dec 1762, MHS; Samuel's reading of the document is described, in his own hand, on the verso of a Salem broadsheet issue of the *Declaration,* MHS. **Cotton Mather died:** CM, *Orphanotrophium* (1711), p. 40; MS document, 22 Jul 1728 ("Mather Adm."), Suffolk County Probate Court, Boston; MS document, 17 Jun 1728 ("Dr Cotton Mather Citation"), New England Historic and Genealogical Society, Boston; Julius Herbert Tuttle, "The Libraries of the Mathers," PAAS, NS XX (1910), 296; MS petition of Samuel Mather to Justices of the Superior Court, SF #26606; MS documents, 24 Apr 1730 ("Mather's Quit Claim") and 25 May 1730 ("Mather's Personal Estate Divided"), Suffolk County Probate Court, Boston (see also Suffolk Probate Records 28.18). **But there was:** MS inventory of CM's estate, 5 Aug 1728, Suffolk County Probate Court, Boston (the inventory was made on 23 Jul but entered on 5 Aug).

Index

Aaron, 45–46
Accomplished Singer, The (Mather), 305
Adams, Samuel, 1
Addison, Joseph, 199, 297
Advice, To the Churches of the Faithful
(Mather), 365
Aeneid (Virgil), 159, 160
"Affectation of Praehiminincies (A.D.
1663–1675)" (Porter), 277
affliction, Puritan views on, 34, 76, 182,
269, 271, 273, 348–349
Africa, inoculation in, 338–339
Agricola (Mather), 412
Ahab, king of Israel, 61
Alden, John and Priscilla, 111
"Alice Doane's Appeal" (Hawthorne), 53
Andover, Mass., witchcraft in, 104–109,
111, 118
Andros, Sir Edmund, 63–74, 78–79, 106,
108, 111, 139, 203, 205, 206, 208, 213,
218, 367
Angel of Bethesda, The (Mather), 406–410
angels:
fallen, *see* devil, devils
as protective spirits, 123–130, 135–137,
311–312, 414, 440*n*
Anglican church, *see* Church of England;
Episcopal church
Anglican Society for the Propagation of
the Gospel, 208, 216, 241–242
Anne, queen of England, 207, 208, 211,
295
Apophthegmata (Lycosthenes), 262
Appleton, Nathaniel, 366
"Apple-Tree Table, The" (Melville), 54
Archeus, 409

Arianism, 328–332, 368, 376, 399
Aristotle, 40, 252
Arius, 328–329
Arminianism, 302
Arndt, John, 231, 232, 235, 289
artillery sermon, 36, 47
Ashurst, Sir Henry, 147, 204–205, 206,
211, 213, 216–217, 220, 240, 294
Ashurst, Sir William, 240, 241–242, 259,
293, 295
astronomy, 22, 40–42, 251–252, 253
see also science
atheism, 92
atomic theory, 167–168
Augustus, emperor of Rome, 309
Autobiography (Franklin), 164, 383
Avery, William, 41–42, 338
Axel, Samuel (Samuel May), 142

Baglivi, Georgi, 233
Balance of the Sanctuary, The (Mather),
400
Ballard, Joseph, 104–105
Bamberg, Germany, witchcraft in, 89
Bancroft, George, 53
Banister, John, 223–224
baptism:
controversy over, 57, 118–120, 153
by devils, 105–106, 118
Baptismal Piety (Mather), 400
Baptists:
in Boston, 69, 111, 302
liberty of conscience for, 141, 161, 302,
332
persecution of, 56
Barker, William, Sr., 106

465